Principled World Politics

Principled World Politics

The Challenge of Normative International Relations

Edited by
PAUL WAPNER
and
LESTER EDWIN J. RUIZ

ROWMAN & LITTLEFIELD PUBLISHERS, INC.
Lanham • Boulder • New York • Oxford

ROWMAN & LITTLEFIELD PUBLISHERS, INC.

Published in the United States of America
by Rowman & Littlefield Publishers, Inc.
4720 Boston Way, Lanham, Maryland 20706
http://www.rowmanlittlefield.com

12 Hid's Copse Road
Cumnor Hill, Oxford OX2 9JJ, England

British Library Cataloguing in Publication Information Available

Library of Congress Cataloging-in-Publication Data

Principled world politics : the challenge of normative international relations / edited by
Paul Wapner and Lester Edwin J. Ruiz
    p. cm.
    Includes bibliographical references and index.
    ISBN 0-7425-0064-0 (cloth : alk. paper)—ISBN 0-7425-0065-9 (paper : alk. paper)
      1. International relations—Philosophy. I. Wapner, Paul Kevin. II. Ruiz, Lester
    Edwin J. III. Falk, Richard A.
JZ1242.P75   2000
327.1'01—dc21   99-053985

Printed in the United States of America

♾ ™ The paper used in this publication meets the minimum requirements of American
National Standard for Information Sciences—Permanence of Paper for Printed Library
Materials, ANSI/NISO Z39.48-1992.

For Richard Falk

Contents

Acknowledgments   xi

Part 1: Introduction

1 The Resurgence and Metamorphosis of Normative International
   Relations: Principled Commitment and Scholarship in a New
   Millennium   1
   Paul Wapner, American University, U.S.A.

Part 2: Critical Perspectives on International Relations

2 Both Globalization and Sovereignty: Re-Imagining the Political   23
   R. B. J. Walker, University of Victoria, Canada

3 Normative and Complexity Theories: Complementary Approaches to
   World Affairs   35
   James N. Rosenau, George Washington University, U.S.A.

4 Theory and Political Practice: Reflections on Theory Building in
   International Relations   50
   Friedrich V. Kratochwil, University of Munich, Germany

5 The Uncertain Reach of Critical Theory   65
   *Radmila Nakarada, Institute for European Studies, Belgrade,
   Yugoslavia*

Part 3: Social Justice

6 Global Economic Inequalities: A Growing Moral Gap   79
   Michael W. Doyle, Princeton University, U.S.A.

7 Social Justice: Growing Consciousness, Receding Prospects   98
   *Rajni Kothari, Centre for the Study of Developing Societies, New
   Delhi, India*

8 Collective Identity, Social Movements, and the Limits of Political
       Dissent in Israel   112
       Simona Sharoni, Evergreen State College U.S.A.

9 Ecological Balance in an Era of Globalization   130
       *Vandana Shiva, Research Foundation for Science, Technology and
       Natural Resource Policy, Dehra Dun, India*

Part 4: Economic Well-Being

10 Markets, Private Property, and the Possibility of Democracy   151
        David Held, The Open University, London, United Kingdom

11 Reconceptualizing Global Poverty: Globalization, Marginalization,
        and Gender   166
        *James H. Mittelman and Ashwini Tambe, American University,
        U.S.A.*

12 The Asian Financial Crisis: Heroes, Villains, and Accomplices   181
        Walden Bello, Focus on the Global South, Thailand

13 Global Backlash: Citizen Initiatives to Counter Corporate-Led
        Globalization   191
        *Robin Broad, American University, U.S.A., and John Cavanagh,
        Institute for Policy Studies, U.S.A.*

Part 5: Peace

14 Enforcing Norms and Normalizing Enforcement for Humane
        Governance   209
        Robert C. Johansen, University of Notre Dame, U.S.A.

15 The Underside of Peace: Reflections on Aum Shinrikyo   231
        *Robert Jay Lifton, John Jay College, City University of New York,
        U.S.A.*

16 An Axial Age? Imagining Peace for the New Millennium   240
        Elise Boulding, Dartmouth College, U.S.A.

17 From a Twentieth Century of War to a Twenty-First Century of
        Peace?   250
        *Johan Galtung, Founder of the International Peace Research Institute,
        Oslo, Norway*

Part 6: Humane Governance

18 The Normative Promise of Nonstate Actors: A Theoretical Account
        of Global Civil Society   261
        Paul Wapner, American University, U.S.A.

19 Technological Underdevelopment in the South: The Continuing
Cold War　　　　275
Ali A. Mazrui, State University of New York at Binghamton, U.S.A.

20 Governance, Legitimacy, and Security: Three Scenarios for the
Twenty-First Century　　　　284
Mary Kaldor, London School of Economics, United Kingdom

21 The Age of Relativization: Toward a Twenty-First Century of Active
Civil Society　　　　300
Yoshikazu Sakamoto, University of Tokyo, Japan

Part 7: Conclusion

22 The Emergence of WOMP in the Normative Tradition: Biography
and Theory　　　　311
Saul Mendlovitz, Rutgers University Law School, U.S.A.

23 Culture, Politics, and the Sense of the Ethical: Challenges for
Normative International Relations　　　　322
Lester Edwin J. Ruiz, New York Theological Seminary, U.S.A.

Bibliography　　　　349

Index　　　　375

About the Contributors　　　　395

Acknowledgments

This book was conceived to honor the work of Richard A. Falk. Richard has been an inspiring teacher, untiring activist, loyal friend, and indispensable colleague to so many of us that we felt it fitting to express a collective sense of appreciation to him. This book is a small gesture toward that end. It presents chapters written by scholars working in the normative tradition of international relations, a discipline that Richard helped establish and develop over the past forty-odd years. Chapter authors push their own work further in a normative direction as a way to honor Richard. There are few moments when we, as academics and practitioners, are able to express our gratitude in a scholarly form. It is a special pleasure to do this for Richard.

Editing a book is like making soup: If you start with good ingredients, you rarely go wrong. As editors, we have benefited from working with a wonderful group of authors, and much of our thanks goes to them. We appreciate their many efforts to bring this project to fruition. We are also grateful to the friends, colleagues, and research assistants who read chapters or helped with the logistics of editing a twenty-three-chapter book with authors from all over the world. Thanks go to Chuck Johnson, Sohini Sarkar, Rob Walker, Ilana Zamonski, and especially Judith Shapiro for reading significant parts of the manuscript and providing helpful comments. We wish also to express our gratitude to Kozue Akibayashi, Natasha Benedicto, Joe Clapper, Ali Ghobadi, and Margo Thoresen for invaluable computer and office support.

Throughout the venture, a number of chapter authors provided wise counsel. A special thanks goes to Bob Johansen, Saul Mendlovitz, Jim Mittelman, and Rob Walker for helping us negotiate our way through the many challenges of such an undertaking. We appreciate their thoughtfulness and commitment. We would also like to thank Jennifer Knerr and Dorothy Bradley of Rowman and Littlefield for the zeal they have brought to the book and their very capable publishing skills.

A number of institutions graciously hosted a surprise dinner for Richard in Washington, D.C., in February 1999 that provided an opportunity to present the manuscript for this book to him. We are grateful to Princeton University's Center for International Studies, the World Order Models Project, the Center for Global Change and Governance at Rutgers University, and the Center for the Global South at American University for their generous contributions to this event. We would also like to thank June Garson, Leeanne Dunsmore, and Hilal Elver for masterfully engineering the surprise.

Closer to our hearts, we have benefited from the warmth, sane insight, and precious comradeship of our spouses. Thanks Diane and Jean.

Finally, our greatest debt goes to Richard for being, well, himself.

1

The Resurgence and Metamorphosis of Normative International Relations: Principled Commitment and Scholarship in a New Millennium

Paul Wapner

Interest in normative international relations (IR) is surging after a half century of neglect and marginalization. There is now an impressive effort, emerging from many different branches of the discipline, to fold ethical concerns into scholarship and use them to fashion intellectual support for achieving a more humane world. Many scholars no longer feel the necessity to hide their moral commitments and, in fact, often see such commitments as important entryways into the study of world politics. The critical moment ushering in the plethora of "new normative approaches" (Brown 1992; see also Smith 1992) is, of course, the end of the Cold War and the new political space within which to focus upon matters not associated with super-power competition and security. However, the opening for normative thought has deeper roots. It is tied up with skepticism about IR as a "scientific" discipline and doubts about political realism that dominated, until recently, IR scholarship in the post-1945 era.

Throughout the latter part of the twentieth century, the study of IR has been fashioned as a scientific discipline in the sense that it tries to provide an objective rendering of world affairs. While some scholars—especially many in North America and parts of Europe—take this to imply a preference for positivist methodologies, overall it means simply an attitude toward scholarship in which researchers study phenomena independent of their own interests and values. The discipline attempts to describe, explain, and at times predict world political phenomena free from the subjective aspirations of researchers. It assumes that there is a political reality "out there" and that the purpose of IR scholarship is to depict it as accurately as possible.

1

One result of this orientation is the belief that inquiry should strive to be indifferent to ethical concerns or human aspirations because these tend to prejudice research, leading to contaminated scholarship and, often, starry-eyed utopianism. To the degree that IR fashions itself as a bona fide science, then, it is uninterested in and often hostile to moral concerns.

A second element of the post-1945 world that marginalized normative thought, until recently, was the dominance of political realism. The scientific aspirations of IR as a discipline found an ally in the tradition of political realism in the sense that the latter prides itself on depicting the actual character of contemporary affairs rather than envisioning preferred arrangements and thus shares a hostile attitude toward the deliberate inclusion of moral sensibilities into scholarship (Frost 1986).[1] Realism tries to maintain a distinction between "what is" and "what ought to be," and asserts that its aim is to understand the former regardless of the compelling character of the latter. Moral considerations blur the distinction between empirical research and aspirations and thus can undermine the effort toward clear-eyed understanding. Of course, realism is not normatively neutral. It believes that the supreme moral act is to safeguard state security and work toward international stability (see Gilpin 1986). It maintains that people and states are fundamentally motivated to seek power and security and thus, while they may seek other ends—of which altruistic or principled goals may be a part—such effort will come to naught if they neglect security concerns. This is especially the case in the international arena, in which there are few reliable mechanisms to ensure international order, thus making the pursuit of security a moral duty. Given the supreme weight of security concerns, realism has little time for broadly conceived ethical thought and belittles any attempt to use such thought as a criterion for informing scholarship or policy.

The alliance between political realism and the scientistic underlay of IR flourished partly because of the plausibility of such an orientation during the Cold War, and this represents the third element responsible for the marginalization of normative IR. In an era of superpower competition in which military security was generally at the forefront of policymakers' minds, realism provided a persuasive conceptual framework for making sense of IR. Its commitment to state security and its practice of analyzing affairs through assessments of relative power provided a prudent formula for acting in the world. It justified the pursuit of self-interest and thereby relieved policymakers and others of attending to nonsecurity issues. Put differently, perceptions of security requirements left little room for envisioning different structural arrangements in the world and thus marginalized broadly conceived ethical concerns. The world was locked in a bipolar situation in which the basic dynamic of all international affairs was seen, at least principally, through the lens of maintaining stability. All other projects were too risky, given Cold War "realities."

With the end of the Cold War, there has been a reevaluation of political realism—not least because of realism's failure, on its own terms, to predict the fall of the Soviet Union (see, e.g., Gaddis 1992–93). Moreover, recent intellectual trends have generated a skeptical view toward the epistemological and ontological foundations of social science as a science and thus have raised doubts about IR as a strictly social scientific endeavor.[2] As a consequence, the edifice that marginalized ethical reflection in IR has fallen, leaving fertile ground for a host of new perspectives toward IR scholarship, especially normative ones.

Tilling the new soil has already ushered in a new moment in IR scholarship and, some would say, world politics. With the invitation to infuse scholarly and political work with moral sensitivity, the actual conditions of suffering—characterized by political oppression, widespread poverty, violence, prejudice, and environmental degradation—are no longer being pushed aside by many IR scholars. This is especially relevant in that the end of the Cold War, despite initial hopes to the contrary, did not herald a new world order. In fact, there has been a rude awakening that some of the most pressing challenges to world order precede and transcend Cold War "realities" and that the end of the Cold War itself unleashed new forces—for example, ones associated with economic globalization—that have their own harsh human costs. The new political environment is allowing observers, for the first time in decades, to perceive the indications of human suffering and analyze them in an unabashed manner. It is in this context that a surge of interest in normative IR is taking place.

What are the "new normative approaches"? How do they differ from previous modes of normative IR scholarship? What impact are they having on the discipline? How are they contributing or not contributing to more humane conditions? *Principled World Politics* sheds light on these questions. It does so not by answering them in an abstract manner but by demonstrating the quality of contemporary normative IR scholarship. The editors have gathered together some of the best minds currently working in the normative IR tradition throughout the world and asked them to illustrate what happens when scholarship is infused with moral passion and a commitment to improve the human prospect. The result is a portrait of normative international scholarship at the millennium. We are now in the first years of the twenty-first century. This historical time provides, if only symbolically, an opportunity to pause from our immediate preoccupations and contemplate the overall character of the human condition and speculate about its future. To put it more poetically, the millennium is "a marker thrown on the shore in the darkness of night while the river of history rushes by" (Falk 1996, 19). This marker casts our gaze long into the past and potentially far into the future. Coming as it does at the end of the Cold War, the millennium is a moment that is ripe for historical reflection, intellectual deliberation, moral consideration, and political imagination. It thus can serve as an appropriate time to understand the challenges and promises of normative IR. This book provides an overview of the discipline and articulates the character of normative work as we live through the first years of the twenty-first century.

RICHARD FALK AND THE NORMATIVE TRADITION

Like any portrait, *Principled World Politics* addresses its subject matter from a particular perspective. While its authors focus on normative commitment at the millennium, they have been brought together not simply to mark the passing of the twentieth century and to chart future terrain but also to celebrate the career of one of the foremost practitioners of normative IR, Richard Falk. Richard Falk is Albert G. Milbank Professor of International Law and Practice at Princeton University. Over the past forty years, he has produced a body of scholarship that aims to advance the achievement of a just, peaceful, ecologically sound, and economically viable world order in which the diversity of people's identities can be respected and drawn upon to enhance the overall quality of life on earth. In an essay on Hugo Grotius, one of Falk's intellectual predecessors, Falk (1983) remarked that Grotius was committed to "leaving the world a better place than he found it" (26). Falk's scholarship and activism have likewise been directed toward this goal. Few scholars have assumed such commitment in the context of academic life, and even fewer have had the talent to translate it into scholarly contribution and political achievement.

The authors of *Principled World Politics* push their own scholarship further in a normative direction as a way of honoring Falk's achievements. They use his work as inspiration to pursue normative studies with more passion and scholarly perspicacity. This book, then, is an effort to take stock of contemporary normative IR on the occasion of celebrating Falk's career. It should come as no surprise, then, that while each chapter makes its own substantive contribution to the discipline, the following pages have a Falkian twist. This is both deliberate and unavoidable. Each of the authors of *Principled World Politics,* in one way or another, shares an intellectual debt to Falk and situates his or her own work within, or at least shows much respect for, a Falkian orientation to normative IR. Additionally, Falk has set into motion a line of scholarship that is now part of the bedrock of normative IR—and whose evolution will greatly inform the discipline's physiognomy in this new century. The authors, as normative scholars, thus cannot ignore a Falkian orientation. This orientation is perhaps best characterized as a sentiment that implicitly emerges as scholars pursue various forms of normative work. There are a number of dimensions to this attitude, four of which are worthy of comment.[3]

Normative IR is made up of various strands, all of which focus on the status of moral responsibility in the world system. Many are purely academic in the sense that they seek merely to *understand* the character of moral argument in the context of world politics. These efforts explore, for example, the logic of moral reasoning as applied to world affairs (e.g., Barry 1982), existing normative commitments by states and other actors (e.g., Bull 1977), the justification for extending ethical consideration at the domestic level to the international one (e.g., Bietz 1979), and intellectual reflection on the meaning of distributive justice, universal human rights, and just-war theory (e.g., Walzer 1992).[4] While having made contributions to these fields, Falk has always maintained that, given the many injustices throughout the world, scholarship must not simply content itself with understanding the place of morality in world affairs but must also bring the demands of moral conscience to the study and practice of world politics. Scholars have a responsibility, in other words, to use their work to leave the world a better place than they found it, and this includes, when possible, translating one's scholarly insights into appropriate political action. The authors of *Principled World Politics* take this commitment seriously and see themselves involved in engaged scholarship. Most of the authors work not only in the academy but also in the street, as it were, negotiating ways to advance certain political agendas. As the following pages demonstrate, this political engagement sharpens the analysis of given authors and highlights the contemporary relevance of their scholarship.

Another orientation that the authors share with Falk is an emphasis on the role of values in scholarly work. Falk has consistently maintained that values inform all scholarship, especially the study of IR. This is at odds with much twentieth-century thought. As mentioned, for decades realists claimed to be value neutral in that they aimed to depict reality as it is rather than as it should be. But, as Falk has pointed out, those who insist on objectivity and claim to exclude normative considerations wittingly or unwittingly endorse the status quo. Their work reflects the value of maintaining the current order in one form or another (Falk 1983, 36). For Falk and the authors of *Principled World Politics,* the current world order supports too many forms of injustice to merit unconditional normative support. The current order legitimates using violence to settle conflicts, tolerates poverty as an inevitable dimension of collective life, endorses the desire to seek material increase through economic growth at the expense of the ecological infrastructure of the earth, and enables the powerful to lord over the weak under the guise of political and economic order. Falk and the authors of *Principled World Politics* criticize the current world system because they are sensitive to the suffering involved with these conditions. This sensitivity comes from cherishing certain values that appear congruent with a quality life.

One of Falk's most noteworthy achievements has been to help establish the World Order Models Project (WOMP), which, since 1966, has worked to stimulate efforts to comprehend and address major problems confronting the people of the world. At the heart of WOMP's work is a set of values that guide scholars and practitioners in assessing contemporary world conditions and through which to envision more humane arrangements. The justification for these so-called world-order values is grounded in Barrington Moore Jr.'s (1972) insight that, "a general opposition to human suffering constitutes a standpoint that both transcends and unites different cultures and historical epochs" (11, quoted in Falk 1975, 4). WOMP's world-order values aim to express, in an encapsulated form, images of trajectories along which human suffering can be relieved if not eliminated. These values include peace, economic well-being, ecological balance, social justice, and humane governance. As general categories of concern, these values not only drive WOMP's activities but had a substantial influence on all normative IR in the latter part of the twentieth century and provide many of the rubrics under which current normative research is conducted. While individual authors of *Principled World Politics* do not necessarily understand their work as based on these values, the editors have asked them to organize their contributions to the book along these lines. These values are taken not as dogma, nor are they themselves immune from criticism. In fact, there is common agreement among the authors that they must be translated into and refracted through the concrete experiences of people living in particular contexts. Nonetheless, the values establish a framework for dialogue among the authors, organizing moral outrage into avenues of critical engagement.

A third element of Falk's orientation at work in these pages is the recognition that much IR scholarship is U.S.-centric and suffers from a tendency to bleach out the insights of scholars from other parts of the world. Although IR has antecedents in Europe and elsewhere, it emerged fully as an academic discipline in the United States shortly after World War I. Moreover, the United States remained the center of IR's intellectual life throughout much of the twentieth century, arguably because of its hegemonic status and the tendency among U.S. scholars to fashion IR into a social science qua science—one of the key elements of IR's staying power throughout the century (see Hoffmann 1977; Holsti 1985; Kahler 1993). Throughout his career, Falk has always resisted the U.S.-centric quality of the discipline, arguing, for example, that some of the most astute insights about the ruling order of world politics come from outside the center of power. Scholars outside U.S. academic circles, according to Falk, are less infected by the privileges that accrue to those who justify and work out the details of continuing U.S. hegemony. Additionally, Falk has always welcomed those insights from outside the United States that were not dressed in the cloak of social science per se, acknowledging that there are various forms of scholarly inquiry, including historical, philosophical, and even literary approaches that contribute to our understanding of world politics. Finally, Falk has insisted on the inclusion of scholarship from around the world because this would respect the genuinely international character of the discipline itself. Neglecting the views of others threatens to collapse IR into the study of U.S. foreign policy, thus creating an almost solipsistic orientation to "world" politics. *Principled World Politics* takes seriously Falk's commitment to international scholarship and thus includes authors from around the world. In the following pages, one will find expressions of the best in normative thought emerging from Japan, India, Germany, Thailand, Yugoslavia, Canada, and the United Kingdom as well as the United States. The international dimension does not, of course, pretend to be representative of worldwide scholarship on normative IR; it merely attempts to broaden the discourse of what is, usually, a U.S.-dominated discipline.

A final aspect of Falk's work that informs *Principled World Politics* is an appreciation for the complexity of the normative enterprise and the idea that normative work is more of a "quest" than a discovery. Normative IR is akin to social criticism in that it begins as a form of complaint. Normative scholars find that the world is not something to be merely described or explained but that it involves widespread suffering from which they cannot turn away. Confronting suffering is no easy matter, however, although the sense of urgency often inspires simplistic reactions. Throughout his career, Falk has warned against being attracted to oversimplified responses and has criticized the political arrogance and kind of confidence that often accompanies prescriptive work. To develop sophisticated normative stances, Falk suggests that the normative thinker see him- or herself inhabiting what he once called the "shadowland." This is that conceptual space wherein one is outraged by contemporary conditions, mindful of past realities, and devoted to exploring future possibilities but cognizant of the speculative nature of the latter enterprise. He calls it the shadowland because it sits in the "shade" of emergent potential structures of power and because one can never see clearly enough from its setting to develop unconditional insight or undertake prophecy (Falk 1983, 25). Speaking of his own work, Falk (1983) once wrote, "These explorations are inevitably tentative. Criticisms are ventured with confidence, large questions are posed with urgency but only the preliminary contours of response are depicted" (15). Such is the nature of normative work. The chapters of *Principled World Politics* share this sense of humility and offer a combination of insightful criticism, urgent concern, and speculative prescription.

Falk's commitments and orientations run throughout *Principled World Politics* insofar as all the authors are part of the tradition of engaged, value-oriented scholarship. The specific contribution of the book is to demonstrate how this tradition is currently undertaking the challenge of normative IR. Individual authors present their most recent and innovative work as a way of advancing normative IR at this particular juncture in world history.

DISCERNING THE CHARACTER OF THE NEW NORMATIVE APPROACHES

The portrait that emerges from the following pages is an orientation that is mindful of recent intellectual developments and real world events. Like any form of thought that wishes to be relevant, contemporary normative scholarship has had to formulate itself to befit current social, economic, and political realities. This means that, while many of the old challenges to normative thought show signs of retreat and opportunities for the flourishing of normative IR abound, there are new challenges that presently engage scholars, and the negotiation of these has much to do with the face of contemporary normative IR thought. In the following, I describe three of these challenges and clarify how the authors of *Principled World Politics* engage them to forge a new mode of normative scholarship. These challenges do not appear in every chapter, nor do they serve as the organizing principle of the book. Rather, they are themes that run throughout the work.

Searching for Humane Governance in a Globalized World

One of the most important challenges, and one that significantly informs the following pages, has to do with the changing character of political demands. Many political problems are no longer primarily domestic or even transnational but increasingly global in scope and character, and this poses particular difficulties for those concerned with improving the quality of life on earth. While the world has always known transboundary trade, collaboration, and communication, the level of transborder interaction has increased and intensified in recent decades such that state boundaries are now easily transgressed and made permeable. Recent innovations in communication and travel technologies have lowered transaction costs, enabling people more easily to engage one another across state boundaries, to pursue joint projects, and to share similar fates. Economic production, distribution, and exchange, for example, increasingly ignore state borders, creating essentially an integrated world economy. Similarly, the traditional boundaries of cultural life are finding themselves permeated by increased social interaction such that many cultural attributes are shared throughout the world (see generally Held et al. 1999).

The extreme level and scope of transnationalism is leading many scholars to characterize contemporary human experience in terms of "globalization," a theme that plays a key role in *Principled World Politics*. Globalization refers to the compression of space and time associated with human interaction (Mittelman 1996). Now goods, services, information, and people flow across state boundaries in an almost instantaneous manner, enabling people to coordinate activities on a global scale. Much collective experience, to put it differently, consists of a type of economic, social, cultural, and political integration that spans the globe and is thus largely indifferent to political borders. The concept of globalization aims to capture the diminished significance of distance and territoriality and the other constructs that are woven around them in contemporary affairs.

Globalization poses significant challenges for the normative thinker insofar as the dynamics that give rise to and fuel political problems, like the dynamics of collective life in general, are increasingly global in character. While political dilemmas were never wholly contained within the territorial jurisdiction of states, many now originate at the interfaces of global collective life and extend their effects throughout the entire world system. That is, global interdependencies are now so tightly woven that many problems emerge out of the countless interactions between states and between societies and then gather steam, evolve, and often intensify along the ligaments of these interdependencies. Many political challenges are thus indifferent to territoriality and develop within innumerable networks sensitive to the dynamics of feedback and the changing character of diverse actors engaging issues from various perspectives, with unequal resources, and with different interpretations of how to define given problems and what is to be done to address such difficulties.[5]

The task for the normative thinker in such a situation involves trying to gain an analytical and prescriptive purchase point on these dynamics. How does one conceptually unpack the complexity of global forces and interpret their character sufficiently to address some of the most obvious pressing challenges? How does one untangle the multifaceted character of contemporary world problems and prescribe forms of political engagement that would actually be effective at changing large-scale structures and widespread practices? How does one see clearly through the complex relationships between global forces and domestic and local political spaces and hope to recommend actions that would successfully negotiate these levels of political life along normative lines?

In the past, normative thinkers answered questions such as these by looking mainly to the state system and, to a lesser extent, the world economy. Normative thinkers traditionally saw the state system as the institutional core of world order and thus the agent of political change. This was in keeping with the long-standing state-centric character of IR itself. Much normative work was thus devoted to developing justifications for, and articulating the character of, obligations, duties, and responsibilities belonging to states. Whether one was trying to think through questions of just-war theory, human rights, distributive justice, or the ethics of intervention, much effort was directed toward enhancing a sense of obligation on the part of states to improve the human prospect.[6]

While the state is still an important focus for many normative thinkers, and while enhancing state responsibility is still a key task for much normative scholarship,[7] many are turning their attention elsewhere as well. They see the state as either unwilling or unable to assume the task of political reform as they envision it, especially given the globalized character of many political problems. Part of this skepticism rests on a long-standing critique of the state system as an imperfect structure within which states must operate, but the critique has taken on new relevance in a globalized age.[8] As is well known, states operate in a self-help system in which actors first seek to promote their own interests before undertaking broader, more collective aims. Moreover, given this self-regarding tendency, states often fail to see how their own interests dovetail with those of other states. Transnational problems become difficult to confront in such a context insofar as they are viewed and refracted through egoistic lenses. This is the central dilemma and, in fact, irony of successful national leadership within a sovereign state system. As Robert C. Tucker (1981) put it years ago, "When it [the state] is most successful at solving problems to the benefits of its own people, it works against the requirements of global life" (29). This dilemma is even more problematic in the contemporary age, when the causes and experiences of human suffering are increasingly global and demand sustained cooperation and collective commitment. In short, while there has always been a fundamental mismatch between the common quality of transnational problems and the fragmentary character of the state system, this mismatch has now taken on a more relevant and poignant meaning, inspiring normative thinkers to grow ever more doubtful of the state system's reformist tendencies.

An alternative to the state system, one that has traditionally appeared promising to normative scholars, is the domain of economic activity—an arena long cherished by those normative thinkers associated with the liberal tradition. Economic activities transcend state boundaries and thus engender loyalties and inspire practices that operate independently of the structural limitations of the state system. This is one reason that economic activities have traditionally been thought able to temper the self-regarding character of states. The "spirit of commerce," as Kant called it, can create economic interdependencies that are believed able to deter international conflict and minimize international competition and animosity (Kant 1963). In a globalized economy, some see the promise associated with the spirit of commerce truly coming of age. In contrast to the state system, there is a comfortable fit between the dynamics of the world economy and the problems that increasingly plague the globe. The liberating dynamics of transnational business enterprises can finally, according to some thinkers, be unleashed everywhere and employed in the service of human betterment (see, e.g., Schmidheiny 1992).

Notwithstanding its transnational dimension, the world economy is a mixed blessing for addressing globalized political problems, and this has made normative thinkers more reticent to embrace it. Indeed, for many thinkers, the world economy looks less like a solution to, than a cause of, contemporary challenges. As a number of the authors of *Principled World Politics* demonstrate, the dynamics of the world economy, especially in their latest globalized incarnation, are responsible for aggravating much human suffering. For example, economic globalization is associated with social dislocation, a widening of the gap between the rich and the poor, a deepening of gender inequalities, and the breakup of communities that have been long held together by forms of economic exchange that were sufficiently autonomous from global economic forces. Globalization is fundamentally about the marketization of the world. The market is not, however, a neutral mechanism that rewards all who play by its rules but is itself embedded in normative structures that privilege certain actors and forms of activities over others. As the chapters that follow demonstrate, these structures tend to accentuate the commercialization of human relations, class distinctions, patriarchal patterns of privilege, and individual autonomy over group solidarity.

In addition to the social ramifications, the authors of *Principle World Politics* are also mindful of globalization's ecological consequences. The promises of economic globalization rest on a belief in the possibility and desirability of infinite material progress achieved through sustained economic growth. The idea that human societies can and should pursue material increase through economic growth is considered one of the foundational ideas animating modern and contemporary life, and it has become arguably more entrenched in the era of globalization (Dryzek 1997; Spretnak 1999). But, as global capital opens up all parts of the earth to resource extraction, enables companies to cruise the globe in search of the least restrictive environmental regulations, and increases consumer demand everywhere, the earth's ability to provide resources, absorb waste, and maintain biological diversity is called into question. According to many, there is a strong correlation between accelerated economic output and dwindling resources, an overtaxing of nature's absorptive capacity, and the extinction of species (Dryzek 1997; Brown et al. 1999). Many normative thinkers take this correlation seriously and use it, along with the social implications of globalization, to justify skepticism toward the world economy as a promising realm for reformist or transformative politics. The world economy is unable, itself, to address successfully the many injustices that are a part of current world affairs and thus, like the state system, represents an unlikely candidate for progressive politics.

From States and Markets to Regimes and Societies

The second challenge motivating new normative approaches has to do with the notion of political agency. If the globalized character of contemporary problems makes it difficult for thinkers to look with promise to the state system or the world economy, where can they find forces that can work in the service of human betterment? Where can normatively oriented scholars find actors and orientations that take human suffering seriously and that are actively engaged in improving the human prospect? More specifically, where can scholars find such forces that are not tied structurally to the limiting character of either the state system or the world economy?

This is an extremely difficult task for contemporary normative theorists. Mindful of poststructural insights, which are addressed in the following section, scholars recognize the problems associated with putting trust in any actor or domain to improve conditions, for, as is well known, all attempts to modify human experience possess their own forms of arrogance, hegemony, and injustice. Moreover, the question of agency is wrapped up in understandings of power that have become quite sophisticated in recent social and political theory. Again as the poststructuralists remind us, power does not inhere only in circumscribed actors, nor does it operate in a linear fashion. Power courses through all elements of collective life—through the "capillaries," as Foucault once put it, of human experience—and continually refashions affairs in ways that are significantly unresponsive to the kind of social engineering inherent in much progressive politics. Finally, the idea of identifying an actor or a set of actors or a domain or a set of domains that one can count on for positive normative action is itself problematic insofar as actors and domains are themselves socially constructed and thus always in the process of identity formation. Searching for a politically progressive agent risks essentializing actors or reifying domains, and this can undermine the entire effort.

Notwithstanding these significant impediments, much normative thought cannot resist engaging the question of agency. While some normative thinkers rightly offer criticism as a form of normative work, many feel the need to go further and actually prescribe action to improve conditions. The search for agency is about that impulse.

Principled World Politics offers divergent views on the question of agency, but, overall, one can sense a set of preferences at work. These preferences revolve around the concept of governance. Governance refers to the general practice of shaping, organizing, and conditioning widespread thought and behavior. It is different from government (and thus states) insofar as it refers to a practice rather than an organization. Governments are material entities with bureaucracies, personnel, equipment, and budgets that are themselves engaged in governance. They are institutions endowed with the authority to make binding decisions applicable to territorially situated communities. While the paradigmatic practitioners of governance, governments are only one among many actors engaged in shaping widespread practices. Normative thinkers are open to the panoply of potential and actual governing mechanisms, and it is within this panoply that they direct their attention.

The most obvious place to look for appropriate forms of governance that will operate on behalf of global well-being has been, and continues to be, the so-called suprastatist realm. This refers to institutions and practices operative at the level above the state. The state system is anarchic in that only weak mechanisms exist above the state to coordinate interstate behavior. Suprastatism refers to those mechanisms, however weak, and seeks to understand both their existent and their potential ability to govern world affairs. In its most general form, suprastatism is constituted by international regimes. These are principles, codes of conduct, rules, and so forth that animate much international and even intranational activity. In its more material form, suprastatism refers to international organizations that deliberately undertake the practice of governance in given issue areas. Suprastatism along these lines includes both regional bodies, such as the European Union and Organization of African States, and global ones, such as the United Nations and its specialized agencies. For normative thinkers, international regimes and organizations represent forms of governance that are free from the territorial focus of the state system and the profit-seeking motivation of transnational economic actors. To be sure, many of the members and certainly the decision-making organs of international organizations are staffed by representatives of states, and thus much transnational governance activity remains bound by statist orientations. Moreover, insofar as many international organizations work to facilitate transnational trade and maintain the health of the world economy, they remain appendages to the processes of economic globalization. Nonetheless, many organizations are staffed by international civil servants who have perfected an ability to act on behalf of the goals of the organization rather than those of their particular state of origin and have become sensitive to many noneconomic imperatives.

While international regimes and organizations are imperfect mechanisms, numerous normative thinkers focus on them to inspire and carry out projects in the so-called global interest. As a number of chapters illustrate, there is enough faith in the suprastatist realm to warrant sustained normative reflection. International organizations are, in essence, problem-solving mechanisms. They address the difficulties (and capitalize on the virtues) that arise from international interaction. While fallible, they are arguably the best existing mechanisms to confront political dilemmas in a globalized world. In the following pages, then, one will find a number of proposals for revitalizing international organizations and redirecting international regimes to enhance the prospect of a more humane world order. This line of thought, obviously, has been part of the normative tradition since its inception; the normative tradition can itself be credited with much of the development of international regimes and organizations. The need for further work in this area, however, has taken on renewed urgency, and efforts in this direction have assumed a new character. International organizations are now free from being merely strategic tools of the Cold War. While they are still vulnerable to power relations—especially to the imperatives of U.S. hegemony—they now enjoy a newfound degree of latitude to address issues outside the immediate domain of the most powerful states and a degree of legitimacy based on this freedom to pursue normative agendas in a more aggressive fashion. As a result, normative scholars are calling for an expanded and more invasive role for organizations such as the United Nations and European Union. This includes enabling international organizations to work both within and across societies and to concentrate on both civil and political dilemmas. From a normative perspective, then, the globalized character of political problems demands mechanisms of governance that can rise above the self-regarding character of states and the commercial interests of economic actors to focus squarely on genuinely transnational dilemmas. To be sure, such mechanisms will not exclusively be able to ensure more promising human prospects. According to contemporary normative scholarship, however, they are still very much a part of the equation of humane global governance.

While international regimes and organizations have been part of normative IR fare for decades if not centuries, new entities and domains are arising that present promising objects of analysis. The most celebrated among contemporary normative thinkers is the growing societal dimension of global life. As mentioned, the world is presently experiencing an increasing level of societal interdependence spawned by innovations in transboundary travel and communication technologies. This is enabling people more easily to communicate, organize themselves, and express their aspirations across state boundaries. One result is a thickening of associational life at the global level that is taking place outside the rubric of states and the world economy. That is, there is an intersocietal dimension to globalization that is beginning to come into its own. Social movements, churches, unions, political parties, and clubs of all sorts now transcend state boundaries and foster transnational affiliations. As such, an amorphous yet analytically distinct sphere is beginning to exist at the global level in which people can collectively express their aspirations and pursue joint enterprises independently of their association with a particular state and outside their identity as a producer and consumer. Put in a way more relevant to normative IR, there is a rich associational life at the global level that is sufficiently free from the dynamics of the state system and the global economy to constitute a domain of global collective life unto its own. Although imprecise, scholars have begun to label this domain "global civil society," and normative thinkers have begun to look toward it for promising forces in the service of human good (Shaw 1994; Falk 1995; Wapner 1996).

For centuries, political thinkers have studied and explained the significance of domestic civil society. Domestic civil society is that slice of associational life that exists above the individual and below the state wherein people voluntarily organize themselves to undertake joint aims. While there is some disagreement as to whether civil society includes the economy (many in the liberal tradition see it as doing so), most contemporary renditions distinguish civil society from both the state and the economy (Cohen and Arato 1992). In a useful metaphor, Marc Nerfin (1989) distinguishes these realms by suggesting that the state is the realm of the prince, the economy the realm of the merchant, and civil society the realm of the citizen (4–5, quoted in Korten 1990, 96). His point is that the actions that take place within civil society are qualitatively different from those of the other two realms. Motivated not by economic gain and behaving free from the preordained patterns emanating from official authority, the citizen represents someone who can develop civic-minded orientations. Citizens work, for example, to hold government officials and economic actors accountable to the public at large. They develop philanthropic and public-minded institutions. They establish organizations that, internally, instill habits of cooperation and public spiritedness and, externally, enhance social collaboration and solidarity (Putnam 1993, 89–90). With the rise of global civil society, many normative thinkers see the same benefits accruing to, and tasks being undertaken by, the "global citizen."

Global civil society is constituted by, among other actors and forces, transnational social movements, and these represent the institutional locale of the global citizen. While certainly not benign across the board,[9] many such movements undertake the kind of civic-minded work of their domestic counterparts. The difference is that they must operate in a vastly broader political terrain marked by complexities having to do with multiple layers of authority and community. This, as some of the chapters that follow point out, requires devising innovative strategies that can effectively engage local and national politics, regional economic and political activities, interstate behavior, and transnational social mores. Global citizenship finds its expression in organizations such as Amnesty International, Greenpeace, and Oxfam. These groups work, respectively, for human rights, environmental protection, and the eradication of hunger around the world and thus work with people regardless of their national affiliation or economic status. To be sure, the specific strategies and orientations of particular groups are open to criticism and do not, themselves, instantiate a global interest. But such organizations clearly transcend the self-regarding character of states and the commercialized interests of economic actors. For this reason, normative thinkers consider many of them promising agents of progressive social change.

In addition to transnational social movements and the domain of global civil society, there is renewed normative interest in local movements and small-scale community-based politics. This may seem counterintuitive given the increasing globalized character of world affairs and the seeming need to identify and enlist forms of governance that straddle state boundaries. For many normative thinkers, however, such a focus is a direct consequence of a more globalized political reality. As interests and power consolidate across state boundaries, local practices become threatened and often disappear. There is a homogenization of sorts that takes place with regard to economic, cultural, social, and political life. For normative thinkers, this homogenization supports, and at times causes, many contemporary injustices. In such a world, then, normative thinkers work to preserve and amplify the dissident voices as a way to find patterns of life that may be more just and humane. Like the Falkian injunction to heed those voices outside the main centers of power because they can yield some of the most productive normative insight about the ruling order, contemporary normative thinkers look to local movements and community-based politics for penetrating critiques of globalization and the current world order and for potential models of resistance and reconstruction. To be sure, scholars do not understand such voices necessarily as realistic candidates for global governance—indeed, dissident expression often calls for distancing particular communities from the dynamics of economic and political globalization—but listen carefully to such criticisms for their subversive and imaginative capabilities. As will be seen in a number of the following chapters, investigating the political promise of local life is an important preoccupation of contemporary normative IR.

Taken as a whole, the vision that emerges with regard to political agency is a dual search both below and above the arena of the state system and world economy, with a focus especially on the civil dimension of collective life. In asserting this preference, it must be noted that the civil dimension does not operate in a vacuum but is part and parcel of the state system and the world economy. In fact, the three realms mutually constitute one another. Put differently, the distinction between the state system, world economy, and global civil society is analytic. Empirically, it is virtually impossible to demarcate the edge of one sphere and the beginning of another. As a result, all three spheres are involved in global governance in that activities in each realm shape widespread thought and behavior. For this reason, you will not find an ontological privileging of the civil dimensions of contemporary affairs in *Principled World Politics* even if you will find an ideological one. Moreover, an appreciation for the political promise of civil society does not render the other realms ineffective. As mentioned, and as will be seen, the state system and the world economy are themselves key nodes in global governance, and a number of authors focus their attention on reforming these domains in the service of human betterment.

Traversing the Postmodern Divide

The third challenge, in light of which scholars are fashioning new normative approaches, has to do with intellectual developments associated with poststructuralism. As mentioned, normative IR was marginalized partly because of the scientistic underlay that animated much social inquiry, and new opportunities are now emerging as this underlay erodes in the midst of widespread skepticism about the nature of scientific knowledge. Notwithstanding the benefits this has for normative IR, the tradition of normative thought is not itself immune from this erosion; it cannot simply reemerge intact from under the debris of what marginalized it. Although it does not share all the assumptions that characterize social science as a science, it is still a child of the Enlightenment. Thus, it is subject to much of the poststructural criticism aimed at modern thought in general. The normative IR that is emerging, then, is not simply old wine in a new bottle but has had to innovate itself to be relevant in a postmodern age. Although it is difficult to capture in a phrase, it could be characterized as a complex amalgamation: a combination of the long-standing practice of using moral outrage and progressive commitment to analyze world politics and a postmodern sensitivity to how even the most well intentioned analyses involve social distortion, hegemonic aspiration, and their own forms of injustice.

Modern normative IR theory emerged within two related and overlapping theoretical traditions: idealism and liberalism. While each school of thought has many branches (encouraging one to talk about idealisms[10] and liberalisms[11]), both share an optimistic view of human possibility. That is, both believe that the quality of human life can be continually improved, and both assume that concerted human activity is at the heart of such progress. Given this orientation, normative work has traditionally consisted of identifying certain valued ends whose realization will, it is claimed, improve the human condition or, contrarily, of identifying particular injustices whose eradication would enhance the quality of human life. A prime example of this work is the long-standing focus on the abolition of war. As is well known, idealism emerged out of a normative commitment to remove the "scourge of war" from human experience, and much liberalism has been devoted to identifying emerging forces, such as increased trade or the diffusion of democracy, that may diminish the war-prone character of world politics. War is seen, by both of these schools of thought, as an evil that can and should be eliminated and thus is part of the idealist and liberal normative agenda. The carrying out of such an agenda has a long tradition and can be associated with what some call "explicit normative thought."[12]

In the light of poststructuralism, explicit normative thought appears naive. Poststructural criticism demonstrates that it is impossible to identify a given good, in an absolute sense, and then simply work out strategies for its realization. Scholars have become too clever for such enterprises. Poststructuralism is marked by what Lyotard (1984) calls an "incredulity toward metanarratives" (xxiv). It maintains that all knowledge is socially constructed rather than ascertained by direct, accurate perception of the so-called real world, and thus there is an extreme skepticism about all claims to definitive knowledge. When scholars deliberately advance a notion of the good, then, they are not, according to poststructuralists, providing a vision that clearly improves the human prospect so much as trying to instantiate conditions that more closely approximate their own predilections. This is the case, by the way, not only for normative thought but for all forms of scholarship as well: Poststructuralism reminds us of the implicit prescriptive quality of all intellectual work. But it poses particular challenges to the tradition of normative IR. If normative IR involves bringing moral sensitivity to one's scholarship in the hopes of augmenting the quality of life on earth, and if the mere act of articulating a particular end itself is subject to deconstruction, then the tradition of normative work comes under direct attack. Indeed, many would say that poststructuralism has rendered explicit normative IR excessively incredulous.[13]

How does one proceed in such an intellectual environment? How can a normatively oriented scholar justify one's work in a poststructuralist world? How can one gain a purchase point to analyze political phenomena if any move to do so is fraught

with ontological and epistemological difficulties that can never, seemingly, be overcome? How can one engage in normative IR when all scholarship is normative?
There are, of course, no easy answers to these questions. In fact, the idea of finding answers to such questions may be the wrong way to think about poststructuralism. The poststructural critical challenge is not a puzzle in search of a solution but
rather an invitation to ask new kinds of questions and to assume a position toward
inquiry that is mindful of scholarship's own predispositions and hegemonic effects.
The normatively driven scholar, as illustrated throughout *Principled World Politics,* operates in this environment by engaging in a number of tasks. The first task is
to dismantle the categories of knowledge that presently set the terms for thinking
about social reality. The aim is to demonstrate that current conditions are not, inevitably, meant to be but, rather, are the result of certain historical contingencies. Deconstruction of what we take to be social reality is thus a key task of the normative
thinker. So much contemporary collective life is animated by cultural, economic,
political, and social dynamics that support obvious forms of injustice and yet that
seem necessary or at least unavoidable. Contemporary instances of torture, rape,
hunger, and so forth take place without much critical analysis of the structures that
support such behavior and experience. Yes, people abhor such atrocities and speak
out against particular instances of them, but the atrocities often appear so much a
part of the fabric of what we take to be reality that their root causes and underlying
justifications rarely come under scrutiny. The normative thinker plays an important
role in exposing the constructed quality of such phenomena and the structures that
underlie them. A dimension of the new normative IR involves, then, deconstructing
the social texts that we take for granted and helping people rethink the authority
behind some of our most sacred, but perhaps debilitating, social structures.[14] Almost
all the chapters in this book, to one degree or another, deconstruct the ruling ideas
that currently animate much economic, political, and social life and see this as an
important form of normative scholarship.

The second task involves writing in such a manner that one's analysis remains
constantly open to criticism and revision and invites dialogue. Poststructural thinkers often assume an ironic stance toward their own scholarship because they understand that their work is not "true" in any definitive sense but simply a stance assumed in a given context and informed by certain predispositions (see Rorty 1989;
Thiele 1997). Thus, in addition to writing abstract tracts explaining the critical posture of poststructuralism, many poststructuralists focus on particular events or activities. This particularity grounds the perspective of the theorist in an actual setting
and thus limits the generalizing tendencies inherent in most forms of scholarship. It
reminds the reader that the analysis is subject to the changing interpretive and material contexts of the events or activities under study. Thus, in the following pages,
whether an author is trying to understand the role of norms in reducing the ravages
of war, the promise of social movements in ameliorating the social dislocations associated with economic globalization, or the potential of corporate accountability
schemes to improve environmental quality, he or she generally couches the discus-

sion in a manner mindful of contingency and with a particular empirical focus. Almost all attempts to think carefully about human betterment are grounded in specific contexts, and these provide both the point of departure for insight and the limitations of universalizing tendencies.

In addition to contextualizing one's subject, a sensitivity to the contingent character of phenomena also encourages a dialogue between readers and author. According to many poststructuralists, in a world dominated by people making pronouncements about the character of human experience, it is important to employ forms of expression that attempt not only to persuade readers concerning a given insight but also to empower readers to formulate a response. This is consistent with the poststructuralist appreciation for the constant renegotiation of meaning associated with expression itself and for the necessity of recognizing the so-called other and of being recognized by the other.[15] This orientation is, of course, not unique to poststructuralism but finds some of its clearest justification in a poststructural turn of mind. Plato's use of dialogue is perhaps one of the earliest representatives of this form of expression.[16] The dialogic form itself reflects a quality of openness that forbids definitive conclusion. It is unable to present the world as a fixed, coherent entity in which all elements of a given subject can conceptually be tied neatly together. Rather, dialogue insists on the never-ending quality of judgments, understandings, and actions and works merely to contribute to the ongoing practice of reflection upon, conversation about, and action within the world. The chapters that make up *Principled World Politics* do not themselves use a dialogic form and indeed make pronouncements about contemporary conditions. Yet the reader will also find that the chapters employ a way of relating that is tentative. Almost all the chapters seek more to raise questions than to provide answers. They work to engage the reader's intellectual, emotional, spiritual, and, above all, moral sense, and the authors find that they can do this best by "discussing" topics with their readers rather than "lecturing" to them.

The final task of the normative scholar in a poststructural age comes from the challenge of poststructuralism itself. Let us say that the normative scholar restricts oneself to particular events and actions, is mindful of contingency, invites dialogue, and deconstructs reigning structures of power. One might reasonably ask, however, where the author is standing, as it were, when one does so. How does a given scholar actually take a normative stance in the midst of such openness? How does one formulate a deliberate normative perspective while being sensitive to the relative quality of perception and the constructed quality of knowledge? Indeed, reading the following chapters, one might ask how an author can claim, for example, that the widening divide between the rich and the poor due to globalization is detrimental, that the patenting of life forms associated with the commercialization of biodiversity is an "evil," or that denying people certain so-called "rights" is somehow "wrong."

Taking a normative stand does not mean solving the philosophical puzzles of relativism or the socially constructed quality of human experience. It does not mean, in other words, finding the so-called view from nowhere and positioning oneself at an

Archimedean point. It does require, however, that one make judgments as to which activities appear most oppressive or which speak most closely to one's sense of moral probity. That is, it requires one to *take* a stand rather than to find one already waiting, one endowed with privilege and insuperability. To be sure, in taking a stand, the language and strategies that one uses are, themselves, subject to criticism for being exploitative or unjust, and the choice itself belies the contingent nature of the enterprise. But language and strategy are the only instruments that humans beings have to engage the world, and the activity of making choices is inherent in the human condition. Engaging in normative work, then, is like using a "thorn to remove a thorn." One uses imperfect tools to work on a broken world. The stands that the authors in this book take, then, are not grounded in any metaphysical justification and enjoy no privilege aside from the status of emerging from the honest expression of personal choice. That choice is open to be reflected upon, and others are invited to join in solidarity with the authors' sense of moral outrage or to reject it. The reasoning behind the stances taken in this book, to put it differently, does not come from "on high" but, rather, emerge out of the authors' engagements with various phenomena refracted through their own moral sensibilities.

It is the mark of contemporary normative IR that it does not ignore poststructural quandaries but, rather, emboldens itself by engaging them. Most of the authors represented in *Principled World Politics* are not themselves poststructuralists, but each is keenly aware of the intellectual and political significance of poststructuralism. The following chapters represent encounters with poststructuralism by those who wish to improve the human prospect.

PRINCIPLED WORLD POLITICS

Contemporary normative thought is fashioning itself in light of the challenges of poststructuralism, globalization, and the search for promising political agency. The chapters that follow illustrate the way in which authors wrestle with these challenges and indicate the general character of twentieth-century normative IR. This chapter, then, serves not merely as an exposition on the quality of contemporary normative work but also as a thematic introduction to the book as a whole. The chapters that follow are diverse. They emerge out of the adventuring minds and compassionate hearts of some extraordinary individuals. Distilling and characterizing their work, as I have done here, necessarily requires much simplification and generalization. Individually, perhaps none of the authors stakes out an intellectual terrain identical to the one I have described. Nonetheless, the portrait that I have sketched captures, at least in crude form, the overall quality of the type of thought expressed throughout the book and the type of thought that will construct normative IR as it develops in the new millennium.

The overall structure of the book is organized along different lines. As I explained earlier, this framework emerges out of the occasion of honoring Richard Falk. The first part, "Critical Perspectives on International Relations," examines the role of normative thought within the tradition of IR theory. It consists of chapters that interrogate the tradition of IR and that locate the place and highlight the significance of normative thought. The book begins in this manner to underline the way theory itself constructs political practices. Falk has always maintained that the way in which people comprehend the world has a tremendous impact on how they act within it. That is, categories of thought largely shape widespread human practices. The discipline of IR, in particular, plays an important role on this score insofar as it has a significant impact on the way government officials, international civil servants, activists, and ordinary citizens politically understand and act within the world. Mindful of the discipline's influence, many of Falk's contributions have come in the form of critically evaluating the tradition of IR scholarship and international law. The first part of *Principled World Politics* follows this lead. It assumes that how we think matters for the world that we create and that critical self-understanding, which includes keen analysis of IR as a discipline, is an important component of normative IR.

The following four parts of the book are more empirically based and explore the relationship between normative theory and particular political practices. They do so under the rubric of four world-order values. As mentioned, Falk has always seen scholarship as value oriented and has worked to win widespread acceptance of certain WOMP values for analyzing, critically assessing, and prescribing world affairs. The success of his work is evident in that much contemporary normative IR is organized—to be sure, often implicitly—under the rubric of WOMP values.[17] The core, substantive chapters of *Principled World Politics* are thus organized into the following parts: "Social Justice," "Economic Well-Being," "Peace," and "Humane Governance." The chapters in each part represent efforts to criticize contemporary conditions that frustrate the achievement of such values and envision arrangements that would foster a more just, economically viable, peaceful, and humane world order.

Since this book was conceived to honor Richard Falk, it seemed appropriate to include at least one chapter that focused specifically on his work. In chapter 22, Saul Mendlovitz, a longtime colleague and friend of Falk's, reflects on Falk's contribution to WOMP and the normative tradition.

The final chapter abstracts from the various chapters throughout the book and explains how justice sits at the center of contemporary normative IR. It describes how justice is the underlying theme of *Principled World Politics* and how justice, as a world-order value, is the animating factor of new normative approaches. Indeed, the chapter makes evident how understanding the many faces of justice in a complex world is one of the critical challenges of normative thought in the twenty-first century.

NOTES

1. To be sure, this alliance evolved over time. Early realists of the twentieth century, such as Morgenthau, Spykman, and Herz, often expressed an antipositivistic orientation that com-

plicated realism's embrace of science. Moreover, as is well known, thinkers such as Morgenthau held normative commitments that were freely expressed in his scholarly writings. Over time, however, realism and science became closely affiliated. This association is perhaps most clear in the use of rational choice theory among neorealists, although it implicitly courses through most realist efforts to be value neutral. On the complex relation between realism and science, see Kahler (1997).

2. This is explored later in this chapter.

3. The following is not a review or an analysis of Richard Falk's scholarship. Given the prodigious profusion of Falk's work, such a task would be monumental. The following, rather, provides an outline of how a number of Falk's central concerns inform the book.

4. For an overview of this type of work, see Nardin and Mapel (1992).

5. This is not to say that every problem facing a collectivity is global in scope. See Wapner (1994).

6. Indeed, the substantive agenda of traditional normative thought itself reveals a state-centric orientation. See Mark Hoffman's (1994) review of normative IR.

7. See, for example, chapters 6 and 19 of this book.

8. For earlier expressions of this critique, see Falk (1971), Mische and Mische (1977), and Johansen (1980).

9. Many social movements, for example, are more interested in advancing parochial interests or inciting violence and supporting injustice than in forwarding more humane aims. See, for example, chapter 15 of this book.

10. For a review of idealist thought that begins before World War I and the formal emergence of IR as a discipline, see Schmidt (1995).

11. For a comprehensive treatment of the various strands of international liberal thought, see Zacher and Matthews (1995).

12. Steve Smith (1992) refers to the conventional normative tradition as engaging in "explicit normative discussions" (490). This characterization is similar to the one that Mark Hoffman (1994) calls "overt normative orientations" (28).

13. Of course, as will be seen shortly, poststructuralist IR thought can be seen as the paradigmatic form of normative IR. For an explanation of this and an illustration of poststructuralism as normative IR in general, see Ashley and Walker (1990) and Walker (1993).

14. Deconstruction, along these lines, usually involves performing genealogies of persistent myths that have been reified through ahistorical orientations. Genealogies call into question the essentialized identities, origins, and structural character of the authority systems that animate collective life. On genealogy in general, see Foucault (1980). For an explanation of the importance of genealogy in IR, see Der Derian (1997).

15. For the relevance of acknowledging the "other" in IR scholarship, see Ashley and Walker (1990) and Der Derian (1997).

16. On the quality of dialogue and its engagement with the reader, see Bakhtin (1981).

17. Simply stated, most normative work focuses on issues of peace, economic well-being, social justice, ecological balance, and humane governance.

2

Both Globalization and Sovereignty: Re-Imagining the Political

R. B. J. Walker

This book provides a portrait of normative international relations at the millennium. Many of the chapters analyze the prospects for creating a more humane world order by investigating specific instances of injustice, exploitation, and violence. In this chapter, I want to explore some of the broader theoretical challenges that confront contemporary normative scholarship in general. I especially want to do so by interrogating the meaning of politics, which is now so often counterposed to ethics and moral action and is thereby both ignored and simply taken for granted in so many contemporary accounts of what it means to engage in normative theory or practice.

LOOKING FOR THE POLITICAL

The most challenging political problems of our time, I want to claim, arise primarily from a need to re-imagine what we mean by politics. I make this claim not to deny the pressing importance of other and somehow more tangible political problems, many of them matters of life and death for thousands of people. Rather, I make it to insist that questions about what is to be done about many of these apparently more tangible problems demand serious rethinking about the agencies and authorities that are empowered to act, and the conditions under which their actions carry some legitimacy. While there is obviously no shortage of agencies claiming authority, neither their capacities to act nor their capacities to sustain the legitimacy of their actions are as clear-cut as they would have us believe. More crucially, it is becoming less clear what a capacity to act, or what a capacity to sustain a claim to legitimate authority, could or should mean under contemporary conditions.

This point has often been made in relation to speculations about the declining significance of state sovereignty as the primary principle guiding our prevailing sense of what we mean by power and authority. It has been made with increasing frequency in relation to claims about the significance of what is so awkwardly and promiscuously referred to as globalization. These claims are usually vague and highly contentious. None of us has sufficient historical perspective or epistemological expertise to offer much more than very partially substantiated judgments in this context. But if they do indeed carry some credibility as indicators of ways in which cultures, economies, and societies have been shifted and shaken by the modernities and capitalisms of the twentieth century, then some sense of the need to re-imagine what and where we take politics to be is simply inescapable.

Aristotle was right to insist that we are all political beings. Latter-day Aristotelians are also right to insist that much of what we are now encouraged to call politics, whether in the name of representation, the market, or rational choice, has been profoundly depoliticized. Politics is not reducible to the administration of things or to a rational calculus of individual self-interest. On the contrary, the rationalization of modern capitalism and the hegemony of utilitarianism only make it more difficult to identify what and where politics now occurs. Still, Aristotle's world is increasingly unfamiliar to us. Whether reworked as a theory of states or of republics, whether reclaimed by Jean-Jacques Rousseau, Karl Marx, or Leo Strauss, Aristotle now names a nostalgia for worlds we think we knew. These are the worlds that grant a certain coherence and plausibility to our sense of knowing what we mean when we talk about politics.

Most of us do indeed still think that we know what we are talking about when we speak about politics. Even now, remarkably few political theorists have qualms about replaying the old categories again and again like organ grinders in the street. Politics, we know, has something to do with powers and politicians, with governance and constitutions, with economies, identities, and violence. It is not always a pretty sight. We know it when we see it, however, precisely because we assume that it has a site, a location within which it occurs, or beyond which it can occur only in the most attenuated forms.

Aristotle invoked the polis. We invoke the state. Without the inheritance of the polis or the achievements of the state, we would certainly not speak about politics the way we do now. We might refer to crude indices of power. We might still refer to economies, governance, and the rest, and defer to generalized logics of power and utility. But the most crucial puzzles of politics, we also know, rest less on logics of power and utility than on the possibilities of legitimate authority. It is in this context that the problems of contemporary politics, and not least about the potentialities of democratization, have become most intense. It is in relation to questions about legitimate authority that the difficulties of speaking about and re-imagining the possibilities of politics have become most perplexing. In some respects, in fact, we both think we know what we are talking about when we speak about politics and also have lost much of our capacity to speak about politics precisely because we so readily assume that all questions about legitimate authority are sufficiently answered by reference to the achievements of the state, by the place where politics is supposed to be. It is this assumption that allows us to speak so easily about politics, to take for granted all our received answers to all the hard questions about the sources and agencies of authority, but also to do so in ways that seem increasingly at odds with contemporary articulations of power.

Knowing where we are, we persuade ourselves that pressing problems of public policy can be dealt with by this or that authority here or there representing this or that political community. Then we read the business pages and the words of strategic analysts. We marvel at the flows of trade and capital, the flexible locations of production, the circulations of information, the Groups of Seven or Eight, and the mysteries of the European Community, the North American Free Trade Agreement (NAFTA), or the Association of Southeast Asian Nations (ASEAN). We try to decipher who makes what decisions where, and under what conditions. We try not to think too much about the massive debt burdens that shrivel the lives of the world's poorest peoples. We find scholars talking about human security, global ecologies, or distinctions between an international and a global political economy. We find international lawyers speaking as though states are not the only subjects of international law. We find interdependencies and neocolonialisms, functional regimes, resurgent religious and ethnic communities, and overlapping citizenships. We find local activists acting globally, global cities fusing transnational cultural identities, and the claims of humanitarian intervention conflicting ever more unsatisfactorily with the claims of domestic jurisdiction. Our prevalent maps are elegant, highly detailed, and generally sufficient to forestall vertigo among the more privileged, but the dragons of the unknown world are no longer simply decorous motifs on the margin. The nationalist rhetorics of the commentators and scholars may be difficult to ignore, but the narratives they relate increasingly suggest that it is becoming as futile to look for politics where it is supposed to be as it is to look for power down the barrel of a gun.

BEING WHERE WE SHOULD BE

There are many ways to characterize contemporary struggles to re-imagine politics. Most of them are animated by some sense of a profound historical shift away from a world of more or less sovereign states to a world that is somehow global. Theoretical orientations and the selection and interpretation of empirical trends vary enormously in this context. It may well be that the broad brush and the rhetorical flourish prevail at the expense of close detail and fine distinctions. There is almost certainly an unfortunate tendency to exaggerate the novelty of many contemporary trends. States, nations, great powers, and arms races remain with us, though not as they once may have been. But crucial structures seem to have shifted. Long-standing dynamics have been transformed. It is quite probable that what appear to us to be sharp disjunctions may well come to look like gradual transitions to later generations, like yet another ripple among great transformations that were already well under way over a century ago. But it is now very difficult indeed to avoid concluding that however we characterize the historical and structural transformations that are so casually invoked in references to globalization, they present significant challenges to the primary categories of modern politics, especially as these were laid out in early modern Europe.

It was in early modern Europe, of course, that politics came to be reframed, against the prevailing hierarchies of feudalism, empire, and theology, in relation to the spatial terrain of the modern state, to the polis reborn in an age of modernizing capitalism and global imperialism. This was the context in which the modern world worked out its conceptions of sovereignty, identity, community, subjectivity, obligation, and interest. These were the achievements that permitted subsequent generations to develop practices of nationalism, liberalism, socialism, democracy, and the rest. If the most challenging political problems of our time involve re-imagining what we mean by politics, it is necessary to do so especially in relation to our now almost automatic reversion to the categories and rhetorics of that era. Much of the difficulty with prevailing literatures analyzing contemporary challenges to state sovereignty, for example, is that these literatures so easily revert to the early modern philosophical categories that are themselves part of the practices through which state sovereignty was articulated in the first place. And much of the difficulty with prevailing accounts of globalization as a form of political economy is that they are so easily fractured into, on the one hand, an economic analysis that is explicitly designed to avoid questions about politics entirely and, on the other, a political analysis that also easily reverts to images of politics contained within a sovereign territorial state. Much the same problem has bedeviled attempts to think more creatively about politics in the past, especially under banners proclaiming emancipation and radical change. Even the great nineteenth-century prophets of historical transformation remained entranced by the political wisdom of an earlier age in this respect.

We all now know where we are supposed to be. This is what allows us to persuade ourselves that we know what politics must be as well. Our normative commitments have even been able to masquerade as the necessities of political realism, that account of what must happen when the normative ideals of the modern state reach their territorial limit. Whether the politics of our contemporary situations or our possible futures can be adequately grasped on the basis of normative commitments of this kind, however, remains an open question, though one that is increasingly difficult to answer in the affirmative. But it is also very difficult to answer in any way at all because the terms in which questions about emerging forms of politics continue to be framed are themselves constituted through the very concepts of politics that seem so at odds with so many contemporary circumstances.

SOVEREIGNTY AS DUALISM

It is especially striking that contemporary discussions about state sovereignty and globalization have come to be framed in terms of two seemingly contradictory forms of common sense. On the one hand, state sovereignty and globalization are taken to be incompatible opposites. On the other, they are seen as long-standing complementarities. Each framing comes in both popular and highly sophisticated variants, as statements of the obvious and as assumptions informing elaborately self-conscious theorizations.

We perhaps find it easiest to think about globalization as a simple alternative to, or a negation of, the modern state or system of modern states. This framing is often articulated as an opposition between political realism as a celebration of the necessity of state interests and a political idealism that celebrates the potentiality of some kind of universality, some global or human community. It is a framing that occurs most frequently as a seemingly natural assumption that if the modern state is being challenged, there must be some kind of withering away of the state and the emergence of some kind of supranational authority somewhere "above" the state. Developments in the United Nations, in the European Community, or among multinational corporations, for example, have especially been read and misread on this basis. Globalization, it is said, must imply a decline of the state; as a corollary, evidence of the continuing vitality of states must imply that claims about globalization are merely "globalony." The rhetorical force of this apparently straightforward choice is quite overwhelming, though not because there is a shred of evidence to suggest that this is the most sensible way of posing questions about either the fate of modern states or the potential significance of globalizing tendencies.

This dualistic framing coexists with one that emphasizes complementarity. Several variations on the theme may be identified, especially those that draw our attention to the embeddedness of the modern state within structures that have been in some sense global from the outset and to the paradoxes of universality and particularity that are expressed in the principle of sovereignty itself. It is this pattern of embeddedness, and the paradoxical or dialectical character of state sovereignty that it implies, that produces a rhetoric of alternatives to state sovereignty that already presumes the natural necessity of state sovereignty and thus the impossibility of reimagining politics on any other basis.

We can insist, for example, that the rise of the modern state and the states system has been coextensive with the rise of capitalism as a globalizing form of production, distribution, and exchange. From Marx to Karl Polanyi, Immanuel Wallerstein, Robert Cox, and other contemporary international political economists, we can assume that there is some kind of connection between particularizing states and globalizing capitalism, even though we also know that everyone has found it a bit difficult to say what this connection is with any great precision.

Alternatively, we can insist that the rise of the modern state and states system is coextensive with some kind of overarching cultural community, or sequence of communities, specifically those identified with the pseudo-universalisms of Christianity, Europe, and modernity. The sense that particular states, and the supposedly anarchical structure of the states system, challenge any overarching universality, and that sovereignty is a claim to separation and autonomy from any higher authority, is mitigated by the contrary sense that states nevertheless participate in some more collective order, whether of Christian ethics, European diplomatic culture, or, now, principles of modern reason and processes of modern rationalization. Again, quite how this participation works remains a bit puzzling, generating considerable theoretical controversy, but the need to work with a dialectical or complementary understanding of sovereignty and globalizing tendencies is not controversial at all. The notion that we are the (plural) peoples of the (singular) United Nations, for example, is simply a formal acknowledgment that our sovereign autonomies and our differences are somehow inseparable from our similarities as participants in some broader collective enterprise to which terms such as "humanity" and "global" are easily attached.

Most incisively, we can insist that the principle of sovereignty itself already expresses a necessary relationship between some sort of global or at least general system or structure and the particularity or autonomy of states. This relationship takes the form of a basic contradiction that might be expressed in two forms.

In one form, sovereignty can be read as a claim to a monopoly of legitimate authority in a particular territory, but only while recognizing that this claim already depends on a wider system of states that enables that claim to be recognized and operationalized. This is because sovereignty cannot be simply a claim to a monopoly or a particularity, as the usual definitions would have it, because only in some broader context could such a claim be either plausible or recognized. This is what gives rise to claims about the so-called society of states analyzed by scholars sensitive to the customs, legal regimes, and institutions generated by states to facilitate their mutual relation. In a more minimalist form, it animates some versions of the so-called logic of anarchy that supposedly explains the action of any specific state in a system of states.

In another form, sovereignty can be read as an account of both one system and many states, of both a general and a quasi-universal reason that informs the logic of the system and the many states that may or may not behave in accordance with that general or quasi-universal reason.

In either rendition, far from being an account of a claim to a monopoly, to an affirmation of difference and the absence of commonality, sovereignty expresses and works to reproduce a specific relation between claims to difference and claims about the forms of commonality and structure that permit claims to monopoly to have any meaning at all.

It is in this sense that sovereignty is a principle of modern *politics* and not just a principle of international relations. It is an expression of a politics that works both inside states and outside states, indeed as a principle that tells us why we must put up with a politics that is radically split between statist political communities and relations between such communities. It is in this sense also that sovereignty is a principle of *modern* politics and has to be understood in part as a specifically modern account of what the world is and how it can be known, as well as a specifically political authorization of states as legitimate political authorities.

DRAWING THE LINE

It may be that the most crucial move in thinking about contemporary politics over the past decade or so has been a rather bemused remembering that sovereignty is not simply an abstract principle fit only for constitutional lawyers and rather conservative political theorists. Still less is it simply an obvious assumption that theorists of international relations can use to ground their claims about states and national interests. As with the concept of the modern individual or the modern aesthetics of representation and three-dimensional perspective, we have largely forgotten about the tremendous historical changes and levels of violence that went into making sovereignty seem like a simple theoretical principle. In fact, it expresses, in a highly condensed form, an entire modern cosmology.

The broad outlines of this story are well known. Theological authority and the claims of an overarching empire once came to be challenged by particular powers and, eventually, by claims to monopolistic authority in particular states. This is not an easy story to tell, of course, not least because all the great categories under which some semblance of a coherent narrative has usually been attempted—the Protestant Reformation, the Scientific Revolution, the emergence of modern capitalism and new technologies, and so on—have become exceedingly elusive; but, however one reads this story (or melange of stories), it focuses centrally on the collapse of prevailing forms of legitimate authority expressed as a hierarchy under heaven and the gradual emergence of a different account expressed as sovereign rule over particular territories: sovereign states. The practice was long and violent. The conceptual shift was not easy either. It required a massive transition from thinking about a world of natural hierarchies capped by a great leap of faith from earthly temporality to heavenly eternity to a world of modern subjects separated in a horizontal space. This was the world mapped out by scientists and philosophers such as Galileo, Descartes, and Hobbes. This was the new modern world of spatial separations, of subjects separated from objects, of men separated from nature. It was a world that had to some extent been foreseen both by the Renaissance artists with their representational perspectives and by the late medieval theologians and their nominalist challenges to Aristotelian realism/essentialism.

Crucially, this was a shift that required redrawing the line that was previously drawn between earth and heaven, between the secular city of man and the sacred city of God, a line drawn on a vertical axis of above and below. It was redrawn as a line between man and world, between man and man, and between collections of men and other collections of men, between states. It was a line now drawn on a horizontal rather than a vertical axis. This is how we came to achieve the modern conception of subjectivity, the modern conception of what it means to be a modern self or a modern state, separated from, yet somehow linked to, other selves and other states. And just as the great gap between the temporalities and finitudes of earth and the infinities and eternities of heaven was posed as the great problem for a Christian theological universe, a problem that nonetheless guaranteed the legitimacy of the ranks and orders below, so also the rewritten gap between separated subjectivities has posed the great problem for us moderns, a problem that nonetheless serves to guarantee the legitimacy of modern subjectivities within.

Modern politics has become more a matter of drawing lines in horizontal space than of negotiating hierarchies and preparing for a final leap into infinity/eternity. Not least, it has become a matter of drawing lines between a proper politics within a specific territorial space and an absence of a proper politics beyond that space, whether in the explicitly international space of relations between states, in the time-less spaces reserved for those who inhabit the world beyond modernity, or, more positively, in the potentiality of a universal reason that might finally be brought down to earth, made immanent within modern spatially delineated subjects.

For modern subjects, for modern political theorists, the problem has been to find ways of affirming the possibility of some sort of universality within a particularity. Indeed, we have long been at a point at which the most privileged modern subjects, and not least the political theorists, have been able simply to assume that a particular state can simply be treated as a universal, as the natural ground on which all contra-dictions of human existence can be resolved. It has been the role of theorists of inter-national relations to remind us that the state is not the world, and the existence of particular states in a system of other particular states provides a puzzle that both enables and undermines the highest aspirations of all modern subjects and all politi-cal theories. Unfortunately, in this great division of intellectual labor, the puzzles and contradictions generated by sovereignty as a specifically modern rendition of the appropriate relationship between universality and particularity on the spatial terrain of the modern state have been replaced by crude reifications of the way things are on both sides of the line. The conditions under which this line was once drawn, or what was achieved by doing so, have largely slipped from our memory.

This is why state sovereignty is so easily misconceived as simply a claim to mo-nopolistic authority on the part of a particular state rather than as a specifically mod-ern resolution of a dialectical relationship, a point of both fusion of and demarcation between particularity and universality. The claim to sovereignty already contains within it an account of what the appropriate relationship between universality and particularity or diversity *must* be. Universality, or the possibility of globalization, is already both present and absent in the claim to sovereignty. Universality seems ab-sent because sovereignty seems to express a claim to particularity, to some national interest or nationalist identity. But it is present because it can only express this claim to particularity in a wider world, in a more general system or society or culture that makes this claim possible.

For example, one of the most problematic of contemporary political concepts of politics is that of citizenship. There has been considerable recent debate about whether citizenship makes sense only in relation to specific states or whether we might reasonably talk about some kind of global citizenship. This debate is funda-mentally misconceived, for although it is technically accurate to insist that citizen-ship expresses a claim to membership in a particular community, citizenship also expresses an aspiration to principles that are generally understood in highly universalizing terms. Citizenship expresses the great hope that people can eventually become humans precisely through their participation in particular states. This is the great hope expressed by Kant, the hope that we might be able to achieve a universality in the particular, to act on the basis of a universal law despite all our particularities. But it is no less a hope expressed by writers who are conventionally counterposed to Kant, the supposed idealist, for example, by Hobbes. And it is the hope that seems so utterly beyond the possibility of achievement to those, such as Max Weber, who have been most forthright in acknowledging the violence that results when hopes for universality in the particular turn out to be the celebration of a very parochial and particular understanding of universality.

Sovereignty expresses not only a specific account of the proper relationship between particularity and universality, but also a very specific understanding of space and time. Like the movement of hands across a clock face, sovereignty affirms a set of spatial demarcations. Inside, we can have an ordered space that permits in turn the possibility of a progressive history. Outside, we can have only the inevitability of contingency and the eternal return of primordial conflict, balances of power, and the permanently tragic wisdom of political realism at the limit of our normative ambitions. This is an account that meshes very uneasily with, say, contemporary patterns of internal war. Indeed, it is arguably an account that is difficult to reconcile with almost any credible narrative about the spatiotemporal organization of contemporary human existence.

It is at the limit of our modern normative ambitions, of course, that the common sense of complementarity gives way to the common sense of radical dualism. The latter is an effect of the former. The ease with which we are drawn to counterpose state sovereignty and globalization as mutually exclusive alternatives is a consequence of the way in which we have already framed state sovereignty in relation to a paradigmatic account of what globalization must be. But this framing, this account of the proper relationship between the sovereign state and the states system or society of states that makes this sovereign state possible—or, more generally, the relationship between modern subjectivities and the world that makes modern subjects possible—is always radically unstable. Kantian ethics sketches the abstract principles through which stability might be sustained in principle. Theories of international relations sketch the pragmatic rules of accommodation that have served to sustain some semblance of stability in practice, and to warn of the dire necessities and consequences of thinking that the modern resolution of universality and particularity in a spatial array of different political communities and subjectivities in a quasi-universal order could be anything but radically unstable. Despite all the criticisms that can be directed at the old political realists, it is their insistence on the radical instability of modern resolutions of universality and particularity expressed in the claim to state sovereignty that still forces us to take them seriously as theorists of modern politics. It is, for example, what sets them apart from the thin utilitarianisms of the contemporary neorealists.

While it is enshrined as an almost unchallengeable part of the common sense of our time, it makes little sense to frame questions about the future of either the state or globalization or the possibilities of politics more generally, as if state sovereignty and globalization are mutually exclusive alternatives. Neither political realism nor political idealism can usefully be read as alternative accounts of political possibility, but only as complementary ways of framing the consequences of the same specifically modern account of what politics must be. This framing is already an effect of ways of thinking about politics that assume that some form of globalization is already a precondition for the existence of the sovereign state. It is an effect of the way in which modern subjectivities in general and state sovereignty in particular are set up in a spatially delineated antagonism, as a relation of self and other, man and world, state and system-system that can be sustained only as long as it is possible to draw the line that allows each subjectivity to struggle to achieve universality within itself.

CHALLENGING THE MODERN SUBJECT

What is at stake in contemporary debates about the future of politics is not whether globalization as a process of quasi-universalization is undermining the state as the site of particularity. Rather, it is whether it is still possible to draw the line that has enabled the state to claim to be able to reconcile all contradictions between universality and particularity on a spatial terrain. If it is not possible to sustain a capacity to draw lines in this way, one should expect to see not a grand drift from a world of sovereign states to a world in which states have become defunct but rather a rewriting of the relationship between universality and particularity that states have insisted must be articulated within their territories.

What is arguably at the heart of contemporary transformations of political life, in fact, is neither the weakness of states (which may well be getting both stronger and weaker as they continue to transform along many dimensions) nor the novelty of globalization (although we may well be witnessing some crucially novel features and be in a major phase of accelerations in this respect) but the decreasing capacity of states everywhere to claim a monopoly on the legitimate resolution of all relations of unity and diversity and a decreasing capacity to delineate their subjectivities within from other subjectivities without. Whether or not states have the capacity to sustain their monopoly in this respect perhaps depends most crucially on five interrelated challenges.

First is the challenge of multiple subjectivities. Few states have ever measured up well to the ideal of a modern nation as a more of less homogeneous subjectivity. Most states have experienced enormous difficulty reconciling ethnic and regional differences and molding them into some semblance of a cohesive social order. In most, if not all, cases, the process of nation building has been, and in many places continues to be, spectacularly bloody. As many recent commentators have argued, however, the decade since the fall of the Berlin Wall has witnessed a considerable upsurge of ethnic, religious, and regional differences that have put even the most hard-nosed defenders of nation building on the defensive. Moreover, the very idea of an idealized singular identity, the ambition to turn cultural difference into a unified nation, has been put into suspicion on many fronts, not least because it has been associated with the oppressive forces of colonialism as much as it has with nationalist assaults against colonialism, or with a specifically male understanding of what it means to construct cultural collectivities.

In practice, political life does seem to be characterized increasingly by forms of accommodation to multiple subjectivities: to the functional disaggregation of citizenship in the European Community, to the differential rights and citizenships available to those who can afford to be mobile across borders, to the loosening of regional and national ties within states such as Belgium and Canada, to the elaboration of spheres of autonomy for aboriginal peoples in some countries, to speculations about various "levels" of governance, and so on. Many of the phenomena that are more usually read as symptoms of "failed states" or as the emergence of ethnic conflicts, warlords, and drug cartels in many places could perhaps be understood in this context as well. Whether as a practical matter or as a regulative ideal, the image of the homogeneous nation sustained around a clear identity within the clear territorial borders of a state has become fairly tattered. The idealized self-identical modern subject that informs the claims of state sovereignty, that carries our modern hopes for universality in particularity, may still be celebrated by some of the most eminent social and political theorists of our time, but only against a growing chorus of cynics and critics of its cultural parochialism.

Second, there is the challenge of multiple relationships, of signs of a shift from a world of compartmentalized spaces to a world of networks of connection that elude all containment. The conventional image of politics can be (and very often was) drawn as a system of black boxes, of colored spaces on the map. States were assumed to be homogeneous actors, and the relations that counted were relations between states. But just as the modern subject is being unbundled, so also is the space in which those subjects were contained being disaggregated into multiple sites, each connected to multiple other sites. The lines we draw are increasingly lines of connection between nodes rather than lines of separation between territorial spaces.

These lines of connection, of course, also imply new ways of distinguishing "included" and "excluded," and this suggests a third challenge: Contemporary lines of inclusion and exclusion are increasingly framed in a great many new ways and do not simply converge on the great zones of inclusion/exclusion at the territorial edges of states. Many contemporary patterns of inclusion and exclusion are constructed on the basis of cultural ascription, or around the fringes of large cities, or around free trade zones. The old categories of class and race are likewise failing to come to grips with forms of inclusion/exclusion within states precisely because inclusions/exclusions are articulated in patterns that cut across states. Most sociologists, for example, are in deep trouble in this respect.

Fourth, and similarly, there is the challenge arising from the degree to which contemporary life is characterized by movement and flows rather than attachments to territorial space. From the circulation of capital to the migrations of refugees and tourists and the activities of social movements, the valorization of speed and temporality over spatiality and geopolitics has made it more and more difficult to draw clear lines between here and there.

Finally, there is the challenge of simultaneity, not only in the sense of temporal convergence but also in the sense that states have lost much of their capacity to mediate between both the global and the local and between the outside and the inside. This capacity is crucial to a politics of state sovereignty. The local is that which owes allegiance to the state above it. The global is that which lies outside the state, whether as a system of states or a system of capitalism. And it is the state that seemingly mediates—that controls when inside may go outside, when outside may come inside, when the states system or global capitalism may impinge on its locales. But it is rather difficult to think about the politics of global cities in this way, or many of the practices of globally organized corporations when investing in specific places, or the practices of those diaspora that so confuse sharp distinctions between here and there. In many respects, outside is inside, the local is global. States still try to maintain control over their territorial jurisdictions, to patrol the borders, to orchestrate the nation. In the meantime, our most basic categories of space and time have twisted, contracted, expanded, and fractured.

It is possible, and indeed probable, that none of these challenges is especially novel. It is undoubtedly the case that states will continue to show enormous resilience in meeting these challenges and will insist on their capacity to draw lines in order to resolve all contradictions between universality and particularity on their spatial terrain. But this is where states are most vulnerable, and this is where our prevailing concepts of politics are most vulnerable as well.

There is no point in addressing this vulnerability by framing our future possibilities as a choice between states and globalization, between national citizenship and cosmopolitan ethics, between the dangerous parochialism of particular states and the hopeful universalism of some common humanity. There is no point because these are the choices that are already posed by the politics of state sovereignty, which forces us into an impossible dualism as a consequence of the necessary tragedies that enable our most elevated ambitions as modern subjects. What is at stake in re-imagining politics under contemporary conditions is the possibility that our most elevated (Kantian) ambitions, our impossibly autonomous and spatially monolithic subjectivities, do not have to monopolize our understanding of what it means to shape the claims of universality, difference, spatiality, temporality, or who we are or who we might become.

3

Normative and Complexity Theories: Complementary Approaches to World Affairs

James N. Rosenau

Slowly, hesitantly, and ambivalently, students of international relations (IR) are coming to appreciate the inextricable links between their normative perspectives and their empirical observations and theories. Comprehending these links has been a difficult struggle, hindered by a past in which extreme positions dominated: The first few decades after World War II were marked by scientific modes of inquiry that faltered when they could not resolve the dilemmas posed by nuclear weapons and a tragic and misguided war in Vietnam; then, as the scientific road appeared to be a dead end, many IR scholars turned to poststructural, postpositivist, and post-anything-but-scientific-empiricism approaches that were rooted in normative preoccupations and that also faltered when they seemed to have little impact on the genocidal conflicts that wracked the Balkans and Africa.

The major lesson of this contradictory past now seems obvious, as both extremes are both right and wrong: Human betterment cannot be expanded unless careful and systematic empirical observations are recorded, but at the same time the processes of observation are bound to derive from normative concerns. Since the whole story of any set of circumstances can never be told and explained (there is too much detail), there can be no observations without selecting out some of the circumstances as important and dismissing the others as trivial—that is, without making selections rooted in values preferences (Rosenau 1971, 1989).

In short, both the scientific and the normative enterprises need each other. Neither alone can advance our grasp of IR. Neither alone can come to terms with the enormous challenges of an ever more complex and changing world. Neither alone can make a lasting impact on policymaking processes. Normative judgments may underlie and precede empirical observations, but the judgments take on a fuller meaning only as they are amplified by systematic and reliable data gathered through the application of scientific theory and methods (Rosenau 1992; Rosenau and Durfee 1995). Anecdotes, single-case illustrations, inferences from experience, and critical assessments are not adequate as the bases for effective normative arguments. They may be insightful and supportive, but they are not nearly as persuasive as findings that systematically depict desirable or noxious patterns that can be addressed by the policies of governments or the actions of private organizations.

As necessary as the normative and scientific approaches are to each other, the relationship between them is a delicate and complicated one. Science can be tailored to serve normative preferences, and the latter can be adjusted to support scientific findings. Accordingly, IR analysts, having come to appreciate the inextricable links between the normative and the empirical, have to be clear about both the values that underlie their work and the limits to the truth claims permitted by their scientific inquiries. Accomplishing this clarity has been made all the more difficult by the deepening complexity of world affairs that has accompanied the end of the Cold War, the microelectronic revolution, and the onset of globalization in the economic and cultural realms. These dynamics have posed enormous questions, both normative and empirical: Are the processes of globalization good or bad for humankind? Are the strides in communication provided by the Internet and other technologies facilitating the dominance of the haves over the have-nots? Can viable theories be developed with which to probe empirically the growing complexities of local, national, and global life?

The ensuing discussion addresses only the last of these questions. It outlines a fledgling theory that may eventually serve to uncover and trace the complexities that mark the course of events at the start of a new millennium. And it is founded, to repeat, on the premise that whatever one's normative premises may be, they are better served if incisive empirical theories of how the world works can be developed and applied. Equally important, it cautions against excessive reliance on the fledgling theory, emphasizing that it is premature to reach conclusions as to its utility.

FAMILIAR PREMISES AND FLEDGLING THEORY

Although complexity theory is still very much a newcomer in the storehouse of social scientific tools, its underlying premises (noted shortly) have long been shared by many analysts. What is new is the explicitness and integration of these premises into a coherent whole that facilitates inquiry. Heretofore, social scientists have tended to ignore the premises of complexity theory by employing parsimonious models that treat the premises as exogenous conditions, as background factors rather than as variables that shape the course of events. Today, however, the normative and empirical uncertainties that mark world affairs are so widespread that many analysts no longer shrink from pondering exogenous factors and, instead, are increasingly prepared to build them into their models as endogenous dynamics. In short, while more than a few observers have always been rudimentary complexity theorists, today they are more ready than ever to acknowledge that if the price of relaxing their criteria of parsimony is a greater ability to discern patterns in phenomena that previously seemed too complex to manage analytically, it is a price worth paying.

At the same time, risks attach to the newfound potentials of complexity theory. Although little noticed, one can discern a discrepancy between our intellectual progress toward grasping the underlying complexity of human systems and our emotional expectation that advances in complexity theory may somehow point the way to policies that can ameliorate the uncertainties inherent in a fast-changing world. The links here are profoundly causal: The more uncertainty has spread since the end of the Cold War, the more analysts are inclined to seek panaceas for instability, and thus the more they have latched onto recent strides in complexity theory in the hope that they will yield solutions to the intractable problems that beset us. No less important, all these links—the uncertainty, the search for panaceas, and the strides in complexity theory—are huge, interactive, and still intensifying, thus rendering the causal dynamics ever more relevant to the course of events.

In short, all the circumstances are in place for an eventual disillusionment with complexity theory. For despite the strides, there are severe limits to the extent to which such theory can generate concrete policies that lessen the uncertainties of a rapidly changing world. And as these limits become increasingly evident subsequent to the present period of euphoria over the theory's potential utility, a reaction against it may well set in and encourage a reversion back to simplistic, either/or modes of thought. Such a development would be regrettable. Complexity theory does have insights to offer. It provides a cast of mind that can clarify, that can alert observers to otherwise unrecognized problems, and that can serve as a brake on undue enthusiasm for particular courses of action. But these benefits can be exaggerated and thus disillusioning. Thus, the central purpose of this chapter is to offer a layman's appraisal of both the potentials and the limits of complexity theory—to differentiate what range of issues and processes in world affairs it can be reasonably expected to clarify from those that are likely to remain obscure.

UNCERTAINTIES

That a deep sense of uncertainty should pervade world affairs since the end of the Cold War is hardly surprising. The U.S.-Soviet rivalry, for all its tensions and susceptibility to collapsing into nuclear holocaust, intruded a stability into the course of events that was comprehensible, reliable, and continuous. The enemy was known. The challenges were clear. The dangers seemed obvious. The appropriate responses could readily be calculated. Quite the opposite is the case today, however. If there are enemies to be contested, challenges to be met, dangers to be avoided, and responses to be launched, we are far from sure what they are. Thus, uncertainty is the norm and apprehension, the mood. The sweet moments when the wall came down in Berlin, apartheid ended in South Africa, and aggression was set back in Kuwait seem like fleeting and remote fantasies as the alleged post–Cold War order has emerged as anything but orderly. Whatever may be the arrangements that have replaced the bipolarity of U.S.-Soviet rivalry, they are at best incipient structures and at worst in widespread disarray.

Put differently, a new epoch can be said to be evolving. It is an emergent epoch of multiple contradictions—one that I have labeled "fragmegration" in order to summarily capture the tensions between the fragmenting and integrating forces that sustain world affairs[1]—that are conspicuous and familiar: The international system is less dominant, but it is still powerful. States are changing, but they are not disappearing. State sovereignty has eroded, but it is still vigorously asserted. Governments are weaker, but they can still throw their weight around. At times publics are more demanding, but at other times they are more compliant. Borders still keep out intruders, but they are also more porous. Landscapes are giving way to ethnoscapes, mediascapes, ideoscapes, technoscapes, and finanscapes (Appadurai 1996, 33–36), but territoriality is still a central preoccupation for many people.

Sorting out contradictions such as these poses a number of difficult questions: How do we assess a world pervaded with ambiguities? How do we begin to grasp a political space that is continuously shifting, widening and narrowing, and simultaneously undergoing erosion with respect to many issues and reinforcement with respect to other issues? How do we reconceptualize politics so that it connotes identities and affiliations as well as territorialities? How do we trace the new or transformed authorities that occupy the new political spaces created by shifting and porous boundaries?

The cogency of such questions—and the uncertainty they generate—reinforce the conviction that we are deeply immersed in an epochal transformation sustained by a new worldview about the essential nature of human affairs, a new way of thinking about how global politics unfold. At the center of the emergent worldview lies an understanding that the order that sustains families, communities, countries, and the world through time rests on contradictions, ambiguities, and uncertainties. Where earlier epochs were widely conceived in terms of central tendencies and orderly patterns, the present epoch appears to derive its order from contrary trends and episodic patterns. Where the lives of individuals and societies were once seen as moving along linear and steady trajectories, now their movement seems nonlinear and erratic, with equilibria being momentary and continuously punctuated by sudden accelerations or directional shifts.

Accordingly, the long-standing inclination to think in either/or terms has begun to give way to framing challenges as both/and problems. People now understand, emotionally as well as intellectually, that unexpected events are commonplace, that anomalies are normal occurrences, that minor incidents can mushroom into major outcomes, that fundamental processes trigger opposing forces even as they expand their scope, that what was once transitional may now be enduring, and that the complexities of modern life are so deeply rooted as to infuse ordinariness into the surprising development and the anxieties that attach to it.

To understand that the emergent order is rooted in contradictions and ambiguities, of course, is not to lessen the sense of uncertainty as to where world affairs are headed and how the course of events is likely to impinge on personal affairs. Indeed, the more one appreciates the contradictions and accepts the ambiguities, the greater will be the uncertainty one experiences. And the uncertainty is bound to intensify the more one ponders the multiplicity of reasons why the end of the Cold War has been accompanied by pervasive instabilities. Clearly, the absence of a superpower rivalry is not the only source of complexity. Technological dynamics are also major stimulants, and so are the breakdown of trust, the shrinking of distances, the globalization of economies, the explosive proliferation of organizations, the information revolution, the fragmentation of groups, the integration of regions, the surge of democratic practices, the spread of fundamentalism, the cessation of intense enmities, and the revival of historic animosities—all of which in turn provoke further reactions that add to the complexity and heighten the sense that the uncertainty embedded in nonlinearity has become an enduring way of life.

In some corners of the policymaking community, there would appear to be a shared recognition that the intellectual tools presently available to probe the pervasive uncertainty underlying our emergent epoch may not be sufficient to the task. More than a few analysts could be cited who appreciate that our conceptual equipment needs to be enhanced and refined, that under some conditions nonlinear approaches are more suitable than the linear conceptual equipment that for so long has served as the basis of analysis, that the disciplinary boundaries that have separated the social sciences from one another and from the hard sciences are no longer clear-cut, and that the route to understanding and sound policy initiatives has to be traversed through interdisciplinary undertakings (e.g., Gaddis 1992–93).

It is perhaps a measure of this gap between the transformative dynamics and the conceptual equipment available to comprehend them that our vocabulary for understanding the emergent world lags well behind the changes themselves. However messy the world may have been in the waning epoch, at least we felt that we had incisive tools to analyze it. But today we still do not have ways of talking about the diminished role of states without at the same time privileging them as superior to all the other actors in the global arena. We lack a means for treating the various contradictions as part and parcel of a more coherent order. We do not have techniques for analyzing the simultaneity of events such that the full array of their interconnections and feedback loops are identified.

SEARCHING FOR PANACEAS

Thus, it is understandable that both the academic and the policymaking communities are vulnerable to searching for analytic panaceas. Aware that they are ensconced in an epoch of contradictions, ambiguities, and uncertainties and thus are sensitive to the insufficiency of their conceptual equipment, officials and thoughtful observers alike may be inclined to seek understanding through an overall scheme that seems up to the challenges posed by the emergent epoch. Complexity theory is compelling in this regard. Since "complexity lies somewhere between order and disorder, predictability and surprise" (Johnson 1997), the very fact that a theoretical lens can be focused on such phenomena with the presumption that they are subject to systematic inquiry, thereby implying that complex systems are patterned and ultimately comprehensible, may encourage undue hope that humankind's problems can be unraveled and effective policies pursued to resolve them.

Stirring accounts of the Santa Fe Institute, where complexity theory was nursed into being through the work of economists, statisticians, computer scientists, mathematicians, biologists, physicists, and political scientists in a prolonged and profoundly successful interdisciplinary collaboration, kindled these hopes (Lewin 1992; Waldrop 1992). The stories of how Brian Arthur evolved the notion of increasing returns in economics; of how John H. Holland developed genetic algorithms that could result in a mathematical theory capable of illuminating a wide range of complex adaptive systems; of how Stuart Kauffman generated computer simulations of abstract, interacting agents that might reveal the inner workings of large, complicated systems such as the United States; of how Per Bak discovered self-organized criticality that allowed for inferences as to how social systems might enter on critical states that jeopardize their stability; of how Murray Gell-Mann pressed his colleagues to frame the concept of coevolution wherein agents interact to fashion complex webs of interdependence—these stories suggested that progress toward the comprehension of complex systems was bound to pay off. And to add to the sense of panacea, expectations were heightened by the titles that these scholars gave to work written to make their investigations meaningful for laypeople. Consider, for example, the implications embedded in Holland's *Hidden Order* (1995) and Kauffman's *At Home in the Universe* (1995) that creative persistence is worth the effort in the sense that, eventually, underlying patterns are out there to be discovered.[2]

There are, in short, good reasons to be hopeful: If those on the cutting edge of inquiry can be sure that human affairs rest on knowable foundations, surely there are bases for encouragement that the dilemmas of the post–Cold War world are susceptible to clarification and more effective control. Never mind that societies are increasingly less cohesive and boundaries increasingly more porous; never mind that vast numbers of new actors are becoming relevant to the course of events; never mind that money moves instantaneously along the information highway and that ideas swirl instantaneously in cyberspace; and never mind that the feedback loops generated by societal breakdowns, proliferating actors, and boundary-spanning information are greatly intensifying the complexity of life late in the twentieth century—all such transformative dynamics may complicate the task of analysts, but complexity theory tells us that they are not beyond comprehension, that they can be grasped.

I do not say this sarcastically. Rather, I accept the claims made for complexity theory. Despite conceptual and definitional difficulties,[3] it has made enormous strides, and it does have the potential for clarifying and ultimately ameliorating the human condition. Its progress points to bases for analytically coping with porous boundaries, societal breakdowns, proliferating actors, fast-moving money and ideas, and elaborate feedback loops. But to emphasize these strides is not to delineate a time line when they will reach fruition in terms of policy payoffs, and it is here, in the discrepancy between the theoretical strides and their policy relevance, that the need to highlight theoretical limits arises.

STRIDES IN COMPLEXITY THEORY

Before specifying the limits of complexity theory, let us first acknowledge the claims made for it. This can be accomplished without resort to mathematical models or sophisticated computer simulations. Few of us can comprehend the claims in these terms, but if the theoretical strides that have been made are assessed from the perspective of the philosophical underpinnings of complexity theory, it is possible to identify how the theory can serve the needs of those of us in the academic and policymaking worlds who are not tooled up in mathematics or computer science but who have a felt need for new conceptual equipment. Four underpinnings of the theory are sufficient for this purpose. The four are equally important and closely interrelated, but they are briefly outlined separately here in order to facilitate an assessment of the theory's relevance to the analysis of world affairs.

The core of complexity theory is the complex adaptive system—not a cluster of unrelated activities but a system; not a simple system but a complex one; and not a static, unchanging set of arrangements but a complex, adaptive system. Such a system is distinguished by a set of interrelated parts, each one of which is potentially capable of being an autonomous agent that, through acting autonomously, can impact on the others and all of which either engage in patterned behavior as they sustain day-to-day routines or break with the routines when new challenges require new responses and new patterns. The interrelationships of the agents is what makes them a system. The capacity of the agents to break with routines and thus initiate unfamiliar feedback processes is what makes the system complex (since in a simple system all the agents consistently act in prescribed ways.) The capacity of the agents to cope collectively with the new challenges is what makes them adaptive systems. Such, then, is the modern urban community, the nation-state, and the international system. Like any complex adaptive system in the natural world, the agents that comprise world affairs are brought together into systemic wholes that consist of patterned structures ever subject to transformation as a result of feedback processes from their external environments or from internal stimuli that provoke the agents to break with their established routines. There may have been long periods of stasis in history in which, relatively speaking, each period in the life of a human system was like the one before it; however, for a variety of reasons elaborated elsewhere (Rosenau 1990), the present period is one of turbulence, of social systems and their polities undergoing profound transformations that exhibit all the characteristics of complex adaptive systems.

The four premises of complexity theory build on this conception. They call attention to dimensions of complex adaptive systems that both offer promising insights into world affairs and highlight the difficulties of applying complexity theory to policy problems.

Self-Organization and Emergent Properties

The parts or agents of a complex adaptive system, being related to each other sufficiently to form recurrent patterns, do in fact self-organize their patterned behavior into an orderly whole,[4] and as they do, they begin to acquire new attributes. The essential structures of the system remain intact even as their emergent properties continue to accumulate and mature. Through time the new properties of the system may obscure its original contours, but to treat these processes of emergence as forming a new system is to fail to appreciate a prime dynamic of complexity, namely, the continuities embedded in emergence. As one analyst puts it, the life of any system, "at all levels, is not one damn thing after another, but the result of a common fundamental, internal dynamic" (Lewin 1992, 192). Thus, for example, the NATO of 1999 is very different from the NATO of 1949 and doubtless will be very different from the NATO of 2009, but its emergent properties have not transformed it into an entirely new organization. Rather, its internal dynamic has allowed it to adapt to change, even though it is still in fundamental respects the North Atlantic Treaty Organization.

Adaptation and Coevolution

There is no magic in the processes whereby systems self-organize and develop emergent properties. In the case of human systems, it is presumed that they are composed of learning entities (Holland 1995, 93), with the result that the dynamics of emergence are steered, so to speak, by a capacity for adaptation, by the ability of complex systems to keep their essential structures within acceptable limits or, in the case of nonhuman organisms, within physiological limits.[5] Human systems face challenges from within or without, and the adaptive task is to maintain an acceptable balance between their internal needs and the external demands.[6] At the same time, in the process of changing as they adapt, systems coevolve with their environments. Neither can evolve in response to change without corresponding adjustments on the part of the other. On the other hand, if a system is unable to adjust to its environment's evolutionary dynamics and thus fails to adapt, it collapses into the environment and becomes extinct. To return to the NATO example, the organization managed from its inception to coevolve with the Cold War and post–Cold War environments despite internal developments, such as the 1967 defection of France from the its military command, and external developments, such as the demise of the Soviet Union and the superpower rivalry. Indeed, as the environment evolved subsequent to the end of the Cold War, NATO accepted France's decision to rejoin the military command in 1996. The adaptation of NATO stands in sharp contrast to its Cold War rival, the Warsaw Pact. It could not coevolve with the international environment and failed to adapt; in effect, it collapsed into the environment so fully that its recurrent patterns are no longer discernible.

As the history of France in NATO suggests, the coevolution of systems and their environments is not a straight-line progression. As systems and their environments become ever more complex, feedback loops proliferate and nonlinear dynamics intensify, with the result that it is not necessarily evident how any system evolves from one stage to another. While "no one doubts that a nation-state is more complex than a foraging band," and while the evolution from the latter to the former may include tribal, city-state, and other intermediate forms, the processes of evolution do not follow neat and logical steps (Lewin 1992, 19). Systems are unalike and thus subject to local variations as well as diverse trajectories through time. Equally important, evolution may not occur continuously or evenly. Even the most complex system can maintain long equilibria before undergoing new adaptive transformations, or what complexity theorists call "phase transitions." Put differently, their progression through time can pass through periods of stasis or extremely slow, infinitesimal changes before lurching into a phase transition, thereby tracing a temporal path referred to as "punctuated equilibrium."

The Power of Small Events

It follows from the vulnerability of complex adaptive systems to punctuations of their equilibria and tumultuous phase transitions that small, seemingly minor events can give rise to large outcomes, that systems are sensitive at any moment in time to the conditions prevailing at that moment and can thus initiate processes of change that are substantial and dramatic. Examples of this so-called butterfly effect abound. Perhaps the most obvious concerns the way in which an assassination in 1914 triggered the onset of World War I, but numerous other, more recent illustrations can readily be cited. It is not difficult to reason, for example, that the end of the Cold War began with the election of a Polish pope more than a decade earlier, just as the release of Nelson Mandela from prison was arguably (and in retrospect) an event that triggered the end of apartheid in South Africa.[7]

Sensitivity to Initial Conditions

Closely related to the power of small events is the premise that even the slightest change in initial conditions can lead to very different outcomes for a complex adaptive system. This premise can be readily grasped in the case of human systems when it is appreciated that the processes of emergence pass through a number of irreversible choice points that lead down diverse paths and, thus, to diverse outcomes. This is not to imply, however, that changes in initial conditions necessarily result in unwanted outcomes. As the foregoing examples demonstrate, the power of an altered initial condition can lead to desirable as well as noxious results, an insight that highlights the wisdom of paying close attention to detail in the policymaking process.

THE LIMITS OF COMPLEXITY THEORY

Can complexity theory anticipate precisely how a complex adaptive system in world affairs will organize itself and what trajectory its emergence will follow? Can the theory trace exactly how the system will adapt or how it and its environment will coevolve? Can the theory specify what initial conditions will lead to what large outcomes? No, it cannot perform any of these tasks. Indeed, it cannot even anticipate whether a large outcome will occur or, if it does, the range within which it might fall. Through computer simulations, for example, it has been shown that even the slightest change in an initial condition can result in an enormous deviation from what would have been the outcome in the absence of the change. Two simulations of the solar system are illustrative:

> Both simulations used the same mathematical model on the same computer. Both sought to predict the position of the planets some 850,000,000 years in the future. The first and second simulation differed only in that the second simulation moved the starting position of each planet 0.5 millimeters. With such a small change in the initial conditions, [it is reasonable] to expect that the simulations would yield almost identical outcomes.
>
> Both simulations used the same mathematical model on the same computer. Both sought to predict the position of the planets some 850,000,000 years in the future. The first and second simulation differed only in that the second simulation moved the starting position of each planet 0.5 millimeters. With such a small change in the initial conditions, [it is reasonable] to expect that the simulations would yield almost identical outcomes.
>
> For all but one of the planets this is exactly what happened. Pluto, however, responded differently. The position of Pluto in the second simulation differed from its position in the first by 4 billion miles. Pluto's resting position is, in this mathematical model, extremely sensitive to the initial conditions. (Smith 1995, 22)

Applying these results metaphorically to the global system of concern here, it could well be presumed that the Pluto outcome is the prototype in world politics, that numerous communities and societies could deviate often from their expected trajectories by the political equivalent of four billion miles. The variables comprising human systems at all levels of organizations are so multitudinous and so susceptible to wide variations when their values shift that anticipating the movement of planets through space is easy compared to charting the evolution of human systems through time.

In short, there are strict limits within which theorizing on the basis of the premises of complexity theory must be confined. It cannot presently provide—and is unlikely ever to provide—a method for predicting particular events and specifying the exact shape and nature of developments in the future. As one observer notes, it is a theory "meant for thought experiments rather than for emulation of real systems" (Holland 1995, 98).

Consequently, it is when our panacean impulses turn us toward complexity theory for guidance in the framing of exact predictions that the policy payoffs are least likely to occur and our disillusionment is most likely to intensify, for the strides that complexity theorists have made with their mathematical models and computer simulations are still a long way from amounting to a science that can be relied on for precision in charting the course of human affairs that lies ahead. Although their work has demonstrated the existence of an underlying order, it has also called attention to a variety of ways in which the complexity of that order can collapse into pervasive disorder. Put differently, while human affairs have both linear and nonlinear dimensions, and while there is a range of conditions in which the latter dimensions are inoperative or "well behaved,"[8] it is not known when or where the nonlinear dimensions will appear and trigger inexplicable feedback mechanisms. Such unknowns lead complexity theorists to be as interested in patterns of disorder as in those of order, an orientation that is quite contrary to the concerns of policymakers.

THEORIZING WITHIN THE LIMITS

To acknowledge the limits of complexity theory, however, is not to assert that it is of no value for policymakers and academics charged with comprehending world affairs. Far from it: If the search for panaceas is abandoned and replaced with a nuanced approach, it quickly becomes clear that the underlying premises of complexity theory have a great deal to offer as a perspective or worldview by which to assess and anticipate the course of events. Perhaps most notably, they challenge prevailing assumptions in both academic and policymaking communities that political, economic, and social relationships adhere to patterns traced by linear regressions. Complexity theory asserts that it is not the case, as all too many officials and analysts presume, that "we can get a value for the whole by adding up the values of its parts" (Holland 1995, 15). In the words of one analyst,

> Look out the nearest window. Is there any straight line out there that wasn't man-made? I've been asking the same question of student and professional groups for several years now, and the most common answer is a grin. Occasionally a philosophical person will comment that even the lines that look like straight lines are not straight lines if we look at them through a microscope. But even if we ignore that level of analysis, we are still

stuck with the inevitable observation that natural structures are, at their core, nonlinear. If [this] is true, why do social scientists insist on describing human events as if all the rules that make those events occur are based on straight lines? (Guastello 1995, 1)

A complexity perspective acknowledges the nonlinearity of both natural and human systems. It posits human systems as constantly learning, reacting, adapting, and changing even as they persist, as sustaining continuity and change simultaneously. It is a perspective that embraces nonequilibrium existence. Stated more generally, it is a mental set, a cast of mind that does not specify particular outcomes or solutions but that offers guidelines and lever points that analysts and policymakers alike can employ to more clearly assess the specific problems they seek to comprehend or resolve. Furthermore, the complexity perspective does not neglect the role of history even though it rejects the notion that a single cause has a single effect. Rather, focusing as it does on initial conditions and the paths that they chart for systems, complexity treats the historical context of situations as crucial to comprehension.

The first obstacle to adopting a complexity perspective is to recognize that inevitably we operate with some kind of theory. It is sheer myth to believe that we need merely observe the circumstances of a situation in order to understand them. Facts do not speak for themselves; observers give them voice by sorting out those that are relevant from those that are irrelevant, and, in so doing, they bring a theoretical perspective to bear. Whether it be realism, liberalism, or pragmatism, analysts and policymakers alike must have some theoretical orientation if they are to know anything. Theory provides guidelines; it sensitizes observers to alternative possibilities; it highlights where levers might be pulled and influence wielded; it links ends to means and strategies to resources; and, perhaps most of all, it infuses context and pattern into a welter of seemingly disarrayed and unrelated phenomena.

It follows that the inability of complexity theory to make specific predictions is not a serious drawback. Understanding and not prediction is the task of theory. It provides a basis for grasping and anticipating the general patterns within which specific events occur. The weather offers a good example. It cannot be precisely predicted at any moment in time, but

> there are building blocks—fronts, highs and lows, jet streams, and so on—and our overall understanding of changes in weather has been much advanced by theory based on these building blocks. . . . We understand the larger patterns and (many of) their causes, though the detailed trajectory through the space of weather possibilities is perpetually novel. As a result, we can do far better than the old standby: predict that "tomorrow's weather will be like today's" and you stand a 60 percent probability of being correct. A relevant theory for [complex adaptive systems] should do at least as well. (Holland 1995, 168)

Given the necessity of proceeding from a theoretical standpoint, it ought not be difficult to adopt a complexity perspective. Indeed, as already indicated, most of us have in subtle ways already done so. Even if political analysts are not—as I am not—

tooled up in computer science and mathematics, the premises of complexity theory and the strides in comprehension that they have facilitated are not difficult to grasp. Despite our conceptual insufficiencies, we are not helpless in the face of mounting complexity. Indeed, as the consequences of turbulent change have become more pervasive, so have observers of the global scene become increasingly wiser about the ways of the world, and, to a large degree, we have become, each of us in our own way, complexity theorists. Not only are we getting accustomed to a fragmegrative worldview that accepts contradictions, anomalies, and dialectic processes, but we have also learned that situations are multiply caused, that unintended consequences can accompany those that are intended, that seemingly stable situations can topple under the weight of cumulated grievances, that some situations are ripe for accidents waiting to happen, that expectations can be self-fulfilling, that organizational decisions are driven as much by informal as by formal rules, that feedback loops can redirect the course of events, and so on through an extensive list of understandings that appear so commonplace as to obscure their origins in the social sciences only a few decades ago.[9] Indeed, we now take for granted that learning occurs in social systems, that systems in crisis are vulnerable to sharp turns of directions precipitated by seemingly trivial incidents, that the difference between times 1 and 2 in any situation can often be ascribed to adaptive processes, that the surface appearance of societal tranquillity can mask underlying problems, and that "other things being equal" can be a treacherous phrase if it encourages us to ignore glaring exceptions. In short, we now know that history is not one damn thing after another as much as it is many damn things simultaneously.

And if we ever slip in our understanding of these subtle lessons, if we ever unknowingly revert to simplistic formulations, complexity theory serves to remind us that there are no panaceas. It tells us that there are limits to how much we can comprehend of the complexity that pervades world affairs, that we have to learn to become comfortable living and acting under conditions of uncertainty.

The relevance of this accumulated wisdom—this implicit complexity perspective—can be readily illustrated. It enables us to grasp how an accidental drowning in Hong Kong intensified demonstrations against China, how the opening of a tunnel in Jerusalem could give rise to a major conflagration, how the death of four young girls can foster a "dark and brooding" mood in Brussels, how an "October surprise" might impact strongly on a U.S. presidential election, or how social security funds will be exhausted in the next century unless corrective policies are adopted—to cite three recent events and two long-standing maxims.[10] We know too that while the social security example is different from the others—in that it is founded on a linear projection of demographic change while the other examples involve nonlinear feedback loops—the world is comprised of linear as well as nonlinear dynamics and that this distinction is central to the kind of analysis we undertake.

In other words, while it is understandable that we are vulnerable to the appeal of panaceas, this need not be the case. Our analytic capacities and concepts are not so far removed from complexity theorists that we need be in awe of their accomplishments or be ready to emulate their methods. Few of us have the skills or resources to undertake sophisticated computer simulations—and that may even be an advantage, as greater technical skills might lead us to dismiss complexity theory as inapplicable—but as a philosophical perspective, complexity theory is not out of our reach. None of its premises and concepts is alien to our analytic habits. They sum to a perspective that is consistent with our own and with the transformations that appear to be taking the world into unfamiliar realms. Thus, through its explication, the complexity perspective can serve as a guide both to comprehending a fragmegrated world and to theorizing within its limits.

Even more relevant in the context of this book, complexity theory can be readily put to the service of normative commitments. Even the most passionate crusaders can enhance their chances of improving the human condition by being aware of the power of small events, the properties of situations that can emerge as they coevolve with their environments, the capacities for self-organization that can advance or thwart desired goals, and the links between initial conditions and subsequent outcomes. They may have to suspend their normative impulses while empirically assessing the conditions they seek to promote, but patience in this regard seems bound to pay off. To suspend norms is not to abandon them. To pursue them in the absence of sound empirical understanding is to undermine the prospects for normative progress. Complexity theory, like any social science perspective, can thus serve to discipline our value concerns and, in so doing, enable us to mover closer to realizing them.

NOTES

For an earlier version of this chapter, see Rosenau (1997b), which was translated into Spanish and published in *Nueva Sociedad*, no. 148 (March/April 1997): 70–80. I am grateful to Matthew Hoffmann, David Johnson, and Hongying Wang for their helpful reactions to earlier drafts.

1. The development of the concept of fragmegration has been gradual (Rosenau 1983, 65–82; 1995, 46–64; 1997a, chap. 6).

2. For a title pointing in the opposite direction, see Kelly (1994).

3. Johnson (1997, C7).

4. As one complexity theorist, Stuart Kaufmann, put it, referring to self-organization as a natural property of complex genetic systems, "There is 'order for free' out there" (quoted in Lewin 1992, 25).

5. The notion of physiological constraints setting adaptive limits is developed in Ashby (1960, 58), whereas the substitution of acceptable limits in the case of human systems is developed in Rosenau (1981, 31–40).

6. For a full elaboration of this conception of adaptation, see Rosenau (1981, chap. 4).

7. For an extensive account that traces the end of apartheid back to Mandela's links to South African President F. W. de Klerk while he was still in prison, see Sparks (1994).

8. For the use of this phrase, see Smith (1995, 30).

9. For an eye-opening sense of how rapidly the social sciences have advanced in recent years, consider that it was only some five decades ago that, for the first time, a gifted analyst (Simon 1945) arrested systematic attention to the dynamics of informal patterns of organizations, an insight that today is taken for granted.

10. Accounts of these events can be found in Gargan (1996), Greenberg (1996), and Simons (1996).

4

Theory and Political Practice: Reflections on Theory Building in International Relations

Friedrich V. Kratochwil

The contribution of theory to our understanding of political practice has been one of the perennial issues in debates about the possibilities and limits of a science of politics (Aristotle 1951) and consequently is at the heart of normative international relations analysis. Aside from the thorny epistemological issues—of interest mainly to the academic fraternity—there remains the more general question of how knowledge relates to action as this problem is linked to notions of participation, civic duty, legitimacy, political resistance, and, at the international level, world order. With respect to these concerns, the crucial issue is then no longer one of how the world works—which our theories capture and describe more or less accurately—but of why and how *we have made* the world (Dessler 1989; Wendt 1992) and what possibilities for changing it present themselves to us as acting subjects.

How then is a "theory" of political praxis possible if we are interested in changing the system in which we participate rather than in accepting the constraints it imposes on our freedom of action? If the task of theory is to provide a type of knowledge that "fits" reality, and if the social world is not simply "there" but is continuously made, then providing such knowledge in the sense of a simple "fit" with reality seems indeed a rather problematic undertaking. While I cannot hope to discuss all the implications that result from the co-constitution of actors and social systems and the peculiar recursivity problem that it entails, I want to examine in this chapter two important problems that have a bearing on the issue of theory building in the social sciences and the practice of normative international relations. The first deals with the problem of how one analyzes transformative change. The second deals with the epistemological issue of deciding between different theoretical approaches that explain this phenomenon, especially when traditional or "problem solving" theories seem less appropriate for that purpose (Cox 1986).

As theoretical optimists and adherents of a Popperian epistemology (Popper 1965), we could assume that all theoretical advances occur by conjectures and refutations. Discrepancies between predicted and obtained results provide opportunities for new theoretical efforts, and science can proceed through the *self-correcting* process of hypothesis testing. If we are less optimistic, especially when we take the various defensive gambits into account by which authors "normalize" discordant evidence, things look quite different. On the one hand, we have to take seriously Lakatos's argument that refutations in single cases, or even in repeated trials, might not suffice for rejecting the old theory and its research program (Lakatos 1970). Even worse, we actually would be ill advised to dispense with our theories after the discovery of some refuting evidence because theories are, after all, not simply tested against "reality." Thus, oddly enough, this suggestion seems to give short shrift to our confidence in the self-correcting process of scientific knowledge. Since data are to a large extent theory dependent, empirical tests might mean little unless everyone agrees that we have a "crucial test" for the research program. True, some criteria still exist by which we are able to recognize a superior or "progressive" program. But if its superiority consists in the larger scope and greater generality of the new program, such a "test" will become available only after a considerable amount of research has been done. No noncontroversial criterion for our decision exists at the beginning of new research endeavors when the old program is challenged by a new set of puzzles.

Without wanting to discuss further the Lakatosian position, something rather disquieting has occurred. Not only have we lost a good deal of our optimism, but, in addition, the fit between our theories and the "world" seems increasingly loose. It is not surprising that this give between concepts and reality has to increase still further if we take seriously the previously mentioned problem of recursiveness. When the importance and meaning of disconfirming evidence is at issue, questions of whether an event means that the actors just made a mistake in the otherwise unchanged practice that reproduces the system or of whether this deviation has theoretically important implications raise difficult problems. Since the meaning of an action in the social world is not ascertainable simply through some neutral measurement procedures but is based on complex *appraisals* in which normative concerns also play a role (Kratochwil 1989), we should not expect otherwise. The danger that discordant evidence is swept under the carpet is then not imaginary.

Nowhere does this problem become clearer than in the debates about the nature of change after the demise of the Cold War (Mearsheimer 1990). The catalog of topics might have increased when compared to the formerly austere agenda of neorealism—for example, questions of nationalism, internal decay, and domestic violence have been registered—but these "new" facts are not accorded theoretical status (Lapid and Kratochwil 1996a, b). Rather, they are considered to be epiphenomena of the underlying structure. But the frequent rather summary dismissal of transformative change—since "anarchy" has not mutated into "hierarchy," the structure of international politics is bound to assert itself "when push comes to shove"—might be less than persuasive (Posen 1993). Even some rather surprising "nonevents," such as the nonuse of force by the former Soviet Union for its preservation and that of its empire, are explained away and are thus hardly embarrassing to our hardened realists.

At this point, at first blush, a rather radical idea attains a certain plausibility. Thinking coherently about such problems might have less to do with our ability to produce theories that satisfy the criterion of "correspondence" between the key theoretical concepts and the "world" than with our capacity to develop a critical awareness that choosing certain practices and certain descriptions over others has consequences for our understandings and actions. Thus, a stance seems plausible even if we adhere to a strict correspondence view, as we have to realize that "reality" is a poor philosopher's stone, given the overdetermination of actions and unavailability of direct tests against reality. What is at issue in most theoretical debates is, therefore, the plausibility of criteria in choosing one "description" over another and the consequences that follow from such a choice. Such a debate is then more like one justifying an interpretation than of one judging the correspondence or accuracy of the theory's representations. In this context "nonevents," or hypothetical counterfactuals (Tetlock and Belkin 1996), might be of even greater importance than actual choices, as the previously mentioned example of the nonuse of force indicates. Furthermore, this view suggests that the theoretical terms of politics are not only "fuzzy," as they attain their meaning largely from their links with other concepts and their imbrication with interests and values, but that this fuzziness is due to the contestable nature of the characterization that cannot be reduced by simply looking harder at the "facts."

These are, perhaps, heady claims, and in order to make a persuasive case for them, my argument will take the following steps. In the next section I address the problem of problematic analogies in international relations analysis and the issue of appraising persistence and change in the international system. Here the recent neorealist contention concerning the enduring importance of the "anarchy problematic," as well as Krasner's (1993) argument against viewing the Westphalian settlement as a benchmark of dramatic change, will serve as my foil. The second section is then devoted to a discussion of the resulting important epistemological issues. Here I claim that the undecidability of many of these questions and the resulting theoretical pluralism is not the result of the failure of theorizing that can be overcome by establishing the "truth" of one theory but that pluralism is, as Lapid (1989) suggested, an inevitable and also desirable result of the complications that arise from the multiplicity of theoretical and metatheoretical issues. Furthermore, I argue that the rejection of a correspondence theory of truth does not condemn us, as it is often maintained, to mere "relativism" and/or to endless "deconstruction" in which anything goes but that it leaves us with criteria that allow us to distinguish and evaluate competing theoretical creations. Such a procedure of critical reflection, of translating one theoretical attempt into another, and of seeing the respective strengths and weaknesses of different visions of politics is an important ingredient in learning and in molding political practices.

A short summary outlining the major steps of the argument is provided in the conclusion.

THE PROBLEM OF CHANGE

If the study of politics is not only driven by some abstract definitional exercises but is understood as an attempt at illuminating the problem of order, then the question of action and change are crucial to such an understanding (Falk 1975, 1995; Bull 1977; Schroeder 1994). These two problems are interconnected, as I will argue. The analysis of change poses several conceptual and empirical challenges. Conceptually, the difficulty consists in the logical requirement that without recognizing some identity "underlying" the observed variations, no assertion of change seems possible. Traditionally, the conceptualization of change has therefore invoked an "ontologically" given substratum, be it ideal or material, that is the carrier of certain accidental properties that are then used to explain the observed variations. Since change is, in one most influential conceptualization, the negation of "being," change inevitably becomes another word for "decay" (Plato 1973). Even the more dynamic interpretation of change in terms of a telos by Aristotle resorts to the conceptual dichotomy between "form" and "matter" that seems basic to our ways of analyzing change (Aristotle 1956). Finally, there is the issue of distinguishing different kinds of change, that is, those of a "fundamental" and those of a less transformative nature.

It is in this context that the notion of a "system" and of an "equilibrium" is often introduced in order to make the distinction in terms of changes *within* a system, understood as oscillation around the equilibrium point, and changes *of* the system, conceptualized as the movement of the equilibrium point. Difficulties, however, arise when we give these notions empirical referents. The question of whether an episode is one of "normal" versus "system-transforming" change is different from *dynamic* analysis in physical systems. When we consider social systems evolving or changing, laws that map this historical change do not appear to exist, as Popper (1957) pointed out. To argue that we deal here with some simple dynamic analysis of some physical system is to engage in deliberate equivocation. There are several basic issues that such a story fails to appreciate.

First, objects of investigation in the social world are not simply autonomously given "in the outer world." They do not appear within the categorical framework that constitutes, in Kantian terms, the objects of the physical world. Rather, social phenomena are part of our practices and of our experiences as moral agents who can start new chains of events by our actions. Diagnosing change involves us, therefore, in complicated practical as well as epistemological determinations that are not simply reducible to observation and the "brute facts" of empirical evidence (Kratochwil 1989). Second, and perhaps even more important, since social "systems" are neither closed systems nor simple systems with feedback loops but rather are complicated self-reproducing systems (Luhmann 1984), neither the notion of equilibrium nor that of causality are strictly applicable.

The conceptual confusion that follows from a neglect of these distinctions can be easily seen when for purposes of analysis the notion of equilibrium is used. On the one hand, the term is used to denote "entropy" in natural systems (i.e., the disintegration of the system), while, on the other hand, when the concept of equilibrium is transferred to the social sciences by Spencer, Parsons, and so on, this very concept is used to explain exactly the opposite (i.e., system *integration* and *reproduction*). Consequently, whether an equilibrium such as, for example, a balance in the international system exists has more to do with *a consensus among the actors reproducing the system* than with an objective function specifying the connections between the observed objective factors or variables. Similarly, given that "autopoetic" (i.e., self-reproducing systems) are characterized by equifinality and equifunctionality, neither strict causal analysis (our beloved independent and dependent variables of causal paths) nor traditional functionalist accounts can claim the status of a criterion securing "true" knowledge. Since outcomes can be achieved now by different paths, the Humean "constant" conjunction between cause and effect is, for all intents and purposes, broken. The same is true in functional accounts in which a similar elasticity exists between structures and functions.

It does not take great sagacity to realize that much of the discussion concerning the international system, its persistence and change, is confused and that a clarification can be expected only when the arguments are sensitive not only to data and their theory dependence but also to the theoretical and metatheoretical issues that are thereby raised. However, given the complexities of the problems, it is not surprising that many traditional arguments rely on highly questionable conceptual presuppositions. Two such erroneous presuppositions deserve a brief discussion. They both concern, in one way or another, the problems of change and of our historical understanding. For lack of better terms, we could characterize them as the "denial" of history and the "abuse" of history, as exemplified in "functional" historical accounts.

The Denial of History

If there is one point on which all neorealists are likely to agree, it is that regardless of observable changes, the "underlying" structure is the driving and persistent force in the international system (Waltz 1979). Thus, discordant phenomena are either declared to represent "temporary" lags or are relegated as unimportant nuisance factors to background conditions that do not challenge the central tenets of the theory. Their "correctness" is then proven by a variety of gambits that systematically shield them from refutation.

First, since the structural theory relies on a simple conceptual dichotomy between hierarchy and anarchy, nothing short of the establishment of a world state would qualify as a system-transforming change. Even changes from multipolarity to bipolarity and from bipolarity to unipolarity are supposed to leave the generative structure of anarchy in place. Virtually by definition, everything short of this eschatological moment has to be relegated to "inconsequential" surface phenomena. Consequently, discordant facts are not used as opportunities for theoretical refinement or reconstruction but are thoroughly normalized so as not to disturb the central tenets.

Second, the "system" itself is often so badly conceptualized as to make a stringent analysis virtually impossible. For example, one seeks in Waltz in vain for a specification of the boundary of the system, of the operationalization of the equilibrium, and, as Ruggie (1983) suggested, of the principles of differentiation according to which the anarchical structure develops over time. Instead, mistaken analogies from microeconomics and biology abound. For example, if a system's persistence is connected with evolutionary pressures, it is not clear why the evolutionary path should not lead to *differentiation*. If the logic of evolution shows anything, it is that there is not one simple law determining survival: Niches, devolution, symbiosis, and so on represent different strategies of successful adaptation. Using a type of systemic theory that neither includes these factors nor does justice to issues of emergent properties, such as cognition and learning in the case of social systems, amounts to little more than utilizing metaphorical expressions.

Third, by arguing that this theory provides only for probabilistic predictions and explanations, the theory can nicely immunize itself from criticism. Thus, the end of the Cold War provides no refutation despite the fact that change came about in exactly the opposite way that one would have expected from the logic of the systemic model. Simply aggregating the entire period from 1986 to 1992 into one data point[1] suffices to buttress the claim that single counterfactuals do not prove probabilistic theories wrong.[2] Finally, in a curious reversal of the burden of proof, neorealists seem to suggest that if the world does not transform itself from anarchy to hierarchy, "their" theory has been proven right. But to someone only vaguely familiar with the problem of civil war, it should seem strange to identify the existence of hierarchy simply with "peace" and "order." Similarly, the familiar and largely obnoxious "I told you so" in case something "bad" (forceful or violent) happens (such as the war in Bosnia)[3] masquerades as an insight based on superior theoretical understanding, although it has very little to do with the vigor or strength of the theory itself.

In general, "history" as an "account of things worth remembering" (*prooemium;* Herodotus 1954) is for neorealists not one of changes, surprises, and fortuitous conjunctures that require detailed investigation. Rather, history, if not treated outright as bunk, becomes a curious morality tale of confirming evidence, of the verities long known, only to be retold because of faults of those who fail to appreciate the lessons of a "theory" that collapses all historically grounded praxis and experience into one timeless structure. True to realist premises, this vision of political realities cannot have but nightmarish qualities. Not only does the emergence of "hypernationalism" (Snyder 1990; Posen 1993) bring our unfounded optimism for organizing international life anew to naught, but we are also told that the dilemmas of international politics can be remedied only by "balancing," which, of course, makes nuclear proliferation necessary!

While the latter policy recommendations might not be shared by many neorealists, the denial of fundamental change through the practice of the actors themselves (rather than through shifting capabilities or technology) is common. It is here that Krasner's (1993) work exemplifies some curious equivocations. Having originally maintained the underlying stability of the Westphalian structure, Krasner now has somewhat modified his thesis and argues, if I understand him correctly, that (1) Westphalia was not really a turning point but rather a midway landmark by which medieval practices and modern territorial arrangements coexisted, that (2) notions of sovereignty have always been contested and have not exhibited the exclusivity and absoluteness that we usually associate with it, and that (3) material and not ideal interests explain the changes establishing the Westphalian system. The least controversial point is obviously the second one, as anyone who is remotely acquainted with early modern Europe will agree with most of Krasner's account. The other two points are more curious.

The first is downright mysterious, especially in the light of his second point. "Turning points" in history are virtually always turning points only in retrospect. They are, as crucial experiments in the history of science, crucial only ex post facto when we, with a new vantage point from which to look backward, try to identify those first beginnings. Thus, as every historian knows, the meaning of the events lies not in the events but in their emplotment, that is, the process of becoming embedded in a coherent story (Polkinghorne 1988). Nothing in this view prevents us from realizing that aside from the "new," whose significance arises from its connection with the present, there are plenty of elements that belong to the "past." This defeats, of course, the naive version of historical research, in which history is simply adduced paradigmatically for purposes of instruction (Koselleck 1985) or in which history has become simply a storehouse of unproblematic data that can be used for the verification or corroboration of theories. Being aware of the importance of historical plots and the meaning that they give to the data corrects also the view that there is only one historical development that serves somehow as a hidden key, as the idea of progress seemed to suggest.

If emplotment and interpretation are irreducible elements of our historical understanding, are we then no longer justified in, for example, appraising the Treaty of the Pyrenees, which was the first to conceive of a boundary in linear terms, as a manifestation of territoriality (Sahlins 1984)? After all, most of the text regulated other issues, such as a dynastic marriage and the restitution of a French nobleman, who had defected and fought for the king of Spain, to all his possessions in France. It would indeed be a strange way of handling historical evidence and of assessing the importance of certain new historical facts if we could defeat claims to novelty by pointing to the existence of some traditional elements in the historical record. Furthermore, it is unclear to me how the contestable character of sovereignty, hardly news for historians and political theorists, can be used as an argument against transformative change.

Puzzles also abound regarding the opposition between material and ideal interests. How can "interests," which presuppose actors' conceptions about their goals, be determined without knowing something about the actors' ideas concerning their situation and their world? Why is an interest more real when it is material than when it is ideal? Obviously, such an assessment depends on complicated inferences and the evaluation of counterfactual alternatives (Hawthorne 1991). But is this not an open question? Do we really have to believe that Essex's rebellion, for example, would be better explained if we could find a note that promised him money as opposed to an account that emphasizes the loss of honor and access to the queen? How real is money after all when taken as an *explanans* for action? Is it really more persuasive, in the light of the financial habits of the Tudor period, to talk about a "rising bourgeoisie" when most of its members abandoned their profitable enterprises in order to buy land and live the life of gentry squires, even if such decisions resulted in considerably lower returns than could be earned in trade and manufacturing (Hexter 1961)? And what does the distinction between material and ideal interests really purchase in view of the genocidal politics of a Hitler, Stalin, or Pol Pot?

After all, even rational decision theory admonishes us only to maximize expected utility and probably is rightly agnostic as to the nature of the preferences. The lack of fit between the expected utility models and actual choices lies also not in the failure to distinguish material and ideal interests but in neglecting to explain how the preferences are formed and how they get transformed in the process of interaction. Thus, without the explicit specification of the process by which interests and/ or ideas lead to the aggregate outcomes via the actual choices of the actors, functional accounts, which show that the outcomes are compatible with rationalist equilibrium interpretations based on "as if" assumptions, are little more than assertions of faith.

The Abuse of History: Functional Historical Accounts

There are also serious normative objections to evolutionary arguments, not only in the discipline of history but also in legal analysis and in certain normative arguments. Suppose that we could all agree that the goal of a legal system is indeed "human dignity," which, according to McDougal, underlies the development of law in the world political process (McDougal 1966; McDougal and Lasswell 1966). But knowing this telos does not relieve us from the painful choices that we have to make in terms of competing values, when, for example, individual liberty has to be curtailed for communal security or when welfare overrides liberty by instituting redistributive schemes. If law serves a purpose at all, it does so in making possible the coexistence of different ways of life that embody competing substantive notions of the good (Rawls 1989). Thus, the notion of human dignity that is supposed to provide the yardstick for the legal force of particular prescriptions is strictly opposed by the liberal conception of justice, which is the most important contribution that legal norms can make (Dworkin 1986).

This brief consideration clearly indicates that law, morality, visions of the good life, and human rights are not all of one cloth and cannot be represented as unproblematic goals or results of historical evolution that pulls some retrogrades, be they statist, communitarians, or simple reactionaries, along the path of enlightenment. After all, as Marion Smiley (1992) has shown, ethics itself, understood as a critical reflection on our practices, is based on a wide variety of formal and substantive criteria that cannot be reduced to simple principles, be they justice as fairness, the categorical imperative, or even the judgments of the sympathetic, impersonal observer. Indeed, the abstract principles are of little help in making the practical choices since even our practices of blaming and excusing, assigning responsibility, and choosing among alternatives consist of a variety of complicated and interacting standards. These standards are derived from our conceptions of roles and communal boundaries, from our imagination and the lessons we have learned, as well as from the historically determined distribution of power within the society. All this is a far cry from the notion of purely formal principles determining the nature of our free will or of the cognitive capacity in determining the overall utility of our individual and/or collective choices (Kratochwil 1989).

Thus, the hope to represent changes in ongoing political practices in terms of a de facto evolutionary path of value realizations seems hardly convincing, precisely because such accounts either skirt the issue of competing values or try to base appeals for particular practical choices on criteria that cannot deliver even logically the desired result. I just point to the difficulties in Rawls's contractarian solution, which leaves issues of membership unresolved. A similar argument could be made concerning the emptiness of the categorical imperative, with which I have dealt on another occasion (Kratochwil 1989). Similarly, given the contestable character of the concepts that designate social practices (Connolly 1983), a critical historical examination, although answering some questions, cannot tell us how "things really were." Our reflections make it painfully obvious that the interpretative schemes that designate certain events or eras as benchmarks are the result of the constructive principles underlying the historical narrative rather than intrinsic properties of the historical data themselves.

This is at least one of the reasons for Krasner's puzzle as well as for my argument that our inquiry has to proceed on the theoretical as well as the metatheoretical level. Furthermore, although I have used the metaphor of levels in order to get the point across that empirical evidence will be insufficient to answer our questions about the importance or meaning of a historical datum, something more might be entailed thereby. After all, the metaphor of levels still suggests the existence of some firm ground that is the basis for the levels that run parallel to it. To that extent, in capturing this ground and then explaining all the other phenomena as surface appearances, we are faced again by the issue of allegedly immutable structures that stay stable despite surface appearances. However, the upshot of the previous argument seems to cast serious doubt on the existence of such a ground. It seems that the questions that are raised in this context are not really those of "theory" but rather are the result of a metaphysics and a type of ontological thinking that can no longer be sustained. Is, therefore, everything arbitrary or subjective? By no means! If we started our reflections not with the assumption of permanent identities, which form the core and to which our concepts correspond, but with some notion of "process," we would neither subscribe to a dubious ontology nor believe that "anything goes." Rather, we would find *temporarily stabilized intersubjective meanings* and mediations, not all of which seem, however, to correspond to a common or unalterable core. As in the case of "property," there might exist a certain family resemblance between the various arrangements that we group together under this rubric, but there might not exist one single feature that all these forms share. Wittgenstein used the metaphor of a rope in this context: It too is made up of many strings tied to each other, but there is not necessarily one string that serves as the core throughout its entire length.

UNDERSTANDING PRAXIS

The last remarks have important implications for our understanding of crucial concepts and their history as well as for the whole effort of using theories as our guides for understanding social reality and for directing action. After all, it is the general validity of laws and the notion of an external reality that are supposed to provide the foundation for our conceptual frameworks and their truth, as they seem to provide the only insurance against arbitrary and/or idiosyncratic constructions. However, if we doubt the notion of an external reality analogous to some furniture standing somewhere in space, and if we furthermore entertain the possibility that neither general laws nor abstract principles as maxims for action are of great help for understanding or resolving the practical questions that we face, on what grounds can we make claims, communicate with one another, and decide issues? While I obviously cannot provide unequivocal answers to these questions, the following thoughts provide plausible clues for such an undertaking.

If the concepts in our theories no longer mirror an independent reality, how is one to proceed? If the theoretical terms function not in virtue of their agreement with reality but largely because of their coherence with other terms and with certain principles of construction that inform our narratives, and if the understandings transmitted by our various "disciplines" are not necessarily the result of some immediate intuition but of often forgotten conceptual gambits and practices of normalizing the things and events, what is there besides endless deconstruction and self-serving and, ultimately, logically unsustainable claims to the relativism of all knowledge? I think that neither of these fears is justified, although the antics of some deconstructionists and the nihilism of Foucaultian analysis, devoted to endless critique, exposure, and dissolution, give plenty of grist for the mill to the adherents of traditional "science." There are two interconnected reasons that I reject both the attitude that the world has to be "out there," for otherwise we could not make knowledge claims, and the belief that the nonespousal of "the world as a thing," which is mirrored in our theories, necessarily results in nihilistic relativism.

The first concerns the problematic understanding of truth as correspondence, and the second concerns the realization that what serves as an explanation for a particular phenomenon is not context independent and that, therefore, answers informed by theories often do little for our understanding, especially when practical issues elicit a request for an explanation. In this case, further specifications and elaborations, the deliberation about options helped by analogies, and inferences from case to case, not gnomic laws or the truth of theories, are at issue. Both points deserve further examination.

Is an antirepresentational stance incoherent and/or nihilistic? After all, there is no longer a point by which the concepts in our language can be "compared" to the things out there. A moment's reflection suggests that the negation of an absolute vantage point does not necessarily dispense with truth, only that the criteria of truth are now largely pragmatic rather than iconic. Instead of attempting to compare our conceptual apparatus with something nonlinguistic standing behind all conceptual creations, we are now bound to examine what difference the adoption of one set of concepts makes in our efforts to cope with the problems of praxis compared with another set. Thus, attempting to adjudicate our conceptual frameworks by resorting to some "thing" out there is as conceptually futile as trying "to convert foreign currency into the 'real money' of dollars and gold" (Buscemi 1993, 142).

This pragmatic criterion of truth turns our attention away from representational issues and focuses on the role of new metaphors and new ways of looking at the world that make the resort to some previous vocabulary unnecessary. Thus, the change from a conception of politics communicated by an organic metaphor—the body politic—to one of contract in the seventeenth century is one of the most far-reaching conceptual revolutions for politics, as an entirely new set of significant puzzles emerged. The important point in this context is, as Rorty (1989) suggests, that neither can the new conceptualizations be reached from the old vocabularies and their logic nor can the process of producing a new set of concepts and questions be interpreted as hitting on, or approximating, a "correct" representation of reality. Instead, this method, which Rorty calls "therapeutic redescription," provides us with the possibility of seeing the old things in a new way and of creating new opportunities for practices and experiences that sidestep the old vocabulary that was getting in the way:

> Such creations are not the result of successfully fitting together pieces of a puzzle. They are not discoveries of a reality behind the appearances, of an undistorted view of the whole picture with which to replace myopic views of its parts. The proper analogy is with the invention of new tools to take the place of old tools. To come up with such a vocabulary is more like discarding the lever and the chock because one has envisaged the pulley. (Rorty, 1989, 12)

A perfect example along these lines is the refusal of the founding fathers of the United States to speak the language of sovereignty in the European idiom (Deudney 1995). On the basis of the republican tradition and innovating in their attempts to find a solution to the traditional problems of tyranny and anarchy, they created a constitutional order and a federal form of government. Obviously, the problem of authority and legitimacy was not thereby avoided, but the old puzzles of sovereignty—that is, its indivisibility and its location, which had preoccupied theorists from Bodin to Hobbes and other defenders of absolutism—did not even arise. Now, neither the government per se nor one of its branches nor the people were in possession of, or knew the location for, sovereignty. Rather, the Constitution itself and the political process—described in Lincoln's felicitous phrase as one "of the people for the people and by the people"—was thus legitimated, institutionalized, and exalted as "sovereign."[4]

Similar observations can be made in conjunction with the emerging European Union. It is not so that suddenly the states transferred "some" of their sovereignty to Brussels, where it now "lies around," as Ole Weaver (1994, 11) has so aptly put it. The latter puzzles are not those of praxis but rather of a representational epistemology according to which sovereignty has to stand for something, and if this something is no longer in its old place, it must have moved. This last example has important implications for the question of the development of sovereignty and for the second point mentioned previously: the issue of explanation.

Questions about the changing nature of sovereignty are usually part and parcel of certain practical concerns. Thus, the argument about states having become increasingly price takers rather than price makers (Strange 1993) is animated by the fear that the increasing integration of financial markets has led to a loss of control by public authority. In a way, such inferences might seem exaggerated since even if markets have become more important, it is only states that guarantee the rights on which markets depend. But in addition to issues of responsibility that have become part of our political consensus and our conceptions of legitimacy, there is obviously also the fear that such a step might be costly and unable to accomplish its purported goals. A simple reassertion of sovereignty cannot magically bring us back to a meanwhile increasingly imaginary status quo. As Louis Pauly (1995) shrewdly observed,

> The social and political implications of expanding international capital mobility are not fully understood. The associated obligations of both states and citizens have not been clearly debated if affirmation of relevant governing rules by established political authorities has been limited. In short if a regime of international capital mobility is now commonly depicted as inevitably governing the life of citizens in an increasingly global economy, the consent of the governed has not adequately been sought out . . . at issue is the legitimacy of an emergent regime, not the sovereignty of the states participating in it. (371)

A similar problematic emerges from Ruggie's example of the effects of a redescription of a policy problem on the current account deficit of the United States in 1991.

While trade policy is still predicated on the view that separate economies are dealing with one another at arm's length, the emergence of global production has thoroughly upset this conception. Antidumping charges can now be brought by a Japanese firm producing electronics in the United States against an American firm that imports the same commodity from its offshore facilities in the Third World. The growing divergence between ownership and location has diametrically opposed policy implications if, for example, the state attempts to take measures furthering employment and economic growth. The U.S. Department of Commerce once pointed out "that the country's 1991 trade deficit of 28 billion would have been a 24 billion surplus if measured by US ownership, rather than location of production" (Ruggie 1994). Which of these "descriptions" is appropriate and is taken as a framework for orienting action is obviously not reducible to questions of what lies "behind" the concepts but must be gleaned from the context and the problems that we want to address.

In this view, concepts we use for practical matters are more like signals for action than labels for things. Precisely because we address practical problems with them, judgment rather than the question of the truth of our generalizations or laws is at stake, especially regarding global developments of macropolitical processes. If we work from the assumption that the world in whose making we are involved is contingent, then our reasoning in making choices and in explaining them will be more concerned with the process of deliberation, with the mapping of alternatives, with the plausibility of counterfactuals and the intricacies of the "Cleopatra's nose" problem than with issues of subsumptions and logical necessities. This involves us in a paradox when we view these matters from the vantage point of theory rather than praxis.

The "better" our explanation of a historical phenomenon is in theoretical terms, the better specified must be its causal connections. However, in order to distinguish causation from mere correlation, we have to engage in counterfactual analysis. As Elster (1978) suggests, "We may point out that the former warrants the statement that if a cause had not occurred, then the effect would not have occurred, whereas no such counterfactual is implied by the latter" (175). But this means that the strength of the causal argument concerning choices and praxis in general ultimately does not depend on the necessary connection in the actual world as much as it does on the *plausibility* of comparing the actual with some counterfactuals, that is, with the construction of other "possible worlds." Which of the "possible worlds" are selected as plausible alternatives depends on what we think the agents in question know about their world, what dispositions we impute to them, which factors we hold constant and think of as constraints. Such a deliberation, in turn, justifies our judgments about available alternatives. None of the conditions that provide us with plausible alternatives, however, are specified by a theory or are even specifiable in such terms. Rather, the procedures and inferences that we go through are more akin to a type of Aristotelian deliberation characteristic of practical reasoning than of theoretical reason.

The upshot of this argument is that theories might be of little help in understanding problems of action and their historical reconstruction. Here familiarity with law seems better suited because knowing the rules underlying institutions allows us to examine the world of institutional facts that is of such importance for our understanding of the social world and its changes. Moreover, familiarity with law also provides us with valuable clues as to the methodological requirements and criteria for making judgments, even though it does not prevent derailments when attempts at building comprehensive "theories" of law try to eliminate the jurisprudential elements in our reflections. This was, after all, the criticism of McDougal's attempts to rely on a "policy science" in deciding questions of law. On the other hand, it has become clear from the discussion of sovereignty that debates about this contested concept are not about "sovereignty and all that" but rather about "sovereignty and all what?"

CONCLUSION

This chapter has attempted to contribute to a clarification of the issue of theory building in international relations. Different from the conventional approach, which focuses on issues of methodology, I have argued that understanding praxis represents a more promising avenue to building better theories. Such a critical reflection on practice not only corrects some blind spots and implicit justification of traditional theories but also suggests that most of the time no simple tests are available for adjudicating controversies among competing theoretical enterprises, precisely because the social world is one of artifice and not one that simply exists "out there."

In order to make this point and draw out some of its implications for theory building, I approached the problem indirectly, that is, by means of an inquiry into how we deal with large-scale or transformative change. Since transformative change calls into question the certainties that inform our problem-solving theoretical efforts, it is understandable that some theorists will nevertheless deny the (theoretical) significance of change, if not its apparent existence. Strategies such as distinguishing immutable or "deep" structures from "surface" phenomena are common as gambits that place the phenomena, taken as indicators of change, in an already long existing class, thereby denying their novelty or importance. Here Krasner's attempt to minimize the importance of the Westphalian moment served as a foil that in turn led, via reflections on the teleological abuse of history, to a discussion of the general problem of how we can appraise theoretical constructs in the absence of a fixed reality.

If neither the events themselves (because of their "emplotment") can serve as unproblematic data nor the social world as a whole exist independently of the actors, their ideas, and the projects in which they are engaged, then the conception of a theory as an abstract but nevertheless true representation of reality becomes problematic. In other words, the idea that the fit between a theory and "reality" represents a test of its truth appears to be seriously misleading. However, as I suggested, it is not true that anything goes. We *do* share some common historical templates of meaning that serve as our foundations in our arguments and projects. Although these templates and metaphors are no longer so much the hoped-for Cartesian *fundamenta inconcussa* as they are historical and cultural artifacts, they do provide us with a common, that is, intersubjective reference world without which neither we nor our political communities could exist.

My brief discussion concerning the rootedness of our conceptual framework and theoretical enterprises in intersubjectively shared master metaphors thus indicates a way out of the dilemma of the unavailability of a fixed reality on the one hand and its concomitant danger of total arbitrariness in our theoretical efforts on the other, as was suggested by the discussion of "pragmatic redescriptions." Not only do ideas and their historical changes matter, but a better understanding of political praxis is likely to emerge when the implications of such an approach to social action and its historicity are taken into account. In this context, the importance of counterfactuals and how we reason about them attains particular importance. I have argued not that such a mode of thinking is idle speculation about "roads not taken"—even if it certainly serves this function too—but that even strict causal accounts embodied in conventional theories are always part of judgments about possible worlds.

NOTES

1. This was the argument advocated by Kenneth Waltz, Steve Walt, and Robert Keohane at a 1993 conference in Ithaca, New York, on the implications of the demise of the Cold War.

2. Needless to say, according to the standard epistemology to which neorealists allegedly adhere, even probabilistic statements must rule something out, that is, specify a definite range within which events are supposed to fall so that even single occurrences falling beyond that range do indeed refute the theory. On this point, see Popper (1968).

3. This was Mearsheimer's justification for being a "realist" at the 1993 American Political Science Association Convention in Chicago.

4. This, of course, thereby created its own conceptual puzzles, such as the issue of whether there can be an amendment to the Constitution that is unconstitutional.

5

The Uncertain Reach of Critical Theory

Radmila Nakarada

Normative international relations finds its intellectual foundations largely in the tradition of critical theory. Critical theory is an approach to politics that self-consciously analyzes structures of domination and tries to identify paths toward greater human liberation. In this chapter, I reflect on the tradition of critical theory as a way to understand the prospects of normative international relations. My hope is that by appreciating the "uncertain reach" of critical theory at this particular stage in history, one can more fully understand the contemporary practice and future promise of normative international relations.

Currently, critical theory faces a significant challenge insofar as many global processes reveal a "double movement": They are made up of forces that are both promising and threatening to human welfare. One sees this, for example, in the universalization of democracy and the globalization of the socially insensitive power of the market, the tearing down of the ideological wall and the expansion and solidification of the walls of inequality, and the decreasing danger of major nuclear confrontation and the increasing danger of establishing "peace worse than war" (Deleuze and Guattari 1986, 119). One way to talk about this is in terms of "triumph" and "impasse." We live in a time of triumph of some progressive forces and of stalled efforts to overcome fundamental impasses to change. Critical theory seems paralyzed in the face of these phenomena. Contemporary global bifurcating processes overwhelm the ability to level insightful critique and to suggest directions for achieving a more humane world.

The double movement of global processes overwhelms critical theory in two ways. First, it makes it difficult to find a purchase point on political issues and to articulate a clear critical message that will have transformative power. Critical theorists have traditionally worked to point out egregious instances of injustice and to marshal moral argument against obvious wrongs. In earlier times this practice may have been more effective in that it could align itself with existing cleavages within societies. Transnationalization and globalization—replete with contrasting tendencies—

multiply local cleavages and diffuse the ability for forces of resistance to coalesce. As a result, the message of critical theory—and its strategy of articulating extreme wrongs—seems less potent at this point in time.

Second, the double movement makes it difficult to find a stable position from which to generate critique. The hallmark of critical theory—at least as it has been applied to global issues—is the theorist's ability to remain impartial to context when it comes to identifying injustice. That is, the critical theorist has long prided him- or herself with an ability to look injustice in the eye and criticize it in the service of human betterment no matter where injustice arises. Current bifurcating processes problematize this task by forcing the theorist to confront numerous, interacting issues that, together, create gray areas unamenable to easy moral insight. Rights and wrongs are part of a piece: They cannot easily be extricated from each other. Moreover, local political affairs are now embedded in global ones, and thus it is difficult to unravel knots of responsibility and situate oneself within a coherent moral community. These have implications for critical theory by making it difficult for the theorist to stake out a space wherein one can be impartial with regard to context and where one can generate a consistent line of critique. As the poststructuralists and communitarians tell us, humans are embedded in layers of social life that color our perceptions. The critical theorist must somehow acknowledge this embeddedness while simultaneously working to rise above the distorting sympathies it generates. Current global processes make this difficult by placing the theorist in multiple communities and revealing contrasting moral trajectories.

This chapter examines the problems that the double movement poses for contemporary critical theory and, by extension, normative international relations. It traces the challenge of locating a purchase point on current world affairs and translating insight into effective agency—and of generating consistent critique within a particular context—through a set of issues that have traditionally engaged critical theorists. These include the existence of extreme wrongs, the potential of the rule of law, and the promise of certain forms of political agency. Since these issues have been part of the standard fare of critical theorists for decades, exploring their character in the face of current bifurcating processes will provide important insight into the challenge of critical theory and normative international relations at the millennium.

EXTREME WRONGS

The predicament of critical theory and its limited reach express themselves in the face of extreme wrongs at the global level. One of the most extreme wrongs is the deprivation of millions of human beings marked by starvation, poverty, and early death due to preventable disease among close to one billion of the world's population. These people tend to live in the South, and this has led some scholars to see global deprivation as a matter of a "silent genocide"(Chomsky 1994, 131) or "global apartheid" (Kohler 1982, 315–25; Mazrui 1993, 9; Falk 1995, 49–55). The disparity between such deprivation and privilege is best illustrated by two facts: (1) Despite all the so-called development efforts directed at the South, the North-South gap has continued to widen, and (2) the aid for the least-developed countries has decreased over the years.

Dear Richard,
   For months now I have been attempting to write an article in your honor, but coherency escapes me. Last night, I watched the film "Mother Night," based on the novel of Kurt Vonnegut, and I decided to come down here and as one of the "walking wounded" write a letter instead of continuing to fumble with the article. Although you have been an inspiring author and friend, it seems that I can honor you with nothing else but sincerity.

According to a UN Conference on Trade and Development (UNCTAD) report (reviewed in the Belgrade daily *Politika*), in 1965 the average per capita income of the seven richest countries was twenty times higher than the per capita income of the seven poorest countries. In 1995, it was thirty-nine times higher.[1] However, not only has the gap doubled and incidences of poverty have increased, but the official declared aid (ODA) has stagnated, declining 13 percent between 1992 and 1995. According to a review of the annual report of UNICEF, it now averages 0.27 percent of the gross national product (GNP), although 0.7 percent was the officially declared UN target. The United States is at the bottom of this list its aid having dropped from 0.21 percent in 1990 to 0.1 percent in 1995.[2]
   The persistence of the dramatic gap and the stagnation of aid reflect the causal link between extreme "rights" (privileges) and extreme wrongs (deprivations). This is expressed, among others, in the disproportionate concentration of wealth and use of global resources. While 80 percent of the world's population lives in less developed regions, the richest billion has 75 percent of world wealth (the poorest billion has 1.4 percent) and consumes more than 80 percent of energy resources. The extreme proportions of inequality are well summarized in the fact that the wealth of 345 billionaires is greater than the total income of countries inhabited by 45 percent of the world population (UN Development Program Report, cited in *Politika*, May 5, 1997, 8).

When we last met, in Malta, you suggested that I write a personal account of what happened here. I live this experience daily, I think of little else, and yet writing about this seems as difficult as the above article. I am ushered into silence because the loss is overpowering, the grief is numbing, the agony is unending. Memory is blurred by sadness, humiliation, and a feeling of extreme awkwardness. First, because it is impossible to deal with all the levels, incidents, directions, forms, and victims of tragedy and injustice. I mourn all those who have lost their . . .

Finally, the distribution of inequality confirms that there is a racist dimension to extreme wrongs. Africa is the location of the most extreme wrongs of the global economy, and sub-Saharan Africa is the Third World's Third World, a human and environmental disaster area.[3] Out of forty-eight least-developed countries, thirty-three are in Africa. Close to half (43 percent) of the sub-Saharan population is undernourished. The average life expectancy is lowest in Africa (51.8 years, 22.6 in Rwanda) and highest in Japan (79.5 years). The average infant mortality rate is also the highest in the world, 94 per 1,000 births, compared to 11 per 1,000 in more developed countries. Africa is most affected by AIDS; 70 percent of the total world cases are located there (UN Economic and Social Council 1997, 39–64).

In light of these facts, critical theorists have consistently called for the eradication of extreme poverty and starvation. Yet their efforts have gone unheeded. This is because critical theory nurtures a number of illusions about its political abilities—illusions that misrepresent the challenge of extreme inequality. One illusion refers to the manner in which critical theory addresses the void created between the endless diagnosing of extreme wrongs and the resisting reality. Critical theory de-dramatizes the depth and character of that void when it continues to nurture the potency of the normative argument—when it overestimates the power of its own lines of argument.

> *. . . country, community, family, and identity, who have perished by the hand of their neighbors and friends. Second, because coming from where I do, I am to a large degree disqualified in advance by the silence of many key witnesses, the pressure of too many half-truths and lies, the consequences of too many unfair accounts that have been awarded as intellectual bravery, the reach of too many ready-made labels. It is difficult to speak when the very need to understand has been practically stamped out by dominant interpretations of the conflict. . . .*

Exposing the inconsistencies between the normative, rhetorical, and practical performances of global capitalism has no preventive or transformative capacity. The forces of power have proven to be immune to such exposure; revelations have had no serious political consequences; moral indignation has had a very limited reach.

Expecting effects from revealing the inconsistencies between the rhetorical and practical would imply that the global structures of power are erected on different principles then they really are; that paradoxes, pain, unnecessary deaths of men, women, and children mean something; and that the system can be shocked or shamed into generosity and solidarity. It would mean that one is appealing to a sense of justice that does not rule our world, to a sense of solidarity that is not only very limited but also rapidly eroding. The drastic inconsistencies between the normative promises and the practical performances of capitalism are not a "betrayal of true capitalism" but its underlying assumption. Therefore, exposing the inconsistencies has a very limited empowering potential where extreme wrongs are concerned.

The second illusion evolves from the correct assumption that the (financial) means for resolving the most extreme wrongs are not lacking, for only a minimal increase in aid is necessary. In other words, extreme wrongs are avoidable wrongs, easily correctable if only the goodwill of the governing elites would slightly increase.

This stance, however, fails to deal with the full meaning of the stubborn fact: A minimal increase in aid has been an unresolvable problem for decades. The cynical paradoxes, for example, between the immense amounts of money spent on arms and the few percentages of the world military expenditure needed to eradicate hunger and sickness have been presented and documented countless times, and the result has been a decrease in aid!

> *If you do not join the prepackaged chant about the causes of war (Serbian aggressive expansionism) and who the main villains are (Milosevic and the Serbian people who continue to vote for him), a priori you are discredited whatever your arguments may be. Mentioning the weight of the past is tiresome. Dealing with the interactions of all the essential local actors and their mutually radicalizing moves is an unnecessary complication. Including the systematic application of double standards by the international actors, noting examples of media fabrications, referring to the paradox of the broader European context—Europe is simultaneously seeking to respond to new security challenges and reconstituting very old border lines—is only an attempt to absolve the main culprit. . . .*

Suggesting that a slight increase in aid would be a painless gesture from the standpoint of the system but a gesture with far-reaching positive effects is to a large degree a utopian notion. An increase of aid for the "avoidable wrongs" is highly improbable because it is potentially subversive to the capitalist system. Increased aid would lead to a fundamental questioning of issues that the system cannot resolve: It would force the system to confront the issue of redistribution (equality)—something that it is unwilling and, more fundamentally, unable to do. Although experience has shown that a number of human wrongs (especially in the political realm) can be eased or eradicated, this is not the case with extreme wrongs. Their resolution requires the redefinition of the very foundation of the global order and changes within Western societies—changes that are unlikely to occur.[4]

> *An appeal for a deeper understanding of the roots of conflict simply has little legitimacy. This conflict falls into a completely different interpretative matrix. If you insist on the complexity of the conflict, you are termed as one-sided, biased. If you subscribe to the simplified argumentation of one culprit, one source of evil, you are accused of representing false moral standards. Understanding is dismissed by moralizing and the argument of numbers.*
>
> *Yet, all the most painful aspects of the conflict have been the objects of numerical manipulation. The full truth is reserved perhaps for the future. In the present, you have to bear the weight of simplified interpretations and the brutally complex reality itself. . . .*

In short, extreme wrongs expose an impasse: Change is needed, but it is not possible. In an attempt to maneuver out of this impasse, critical theory typically overestimates the potential of rhetorical critique and offers unrealistic assessments of progressive forces. The problem is that this can only benefit prevailing global power relations, for it obscures the degree of their influence and misrepresents the structural character of the impasse.

Amidst impasse and triumph, then, the tasks of critical theory have to be redefined. At a minimum, critical theory needs to continue to contest the legitimacy of the drastic inequalities but recognize the limited empowering potential of the normative argument.

POWER AND THE RULE OF LAW

Interdependence among states is growing, the sovereignty of the nation-state is shrinking, and this is creating greater possibilities for limiting the repressive practices of national governments, strengthening the relevancy of international law, and globalizing the rule of law. However, strengthening the relevancy of international law is simultaneously occurring with the strengthening of the principle "might makes right" (the transposing of the will of the global elite into international law, to paraphrase Karl Marx). In other words, the sphere of international law is also a location of "double movements."

> *Retelling the story of the Yugoslav tragedy requires, to my mind, speaking in several voices at the same time. You have to deal with the specificity of the Balkan heritage but also with the deeply (sometimes to the point of racism) rooted prejudices according to which the Balkans is perceived as an essentially barbarian region, the non-European part of Europe. One has to deal with the horrifying violence and destruction amongst peoples that were yesterday living in relative normalcy but also with distortions concerning the character and proportions of this violence. In spite of all the atrocities, it is in no way comparable with the Holocaust. That analogy is an attempt to reconstruct historical responsibilities. . . .*

New patterns of domination integrate the ingredients of power and emancipation into an amalgam, in this case, the principles of the rule of law and might make right. The strengthening of the rule of law is occurring together with the unprecedented capabilities of new structures of power to contain rational resistance to domination. Therefore, the voice of critical theory cannot set aside the schizophrenic tensions created by the double movement of the global processes. This means that critical theory cannot celebrate the strengthening of the international law as if it does not recognize the inequality of states before the law. However, while recognizing the lack of objectivity, it cannot ignore concrete violations of the international law. But then again, it can not speak of concrete violations apart from the practice of double standards present in the implementation of the international law. The challenge is misrepresented when elements of the amalgam are taken as separate, disconnected chapters of analyses.

The issue of double standards, for example, cannot be resolved by giving selective support to the actions of the most powerful states when their particular interests and international law happen to coincide. This undermines the position of critical theory, as it requires critical theorists to deal only with fragments and incidences and contributes to the legitimization of coincidences as unconditionally progressive steps leading toward the strengthening of the rule of law. Adding up "coincidences," however, cannot result in legal coherence. When the "rule of law" does not mean that the same norms apply equally to the most powerful and the least powerful states, critical analysis is undermined.

> *You have to deal with the responsibility of your own state, nation, in bringing about the tragedy but also with the injustice of unprecedented satanization of a whole nation (that cannot be explained by the committed misdeeds) and concentrated efforts to deprive it of a place in the international community. You have to bear the cross of the crimes some members of your nation have committed but also suffer because of the cold indifference to the violence that other members of your peoples have been exposed to. . . .*

Because of the double movements in the realm of international law, critical theory cannot speak in the same voice as the governing elites, even when the issue seems self-evident, as in the case, for example, of protecting individual and collective rights. Yes, of course the protection of human rights should be promoted; this is an unquestionable axiom. However, even such an issue needs to be situated; the strength and direction of external pressures must be measured according to the possibilities within concrete societies and the magnitude of their internal challenges. Unsituated celebration of the right to self-determination, for example, may result in civil wars, the breakdown of states, the economic massacre of large segments of the population, and the transition from independence to clientelism. Pressing the question of human rights can be part of geostrategic interest, as testified to by their uneven problematization, depending on whether a "friend or a foe" is in question.[5] Critical theory, therefore, cannot be a partner to the double standards of geopolitics nor to the geopolitical trade-offs. Rather, it must find its own convincing and consistent voice amidst these ambivalences, or double movements. The promotion of pressing issues by critical, concerned intellectuals should contribute to the constitution of internal consensus for change and not to the breakdown of societies; it should be the material force of conflict resolution, not conflict production. Let me attempt to clarify the ambiguity of the situation by two examples.

> *Yes, certainly the Serbian political elite contributed significantly to the violent breakdown of Yugoslavia, but so did the other national elites. Yes, the armed forces of Yugoslavia were involved in the Bosnian conflict, but so were the Croatian*

regular army and the mujahideens. Yes, the Bosnian Serbs took part in the ethnic cleansing of the Muslims, but they were also the object of ethnic cleansing, particularly in Croatia, . . .

Sanctions

Sanctions have gained wide acclaim as an appropriate instrument of restoring law when gross violations are committed, such as aggression terrorism and severe violations of human rights. Setting aside the social consequences of sanctions, the politics of sanctions has, however, demonstrated drastic arbitrariness in terms of the target of sanctions, the procedures involved in their implementation and suspension. The main criteria have not been what offense was committed but *who* committed it. For the same offense, some are punished, and others are not. Because of the unequal dependency, some countries are in the position to introduce (unilateral) sanctions, and others are not.

> *. . . where the most extensive ethnic cleansing after the Second World War has been carried out by a European state. If the whole ordeal is explained as the doing of one (evil) nation, one (evil) national leader, secession and nationalism of others only as a reactive phenomena, then how are we to explain the nationalist movements in Slovenia and Croatia in the seventies during the reign of Tito (incidentally, a Croat), the breakdown of two other (multiethnic) federations—the Soviet Union and Czechoslovakia—and the general upsurge of the problem of ethnicity and state formation after the end of the Cold War? Furthermore, such an approach has to disguise the evident tension between the principles of self-determination and inviolability of borders and ignore the fact that the consequences of the breakdown of a multiethnic country and the . . .*

Some can violate UN sanctions without consequences, and others cannot, and some can be under illegal sanctions for decades while others are militarily destroyed after a few months of sanctions by the most powerful nations; sanctions continue when the initial conditions for their suspension have been met (e.g., Yugoslavia). Can this broad range of arbitrariness be simply dismissed because of their alleged ineffectiveness? Sanctions have not been introduced when there was reason to do so (e.g., the Indonesian massacre in East Timor, the U.S. attack on Panama, the violation of the border of Iraq by Turkey, and the operation of Croatian regular troops in Bosnia.), and sanctions have been violated (e.g., against South Africa and Haiti) when there were higher (economic) interests of the "imperfection of the world." Is it an expression of the structural limits to the rule of law under the present global order of power? Arguing persistently that law is implemented selectively does not annul the responsibility of concrete actors (e.g., if the United States is not punished for its intervention in Panama, it does not make Iraq innocent), but it does not allow the responsibility of others (i.e., of the powerful) to be forgotten either. If all violations of international law cannot be sanctioned, they should not be amnestied, or legitimized. This is one of the tasks of critical theory—to delegitimize persistently all violations and resist the manifestations of realpolitik.

War Crimes

Clearly, war crimes should be punished, justice should be served, and if national courts are not willing to fulfill this task, the international community should have the power to intervene. Against this background, the Hague tribunal for the war crimes committed in the former Yugoslavia is hailed as a milestone in strengthening the implementation of international law, a step toward the establishment of a permanent Criminal Court.[6] If critical thinkers are to take part in the celebration of the Hague tribunal, they have to address, at a minimum, the following questions. First, are the legal grounds for the constitution of the Hague tribunal unambiguous since the Security Council, according to the UN Charter, does not have a clear mandate to constitute such a court and it has not in the past assumed judicial capacities? What are the implications of the fact that the legitimacy of the Court is generated primarily by the political power of the UN Security Council?

> . . . *problem of new minorities (according to U.S. General Boyd, no one wanted to be a minority in Yugoslavia) were predictable, and it has to distort the proportions of violence. (As far as the nature of violence is concerned, one should look once again at Lincoln's description of the U.S. Civil War, quoted by Hayden (1997), and discover surprising similarities among civil wars as such.) Unfortunately, many have invested their energy to celebrate this Manichaean image and the easy moral heroism it allows. However, the understanding of the conflict is not possible on the basis of a simplified Manichaean matrix; and the truth of the tragedy cannot be reduced to a bitter battle between the good and evil side. Burying the truth under the Manichaean matrix leads to modes of resolution that cannot be the basis of reconciliation and stability. . . .*

Second, do the procedures, rules, and method of the Court[7] depart from those that would be considered acceptable if they were to be applied within Western states? Third, is the Court an instrument of individualizing guilt, or more of an instrument of collective punishment? The crime of genocide inevitably presupposes collective responsibility (only a collectivity can endanger another collectivity, not an individual) (Hayden 1997, 57), and only the *leaders* of one out of the three ethnic groups involved in the conflict are indicted for war crimes. Finally, despite the bloodiness of the war in Bosnia, ethnic cleansing, and the uneven distribution of victims, are there convincing arguments that the crime of genocide has been committed? As a consequence of the breakdown of multiethnic Yugoslavia, ethnic cleansing has been practiced by all three sides (albeit unevenly) in order to create homogenized territories. How should we think about this? Furthermore, retired

U.S. General Charles Boyd and Sadako Ogata, former UN high commissioner for refugees, estimate that between 75,000 and 100,000 people have been killed in Bosnia, and this includes victims on all sides.[8] More civilians have died because of UN sanctions against Iraq than in the civil war in Bosnia. In addition, even more Vietnamese have been killed in the war in Vietnam, but Hannah Arendt argues that Vietnam, despite all the crimes committed by the United States, is not a case of genocide.[9] Having all these ambivalences in mind, it is important to reassert that all unpunished war crimes are a source of moral scandal. Should not critical theory then be obliged to nurture a consistent memory of *all scandals* if it is not going to become an additional force of legitimizing the principle of "might makes right?" If the argument that "you have to begin somewhere" is used, then it is of profound importance that the "beginning" is not based on the dominant political matrix: double standards, inconsistency, misproportions, false analogies, and political instrumentalization. Otherwise, it is not a "beginning" but rather the continuation of the well-established practice of inequality, or selectivity—of "might makes right." Critical theory has to be able to make the distinction without undermining the rule of law and without rationalizing the bias of power.

> *However, no one will ever be held responsible for such gross simplifications because the Serbs have been successfully reduced to an insult of the civilized world. The fact that this Manichaean exercise is carried out with few murmurs, whispers of doubt is an expression not only of a relationship toward a "barbarian region" but of a widespread propensity to betray the search when truth is not easily accessible. Those who attempted to salvage the complexity of the conflict, to understand at least the legitimate fears of all ethnic groups involved, have been intellectually ostracized. . . .*

The task of critical theory is to pursue justice without becoming (unwillingly) part of the forces legitimizing the double standards, without expressing fragmented concerns and partial coherency. The task of the critical theory is to search for the local/global truth as the foundation of justice.

THE CRISIS OF AGENCY

The uncertain reach of critical theory is painfully evident when the question of subjective forces (political agency) is taken up. Critical theory is confronted with an enormous disproportion between its description and diagnoses of the challenges, especially those related to state and market forces, and the lame hope that it expresses in the potentiality of resistance. There is no countervailing power to the multinationals, to the reach of the established coalition of the most privileged and powerful, and to the emerging global media order. There are no coherent and politically effective alternatives, theoretically plausible and at the same time promoted by an institutional and intellectual apparatus.[10]

That is one pole of the problem. The internal turmoil is equally disquieting. The local political power holders have demonstrated the lack of capability to perceive reality (global relations of power after the Cold war), to rationally articulate the national/state problem, to contribute to the creation of an internal consensus, and to embark on the path of development and democratization. On the other hand, the opposition has not presented a convincing alternative. . . .

Contestation is inhibited by the fact that issues have changed and have become more complex and diffuse. The overriding issue—the nuclear threat—has been replaced by an extensive agenda including ecocide, drugs, Mafia, terrorism, microviolence, and ethnic wars. Contributing to the inhibition is also the grand consensus in major Western countries that surpasses party divisions and limits the forces of civil society. The pressure of the system has ironed out the left/right party divisions on a number of major issues (especially on peace and security and economic issues), reducing the space for contestation to powerless, symbolic gestures.

The present crisis of actors is clearer when we compare, for example, the situation of peace movements during and after the end of the Cold War. The threat of nuclear war brought together peace activists all over the world. Now the dangerous implication of the extension of NATO to the East, not to say its very raison d'être after the end of Cold War and the dismantling of the Warsaw Pact, is not problematized by transnational peace movements. During the Cold War, links were developed between the Western peace movements and the Eastern human right movements. Together they contested the ideological boundaries of the two Europes and celebrated the tearing down of the Berlin Wall. Energies resisting the erection of new post–Cold War boundaries, if not walls, however, have not emerged. Those voices contesting, for example, the extension of NATO come paradoxically from parts of the U.S. establishment.[11]

It has either shared the weaknesses of those in power, or it has failed to present a formula that bridges the national, democratic, and social concerns of the citizens. In such a difficult moment for the state and society, the scene is governed by political midgets.

There is no actor sufficiently rooted in the social reality that respects those who yearn for the times past, that can heal those struck down by the present or support those who are purveyors of the future. I see no one capable of responding rationally to the challenges confronting this mutilated society, for I see no one with a consensus-creating capability. There is very little political wisdom that distinguishes the real problems from the wrong answers, that recognizes moral responsibilities and legitimate rights, needs, and fears, a position that does justice to the victimization and losses of all sides, including one's own, a position that can resist the temptations of vanity, immediate gains. That is why the majority of the population is silenced (not silent). They are blackmailed. . . .

Contestation is diluted by the radical erosion of solidarity. The race of the Eastern European countries to become members of the "chosen" (NATO and the European Union) and the tensions to preserve the privileges of the West have to a large degree replaced previous inclinations toward solidarity.

Furthermore, the response of a number peace movement activists themselves to the conflicts in the post–Cold War period has been inconsistent. They have celebrated the principle of self-determination irresponsibly—disregarding the fact that it can, as it did, lead to bloodshed in multiethnic countries—and inconsistently in that they supported some in their struggle for self-determination while ignoring and at times castigating others. Moreover, they have abandoned the basic premises of "peace by peaceful means" and have become an additional force of legitimizing military intervention as an instrument of conflict resolution (e.g., in Bosnia).[12]

> . . . *into silence by having no real option to choose from, by the incompetence, irrationalities, biases, injustices from within and without. That is, they can only choose among various forms of self-betrayal. Incompetent internal actors and defeat, together with gestures of collective punishment (like sanctions), have erased the dignity of the citizens. Some have turned to nurturing revengeful feelings, others to a masochistic catharsis; the majority has sunk into apathy. The society itself is looted, fragmented, disfigured. Yugoslavia today is irreparably damaged, battered, a melting pot of frustrations and bizarre contrasts! It is a society where you can run into both skinheads and Chetniks, Mafia and refugees, where the breakdown of city transportation is occurring among electronic highways (Internet, e-mail, satellite lines), where cultural links with the world coexist with visible scars of banishment from the international community, where both incidences of poverty and luxury are surpassing all previously known boundaries. The society is colored by street violence, greed of the privileged, mass confusion, and general mistrust. Children are fainting in school because of hunger, retired people and refugees are committing suicide in alarming numbers. Cities, hospitals, schools are in a state of decay.*

The crisis of actors may be a temporary phase, a phase of fermentation, or a symptom of an entirely new situation evolving in which contestation will be limited only to the local, microlevel. The uncertainty of the answer is why responsible realism of critical theory is necessary, why it is an act of contestation.

Critical theory is confronted with a major challenge, and that is to define and not misrepresent conditions. This means that it has to recognize the double movements of global processes and carefully distinguish between their hegemonic and transformative ingredients. Moreover, it has to refrain from unrealistic assessment of forces of contestation in order not to obscure the unprecedented reach of global power. Facing all the uncertainties and limits, critical theory has to redefine, not abandon, its tasks.

> *I watch all this with great sorrow and see no possibilities for some substantial betterment in the near future. Personally, I have felt all these years extremely lonely*

outside the boundaries of my family. I have been marginalized by the naive expectation that analysis, judgments, opinions, political programs should articulate not only the "A" or only the "B" part of the story, but both. But you can be heard only if you unconditionally subscribe to one position, one side, one part of the story. The choice is between being designated as a nationalist or a traitor. If you criticize the local scene, above all Milosevic, you are a traitor; if you criticize the external actors, you are a nationalist; if you criticize both, you are irrelevant. The imperative that all actors, internal and external, should be subjected to the same critical analysis is not a widely shared view. I have doubted myself countless times, but I have not found good arguments to join the voices of nationalism, or the crudest anticommunism, although I believe that the Serb nation was facing an extremely difficult challenge. Nor did I choose to be submissive to the uncritical legitimization of the biased relation of global powers to the drama of Yugoslavia, even though I was painfully aware of the benefits of such a position. Healing requires evenhandedness, consistency, recognizing the importance of individual autonomy. But in times of intense conflicts and fragmentation, ardent submissive followers are only needed.

I really do not know whether the end of Yugoslavia is a symptom confirming that "the catastrophe has already occurred," as Baudrillard says, but I know that I have lost a country and a world. I fear that I have also lost in some ways my dear WOMPers. Although our worlds and concerns are intertwined, we are not looking through the same window. I suspect you cannot share (perhaps even trust) my insights and intuitions, nor can I fully share your hopes for a better world. As much as my outlook is marked by the misfortunes of the local context, I am convinced that the potential for consolidating the global order on authoritarian premises has increased, the space for dissenting voices has diminished.

Dear friend, I have tried to tell you many things and have probably said little. It is difficult to tame countless images and feelings, balance insights and uncertainties, bear the hollowness of one's own words in face of an immense tragedy. Nevertheless, I feel that I will be writing this letter, in one form or the other, over and over again, for the story has not come to its end, the pain is not extinguished, and questions continue to haunt me. With deep friendship and respect,

Radmila

NOTES

1. "Paradise for Some, Inferno for Others," *Politika*, October 6, 1997, 8. See also UN Economic and Social Council (1997).

2. "The Rich Have Reduced Their Assistance to the Poor," *Politika*, July 24, 1997, 9. In contrast, the Social Summit emphasized increasing official development assistance as one of the key assumptions of eradicating poverty ("Report of the World Summit for Social Development," Copenhagen, preliminary version, UN Document A/Conf.166/9, April 1995,

19). However, the immediate U.S. official reaction was that an increase in assistance was not possible because of its internal financial constraints.

3. For example, Paul Kennedy (1993) describes Africa in such a manner: "The condition of sub-Saharan Africa—'the Third World's Third World,' as it has been described—is even more desperate" (211).

4. "That the Cold War came to an end essentially through the unilateral acts of the Soviet Union also helps to explain why the American projects of global hegemony and allied containment continue: Nothing really changed in American policy" (Cummings 1993, 28).

5. The predicament of the Kurds illustrates this. In Iraq they are victims protected by the international community; in Turkey they are hunted terrorists.

6. "The International Tribunal for the Prosecution of Persons Responsible for Serious Violations of the International Humanitarian Law Committed on the Territory of Former Yugoslavia Since 1991" was established in 1993 by UN Resolution 827.

7. This includes the privileged position of the prosecutor (see, e.g., Rules 33 and 39), secret indictments, permanent hidden identity of witnesses, kidnapping, violation of habeas corpus, different treatment of those indicted, and the fact that some are in comfortable apartments, and others are in jail cells, and so on.

8. The June 6 statement of Sadako Ogata is quoted in Kovacevic and Dajic (1997, 84). General Charles Boyd, who was the deputy commander-in-chief of the U.S. European Command from November 1992 to July 1995, poses the following question: "In April the (Bosnian) government lowered its estimate to just over 145,000, about 3 percent of the prewar population. That is a sobering number, but even accepting it at face value and granting that it is unevenly distributed across the population, does that total after 38 months of warfare make charges of genocide a meaningful contribution to policy debate?" (Boyd 1995).

9. Arendt (1994, 77).

10. Gill (1996, 180–81).

11. The revelations by the American press that the United States is building a new nuclear bomb have not become a major issue for the transnational forces of global civil society either. Land mines have become a major issue, thanks to the support of a number of governments.

12. For more about the relationship of peace movements toward the Yugoslav crisis, see Nakarada (1995, 473–89).

6

Global Economic Inequalities:
A Growing Moral Gap

Michael W. Doyle

> Were all humanity a single nation state, the present North/South divide would
> make it an unviable, semi-feudal entity, split by internal conflicts. Its small part
> [one-fifth] is advanced, prosperous, powerful; its much bigger part [the other
> four-fifths] is underdeveloped, poor, powerless. A nation so divided within itself
> would be recognized as inherently unstable. A world so divided should likewise
> be recognized as inherently unstable. And the position is worsening, not im-
> proving.
>
> South Commission (1990, quoted in Falk 1995, 50)

The problem of global economic inequality is even worse than the plight that the
South Commission highlighted. Not only is global economic inequality growing,
but the old excuses for inaction (none of which were fully exculpatory) are even less
credible and the willlingness to act even less evident. We might blame the moral gap
on the newness of the issue. Indeed, the debate over global economic inequality is a
relatively new issue in world politics. While the fact of global inequality is old, as
old as the modern international system (Wallerstein 1974), it is only since the 1970s
that international distribution became a prominent, contentious issue in interstate
diplomacy. It came to prominence with the debate over the New International Economic Order, when "Southern" (Third World) countries sought to renegotiate the
distribution of control and income in the world economy.[1] But, twenty years later,
the prominence of distributional issues in world politics has declined, not advanced.
Today, global distribution should be an issue because of what appears to be an unprecedented degree of economic inequality in the world economy. It thus has engaged a key part of the global "sustainability" and "decency" that are the core principles at the heart of the research and policy agenda that Richard Falk has outlined
throughout his career, recently in *On Humane Governance* (1995, 16). In this chapter, I would like to take up that agenda, explaining how global economic inequality

is discussed in the current debate. I will conclude that, first, inequality is becoming more, not less, significant but that, second, while our obligations are rising, our wills appear to be flagging.

Not all economic inequalities raise issues of moral concern. Differences of income among individuals might, as some laissez-faire liberals suggest, simply reflect differences in preference for leisure or differences attributable to talent or inheritance within the scope of a just society. What determines the moral issue is the nature of the relationship between the parties, not the level of income, unless, of course, that income does not provide for healthy subsistence. Above the natural floor of subsistence, just relationships depend on the society. Equal citizenship may need, for example, a certain degree of additional income, education, and perhaps equality.

In international politics, the society of states makes national, and not just personal, income a moral issue. Even wealthy individuals in poor societies may be vulnerable to violence and conquest since their wealth (unless they emigrate) does not exempt them from a common external danger. Poor individuals in poor societies are doubly vulnerable. Correspondingly, the very poor in wealthy societies must first claim redistribution against national resources because the states system lacks the security and solidarity that would make global justice the principle of first resort. In any case, the unit—state or nation—has a claim to distributive consideration because the society of states does not allow for complete independence, and individuals depend on their states for both security and welfare.

In this chapter, I propose to examine global inequality in both its individual and its international aspects. I will focus especially on the responses that international political philosophies make to global inequality and explore the current obligations highlighted by the end of the Cold War. Do the rich have a right to what they now own? Do global inequality and the end of the Cold War warrant a global New Deal?

GLOBAL INEQUALITY

How unequal is the world? A provocative (and impressionistic) metaphor in *Fellowship* magazine in February 1974 stirred considerable original interest in the issue. It asked its readers to imagine the world—without borders—as a statistically sampled village of 100 human beings. In that village of 100, it noted, six would be North Americans, nine Europeans, and three Japanese. They would have more than half the total village (global) income. The other eighty-two villagers would live on less than the other half. Sixty to seventy villagers (few in North America, Europe, or Japan) would be illiterate. Fifty villagers would be undernourished. The village would have the equivalent of one college education.

While impressive, such comparisons exaggerate the real purchasing-power effect of differences in monetary income. One hundred dollars delivers more necessary goods in a very poor economy than it does in a rich one. A 1989 World Bank study that attempted to control for that exaggeration by using purchasing-power measures of real income nonetheless found that the differences in per capita national income (as gross domestic product [GDP]) between the poorest and the richest economies were on the order of 50 to 1. This ratio is double the greatest disparities found within even the most unequal countries, between the richest and the poorest fractions of the population (highest 10 percent and lowest 20 percent; 25 to 1 in Brazil in 1989) (World Bank 1989, 222–23). In 1992, some 1.4 billion people lived in "absolute poverty," more than a quarter of the world's population. This is 400 million (40 percent) more poor than fifteen years ago. One in four live without the regular food, health care, and shelter that they need to have productive lives. In 1998, despite all the economic growth of the past decade, 1.3 billion people live on less than a dollar a day, and three billion live on less than $2 per day (World Bank 1998). In 1960, the richest one-fifth of world population had thirty times the income of the poorest fifth; by 1989, the ratio was 60 to 1 (UN Development Program 1992). Population growth, at 90 million per year, and unemployment, at 400 million in the South, compound these problems. Merely to maintain the status quo thus requires 40 million new jobs per year, far beyond the current rate, while failure to contain population growth in the next ten years will result in an additional four billion human beings in the year 2050 (UN Fund for Population Activities 1992b).

The world was not always this way. The fourteenth-century Arab traveler, Ibn Batutah highlighted Cairo, Toledo, Damascus, Delhi, and Cambay in China (all of which he visited) and mentioned the fame of the cities of Milan and Venice in Europe when he discussed the leading cities of the world. But he also noted the beauty and comfort and safety of Timbuktu in the Sahel of West Africa. Would anyone describe so equal or homogeneous civilizations today (Batutah 1958)? While few (none) advocate a return to the material conditions of past civilizations, the historical development of international inequality adds wounded prestige to the list of material deprivations and stimulates searches for who was responsible.

REDISTRIBUTION: THE DEBATES FOR AND AGAINST

For contemporary realist (and for some Marxist) scholars, international economic justice among existing nations is not an important normative issue. They doubt the basis for global, cosmopolitan international morality in the first place, finding international redistribution somewhat utopian, as we shall hear. Thus, the issue has devolved almost by default primarily to the liberals, with the other scholars serving, occasionally, as very effective critics.

Liberals

The liberals present us with three major views. The first portrays inequalities as the product of imperial theft, a violation of global common law that then requires reparations. The second, a utilitarian view, focuses on global humanitarianism. The third examines international justice as an implicit contract among free individuals that should be judged by the standards of fairness.

Global Common Law

Drawing on ideas articulated by John Locke, radical neo-Lockeans portray present inequalities as the result of imperialistic theft. In the state of nature, individuals have a right to acquire property by mixing their labor with it. As long as they (1) do not waste and (2) leave "enough . . ." and (3) "and as good" for others, all others must respect those property rights (Locke 1988, paras. 28–33). The "tacit and voluntary" establishment of money alters all three restrictions just as it alters the incentives to acquire that individuals experience.

The value of primitive commodities—such as apples picked from trees in the state of nature—has limits. There are only so many apples that an individual can want to acquire because our demand (use value) for them is limited and an excess will rot. The incentive to save, invest, and develop productive capacities is consequently also limited. But the value of money is unlimited. Money (e.g., gold and silver) can neither rot, nor be subject to the inherent limits of use value; it has exchange value. Accumulating money produces no inherent "waste," and its accumulation has social effects that can generate "enough and as good" for others. Money can turn into savings and savings into investment, and this can generate employment. Provided that an otherwise deprived individual can find employment (literally, at a living wage), then there is "enough" and, with enterprise and hard work, presumably as "good" an opportunity to acquire wealth as the original possessor (Locke 1988, para. 50).

What are the implications for international relations and the justice of the international distribution of property? Curiously, we find a contradiction, an odd combination of liberal conservatism and radicalism.

On the one hand, the informal tacit process of justification of both physical and monetary property indicate that the lack of global institutionalization is little bar to just differences in distributions of wealth and income that are large. The rich can justly enrich themselves while the poor remain, therefore, justly poor. There are no barriers here that would not also be present in the state of nature, and so both can be justified. Demands for redistribution based on egalitarianism or gaps in the standard of living have no place in a Lockean ethic.

On the other hand, the priority of the right to life makes equivalent demands. Individuals have a right to life, effectively a right to employment somewhere, and, if not available at home, they would have right to emigrate to find work at a living wage. Barriers to immigration from the poorest of the developing countries, where starvation is rife, would on the surface be suspect in this Lockean ethic.

In addition, that absolute prohibition of waste offers a powerful, moral foundation for an environmentalist's ethic. Either God or we collectively own the "commons" unless they are justly appropriated by individuals, that is, without waste. Pollution and other forms of waste violate our rights. It is then *our* commons that are being polluted, and this gives us a right, whenever and wherever it occurs, to defend the health of the earth.

Some radical Lockeans highlight international theft. The victims or their grandchildren demand reparations. This view, once held by many Third World radicals (among them the eminent Guyanese historian Walter Rodney), draw to our attention the documented history of slavery, land seizure in South Africa and Rhodesia, the widespread appropriation of mines and plantations, and the exploitation of cheap produce and products for consumers of Europe and North America (Rodney 1981). Famous cases such as the theft of Aztec and Inca gold, the crops produced by slave labor, and other indentured and underpaid labor are too numerous to detail. Even where colonialism did produce some benefits, such as in education, these were designed in the first instance to serve the imperialists.

In the name of the descendants of those who suffered, contemporary Third World intellectuals demand reparations for theft and kidnap. Their great-great grandfathers were done wrong; their great-great grandchildren seek recompense—with, on the conventional international lending principle, compounded interest. This recompense, we should note, will be a large sum (almost any sum long ago will compound into a large sum now). This presents a plausible moral case, especially given the current poverty of some of the most exploited areas, such as northeastern Brazil, Congo, Bangladesh, and parts of Indonesia.

But claims are complex for the following reasons:

1. Is there an international statute of limitations? Are we (citizens of the wealthy North) responsible for the crimes of our great-great grandfathers? If so, on this principle, does England also owe reparations to the United States for colonialism? Does Rome to Britain? Do the Mongols to the Ukrainians?
2. If we do owe, how much do we owe? Consider what small sums borrowed in 1800 are now worth with compounded interest. For example, the real estate value of Manhattan (bought for $24 in the 1640s) would now, one economist has calculated, be worth less than the value compounded annually at current interest rates of $24 over 350 years.
3. To whom do we pay? Do you pay elites, who may be wealthier than U.S. or French or British taxpayers (Cooper 1977)?
4. If identifying specific heirs is impossible and one tries to identify those most in need today, how much interference is tolerable? Should we also make sure that those in the North most connected to the theft pay (e.g., those who are descended from slave owners or slave merchants)?

Drawing on another radical interpretation of Locke, Brian Barry (1982) has highlighted the lack of just titles to property, regardless of whether actual theft can be proved. After rejecting "just requitals" (just prices) for past exploitation as being inadequate justice for poor societies lacking resources and after rejecting justice as "fair play" (reciprocal obligations) as ill-suited to the minimally integrated international economy, he settles on justice as equal rights (Barry 1982, 234).[2] He follows H. L. A. Hart's argument that special rights (e.g., to a piece of property) presuppose general rights (to property) and that natural resources (or inherited endowments) cannot be justly acquired without consent. Echoing Locke, he argues that, without consent, all have an equal right to global resources. The contemporary rich countries, therefore, owe a share of their income or resources to poor countries. Moreover, they owe this share without the requirement that it be directed to the poorest individuals in the poor countries because the rich have no right to impose conditions on income or property to which all have an equal right. If rich countries can dispose of global income autonomously, poor countries should have the same right (Barry 1982, 248). These are powerful arguments to which I return shortly.

The complications of international ownership led one U.S. Senator (Hayakawa) to dismiss claims to the Panama Canal with the widely quoted remark, "We stole it fair and square." Liberal Lockean values do not permit fair-and-square thefts. Both sides of the debate score points. The absolute status of international property is far from morally secure, yet the moral complexity of reparations does recommend that we consider other avenues toward justice.

Utilitarianism

Utilitarianism offers a recrimination-free approach that focuses on the needs of the destitute. Peter Singer (1972), in a classic article, argues that we should base our distribution of goods on values that are common to all mankind (i.e., saving lives, avoiding harm). Liberal and cosmopolitan in its assumptions, it treats all humanity as ends, regardless of state borders or class division.

Singer focuses on the most desperate problem of international distributive justice: the plight of the starving. He wrote in 1971, in the midst of the famine in Bengal, but of course many other disasters have come since, and there are more than enough crises to spark our continuing concern. He says that charity is not a sign of generosity but rather an imperative duty of justice. And this point he makes in an unforgettable analogy.

Imagine walking by a shallow pool of water and seeing a two-year-old child drowning in it. What should you do? Obviously, you should walk in and save the child. And so, just that simply, you should aid people starving in the world.[3] But many would object with the following:

1. Starving people are foreigners, or are on the other side of the world.
2. Other people don not provide aid; why should I?
3. I cannot end the starvation unless all the rich also aid.
4. Aid is costly; I do not have enough to spare and still meet its other needs.
5. It is government's—my country's—responsibility, not my personal responsibility.

Singer takes up each of these objections in turn:

1. Foreigners: Would it make a difference if it is not your child in the pool, or if it takes place not in your hometown? Obviously not.
2. Other people do not aid the starving, so why should I? Would it make a difference if three other people were standing around doing nothing?
3. Too many people are starving—cannot save them all? What if there are ten children drowning and you cannot save them all. Should you not save as many as you can?
4. Too costly to aid the starving? What if you are wearing your best dress or suit? Should you still jump in? Of course.
5. It is a government responsibility? Yes, but if lifeguards are not present, should you shrug your shoulders?

A stronger objection: What if it is truly costly? Suppose the children are swept away in a deep, raging river, and rescue is a risk to your own life. Then, Singer at last acknowledges, it seems different. There is no moral obligation; instead, rescue becomes an act for heroes. But how much risk, or cost, is less than life threatening? Singer argues that for a pure utilitarian, it is up to the point that your own life is also at risk. This means that one should, if necessary, reduce one's real income to the poverty or starvation level. Mother Theresa, thus, did the right thing, but do any of the rest of us? Singer then provides a more accommodating version of his ethic. He suggests that at least we should reduce our income significantly in order to offer assistance—that is, by 40, 30, or 20 percent—or, at the very least, we should do something—agitate, petition, or try to persuade the government to supplement our efforts to aid the world's desperate.

Powerful as this ethic is, it leaves many questions, even for the well intentioned. Does it apply to lesser inequality, or does it hold only in an emergency?[4] To state the charge provocatively, do we have a moral obligation to act in order to prevent children from perhaps catching a cold when their parents do not take them out of the safe but chilly pool of water? Moreover, in the less-than-clear emergencies, do not other principles begin to have relevant weight? For example, does foreign assistance disrupt local cultural stability? Are the right people being taxed to pay for the assistance (rich more than poor)? Is there an appropriate international institution to distribute the aid in a way that discourages paternalism, ensures that no one state acquires unmerited international influence, and avoids coercion in the raising of aid and also exploitation of the generous? These problems are the typical concerns that arise in moral political practice; they acquire additional weight as one moves away from emergency, life-and-death to situations of "merely" chronic deprivation.

International "Justice as Fairness"

Utilitarians appeal to preexisting common moral standards that should apply to each individual. Advocates of rights-based "justice as fairness" explain how separate individuals could converge on agreed standards for what is fair for the overall distribution of rights and valued primary goods.

How do we decide what is a fair set of standards? John Rawls (1989), in *A Theory of Justice,* said, as did Immanuel Kant, that we should contemplate a hypothetical contract. That is, what would be agreed to by free individuals under conditions of impartiality: the Rawlsian "veil of ignorance"? If individuals had to agree to govern their lives and prospects, not knowing one another's identities—class, talents, race, religion, tastes—and yet knew that they would have to live together and be dependent on one another for protection, economic production, and the products of social cooperation, what principles of justice would they choose to regulate the basic features of public life?

Rawls says that we would choose two basic principles, the first being maximum equal liberty. Even from a self-interested point of view, we have a stake in equal liberty for all. In case it turned out that, after the veil of ignorance was lifted, we were part of a minority, we would not want to be oppressed by tyranny, even by democratic majority tyranny. So we would insist on civil liberties, such as constitutional protections of free speech, religion, assembly, trial by jury, and habeas corpus. For matters not protected by basic liberties, we would want democratic government so that our voices would be equal. Second, we would require equal opportunity and the difference principle. We would want income distributed so that (1) it was open to fair competition (no discrimination), and (2) we would all receive equal income, unless differences in income helped the people at the bottom of the social ladder improve their condition. That is, we would reward the long, hard work of surgeons with an income high enough to attract enough skilled practitioners away from sunbathing into surgery (because, unlike sunbathing, surgery helps unfortunates needing medical care). We all would want the "difference principle" as well, however, because we too might turn out to be among the poorest, least able, severely ill, or handicapped after the lifting of the veil.

These highly egalitarian principles, Rawlsians say, apply only to domestic society. International relations should be governed by traditional international law (the legalist paradigm, no aggression, and so on) and save just redistribution for domestic consumption (Rawls 1993).

However, Charles Beitz, Thomas Pogge, and others have objected that Rawls assumes unwarrantedly that societies are self-sufficient in international relations. Instead, they argue, societies are interdependent. So, like interdependent individuals, nations who trade, invest, borrow, and yet are unequal must redistribute goods fairly. Moreover, they must consider that—like the endowments or talents of the hypothetical domestic original condition—national natural resources are arbitrary from a moral point of view (Beitz 1975; Pogge 1994). The United States has done nothing to deserve ownership of the fertile Great Plains, Mesabi iron range, and West Virginia coal fields, while the Sahelians deserve only the desert sands.

By analogy, the world, too, needs a hypothetical social contract in order to redistribute justly the products of social interdependence. We then should distribute goods as if we also did not know of which *country* we would find ourselves a citizen. The implications are unclear. How much would the wealthy have to tax themselves to implement a global difference principle in which all incomes were distributed in such a fashion that inequalities were permitted only to the extent that they served the needs of the *world's* least advantaged? Such a calculus would, however, seem to give rise to a large duty to redistribute income to the poor around the world.

These are the major liberal justifications for international distributive justice. Together they make strong claims. While claims to reparations for past theft are problematic in application, they are strong enough to undermine a complacent enjoyment of international ownership. Some of the wealth of the rich is tainted by origins in force, fraud, and theft. While the utilitarian argument mandating a duty of achieving equal happiness strains our common notions of the actual reach of human generosity, it successfully undermines a claim that neglect in the face of suffering can claim to be benign. The international Kantian claim for global social justice is the most systematic, addressing the weaknesses of the first two by articulating a political answer to a political question, but can it answer the criticisms of the realists?

Realist Criticisms

The most famous realist criticism of global redistribution must be Garret Hardin's (1974) "Living on a Lifeboat." Rather than a global village, our metaphorical condition, according to Hardin, is that of survivors on a lifeboat after a shipwreck. These lifeboats happen to be nationally distributed, and those objecting to that distribution are free to surrender their seats to the many who are struggling in the water. But no one has a duty to surrender space or the provisions. To do so might erode the "safety margin" on which all in the boat depend. Even for a well-equipped boat, charity leads to long-run disaster through a "ratchet effect," as more consumers are saved, thus increasing the burden on the next round of distributions. Moreover, any mutual sharing of resources will produce a long-run "tragedy of the commons." If resources (such as grazing on a village "common") are shared, no one (no "owner") has an incentive to save or invest since the product of any investment would be shared by all. Pooling lifeboat supplies, Hardin suggests, produces a similar tragedy of excess consumption. Associated with these catastrophes is the potential for the outbreak of plagues that may spread globally.[5]

The ethics of realism inform Hardin's lifeboat.[6] All states are at sea in some degree of peril—boats in a storm in various degrees of proximity to sinking or starvation. Realists ask, "Do we in the better national boats have the obligation to aid those in the more desperate or sinking craft?" What if the foreign boats are poorly managed or reluctant to rely on our assistance? What if, even if the foreign boats are well managed and willing to accept assistance, taking in too many will sink our boat? Do we not have the right to aid our own first, or must we aid all in all boats at the same time? Have not our passengers commissioned us to consider their care first, and is that not a duty that should govern the conduct of crew and captain?

Furthermore, the world, according to the realist, is not composed of children falling into shallow pools of water or out of well-provisioned lifeboats. Nor is it governed by a global social contract among free and rational individuals. That is, while children do fall into pools of water, people do face starvation, and we can think of contractual justice, those images are not accurate models of the international world. National lifeboats are more likely to confront than to aid other national lifeboats, and both may prefer plunder to relying on charity.

R. W. Tucker, who exemplifies realist thinking on international economic justice, argues that the real world is not the global village of 100 described previously but instead a system of 180 or so interdependent, sovereign states. These states interact in an anarchic system, each protecting its own territory and sovereignty, each suspicious of interference from others. Fear, relative power, insecurity, a state of war, anarchy, and real power shape the actions of states. Therefore, aid rarely reaches directly to the children or the starving. Instead, between them and all who would help—or harm—stand state institutions. It is through states that one must act, and therefore it is only through addressing the needs or goals of states that one can have any impact on individuals (Tucker 1975, chaps. 4–5; Krasner 1985).

Tucker adds that we misconstrue the South (the Third World) where the needy live if we think of them according to the "New Sensibility"—a human rights ideology that focuses on the global needs and rights of all individuals worldwide. Instead, states in the Third World are driven not by the New Sensibility but by a "New Egalitarianism." They seek not an equality of all individuals, themselves becoming one minor part of worldwide liberal social democracy. Rather, they seek an egalitarian order of states in which they equal the superpowers.

Many Southern statesmen may welcome the alleviation of poverty within their societies, but what, in the realist view, they in fact demand is an equal status, equal power, and equal development of their state—becoming not like us domestically but taking our place internationally. Northern (First, Industrial World) New Sensibility statesmen, who think otherwise, are therefore irresponsible and are failing to protect the security or welfare of their populations against the threat of the next turn in the international cycle of hierarchy.

This is where and why Tucker came into the debate on the just structure of the international economic order, as a Cassandra who wanted to be Paul Revere—whose warning to the West in 1973 to restore international hierarchy over the Persian Gulf in response to the "rebellion" of the Organization of Petroleum Exporting Countries (OPEC) (its embargo and price raises) went unheeded. He laments our lack of intestinal fortitude and writes to educate us as to how the world truly is—a world of order before justice, where you are neither right nor wrong, good nor evil, but instead up or down, rulers or ruled.[7]

Liberal Criticisms

Unlike the realist critics, the liberal critics agree with their fellow liberals that one must justify who has a right to what in what boat but insist that we need not all wind up in the same one. This debate over the moral significance of national borders has both moral and political aspects.

Liberal moral criticisms fall into differing camps, two of the most prominent of which draw their inspiration from Locke and Kant. As noted previously, conservative neo-Lockeans, or laissez-faire liberals, have argued that property could be justly acquired without a state to authorize acquisition and that states that instituted money further solidified the ownership of property, however unequal the distribution. International property rights for a pure Lockean might now be regarded as ambiguous because land is no longer abundant, pollution (Lockean "waste") is widespread, and international money is thinly instituted. Locke is also famous for recommending the export of labor to labor-scarce countries as a solution to distributive concerns in overpopulated ones. Laissez-faire Lockeans thus concentrate on opportunity to work and blame unjust inequality primarily on restrictions on labor mobility *within* Third World economies and, only secondarily, on international restrictions.[8] But practically, the commitment of liberals—especially laissez-faire liberals—to the efficiency and the advantages of international free trade tend to be severely tested by the inflow of low-cost imports from newly industrializing countries of the Third World. These imports threaten politically active domestic industries.[9]

Differing from both the Lockeans, the neo-Kantians raise a more fundamental set of moral concerns that limit all politically indiscriminate distributional claims founded on liberal principles. International rights, they argue, must be founded on moral freedom and individual self-determination. One cannot separate the economic from the political features of a just social order, but freedom, overall, is prior to wealth, just as Rawls's maximum equal liberty is prior to the difference principle. They do not want to sacrifice freedom and democratic self-determination for material well-being unless, Rawls and others have argued, the community finds itself in a state of desperation, such that the natural principle of justice should operate, determining that the basic minimum subsistence of all is the first duty of public justice.[10] Thus, in cases of extreme inequality and political anarchy within a country, the welfare liberals find justifiable a developmental, redistributing dictatorship to equalize opportunity as a necessary foundation for an eventually just liberal society (Rawls 1989, 252–53).

Neo-Kantian liberals also focus on the practical difficulty of establishing a just global society. At the public, constitutional level, the liberal justification for a dictatorial redistribution on a national scale is that, without it, authentically democratic liberal politics and social economy are rendered ineffective. The enormous social inequalities of the international order might, however implausibly, suggest that the same prescription should apply to the international order. But extended to global scale, this prescription runs up against a fundamental liberal constraint. It is not clear that an effective global, liberal polity can be formed. Kant, for example, regarded global sovereignty, whether liberal in aim or not, as equivalent to global tyranny because of the remoteness of the representation that it would entail. Differing from the utilitarians, no Rawlsian or neo-Kantian liberal would want to join a

"Scheme of Global Social Cooperation" unless it included a complete global social contract.[11] This would need to cover a polity establishing order and maximum equal liberty. But under the present regime of global intentions characterized by national independence and cultural diversity, this may not be possible. We then have no duty to ensure a global difference principle without a global polity guaranteeing maximum equal liberty. If the maximum effective size of a deliberative legislature is the conventional 500 or so, a global constituency would have to be of the order of eight million persons. The other alternative to direct representation—confederal solutions that mix direct and indirect elections—also attenuate the political life of the citizen or create grounds for serious conflict between the local government and the remote confederation.

Additional concerns arise at the individual level. The priority of freedom reflects the assumption that it is freedom that makes life subjectively valuable. We re-create ourselves, and this is the highest human faculty. Thus, obligations incurred in the name of freedom to distribute to the destitute at home or abroad have to have a cutoff that allows individuals to pursue a self-determining life. They should not be forced to be "moral saints" or be subject to "moral tyranny."[12]

In short, the redistribution that can be justified on liberal-contractarian grounds does not stretch beyond liberal government. Modern states may already be too large for effective liberal politics; it is even more difficult to argue that global government can be a liberal aim. Global reformers need to be able to guarantee that a scheme of global natural justice to assist the poor will end in effective, global equal liberty. Without the prospect of moral autonomy through representative government, this form of international redistribution is not justified on liberal grounds.

Thus, neo-Kantians object against accepting any principle of indiscriminate utilitarian or radical Lockean interstate justice, even when they accept (as argued by Barry, for example) the view that international property rights are not morally secure. First, if justice is determined by the equal rights of individuals to global resources or inheritances, then rich countries acquire income justly only when they acquire it justly from individuals (e.g., by international trade and democratically legislated taxation). Only just countries have rights over the autonomous disposition of national income. An unjust rich state has no right to dispose or hold income. A just rich country, conversely, has the right to dispose autonomously of national income, provided that national income represents its just share of global income. Any surplus is owed to individuals who are poor or to (just) poor states that have acquired a right to dispose of income or resources by the consent of their citizens. Neither unjust poor states nor unjust rich states should (by the argument of equal rights of individuals) have rights over global income. If there were justice among "thieves," it might call for distribution without condition from unjust rich states to unjust poor states. It is difficult to see, however, why that scheme should apply to the surplus of just rich states beyond what they distribute to just poor states. It is important, however, to remember that there do exist international and nongovernmental organizations (IGOs and NGOs), such as UNICEF and OXFAM, that form a trust for the global poor channeling some money successfully even to poor individuals living in unjust poor states.[13] The point is that an obligation of equal justice that would have required, say, Norway or Sweden to tax its citizens to provide direct transfers to a Somoza (Nicaragua) or Duvalier (Haiti) or Mobutu (former Zaire) in preference to funding the World Bank or UNICEF is morally unconvincing.

The second objection reflects the residual insecurity of the contemporary order. As long as there is no guarantee of international security, indiscriminate obligations of justice to redistribute substantial amounts income and resources (including redistribution to potential security threats) cannot be justified.[14] Obliging Japan to tax itself for China, or Israel for Syria, or even the United States for Cuba threatens the rights of individuals within these states to promote their territorial integrity and political independence.

It should be emphasized that these two objections to the application of just redistribution should not apply to (1) cases of assistance to the destitute, especially when they are reachable by neutral nonpolitical agencies, such as developmental NGOs, or (2) to social justice within the pacific union of liberal states.[15]

The priority that liberals give to freedom thus raises troubling implications for global justice of both the individual and the public variety. A neo-Kantian ethic could argue that we can do our personal reasonable bit in assisting the destitute and then shift obligations to a state that makes moral political decisions that take into account national security and welfare in a world where both are goods that need protection. Liberal states have a hierarchy of duties of global justice. First, they do have duties to aid the truly destitute everywhere in the world within the limits of guaranteeing the national security of their citizens. Second, they thus do not have universal obligations to institute a global scheme of distributive justice that would aid potential enemies. Third, for liberals, states within the liberal Pacific Union do rest on sufficient consent and do not constitute threats to one another. Between the union's rich and poor members, some obligation of justice to distribute global resources and income should supplement universal humanitarian obligations that are applicable globally to aid those whose poverty threatens their life. This is because of basic human solidarity and reciprocal interdependence under conditions of safety. It might reasonably extend to assistance directed toward achieving international basic opportunity (minimum adequate health care, basic education, and so on). Fourth, but those obligations need not include a complete difference principle because even within the Pacific Union liberal states can legitimately choose to reject a global polity and thus cherish a form of independent difference that does not allow a global scheme of cooperation.[16]

In addition, there are unresolved practical questions, including how to raise international revenue in a just fashion, how to distribute this revenue in an efficient manner such that it actually reaches those in need, and how to maintain the support of democratic citizens for lengthy programs when some mismanagement is likely and when strategic ties to authoritarian allies make competitive demands on aid revenues. These not insignificant obstacles and the competitive moral logic of realism enter the moral politics of actual foreign aid. Together they can identify the moral and political contours of international distributive reform.

Mixed Views

In theory, the trade-offs among basic national purposes as revealed by philosophic worldviews need not be large. We can, for example, conceive of mixed views that satisfy many objections to extensive redistribution but that still include real duties to redistribute wealth or aid the starving.

If a prudent realist puts security first and relative power of state next but yet acknowledges a residual duty to aid the desperate, then they should follow Robert Gilpin's suggestion (Doyle 1986). Gilpin notes that you can help the global poor in three ways: (1) exporting capital (but this weakens the economy at home), (2) importing products (but this puts domestic corporations out of business and workers out of jobs and may increase dangerous dependence), or (3) importing the global poor. If you will not bring jobs to the global poor, bring them to the jobs. It adds population, which adds to national power (reserve soldiers), and this is good realism. Immigration was once thought to be economically disruptive and harmful to the domestic poor through additional unemployment, but recent studies indicate that this is not the case. The Cuban influx into Miami in the 1980s, for example, produced growth and no extra unemployment other than that borne temporarily by the immigrants themselves (Passell 1990, E4).

Another possibility is a liberal view that responds to realist objections. If you accept the neo-Kantian critique of liberal universalism—no global "difference principle" without a global polity—then the four principles described previously should apply. After you tithe yourself 5 to 10 percent of your income, states have the residual obligation to alleviate suffering. States can legitimately infer that their obligation is owed to the global poor, not to rival states. Since, however, they can reach the poor only through just states, wealthy states are obliged to aid only to the extent that the money actually reaches the poor. They can, therefore, discriminate both against unjust countries and (accepting the realist consideration of protecting national security) against hostile, threatening countries (a Kantian can assume that all liberal states are not threatening). In periods of great danger, moreover, just wealthy states can discriminate against all, including the just and desperate, in favor of preserving survival first.

Responding to realist objections, this amounts to liberal discriminate justice. But this position still leaves firm duties to aid the desperately poor when danger is low, when the poor inhabit pacific or nonthreatening states, and when they can do so effectively. The current spread of democracy and security among democracies in the world may thus raise, not lower, international moral obligations. Ironically, the peace dividend *should*, by this logic, become an aid dividend. In short, mixing liberalism and realism produces less obligation to cure the world's poverty but a better prospect of alleviating some suffering.

These realist and liberal combinations could be politically viable, even in a conservative capitalist liberalism, such as that of the United States. One can see clearly that there is now a minimum amount of aid that all wealthy states are expected to contribute to poor ones. Likewise, it is obvious that such a system did not spring up overnight. Equally encouraging (and perhaps the best model for aid improvement for countries such as the United States and Germany) is the move toward greater attentiveness to domestic public opinion on aid, as exemplified recently by the Australian government. If they so choose, Australia's leaders can now explicitly alter policies in response to public demand—a rare foreign policy mandate. Of course, rather than running roughshod over public opinion if and when it does fall short on altruism, liberals advocate a program of popular education, which seems beyond reproach. Yet in regard to foreign aid, certain liberals argue correctly that most governments have a long way to go before they overreach the humanitarianism of their societies (Contee 1987). Moreover, there seems to be little disagreement that the all-important softer components of aid are best handled by NGOs and that local development is best initiated and directed locally. Yet there are also things that community groups cannot do as well as governments can, and this is where a public economic/infrastructure-centered program will continue to be of great value. In any case, there seems to be strong support in almost all countries for a further channeling of assistance through nongovernmental bodies, and it is arguably more in soft aid than in hard aid that the current system is lacking.

POST–COLD WAR DUTIES

The end of the Cold War presents a striking opportunity for the wealthy countries to meet their obligations toward the world's poor. But, ironically, it also may make it less likely that they will actually do so. Indeed, we seem to be approaching what might be called a widening international legitimacy gap of the sort referred to by Richard Falk and the South Commission in the quotation that began this chapter. Claims are legitimately rising, and the prospect of meeting them is falling.

The number of reachable claimants has increased, and their security needs have risen. As more governments become more representative, they increase the legitimacy of their claim to be representing their citizens. Liberal governments in the wealthy North should recognize that those new governments pose less of a security threat, so the security exception also becomes even less credible or justifiable. Moreover, while the spread of democracy seems to have improved the security of many individuals in the global North (with the end of the Cold War), the collapse of multinational states in the former Yugoslavia, the former Soviet Union, Somalia, Rwanda, and Sudan has greatly increased the vulnerability of these populations and the risks borne by their neighbors.

The continuing growth of NGOs also provides increased reliable access to the world's poor, even in those countries lacking a responsible government. The worldwide growth of democracy and global civil society thus has distributive significance even if the needs of the world's poor remained the same.

However, the number of the world's desperate has continued to increase. On the positive side of the news, life expectancy continues to rise, increasing one-third in the past thirty years. Yet only 20 percent of the aged have income security. Infant and under-five mortality has more than halved in the same period, yet 34,000 children die of malnutrition and disease each year. Although the number of poor countries able to meet the minimum nutritional requirements of their population has doubled, from twenty-five to fifty, since 1965, over 800 million people go hungry every day. The absolute number of those in poverty continues to increase—to 1.4 billion, one-quarter of the world, 400 million more than in 1980—and these people lack the reliable nutrition, health care, and shelter needed for safe, healthy, and productive lives. Relatively, the gap between the richest 20 percent and the poorest 20 percent of individuals in the world doubled between 1960 and 1991, from 30 to 1 to 60 to 1 (Wijkman 1996).

The wealthy countries, and especially the United States, are intellectually poorly equipped and politically handicapped in any effort to meet rising responsibilities. Intellectually, the current taste for national and market solutions to social problems makes it less likely, though not less justifiable, that global responsibilities will be addressed. The market has been hailed as the cure-all for the ills attributed to the inefficiencies of state socialism, and the evidence of the collapse of communist governments has advertised the proposition. The striking success of the East Asian economies makes it appear that national, bootstrap strategies are sufficient to eradicate poverty and inequality. The more successful Asian developers have moved toward democratic rule, as in South Korea, Taiwan, Thailand, and the Philippines. Indeed, the success of those countries is heartening and should give pause to those inclined to despair. But, together, these trends have unduly undercut much of the public rationale for global Keynesianism. It is often forgotten that the success of the East Asian economies is not free-market driven; the state has played a vital directing role. On top of that, some of the social reformist policies now under a cloud, including agricultural reform and investment in education, are widely seen as key elements of their success. Moreover, some of their success is attributable to the very international Keynesianism now so maligned. Both the Korean War and the Vietnam War provided extensive war-Keynesian stimuli for the regional miracles (Wade 1992).

Politically, additional constraints come into play. The first is increasing inequality in the United States and persistent unemployment across much of Europe. In the United States, three-quarters of households have not gained in real income (inflation adjusted) since the 1970s. The number of workers below the $12,000 poverty line almost doubled in the 1980s, and the number of incomes over $1 million increased 100-fold. In 1980, chief executive officers made 40 times the average income of factory workers; by 1996 the multiple was over 100 times (Wijkman 1996, 182). None of the rich industrial economies are overburdened, and yet they are failing to offer substantial assistance, the United States most strikingly. French aid is at 0.55

percent of GDP; Germany and Japan offer 0.31 and 0.28 percent, respectively. The U.S. figure is an astounding 0.1 percent. The German deficit is 3.6 percent of GDP; and Japan's is 3.1 percent. The U.S. deficit is only 1.9 percent of GDP (Gotz-Rechter 1996, A17). Yet U.S. foreign aid policy, if current trends continue, is unlikely to respond. Foreign aid, unlike defense, is "on the table" for further cuts stimulated by efforts to balance the budget. Although some reductions can legitimately be made in the years ahead (transition funding for the East European economies should phase out, and aid for Israel and Egypt can fall as, or if, the peace process proceeds), the dominant need is an increase, and that is not under consideration (Gordon and O'Hanlon 1996).

Together these trends suggest a crisis of obligations. Legitimate demands are rising. Justifications for not meeting them are becoming less credible. But policy reform that is designed to marshal the resources to address them is nowhere on the horizon.

NOTES

This chapter draws on parts of a chapter of my *Ways of War and Peace* (New York: W. W. Norton, 1997). I am grateful to Peter Furia and Paul Wapner for their suggestions.

1. We can, however, trace aspects of the debate back somewhat earlier, to World War II and to diplomatic demands of Latin America, Nazi Germany, and Fascist Italy in the 1930s for a larger share, for a redistribution to the then "have-not" nations from the "haves."

2. For additional considerations on the difficulties of extending Rawlsian justice to the international arena, see Brewin (1978, 151–52) and Amdur (1977).

3. Singer also grounds his argument in a utilitarian critique of Northern government expenditures in 1971, the crucial famine year. What is the implication, he asks, given that Australia spent more money on the Sydney Opera House than on famine relief or England more on the SST?

4. While Singer formulates his ethic only in terms of emergencies and not in terms of lesser inequalities, the two are quite closely related in practice. Perhaps the most simple way to see this is to consider that even given a severe drought in the United States, there is little (if any) chance of Americans experiencing famine conditions. Utilitarians should have no problem imploring us to care about the 90 percent of the 40,000 deaths per day due to non-emergency chronic hunger conditions.

5. Some recent commentary suggests that these problems of social decay, environmental stress, and mass starvation are multiplying across the less developed world, especially in Africa. It must be noted, however, that the broader predictions of Hardin's and Paul Ehrlich's "neo-Malthusian" view of population growth have not come to fruition.

6. Onora O'Neill (1975), however, challenges Hardin's moral reasoning. Going a step further, pursuing the implications of Singer and Beitz, and questioning the basic assumptions of Hardin, O'Neill concludes that inequalities that result in starvation in today's world are like murder in a "lifeboat" if others on other "boats" have enough to survive. Even if others do not have enough to survive, if the procedures governing the determination of those who die are not fair (e.g., if not by lot), then even in this circumstance, deaths are murders.

7. Many Marxist also object to liberal distributive justice across international borders on the grounds that redistribution may be counterproductive. If substantial, redistribution of income to the very poor may serve to reinforce the unjust social order of world capitalism by assuaging—or buying off—dissent; reforms thereby prolong oppression. But capitalists are unlikely in any case to be so redistributive, and most Marxists argue that aid does not reach the poor in the first place. Besides, according to these critics, it took massive rearmament (i.e., much more than Marshall Plan assistance) to achieve the stable reintegration of war-devastated Europe into the postwar, capitalist order dominated by the United States (Block 1977, 103–4). The Asian case involving massive U.S. purchases in East Asia in support of the Korean War is well documented (Cumings 1987, 67). In addition, the United States spent $500 million per year in aid for Japan between 1950 and 1970. Between 1946 and 1978, the aid figures are $600 per capita for South Korea and $425 per capita for Taiwan, both of which also became part of the order of postwar U.S. capitalism. Therefore, only when power—through social revolution-changes and liberates and equalizes social interaction will redistribution be useful, namely, to mop up leftover inequalities. For insightful remarks on the significance of these issues in Marxist theory, see the comments from an American Political Science Association roundtable by Alan Cafruny (in Doyle 1986, 857–59). But many Marxists likewise have no patience with realist views of New Egalitarianism, Third World nationalism, and international pecking orders; they often feel that the national ambitions of Third World developmentalists are no more than a fig leaf for the private ambitions of the Third World elites—lining their own pockets and those of their relatives is much more important than developing their countries. With the exception of a small authentically revolutionary set of communist leaders (Mao, Ho Chi Minh, and Castro) and (at least for some Marxists) an equally small set of revolutionary capitalist national bourgeoisie (South Korea, Taiwan, and Singapore), the Marxist commentators see Third World leaders as marrying a rhetoric of nationalism to a reality of collaboration with multinational corporations and plundering of their economies. These harsh criticisms were first and most eloquently presented in Fanon (1968).

8. An example of this line of reasoning would be Loehr and Powelson (1983). But, for an insightful discussion of the ethics of immigration restrictions, see Carens (1989).

9. The welfare liberals face similar political dilemmas in their association with well-organized labor in related industries (e.g., the garment industry) or in industries just recently threatened by imports (e.g., steel or automobiles). Two classic sources on economic policy and pressure groups are Pincus (1975) and Salamon and Siegfried (1977).

10. Isaiah Berlin, for example, suggests the prior importance of at least a minimum level of subsistence before personal and political liberty can be enjoyed (Berlin 1969, introduction).

11. Rawls's position is, however, complex, resting as much as anything on his view that peoples from different cultures do not possess the (nonpolitical) cultural common ground to "construct" a just cosmopolitan order. Here a dissenting line of liberal thought (one distinct from both utilitarianism and global common law) is worth mentioning: Explicitly motivated by questions of development in the global South, Martha Nussbaum, Amartya Sen, and others have recently attempted to construct a universalistic philosophy of "human capabilities." The group's most recent edited volume includes an essay by Seyla Benhabib that stakes out what might be called the middle ground between Rawls and the a priori cosmopolitanism of Pogge and Beitz (Benhabib 1995).

12. See the classic article by Wolf (1982). For useful critical reviews of the literature, see Findlay (1982) and Walter (1983).

13. The very existence of such institutions thus can expand the range of obligations of distributive justice, a point that has been developed by Martha Nussbaum among others.

14. This prohibition need not include small payments into multilateral institutions that (albeit via a middleman) already result in some minor such redistributions; for example, some of Israel's contributions to UN institutions actually end up funding projects that benefit its enemies. The question of "where to draw the line" as it relates to the still simmering debate over a more significant multilateral tax in exchange for the privilege of UN membership is an interesting one indeed.

15. Kant's argument for the mutual security that should be established among fellow liberal republican states is in "Perpetual Peace" (Kant 1970). I and many others have argued that his proposition has significance in the tendency for actual liberal republics to maintain peace with one another (for a review of the literature, see Doyle 1997, chap. 8).

16. Beyond the moral uncertainties of distributive duties, political obstacles are also daunting. If the disadvantaged are rightly the objects of social welfare, redistribution should be directed toward the vast preponderance of the world's poor who are in the developing countries of the global South, primarily in Africa and Asia. Since this aid is required by needy individuals (mostly) in the poorer developing countries of the South and not clearly owed to their states, the political logistics of distributing humanitarian aid, short of imperial control, will prove difficult. Political obstacles to taxing rich liberal societies for humanitarian aid are also evident. The income of the Northern poor places them among the world's more advantaged few. But the demand for redistributing income from the industrialized countries to the Southern poor meets two domestic barriers: the poor within the North are clearly disadvantaged, and our democratic politics places the needs of disadvantaged voting citizens above those of more disadvantaged but foreign people. That said, in practice support for genuinely redistributive foreign aid is high among Northern publics, and it may even be among disadvantaged groups within the North that such support is the highest. Throughout most of the Northern countries, public support for economic aid generally hovers around 75 percent. The case of the United States, where support for aid has historically been around only 55 percent, nonetheless also turns up some interesting findings, First, even a Cold War–era Chicago Council on Foreign Relations (1983) study found support strong (68 percent) for aid that "helps the economies of other countries" but weak (30 percent) for aid that "helps our economy at home" or that "helps our national security" (44 percent). The most comprehensive survey ever undertaken on U.S. public attitudes toward aid, the ODC–Interaction Survey, prepared by Contee (1987), adds that American blacks support aid more highly than do whites and for much more strongly felt humanitarian reasons. (Support for aid also correlates consistently with youth and with femaleness and perhaps even inversely with wealth—albeit here the results for purely humanitarian aid are ambiguous.) Finally, it seems that a majority of all Northern publics are opposed to military aid, albeit only slightly (51 percent) in countries such as the United States.

7

Social Justice: Growing Consciousness, Receding Prospects

Rajni Kothari

> There is no justice in this world.
>
> An epitaph on the human condition,
> expressed by a wide range of humans,
> from philosophers to plebeians

In this chapter, I consider the idea of justice (social justice included) in "global" terms. By global, however, I do not mean some elitist conception imposed by some transnational ideology or institutional structure. I think of it as a preferred value that permeates all social levels and historical contexts, as a deeply inlaid normative impulse that might move large masses of humankind to reverse many contemporary trends.

Such an understanding of justice in global terms pursued through a variety of practical engagements must be thought of in multidimensional space. It is not just a matter of gaps between rich and poor, between affluent nations and "poverty-stricken" countries, or between North and South. Nor is it simply a matter of public policy, even those aimed at the fulfillment of "basic needs." It has to do with much more: with the movement of sociopolitical structures over time, with the way in which minorities of various kinds are treated, with the way in which more and more sections of society are becoming vulnerable, and with a growing divide between an organized sector and an unorganized sector underclass. It has to do with the role of the state in all this, the nature of governance, the fulfillment or violation of human rights, the general disposition of elites toward the creation of a properly democratic social order, and the emerging outbreaks of strife and violence resulting from their failure to create one. Such a conception includes the variables of gender, generations, aging, health, shelter, and access to education and social mobility. It includes attitudes to migrants, refugees, unmarried mothers, those living on tiny pensions and poverty relief, masses of the forcibly displaced and evicted victims of "development" placed in "rehabilitation" camps, those who are in consequence physically disabled and mentally distressed, and those driven to drowning their solitary beings in liquor, drugs, promiscuity, and sexual violence. It also involves the way in which entire communities are being rendered rootless and culturally denuded, their collective memories and heritages enfeebled through the relentless growth of economic development (despite all the bold talk of alternative development).

If the quotation that opens this chapter has a certain resonance now, it is because the erosion of justice has acquired a deep structure that may well prove irreversible. Reversing it will call for a major revolution in both the structure of human thought and the world of practical politics, at global as well as national, regional, and local levels. The same extends to those instrumentalities and institutions on which our conventional accounts of justice depend—the paternal state, the market and the "hidden hand" mediating between competing interests for the good of all, the international system, and, above all, law. Moreover, the pursuit of justice ought not to be confused with the achievement of equality, at any rate not equality as has been conceived ever since the French Revolution. Left to itself, the concept of equality can become a dogma, lead to demagogy and tyranny from above, and reduce individual human beings into uniform entities, those masses in whose name power is concentrated in the hands of a few. This is especially true in our time in which the state, supposedly the principal equalizer, has generated so much homogenization and standardization, as well as a competitive ethics, and threatens to undermine basic freedoms. A proper concept of justice, in contrast, should foster respect for and preserve diversities in human propensities and preferred social arrangements, creating an awareness that whatever one does, individually or socially, is bound to be imperfect and that those who enjoy power must also exercise self-control and act with humility toward others.

In short, the growing erosion of justice is a result of a variety of normative pursuits that are the hallmark of modernity itself. If "there is no justice in this world," it is because the structures of injustice have become so deeply entrenched over time. The "brave new world" of which we were warned decades ago is at last here, leaving behind a very large part of humanity.[1] The passion for justice is reverberating in the hearts and souls of large sections of humanity alongside a sociopolitical-ecological-ethical thrust toward injustice that seems to be growing apace, the two coexisting almost in the fashion of an organic tie, not just following some dialectic of history.

DEMOCRACY AND SOCIAL JUSTICE

We live in an age of democratic consciousness. People are "on the move" everywhere. Old hegemonies have either crumbled or are being challenged. Ideological doctrines fashioned to perpetuate dominance and control are being widely questioned. All this is known and is gaining recognition. What is not equally well recognized is that the age we live in is also one of growing backlash against the democratic forces. It is also one of growing co-optation of voices of protest and intellectual dissent. While old hegemonies might be crumbling, new ones are being formed and perpetuated. There is also a slow but seductive crystallization of doctrines—about security, of stability, of unity—that are all being used to legitimize patterns of governance that are clearly antidemocratic. Even less clearly recognized is the fact that the very structures that had been conceived for promoting the democratic process and providing liberation from traditional constraints—political parties, representative institutions, the judiciary—are producing conditions not just of political instability but of incipient breakdowns of the social order. The result is large-scale social violence, the rise of negativist identities (sectarian and otherwise), and doctrines of exclusion and dispensability according to which entire populations are looked upon as undesirable and unwanted.

There has been, not least, a basic shift of focus and a fundamental inversion of priorities in the prevailing account of development. Problems of the world are no longer seen in terms of the possibility of bridging chasms between rich and poor. Instead, the new vision seeks to provide—to the exclusion of all humanist considerations—for the unhindered advance of technology that would integrate the world into a single unified world political economy. Large segments of the powerless and backward, comprising a variety of emerging nations, traditional communities, and cultures, are incapable of keeping pace with or finding a place in this rapidly transforming world. This fact is not easy for them to accept. However, they have to be made to accept it. The best one can do is to offer, to a limited extent, certain palliatives, such as state assistance to the poor and the victimized. Even this is currently under attack.

Gradually, such a shift in thinking has given rise to a tendency to underplay the very problems of poverty and victimization and to act as if they did not exist. The new penchant for turning away from the past and forging ahead into the future and joining the global march toward progress and affluence also involves forgetting the poor and the oppressed, the women and the aged. There is declining concern for the coming generations and little sense of embarrassment or guilt (not to speak of anger and outrage) at the continuing exploitation and blatant violation of people's rights and dignities. Poverty is fast becoming a forgotten issue while describing the human condition. Key headlines in the media, the new slogans, and the emerging prognoses put out by those in authority are no longer concerned with the absolute poverty or ill-health in which a large part of humanity lives. Even ordinary people have been brainwashed by new desires and expectations, by new consumer needs, that have been planted in their minds by the mass media and ad agencies. This in turn has resulted in deepening relative poverty as well. For most of the elite, neither absolute nor relative poverty is any longer a matter of primary concern. The result is an increasingly disenchanted, insecure, and angry youth; a rapid breakdown in living conditions; a growing decay of the physical environment; and an increasing incidence of squalor and disease and insufferable surroundings in both rural habitats and urban ghettos to which this youth is forced to migrate.

Those engaged in a systematic onslaught on the poor and deprived sections of society do not seem to realize the costs of what they are doing. As the sense of insecurity among the people grows alongside persisting poverty, unemployment, and increasing injustice and discrimination, the poor and the unemployed are pushed into a culture of protest, anger, and desperation, contributing further to an overall condition of insecurity that is then exploited by sectarian politicians and is sought to be put down by a criminalized police and paramilitary establishment. Slowly and without their knowing it, the poor are being pushed into a world of crime and criminality, of interethnic violence and militancy against the state.

It is this wanton criminalization of poverty spurred on by the politics of the elite that poses the most fundamental crisis of survival. It also poses a crisis in the system and its stability. If the poor have no recognized institutional channels through which to take up their grievances against the continuous injustices that they face, and if the elite no longer considers it necessary to act through the same institutions and their systems of accountability—they already seem to be acting more and more outside the institutional framework, thereby reducing their legitimacy—there seems to be less and less scope for improving the condition of the people through the operation of the existing order.

It is not just that the poor are pitched against the rich and the rich against the poor. The poor also fight against other poor, faced as they all are by an overall climate of deprivation and a growing sense of insecurity among various subgroups. But such a combination of deprivation and sense of insecurity—getting worse because of inflation and unemployment—is also hurting the less poor sections of society. It is producing divisions among the middle classes and even sections of the rich.

Even more basic than this cultural syndrome of poverty, the modernist idea that economic growth will create wealth and that this will in turn "trickle down" does not take account of the wealth that had already existed through long periods of history and that is now being destroyed in the process of creating new wealth (agricultural land, forests, and common property resources). We are already slowly eating away the capital created over the centuries by our forebears that, it is now discovered, is being depleted at a much faster rate and can perhaps never be replenished. The ecological dimension of poverty is not even touched upon by those who offer us "global" solutions. Examples of this are the destruction of forest and water resources that once abounded in plenty, the growing incidence of famines and floods, and the growing desertification on the one hand and growth in malnutrition, hunger, and starvation on the other. Much if not most of this is caused by massive imbalances generated by modern industrialization, the building of gigantic hydroelectric projects (which are also displacing entire communities and tribal homelands), and the craze for runaway urbanization and enclosures of rural commons for expropriating from them goods and services meant to feed into ever rising levels of consumerism. The steady growth of the unorganized sector in which migrants, women, and child labor are ghettoized is another instance of ecologically caused exclusions of the poor from the social arena.

It is a mistake to think of poverty as the absence of wealth. Nor is poverty by itself to be bemoaned. So many civilizations and communities have lived in "poverty" without becoming destitute and driven to misery. It is only when they are denuded of their basic resource base in nature and ecology that "poverty" of the modern exploitative variety takes roots in which the social base of the economy is riven apart and civil society rendered incapable of sustaining itself.

In sum, what are neglected in the prevailing approach to poverty are social and ecological dimensions, that the poor—as poor—are a social class, not just an economic or statistical category. Even if economic or financial supports are provided, several sections of the poor could continue to be socially backward, underprivileged, discriminated against, perceived as backward by society at large, and, as a result of this, oppressed in many ways. The scavengers and the carriers of night soil may make money, but they do not cease to be poor. This phenomenon of social poverty (as distinct from economic poverty) needs to be fully examined if we are to get out of the vicious cycle of poverty–development–poverty.

Especially serious is the condition of those who have been forcibly physically dislocated and uprooted, disinherited in both space and livelihood, and then thrown into a vortex of slums and ghettos from which the only "exit" point is crime and terrorism and, for some, social militancy. Taking place here is not only the criminalization of the poor because of their condition of poverty but also the rendering of people who were not poor, such as the tribals who have been forced out of their habitats and cultural inheritance wherever large dams have been built, into becoming poor, forcing them to participate in criminal or paracriminal activities.

A CRISIS OF THEORY

Meanwhile, major efforts to challenge hegemonic structures and patterns of domination—institutional, ideological, mobilizational—that were at work both at the grassroots and in intellectual thinking have been weakened and, to a considerable extent, delegitimized. One reason why these "movements" have failed to generate an alternative combination of theory and praxis, and the reason why "new visions" in the form of right-wing reactions and "fundamentalist" onslaughts seem to be casting a spell on the middle-class mind and large sections of the mass media, may lie in what needs to be clearly grasped and boldly stated: the failure of major theoretical conceptions of historical change that have ruled the roost for a long time now. These include modern science, which lies at the root of the promise of the European Enlightenment; the modern state, which was supposed to liberate the human spirit from both tradition and the "state of nature" that had for long held back the human potential from realizing itself; class and class consciousness, which were supposed to deal with the inequities and injustices produced by the role of certain vested interests that had taken control of the state; and in recent decades the notion of "development," principally economic development but social development as well, which was to catalyze the human urge to prosper and excel and accumulate through the mechanisms of the state and the market.

Powerful as the grand theory and vision that emerged out of these various constructs was, it failed to provide the basis of social transformation and justice. Science degenerated into a monolithic, elitist technological fix in the hands of a class of technocrats and experts and economists. The state became a corrupt bureaucratic enterprise that failed to carry out its original mission of controlling strife and criminality. And, instead of steering the full dialectic of human history through the instrumentality of modern science and technology, as had been envisaged by Marx, class and class consciousness got sidetracked into an apolitical vision of "development" that has been hijacked by a bloated and parasitic presence of a middle class, the only world class that there is.

In the "socialist" countries, instead of class formations of "workers and peasants" releasing the social dialectic inherent in civil society utilizing both modern science and technology and the modern state, the domination of a so-called vanguard overlay the citizenry through the machinations of a relatively close and straitjacketed party that has smothered civil spaces and diverse cultural, craft, and other autonomous formations. This has further led to a delegitimization of the modern state in the eyes of the people, especially the working class and the peasantry.

TOWARD A NEW CONCEPTION OF CIVIL SOCIETY

It is against this erosion of civil society as the primary catalyst of both the modern state and the national market, the erosion of its voluntaristic ethos, and the gradual withdrawal from distributive justice both through the instrumentalities of the welfare state and through the organization of citizen groups and movements that a completely new model of "civil society" is making itself felt.

This is civil society not as *civitas* but as *communitas*, taking religious, ethnic, communal, and other sectarian forms. *Civitas* implies pluralism and diversity; *communitas* brings forth monolithic, homogenizing dimensions. *Civitas,* on the one hand, is nondichotomous vis-à-vis the state, pluralizing vis-à-vis the market, and decentralizing vis-à-vis global structures as well as vis-à-vis the mass media and communication networks. *Communitas,* on the other hand, is dichotomous vis-à-vis the state (religion versus politics), reinforces neo-orthodox thinking in the economic sphere, and borrows heavily on the new trends and fashions in communications. It utilizes commercial methods, both co-opting and intimidating adversaries and, through a determined ideological onslaught, creating an atmosphere of growing polarization and forcing people to take positions. Furthermore, *communitas* generates a structure of feuds and factions within civil society, forces them to seek legitimization through politicization of existing or new cleavages that then impels the state to treat the various movements of dissent and upsurges from the grassroots as defiance of law and order, and to adopt repressive measures against them. The capacity to protest and resist such manipulation has become weak and increasingly ineffective.

This is particularly true in relation to the condition of vulnerable sections of civil society, especially the lower classes, the tribals, the women, and the children. It is particularly bleak for the younger generation of each, especially the children and women. Today's children have at least child labor to offer, regrettable though this is. Many of them support entire families, though they may not always get the best of the bargain. Soon, however, under the impact of growing technologization of the tertiary sector, they will just not be needed. The process of not being needed has already begun. The modern child, especially from the poorer strata, faces deep loneliness and often expresses this loneliness through an increasing incidence of crime, violence, and drugs. We are living through a period of growing criminalization of youth. The state has ceased to provide minimum protection or security, not to speak of social security. The "new" economic thinking is underplaying welfare, compassion, patronage, and affirmative action in the form of subsidies and reservations. The emphasis is instead on meritocracy. The overall framework consists of the political economy of colonization and the sociology of fundamentalism, of the entrenchment of exploitative structures, of poverty turning into destitution, of women and children being made into commodities, and all of this shot through by the growing virus of consumerism, which seems to flatten out all choices and alternatives. The so-called nongovernmental organizations (NGOs) are unable to stem this tide, besieged as they themselves often are by internal feuds, declining accountability, and the growth of undemocratic practices within many of them, as well as by a high incidence of the commercial ethic and the susceptibility for more and more incomes and perks.

Women are victims of exploitation not just in bureaucratic structures and development projects, not just in civil society at large (including the NGOs), but within families and communities as well. Exploitation of men also leads to cruelty on women, men being both exploited and exploiters. The crisis of civil society becomes especially onerous for women who are traditionally supposed to manage family and community affairs through a simultaneous exercise of both control and self-denial, of suffering while holding things together. This predicament is becoming more acute. With all the confidence and boldness displayed by modern women, they are still expected to have an infinite capacity to cope with oppression and pain through various stages of life. Increasingly, modern men are found to be exhausted, unable to stand up to any real challenge in life, at worst getting drunk and beating up their wives and children, continuously marginalizing themselves, sinking in self-esteem and becoming doubly dependent, and doubly lacking in dignity, courage, and confidence. As for children, their traditional incapacitation (except in laboring classes) through indulgence in an early age and being thrown to a heartless future later is getting reinforced by new sources of incapacitation, especially female children, but male children as well.

All of this applies more and more as we move down the social ladder and as we confront the growth of political and social fragmentation created by social disintegration, by multiethnic polities, and by the mounting backlash on minority communities, all by the various ethnic and linguistic identities being manipulated by local chieftains, who in turn are becoming criminal and corrupt warlords. The latter are especially merciless on children, who are at once being commodified and brutalized, growing up into brutes themselves who have been socialized into dealing with the world the hard way, including carrying AK-47s and explosives both as instruments of self-defense and as a matter of sheer style.

How will civil society manage both its own backyard—family and community—and the political and economic burdens increasingly brought to it with the decline of the state and the erosion of the pluralistic democratic process? Is it at all likely that from the very excesses of modernity turning more and more inward, from the political arena to the communitarian and familial, to the real core of civil society and its innermost recesses, new agendas of response to the diverse crises facing humanity may well emerge? In addition, as these surface, will they draw on potentialities that exist within more macrostructures of polity, economy, and world affairs?

Despite the growth of atomizing tendencies, there exists a wide arena of plural identities and structures, and these are likely to grow, giving rise to both new possibilities and new vulnerabilities. Globally, the inherent multilateralism provides a broad arena of pluralism despite recent deformities based on various modes of centralization and globalization. To this is being added, by leading exponents of world order, a "regional alternative."[2] Within individual nations (I deliberately avoid tagging statehood to nations) there exist—and these are growing—the various federal and federating (and confederating) structures and, within these, diverse regional and social units, communities, castes, and ethnically and ecologically based habitats, all of them seeking a place under the sun as part of a larger, more inclusive and plural structure. Traversing the diverse spatial, social, ecological, and gender components of these pluralities are various "grassroots" structures outside the traditional formations based on caste and village identities. In the last few years, these have been conceptualized in the form of diverse "movements," of people setting their own agendas, both fighting against dominant tendencies and generating their own demands. Even as the voluntary organizations and the NGOs falter, one pins one's hopes on "people" at large.[3]

There are obvious dangers inherent in any exaggerated interpretation of peoples' movements, of activists and militants organizing them, of counting so much on people's own initiatives. We have long romanticized the state (in my view the original sin of political science and, without our knowing so, of economics as well), the market, and science and technology, and now we romanticize "religion" as well by referring all the time to its "fundamentals." As we move into the twenty-first century, we certainly cannot afford to romanticize the people in any populist way.

Even so, the only striving that has survived the decline in legitimacy of each of these arenas of the mass age is that of democracy. This is why we may be standing at the threshold of a new democratic era: of the transformation of a "mass age" into a "democratic age," of the state as deliverer into the state as responder to the churnings of civil society, of science with a capital "S" providing some kind of a magic wand into science with a small "s"—and technology with a small "t"—serving the small and medium aspirations of people living in diverse social and economic settings, seeking technical inputs in their decentralized and pluralistic strivings and their many "agroclimatic" and "biomedical" terrains.

Such an agenda is primarily one in which "Glasnost" becomes a condition of "Perestroika," not a "Thing-In-Itself." To a considerable extent, the agenda posed by the democratic resurgences of our time includes the deeper mainsprings of human livelihood.[4] This agenda also entails those economic and technical issues that have arisen in the wake of decades of maldevelopment and skewed priorities that can no longer be left to experts and technicians, planners, and planning bodies. Problems of poverty and destitution, disparities and inequities, are at bottom political problems. Moreover, they need to be viewed not only as political problems but also as ones in which large numbers of people at different levels of social existence need to play a variety of roles. The social urge toward equity has to be conceived as a political urge. Similarly, the cultural craving for diversity and pluralism must be conceived so that equity does not degenerate into equality and becomes a basis for social justice, politically conceived.

It will not do, for example, to think of decentralization of rural life in terms of bureaucratic reorganization or the transfer of resources. Any step toward decentralization without enlisting the support and struggles of the mass of the people—indeed their direct involvement—is bound to land in the hands of bureaucracies, contractors, or organized crime, as this opened up for corporate and transnational penetration. Nor will it prevent us from the deeper malaise of conflicts and violence and protect various types of minorities—religious, ethnic, and gender based—from even more brutal invasions than is presently the case. The real kernel of decentralization lies in the interplay between the institutions of the state and the structures of civil society (including deeply laid and historically legitimate traditional structures). The worst forms of exploitation and repression that have surfaced in recent times are to be found at the grassroots, often between adjacent social classes and communities. It is only by conceiving decentralization in at once political, social, and cultural terms that the hold of entrenched interests and their intimate nexus at the grassroots can be challenged.

All this is not merely a matter of positing a set of normative considerations and a desired set of ideas. It is also one of recognizing the forces at work from below as well as from the large horizontal space of a geopolitical and geosocial kind. Not to recognize the emerging and restive aspirations of the mass of the people, not to accredit their real representatives with legitimate standing, not to reconcile interests and provide a just resolution of them, and not to respond to genuine, even if modest, claims and demands would be flying against the face of reality.

EMERGING DILEMMAS

In this chapter, I have offered an intellectual and theoretical perspective for grappling with these varied dimensions, both globally and nationally, by enhancing my own concerns with civil society, pluralism, and a model of secularism that is rooted in a pluralist framework of society and, consequently, of the state as well. Moreover, it is on this basis that I want to claim that it is possible to confront the centralizing tendencies of the modern polity. Much of the contemporary turbulence at various levels is a direct consequence of a growing lack of fit between a plural society and an unplural polity. This emerging incongruity has in turn received further impetus from global tendencies in the economy, modern communications, and the steamroller of a consumerist culture. Claims of democracy, human rights, and the legitimate aspirations that move people around the world are increasingly being used to legitimize a universal and homogeneous model of governance, thereby opening new frontiers for both world capitalism and the so-called "new world order." This is happening in large parts of the world, including in countries that had hitherto sought to pursue alternative paths to development, nation building, and people's participation, which believed in distinctive social philosophies, and were especially keen on national self-reliance. India, long an advocate of self-reliant nationhood, has now become a willing candidate for such globalization. So has China, though in ways quite different from India.[5]

As we move forward in the twenty-first century, two opposite pressures will be at work on democracies. There is, first, the global setting of economic integration, cultural homogenization, global trade regimes, and massive displacement, marginalization, exclusion, and an easing out of larger and larger sections of "the people." This also feeds into hegemonic, monotheistic, and "fundamentalist" agendas. But there is also the local, national, regional, ethnic, and community settings that will, in the years to come, press on with completely opposite agendas—of autonomy, pluralization, national and local development regimes, indigenization of knowledge and belief systems, and new and varied experiments from the "grassroots." The interaction between the two could well be resolved "democratically." Much will depend on the extent to which hegemonic structures are made to bow to the compulsions of democratic politics. In the words of Richard Falk (1994), since 1991 it has become evident that "the unipolar moment" was only a brief interregnum. If this reading of the situation is correct, the democratic impulse that lies at the bottom of the upsurges of civil society could also join the battle against global hegemonic forces, though the outcome may still be uncertain.

AGE OF UNCERTAINTY

Central to the new churnings of civil society is the emerging response of the people at large to the age of uncertainty on which we seem to be embarking as we face an increasingly uncertain future. As the world falters along after the end of both the century and the millennium, little seems to be clear. All kinds of scenarios have been visualized—from Francis Fukuyama's (1992) *The End of History* and the "defeat" of communism to his compatriot Samuel Huntington's (1993) coming clash of civilizations. Having run over the East, the sights have now shifted to the conquest of Islam and the Confucian Far East.[6] The European think tanks too are nervously depicting the dawn of the "Pacific Century," the Third Worldists widowed by the demise of the Soviet Union are bemoaning the advent of a unipolar world, while the beaming Chinese continue to find multilateralism at work, and the confused and diabolical Indians expressing one view, meaning another, and hoping for yet another one. Nothing seems clear. We all seem to be swimming together in a vast ocean of uncertainty.

Not only is the system learning to live with uncertainty, it is also accepting it as the normal state of affairs and, to an extent, institutionalizing it, getting suspicious about anyone coming forward with clear-cut or positive answers to problems—in fact, not believing that there can ever really be such answers. With this is born not just the phenomenon of uncertainty but what can be called a *cult of uncertainty.*

Why so much uncertainty, such great disbelief in anything working? Two factors seem to be at work. First, the dominant structure, the ordering mechanism that had been around for a long time, is not functioning any more and has suffered deep erosion. Second, the alternatives that came up proved illusory and created even greater uncertainty than before. In addition, as the people prefer neither the old nor the attempted new, and as neither works anyway, the sense of uncertainty grows even more.

Alternatively, is it the case that moving out of a single hegemonic center and a homogeneous ruling set necessarily leads to uncertainty—at least, to a widespread feeling of uncertainty? If it is the latter, can not uncertainty be creative, indeed necessary, before moving on to a new era? Perhaps the age of uncertainty will see people coming into their own, handling things on their own, relying less and less on rulers and more and more on themselves.

In fact, problems have a way of handling themselves, without any externally determined intervention in the direction of some clear "solution," and yet shifting the ground forces, allowing those very forces to express themselves in completely new, complex, and apparently anarchic ways, in the process at once marginalizing the state and making its operators suffer from the illusion of their having resolved matters. Seen in this way, indecision among rulers becomes a consequence of their disempowerment—not disempowerment of the people but of the elite. The media have a tendency to criticize the various elites, governmental and otherwise, all the time and demand decisive action from them. However, they do not know that over time these elites have been denuded of their power to intervene in the social terrain.

"Problem solving" is a peculiarly modern mentality, a managerial syndrome, as if some people—administrators, politicos, and experts—can make things work, and when things do not work, we are up against "problems," which again only the same set of people could put right. Traditional societies had problems as well, but these were never "solved" for good, nor were attempts made to do so. States of tension and disequilibrium were brought under control, but the problems continued to exist. They recurred at regular intervals, and adjudication thereof was a continuing task. There was no general peace or even "harmony" in traditional civil society, but there were constant adjustments of rival claims for which there were available loci of power and authority, in fact several of them, not one centralized one.

It is the coming of the modern state that led to the compulsion among the new rulers to "sort things out," to "move along," to "change things around," and through all that movement to consolidate their legitimacy and displace traditional centers of authority. It now seems that this project of the modern state has created its own "problems." The "people" too—mobilized along unprecedented paths—believed for a while in this magic of the modern state, in the superiority of the new and the modern over old and tried-out ways. Only now, in the last few years, people seem to be losing that faith and moving toward wresting things once again from alien centers of authority and governance (including in their own societies) for themselves. The process is still under way. People's empowerment, through a variety of affirmative devices, is already under attack. This is partly because they have relied far too much on the machinery of the state. They have yet to come into their own and decentralize power, not just politically but also socially and in terms of a diversity of cultural domains. This will not be easy, for the new inheritors of power from the colonial masters, despite the democratic rhetoric, would not easily move things over to the people or even lower the scale and intensity of their present dominant roles and the institutional structures that sustain those roles. Their legitimacy will need to get a few more knocks before this could really happen. However, the process has begun.

Meanwhile, the capacity of nonmodern societies, such as India, for individual survival when faced by institutional erosion, abnegation of responsibility by the rulers, and surrender of the self before the greater sweep of "global" and cosmic forces continues unabated—for the individual as well as the state. For them, there never was any "history" to make or unmake. It ended before it began. Perhaps we should leave it to the Fukuyamas and the Huntingtons to worry about history and how it will proceed. We shall see what they make of it. As for ourselves, we will seek to cull out wisdom from the uncertainty that surrounds us. This, for us, is our "normative" choice—the basis on which to erect a truly humane future.

NOTES

1. Over the years I have worked on this phenomenon of "two worlds," largely within India (in an analysis of two Indias) but also globally. For example, in my acceptance speech for the Right Livelihood Award on behalf of Lokayan in 1985 at Stockholm, "Bridging Two Worlds," I argued that "we live in a deeply divided world with increasing loss of contact

between the divisions an growing estrangement between them", and that it is an estrangement that not only promotes ignorance and loss of empathy but also creates a psychic condition of growing immunization, apathy and amnesia. See "Two Worlds within Each Society: Lokayan's Efforts to Overcome the New Rift" (text of the Right Livelihood acceptance speech, International Foundation for Development Alternatives (IFDA) dossier, March–April 1986, xx). On India, see Rajni Kothari, *State against Democracy: In Search of Human Governance* (Delhi: Ajanta Publishers, 1988; New York: New Horizons, 1989).

2. See especially Bjorn Hettne (1994a, b).

3. I have argued this point at length in many of my recent writings, in particular in the chapter "Ethical Imperatives," in *Growing Amnesia: An Essay on Poverty and the Human Consciousness* (Delhi: Penguin, Viking, 1993; London: Zed Books, 1995); see also "Globalisation: A World Adrift," *Alternatives: Social Transformation and Humane Governance* 22, no. 2 (April–June 1997): 227–67; "Towards a People's Democracy," *Biblio: A Review of Books* 3, nos. 7–8 (July–August 1997): xx; and "India: The Growing Confidence of the Poor," *The Times of India*, July 28, 1997.

4. Unfortunately, modern society has a record of dismal failures and painful betrayals of basic mass aspirations—not just betrayals but increasing indifference to the exclusion of millions and millions of people as a given, considering them as dispensable, a burden, an embarrassment. Poverty and destitution that should provoke our cultural values have instead produced a mood of cynical withdrawal and dehumanization. Indeed, the most pathetic aspect of current states of consciousness that need to be resolutely fought against is our growing indifference to misery among large sections of the people, especially in formerly colonized societies where decolonization has brought little by way of emancipation or justice, "independence" has proved illusory, and the elites that have assumed power seem to be even more indifferent to the plight of their poor than are some distant observers who are possessed by humane values and a democratic commitment. With the dramatic collapse of the socialist world and the growing erosion of the very idea of the "Third World," there has emerged an unnerving and frightening ethical vacuum, both in the conduct of international affairs and in the positioning of governments almost all around the world. In this vacuum, the only recourse and stratagem left to governments and other centers of power will be that of realpolitik. And this time around (unlike during the long transition after the Congress of Vienna), it is going to be realpolitik without a framework of norms and conventions and an overarching liberal set of values and limits, giving rise to growing normlessness and an insensitivity to the human condition. This poses the greatest challenge to the democratic agenda.

5. The Chinese model—and to a large extent the model followed by other East Asian countries, from Japan to Malaysia—is different from that followed by India and other South Asian countries in that, while accepting elements of liberalization and even certain aspects of globalization, they have not permitted scaling down of their autonomy and sovereignty as nation-states, so much so that in many of them, especially China, the Communist Party has continued to retain its dominance. Even more pertinent, most of them have remained autocratic regimes and have violated democratic norms without paying any heed to Western pressures for human rights. "Self-reliance" for them includes the freedom to suppress dissent not just at home but, as the admission of Burma into the Association of Southeast Asian Nations (ASEAN) shows, elsewhere too. India's economic self-reliance, hoping to regain it through its own brand of pragmatism, is altogether different.

6. While the former was more in the nature of celebrating the end of world communism

and the triumph of a unipolar, corporate world order, the latter was less sanguine about the collapse of a bipolar world and the stability that went along with it and, instead, concerned with a new structure of challenges to U.S. hegemony, namely, that represented by non-Western civilizations as practiced by West and East Asian nations. This represented, geopolitically speaking, a return to managing outlying regions and states, as used to be the case in the early years of the Cold War. Huntington's more recent *The Clash of Civilizations and the Remaking of World Order* (1997) seems like an effort to realistically accept the new reality of a multipolar and multicivilizational trend of world politics while still being concerned with how the West will manage the new challenges that are emerging, especially China, which he considers inimical to U.S. interests.

8

Collective Identity, Social Movements, and the Limits of Political Dissent in Israel

Simona Sharoni

INTRODUCTION

It would be an understatement to say that the Arab-Israeli conflict has shaped the lives of at least three generations of Israeli-Jews and Palestinians. The conflict has served as both the catalyst and the touchstone for the consolidation of particular notions of a national "imagined community" for Palestinians and for Israeli-Jews, respectively. For Palestinians, the imagined community came to be seen as a future sovereign Palestinian state. Apart from differences concerning the territorial boundaries and the political and social character of their future state, a broad consensus emerged among Palestinians that the principles of national self-determination and territorial sovereignty are inseparable and crucial to the survival of the Palestinian people. A consensus around the same principles has served as the basis for the Israeli-Jewish imagined community. But, while Jews realized their dream and established a Jewish state, this has come at the expense of Palestinians, whose desire to fuse national self-determination with territorial sovereignty remains unfulfilled. This outcome has in many ways formed the basis for the Palestinian-Israeli conflict.

The centrality of the Israeli-Palestinian conflict in the daily lives of Israeli-Jews and Palestinians since that time has helped generate particular answers to the question "Who are we?" These answers, rooted in the rigid distinction between "us" and "them," played an important role in shaping Palestinian and Israeli-Jewish collectivities. But an overemphasis on this distinction has often overlooked differences within each community and thus other possible answers to the question "Who are we?" Just as Palestinians and Israeli-Jews have articulated different and often competing answers to this question, there have been multiple answers within each national collectivity. The persistence of the conflict, however, has undermined differences within the communities and helped consolidate what have appeared to be cohesive, stable notions of collective identity.

This fact became more evident with the September 1993 signing of the Oslo Accords, which destabilized many of the previously taken-for-granted meanings of Israeli-Jewish collective identity. The unexpected signing of the historical agreement confronted many Israeli-Jews with a double challenge. One the one hand, it forced them to rethink their relationship to the "other"—that is, to the Palestinians and to Arabs more generally. On the other hand, Oslo made inevitable the exploration of new answers to the question "Who are we?," which until then had yielded fairly simple and clear answers grounded in the crude distinction between "us" and "them." Israeli liberal novelist David Grossman grappled with this challenge and its implications a few weeks after the signing of the agreement. Utilizing the pages of one of Israel's mass-circulation papers to open a public debate on this issue, he wondered, "How are we going to live and function without a clearly defined enemy against whom we can unite and direct our aggressions?" [and] "What does it mean to live without an enemy" (Grossman 1993, 5–6)?

The unanticipated peace agreement, coupled with the prospects of living without an enemy on the one hand and having to deal with internal divisions on the other, triggered a serious identity crisis for many Israeli-Jews. This crisis became especially acute following the November 1995 assassination of Israeli Prime Minister Yitzhak Rabin by a fellow Israeli-Jew opposed to the Oslo Accords. But the victory of the right-wing Likud Party in the May 1996 elections and the subsequent stalemate in the peace process have diverted attention away from Israel's identity crisis to a more familiar realm: the relations with Palestinians. Ironically, it was Israel's fiftieth-anniversary celebrations, designed to underscore the achievements and unity of the Jewish state, that highlighted once again its internal fragmentation, triggering an unprecedented public debate about the character of the state, its contested history, and its relationship to its citizenry.

Nevertheless, while many reports commented on such internal divisions as between secular and religious Jews, Left and Right, or immigrants and "native" Israelis, their analysis remained superficial. There was little or no attempt, including on the pages of such progressive magazines as *The Nation* and *Tikkun,* to examine how the Zionist project and the persistence of the Arab-Israeli conflict reinforced multiple distinctions between "us" and "them." These distinctions were based upon, and at the same time masked, structured inequalities and discriminatory practices based on such differences as race, ethnicity, nationality, gender, and sexuality that presently divide the Israeli-Jewish collectivity. Another blind spot in the prominent coverage of these celebrations involved the role of ordinary citizens and social movements in forming and transforming Israel and their perspectives on and ways of coping with Israel's identity crisis.

This chapter is designed to shed some light on Israel's identity crisis by examining it from the perspectives of two social movements in Israel: Yesh Gvul (Hebrew for "there is a limit" and "there is a border"), a movement of Israeli soldiers who refuse to serve in the Israeli-occupied West Bank and Gaza Strip, and the Israeli women's peace movement. Inspired by the growing body of literature on new social movements and collective identity, the chapter is designed to assess the potential of these movements to introduce new notions of identity and community. Such notions may inspire a new vision of Israeli society, reflecting its diversity and structured inequalities on the one hand and the changes in the political context on the other.

The most common tendency is to view social movements as agents of social and political change and to examine their responses to contemporary political developments and global changes (Gusfield 1981; Alger and Mendlovitz 1987; Basu 1990; Smoker 1992; Wallerstein 1991). Another tendency has been to present social movements as transnational actors who challenge the centrality of state sovereignty in international politics (Walker 1990b; Falk 1992). A third tendency treats social movements as contexts for the exploration of new ideas about political identity and community and alternative answers to the question "Who are we?" that heretofore have been answered by the claims of sovereign states (Ruiz 1990; Walker 1990b).

This chapter touches upon the first two themes by pointing to the role of social movements in fostering social and political change and to the ways in which they transgress conventional understandings of state sovereignty by forging new bonds and solidarities across state boundaries. My primary focus, however, is on the third theme, which examines the role of social movements in challenging taken-for-granted notions of identity and community and in the process transforming the state and its relationship to its citizens. This includes paying attention to attempts by social movements to challenge the primacy of national identity by coalescing around other modalities of identity, such as gender, race, class, ethnicity, or sexuality, or by transforming the meanings of collective identity altogether. In addition, this chapter examines the discourses and strategies of struggle utilized by social movements in Israel to both respond to and promote political change.

SOCIAL MOVEMENTS AND POLITICAL CHANGE

Social movements in Israel have a relatively short history. As mentioned earlier, this is primarily because the Arab-Israeli/Israeli-Palestinian conflict inspired the crystallization of a strong national consensus that emphasized rigid distinctions between Israelis and Palestinians, Arabs and Jews, and at the same time rendered internal divisions and structured inequalities invisible or unimportant. Moreover, the persistence of the conflict enabled Israeli-Jewish politicians to ignore altogether or at least blur the boundaries between the state and civil society, thus discouraging various disenfranchised constituencies from challenging the state. Under the pretext of unity in the face of the enemy, existing social and political institutions in Israel remained unchallenged. Challenging the state or any of its institutions or practices implied risking being perceived not only as undermining the national consensus and shattering the illusion of national unity but also as posing a direct threat to the security of the state and fellow citizens (Sharoni 1993).

Despite the constraints that states such as Israel have imposed on social movements, major political developments triggered primarily by the end of the Cold War have called into question the role of states as the primary actors in the international arena. It finally became evident that social movements can play a key role in transforming both the state and its relations with its citizens as well as with other actors in the arena of world politics. This is especially true during periods of intense political change when rigid constructions of collective identity tend to get destabilized. Three such periods come to mind when examining the history and contemporary interventions of social movements in Israel: the 1982 invasion of Lebanon; the Palestinian uprising, known as the intifada, which began in December 1987; and the signing of the September 1993 Oslo Accords and their aftermath. Following is a partial account, focusing primarily on the activities of and challenges facing Yesh Gvul and the women's peace movement during these historical turning points.

The 1982 Invasion of Lebanon

The Israeli invasion of Lebanon in 1982 marked the beginning of an erosion in the Israeli national consensus. For the first time since the establishment of the state, individuals and groups dared to challenge government policies and publicly voice dissent. Within days there emerged a distinctive peace movement in Israel, providing a loose organizational structure for citizens and groups who were outraged by the senseless war. Peace Now, founded in 1978 by a group of Israeli reserve officers and soldiers, situated itself at the center of the emerging peace movement through its superior resources and its ability to define peace as inextricably linked to the hegemonic discourse of national security (Sharoni 1995; Kaminer 1996).

A more radical intervention was that of Yesh Gvul, a group of Israeli-Jewish men who explicitly challenged the discourse of national security by refusing to serve in Lebanon. This movement of Israeli-style conscientious objectors, comprised primarily of reserve soldiers, forced the Israeli public for the first time since the establishment of the state to question the right of the government to send people to fight a war that they consider illegal from its inception (Shnitzer 1993; Kaminer 1996). During the Israeli invasion of Lebanon, over 2,000 Israeli reserve soldiers signed the Yesh Gvul petition asking the government not to be sent to serve in Lebanon, and 150 of them were court-martialed and sentenced to military prison. During this period, Yesh Gvul confined its objection to service in Lebanon and avoided the issue of military service in the territories occupied by Israel in 1967. Nevertheless, the existence and raison d'être of the organization gave rise to serious public debate about the conditions under which a state is justified to send its army to war.

Although women in Israel, as in other parts of the world, have been at the forefront of the peace movement, the Israeli invasion of Lebanon prompted some women to organize exclusively as women. Two major women's protest groups emerged during this period: Women Against the Invasion of Lebanon and Parents Against Silence. Both groups opposed the Israeli invasion and demanded an immediate withdrawal of Israeli forces. The most striking difference between the two groups, however, was their relationship to feminism. The members of Parents Against Silence, which the Israeli public referred to as Mothers Against Silence, publicly disassociated themselves from feminism and insisted that they were simply mothers (and fathers) worried about their sons in combat. Women Against the Invasion of Lebanon, on the other hand, was made up of women who had been active in the Israeli feminist movement; their protest against the war explicitly opposed Israeli sexism and militarism. Israeli society and its mainstream media were sympathetic to Parents Against Silence but did not tolerate the feminist antiwar and anti-occupation positions articulated by Women Against the Invasion of Lebanon.

Taken together, these groups and others, despite apparent differences in their broader political platforms, were consistent in expressing their opposition to the unnecessary war. The peace movement, with its large-scale protest activities, was instrumental in forcing then Israeli Prime Minister Menachem Begin to resign in September 1983. The movement also played a very important role in forcing the decision of the Israeli government to finally withdraw from Lebanon, if only partially, in 1985 (Bar-On 1985; Wolfsfeld 1988; Kaminer 1989). In sum, the invasion triggered the emergence of a distinct peace movement in Israel and created numerous venues for the articulation of political dissent. This surge of activism and public protest spread and grew stronger with the outbreak of the Palestinian intifada in December 1987.

The Intifada

The intifada is an important milestone in the history of the Israeli peace movement. The massive Palestinian revolt and large-scale mobilization against the Israeli occupation of the West Bank and Gaza Strip forced the Israeli peace movement to take an unequivocal position against the occupation. According to Kaminer (1996), the intifada "made it clear to the Israelis and the international community that there just was not going to be a new status quo despite Israeli control of the territories for more than twenty odd years" (42).

Since the intifada was neither planned ahead of time nor orchestrated by a central coordinating body, it caught Israel, including the peace camp, by surprise. It soon became apparent, however, that the intifada was characterized primarily by large-scale nonviolent resistance of an unarmed civilian population against an army of occupation. In a matter of weeks, this courageous struggle for self-determination resonated with large segments of the Israeli peace movement, triggering massive protest, solidarity visits, and the establishment of new protest groups. Robert Rosenberg, a *Jerusalem Post* reporter, characterized these mobilization efforts as unprecedented, describing how "dozens of groups . . . have sprung into action, each looking for a slogan that will draw the largest number of supporters, each seriously preserving the semantics that distinguish it from others, and each searching for contact with other groups in the hope of forming a single mass movement" (quoted in Kaminer 1996, 48).

While new groups and initiatives burst onto the scene, existing groups, such as Yesh Gvul, were forced to reevaluate their political platforms. Discussions about extending Yesh Gvul's opposition to service in Lebanon to reserve duty in the Occupied Territories started long before the intifada. After Israel's partial withdrawal from Lebanon and especially following the outbreak of the intifada, the West Bank and Gaza Strip became the focal point of Yesh Gvul's resistance. A few months after the beginning of the intifada, the movement published a new petition titled "There Is a Limit to the Oppression" (Spiro 1988). It is estimated that more than 150 soldiers served prison sentences and more than 2,000 people (men and women) signed the Yesh Gvul petition. In addition, for every declared "refusnik," there were ten soldiers who evaded service on various pretexts in order to avoid political confrontation and possible imprisonment. Others came to terms with their commanding officers and struck unofficial compromises. In most cases, the army preferred to make a deal in order to portray the phenomenon of refusal to serve in the West Bank and Gaza Strip as a marginal one rather than to confront it head-on and focus public attention on such a sensitive issue (Kaminer 1996).

While Yesh Gvul managed to play a key role during the intifada by reformulating its basic ideas and adopting them to the new circumstances, women, many of whom had not been previously involved in the Israeli peace movement, responded to the intifada with new and original forms of protest. Whereas pre-intifada attempts by Israeli women to organize *as women* were unable to seriously challenge the prevailing patriarchal order and mobilize large numbers of women, the intifada sparked the emergence of numerous exclusively female peace groups. Groups such as Women in Black, the Women's Organizations for Women Political Prisoners, Shani-Israeli Women Against the Occupation, the Women and Peace Coalition, and the Israeli Women's Peace Net initiated demonstrations, letter campaigns, local and international peace conferences, and solidarity visits to the West Bank and Gaza Strip. The emergence of a multitude of women's peace groups provided some Israeli women with new opportunities to step out of their prescribed roles as mothers and keepers of the home front and to take positions on what was the most crucial matter in Israeli politics: the Israeli-Palestinian conflict (Sharoni 1995).

Women in Black, a weekly women's vigil, soon became the most visible segment of the women's peace movement. In January 1988, women in Jerusalem, and soon thereafter throughout the country, began holding silent vigils on Friday afternoons. The women dressed in black to symbolize the tragedy of both Israeli and Palestinian peoples and held signs in Hebrew, Arabic, and English, calling for an end to the Israeli occupation of the West Bank and Gaza Strip (Sharoni 1995). Within weeks the vigils spread to other towns and major intersections throughout Israel, reaching a record number of thirty-three vigils in the summer of 1989. Only one slogan, "End the Occupation," was kept by all the vigils while women across the country added slogans such as "Two States for Two People" or "No to Violence." In a few places, women added such slogans as "Listen to Women, Speak Peace" or "Women Demand an End to the Occupation" (Sharoni 1993).

In addition to consistent protest against the occupation, women also began to address the particular implications of the occupation for women's lives. The Women's Organizations for Female Political Prisoners (WOFPP) was established in Tel-Aviv and in Jerusalem to confront the harassment and political detention of Palestinian women—aimed at inhibiting the vital role played by Palestinian women's organizations during that period. The main objective of WOFPP was to offer support to Palestinian women political prisoners and at the same time to challenge the policies that violate their basic civil and human rights. In addition to delivering cloths and other necessities to the women and acting as liaisons between them and their families and lawyers, the groups intervened legally on behalf of Palestinian women around such issues as sexual harassment, assaults, torture, and inappropriate prison conditions. WOFPP also mobilized public opinion nationally and internationally through press releases and demonstrations and put pressure on members of the Israeli parliament.

Despite its original ideas and efforts, the women's peace movement was not treated as an important political force in Israel. In fact, it received more favorable media coverage outside Israel. The far-from-welcoming reception that women's peace groups received in Israel was also characterized at times by open hostility. Women's peace initiatives, especially Women in Black, were favorite targets for verbal and physical violence that was almost always laced with sexual and sexist innuendoes. The men's backlash was fueled by the omnipresent discourse of national security that informs a belief that the political mobilization of women against government policies represents a serious social and political threat. The threat is twofold. First, women challenge their socially assigned roles by stepping into the public–political arena and taking a position on the Israeli-Palestinian conflict, which is considered the most important matter in Israeli politics. Second, their position stands in opposition to the national consensus and disrupts prevailing understandings of womanhood and manhood in Israeli society. By trying to keep women's perspectives out of the official political debate and by using sexist and sexually loaded terminology and threats of physical intimidation, many Israeli men expressed their fears, frustrations, and inability to cope with new conceptions of womanhood and gender relations. These systematic attempts to intimidate women were generally unsuccessful, but the outbreak of the Persian Gulf crisis and the subsequent war confronted the women's peace movement with a challenge that proved more difficult to overcome.

Like most segments of the Israeli peace movement, the women's peace movement was not able to articulate a unanimous antiwar position. For the first time since the beginning of the intifada, Women in Black suspended for a while their weekly vigils. The Gulf crisis also interrupted the planning of an international women's peace conference jointly organized by Palestinian and Israeli women and scheduled to take place in Jerusalem in December 1990. As the level of repression against Palestinians increased with events such as the Haram-al-Sharif massacre in Jerusalem and long curfews that were imposed on the entire West Bank and Gaza Strip, joint planning meetings for the conference were postponed and never resumed in the same format. In the aftermath of the Gulf War, many women peace activists in Israel tried to overcome the numbness of the movement during the war, but within a short while they were confronted by new challenges. The movement was unable to mobilize against the massive deportations of 415 Palestinians, the blockade-style closure imposed on the Occupied Territories, and the July 1993 Israeli attack on southern Lebanon. Many women peace activists felt reluctant to criticize the national consensus on peace and security issues, especially since the Meretz Party, the prominent representative of the Israeli Left, joined the Labor-led Rabin government. This reluctance, however, triggered in many women feelings of frustration, burnout, and helplessness. During the summer of 1993, almost six years after the start of the intifada, the women's peace movement faced a major crisis. Women in Black decreased from thirty-three to about twelve permanent vigils and a few sporadic ones. Encounters with Palestinian women in the West Bank and Gaza Strip were almost nonexistent, and the few that did take place involved only Palestinian and Israeli-Jewish women who explicitly supported the peace overtures (Sharoni 1993).

In sum, the large-scale political mobilization triggered by the intifada reached a major crisis during the Gulf crisis and war. Before they were able to overcome the crisis of war, peace activists in Israel were confronted with a crisis of peace prompted by new political developments—first the 1991 Madrid peace conference and later the September 1993 signing of the Oslo Accords.

The Oslo Accords and Their Aftermath

Soon after the signing of the Oslo Accords, it became evident that Israeli society was deeply divided about both the content and the implementation of the accords. While some were convinced that the Oslo Accords were an important step toward a comprehensive peace with the Palestinians, others argued that far from representing a move toward a just and lasting peace, the accords perpetuated Israeli domination of Palestinians. In addition, there was a sizable group of longtime activists who agreed with Stan Cohen (1993) that "it makes little sense for us to oppose the peace agreement (whatever that means), or to pretend that nothing has happened. We have to do what we've always done—criticize the Israeli government, and now the emerging Palestinian authorities, and support the more democratic forces in our two societies, but within a new political reality" (17).

But the internal divisions were not simply a result of difficulties in comprehending the new political reality. Rather, they were fueled to a large extent by feelings of both burnout and frustration; while Rabin, Peres, and Arafat were nominated for a Nobel Peace Prize, the tireless work of the Israeli peace movement remained largely unacknowledged. Adding to the frustration was a realization on the part of the more progressive segments of the peace movement that peace once again had been defined "from above" by powerful people who were not interested in radically challenging the status quo of power relations in the Middle East. Rather than articulating a different vision of peace that social movements can work to make a reality within or despite the framework of the Oslo Accords, most segments of the Israeli peace movement took a "time-out."

Yesh Gvul was no exception. Despite the fact that the occupation of large segments of the West Bank and Gaza Strip continued, many Yesh Gvul activists were either burnt out or felt compelled to support (or at least not to directly oppose) the Labor government's interpretation of peace. Instead of continuing to struggle for a complete withdrawal of the Israeli army from the Occupied Territories, Yesh Gvul, like other segments of the Israeli peace movement, was convinced, or at least hoped, that the implementation of the Oslo Accords would eventually bring an end to the occupation. As a result, Yesh Gvul kept an extremely low profile during this period.

Similar dynamics took place within the women's peace movements. The signing of the Oslo Accords triggered intense debates and brought to the fore serious political divisions. Because of these divisions, the women's peace movement, unable to reach consensus, began to founder. Women in Black, once the most visible segment of the Israeli peace movement, decreased the number of its vigils and gradually abandoned the idea of holding them every week. Other groups, such as the Women and Peace Coalition, an umbrella organization for the women's peace movement, were unable to transcend these divisions and halted their work as a result.

At the same time, the uncritical embrace of the Oslo Accords by the international community gave rise to the establishment in 1994 of a new institutional framework, the Jerusalem Link, funded by the European Community. It served as the coordinating body of two independent women's centers: a Palestinian center, The Jerusalem Center for Women, located in East Jerusalem, and an Israeli center, Bat-Shalom (Hebrew for "daughter of peace"), in West Jerusalem. Bat-Shalom soon became a regular meeting place of the Israeli women's peace movement. Yet its sudden emergence as a center of political organizing and its close links to several Knesset members from the Labor and Meretz parties has received mixed reactions from some veteran women peace activists. Bat-Shalom has been criticized for its unequivocal endorsement of the Oslo process, its failure to criticize Labor and Meretz policies, and its patronizing approach toward Palestinian women. In response to these criticisms, Bat-Shalom has capitalized on its organizational base and financial strength to put together demonstrations and public forums dealing with such issues as Jewish settlements, the torture of Palestinian political prisoners, and the closure and annexation of Jerusalem.

Another interesting post-Oslo phenomenon involves the emergence of a number of new women's groups who have successfully mobilized the discourse of motherhood to challenge Israeli government policies against Palestinians in the West Bank and especially in southern Lebanon. Women with no previous involvement in the women's peace movement or in official Israeli politics founded such groups as Women and Mothers for Peace and Four Mothers. These groups received prominent coverage in both Israeli and international media and a relatively warm reception from the Israeli public, including many elected officials. This is especially true of Four Mothers, which was established in February 1997 by four mothers who live in northern Israel with sons on active duty in Lebanon. The catalyst for the establishment of the movement was a helicopter crash that killed seventy-three Israeli soldiers on their way to Lebanon. The movement, which currently has hundreds of active members across Israel and thousands of supporters worldwide, calls for a unilateral Israeli withdrawal from Lebanon. Its immediate goal has been to put the Lebanon issue back on the public agenda by impressing upon both the general public and political and military decision makers that Israeli citizens are paying an unconscionable price for the questionable security that they receive from Israel's self-proclaimed security zone. Four Mothers played an instrumental role in reopening the public political debate in Israel on Lebanon (Becker 1998).

In sum, despite the prevalent interpretation of the Oslo Accords as an important step toward peace in the Middle East, it confronted the Israeli peace movement with a serious crisis of both identity and direction. Groups such as Yesh Gvul and the women's peace movement, which have been at the forefront of the Israeli peace movement, were unable to articulate a clear position vis-à-vis the accords or to reformulate their platform so that it reflects the new political reality. Ironically, at a time when the Israeli-Palestinian conflict lost some of its power to freeze the meanings of Israeli-Jewish collectivity, social movements were unable to articulate their own vision for peace and justice in the region. Such a vision could have had the potential to transform the contours of Israeli-Jewish collective identity. Instead, the Israeli peace movement in general and the groups examined in this chapter in particular seemed paralyzed. A careful examination of the discourses of identity that have informed these groups' activities over the years may shed some light on this phenomenon and possible ways to overcome similar challenges in the future.

SOCIAL MOVEMENTS AND THE POLITICS OF IDENTITY IN ISRAEL

Social movements offer a susceptible environment for the exploration of questions about individual and collective identity and for the emergence of daily practices of struggle and resistance, which are central to processes of identity formation and transformation. One of the underlying assumptions of the body of literature on identity and social movements is that "the collective search for identity is a central aspect of movement formation" (Johnston et al. 1994, 6). Along these lines, Alberto Melucci (1980) suggests that "what individuals are claiming collectively is the right to realize their own identity" (218). Social movements, according to this thesis, arise "in defense of identity," providing a safe space for their members and empowering them to "name themselves" (Johnston et al. 1994, 10). Yet the reassertion of identity should not be viewed as an end in and of itself but rather as a means to an end. The search for and articulation of collective identity can be viewed strategically as part of the movement's struggle. Thus, the group's identity is formed and transformed in direct relation to the struggle in which it is involved and in response to particular political events.

During the first years following its establishment, Yesh Gvul focused on mobilizing support for its cause and on creating a support group for men who refused to serve in the Occupied Territories. In addition to creating a group identity, an "us" based on a shared experience and shared political goal, the movement has gradually begun to distinguish itself from other segments within Israeli society as well as within the peace movement. According to Yishai Menuhin, Yesh Gvul's spokesman, the movement has provided "a moral political alternative to the traditional model of blindly following and obeying orders . . . [and accepting] the process of oppressing and dominating the Palestinian people [which] has become a fundamental factor in the psyche of Israeli society and [a] component of the personal identity of its citizens" (Shnitzer 1993, 36). In this particular case, Yesh Gvul defined its collective identity in opposition to the dominant model prevalent in Israel at the time. This was a clear attempt to challenge the rigid distinctions between "us" and "them," Israeli-Jews and Palestinians, which legitimized the political status quo.

Yesh Gvul has also challenged the almost natural link that has been established in Israel between masculinity, military service, and a complete acceptance of the state's imperatives of "national security." Yesh Gvul members, most of whom are high-ranking reserves officers, have demonstrated that you can still be a man even if you refuse to serve in the West Bank and Gaza Strip and feel responsible to question the legitimacy of military and government policies when necessary. At the same time, Yesh Gvul's public statements reflected some reluctance to directly challenge the national consensus. In fact, as if to preempt accusations of treason and disloyalty that have often been directed against individuals and groups on the Israeli Left, Yesh Gvul "refusniks" have tried to voice their critique from "inside," emphasizing their military careers and their commitment to secure Israel's existence. This is evident in a Yesh Gvul leaflet, distributed in March 1986, that states,

> We the undersigned serve, all of us, in the IDF reserves, and many of us have taken part in Israel's wars. We have different ideological outlooks . . . but *we are united by our concern for the existence and the character of Israeli society.* (emphasis added) (Kaminer 1996, 67)

Another important feature of Yesh Gvul that sets it apart from many social movements has been its insistence that the decision not to cooperate with the occupation is an individual decision, not a collective act. According to an official Yesh Gvul statement,

> Each member of Yesh Gvul determines on his own what actions will define his refusal. For example, some might decide not to cross the 1967 borders . . . others might decide to serve in non-populated areas in the Territories but will refuse to participate in any

police-like operations against the Palestinian civilian population; some might decide not to receive a riot stick, demonstrating their refusal to participate in the breaking-bones policy against Palestinians; and others might decide to serve in the Occupied Territories but refuse to carry any type of weapon. All these forms of refusal are accepted and respected by Yesh Gvul. (Spiro 1988, 3)

By framing the act of refusal an individual act, Yesh Gvul as a movement tried to avoid dealing explicitly with the primacy of "national security" and with the unchallenged centrality of the military in Israeli society. Yesh Gvul members and supporters continue to emphasize that they are not a pacifist movement and that they question the occupation, not the necessity of an army for Israel's defense. The focus on the moral authority of the individual shifts the burden and responsibility from the state and its institutions to its (male) citizens. The group appeared to be more comfortable with its identity as a support group for men who decide to refuse military service in the Occupied Territories than as an advocacy group that is actively trying to convince men to consider this option.

Nevertheless, in the eyes of the Israeli-Jewish public, the act of refusal to serve in the Occupied Territories was viewed as both a collective and an individual threat. Yesh Gvul members forced many Israelis, especially men, to come to terms with their identities as occupiers. By pointing out that the acceptance of an occupier's identity is neither natural nor inevitable, Yesh Gvul created a context in which Israeli men, including many in the peace movement, were forced to either choose or reject that part of their identity. In order to avoid this moral dilemma, the movement's opponents have focused their efforts on portraying Yesh Gvul as a threat to national security, to democracy, and to the stability of Israeli society. In this context, the most common question became: What if more soldiers refuse to fulfil military orders and serve in certain locations? In the eyes of the Israeli public, Yesh Gvul's departure from familiar tenants of Israeli collectivity was interpreted as men's rejection of their duties both as members of the Israeli-Jewish citizenry and as men.

Two major labels have been used to counteract Yesh Gvul's resistance: "traitors" and "faggots." The label "traitor" reflected dismay and anger at men's refusal to fulfil the often taken-for-granted duties that accompany their membership in the national collectivity. The second label, "faggots," aside from reflecting the homophobic climate in Israel, reprimands Israeli-Jewish men for failing to comply with the gendered division of power and labor and to act like Israeli-Jewish men are supposed to act, that is, to obey any order and never challenge the imperative of "national security." In addition to representing discontent with the disruptions of dominant constructions of personal and collective identity, the hostile public reaction in Israel toward Yesh Gvul points to the central role of the soldier as a crucial signifier of Israeli identity and Jewish survival.

It is precisely this centrality of militarized masculinity in Israel that has made women's political mobilization so difficult and full of contradictions. According to Yael Yishai (1997), "Women in Israel have vacillated between the two alternatives:

mobilization to the feminist banner or integration with institutions associated with the national flag" (232). Yishai argues that Israeli women's involvement in politics is marked by an irreconcilable tension between efforts to advance their own social, political, and legal status as women and their mobilization in the service of the state and its male-dominated political elite. This tension may partially explain the marginalization of women in the official political arena in Israel. Despite this tension, the political involvement at the grassroots level has increased in the past two decades. With the emergence of women's peace groups in Israel in the early 1980s, Israeli women have become more aware of the tension between the national flag and the feminist banner.

In the 1980s, the Israeli public's general view of feminism as a threat to the state, coupled with the crisis atmosphere triggered by the invasion, helped generate public hostility toward Women Against the Invasion of Lebanon. In contrast, the public's reaction toward Parents Against Silence was mostly sympathetic. The divergent public reactions suggest that women in Israel still had very little room to become politically active as women, let alone as feminists. The only legitimate articulation of political dissent for women was to embrace motherhood and to emphasize care and protection, clearly in compliance with conventional notions of femininity and gender relations (Sharoni 1997).

On the surface, the intifada seemed to create more space for women's involvement in the Israeli political arena. During the intifada, Israeli women have gradually come to realize, if not always publicly acknowledge, that the broad array of problems often defined as "women's issues" cannot be treated in isolation from structures of militarization, inequality, and oppression reinforced by the Israeli military occupation of the Palestinians. Informed by implicit feminist principles, women peace activists in Israel articulated important connections: (1) between different systems of domination and structured inequalities, (2) between practices of violence used against Palestinians and the unprecedented rise in violence against women in Israel, and (3) between the struggles of Palestinians for liberation and self-determination and those of women throughout the world, including in Israel. Many women activists acknowledged in public that these connections have solid grounding in feminist theories and praxis. Nevertheless, the movement was reluctant to overtly identify its message as feminist, fearing that a backlash would hamper its objective to reach a broad segment of Israeli society.

Ironically, despite the movement's cautious relationship with feminism, the magnitude of women's political organizing triggered a serious backlash within Israeli society. Women involved in various peace initiatives, especially Women in Black, became targets for verbal and sometimes physical abuse that was almost always laced with both sexual and sexist innuendoes. This backlash against women peace activists once again underscored the little space available for women's political activism and dissent in Israel. Although Israeli women did not explicitly carry a feminist banner, any attempt on their part to introduce new frameworks for women's political mobilization was perceived as a threat. By publicly taking a position on the Israeli-Palestinian conflict, women challenged their socially assigned gender roles. Equally, if not more threateningly, was their departure from the national consensus in Israel through their forthright opposition to the Israeli military occupation and oppression of Palestinians.

By opposing the occupation and taking positions *as women* on the Israeli-Palestinian conflict, women peace activists have transgressed the distinction between so-called women's issues and political issues, crossing the border that kept women out of the public political arena and excluded their potential contributions to debates concerning peace, security, and foreign policy. Moreover, women not only "invaded" a domain from which they were previously excluded, they dared challenge the public consensus in Israel on questions of peace and security, using strategies of struggle that called into question the boundaries between "us" and "them" (i.e., Israelis and Palestinians) that lend the Israeli-Jewish collectivity its imagined stability.

Moreover, through solidarity work, groups such as the Women's Organizations of Political Prisoners in Tel-Aviv and in Jerusalem have utilized the power and privileges that accompany their membership in the Israeli-Jewish collectivity to act as strong advocates on behalf of Palestinian women prisoners. In so doing, they were able to challenge not only the boundaries between "us" and "them" but also the primacy of national identity as the most important web of meaning that underlies dominant understandings of Israeli-Jewish collective identity. To be able to do that, they had to create for themselves a kind of experience that their "original" identity—bound by the dominant narrative of Israeli national identity and "national security"—had forbidden (Sharoni 1993).

But the Gulf crisis and subsequent war reinforced the common divisions between "us" and "them," and confronted the women's peace movement with a serious challenge. Despite its clear opposition to the Israeli occupation and support for peace, the women's peace movement, like other segments of the Israeli peace movement, was not able to articulate a unanimous antiwar position. There is no doubt that the crisis in the women's peace movement has been prompted, among other things, by the change in government from Likud to Labor and by the narrowing of political discussions to statements for or against the Madrid peace process or the Oslo Accords. Given the new political reality, the discourse of "us" versus "them," dissident peace activists versus government officials, seemed inappropriate. Yet, instead of taking advantage of the change in government and utilizing a discourse of identity and strategies of struggle that seek to transform both "us" and "them," the women's peace movement has began to slowly lose its sense of identity.

The crisis intensified significantly following the signing of the Oslo Accords. In September 1993, the accords were interpreted by some women peace activists as an opportunity to rejoin the Israeli national consensus. Indeed, the new modes of women's peace activism that have emerged after Oslo reveal that very little has changed in Israel in the past two decades: Women who want to get involved in politics still have to choose between adhering to the national flag and carrying a feminist banner.

For example, despite the fact that Bat-Shalom's leadership and core members include many feminists and that the center regularly features discussions that link gender to other political issues, there has been a clear reluctance to use feminism as a public political discourse to articulate the center's mission statement and objectives. While this reluctance to carry feminist banners is no doubt strategic, designed not to alienate the Israeli public, it helps reinforce the public's view of feminism as a threat and forces women to embrace modes of political mobilization that do not challenge conventional gender roles.

The search for nonthreatening banners is evident in the discourses of some of the women's groups that have burst onto the Israeli political scene after the signing of the Oslo Accords and especially in the past two years. Groups such as Women and Mothers for Peace and Four Mothers have explicitly utilized the discourse of motherhood to challenge government policies against Palestinians and in southern Lebanon. Given the history and dynamics of women's political mobilization in Israel, there is no doubt that part of the success of Four Mothers can be attributed to their conscious embrace of motherhood as a principle discourse. Careful not to appear threatening, the movement's leaders have emphasized that they do not see themselves as feminists or as an exclusively women's movement. These women are well aware that if they are to successfully challenge the Israeli national consensus on Lebanon, they must do so by embracing their traditionally praised roles as mothers of their own sons and their moral authoritative status as mothers of the nation (Sharoni 1997).

At the same time, while working within the confines of the national consensus, Four Mothers do so subversively and on their own terms. As Irit Letzter, one of the women in the group, pointed out,

When God said to Abraham, "Please take your son, your only one, whom you love, Isaac," Abraham did not argue. We believe that if God had approached Sarah, she would have replied, "Forget it. I'm not sacrificing this child." She would never have submissively accepted the order. I believe the meaning of our movement is much deeper than meets the eye. From now on, the soldiers' mothers will be an inseparable part of the decision making. It's impossible to ignore us. I'm not naive, I don't bury my head in the sand, but I don't agree with the warped male notion that war is somehow a challenge, a project, heroic. We're not planning a revolt, but we won't let the government continue in its complacency. (quoted in Becker 1998, 5)

In sum, the examples of political organizing discussed here and the backlash atmosphere within which they have operated demonstrate the particular challenges that have limited the ability of such movements to transform both their own position in society and the broader collectivity of which they are a part. Soldiers who refuse to serve in the Israeli-occupied West Bank and Gaza Strip and women peace activists are examples of social groups that have attempted to challenge the boundaries of Israeli-Jewish collectivity. While none of these groups explicitly identified the expansion of Israeli-Jewish collectivity as one of its stated objectives, their social and political interventions have opened up space for the critical rethinking of the question "Who are we?" Another common characteristic these groups share is their often implicit challenge to dominant constructions of masculinity, femininity, and gender relations in Israel. Finally, while the political interventions of Yesh Gvul and women peace activists in Israel have not directly challenged the boundaries of Israeli-Jewish collectivity, they have destabilized, though not explicitly, dominant constructions of masculinity and femininity in Israel and thus opened up space in which new answers to the question "Who are we?" may emerge.

CONCLUSION

The spontaneous large-scale political mobilization of both Yesh Gvul and the women's peace movement in Israel during the first years of the intifada confirms that activists in Israeli are ready and determined to struggle for a distinct voice and place within the peace movement and in the broader political arena in Israel. It would be a grave mistake, therefore, to interpret the inability of these groups to respond to the unexpected signing of the Oslo Accords simply as a sign of failure or burnout. Such an interpretation, which is common among activists themselves, is indicative of the reactive nature of peace activism in Israel; the common view is that it is the task of grassroots activists to immediately respond to events unfolding in the official political arena. This limited understanding of resistance narrows the parameters of possible responses by social movements.

At the same time, it is imperative that such movements engage in critical self-reflection designed to make sense of new political developments and search for new and creative ways to effect social and political change and transform dominant notions of collective identity. Indeed, Alberto Melucci (1994) suggests that "collective identity is becoming the product of conscious action and the outcome of self-reflection more than a set of given or structural characteristics" (50–51). Such action-orientated self-reflection was largely missing within the Israeli peace movement in the aftermath of Oslo. As a result, groups such as Yesh Gvul and the women's peace movement found themselves confronted with an uneasy choice: either support the Oslo Accords and back the Labor government or adopt a more critical interpretation of the Oslo Accords and continue to struggle against the occupation. Neither option was attractive because, in addition to requiring some reformulation of the movements' identity and strategies of struggle, it also exposed inevitable divisions within the movements. These divisions, which mirrored the internal fragmentation at that time within the broader Israeli society, were viewed by many peace activists as a sign of weakness and thus triggered frustration and hampered the movements' ability to engage in critical self-reflection and creative collective action.

The crisis of identity and direction experienced by the broader Israeli collectivity had different implications for the Israeli peace movement. The movement in general and Yesh Gvul and women peace activists in particular have long moved beyond the rigid distinctions between "us" and "them" and the need to maintain "unity in the face of the enemy." Thus, theoretically, this constituency could have played a major role in interpreting the Oslo Accords for the Israeli collectivity, a task neglected by the Rabin-led government. Such an interpretation should have underscored the fact that the Oslo Accords were far from representing an agreement between two equal partners. Rather, the accords reflected most if not all Israeli security needs and concerns, forcing Palestinians to make more concessions than they were ever prepared to do throughout their struggle for self-determination and territorial sovereignty.

In the aftermath of the signing ceremony, it was crucial to assure Israeli-Jews not only that the Oslo Accords provided ample safeguards for their personal and collective security but also that their security is inextricably linked to the national liberation of Palestinians. Such an intervention on the part of the Israeli peace movement could have had the potential to prevent the assassination of Yitzhak Rabin in November 1995, the series of suicide bombings in 1995 and 1996, and the subsequent election of Benjamin Netanyahu as Israel's prime minister in May 1996. This thesis is not designed to assign the blame or responsibility for these crucial events to the peace movement. Rather, it seeks to underscore the fact that because of the top-down nature of the Oslo process, the peace movement, with its experience and resources, was completely marginalized and overlooked as a constituency that could have played a crucial role in the implementation of the accords. Instead of forcing the Rabin-led government, whose interpretation of peace did not go far beyond the absence of direct confrontations with Palestinians, to follow its lead, the movement opted to take a time-out and follow its reluctant leaders. As a result, groups such as Yesh Gvul and the women's peace movement missed an important opportunity not only to effect serious political change but also to play a key role in the transformation of Israeli collective identity.

Ironically, Netanyahu's election and the subsequent stalemate in the peace process, while creating serious instability in the Middle East, eased, if only temporarily, some of the pressure felt by many Israeli-Jews in the aftermath of Oslo. But the old rhetoric of "us" and "them" and the need to maintain unity in the face of the enemy is gradually losing some of its power. As the public debate in Israel around it fiftieth-anniversary celebrations underscores, many Israeli-Jews seem ready to critically reflect on the construction of their collective identity and its implications. Social movements in Israel must take advantage of this opening and seriously consider not only whether to challenge explicitly or implicitly existing notions of collective identity but also how to be most effective in this struggle.

The groups discussed in this chapter have operated primarily within the confines of "identity politics," struggling for the voice and visibility for their own group while overlooking differences within the movement and leaving unchallenged the dominant assumptions that underlie the broader Israeli-Jewish collectivity. While this phenomenon is not surprising, given the limited space for dissent in the hegemonic discourse of national security, it has serious implications for the movements' potential to achieve their own objectives if not to play a significant role in transforming Israeli society.

New understandings of identity and community ought to call into question the core assumptions and practices that form the basis of Israeli-Jewish collectivity. No group in Israel can undertake this task alone. But, taken together, individuals and groups who have either endured discrimination and injustice themselves or realized that others have constitute a powerful majority that can not only disrupt but also transform the meaning of Israeli collective identity. To move in that direction, social movements in Israel, like elsewhere, must recognize the limitations of identity politics and the necessity for alliances and coalitions. Some individuals and groups fear that such a transition may dilute a group's distinct identity and as such hamper its political efficacy. But, as Judith Butler (1990) points out, "The deconstruction of identity is not the deconstruction of politics; rather, it establishes as political the very terms through which identity is articulated" (148). Rather, such a move from identity politics to coalition politics has the potential to increase a group's overall efficacy.

The potential of coalition politics and of contingent alliances between various social and political movements in Israel lies in their ability to decenter and displace the hegemonic discourse of "national security." Such a project would also involve challenging conventional conceptions of collective identity that allowed a particular notion of militarized masculinity to become the center of Israeli collectivity. More specifically, such a project entails a conscious effort not simply to expand the boundaries of the existing collectivity but rather to create an alternative one, grounded in mobile identifications and acknowledgment and appreciation of difference. Recently, Yesh Gvul provided an example of how these abstract ideas could be put into practice. The movement marked Israel's fiftieth-anniversary with an alternative torch-lighting ceremony. Although this ceremony was attended by only 200 people and, unlike the state-sponsored one, was not broadcast on national television, it is nevertheless significant.

As the recent example of the intervention by Yesh Gvul underscores, to challenge the national consensus in Israel and transform existing notions of Israeli-Jewish collective identity, one must critically examine the Zionist project from the perspectives of both its Palestinian and its Jewish victims. This examination should form the basis for a new vision of society and politics based on the principle of equality and justice for all, which could inform progressive struggles for social and political change in Israel/Palestine.

9

Ecological Balance in an Era of Globalization

Vandana Shiva

In 1992, the Earth Summit in Rio marked the maturing of ecological awareness on a global scale. The world was poised to make a shift to sustainability. However, the Rio process and the sustainability agenda were subverted by the free-trade agenda. In 1993, the Uruguay Round of the General Agreement on Tariffs and Trade (GATT) was completed, in 1995 the World Trade Organization (WTO) was established, and world affairs grew increasingly dictated by trade and commerce. The normative political commitment to sustainability and justice was replaced by the rule of trade and the elevation of exploitation, greed, and profit maximization as the organizing principles of the market, the state, and society. Instead of the state regulating the market for the good of society, global economic powers and commercial forces are now regulating the state and society for the benefit of corporations. Instead of commerce being accountable to state and society, economic globalization is making citizens and their governments accountable to corporations and global economic bodies.

Economic globalization is not merely an economic phenomenon related to reduction of tariff barriers and removal of "protectionist" policies. It is in fact a normative process that reduces all value by commercial value. Free trade is, in reality, the rule of commerce. Both GATT and WTO basically undo the Rio agenda. Five years after Rio, we do not have Rio plus five but Rio minus five.

On the one hand, the search for ecological balance in an era of globalization requires an assessment of the social and ecological impact of globalization. On the other hand, it requires an imagination and a realization of an alternative order that puts ecological balance and social and economic justice rather than trade at the center of economic policy.

Globalization is not a natural, evolutionary, or inevitable phenomenon, as is often argued. Globalization is a political process that has been forced on the weak by the powerful. Globalization is not the cross-cultural interaction of diverse societies. It is the imposition of a particular culture on all others. Nor is globalization the search for ecological balance on a planetary scale. It is the predation of one class, one race, and often one gender of a single species on all others. "Global" in the dominant discourse is the political space in which the dominant local seeks control, freeing itself from local, regional, and global sources of accountability arising from the imperatives of ecological sustainability and social justice. "Global" in this sense does not represent the universal human interest; it represents a particular local and parochial interest and culture that has been globalized through its reach and control, irresponsibility, and lack of reciprocity.

THE THREE WAVES OF GLOBALIZATION

Globalization has come in three waves. The first wave was the colonization of the Americas, Africa, Asia, and Australia by European powers over the course of 1,500 years. The second wave was the imposition of the West's idea of "development" on non-Western cultures in the postcolonial era of the past five decades. The third wave of globalization was unleashed approximately five years ago as the era of "free trade," which for some commentators implies an end to history, but for us in the Third World is a repeat of history through recolonization. Each wave of globalization is cumulative in its impact, even while it creates a discontinuity in the dominant metaphors and actors. Each wave of globalization has served Western interests, and each wave has created deeper colonization of other cultures and of the planet's life.

Colonization involves violence when it replaces the self-organizing capacity and order of diverse social and natural systems with an externally controlled global order that is unstable and is maintained only through coercion and force. Indeed, each time a global order has tried to wipe out diversity and impose a homogeneity, disorder and disintegration have been induced, not removed. Among examples of violence in the current free-trade era is the U.S. Trade Act, especially the Super and Special 301 clauses, which allow the United States to take unilateral action against any country that does not open up its market to U.S. corporations. Super 301 is used to force freedom for investment. Special 301 is used to force freedom for monopoly control of markets through intellectual property rights protection. Free trade is, in fact, an asymmetric arrangement that combines liberalization and protectionism for Northern interests. While not implemented with tanks and bullets, the coercive element at work is a type of violence.

Such brute force has continued to be used against the Third World, even in multilateral negotiations of the Uruguay Round of GATT. In a speech on January 14, 1995, Fernando Jaramillo, chairman of the Group of 77 and Colombia's permanent representative in the United Nations, said, "The Uruguay Round is proof again that the developing world continues to be sidelined and rejected when it comes to defining areas of vital importance to their survival" (quoted in Raghavan 1995).

Free-trade treaties such as GATT are not expressions of freedom for all because of the process through which they have been arrived at. They have been forced on citizens and on weaker trading partners, namely, the countries of the Third World. Multilateral treaties such as GATT are not really multilateral. Nothing makes this clearer than the fact that in 1991 a take-it-or-leave-it draft was prepared by GATT's secretary-general, Arthur Dunkel, which in India has taken on the not so pleasant acronym of the DDT (Dunkel Draft Text), suggesting toxic chemicals. An even more blatant expression of undemocratic decision making and nontransparency was the last stages of GATT negotiations, in which two men, Mickey Kantor, the U.S. trade representative, and Leon Brittany, the European Community negotiator, sat behind closed doors and then presented the world with a "free trade" treaty that was supposed to have been negotiated multilaterally. This is neither multilateralism nor global democracy.

Despite insisting that the negotiations were global, the countries of the North refused, in the end, to accept any discussions, even bilaterally, with the countries of the Third World, illustrating once again that globalization is the imposition of the will of the economic powers of the North on the rest on the world.

A new authoritarian structure emerges, as Ambassador Jaramillo of Colombia observed in his speech in Geneva:

> The Bretton Woods Institutions continue to be made the center of gravity for the principal economic decisions that affect the developing countries. We have all been witnesses to the conditionalities of the World Bank and the IMF. We all know the nature of the decision-making system in such institutions; their undemocratic character, their lack of transparency, their dogmatic principles, their lack of pluralism in the debate of ideas, and their impotence to influence the policies of the industrialized countries. . . . This also seems to be applicable to the new World Trade Organization. The terms of its creation suggest that this will be dominated by the industrialized countries and that its fate will be to align itself with the World Bank and IMF. . . . We could announce in advance the birth of a New Institutional Trinity which would have as its specific function to control and dominate the economic relations that commit the developing world. (quoted in Raghavan 1995, 40)

Free trade has come to mean, in reality, the vastly expanded freedom and powers of transnational corporations to trade and invest in most countries of the world, with first-world states and associated international financial institutions paving the way for such activity and, in the process, reducing their own regulatory relevance. Transnational corporations (TNCs), which have been the real power in the Uruguay Round, have gained new rights and given up old obligations to protect workers' rights and environmental well-being.

THE COMMUNITY, THE STATE, AND THE CORPORATION

Globalization has distorted the relationship between the community, the state, and the economy, or, to use Marc Nerfin's more colorful categories, the relationship between the citizen, the prince, and the merchant. It is privileging the economy and its key actor, the corporation, insofar as the state and the community are increasingly becoming mere instruments of global capital.

The appeal of globalization is usually based on the idea that it implies less red tape, less centralization, and less bureaucratic control. It is celebrated because it implies the erosion of those bureaucratic impediments that drive up the ecological costs of trade and exchange in general.

During the past fifty years, the state has increasingly taken over the functions of the community and the self-organizing capacity of citizens. Through globalization, corporations are taking over the functions of the state and citizens. Food provisioning, health care, education, and social security are all being transformed into corporate projects under the code words of "competitiveness" and "efficiency." People's rights and the public domain are being eroded by exporting the economic label of "protectionism" to cover all domains: ethical, social, and political. The protection of the environment and the protection of people's security are treated as nontariff trade barriers that need to be dismantled.

While the state is being required to step back from the regulation of trade and commerce, it is being increasingly called in to regulate citizens and remove communities that are an "obstruction" to free trade. Thus, the state is becoming leaner in dealing with big business and global industry, and it is becoming meaner in dealing with people.

In the North and in the South, the principle of "eminent domain" is still applied to the state takeover of people's land and resources, which are then handed over to global corporations. For example, in India, under the new infrastructure policies, foreign companies can enjoy up to 100 percent equity participation, but the government will acquire the land, displace people, and deal with "law and order" problems created by displacements.

In the United States, the federal, state, and local governments are appropriating citizens' homes and farms to hand over to large corporations. In Hurst, Texas, a suburb of Fort Worth, the government appropriated the land of more than 100 home owners, handing it over to its largest taxpayer, the Northeast Mall. Additionally, 4,200 residences were destroyed in Detroit, Michigan, so that General Motors could build a new plant. Quite clearly, it is the property of the powerful corporations that is being protected by the state in every part of the world under the new free-trade regimes, while the property of the ordinary citizen has no protection.

Another area in which the role of the state is actually increasing is in intellectual property rights (IPRs). As larger areas are being converted into "intellectual property" through patents—from microbes to mice, from seeds to human cell lines—the state is being increasingly called on to police citizens to prevent them from engaging in everyday activities, such as saving seeds and exchanging knowledge. Our most human acts have been criminalized—in relationship to ourselves, to one another, and to other species through IPR legislation that is being forced on all countries and all people.

The inverted role of the state with respect to citizens is exemplified in the concrete cases of John Moore, Peter Toborsky, and Josef Albrecht.

John Moore, a cancer patient, went to court when he discovered that his own doctor, Dr. Golde, had patented his cell line as the Mo-cell line. However, the California Supreme Court ruled that Moore could not have autonomy and integrity with respect to his own body since this would interfere in trade and scientific progress (Research Foundation for Science, Technology and Natural Resource Policy 1995).

Peter Taborsky worked as a lab assistant at the University of Florida on a project funded by Progressive Technologies Corporation. Outside his scheduled work hours, Taborsky did research of his own, for which he obtained a patent. He was accused of "theft" by the corporation and arrested. His arrest dramatizes the problems of IPRs linked to private funding of public institutions. Most labs and research facilities have been built by public funds. When a corporation finances a project and the research product becomes its intellectual property, it is forgotten that the facilities that make knowledge production possible were built as a public resource. Later, when someone uses that public resource to generate new ideas, it is treated as theft, as in Taborsky's case (Shiva 1996).

The case of farmer Josef Albrecht in Germany and potato seed farmers in Scotland are examples of how seed acts prevent farmers from engaging in their own seed production. Albrecht is an organic farmer in the village of Oberding in Bavaria. Not satisfied with commercially available seed, he developed his own ecological varieties of wheat. Ten other organic farmers from neighboring villages took his wheat seeds. Farmer Albrecht was fined by the government of Upper Bavaria because he traded in uncertified seed. He has challenged the penalty and the Seed Act because he feels restricted in freely exercising his occupation as an organic farmer by this law. During the Leipzig Conference on Plant Genetic Resources, Albrecht initiated a noncooperation movement against seed legislation that denies farmers the right to freely breed and exchange their seeds in the same church from which the democracy movement against the erstwhile communist state of East Germany was organized in Leipzig (Research Foundation for Science, Technology and Natural Resource Policy 1996).

Globalization does mean "less government" for regulation of business and commerce. But less government for commerce and corporations can go hand in hand with more government in the lives of people. As globalization allows an increasing transfer of wealth and resources from the public domain—under the control of communities or the state—the result is often increasing poverty and insecurity. Discontent and dissent necessarily increase, leading to law-and-order problems. In such a situation, even a minimalist state restricted only to policing law and order will become enormously large and all-pervasive, devouring much of the wealth of society and intruding into every aspect of citizens' lives.

Most of the ideological projection of globalization has focused on the new relationship of the prince and the merchant, the state and the corporation, the government and the market. The state has been stepping back more and more from the regulation of commerce and capital. However, the shift from the rule of the nation-state to the rule of the corporations does not imply more power to the people. If anything, it implies less power in the hands of people because corporations, especially TNCs, are often more powerful than governments and less accountable than governments to democratic control.

For these reasons, it is clear that globalization runs into conflict with the democratic space for citizens to determine and influence the conditions for their health and well-being and to elect governments that protect the public interest. In country after country, governments are elected on the basis of manifestos that expose the social and ecological destruction inherent to processes of globalization. However, in every country, governments of every shade in the political spectrum enforce the free-trade agenda more forcefully than their predecessors and act against the citizens who have put them in power.

In India, the Bharatiya Janata Party won the Maharashtra elections by criticizing the Congress Party for giving clearance to the Enron power project. They came to power on the anti-Enron slogan. But the first thing they did was clear the power project, even though it involved human rights violations against their own supporters at the grassroots (Amnesty International 1997).

It is not just in the Third World that democracy is being eroded by globalization. In Denmark, people voted against joining the European Union, but their vote was brushed aside and a second referendum organized. In Austria, 1.4 million people voted against the import of genetically engineered food, but the European Union has ruled against the democratic vote. In the European Union, the parliament rejected a law that allowed patenting of life, but the bureaucracy of the European Commission bulldozed the patent directive despite the vote (Raghavan 1997).

Globalization and democracy are therefore mutually exclusive, both in the deeper sense of democracy as people's control over their lives as well as in the shallower sense of people's control over their elected representatives. The expansion of corporate control is often made to appear as the expansion of the democratic space for citizens on the basis of "consumer choice." However, such choice is based on increasingly narrowing alternatives. Choice within a narrow, predetermined set of options of corporate rule is not freedom because it involves the surrender of the right to determine the context of living and the values that govern society. The apparent widening of individual consumer choice for the elite in matters of automobiles and junk foods is based on the shrinking of the rights of communities to control their local natural resources, the shrinking of work opportunities for large numbers of people, and the shrinking of social and political choice through democratic public process. Globalization is creating more freedom for corporations, but this is not translating into more freedom for citizens.

GLOBALIZATION AS ENVIRONMENTAL APARTHEID

"Apartheid" literally means "separate development." However, in practice, apartheid is more appropriately a regime of exclusion. It is based on legislation that protects a privileged minority and that excludes the majority. It is characterized by the appropriation of the resources and wealth of society by a small minority based on privileges of race or class. The majority is then pushed into a marginalized existence without access to resources necessary for well-being and survival.

Erstwhile South Africa is the most dramatic example of a society based on racial apartheid. Globalization has in a deep sense been a globalization of apartheid. This apartheid is especially glaring in the context of the environment. Globalization is restructuring the control over resources in such a way that the natural resources of the poor are systematically taken over by the rich and the pollution of the rich is systematically dumped on the poor.

In the pre-Rio period, it was the North that contributed most to the destruction of the environment. For example, 90 percent of historic carbon dioxide emissions have been by the industrialized countries. The developed countries produce 90 percent of the hazardous wastes produced around the world every year. Global free trade has globalized this environmental destruction in an asymmetric pattern. While the economy is controlled by Northern corporations, they are increasingly exploiting Third World resources for their global activities. It is the South that is disproportionately bearing the environmental burden of the globalized economy. Globalization is thus leading to an environmental apartheid.

The current environmental and social crisis demands that the world economy adjust to ecological limits and the needs of human survival. Instead, global institutions, such as the World Bank and the International Monetary Fund and the WTO, are forcing the costs of adjustment on nature and women and the Third World. Across the Third World, structural adjustment and trade liberalization measures are becoming the most serious threat to the survival of the people.

While the last five decades have been characterized by the "globalization" of maldevelopment and the spread of a nonsustainable Western industrial paradigm in the name of development, the recent trends are toward an environmental apartheid in which, through global policy set by the holy trinity, the Western TNCs, supported by the governments of the economically powerful countries, attempt to maintain the North's economic power and wasteful lifestyles of the rich by exporting the environmental costs to the Third World. Resource- and pollution-intensive industries are being relocated in the South through the economics of free trade.

Lawrence Summers, who was the World Bank's chief economist and was responsible for the *1992 World Development Report*, which was devoted to the economics of the environment, actually suggested that it makes economic sense to shift polluting industries to Third World countries. In a memo dated December 12, 1991, to senior World Bank staff, he wrote, "Just between you and me, shouldn't the World Bank be encouraging more migration of the dirty industries to the LDC?" Summers justified his economic logic of increasing pollution in the Third World on three grounds. First, since wages are low in the Third World, the economic costs of pollution arising from increased illness and death are the least in the poorest countries. According to Summers, "Relocation of pollutants to the lowest wage country is impeccable and we should face up to that." Second, since in large parts of the Third World pollution is still low, it makes economic sense to Summers to introduce pollution: "I've always thought that countries in Africa are vastly under polluted; their air quality is probably vastly inefficiently low compared to Los Angeles or Mexico City." Finally, since the poor are poor, they cannot possibly worry about environmental problems: "The concern over an agent that causes a one in a million change in the odds of prostate cancer is obviously going to be much higher in a country where people survive to get prostate cancer than in a country where under five mortality is 200 per thousand." He recommended the relocation of hazardous and polluting industries to the Third World because, in narrow economic terms, life is cheaper in the poorer countries. The economists' logic might value life differentially in the rich North and the poor South. However, all life is precious. It is equally precious to the rich and the poor, to the white and the black, to men and women.

In this context, recent attempts of the North to link trade conditionalities with the environment in platforms such as WTO need to be viewed as an attempt to build on environmental and economic apartheid. The destruction of ecosystems and livelihoods as a result of trade liberalization is a major environmental and social subsidy to global trade and commerce and those who control it. The main mantra of globalization is "international competitiveness." In the context of the environment, this translates into the largest corporations competing for the natural resources that the poor people in the Third World need for their survival. This competition is highly unequal not only because the corporations are powerful and the poor are not but also because the rules of free trade allow corporations to use the machinery of the nation-state to appropriate resources from the people and prevent people from asserting and exercising their rights.

It is often argued that globalization will create more trade, which will create growth, which will remove poverty. What is overlooked in this myth is that globalization and liberalized trade and investment create growth by destroying the environment and local, sustainable livelihoods. They, therefore, create poverty instead of removing it. The new globalization policies have accelerated and expanded environmental destruction and displaced millions of people from their homes and their sustenance base. The broad dynamics of globalization are coursing throughout India's collective life. In the following sections, I outline the character of some of the colonizations taking place in particular social sectors and the resistances that such impositions are generating.

IMPORTING POLLUTION AND TOXINS

Globalization has implied that toxic waste, like anything else in the context of free trade, is treated as a commodity that shifts around the world to those countries in which the economic costs of internalizing, processing, and disposing it are the lowest and in which the economic and political clout to resist is the lowest. This was, after all, the ineluctable logic propounded by Lawrence Summers in 1991. Thus, under trade liberalization, India has become a dumping ground for industrial toxic wastes from the North as well as a target for deceptive marketing, double standards, and dangerous exports of rejected goods.

Under the new economic trade recipes of the WTO, structural adjustment programs and unilateral trade threats from the United States under the 301 clauses of its trade laws—which allow the United States to take unilateral action against countries that do not open up to U.S. TNCs—are seeking freedom to relocate toxic and polluting industries to India. Drawn by our cheap raw materials, minimal labor costs, pliant bureaucracy, lax environmental standards, and, importantly, low processing and disposal costs for waste, TNCs find India an attractive option. Free trade translates into the right to the free and unrestrained export of hazardous wastes, products, and industry to countries where life is considered cheaper because the people are poorer.

The Case of Thapur and DuPont

Since 1985, DuPont had been attempting to relocate a hazardous nylon 6,6 plant from the United States to the picturesque state of Goa. It was to be established at a cost of rupees (Rs) 600 crore (1 crore = 10 million rupees) to produce 18,500 tons of nylon 6,6 per year. They were forced to give up their plans and move to Tamil Nadu because of sustained agitation launched by the villagers of the area where the factory was to be located.

The House Committee of the Goa Assembly that was set up to look at the environmental implications of the nylon 6,6 plant stated that

> it would be an ill-advised move to allow large chemical industries to discharge even their treated effluents into our eco-rich and virgin rivers. We have to safeguard our rivers against any conceivable environmental and pollution threat. . . . While deciding on the establishment of large chemical industries in a small relatively densely populated and socio-economical rich state as ours, we should consider not only the statistical probability of a possible industrial accident but also the disastrous danger to humans and ecology that may result from such an accident. It is also imperative to realize that in a tiny state like Goa, any large capital intensive industry is bound to consume/utilize a very significant percentage of available natural resources and infrastructural facilities, but in turn, contribute negligibly to the local economy. (Alvares 1996)

The Federal Ministry of Environment also did not give clearance to DuPont. However, in mid-December 1991, Gaza Feketekutty, the U.S. trade representative, made a special trip to India to put pressure on the government to give clearance to DuPont. Key officials in the U.S. government gave hints that DuPont was being treated as a test case for the new trade liberalization policies. On January 1, 1992, the Cabinet cleared the project. Then, under the guise of public purpose, the central government acquired grazing land for the DuPont plant and authorized building work to commence without local Panchayat consultation. This was possible under the Industrial Development Act, which empowers governments to grant special favors to industry in the interests of development.

However, people did not accept the DuPont plant. Protests were initiated, and an Anti-Enron Committee was formed. People were arrested repeatedly during protests. One youth, Nilesh Naik, was shot at point-blank range, and many others were injured in clashes with the police. Even the chief minister was forced to admit that "if the people do not want the project, how can we force it?" The Panchayati Raj Act became effective in Goa only subsequent to this land acquisition. At its monthly meeting, the Panchayat (the locally elected body for village governance accountable to the village community who have elected it) resolved unanimously that local public opinion should be sought prior to granting DuPont permission to continue with its development. In brazen defiance of the Panchayat's decision, DuPont's construction program continued unabated while the Panchayat was still considering the pending application. Anticipating that the director of Panchayats, a government employee, would not uphold the local Panchayat's decision, villagers clashed violently with police and DuPont representatives. However, the decision of the Panchayat, which subsequently and unanimously resolved that the planning application should be quashed, was honored by the High Court. Even before the High Court decision, it was obvious that the site acquired by the government for the factory had returned into the possession of the villagers because of the anti-DuPont movement. Village animals, including goats and cows, prevented for several months from entering the area, were now seen once again freely browsing all over the plot.

This represents an important precedent for the reversal of the logic of globalization and the establishment of local democracy. The rejection of planning permission by a Panchayat, following intense local opposition, even after the approval of central and state governments and despite the global power of DuPont and the global pressure it had mobilized, is evidence that even in an age of globalization, people's power can sometimes overcome the power of TNCs.

NORTHERN DUMPING IN THE SOUTH

The United States generates more than 275 million tons of toxic waste every year and is the leading waste-exporting country in the world. The United States is one of the 161 countries that has signed the Basel International Convention but has not ratified it (along with fifty-eight other countries); parties to the convention, such as India, are not allowed to trade in hazardous wastes with nonparties to the convention. However, notwithstanding the convention, the United States continues its long tradition of exporting its toxic wastes, finding loopholes for dumping them on the South. The United States is thus violating international law in sending shipments of its waste, often mislabeled as recyclables, to India.

In the first half of 1996, approximately 1,500 tons of lead wastes were imported to India. Greenpeace findings state that the amount of toxic lead waste imported from industrialized countries into India has doubled since 1995. Imports from the United States, Australia, South Korea, Germany, the Netherlands, France, Japan, and the United Kingdom account for about 67 percent of the total import of lead wastes to India. The Organization of Economic Cooperation and Development (OECD) accounted for 98 percent of the 400 million metric tons of toxic waste generated worldwide.

Toxic waste such as cyanide, mercury, and arsenic is being shipped as "recyclable waste"—a deliberate attempt to mislead and disguise the true nature of the wastes. In reality, there is no such use or demand to recover such toxic chemicals because it is pure waste. The imported waste often ends up in backyard smelting organizations, not the commercial sector as stated by the government. Many of the importing units do not possess the technology or the expertise to process the chemicals they are importing; therefore, they inadvertently cause more harm to the environment and their communities because of their ignorance concerning the chemicals that they are dealing with. Eight-five hundred such units operate in Maharashtra alone.

Developed countries are offering lucrative prices (in Indian terms) to Indian "recycling" companies to take their material for "processing." India is being used as a dumping ground by the Northern industrialized countries because the cost of treating and disposing waste in a sustainable manner in the North has become highly expensive. Costs have become so high because of stringent laws that ban dumping, burning, and burying waste. Dumping in the developing world therefore becomes justified on grounds of economic efficiency.

The cost of burying one ton of hazardous waste in the United States rose from $15 in 1980 to $350 in 1992. In Germany, it is cheaper, by $2,500, to ship a ton of waste to a developing country than to dispose of it in Europe. Countries such as Germany find it cheaper to export their waste to a landfill than to recycle it themselves. Because India does not charge any landfill costs, the profits made in waste trade has made the industry even more attractive.

In 1966, the Research Foundation for Science, Technology and Ecology (RFSTE) filed public interest litigation seeking a ban on all hazardous and toxic wastes into India. In response, on May 6, 1997, the Supreme Court of India imposed a blanket ban on the import of all kinds of hazardous and toxic wastes into the country. The court also directed state governments to show cause why immediate orders should not be passed for the closure of more than 2,000 unauthorized waste-handling units identified by the central government in various parts of the country. The Supreme Court directed that no import be made or permitted of any hazardous waste that is already banned under the Basel International Convention, or to be banned after the date specified therein by the court.

A court statement established that 2,000 tons of hazardous wastes were being generated every day in India without adequate safe disposal sites. This ban applies to state governments as well as the central government to give authorization for the importation of hazardous wastes.

Today, toxic waste dumping has become a national issue, and several nongovernmental organizations are working specifically on the banning of toxic waste import and dumping and related issues. Srishti, Greenpeace, Toxics Link Exchange, Public Interest Research Group, WWF-India, and the RFSTE are Delhi-based movements that are concerned with hazardous wastes and toxics issues and that, in particular, are opposing the importation of toxic wastes. Furthermore, some of us are involved in creating awareness within India as to the actions of transnational and local industries who often openly defy existing environmental laws regarding importation, treatment, handling, and disposal of hazardous wastes.

EXPORTING OUR BIOLOGICAL WEALTH

Cattle: The Case of Al-Kabeer

The focus on meat production and meat exports in the New Livestock Policy is in fact an export of our ecological capital in the form of animal wealth. It has led to a mushrooming of slaughterhouses. The largest export-oriented slaughterhouse is the Al-Kabeer Slaughterhouse.

People's movements toward conserving livestock diversity and protecting the basis of sustainable agriculture are slowly emerging as the impact of slaughterhouses and meat exports becomes apparent. The courts are playing a significant role in this awareness.

A much awaited judgment was received from the Supreme Court on March 12, 1997, regarding the Al-Kabeer Slaughterhouse case. The interim judgment calls for Al-Kabeer Exports Ltd. to reduce its operation to 50 percent of its installed capacity by April 1, 1997. The judgment came as a response to the severe decline in cattle and buffalo numbers in the vicinity of the Al-Kabeer Slaughterhouse in Andhra Pradesh over the last two years.

At the national level, while animal exports are earning the country Rs10 million, the destruction of animal wealth is costing the country Rs150 million. Examining the dung economy reveals the problem of exporting our animal wealth. A buffalo produces around 12 kilograms of wet dung every day as fuel. This converts to 6 kilograms of dry dung. An average Indian family of five members needs 12 kilograms of dung cakes every day as cooking fuel, which translates into a pair of buffalo. The 182,400 buffalo that Al-Kabeer kills every year can satisfy the fuel needs of 91,200 families in India (Gandhi 1995).

The depletion of cattle and buffalo leads to the decline in availability of dung. The government therefore has to supply kerosene or liquid petroleum gas. The transport cost of this runs into crores of rupees, which means that poor people pay vastly higher fuel expenses. The import of liquid petroleum gas and kerosene increases every year; Rs 547.49 crore of kerosene was imported in the period 1987–

1988. By the period 1992–1993, this had increased to Rs2,008.97 crore, almost a fourfold increase in five years. Thus, the 91,200 families whose fuel requirements have been forcefully altered by the killing of 182,400 buffalo per year in Al-Kabeer will now spend Rs1,440 × 91,200 = Rs13.13 crore on buying fuel. This fuel has to be imported by the government's paying foreign exchange.

The return from this gigantic capital, which the state gets, is as follows. If animals were allowed to live in the state of Andhra Pradesh, we would get 1,918,562 tons of farmyard manure with the help of their dung and urine every year. This farmyard manure would cultivate 383,712 hectares. In 1991, the average food grain produced per hectare was 1.382 tons. Therefore, the food grain produced would be 5.30 lakh tons (1 lakh = 100,000).

Additionally, if the animals were allowed to live out their natural lives instead of being slaughtered by the Al-Kabeer Slaughterhouse, they would save foreign exchange worth Rs910.25 crore from the state of Andhra Pradesh. The calculation based on data from Andhra Pradesh goes as follows. The annual availability of major nutrients in farmyard manure, from the dung and urine of 1,924,000 buffalo and 570,000 sheep per year, works out to the following:

- 11,171,79 tons of nitrogen, which at the current price of Rs20.97 per kilogram at unsubsidized rates, adds up to Rs23.42 crore
- 2,164,15 tons of phosphorus, which at the current price of Rs21.25 per kilogram at unsubsidized rates, adds up to Rs4.6 crore
- 10,069,29 tons of potash, which at the current price of Rs8.33 per kilogram at unsubsidized rates, adds up to Rs8.39 crore

Total value of nitrogen + phosphorus + potash = Rs36.41 crore

All these items are now imported. Thus, Andhra Pradesh would save foreign exchange worth Rs36.41 crore per year from the first lot of animals that are going to be killed. Taking into account their average remaining life span to be five years more, they would save Rs36.41 × 5 = Rs182.05 crore in foreign exchange.

Following the same argument, if all the animals that are going to be killed during, say, five years of Al-Kabeer's operation live out their natural life span, then they will be able to save Rs182.05 × 5 = Rs910.25 crore in foreign exchange. This means that against a projected earning of Rs20 crore by Al-Kabeer through the killings, the state can actually save Rs910 crore in foreign exchange by not killing.

Cattle have long been sacred in India. Today, under the impact of globalization, this conservation culture, which is necessary for the survival of the people, is being perceived as an obstruction to the production and trade of meat. Livestock policies are being rewritten with the objective of exporting cattle for meat. As the new livestock policy states, religious sentiments (especially in the northern and western parts of India) against cattle slaughter prevent the use of many surplus male calves.

In industrial livestock systems, cattle are bred either for milk or for meat. The male calves of milk breeds are thus treated as "surplus." However, in India, the diverse cattle breeds, such as Ongole, Hallihar, Haryana, Tharparhar, and Sindhi, are dual purpose breeds, bred for both milk and drought power. Both male and female offspring are therefore useful and essential for sustainable agriculture. Such usefulness complements the sacred character of the cow in India and reflects a conservationist orientation.

In the last decade, there has been a significant decline of livestock in India, especially the indigenous breeds known for their hardiness, milk production, and draft power. The decline in livestock is due primarily to illegal slaughtering of cattle and buffalo for meat export. Throughout the world domestic animal breeds are disappearing, taking with them irreplaceable genetic traits that often hold the key to resisting disease, not to mention productivity and survival under conditions of adversity (Food and Agriculture Organization 1996). For example, some of the declining indigenous breeds today are Pangunur, Red Kandhari, Vechur, Bhangnari, Dhenani, Lohani, Rojhan, Bengal, Chittagong Red, Napalees Hill, Kachah, Siri, Tarai, Lulu, and Sinhala. The dramatic decline in livestock population in India has reached rave proportions. If measures to arrest this trend are not taken now, most of us will witness the extinction of many breeds of livestock within our lifetime and with it much of the foundation for sustainable agriculture.

In a judgment given in a Delhi court, the protection of cattle and the prevention of slaughter were upheld as a duty of citizens and the state. The judgment stated,

This fundamental Duty in the Constitution to have compassion for all living creatures, thus determines the legal relation between Indian Citizens and animals on Indian soil, whether small ones or large ones. This gives legal status to the view of ancient sages down the generations to cultivate a way of life to live in harmony with nature. Since animals are dumb and helpless and unable to exercise their rights, their rights have been expressed in terms of duties of citizens towards them. (S. 93)

In addition,

Their place in the Constitutional Law of the land, is thus a fountain head of total rule of law for the protection of animals and provides not only against their ill treatment, but from it also springs a right to life in harmony with human beings.

If this enforceable obligation of State is understood, certain results will follow. First, the Indian state cannot export live animals for killing: and second, cannot become a party to the killing of animals by sanctioning exports in the casings and cans stuffed with dead animals after slaughter. Avoidance of this is preserving the Indian Cultural Heritage, of which we claim proud by claiming India as the land of Gandhi, Buddha and Mahavir. India can only export a message of compassion towards all living creatures of the world, as a beacon to preserve ecology, which is the true and common Dharma for all civilizations. This is keeping with the culture of living in harmony with nature by showing respect to all life; and that is Vasudhaiv Kutumbakam [the earth family] referred by our Minister of Environment, Mr. Kamal Nath, at the Environment Conference at Rio, June 1992. (S. 98)

PLANTS AND BIOPIRACY

India is a major region of biodiversity. It is recognized as a country that is uniquely rich in all aspects of biological diversity—from the ecosystem level to the species and genetic levels. It is estimated that more than 75,000 species of fauna and 45,000 of flora are found in India. Of the estimated 45,000 plant species, about 15,000 species of flowering plants are endemic to India. Estimates of other plant taxa include 5,000 species of algae, 1,600 lichens, 20,000 fungi, 2,700 bryophytes, and 600 pteridophytes. The 75,000 species of animals include 50,000 insects, 4,000 mollusks, 200 fish, 140 amphibians, 420 reptiles, 1,200 birds, and 340 mammals and other invertebrates Thus, India is home to about two lakh species of living organisms.

Most of the people in our country derive their livelihood and meet their survival needs from the diversity of living resources—as forest dwellers, farmers, fisherfolk, healers, and livestock owners. The indigenous knowledge systems existing in medicine, agriculture, and fisheries are the primary base for meeting the food and health needs of the majority of our people. This immense resource of natural heritage has been protected, preserved, and conserved by India's indigenous people over the years who have had a reverence for this natural heritage. This knowledge also reflects the continuous, cumulative, collective innovation of the people of India in all their diversity. Conservation and utilization have been delicately, sensitively, and equitably combined in the indigenous knowledge systems and cultures of India.

The sharing and exchange of biodiversity and knowledge of its properties and use have been the norm in all indigenous societies and continue to be the norm in most communities, including the modern scientific community. Sharing and exchange get converted to "piracy," however, when individuals, organizations, or corporations who freely receive biodiversity from indigenous communities and knowledge convert such gifts into private property through IPR claims. This blocks the continuity of free exchange and leads to an "enclosure of the commons."

Biopiracy refers to the process through which the rights of indigenous cultures to these resources and knowledge are erased and replaced by monopoly rights for those who have exploited indigenous knowledge and biodiversity. Indeed, biodiversity-based traditional knowledge systems of the forests dwellers, farmers, and healers are fast becoming the private property of the TNCs. The TNCs are usurping these systems from the domain of common knowledge through IPRs, which in essence promote resource piracy and intellectual piracy. In the present world-market economy, where knowledge represents money, capital represents power, and profit earning is the sole aim, those who own capital seek IPRs to protect their "discoveries," which often are based on the cumulative and collective innovation of traditional societies.

The system of IPRs expanded the domain of intellectual property to biodiversity.

However, these IPR regimes, as provided under trade-related intellectual property rights, recognize and provide protection only to the formal innovators, not to the informal indigenous innovators. The traditional knowledge of informal innovators (farmers, indigenous medical practitioners, and forest dwellers) is being pirated by the formal innovators (scientists, plant breeders, and technologists) who make minor modifications or advances and then seek patents, thereby claiming the knowledge as their private property.

Biopiracy leaves the donors poorer both materially and intellectually, as they are excluded from sharing in the benefits of their own resources and knowledge. As we enter the third millennium, we need to find ways to protect biological diversity and the intellectual heritage of India for the future of India's people and the world as a whole. Emergent ecological concern for the conservation of biological diversity provides a new opportunity to value our biological and intellectual wealth and to use and conserve it for sustainable human use.

PEOPLE'S MOVEMENTS FOR THE PROTECTION OF BIODIVERSITY AND COLLECTIVE RIGHTS

New social and environmental movements are emerging everywhere in response to the widespread destruction of the environment and of the livelihoods that depend on biodiversity and in response to piracy of our indigenous resources and indigenous innovation. In India, the intricate link between people's livelihoods and biodiversity has evolved over centuries. Economic liberalization is threatening to sever this link by treating biodiversity as a raw material for exploitation of life forms as property and of people's livelihoods as an inevitable sacrifice for national economic growth and development. It is also eroding the level of governing control that people have over their lives.

In February 1995, the tribal people from different parts of India were in Delhi on an indefinite fast to force the government to recognize their declaration of "self-rule." The National Front for Tribal Self-Rule, a national organization of organizations of tribal people, has conducted a civil disobedience movement since October 2, 1995, for the establishment of self-rule. As they state,

> We have carried the cross of virtual slavery for much too long in spite of independence. Other rural folks are also in a similar state. Yet, now that everything is clear and there is unanimity in the establishment as also among members of parliament and experts, the change must not be delayed. We will not tolerate this. Even otherwise, on the issue of self-governance we need not be solicitous. It is a natural right. In the hierarchy of democratic institutions gram-sabha is above all, even parliament. This is what Gandhi preached; we will not obey any law which compromises the position of gram-sabha. In any case we resolve to establish self-rule with effect from October 2, 1995. We will have command over our resources and will manage our affairs thereafter. (Declaration, "Front for Tribal Self-Rule," Delhi, February 1995)

The struggle of the tribal people was successful.

The passing of the Provisions of the Panchayats (Extension to the Scheduled Areas) Act that came into effect in December 1996 represents a landmark piece of legislation as far as acknowledging the legal rights to self-rule of the tribal people are concerned. Section 4(b) and (d) of the act state the following:

- A village shall ordinarily consist of a habitation or a group of habitations, or a hamlet or a group of hamlets comprising a community and managing its affairs in accordance with traditions and customs.
- Each gram-sabha shall be competent to safeguard and preserve the traditions and customs of the people, their cultural identity, community resources and the customary mode of dispute resolution.

The implementation of the Panchayati Raj Act in Scheduled Areas has already set the precedent for the recognition of communities as competent authorities for decision making on resource use, cultural values and traditions, and community rights to common resources as the building block of a decentralized democracy (Research Foundation for Science, Technology and Ecology 1997).

More than 100 villages in and around the thick forests of Nagarhole in Karnataka have established self-governments to safeguard their livelihood under the provisions of a law passed by the Parliament that came into effect on December 24, 1996: the Provisions of the Panchayats (Extension to the Scheduled Areas) Act, 1996. However, this law has yet to be passed by the Karnataka Assembly to implement it in that state.

The people have formed gram-sabhas and established task forces to implement the self-rule program. In some of the villages, they have erected gates at the entrance, and only the chief of the tribal community/village has been entrusted with the power to give permission to any outsider to enter their village. The villagers are freely collecting the minor forest produce, and even they are adjudicating the problems themselves rather than going to the police or court.

THE MOVEMENT FOR DECLARATION OF COMMUNITY RIGHTS TO BIODIVERSITY: THE CASE OF PATTUVAM PANCHAYAT

Nationwide people's movements have succeeded to date in stalling any legislation passing parliament that would promote IPRs over biodiversity. Such opposition signifies the degree of democratic dissent being generated at the grassroots level to laws affecting people's livelihoods and rights over their resources. People's movements against erosion, exploitation, and usurpation of biodiversity are numerous and widespread throughout the country. A small community in southern Kerala has taken a bold step to protect its biodiversity. On April 9, 1997, in a remote part of Kerala, hundreds of local people gathered to declare their local biodiversity as a community-owned resource that they will collectively protect and that they will not allow to be privatized through patents on derived products or varieties.

The community is known as the Pattuvam Panchayat. The Panchayat has set up its own biodiversity register to record all biodiversity of species in the region. It has stated that no individual, TNC, or state or central government can use their biodiversity without the permission of the Pattuvam Panchayat. The people of Pattuvam have taken a pathbreaking step by declaring their biodiversity a community resource over which the community as a whole has rights. This step demonstrates a commitment to rejuvenating and protecting their biodiversity and knowledge systems from the exploitative forces of economic liberalization.

Movements are occurring in other parts of India as well whereby communities are declaring the biodiversity and knowledge as the common heritage of local communities. For example, in Dharward in Karnataka and in Chattisgarh, Madhya Pradesh, declaration ceremonies have been held announcing that biodiversity is a community resource and that privatization of biodiversity and indigenous knowledge through patents is theft.

THE PEOPLE'S COMMISSION ON BIODIVERSITY AND INDIGENOUS KNOWLEDGE AND PEOPLE'S RIGHTS

The People's Commission on Biodiversity and Indigenous Knowledge and People's Rights was launched, on the initiative of the Research Foundation for Science, Technology and Natural Resource Policy, on March 17, 1997, under the Chairmanship of Justice V. R. Krishna Iyer. The commission consists of Justice R. S. Sarkaria and Justice Kuldeep Singh, retired judges of the Supreme Court of India, as members and Afsar H. Jafri, research officer in the RFSTE, as secretary. The commission's basic task is to inquire into the piracy of India's rich biodiversity so as to assist the country and the government in taking appropriate measures to preserve our rich biological and genetic resources.

The commission will carry out wide-ranging consultations and public hearings in order to provide legal guidelines to ensure that our national laws protect the national and the public interests and then will submit its findings and recommendations to the government in its effort to frame new laws on patents and plant varieties protection. The commission held the first phase of the public hearing on August 5 to 7, 1997, at India International Center, New Delhi. The commission has requested the Indian government to wait for this democratic process to be completed before introducing any changes in our existing laws related to IPRs. At present the commission has been engaged in the collection of relevant data and materials on the nation's biological wealth. The chairman has also requested people to help and cooperate with the commission by providing relevant copies of the books, articles, papers, and data on India's natural and biological wealth and its loss.

NAVDANYA: SEEDS OF FREEDOM

I have started a national movement for the recovery of the biological and intellectual commons by saving native seeds from extinction. Seed is the first link in the food chain. It is also the first step toward freedom in food. Globalization is leading to total control over what we eat and what we grow. The tiny seed is becoming an instrument of freedom in this emerging era of total control. Our slogan is, "Native seed—indigenous agriculture—local markets."

Through saving the native seed, we are becoming free of chemicals. By practicing a "free" agriculture, we are saying no to patents on life and to biopiracy. Gandhi called such resistance "Satyagraha": the struggle for truth. Navdanya is a "Seed Satyagraha" in which it is the most marginal and poor peasants who are finding new hope.

A central part of the Seed Satyagraha is to declare the "common intellectual rights" of Third World communities who have gifted the world the knowledge of the rich bounties of nature's diversity. The innovations of Third World communities might differ in process and objectives from the innovations in the commercial world of the West, but they cannot be discounted just because they are different. But we are going beyond just saying no. We are creating alternatives by building community seed banks, strengthening farmers' seed supplies, and searching for sustainable agriculture options that are suitable for different regions.

The seed has become, for us, the site and the symbol of freedom in the age of manipulation and monopoly of its diversity. It plays the role of Gandhi's spinning wheel in this period of recolonization through free trade. The "Charkha" (spinning wheel) became an important symbol of freedom not because it was big and powerful but because it was small and could come alive as a sign of resistance and creativity in the smallest of huts and poorest of families. In smallness lay its power. The seed too is small. It embodies diversity. It embodies the freedom to stay alive. And seed is still the common property of small farmers in India. In the seed, cultural diversity converges with biological diversity. Ecological issues combine with social justice, peace, and democracy.

CONCLUSION

The dynamics of globalization and their associated violence are posing some of the most severe challenges to ordinary people in India and throughout the world. While this chapter has been pessimistic, outlining the character and strength of globalization and its ability to thwart citizen accountability, I take heart in the resistance movements mentioned in the last few sections. Continuous globalizing efforts may threaten democracy, the vibrancy and diversity of life forms, and ecological well-being in general. However, the human spirit, inspired by justice and environmental protection, can never be fully repressed. Despite the brutal violence of globalization, we have hope because we build alternatives in partnership with nature and people. As a Palestinian poem called the "Seed Keepers" has stated,[1]

Burn our land
burn our dreams
pour acid on to our songs
cover with saw dust
the blood of our massacred people
muffle with your technology
the screams of all that is free,
wild and indigenous.
Destroy
Destroy
our grass and soil
raze to the ground
every farm and every village
our ancestors had built
every tree, every home
every book, every law
and all the equity and harmony.
Flatten with your bombs
every valley; erase with your edits
our past,
our literature; our metaphor.
Denude the forests
and the earth
till no insect,
no bird
no word
can find a place to hide.
Do that and more.
I do not fear your tyranny
I do not despair ever
for I guard one seed
a little live seed
that I shall safeguard
and plant again

NOTE

1. "Seed Keepers," an unpublished poem, has come to me through the oral tradition, part of the popular culture in Palestine.

10

Markets, Private Property, and the Possibility of Democracy

David Held

This chapter focuses on a much debated theme in political thought: the relationship of democracy to the "free market" and private property. While the chapter rehearses a number of familiar positions in this debate, it develops a distinctive position by arguing that, if different kinds of markets are to flourish within the constraints of democratic processes and outcomes, democratic rules and procedures must be entrenched in market mechanisms and relationships. In presenting this case, the democratic justification for political intervention in the economy at the national, regional, and global levels is also set forth.

The backdrop of the chapter is the neoliberal argument that only individuals can judge what they want and, therefore, that the less the state interferes in their lives, the more freedom they will have to set their own objectives (Falk 1995). In the first section of the chapter, I explore this argument as it is unfolded in the work of Robert Nozick and Friedrich Hayek. In the second section, I assess this argument critically by examining whether there are economic limits to freedom and democracy. After showing that there are distinctive tensions between democracy and capitalism, I emphasize that the implications of these—in the context of the end of the Cold War and the collapse of Soviet communism—are by no means straightforward. In the third section, I explore further the terms of this analysis and examine the rationale of democratic political intervention in the economy. In the fourth and fifth sections, I turn to how, and at what levels, democracy might be "deepened" and more extensively entrenched in economic life. Different forms of political intervention are discussed, and I make the case for what I call "reframing" the market. Finally, I offer a few concluding reflections on a cosmopolitan democratic program for the regulation of the economy.

THE FRAMEWORK FOR UTOPIA: NEOLIBERALISM?

The least intrusive form of public power commensurate with the defense of individual rights, it has been argued, is the "framework for utopia." The author of this view,

Robert Nozick, holds that we must get away from the idea that utopia represents a single conception of the best of all social and political arrangements (Nozick 1974). There is no one type of community that will serve as an ideal for all people because a wide range of conceptions of utopia exists. Provocatively, he wrote,

> Wittgenstein, Elizabeth Taylor, Bertrand Russell, Thomas Merton, Yogi Berra, Allen Ginsburg, Harry Wolfson, Thoreau, Casey Stengel, The Lubavitcher Rebbe, Picasso, Moses, Einstein, Hugh Heffner, Socrates, Henry Ford, Lenny Bruce, Bab Ram Dass . . . Emma Goldman, Peter Kropotkin, you, and your parents. Is there really one kind of life which is best for each of these people? (Nozick 1974, 310)

A society in which utopian experimentation can be tried should be thought of as utopia; or, to put it another way, utopia is the framework for liberty and experimentation (Nozick 1974, 333–34).

There is much to recommend this view; since individuals and peoples are extraordinarily diverse, no one kind of life seems best for all of them. An institutional arrangement that creates maximum space for initiative and autonomy and minimum space for restriction and coercion, is, prima facie, highly appealing. However, the questions are the following: How can radically different aspirations be both articulated and reconciled? How can self-determination be achieved without a framework of mutual accommodation? If people are to be self-determining, do they not require a common structure of political action to protect themselves as agents with an equal entitlement to self-determination? According to Nozick, the grounds for any such suggestion are deeply suspect; the framework for utopia is properly conceived as "libertarian and laissez-faire." The framework is inconsistent with "planning in detail" and the active redistribution of resources.

Developing a parallel theme, Friedrich Hayek insists that a free society is incompatible with the enactment of rules that specify how people should use the means at their disposal (Hayek 1960, 231–32). The value of individuals' services can be determined justly by their fellows only in and through a decision-making system that does not interfere with their knowledge, choices, and decisions. And there is only one sufficiently sensitive mechanism for determining "collective" choice on an individual basis: the free market.

The free market does not always operate perfectly, but, Hayek insists, its benefits radically outweigh its disadvantages (Hayek 1960, 1976; Rutland 1985). The market system is the basis for a genuinely free order, for economic freedom is "an essential requisite for political freedom" (Friedman 1980, 21). Thus, "politics" or "state action" should be kept to a minimum—to the sphere of an "ultra-liberal" state (Hayek 1976, 172). An "oppressive bureaucratic government" is the almost inevitable result of deviation from this prescription. By contrast, a public authority that acts within this framework—preserving the rule of law, providing a "safety net" for the clearly destitute, and maintaining collective security against internal or external threats—will be not only a "limited government" but a "decent government" as well (Hayek 1982, vol. 2, 102; cf. 1982, vol. 3, 102–27). The framework for utopia is limited and decent government; it can be referred to as "legal democracy"—a democracy circumscribed by the rule of law that prohibits the making of general, (i.e., redistributive) rules.

THE ECONOMIC LIMITS TO DEMOCRACY?

The arguments just outlined include a number of elements that are important to consider. Those of particular note include the emphasis on protecting individual autonomy against coercive political power in all its forms and limiting the scope and form of state action by means of the rule of law. However, there are many reasons for pausing before equating the framework for utopia with "legal democracy." The idea that modern society approximates, or could progressively approximate, a world in which producers and consumer meet on an equal basis seems implausible, to say the least. Hayek in particular and neoliberalism in general project an image of markets as "powerless" mechanisms of coordination and in so doing neglect the distorting nature of economic power in relation to democracy (Vajda 1978; Falk 1995, 47–48).

These general reflections can be broken down further into a number of different elements. First, there are significant areas of market failure, recognized by many conventional economists, that need to be borne in mind when analyzing the relationship of democracy to market forces, including the problem of externalities (e.g., the environmental externalities produced by economic growth), the persistent dependence of market economies on nonmarket social factors that alone can provide an effective balance between "competition" and "cooperation" (and, thus, ensure an adequate supply of necessary "public goods," such as education, trained labor, and market information), the tendency to the "concentration" and "centralization" of economic life (marked by patterns of oligopoly and monopoly), the propensity to "short-termism" in investment strategy as fund holders and fund corporations operate policies aimed at maximizing immediate income return and dividend results, and the underemployment or unemployment of productive resources in the context of the demonstrable existence of urgent and unmet need (Miller 1989; Cohen 1991; Evans 1992; Hirst 1993; Pierson 1993).

Second, some of the main threats to democracy and political freedom in the contemporary world be can be related not to demands for equality or the ambitions of the majority to level social difference, as thinkers from Tocqueville to Hayek have feared, but to inequality—inequality of such magnitude as to create significant violations of political liberty and democratic politics (Held 1993c, pt. 2, 1996, chap. 3; see also Dahl 1985, 50, 60). Nozick and Hayek, and neoliberalism in general, neglect to inquire into the extent to which market relations are themselves power relations that can constrain the democratic process. They do not ask whether systematic asymmetries in income, wealth, and opportunity may be the outcome of the existing form of market relations and whether one particular form of autonomy—the autonomy to accumulate unlimited economic resources and to organize productive activity into hierarchically governed enterprise and highly mobile units—poses a fundamental challenge to the extent to which autonomy can be enjoyed by all citizens, that is, the extent to which citizens can act as equals in the political process. Economic organizations are cooperative ventures governed by rules, policies, and strategies, but they remain ventures in which most employees have no democratic stake despite the fact that each employee is expected to operate for the mutual advantage of all others and that the decisions, policies, and strategies of these ventures have a major influence on other sites of power, from health and welfare to politics (J. Cohen 1988).

Third, the stratification of democratic systems produced by modern corporate capitalism goes beyond the immediate impact of economic inequalities, for the very capacity of governments to act in ways that interest groups may legitimately desire is constrained. Lindblom (1977) has explained the point simply:

> Because public functions in the market system rest in the hands of businessmen, it follows that jobs, prices, production, growth, the standard of living, and the economic security of everyone all rest in their hands. Consequently, government officials cannot be indifferent to how well business performs its functions. Depression, inflation, or other economic disasters can bring down a government. A major function of government, therefore, is to see to it that businessmen perform their tasks. (122–23)

The constraints on governments and state institutions systematically limit policy options. The system of private property and investments creates objective exigencies that must be met if economic growth and development are to be sustained. Accordingly, governments must take action to help secure the profitability and prosperity of the private sector; they are dependent on the process of capital accumulation, which, for their own sustainability, they have to maintain, and this means, at the minimum, ensuring the compatibility of economic policies with the imperatives of the corporate sector and/or with the imperatives of the international capital markets.

Another way to put this is to note that the possibility of managing a national economy and of "bucking" international economic trends has become more difficult. In an international economic system that fosters vast, instantaneous movements of short-term capital—over a trillion dollars a day is dispatched across borders—a government's capacity to reflate its economy at a time of its own choosing has become problematic, although it retains deflationary options in order to bring its economy into line with wider market trends—options, however, with high social costs measured in terms of unemployment and crime (Hutton 1993).

Government legitimacy, furthermore, is thoroughly bound up with the success of its economic measures, for governments are also dependent on the private sector to meet the demands of their consumers (Evans 1992). If governments fail in this regard, their electoral support can quickly melt away. A government's policies must, thereby, follow a political agenda that is at least favorable to (i.e., biased toward) the development of the system of private enterprise and corporate power, national and international.

Democratic theory and practice is, thus, faced with a major challenge; the business corporation or multinational bank enjoy a disproportionate "structural influence" over the polity and, therefore, over the nature of democratic outcomes. Political representatives would find it extremely difficult to carry out the wishes of an electorate committed to reducing the adverse effects on democracy and political equality of corporate capitalism. (For an account of some past attempts, see Coates 1980; Ross et al. 1987; cf. Hall 1986.) Democracy is embedded in a socioeconomic system that grants a "privileged position" to certain interests.

If a state or a set of regulative agencies is separate from the associations and practices of everyday life, then it is plausible to see it as a special kind of apparatus—a "protective knight," "umpire," or "judge"—that the citizen ought to respect and obey. But if states and governing agencies are enmeshed in these associations and practices, then the claim that they constitute "independent authorities" or "circumscribed impartial powers" is compromised, as thinkers on the left of the political spectrum have traditionally maintained. This is unsettling for a whole range of questions concerning the nature of public power, the relation between the "public" and the "private," the proper scope of politics, and the appropriate reach of democratic governments (Pateman 1985, 172ff).

Furthermore, if states are, as a matter of routine, neither "separate" nor "impartial" with respect to society, then citizens will not be treated as equally free. If the "public" and the "private" are interlocked in complex ways, then formal elections will always be insufficient as mechanisms to ensure the accountability of the forces actually involved in the "governing" process. Moreover, since the "meshing" of state and civil society leaves few, if any, realms of "private life" untouched by "politics" and vice versa, the question of the proper form of the state, law, and democratic regulation is posed acutely. Pace Nozick and Hayek, if the rule of law does not involve a central concern with distributional questions and matters of social justice, it cannot be satisfactorily entrenched, and democratic accountability cannot be, as Falk has always emphasized, adequately realized (Falk 1995).

The arguments outlined here emphasize a number of sources of tension between democracy and capitalism. Even when taken together, however, they by no means amount to a straightforward critique of the latter. While granting priority to the right to self-determination entails recognizing the importance of introducing limits on the right to, and on the rights of, productive and financial property, the exact implications of this viewpoint remain obscure. It would be quite foolish to suggest that there are simple alternatives that are both feasible and desirable to the existing system of corporate capitalism. For example, the notion that the tensions between democracy and capitalism can be overcome by the introduction of a planned economy, as classical Marxists have traditionally argued, suffers from two decisive problems that render it implausible and, for most people, unappealing. To begin with, in its technocratic-elitist form, expressed most clearly in the Soviet conception of a command economy, the planned economy has failed as a political and economic project. This is so for many of the reasons that Hayek proffered, including an arrogant and misplaced presumption of knowledge about people's needs and wants, a crisis of "excessive information" that could not be properly evaluated in the absence of market prices and costs, and the pursuit of coercive political programs in diverse domains, from economic management to cultural life (Hayek 1960, 1976, 1978). The command economy was the epitome of the "oppressive bureaucratic state." In addition, those who have sought to articulate the notion of a planned economy with democracy—defending the idea of self-managed economic system, for example— have so far failed to elaborate a fully convincing alternative political economy to capitalism (cf. Callinicos 1993; Held 1993a, b). At the present juncture, there does not seem to be a viable alternative economics to capitalism, but this does not mean, of course, that one might not be forthcoming. Nor does it mean that the question of "alternatives" is an insignificant matter.

However, the whole question of capitalism and its alternatives is wholly misstated by putting the issue as one between capitalism and something different in all fundamental respects. Just as there is more than one socialism, there is more than one capitalism. Capitalism is not a single, homogeneous system the world over; there are different capitalisms with different capacities for reform and adaptation. The United States, Japan, and Sweden, for example, embody quite different models of economic development, production, labor market regulation, and welfare regimes (Esping-Andersen 1990; Allen 1992). In addition, capitalism, in the context of democratic constitutional societies, has strengths as well as weaknesses—strengths that need to be recognized and defended as well as extended and developed (cf. Habermas 1992).

Accordingly, if the implications of the arguments about the tensions between democracy and capitalism are to be pursued, it needs to be on terms that break with the simple and crude juxtaposition of capitalism with planning or of capitalism with systems of collective ownership and control and in terms that are more cautious and, I should add, experimental. In order to consider these matters further, it is necessary to relate them to a broader and more systematic framework of assessment—that provided by the arguments for democracy and what I call "democratic autonomy." By democratic autonomy, I mean the capacity of all persons as citizens to, in principle, enjoy autonomy in equal measure. I take a commitment to democratic autonomy to be at the core of democracy. More formally stated, I take such a commitment to mean

> that persons should enjoy equal rights (and, accordingly, equal obligations) in the specification of the framework which generates and limits the opportunities available to them; that is, they should be free and equal in the determination of the conditions of their own lives, so long as they do not deploy this framework to negate the rights of others. (Held 1995, 147)

Any power system that systematically violates or undermines this principle can be regarded as an illegitimate restriction on democracy's proper form and scope (Held 1995, pt. 3, where this issue is explored in some depth).

THE RATIONALE OF POLITICAL INTERVENTION IN THE ECONOMY

To create a framework for utopia demands not an abdication of politics in the name of liberty and experimentation but, on the contrary, a distinctive logic of political intervention. The rationale for this logic does not derive primarily from the domain of political control, that is, from a desire to plan and regulate economic and social affairs. Rather, the rationale derives from the requirement to ensure that the conditions are met for the democratic regulation of sites of power in all their forms. The requirement of democratic autonomy provides a direction for public policy and for its proper form and limits. Political intervention is justified when it upholds and furthers this objective.

A "legal democracy," therefore, can never simply be a minimum national state or a federation of minimal states, for the rationale of political intervention lays on the polity—at the local, national, regional, and global levels—the responsibility to promote and defend democratic autonomy. Within the economy, thus, political intervention is warranted when it is driven by the objective of overcoming those consequences of economic interaction, whether intended or unintended, and this generates damaging externalities, such as environmental pollution threatening to citizens. In addition, it is warranted when it is driven by the need to ensure that the basic requirements of autonomy are met for each and all both within and outside the firm. None of this is a case for abandoning the market system. The latter has distinct advantages, as Hayek has emphasized, over all known alternative economic systems as an effective mechanism to coordinate the knowledgeable decisions of producers and consumers over extended territories. However, it is an argument for "reframing" the market.

THE ENTRENCHMENT OF DEMOCRACY IN ECONOMIC LIFE: REFRAMING THE MARKET

Democracy is challenged by powerful sets of economic relations and organizations that can—by virtue of the bases of their operations—systematically distort democratic processes and outcomes. Accordingly, there is a case that, if democracy is to prevail, the key groups and associations of the economy will have to be rearticulated with political institutions so that they become part of the democratic process—adopting, within their very modus operandi, a structure of rules, principles, and practices compatible with democracy. The possibility of such a structure depends on groups and economic associations functioning within agreed and delimited frameworks. Companies may be conceived as real entities or "legal persons" with legitimate purposes of their own without surrendering the idea of a shared framework of political action (Hirst 1990, 75–78). In the first instance, what is at issue is the inscription of the principles, rules, and procedures of democracy and democratic autonomy into the organizational rules and procedures of companies and of all other forms of economic association.

If democratic processes and relations are to be sustained, corporations will have to uphold de jure and de facto a commitment to the requirements of democratic autonomy. What this entails is that companies, while pursuing strategic objectives and profit goals, must operate within a framework that does not violate the requirement to treat their employees and customers as free and equal persons. Within their sphere of competence, that is to say, companies would have to pursue working conditions and practices that sustained health and safety, learning and welfare, the ability to engage in discussion and criticism (including of the company and its staff), the capacity to join independent associations (in this case, trade unions and professional organizations), and the capacity for economic independence and involvement in decision making (i.e., most of the basic requirements of democratic citizenship). I do not have the opportunity here to justify the inclusion of all these elements in economic associations, but I would like to dwell on a few ingredients of democratic autonomy in the sphere of work. These include rights to a "basic income" and "access avenues" to productive and financial property.

A commitment to basic income is a commitment to the conditions for each employee's economic independence, that is, the conditions that are commensurate with an individual's need for material security and the independence of mind that follows from it (Rousseau 1968, 96; Connolly 1981, chap. 7). Without a resource base of this kind, people remain highly vulnerable, dependent on others and unable to exercise fully their capacity to pursue different courses of action. The requirements of economic independence include a firm policy of "minimum wages" at work, politically determined intervention to uphold such levels, and a wider collective provision for those who fall outside the income-generating mechanisms of the market (Jordan 1985; Rogers and Streeck 1994). However, even more important for the form and character of economic associations is the commitment to "access avenues" to the decision-making apparatus of productive and financial property, that is, to the creation of participative opportunities in firms and in other types of economic organization. Such opportunities do not translate straightforwardly into a right to social or collective ownership, for what is centrally at issue is an opportunity for involvement in the determination of the regulative rules of work organizations, the broad allocation of resources within them, and the relations of economic enterprises to other sites of power (Pierson 1995). The question of particular forms of property right is not in itself the primary consideration (see the following discussion).

Furthermore, the transaction of all business would, within this conception, have to be conducted in a manner that respects each and every person's right to lawful political relations and upholds a wider framework of international law. This means that companies ought not engage in activities, openly or covertly, that undermine the political choices of peoples as, for example, some North American companies did in Chile in 1973 when they colluded in the downfall of the Allende regime or as many companies do when they fund (typically center-right) political parties in order to ensure electoral outcomes favorable to their interests. The private determination of election results, whether by force, fraud, or funding, should be ruled out by the requirements of democracy, with its insistence, in principle, on free and equal participative opportunities for all parties in the democratic process.

The entrenchment of democratic rights and obligations within economic organizations represents an extension of an established idea of using legislation to alter the background conditions of firms in the marketplace. The Social Chapter of the European Maastricht Agreement, for example, embodies principles and rules that are compatible with the notion of generating elements of a common framework of democratic action. If operationalized, the Social Chapter could, in principle, alter the structure and functioning of market processes in a number of distinct ways (Lebrun 1990; Addison and Siebert 1993). However, its provisions fall far short of the determination of what is necessary to secure a democratic framework of economic action (see Hepple 1993). In addition, the intensive arguments about the Social Chapter in Europe highlight a legitimate concern about a European attempt to address the social conditions of the market. It has rightly been argued that a European social initiative of this kind that did not lead to parallel reforms and developments elsewhere might disadvantage European capital in competition with other regional economic zones and/or so weaken the European initiative that it would become either ineffective or unenforceable over time (Addison and Siebert 1993, 29ff; Balls 1994).

It is desirable, therefore, that markets are framed by a democratic law, especially an international democratic law, that could entrench and enforce its provisions—concerning rights and obligations with respect to health, welfare, learning, participation, and a basic income—across economic life, nationally, regionally, and globally. What is required, in essence, is the introduction of new clauses into the ground rules or basic laws of the free-market and free-trade system. Ultimately, this necessitates the stipulation of new democratic terms of economic organization and trade. While the advocacy of such a position would clearly raise enormous political, diplomatic, and technical difficulties and would need a substantial period to pursue and, of course, implement, this is a challenge that cannot be avoided if people's equal interest in self-determination is to be nurtured and fulfilled. Only by introducing new terms of empowerment and accountability throughout the global economic system, as a supplement and complement to collective agreements and welfare measures in national and regional contexts, can a new settlement be created between economic power and democracy (Lipietz 1992, 119–24).

A new agreement of this kind—a new "Bretton Woods" as it were—would seek to entrench not only the general conditions that are necessary for a common structure of democratic life but also the conditions necessary for the pursuit of policies aimed at alleviating, in the short and medium term, the most pressing cases of avoidable economic suffering and harm, for a common structure of democratic life cannot be achieved without the transformation of the conditions of "the disadvantaged," that is, those whose very political agency is impaired by need. Without such a transformation, these people's equal interest in democracy—their equal entitlement as a citizen to self-determination—cannot be protected. Therefore, at a minimum, a democratic process of change would involve negotiation to reduce the economic vulnerability of many developing countries by reducing debt, decreasing the outflow of net capital assets from the South to the North, and creating new economic facilities at organizations such as the World Bank and the International Monetary Fund for development purposes (Lipietz 1992, 116ff; Falk 1995, chap. 6). In addition, if such measures were combined with a consumption tax on energy usage and/or a shift of priorities from military expenditure to the alleviation of severe need, then the developmental context of Western and Northern nation-states could begin to be accommodated to those nations struggling for survival and minimum welfare. It has been estimated, for example, that a consumption tax "of a dollar per barrel of oil, collected at source, would yield around $24 billion a year (73% from the industrial nations). An equivalent tax on coal would yield around $16 billion" (UN Development Program 1992, 90). These are clearly substantial sums, reinforcing the view that development assistance is more a question of political will and judgment than of monetary resources per se.

Moreover, "zones of development," areas defined by the extensiveness of cases of urgent need (typically found in the South but also in parts of the North), could be established and formally demarcated. In such zones, the responsibility for the nurturing and enforcement of urgent levels of autonomy would not be left to the countries alone in which the zones were located, especially if particular democratic rights clusters—for example, aspects of safety, welfare, and basic income—were demonstrably unfundable by those countries. If this were the case, urgent levels of autonomy would have to be treated as targets for attainment by developing areas rather than as obligations that were legally binding and capable of immediate enforcement. However, such limited suspension of the enforcement of certain rights would need to be linked directly to the provision of additional resources by the international community to help promote local forms of industry and work. Such a "double-sided" strategy could be expected to provide a significant impetus to self-generative activities; thus, hard-pressed nations or regions could find support from a policy context oriented toward mutual responsibility for democracy and autonomy, in the short and long run.

Entrepreneurs and executives appear to object less to regulation or reform per se than to the intrusion of regulatory mechanisms that upset "the rules of the game" in some particular places or countries only. High direct-tax levels or tough equal-opportunities legislation, for example, are objectionable to companies if they handicap their competitive edge with other companies from areas not subject to similar regulations. Under such circumstances, companies will do what they can to resist regulation or depart for more "hospitable shores." Accordingly, the rules of the game have, in principle, to be altered tout court, at regional and global levels, if capitalism is to be democratized and entrenched in a set of mechanisms and procedures that allow different kinds of markets to flourish within the constraints of democratic processes. A democratic political economy can be envisaged as part of a "democratic alternative" to both state socialism and liberal democratic capitalist economies.

FORMS AND LEVELS OF INTERVENTION

Against this background, international organizations would be given new responsibilities to oversee the process of democratic entrenchment. Among their objectives would be to reduce the role of economic forces in delimiting democratic conditions and outcomes while not eroding the role of market exchange, that is, the orientation of enterprises toward the effective use of their capacity to meet market demands (Devine 1991, 211). To enhance the prospects of attaining this result, levels of public expenditure and public investment would need to be subject to public deliberation and decision, as would the broad aims of such investment. For example, the amount spent on the world's military exceeds the combined incomes of the poorest half of humanity (see, e.g., UNICEF 1992). Accordingly, less investment in the arms industry and more spent directly on human capital would be a significant shift in the direction of the widespread development of some of the key conditions of human autonomy. Trade-offs such as these could be publicized and debated. In the context of public decision making orientated to the democratic good, priorities might be renegotiated and changed.

Furthermore, decisions could be implemented by fixing the areas in which capital could be encouraged to deploy and the terms on which it could be "rented" (Cohen 1988, 16–17). The management of interest rate levels to induce capital to invest in certain areas is clearly more justifiable in the case of social investment projects—or in what I would prefer to call "social framework investments in the conditions of autonomy"—than in the case of particular economic sectors or industrial areas where the track record of political bodies for second-guessing economic and technical change has generally been unimpressive. The management of social and public investment in the infrastructure of autonomy is rightly undertaken publicly, whereas private investment in economic sectors is, as a working rule, best left to those in those sectors with the practical knowledge to make such decisions. Of course, it is likely that there would be strong differences of view as to the scope and direction of public investment, but in a political system that welcomes open debate, these differences could be discussed and examined. If pressing cases of need or autonomy are to be addressed, the scope and direction of such investment must be brought into the center of democratic processes. In the absence of this, democracy is fundamentally handicapped.

It is hard to imagine how public expenditure and investment coordination could take place without a new high level, cooperative organization operating as a complement to, but reaching beyond, existing economic structures. New forms of economic coordination would be indispensable to overcome the fragmentation of policymaking that emerge in the context of organizations such as the International Monetary Fund, the World Bank, the Bank for European Construction and Development, the Organization for Economic Cooperation and Development, and the Group of Seven all operating with separate briefs. Where exactly a new economic coordinator should be located (e.g., whether it should be some form of economic security council working at the United Nations) would need to be debated (UN Development Program 1993). However, this debate is of secondary importance. The primary issue is to recognize the need for a new transnational authority capable of deliberation about the broad balance of public investment priorities, expenditure patterns, and emergency economic situations. The brief of such a body would be to fill a vacuum, that is, to become the coordinator for economic policy that is set at either global or regional levels or is not set at all. It could, thereby, help establish targets for the deployment of funds in various policy areas as well as create policies for economic domains that escape the jurisdiction of existing regulatory spheres, for example, short-term international capital markets. Its task, therefore, would be to lay out broad policy frameworks that could act as points of orientation for those working at other levels of governance.

Nonetheless, even with widespread support for a set of public investment priorities, it would be foolish to presuppose that major capital markets would simply accept and go along with these priorities. There has been many a reaction—including the flight of capital to "safe havens"—against governments seeking to pursue social priorities for investment, sometimes despite clear mandates for such programs. Further, in the era of the twilight of communism, it would also be unwise to think that there would not be clear and popular instances of resistance to programs of public investment, especially if they involved a requirement to raise additional revenue. It is essential, therefore, that strategies of economic democratization, if they are to be feasible strategies, work, wherever possible, "with the grain of private property rather than against it" (Beetham 1993, 69). Examples of such strategies include, for example, the formulation of a general incomes policy that allows profits to rise while using increased taxation on a percentage of these to create social investment funds on a local, national, or regional basis (Korpi 1978) and/or the creation of special representative bodies at the local, national, and regional levels to control the investment of pension funds and/or the alteration of company dividend policy to allow a proportion of profits to be set aside as shares or income for the collective control and future benefit of employees (Dahl 1985; cf. Adamson 1990, 56–71; Beetham 1993). Individually or together, such proposals would increase the possibility of social determination of investment by creating further "access avenues" to productive and financial resources.

Within the context of national, subnational, and local markets, to the extent that they retain their separate identities, the erosion and breakup of coercive economic structures could be encouraged further by the development of the nonmarket factors that impinge directly on the dynamics of market forces (Reich 1993). Such factors include the provision of public goods such as education, the training of labor, and market information. In addition, the nurturing of subnational and local institutional contexts for the organization of economic activity, including the development of community-based mutual financial institutions (savings banks, local pension funds, and industrial credit unions), provides a positive background for small- and medium-size firms to develop (Piore and Sabel 1984; Best 1990). Combined with effective local regulations, these firms can, individually and in combination, help generate the means for economic autonomy (Hirst 1993, 125–30). In short, cooperation to enhance supply-side economic performance (nationally, subnationally, and locally), commitment to policies that allow the adequate provision of public goods, and investment in human capital (alongside strategies of restraint in wage bargaining linked to investment in local areas) can aid the development of the economic capacities of communities in an age in which national economic regulation and national demand management are increasingly ineffective alone. Along with the pursuit of greater political equity within companies and other forms of economic association, economies might be rebuilt or expanded not simply from "above" or from "below" but from within the framework of democratic law. Although none of this amounts, of course, to an economic policy per se, it does amount to the specification of certain parameters for economic activity, if the latter is to become part of the sphere of the political, that is, embedded in a framework for public deliberation and decision about the conditions of economic prosperity.

CONCLUDING REFLECTIONS

The program of bringing the economy into the "sphere of democracy" creates new possible avenues of political participation, but it also raises a number of new risks for political life. Joseph Schumpeter (1976, 296–302) rightly warned that an "unbounded" concept of politics provides no clear-cut barrier between the polity on the one hand and the everyday life of citizens on the other. Broad concepts of politics, he suggested, may become connected for many, in practice, to a diminution of freedom. Nevertheless, real though this risk is, the preference for democracy contains within itself obstacles to political hierarchy and unwarranted intrusion. It does so by the insistence that decisions be debated and taken by those who are immediately affected by them and by the insistence that this process is compatible with respect for the rights and obligations of others. Accordingly, issues and problems ought only be pursued within and beyond particular associations if, by so doing, they deepen the entrenchment of democratic rights and obligations. Thus, the framework for utopia is the rule of democratic public spheres, shaped by democratic rights and obligations (democratic public law), and enhanced through their extension to the agencies and organizations of economic life; through deliberation over and coordination of public investment priorities; through the pursuit of nonmarket policies to aid fair outcomes in market exchange, and, it should be added, through experimentation with different forms of the ownership and control of capital to facilitate the attainment of equal opportunities for all citizens in the governance of their common affairs—the ultimate purpose of democracy.

Recent economic transformations have, however, further implications for our understanding of the proper nature and form of democratic life. We readily understand that the quality of democracy depends on rendering political decision making accountable to citizens in a delimited political community. We readily understand, moreover, that the quality of democracy depends on more than merely the formal access that citizens have to the public sphere and the polity—to public deliberation and decision making. However, it is rarely acknowledged that the nature, form, and prospects of democratic life are clouded by multiplying interconnections among political communities. While more countries seek to establish robust national democracies, powerful forces affecting our economic and social welfare now transcend the boundaries of nation-states. What should democracy and citizenship mean in this context?

In the millennium ahead, it must be recognized, each citizen of a state must learn as well become a "cosmopolitan citizen," that is, a person capable of mediating between national traditions, communities, and alternative forms of life. Citizenship in a democratic polity of the future must increasingly involve a mediating role: a role that encompasses dialogue with the traditions and discourses of others with the aim of expanding the horizons of one's own framework of meaning and prejudice and increasing the scope of mutual understanding. Political agents who can "reason from the point of view of others" are likely to be better equipped to resolve, and resolve fairly, the new and challenging transboundary issues and processes that create overlapping national fortunes. If many contemporary forms of power are to become accountable, and if many of the complex issues that affect us all—locally, nationally, regionally, and globally—are to be democratically regulated, people must have access to, and membership in, diverse political communities. Put differently, democracy for the new millenium should describe a world in which citizens enjoy multiple citizenships. They should be citizens of their own communities, of the wider regions in which they live, and of a cosmopolitan global community. We need to develop institutions that reflect the multiple issues, questions, and problems that link people together regardless of their particular nation-states in which they were born or brought up.

Against this background, democracy must be thought of as a "double-sided process" (Held 1996). By a double-sided process—or a process of double democratization—I mean not just the deepening of democracy within a national community, involving the democratization of states and civil societies over time, but also the extension of democratic forms and processes across territorial borders. Democracy for the new millenium must involve cosmopolitan citizens able to gain access to, mediate between, and render accountable the economic and political processes and flows that cut across and transform their traditional community boundaries.

The notion of "cosmopolitan democracy" that I have set out and explored elsewhere (Held 1995, 1996), recognizes our complex, interconnected world. It recognizes, of course, certain problems and policies as appropriate for local governments and national states, but it also recognizes others as appropriate for specific regions and still others—such as global security concerns, world health questions, and economic regulation—that need new institutions to address them. Deliberative and political decision-making centers beyond national territories are justified when cross-border or transnational groups are affected by a public matter, when "lower" levels of decision making cannot resolve the issues in question and when the issue of accountability of a matter in hand can be understood and redeemed only in a transnational, cross-border context. Such political arrangements are not only a necessity but also a possibility in light of the changing organization of regional and global processes, evolving political decision-making centers such as the European Union, and growing political demands for new forms of political deliberation, conflict resolution, and decision making. In such a world, cities, national parliaments, regional assemblies, and global authorities could all have distinctive but interlinked roles within a framework for democratic accountability and public decision making.

NOTE

This is a revised and adapted version of an essay that first appeared in *Theoria* 85 (May 1995). Some of its themes are explored at greater length in my *Democracy and the Global Order: From the Modern State to Cosmopolitan Governance* (Cambridge: Polity Press, 1995).

11

Reconceptualizing Global Poverty: Globalization, Marginalization, and Gender

James H. Mittelman and Ashwini Tambe

In the post–Cold War era, a major normative commitment in world politics is encapsulated in neoliberal globalization. On the altar of a benevolent market rests the promise that economic gain can benefit all who are faithful to its principles. Neoliberal globalization's normative appeal lies in the vision it offers of the opportunity to ascend the global hierarchy of power and production. This model of world order is not only a set of policies about economic well-being but also an ethical claim with real implications for distributive justice. Implicit in this value system is the express assurance that neoliberalism will lift millions of people out of poverty, embracing them in a win-win situation rather than a winner-take-all dynamic.

From a neoliberal perspective, it is argued that as a percentage of world population, poverty is decreasing; thus, the existing pattern of poverty alleviation conforms to the neoliberal promise. This argument, however, invites debates over the most appropriate measures of poverty—mine fields that we do not wish to enter. Suffice it to say that, among analysts, there is no consensus in this regard.[1] Acknowledging that social scientists do not endorse a widely shared definition of poverty, Mary Durfee and James Rosenau (1996, 523), for example, settle on the formulation "realities and fears of substandard living conditions," including inadequate disposable income, housing, clothing, and employment. This formulation is especially useful in its coupling of both the objective and the subjective dimensions of poverty. Even without engaging the methodological issue, it follows that a wide range of empirical indicators may then be employed to gauge the changing incidence of poverty.

There exists evidence to counter the claims of neoliberalism, to argue instead that higher levels of globalization mean more poverty. While average incomes have increased worldwide, the total number of poor people (defined as those who earn less than $1 per day) grew from 1.23 billion in 1987 to 1.31 billion in 1993. This has occurred with large inter- and intraregional variance: The rate of poverty is declining in East and Southeast Asia (a pattern now changing as the market turbulence of the late 1990s is becoming fully felt) but is remaining steady at 39 percent in sub-Saharan Africa, where there is a rise in the total number of poor people (World Bank 1996, 7–9). In addition, the assets of the world's 358 billionaires now exceed the combined annual incomes of countries with 45 percent of the world's poor people (UN Development Program 1996, 2). How can this be? How is it that globalization, which helps alleviate poverty in some parts of the world, is antithetical to poverty reduction on a world scale? It appears antithetical to poverty reduction because there is a shifting incidence of poverty, a growing polarization among and within regions, and a reconcentration of wealth. In other words, global poverty comprises a downward spiral of economic conditions in some countries and elsewhere a sense of the disjuncture between macroeconomic growth and persistent material deprivation for the many.

Against this backdrop, the central questions that frame this chapter are: What are the evolving linkages between globalization and poverty? In light of changing global structures, what is the analytical key to understanding poverty?

The purpose of this chapter, then, is to confront neoliberal claims about poverty and to offer, if only in a preliminary manner, an alternative conceptualization. The focus is on the *production* of poverty but not on political and cultural resistance to the globalizing structures that underpin it, a topic of another study (Chin and Mittelman 1997). Our core hypothesis is that although poverty is an age-old phenomenon, today it may be best understood as an outcome of the interactions among globalization, marginalization, and gender. We attempt to delineate the linkages in this multifaceted process. Central to the chain of relationships are the varied ways in which economic globalization marginalizes large numbers of people by reducing public spending on social services and delinks economic reform from social policy. This type of marginalization manifests a gendered dimension inasmuch as women constitute those principally affected by it.

With economic restructuring, it is women who take on most responsibilities jettisoned by the state, in its response to globalization, and still carry out traditionally defined work in the household. Notwithstanding new sources of income for some women, traditional tasks become more arduous because globalizing processes, such as the incorporation of women into the formal labor force through the spatial reorganization of production, have an uneven and disruptive impact on ways of life. By delimiting the ways in which everyday life is transformed by the concomitant processes of neoliberal globalization and marginalization and the ways in which gender is implicated in marginalization, this chapter not only questions the basic promise of neoliberalism but also shows its limits.

Without grounding, however, structural explanations of this genre would also have their shortcomings. It is therefore beneficial to explore gendered marginalization through the use of case studies, which provide fine-grained evidence of increasing poverty amid neoliberal globalization. A central argument here is that the rise in the number of people living under poverty is attributable to the delinking of society and economy—a *disembedding* of economy from society.

In terms of operational definitions, *globalization* may be understood as a historical transformation, extending and accelerating interactions across time and space, with profound implications in terms of changing power relations as well as for the capacity of a community to determine its own fate (Mittelman 2000). Higher levels of globalization further marginalization both within and between territorial units. In order to comprehend *marginalization,* one may combine the visual sense of the term "margin"—an outer edge viewed from a center—with the economic usage of the word "margin," that is, the point at which the returns from an activity barely cover its cost. Especially important to our argument is the *gender* division of labor: a key social stratification system that places most women in subordinate positions. Gender is fundamentally a relationship of power.

Gender ideology consists of ingrained beliefs that order power relations between men and women. As with other kinds of ideologies, structures of domination are preserved in an often unconscious manner through commonsense assumptions. In the case of gender ideology, some common assumptions are that household work is the natural domain of women and that women are nonproductive social actors. A proposition to be advanced here is that gender ideology not only structures power within social relations but also articulates with—connects in distinctive ways to— the ideology of globalization. The ideology of globalization lends legitimacy to shifting functions in the realm of social services from the state to women as well as to prying open markets, liberalizing trade, and reducing state intervention in the economy. In economies that structurally restrict women's economic participation to subsistence activities, the paring down of the state, which is sometimes theorized as the institutionalization of patriarchal power, in fact works against augmenting this participation. Even in economies in which women's economic participation has increased under pressures arising out of the liberalization of trade and industry, the terms of this participation are often highly exploitative. Thus, although there may seem to be nothing patently masculinist about the ideology of globalization, its specific articulation with gender ideology sustains the marginalization of women. The gender division of labor is actually one of the conditions that makes globalization possible.

Our case studies will illustrate the previously mentioned features of this articulation in two contexts—the informal farming sector and export-processing zones. This chapter offers a cross-regional analysis of countries where these sectors represent important components of the national economy. The poverty-generating implications of the deepening of a market economy for women are explored in both cases. We focus on women in the informal farming sector in Mozambique, often cited as the world's poorest country (World Bank 1990–99),[2] where women's work in the fields provides much of the sustenance for families (Marshall 1990, 33). For export-processing industries, we anchor our concepts in the case of the Philippines, where export-oriented and female-led industrialization (i.e., with low-paid female labor being a prime component) was the engine of economic growth in the 1990s. Notwithstanding many dissimilarities, both countries were economic laggards in their respective regions until the recent growth spurt in the Philippines and Mozambique. Although it is not central to our argument, both countries are also former colonies sharing the imprint of an Iberian and Catholic heritage. Importantly, both countries are undergoing structural adjustment programs. These globalizing programs are aimed at alleviating poverty but are not gender neutral in conception or effect.

In both cases, structural adjustment is but one aspect of neoliberal policies aimed at denationalizing economies as well as spreading and deepening the market. Not only does evidence challenge the neoliberal promise, but Karl Polanyi's (1957) theoretical insights into market economies may also be enlisted to help explain this disjuncture. Whereas Polanyi focused on the growth of markets in nineteenth-century England (as well as on premarket societies), his notion of "the great transformation" may be extended to understand the dynamics of global poverty at the turn of the millennium. Polanyi held that the onset of "the self-regulating market"—for him, a normative construct—reversed the long-standing relationship between society and economy and, for the first time in history, *disembedded* the latter from its sociocultural foundations. Before the rise of market societies, production, as Aristotle maintained, was for use—a principle the Greeks called *householding*—not primarily for gain. Men and women, bound together in families, treated markets and money as "mere accessories to an otherwise self-sufficient household" (Polanyi 1968, 16–17). In other words, Polanyi's concept of the *embeddedness* of economic systems in—and subsequent disembeddedness from—society anticipates one form of gender analysis and even offers a mode of inquiry for examining the ways that globalization has disrupted and redirected existing socioeconomic arrangements. To develop this conceptualization, we first offer a critique of the neoliberal framework for poverty eradication and then from an alternative entry point extend our own formulation.

RECONCEPTUALIZING POVERTY

The Neoliberal Perspective

Neoliberalism provides the rationale for measures that propel globalization, such as structural adjustment policies. From this perspective, a commitment to reducing poverty can be displayed only by integration into the international capitalist economy. Neoliberal globalization is thus presented as the antidote to the problem of poverty instead of also being implicated in generating it. Furthermore, neoliberal ideology promotes the expansion of markets as natural and inevitable, while existing social arrangements within which economies are still partially embedded are seen as chains that need to be unshackled. Polanyi (1957) would regard such a view as ahistorical, as suggested in the following passage:

Economic history reveals that the emergence of national markets was in no way the result of the gradual and spontaneous emancipation of the economic sphere from governmental control. On the contrary, the market has been the outcome of a conscious and often violent intervention on the part of governments which imposed the market organization on society for non-economic ends. And the self-regulating market of the nineteenth century turns out upon closer inspection to be radically different from even its immediate predecessor in that it relied for its regulation upon economic self-interest. (250)

The notion of a self-regulating market is most fundamentally misapplied to labor when labor is assumed to be a commodity in abundant and variable supply that responds primarily to market signals. Poverty is then explained as a preponderance of underutilized labor, the solution to which is increased employment through macroeconomic growth. The poor are asked to take heart, for they have an asset in the global economy, their labor potential. Nonetheless, the actual erosion of much secure employment in the context of structural adjustment programs brings forth a new contradictory demand. Labor must now "diversify" and "adjust." The speed and the flexibility of capital in the context of globalization are thus projected onto labor. Labor, too, is expected to be flexible and mobile. The result is new winners and new losers, with some segments of the labor force adjusting speedily into poverty.

Poverty and Social Relations of Production

A common pitfall is treating poverty as a static category, fixed in specific regions or in particular social strata. While it is true that processes ingrain it in certain regions, countries, and enclaves, this should be understood as part of a global problem of poverty generation. In much social scientific analysis, the poor are contained in identifiable and fixed units of society through the drawing of poverty lines. Such lines, although useful in a preliminary way, represent poverty with a false clarity, obfuscating the relationships that generate it. The basis on which these lines are mapped reflect reigning intellectual frameworks. The dominant paradigm in poverty analysis, encompassing at first the modernization school and neoclassical economics and now extended by neoliberalism, tends to explain poverty on the basis of consumption levels. Emphasis is one-sidedly accorded to underconsumption, not overconsumption. Focusing on the realm of consumption begets policies primarily aimed at raising consumption levels. Typically, these policies are instruments meant to achieve greater market integration, which may actually accentuate marginalization, worsen inequalities, and heighten political conflict.

An example of this manner of approaching poverty is the World Bank's analysis. The World Bank defines poverty as the inability to attain a minimum standard of living, with poverty gauged in terms of the expenditure necessary to procure nutrition and basic necessities and, at a more country-specific level, the cost of participating in everyday life. How the poor derive and spend their income is the stated focus of the World Bank *World Development Report,* subtitled *Poverty* (1990–99, 6). The follow-up report on poverty reduction (World Bank 1996, 2) also centers on income and consumption. In both documents, the use of expenditure as a starting point in measuring poverty betrays the bank's own interest in international market integration and the generation of "effective" demand for products in global commodity markets.

Entertaining a different entry point, one based on production relations, may invite easy accusations of economic reductionism in the post–Cold War intellectual climate. However, we hold that the mainstream treatment of poverty within the analytical realm of consumption fixes it as a statistical or gradational measure; the social relations that maintain and, in some cases, extend it are thereby neglected. Poverty needs to be recast as an outcome of the interactions among globalization, marginalization in the production process, and gendered social relations.

In the context of globalization, to be marginalized is to be pushed to the edges of the economy beyond which returns from work are lower than the effort expended. Poverty, then, is the experience and perception of marginalization that have been locked in through structural pressure. When people live in poverty, their work consistently incurs a higher cost than its return. Implied here is all work, whether wage-earning or not, and all costs, especially those of health and the ability to survive. Both formally and informally employed workers as well as the unemployed may well be living in varied degrees of poverty.

This conceptualization of poverty departs from mainstream writing on the subject in two ways. First, it focuses on production in order to portray poverty as arising within work relations, however constrained, and not simply occurring simultaneously with unemployment and underemployment. Second, it links poverty to the process of marginalization rather than limiting it to a category of people. It performs the preliminary move of dissociating poverty from static geographic and cultural categories to conceive it in relational terms. Such a departure is necessary in order to place poverty within the same framework as that used to understand globalization and the language of changed spatiotemporal relations. Poverty, too, is transnational; its margins cut across states and regions of the world.

The powerlessness of the poor may then be partly explained by the disembedding of markets from society. They are excluded from the processes that determine what will be produced. The rigidity of the structures of authority in work relations are important because these sustain marginalization. Referring back to the earlier conceptualization of marginalization, the poor may be identified as those for whom the rewards from work are lower than the effort expended. What distinguishes the relations of poverty from other kinds of top-down relations of production is precisely the high degree of social constraints against escaping those structures. For the poor, individual resources are insufficient for surmounting social forces that maintain their marginalized relations of production.

Gender ideologies pervade social relations of production. Women generally have less access to and control over means of production than do men. The undervaluation of socially productive work by women keeps them working harder for longer hours. The marginalization of women arises from social forces that organize and segment production. Women's economic impoverishment is accentuated by the workings of supposedly self-regulating markets. This articulation of gender ideology with globalization ideology creates and sustains painful experiences of poverty, as the following brief case studies show.

POVERTY IN MOZAMBIQUE

Although Mozambique exemplifies "involuntary delinkage" from the global manufacturing system, it is all but delinked from the global financial system. Mozambique's debt amounted to $5.4 billion in 1994, which is four and a half times its GNP (World Bank 1996, 220). Much of its foreign aid is drained back into donor pockets through debt payments. The International Monetary Fund (IMF) and the World Bank not only condition the macroeconomy but also intervene in all sectors: project units—monitors—have been set up in each ministry (Mittelman 1991).

Two events from Mozambique's recent history demonstrate the conditions that reinforce poverty there. In March 1993, 12,000 tons of food aid that had been stockpiled for sale were sold as animal feed because they had rotted while waiting in a port warehouse in Maputo. The reasons given by Trade Minister Daniel Gabriel for this occurrence was "market saturation" in southern Mozambique and the inability of companies to sell existing stocks of maize (Mozambiquefile 1993a, 21). The food aid was part of a donation that designated 200,000 tons for free distribution and 100,000 tons for sale. While the 200,000 tons of free maize had been easily disbursed, the remaining amount was left to deteriorate. The so-called saturation in the market was clearly at odds with prevailing hunger caused by drought and the ongoing civil war between the governing Mozambique Liberation Front (FRELIMO) and a contra group, known as the Mozambique National Resistance Movement (RENAMO). The theft of other food aid in the following month attested to this problem (Mozambiquefile 1993b, 21).

In another incident, in October 1995, food riots rocked the capital city, Maputo. Hundreds of people blocked roads, stoned vehicles, and rampaged through marketplaces in response to an escalation in food prices. In a sudden increase driven by the need to align domestic prices with international ones, the cost of a 50-kilogram bag of rice had gone up from $15 to $50 ("Disquieting Signs in Mozambique One Year On" 1995, 11). The annual purchasing power per person being barely $90 at the time, a price hike of this magnitude spelled massive hunger. Both of these events illustrate the harmful dissonance between the workings of the market and actual conditions of hardship; they signal the disembedding of the market from social control.

That women farmers are found to be among the poorest people in Africa is well known. Currently, this poverty is becoming entrenched as a structural relationship through globalizing forces. Mozambique's proportion of women in the labor force is among the highest in Africa, 49 percent in 1990 (UN Development Program 1996, 169). Owing to male migration to cities and to neighboring states, women head 60 percent of Mozambican households, which is well over the average of 43 percent for the rest of sub-Saharan Africa (James 1995, 6–7). Nevertheless, women's access to land and credit is limited, and much of their labor cannot be diverted from subsistence. Let us turn to how structural adjustment works in regard to these social relations.

Pricing Mechanisms and the Persistence of Food Insecurity

Hunger is a most urgent social problem in Mozambique. Not only is there restricted access to arable land for food production, but existing methods of cultivation also have low yields. This creates the need for a market to obtain food from other sources. In modern economic terms, the existence of a food market depends on cash income being available to create effective demand. Cash income can be generated through cash-crop sales or off-farm work, but each of these activities takes away from the subsistence base of households. Off-farm work decreases food production and the possibility of surpluses arising for sale on the market.

Pressure on rural land has been increased by two facets of structural adjustment: the promotion of cash crops and exportables, such as cashew nuts and cotton, and the drive to privatize landholdings. The problem is rooted in the colonial political economy because the metropole, Portugal, designated areas for exclusive commercial cultivation and provided incentives for growing cash crops. Although most of these commercial lands were placed under state farm control after Mozambique graduated to political independence in 1975, many of them have been privatized. Land intended for redistribution is being sold, often to large-scale commercial producers. Most recently, schemes to sell land to groups of white South African farmers in the northern provinces have been negotiated (Economic Intelligence Unit 1996, 10). In irrigated areas, some poor peasant families, especially those headed by women, have lost or sublet their holdings (O'Laughlin 1995, 105).

Owing to low wages and high food prices, even urban households depend on farming by wives to bring in substantial provisions of food. In many urban families, women work on the *machamba* (small farms) adjacent to Maputo. Such labor is regarded as obligatory for women. In fact, Marshall's (1990) interviews with male workers in Maputo reveal that wives who farm are considered as not working and "doing nothing" (33). The pressure on periurban land is increasing markedly as a result of both high food prices and the incentives for cash-crop cultivation. Only an estimated 30 percent of families today have access to an agricultural plot in Maputo (O'Laughlin 1995, 105).

On the question of higher food production, Diane Elson (1994) points out that there are two contrasting ways in which poverty can be tackled:

> [O]ne seeks to reduce the power of money through extending social provision; the other seeks to extend the power of money by introducing financial criteria into the operation of all public services, and by deregulating labor markets. (517)

Under a neoliberal reform program in Mozambique, it is clearly the latter that has been followed. In 1988, under the IMF/World Bank–sponsored Economic and Rehabilitation Program (PRE)-2, the removal of subsidies for food prices was an attack on a vital social provision for urban dwellers. The logic of raising food prices in order to stimulate agricultural production was misplaced since the bulk of farming is for subsistence. Because food markets do not play a preponderant role in ensuring food security in rural households, the hike in prices simply meant hardship in both rural and urban areas (Tschirley and Weber 1994, 159–73).

Gender and Food Security

As in many parts of the world, women in Mozambique have access to land only through their husbands or male relatives. Food crops are customarily the domain of women; gender ideology militates against food cultivation by men, for whom the call to grow cash crops is compelling. In recent times, land used by women for food growing has been appropriated by men for cultivating cash crops. This increases the pressure on women's labor on marginal food-growing land. The privatization of land often means closing doors to women who head households; the drive to commercialize land in fact frequently forces rural women off the land. Price signals in the food market do not evoke the response presumed by macroeconomic monetarist policy since they do not reach subsistence farming by women. Thus, the dual pressure of privatizing land and raising cash crops works against the interests of women farmers. Inasmuch as resources to produce food are taken away from women while the need to provide sustenance remains, one may expect continued food insecurity.

Poverty and the Paring Down of State Spending

Within the household, there is no decline in the time spent by women on child rearing, food preparation, and care of the elderly. Even women's claims on food are subordinated to those of other family members in the hierarchy of the household. Current social provisions in Mozambique do not redress the high toll on women's health taken by this combination of increased labor and food scarcity. Instead, under PRE-2, privatization of health care drove up the cost of medical services, in turn resulting in an immediate 50 to 80 percent drop in attendance at local clinics and hospitals, especially by women (Marshall 1990, 36). A downward spiral of poor nutrition and lack of health care for women has been accelerated by structural adjustment.

Rural infrastructure recovery after the end of the seventeen-year civil war is urgently required, but structural adjustment has meant that spending by provincial governments is highly constrained. Reductions in expenditure on rural transport have serious consequences for women, whose chores include gathering fuel and water. According to the Ministry of Agriculture, women spend an average of four and a half hours daily just on transport (Berman 1996, 9). But it is not all expenditure on transport that has been curtailed. For its landlocked neighbors, Mozambique's location is strategic in providing railroads to the sea. Whereas many east-to-west links exist, few north-to-south ones do. Recent development efforts have concentrated on rebuilding regional railways but not on new spurs connecting outlying areas to major cities and ports. The creation of wage-labor employment through rural rebuilding, including transport, is necessary for improving the conditions for demobilized soldiers. Increased spending on regional infrastructure to facilitate trade, however, means decreased spending on domestic transportation, which women need. Yet the priorities of structural adjustment work actively against such social provisions.

The impact of reductions in the face of social need is also evident in the realm of education. There is currently a shortage of teachers, and this will undoubtedly get worse because programs for in-service training of teachers have largely been terminated since the late 1980s (Marshall 1990, 36). Decreased expenditure on education entrenches women's marginal economic position. This occurs in two ways: Women have to take on child-rearing responsibilities for longer periods, and their own access to education as a means of opening new productive opportunities is limited.

The argument here is that globalizing tendencies—notably, deregulation, liberalization, and privatization—are gendered in conceptualization and effect. In conceptualization, they assume women's ability to bear increasing demands on their labor in household obligations of food provision, child rearing and education, and caregiving for the elderly. They are also gendered in their effect inasmuch as "self-regulating" markets and privatization of land restrain women's access to productive resources. In an already impoverished country such as Mozambique, these tendencies consign most women to relations of poverty within a highly hierarchical society.

In a Polanyian sense, women are experiencing the instituting of a market in ways that disembed their claims to well-being in terms of health, land, and education. Women farmers have been marginalized, pushed to labor in conditions in which the returns barely cover or fail to meet the costs to their well-being. According to the ideology of women's domestic duty, food provision and caregiving for the family are activities whose "rewards" are intersubjectively produced through love and the gratitude of family members. However, no amount of love or gratefulness can substitute for adequate food and medication to counter women's hunger and ill health, a proposition that applies across regions.

POVERTY IN THE PHILIPPINES

Prescriptions for a globalized economy have long been followed in the Philippines, a country that has been through twenty adjustment programs. Forty percent of its annual budget is spent on repayment of foreign debt, which amounted to $39 billion in 1994 (World Bank 1996, 220). During the mid-1990s, annual economic growth figures in the range of 5 percent would lead one to think that the Philippines was experiencing a boom. Persistent poverty, however, was and is the actual experience of large portions of its population. Only 9 percent of respondents to a nationwide survey in 1994 felt that they were "not poor," even fewer than in 1992, when 19 percent made the same claim (Social Weather Station 1994). What explains this contradiction between macroeconomic gains and deepening poverty is scant spending on social policy and the mainly enclave-based growth in the country. Gauged in terms of a "social allocation ratio" (public expenditure on health and education as a share of total central government spending), the Philippines, at 20 percent, trails such countries as Mauritius's nearly 60 percent, Zimbabwe's 40 percent, Pakistan's more than 50 percent, and Trinidad and Tobago's 33 percent (UN Development Program 1996, 71). Furthermore, the notion that growth channeled by international financial institutions filters down is a premise embraced by successive Philippine regimes, whose support has been directed to specific sectors, such as electronics, garments, and finance, with few domestic linkages, most often located in geographically distinct export-based enclaves.

The first export-processing zone (EPZ) in the Philippines was established in the early 1970s in Bataan province. Incentives offered to foreign firms by the Philippine state included 100 percent ownership backed by the right to borrow within the country, with government guarantees for foreign loans. No taxes were placed on imports or exports, and there was no minimum investment requirement. The EPZs attracted "quota refugees" (investors from countries with export restrictions to the United States), such as Japan, South Korea, Hong Kong, and Taiwan. By basing themselves in the Philippines, foreign firms were able to secure U.S. markets through Philippine export quotas. Light manufacturing, electronics, garments, and heavy fabrication form the bulk of the activities of the firms, with electronics on the rise and garments on the decline. The Bataan EPZ is the most export oriented, world-market dependent of the country's economic ventures. It represents the classic disembedded enclave, in which the neoliberal economic logic that sustains the zone lifts it away from the context surrounding it.

Female-Led Growth and Female Poverty

The economic growth experienced by the Philippines is fueled by women workers. Eighty-five percent to 90 percent of the workforce employed in EPZs are women, and much of the economy is buoyed by remittances from overseas contract workers, over half of whom are women. The workforce in EPZs is usually drawn from neighboring rural areas, most of the laborers being between the ages of seventeen and twenty-nine. In the case of the Bataan EPZ, high unemployment marks the adjacent areas. Supporting families is therefore an important reason for taking up employment there (Rosa 1994, 77).

One would think that because EPZs offer jobs, they help to eradicate poverty. However, wages are low in the EPZs relative to other industrial areas, for example, around the capital, Manila. In addition, gender differentiation segments the workforce such that 40 percent of the women employed in EPZs receive less than the legal minimum wage, compared with 17 percent of the men. As one manager in the Bataan EPZ put it, women were recruited because they "endure poverty well" (Eviota 1992, 121). If the criteria for their recruitment are poverty and "low skill," what results is a downward pressure on women to remain poor and low skilled. Living conditions in the zones are also reported to be spartan; food prices are higher than in nearby areas, and boarding houses for the women are often overcrowded and costly. Moreover, unsafe working conditions threaten the women's future. In the microelectronics industry, for example, blurred vision is a common ailment among workers. These pressures, combined with the fact that they often have to remit a portion of their wages to their families, means that the women, though wage earners, live in persistent poverty.

Gender relations merit careful consideration because they are a major means by which male managers and supervisors subject labor to authority. A regime of patriarchal discipline is reproduced in the factories, with managers presented as father figures to the young women employed there. Strict control of the workers' time is attempted, down to rules regarding the use of the bathroom. In some cases, looming over this disciplinary pattern is the threat of sexual coercion—job security often depends on the exchange of sexual services (Eviota 1992, 123). Recreational activities initiated by the company preserve or inculcate sexual stereotypes (e.g., cosmetic product promotions and company-sponsored beauty contests). Such contests are especially common in the microelectronics industry, in which an explicit effort has been made to construct the assembling of semiconductors as "women's work" (Eviota 1992, 120).

It is gender ideology, not the intrinsic quality of the labor, that structures hiring policies. It is who does the work, not the work itself, that leads to its identification as "high" or "low" skilled labor. Maintaining the category of low-wage work as women's work is the dynamic. The treatment of women as secondary workers originates in the concept of women as temporary workers for whom waged work is a source of income in addition to an already ensured dependent livelihood. Although it is sometimes argued that EPZs enable women workers to escape patriarchal rural life, they do come under wage discipline. As a result of the high cost of living under structural adjustment, it is not supplemental income but rather basic sustenance that women are trying to ensure. Marriage is not necessarily a way out, for many women continue to have to earn wages, often working harder after marriage.

Although the justification for hiring women by naturalizing—that is, referring to the supposed natural qualities of—women's labor is common, slippage occurs when this assumption is also accepted by observers of globalization. The same ideology that threatens women in the workplace keeps up demands on their labor in the household. The expectation that women perform multiple duties, as well as the rising cost of food and health care, drive women to seek waged jobs. Single women seek jobs as a means to gain some measure of independence from restrictive conditions at home. Whereas the experience of women in EPZs is often an alienating one, with workers' connections to society forcibly changed, it is improved relations of production that they struggle for, not a return to their former conditions of dependence. Thus, any escape from their existing marginalized social relations of production, and any reembedding of the local economy within the society, necessarily involve challenging the prevailing norms produced by gender ideology.

THE MATRIX OF GLOBALIZATION, MARGINALIZATION, AND GENDER

We have argued that neoliberalism concentrates on categorizing poverty according to aggregate growth, individual expenditure, and other symptomatic indicators rather than the relational and more fundamentally structural factors and thus fails to tug at the deepest roots of poverty. Whereas globalization offers unparalleled economic opportunities for some, it also reconfigures the incidence of poverty within and between countries. That is, globalization and marginalization are interconnected processes, the former driving the latter. Propelled by higher levels of competitiveness, globalization pushes some groups, typically women, to the margins, further entrenching poverty. Inasmuch as gender ideology helps to segment women in particular positions in the production process, it is important for analysts to overcome the separation between structures of class and gender and to examine the varied ways in which they are interrelated. Our thesis, then, is that the interactions among these processes—globalization, marginalization, and social forces—shape patterns of poverty as well as other distributional outcomes. In this context, it is important to conceptualize poverty in terms of social relations of production.

Moving to the question of remedies, it would be wrong to trivialize the pain of poverty, but there is a danger in some attempts to suppress it. The supposed suppressant of neoliberalism only perpetuates poverty by reconcentrating it. While neoliberal policies pull many people out of poverty in some regions, they also lodge women in its mechanisms. Not only does neoliberalism worsen inequality, but it also breeds consumerism. The neoliberal strategy conflates a would-be solution to poverty and an underlying cause of it. But is there an alternative poverty suppressant? If our approach to the structuring of poverty is correct, the problem of poverty suppression is transposed into the question of how to challenge underlying structures. To answer this question, it is instructive to draw on the case studies. Mozambique, the poorest country on the poorest continent, and the Philippines, for long the most poverty-stricken and, until recently, the most marginalized country in a subregion that experienced explosive economic growth, appear dissimilar in terms of their resource endowments, historical trajectories, social structures, and cultural mosaics. Yet, when taken together, these countries embody dynamics that are similar and telling about the structuring of poverty: While an economic condition, poverty is also integrated with other forms of social discrimination, frequently but not exclusively gender; the rigid hierarchies of patriarchy work to impoverish women. In other words, the structures of poverty comprise parallel and mutually reinforcing processes.

With neoliberal globalization, it is ever more difficult to dislodge this structure because the technical caliber of production—organized not primarily on a national but now on a worldwide scale—seems to exceed the capacity for social control. In this sense, neoliberal globalization is a development anticipated (but of course not delimited) in Polanyi's seminal analysis of the disembedding of unfettered market forces from society. In an age of globalization, poverty is not only set in a rather different constellation of market forces from those examined in Polanyi's studies but also must be construed as a political condition. In more graphic terms, poverty becomes a crucible in which social discrimination, including the degradation of institutions such as health care and education, and the arbitrariness of power fester and become self-sustaining. "Growth," often presented as a cure-all in dominant policies of poverty alleviation, appears a faint solution to this deeper political condition.

If the challenge is to alleviate poverty, the first step is to create new knowledge and norms about the problem in specific contexts and also to locate them within the globalization process. Inasmuch as neoliberal globalization diminishes the state's role in combating structures of gendered marginalization, it entrenches poverty while further opening the market. Markets have ingrained poverty on a gendered basis partly because of a lack of popular control over them. To mitigate poverty, political interventions must pull at the roots of the problem of how to reembed the economy in society. At present, society still takes the national framework as its main point of reference and is itself pocked with gendered and other forms of inequality. In the absence of fundamental social change within this complex, to reembed globalizing markets would not ipso facto solve the problem of poverty generation. As a precaution about the peril of a Polanyian prescription of reembedding, it must be emphasized that different societies bear their own forms of patriarchy and distinctive dynamics of poverty. The interplay of neoliberal globalization and local, historical structures produces varied permutations, as our case studies demonstrate. Nonetheless, in the final analysis, the resolution of poverty lies in establishing a social market—resubordinating economies to society but without maintaining the gender ideologies that helped animate these inegalitarian and hierarchical societal structures in the first place.

NOTES

While we accept responsibility for the analysis developed here, we owe a debt of gratitude to Nancy Hirschmann and Paul Wapner for their constructive criticism of earlier drafts of this chapter.

1. For citations on poverty and a broader discussion of different scholarly traditions, see Mittelman and Pasha (1997).

2. According to World Bank reports (1990–95), Mozambique had the lowest per capita gross national product (GNP) in the late 1980s and early 1990s. Although Rwanda's 1994 average per capita income of $80 was below that of Mozambique's at $90 (World Bank 1996, 188), the most recent figures, for 1997, place Mozambique, with $90 per capita, at the very bottom (World Bank 1999, 191). For a critical evaluation of data suggesting that in the mid and late 1990s, Mozambique attained the highest economic growth rate in Africa, see Mittelman (2000, 103–4).

12

The Asian Financial Crisis: Heroes, Villains, and Accomplices

Walden Bello

The volatile character of the so-called Asian financial crisis that exploded in mid-1997—but has its roots in the postwar struggle for dominance by what is now commonly known as the G-7 countries—poses both a theoretical and a practical dilemma for those in the field of normative international relations who understand, on the one hand, the importance of theory and, on the other, the necessity of analysis and action. In this context, normative international relations theory—the substance of this book—turns out as always being done "on the run"; that is, it is articulated in the everyday encounters of contested goals, interests, and values of individuals, collectivities, and institutions. Indeed, normative international relations theory turns out to be what poststructuralists today call "practice."

For this reason, normative international relations requires itself to be made understandable and comprehensible not only to the theorists but also to the "practitioners"—those who are seeking ways to transform the intolerable situations in which they find themselves in the light of what they understand to be the "good, the true, and the beautiful." This, in turn, requires a plurality of genres, modes of interpretation, and analyses that could open up what often appears to be convoluted, incomprehensible realities to understanding and action. In this context, it may be useful to interpret the Asian financial crisis as an ongoing drama of shifting characters (heroes, villains, and accomplices)—to identify plots and subplots and to analyze problems, prospects, and possibilities—but to do these as they unfold "on the ground," placing, as it were, the interpretation of the crisis in the context of practice.

HEROES

First of all, there are no heroes. The Japanese could have played the role of "knight in shining armor" as early as 1996, when they had the chance to reverse the descent into depression via the proposed Asian Monetary Fund (AMF)—a mechanism capitalized to the tune of $100 billion that was designed to defend the region's currencies from speculative attacks. Unfortunately, in typical fashion, they shelved their proposal when Washington opposed it. Although the AMF is now resurrected as the Miyazawa Plan, which would give the troubled Asian economies $30 billion in financial aid, it is too little and too late.

VILLAINS: CRONY CAPITALISTS OR FOREIGN SPECULATIVE INVESTORS?

In contrast, there are a number of candidates for the role of principal villain. Taking our cue from the Western press, one might begin with the practices and institutions that are usually presented to the public as the villains of the crisis—that is, aside from Prime Minister Mohamad Mahathir of Malaysia, who has become the U.S. media's favorite whipping boy—at the same time that they are elevating Philippine actor-president Joseph Estrada to the status of Asia's new hero.

One might begin by quoting a person who has come to be the chief director of one version of the crisis: U.S. Treasury Secretary Robert Rubin. In assigning the blame for the financial crisis, Rubin assigned pride of place to a lack of information on the part of investors. In a speech that he gave at the Brookings Institution in April 1998, Rubin said,

> There are obstacles to getting good information about economic and financial matters. One is the temptation—in the private sector and in government—to avoid disclosing problems. But sooner or later, as we have seen in Asia, the problems will make themselves known. . . . In many cases, lack of data meant that no one had a true understanding of this build-up or of these economies' vulnerabilities. (Rubin 1998b)

This lack of transparency on the part of financial institutions went hand in hand with distorted incentives, lack of supervision, and the absence of so-called prudential regulation. All this is, in turn, part of a witch's brew of unsound and corrupt practices known as "crony capitalism," which Larry Summers, the famous economist who is Rubin's undersecretary, says is "at the heart of the crisis" (Summers 1998). Interestingly, it might be pointed out, Summers and others picked up a term—crony capitalism—that we Filipinos coined during the Marcos period to characterize the Marcos regime.

One might also briefly note here that this is a massive reversal of the view that held sway at the World Bank when Summers, who now plays an overweight, over-the-hill Sundance Kid to Rubin's Butch Cassidy on CNN, was that institution's chief economist in the late 1980s and early 1990s. For those too young to remember what the orthodoxy was then, one might cite the World Bank's (1993) famous *East Asian Miracle:*

In each HPAE [high-performing Asian economy], a technocratic elite insulated to a degree from excessive political pressure supervised macroeconomic management. The insulation mechanisms ranged from legislation, such as balanced budget laws in Indonesia, Singapore, and Thailand, to custom and practice in Japan and Korea. All protected essentially conservative macroeconomic policies by limiting the scope for politicians and interest groups to derail those policies. (348–49)

To repeat, economic policymaking by Asian technocrats, in this view, was largely insulated from political and business pressures, and this was a large part of the explanation for the so-called Asian miracle. Every mortal is, of course, entitled to an about-face. But the problem with the latest intellectual fashion from the Summers salon is that the practices of "crony capitalism" were very much part of economic life in the three decades that East Asian countries led the world in the rate of growth of gross national product (GNP). If, indeed, crony capitalism was the chief cause of the Asian collapse, why did it not bring it about much sooner? How could economies dominated by these practices of rent seeking that supposedly suffocate the dynamism of the market—including Japan and South Korea—even take off in the first place?

Moreover, "crony capitalism" has become so elastic in its connotations—which range from corruption to any kind of government activism in economic policymaking—as to become useless as an explanatory construct. It is one thing to say that corruption has pervaded relations between government and business in East Asia, as it has, in the Philippines, Italy, and the United States, where it is legalized through such mechanisms as political action committees (PACs), which make politicians' electoral fortunes dependent on favorable treatment of corporate interests. It is quite another thing to say that corruption and its companions—lack of regulation and lack of transparency—constitute the principal reason for the downfall of the East Asian economies.

Now, in light of the developments of the last half of 1998, criticizing the crony capitalist thesis might strike those who have followed recent events closely as beating a dead horse. It is, but this dead horse deserves to be beaten and buried because it has a way of resurrecting periodically in Dracula fashion. In any event, after the latest Russian "crash," the recent bailout of the hedge fund Long-Term Capital by the U.S. Federal Reserve, and Brazil's teetering on the edge, there is now little doubt that the central cause of the financial crisis was the quick, massive flow of global speculative capital and bank capital into East Asia in the early 1990s and its even more massive and even swifter exit in 1997.

Moreover, there seems to be little doubt as well that the multilateral institutions, especially the International Monetary Fund (IMF), played a key facilitating role by pressing the Asian governments incessantly to liberalize their capital accounts in order precisely to encourage massive foreign capital inflows into their economies in the belief that foreign capital was the strategic factor in development. Indeed, one can say that the IMF has been the cutting edge of globalization in the region, since it is financial liberalization that is the cutting edge of the integration of these national economies into the global economy.

It has been suggested as well that Northern speculative funds came to Asia because investors were conned by crafty and dishonest Asian financial operators. To be sure, Asia was swarming with crooked financial operators. However, to insist that these Western investors were conned or fooled borders on the ridiculous. In fact, speculative investors came into Asia because they perceived the opportunities to gain greater margins of profit on financial investments here to be greater than those in the Northern money centers in the early 1990s, owing to the much higher interest rates, the low stock prices, and—not to be underestimated—the incredible hype created around the so-called Asian economic miracle.

The fact is, Northern money was very eager to get into Asian capital markets in the early 1990s, and whether or not the information was available, investors and fund managers were quite nondiscriminating in their moves into these markets. As Rubin himself admitted in a speech at Chulalongkorn University in June 1998,

> One of the things that has most struck us about the Asian crisis, is that after the problems began to develop and we spoke to the institutions that had extended credit or invested in the region, so often we found these institutions had engaged in relatively little analysis and relatively little weighting of the risks that were appropriate to the decisions. (Rubin 1998a)

The fund managers were going to see what they wanted to see. Not only did many not assess their investments and local partners or borrowers, but they actually made their moves mainly by keeping an eagle eye on the moves of other investors, especially those with great reputations for uncanny investing, such as George Soros or Long-Term Capital's John Merriwether. But if there was little room or desire for serious analysis of markets in the entry phase, there was even less in the exit phase, as the rush of investment leaders communicated panic to one and all.

Indeed, in the first months of the crisis, Stanley Fischer, the U.S. deputy managing director of the IMF, was attributing the crisis not to politicians, a lack of transparency, or crony capitalism but to the investors' herd behavior.[1]

Bangkok, for example, was a debtor's rather than a creditor's market in the early 1990s, with so many foreign banks and funds falling over themselves to lend to Thai enterprises, banks, and finance companies, even willing to forgo the rigorous checks on borrowers for which Western banks and financial institutions are supposedly famous. The bad, indeed shady, financial history of the Thai finance companies was not a secret (Vichyanond 1994). In the 1970s and 1980s, many finance companies resorted to questionable business practices to raise capital, including widespread speculation and manipulation of stock prices, leading to the closure of some of them. Any neophyte in Bangkok's financial club knew this history. Yet the finance companies were flush with foreign cash, oftentimes urged on to them by foreign lenders unwilling to forgo what could turn out to be a gold mine.

Throughout Asia, U.S. chambers of commerce, foreign correspondents' clubs, and expatriate circles were replete with stories of rigged bids, double (sometimes triple), accounting, false statistics, and cronyism in high places, but everyone accepted that these were the risks of doing business in Asia: You had to live with them if you were going to have your share of the bonanza. In the end, what really served as the ultimate collateral or guarantee for the investments that foreign operators made in Asian enterprises and banks was the 6 to 10 percent growth rates that they expected to go on far into the future. Now you might end up with some duds, but if you spread your investments around in this region of limitless growth, you were likely to come out a winner.

SUPPORTING CAST

This fact underscores the role of strategic expectations and the role of certain players and institutions that encouraged and maintained those expectations. In other words, there was a whole set of actors that played a supporting but critical role in this crisis. Speculative investors were operating in a context in which they were locked into a mutually reinforcing psychology of permanent boom with these other players.

A key player here is much of the business press. Business publications proliferated in the region, beginning in the mid-1980s. However, proliferation alone is not adequate to convey the dynamics of the business press since there was a also a process of monopolization at work. Asian prosperity started attracting the big players from the West, and among the more momentous deals were the purchases of the famous *Far Eastern Economic Review* by Dow Jones, of *Asiaweek* by Time Warner, and of Star Television in Hong Kong by Rubert Murdoch; CNN, another Time Warner subsidiary, and CNBC also moved in, with much of their programming devoted to business news. These news agents became critical interpreters of the news in Asia to investors located all over the world and served as a vital supplement to the electronic linkages that made real-time transactions possible among the key stock exchanges of Singapore, Hong Kong, Tokyo, Osaka, New York, London, and Frankfurt (Gapper and Denton 1996).

For the most part, these publications and media, whether they were independent or part of the big chains, highlighted the boom, glorified the high growth rates, and reported uncritically on so-called success stories, mainly because their own success as publications was tied to the perpetuation of the psychology of boom. A number of writers writing critical stories on questionable business practices, alarming developments, or failed enterprises complained that they could not place their stories or that their editors told them to accentuate the positive.

Parachute journalism—a phrase applied to writers who flew in, became instant experts on the Vietnam War or the Philippines under Marcos, and then left after filing their big stories—became a practice as well in economic journalism in the 1990s, with *Fortune, Business Week, Newsweek,* and *Time* setting the pace. It was,

for example, Dorinda Elliot of the *Newsweek* airborne brigade who, more than anyone else, sanctified the Philippines' status as Asia's newest tiger during the Subic
Asian Pacific Economic Cooperation (APEC) Summit of November 1996—a status
that lasted less than eight months, with the collapse of the peso in July 1997.

Many of these business publications, in turn, developed an unwholesome reliance
on a character type that proliferated in the region in the early 1990s: the investment
adviser or strategist—an "expert" connected with the research arms of banks, investment houses, brokerage houses, mutual funds, and hedge funds. Indeed, in many
instances, notes Philip Bowring (1998), former editor of *Far Eastern Economic Review,* economic journalism degenerated into just stringing along quotes from different investment authorities.

Interestingly enough, many of these people were expatriates (or "expats," to use
a Bangkok term), some of whom were refugees from the collapse of stock markets
in New York and London in the late 1980s. Some of them were Generation X or
pre–Generation X types who had been too young to participate in the junk bond
frenzy on Wall Street in the Reagan years but who discovered similar highs in the
East. Many of these people were as young as Nick Leeson, the twenty-six-year-old
broker who brought down the venerable Baring Brothers; however, to the reporters
in the business press, their advice on going underweight or overweight in certain
countries, on taking short or long positions in dollars, or on moving into equities
and out of bonds and vice versa was dispensed to readers as gospel truth. This is not
to say that all these actors dispensed uniformly optimistic advice to investors playing
the region. It did mean, however, that they could not afford to paint too pessimistic
a picture of any country in the region since all their bread and butter came from
bringing global capital into Asia.

A good illustration of the modus operandi of these operators is provided by a
prominent Singapore-based expat expert who was widely cited in the *Economist, Far
Eastern Economic Review, Financial Times,* Reuters, and the *Asian Wall Street Journal*
as the last word on the Southeast Asian investment scene. This is how this expert
assessed Thailand in December 1996, when it was becoming clear to the rest of us
mortals in Bangkok that the economy was in real deep trouble:

> We believe that current pessimism about the Thai economy is based on a number of
> key misconceptions. We do not believe any of the following:
>
> • Thailand is entering a recession.
> • Investment is collapsing.
> • Export growth is collapsing.
> • The Bank of Thailand has lost control.
> • Current account deficit is unsustainable.
>
> Economic prospects for 1997: expect a rebound. (Saker 1996, 4)

The reason for focusing on Neil Saker of Singapore's SocGen Crosby Securities
is that he is one of the best examples of the way in which markets operate in East

Asia. One would have expected that after such a massive misreading of the situation, he would have been run out of Asia by irate investors. But, lo and behold, Saker was able to transform himself from the prophet of permanent boom into the prophet of doom after the financial collapse of 1997, this time issuing statements about how investors would be wise to go underweight in their investments in the region for a long time to come. Lately, he has again reinvented himself, this time as the prophet of the "Asian recovery," advising investors to go "overweight" in Thailand and Singapore, which so happened to move into recession on the day he issued his recommendation (Reuters 1998). And, worse, he is quoted just as frequently today in the *Financial Times, Far Eastern Economic Review, Asiaweek,* and the *Asian Wall Street Journal.* The market has such a short memory that it rewards charlatans instead of punishing them.

ACADEMICS: BYSTANDERS OR ACCOMPLICES?

However, to lay the blame only on the business press and the investment advisers for the creation of an atmosphere of inflated expectations would not be fair. In fact, the academic world played a key role in this crisis. Indeed, it was economists and political scientists in the West who, when seeking to explain the high growth rates of the Asian countries from the 1960s on, formulated the interrelated propositions that an economic miracle had come about in Asia, that high growth was likely to mark the region in the foreseeable future, and that Asia would be the engine of the world economy far into the twenty-first century. What is even more amazing is that there was a remarkable consensus between the left and the right in the academic world that Asian growth was exceptional—though for diametrically opposite reasons. The right insisted that it was because of free markets, the left because of the role of the interventionist state (Little 1982; Amsden 1989; Wade 1990; Hughes 1992; Kreuger 1993).

Writing on why and how the tigers evolved and why Asia would be the center of the world economy in the twenty-first century became big business, and here the most thriving business were those books that sought to equip U.S. businessmen and politicians with insights on how to deal with those formidable Asians, such as James Fallows's *Looking at the Sun.* Not to be left out of the boom, the security experts sought to cash in on the Asian miracle mania by writing on how Asian prosperity could produce either peace or war, with crass pop analysts writing on "the coming war with Japan," "the coming war with China," or, like Harvard guru Samuel Huntington, expatiating on the long twilight struggle against the "Islamic Confucian Connection." But whether they liked Asia or saw it as a threat, most academics and policy analysts believed in the long Asian boom.

The few of us who dissented from this consensus were attacked by both sides. Our critique of the increasing stresses of the newly industrialized countries (NIC) growth model on account of collateral damage in the form of environmental devastation, the subjugation of agriculture to industry, the growing income disparities, and the growing technological dependency that was behind the creation of structurally determined trade deficits was dismissed by the Right, as well as by the academic liberal center, as a case of "leftist pessimism." We were also dismissed by the academic left, who saw us as adhering to old-fashioned dependency theory or to obsolete variants of Marxism. Indeed, the most savage criticisms sometimes came from the left.

In any event, the World Bank stepped in to serve as arbiter between the Left and Right interpretations in the early 1990s and found merit on both sides of the argument—though more merits, it said, resided on the right than on the left. What is especially significant for this discussion is that the World Bank declared that, despite slight deviations here and there, the Asian tigers had the economic fundamentals right and were thus geared to enter a period of even greater prosperity. Since the World Bank is the equivalent in development circles of the papacy in the Roman Catholic Church, the World Bank's *The East Asian Miracle*, published in 1993, became a kind of Bible not only in the academic world but in financial and corporate circles as well. The rush into Asia of speculative capital in the next few years that followed must certainly be at least partly tied to its thesis of Asian exceptionalism, to Asia as the land of the never-ending bonanza.

Let me recapitulate the main points of this drama:

1. Crony capitalist practices pervaded Asian capitalism, but they were definitely not the cause of the financial collapse.

2. Northern finance capital was not conned into investing in the region by dishonest Asian banks and enterprises that concealed the actual state of their finances. That is, they cooked their books, but they fooled no one.

3. Portfolio investors and banks moved vast quantities in and out of the region, often without any real effort to arrive at an assessment of local conditions and borrowers and largely as a result of herd behavior.

4. The fundamentals of borrowers were often ignored in favor of what many investors and lenders saw as the real collateral or guarantee that they would eventually get a high rate of return from their investments, which was the 8 to 10 percent growth rate of the country, and that that was expected to extend far into the future. Now with such a perspective, you should expect to end up with some bad eggs among your debtors, but if you spread your investment around in this region of everlasting prosperity, you were likely to come out ahead in the end.

5. Also playing a critical role as accomplices in the Asian financial crisis were three institutional actors: the business press, the investment analysts, and, last but not least, the majority of academic specialists on the East Asian economies and political systems. To reiterate, a global network of investors, journalists, investment analysts, and academics were locked into a psychology of boom in which growth rates, expectations, analysis, advice, and reporting interacted in

a mutually reinforcing, inflationary fashion characteristic of manic situations. Just as in the case of the Cold War lobby in the United States, there was a whole set of actors that—perhaps half-consciously, one must concede—developed an institutional interest in the maintenance of the illusion of a never-ending Asian bonanza so that, whether in the press, in the boardroom, or in the academy, alternative viewpoints were given short shrift.

QUO VADIS, ASIAN FINANCIAL CRISIS?

Happily, many of the prophets of boom quickly adjusted and became prophets of doom, not to mention sanctimonious exponents of the crony capitalist explanation for Asia's problems. Many are coming through with their reputations intact, and some are realizing that books on why Asia collapsed can be just as profitable as books on why Asia was going to be the driver of the twenty-first century during the boom.

But this only brings the drama to July 1997, when the floating of the Thai baht triggered the crisis. The story from July 1997 until today still needs to be written. For this part of the drama, the story line is much clearer, with the IMF and the U.S. Treasury, Japan, and Prime Minister Mahathir serving as chief protagonists, with brief walk-in performances by China, Hong Kong, and the World Bank.

How will this drama end? That part of the story remains to be written by the peoples of East and Southeast Asia.

In this connection, one might note that in the script for the first part, quite a number of characters—indeed, hundreds of millions of ordinary Asians—have not been brought in. This is because they were largely passive participants in this drama. Rather than acting, they were acted upon. That may no longer be the case, judging from events in the streets of Jakarta, Kuala Lumpur, and Bangkok. In the coming period, the region is likely to see the emergence of movements motivated by resistance not only to indiscriminate financial and economic globalization but to its cultural and political aspects as well.

Within the region, we are likely to see a move away from dependence on foreign financial flows and foreign markets toward economic strategies based principally on domestic financial resources and the local market. That means greater pressure on governments for redistribution of assets and income in order to create the dynamic domestic market that can serve as the engine of growth in place of the roller-coaster global economy.

Elements of the domestic alternative are already being discussed actively throughout the region. What is still unclear, however, is how these elements will hang together. The new political economy may be embedded in religious or secular discourse and language. Its coherence is likely to rest less on considerations of narrow efficiency than on a stated ethical priority given to community solidarity and security.

Moreover, the new economic order is unlikely to be imposed from above in

Keynesian technocratic style but is likely to be forged in social and political struggles. One thing is certain: Mass politics with a class edge—frozen by the superficial prosperity before the crash of 1997—is about to return to center stage in Asia.

In short, the Asian financial crisis is likely to end with a bang, not a whimper.

NOTE

1. For a thorough analysis of Fischer's views on the subject, see Fischer (1997).

13

Global Backlash: Citizen Initiatives to Counter Corporate-Led Globalization

Robin Broad and John Cavanagh

INTRODUCTION

The end of the Cold War has yielded unforeseen opportunities for global corporations. As Russia and China compete with Mexico and Indonesia to lure investors of every sort, today's world is one in which literally no country stands off limits to corporate intrusions. To the contrary, governments around the world, almost without exception, have actively accelerated this global spread both by lowering barriers to corporate penetration and by backing new regional and global rules to facilitate the flow of goods and capital. Indeed, the 1990s has become a golden age for global corporations, an era in which new global and regional attempts at governance provide not the more restrictive rules envisioned by the "new international economic order" of two decades past but rather what Canadian citizen leader Maude Barlow (1997) has termed "corporate bills of rights."

Yet barely beneath the surface of rapid corporate-driven economic globalization percolate a host of problems that emerge with increasing regularity in almost every nation around the world: a jobs crisis, rising inequalities, and severe ecological imbalances, to name but three. Although the root of these problems is impossible to pinpoint with empirical rigor, they are increasingly viewed at least partially as consequences of deregulated corporate-led globalization.

As the problems fester, so too have they touched off a backlash against globalization that spans numerous countries, classes, ideologies, and religions. Richard Falk (1993) has offered a fitting label to this global wave of resistance: "globalization from below." From North American activists who came close to defeating the North American Free Trade Agreement (NAFTA) in 1993 to Indian peasants rallying against Colonel Sanders's brand of fried chicken and Cargill's attempts to patent traditional seeds, millions of people have joined in thousands of local, national, regional, and transnational campaigns to stop, slow down, or reshape corporate-led globalization.

Documentation of this backlash has been growing in both mainstream and scholarly publications. Yet, while chronicling the growth of the backlash is useful, it is more important to assess its potential actually to redraw the rules of the global economy and to change the nature or behavior of its major private actors: transnational corporations and banks. Does Falk's globalization from below hold the potential to be an effective countervailing power to the corporate-led "globalization from above?" On what does the former's ultimate ability to become an effective countervailing power and to change globalization in a socially and environmentally positive way depend? What challenges must the globalization-from-below movement meet, and what tensions must it overcome? These are among the questions that we attempt to grapple with in the pages that follow.

GLOBAL CORPORATE POWER AND THE SEEDS OF OPPOSITION

Whereas economic globalization is thousands of years old, the size, speed, and scope of the newest wave of global corporate expansion are unprecedented. The end of the Cold War has unlocked the markets of China, the former Soviet republics, and Eastern Europe to corporate intrusions. The World Trade Organization and its new trading rules are prying open more and more sectors of economies to foreign investment, moving closer toward the goal of equal "national treatment" for all firms. And new information technologies have increased the speed and ease with which capital can flow from one stock market to another around the world.

The prime beneficiaries of these changes have been the world's largest corporations. According to UN calculations, there are now some 40,000 corporations with activities that cross national boundaries; these firms ply overseas markets through some 250,000 foreign affiliates (UN Conference on Trade and Development 1996). At the apex of this corporate empire stand 200 firms, most of them headquartered in the United States, Japan, Germany, the United Kingdom, and France. In 1995, the combined sales of these top 200 exceeded $7.1 trillion, a figure equivalent to a staggering 28.3 percent of the world's gross domestic product; this share rose from 24.2 percent in 1982 (Anderson and Cavanagh 1996).

As the numbers and size of transnational corporations grow, so too does their reach. In addition to organizing their production processes among tens of thousands of global assembly lines, these firms are wooing consumers around the world with nearly identical merchandise sold in nearly identical shopping malls. Global banks are offering services that hold the potential to create billions of new credit-card holders and borrowers in the next century. Perhaps the most penetrating "global reach" has been that of Sony, Bertelsmann, Time Warner, and the culture conglomerates, spreading Hollywood sounds, images, and wants into even the most remote rural villages of the Third World (Barnet and Muller 1974; Barnet and Cavanagh 1994).

In recent years, researchers and activists around the world have detailed what could be grouped as six broad problems that the swath of corporate-driven globalization from above leaves in its wake: rise in inequality, erosion of jobs and wages, increasing vulnerability of "casino" economies, plunder of natural resources, destruction of community, and deterioration of democracy.

Growing Inequalities

Rather than create an integrated global village, these corporations are weaving webs of production, consumption, finance, and culture that incorporate billions of people but leave out billions more. This globalized economy is assisting the rich to get richer and leaving the poor with a smaller percentage of the world's wealth. For example, researchers at the Institute for Policy Studies calculate that the combined wealth of the world's 447 billionaires is greater than the income of the poorest half the world's people ("Richie Rich" 1997). These and similar calculations show that at least two-thirds of the world's people are left out, hurt, or marginalized by globalization (Barnet and Cavanagh 1994; Broad and Cavanagh 1995).

The inequalities are growing within nations as well as between blocks of nations. Roughly three-quarters of the new private financial flows into the developing world are going to just ten countries; in 1996, these were China, Indonesia, Mexico, Malaysia, Brazil, Thailand, Argentina, India, Turkey, and Chile (World Bank 1997). The resulting configuration could be called a new global economic apartheid: 24 richer countries growing slowly, 10 to 12 rapidly growing developing countries, and 140 others that are growing slower, not at all, or actually falling backward (Broad and Cavanagh 1995; Broad and Landi 1996).

Eroding Jobs, Wages, and Working Conditions

Corporate-driven globalization advocates often point to clean global factories where workers are relatively well paid; they typically suggest that a sizable share of Third World workers are entering this world (Richburg 1996). They invariably fail to mention such realities as rampant subcontracting of clothing and footwear to people's homes where child labor sometimes exists or the subhuman living conditions that accompany many of the factory jobs. And, while the world's top 200 corporations have sales equivalent to over a quarter of the world's measured economic activity, their employment impact is shockingly small: They employ well under 1 percent of the world's workers (Anderson and Cavanagh 1996).

Workers in many of the Third World's new global factories are denied what the International Labor Organization has deemed core workers' rights, including the rights to organize and strike. Moreover, companies use the threat of moving production to China or Mexico or Vietnam to pressure workers in countries offering higher wages and better benefits, such as the United States, to accept lower wages and reduced benefits (Bronfenbronner 1997).

Casino Economies

One of the pillars of the most recent wave of corporate-led economic globalization has been pressure from the U.S. government, the World Bank, and other multilateral institutions on poorer governments to open up their stock and financial markets to foreign capital. While offering new profit opportunities to global investors, these measures are turning Third World economies into casinos vulnerable to the whims of the twenty-somethings who manage many of the world's mutual and other investment funds.

This vulnerability and volatility left Mexico open to massive capital flight in late 1994 and precipitated the Thai, Philippine, and Malaysian currency crises of 1997–1998. Dozens of other countries have Mexican-style crises waiting to happen as nervous investors move their money elsewhere at the touch of a computer key. The domino effect has brought even such supposed "success stories" as South Korea and Indonesia to their knees, leaving the conventional economic pundits at a loss.

Environmental Plunder

Corporate-led economic globalization is also twisting economies toward the accelerated plunder of fragile natural resources. From China and Chile to Indonesia and the Philippines, "development" has been squarely centered on some combination of tearing down forests, overfishing, open-pit mining, and the poisoning of land by agrichemicals (Goldsmith et al. 1990; Broad and Cavanagh 1993; Rich 1994; Collins and Lear 1995; Shiva 1995; Mander and Goldsmith 1996). Undoubtedly the most striking example of the costs of this profit-by-plunder development is the haze that settled over much of Southeast Asia in mid-1997, primarily the result of the burning of land to make way for palm oil plantations (after the increased price for palm oil on world markets led the Indonesian government to encourage their expansion) (Cohen and Hiebert 1997; Kaiser 1997).

Adverse environmental (and social) consequences from investment flows are likely to increase as China and India build more coal-fired power plants, Indonesia encourages the further expansion of plantations, corporations expand the *maquiladora* zone on the U.S.–Mexico border, and the subcontracting of footwear, apparel, and toys spreads to more countries. The long-term costs of this brand of growth are not factored into the various measures of success, yet the next generation in these plundered economies will spend much of its energy coping with the after-effects of erosion, depleted fishing banks, and increasingly unproductive soil.

Community Collapse

Globalization proponents often equate progress with poor people landing jobs in global factories, entering the cash economy, and purchasing their first television. There is no denying that corporate-led economic globalization has offered this path to millions of people. Yet many of the rural communities that have been bypassed or undermined by globalization were well-functioning social units where hundreds of millions of subsistence farmers and fisherfolk earned a livelihood for decades. While poor in terms of cash income (and therefore by Western definitions), these functioning subsistence communities often scored high in terms of nutrition, social peace, and even education.

When the large corporate fishing fleets and agribusiness firms that are the engines of globalization devastate such communities, a few people land jobs in the new factories, but many more join the growing ranks of the hungry and unemployed in the crumbling urban sprawl of Mexico City, Lagos, and Manila. In this sense, globalization is destroying "poor" but viable rural communities, offering wages to a few in global factories, and delivering grinding urban poverty to the many.

Democracy in Danger

As global firms grow in power, so too do both their control over government agendas and the spoils they receive from government "corporate welfare" (Clarke 1996). In country after country, rich and poor alike, policies have been adapted to serve the needs of global firms, often undermining stable communities, a clean environment, and dignified jobs. As corporate contributions become the determining factor in elections the world over, governments' ability to serve the needs of their people diminishes.

GROWING BACKLASH: THE BROAD SPECTRUM AND THE "THIRD WAY"

Inasmuch as corporate-led globalization hurts, leaves out, marginalizes, or culturally alienates roughly two-thirds of the world's people, a citizen backlash is on the rise around the world. This backlash is complex and varied. Part is rooted in religious and cultural beliefs and traditions: Iran, Saudi Arabia, and even Canada, for example, have attempted to stop the intrusion of U.S. videos and other "cultural" products. In the United States and parts of Europe, strong opposition has emerged among nationalistic—and often racist and jingoistic—politicians and movements that seek to exclude foreigners from native soil and prevent the diffusion of sovereign political power. But in these same countries, growing numbers of workers, farmers, and environmentalists are building cross-sectoral and, at times, transnational coalitions to fight the new corporate-oriented rules of the global economy.

Indeed, recent battles over the rules of corporate-led globalization are transforming the boundaries of the traditional political debate around trade and investment in a number of other countries. Let us focus for a moment on this transformation in the United States, where, for most of the twentieth century, the Republican Party worked with big business to win expanded opportunities for production and trade throughout the world. This quest was viewed as synonymous with U.S. national interests; as the cliche had it, what was good for General Motors was good for the United States. Toward the other end of the traditional "free trade" versus "protectionism" spectrum, many in the Democratic Party, along with small business and labor (pejoratively termed "special interests"), argued for some protections of the domestic economy.

In the 1990s, the protectionism end of the spectrum became murkier. Small-business Republicans clung to protectionist solutions while much of the labor and environmental movement embraced notions of "fair trade."

Today, that divide between free trade and protectionism/fair trade no longer splits Democrats from Republicans; rather, the split is within both parties. In the 1996 presidential primaries, rhetoric aside, Bob Dole and Bill Clinton stood in favor of corporate-led globalization; only Pat Buchanan championed the protectionist position. His nationalistic rhetoric, aimed at small-business owners and workers, had distinct and vicious anti-immigrant and racist undercurrents. His pronouncements, however, were clear in pinpointing trade agreements such as NAFTA and the new international institutions such as the World Trade Organization (WTO) as among the culprits responsible for speeding up corporate globalization without any protections for the workers who watch wages and benefits eroded by mobile firms. House Democratic Party leaders Richard Gephardt and David Bonior rallied the majority of party members around a fair trade agenda while Bill Clinton argued for free trade.

The key development of the 1990s was that the debate became much wider than Clinton or Dole's free trade versus Buchanan's nationalist protectionism, thanks to thousands of citizen efforts within countries and across borders striving to address the negative impacts of corporate-driven globalization and to propose alternatives. Although conventional pundits and daily newspaper reporting strive to reduce these positions to either the "free trade" or the "protectionism" pole of the spectrum, the emergence of this "third way" offers a pathway forward between the extremes of free trade and nationalistic protectionism. In so doing, it also provides the hope of a swath of global civil society broad enough to serve as a countervailing power to globalization from above.

Actors promoting a third way do not, however, constitute an undifferentiated, amorphous body politic. This third way includes three prominent, often overlapping tendencies. Closest in certain respects to the Buchanan end of the spectrum are "radical" environmentalists and localization advocates who say "no" to large corporations and globalization through campaigns to kick Kentucky Fried Chicken out of India, to keep Wal-Mart out of small-town America, and to prevent pharmaceutical firms from patenting products derived from trees and other life forms. A second tendency includes Ralph Nader and much of the anti-NAFTA and anti-WTO coalitions working to "slow down" corporate-led globalization by such tactics as defeating trade and investment agreements whose impact would be to accelerate trade and investment flows by lowering existing barriers.

Finally, there is a third tendency within this third way: an array of citizen movements seeking not to *roll back* globalization and not necessarily to *slow it down* but to *rewrite the rules* under which corporate-led globalization occurs and thereby render it more "socially and/or environmentally responsible." This third tendency includes the relatively recent campaigns to add enforceable labor and environmental standards to trade and investment agreements; those pressuring Nike, Gap, Starbucks, and other firms for tough and enforceable corporate codes of conduct; and the growing alternative trading movement that bypasses large corporate channels to deliver products made under more humane and sustainable conditions from cooperatives directly to consumers.

While analytically useful, this disaggregation of the third way is not meant to suggest that there are insurmountable divisions among the three tendencies. This is a point to which we return later. Part of what unites these forces is an internationalist, anticorporate stance that counters the nationalistic populism of Buchanan or Ross Perot (who, unfortunately, became the most prominent face of the anti–free trade forces in the United States in the 1993 debate over NAFTA). Indeed, despite some tensions, these various tendencies of a third way came together dramatically in North America in the grassroots, cross-sectoral, and cross-border alliances that opposed NAFTA. Since then, these forces have linked together with other citizen movements in Europe and parts of the Third World through fora such as the San Francisco–based International Forum on Globalization (1995). With participants from nineteen countries, the Forum has organized teach-ins on globalization in Toronto, Paris, Santiago, New York, Washington, D.C., Berkeley, and Seattle.

This full spectrum of forces—from protectionist to third way to free trade—sets the stage for the economic battleground of the twenty-first century. On one side, large global corporations are attempting to establish international rules to amplify their mobility, their protections from government intervention, and their ability to maximize global profits. Their intent is to speed up a corporate-led globalization from above. On the other side are two widely divergent forces attempting to slow down corporate globalization: the nationalist, xenophobic, often culturally isolationist forces at the protectionist pole of the spectrum and the internationally oriented citizens' groups that are part of the third way.

Ignoring for the moment the fact that the two sets of forces against globalization from above are themselves fighting for different strategic goals, the outcome of the battle between globalization from above and globalization from below is, at this moment, difficult to predict. One can point to anecdotal evidence of third-way citizen forces appearing to have slowed the rapid momentum toward deregulated globalization of the early 1990s. For example, U.S. citizen pressure to include labor and environmental language in trade agreements has prevented any U.S. congressional consensus on granting the president new authority to negotiate trade agreements since 1994. Indeed, in November 1997, President Clinton was unable to counter this pressure as the majority of members of Congress opposed a bill to extend "fast track" trade negotiating authority. Likewise, in late 1995, Northern governments began discussions to expand the powers of the WTO into the field of investments in a "Multilateral Agreement on Investments" (MAI); a Third World–initiated citizen mobilization of several Southern governments stymied negotiations and forced Northern governments to shift MAI discussions into the friendlier confines of the Organization for Economic Cooperation and Development (OECD) (Third World Network 1997). And, in 1996 and 1997, large worker mobilizations in France and Korea prevented governments from adopting legislation that was to have enhanced the nations' "global competitiveness" at the expense of workers.

In order to move beyond such seemingly anecdotal evidence, we shift to two of the main arenas where third-way forces have begun to challenge globalization from above. These involve activities to advance the rights of workers and the environment through one of two instruments: corporate codes of conduct and trade agreements. After looking at these two initiatives in somewhat greater detail, we will then be in a position to assess the challenges that will determine the extent to which the third way effectively confronts corporate-led globalization.

Corporate Codes of Conduct

One cannot discuss the corporate codes of the 1990s without at least a brief acknowledgment that it has been a full quarter of a century since governments, corporations, and citizens' groups began to negotiate corporate codes of conduct. In the wake of revelations that the U.S. corporation AT&T assisted in the coup that toppled the Allende government in Chile in 1973, a strong movement emerged among nongovernmental organizations, North and South, and among Third World governments advocating greater corporate accountability around the world. With Third World governments unified in their support, in 1975 the United Nations created the Commission on Transnational Corporations, which was handed the mission of negotiating a UN code of conduct on transnational corporations.

Alongside this UN level of governmental codes, in the 1970s nongovernmental citizen campaigns for more specific corporate codes grew rapidly to challenge certain instances of egregious corporate abuse: corporate support for apartheid, unethical marketing practices by infant formula corporations, and abusive practices by the global pesticide, alcohol, soft drink, and tobacco industries, to name a few of the key campaigns. While some of these campaigns were local and most were less grandiose than the UN code initiative, several were sophisticated global efforts that fundamentally changed the way consumers would see infant formula or corporations investing in an apartheid regime (Sikkink 1986; Broad and Cavanagh 1997).

But the 1980s and the free-market triumphalism that marked the Reagan, Bush, Thatcher, and Kohl administrations ushered in a less propitious environment for the development of codes. Within the United Nations, momentum toward a UN code of conduct was effectively halted when the Reagan administration, along with some European governments and Japan, vehemently opposed the effort. Negotiations collapsed, and eventually even the commission itself was dismantled. During this period, when the very legitimacy of governmental oversight of corporate affairs was called into question, the movement to enhance global governance of corporations was significantly set back. To this day, UN-level corporate code work has not recovered.

By the mid-1990s, however, as the set of global crises (detailed previously) emerged, the triumphalism became more muted, and the corporate code movement was reborn. In its 1990s reincarnation, however, it was a different movement: The retreat of governments during the 1980s, alongside the growth of nongovernmental organizations (NGOs) in that decade, set the context for a shift in emphasis in the movement toward nongovernmental actors as the main countervailing power to corporations.

Campaigns in the 1990s by human rights, labor, and other groups led relatively quickly to some individual U.S. firms adopting their own voluntary codes of conduct for themselves and their subcontractors. This was typically done under pressure from citizen campaigns, but, on occasion, firms considering themselves more "socially responsible" took the initiative. The initial focus of campaigns was, for the most part, labor conditions—often involving child labor—in apparel and footwear firms in which sweatshop conditions made for easy targets and public outrage. In both the United States and Europe, citizen campaigns against Nike and other footwear companies resulted in some adopting their own corporate codes of conduct. Sears and Levi Strauss agreed not to contract production to firms that used prison labor or that committed other specified violations of workers' rights. Persistent violations in China prompted Levi Strauss to announce that it would phase out all production contracts in that country. Eddie Bauer, Levi Strauss, and Liz Claiborne stopped subcontracting in Burma because of flagrant Burmese violations of human rights.

As other citizen organizations joined the work on codes, they have added consumer pressure to help convince firms to adopt codes. A case in point was the mid-1990s campaign led by the Chicago-based Guatemalan Labor Education Project and allied groups, working with organizations in Guatemala, to push Starbucks to adopt a code to govern conditions under which the coffee that it sells is grown. After minimal consumer pressure, the image-conscious Starbucks management, which saw itself as socially responsible, agreed to adopt what would be the first code of conduct to govern the production of an agricultural commodity. (Compa and Hinchliffe-Darricarrere 1995).

The mid-1990s saw a number of such code campaigns. While many of the code initiatives grew from consumer concerns in the North, some initiatives took the lead from groups in the South. A notable example is toys: In July 1995, several European and Asian organizations responded to fires and exploitative work conditions in Asian toy factories with a call on toy firms to adopt a model "Charter on the Safe Production of Toys." The charter is significant in that it was drafted by groups in Hong Kong and in that the goal is to move beyond individual company codes of conduct into a sectoral code (Asia Monitor Resource Center 1996). It also moved beyond a

: on child labor to a broader set of workers' rights. Leading toy manufacturers
nded by announcing their own narrower code (Islam 1996).
the mid-1990s, it was becoming clear in the code campaigns that—with the
:r mix of media work and a company or sector (i.e., toys) that depended on
ood" brand name—even a small amount of consumer pressure could succeed
ely quickly at getting a company to promulgate its own code of conduct for
rights. The weak implementation of these codes and the ease with which in-
tive reporters and NGOs were able to find blatant abuse of these codes by
ntractors, prompted many groups to begin pressing for new enforcement
nisms that built on "independent" and "external" monitoring.
ε initiative in particular advanced this "independent monitoring" approach.
)5, a small New York–based NGO called the National Labor Committee
, which had a history of working with groups in Central America, along with
tile union UNITE, religious groups, and allies in Central America launched
aign against the Gap. Gap was a company that viewed itself as being socially
ible and that had its own voluntary code of conduct. The NLC sought to
e widespread publicity around Gap's inability and/or unwillingness to en-
ς code in one large subcontractor in El Salvador. To help the effort, the NLC
ed a tour through the United States by two young Central American women
ved clothes for the Gap and other U.S. firms. As religious, student, and other
in both the United States and El Salvador joined the chorus of disapproval
ns and picket lines, Gap announced its intent to move out of El Salvador
iers in other countries. To Gap's surprise, activists responded by broadening
paign, demanding that Gap stay in El Salvador, pressure its contractors to
asic workers' rights, and allow independent, NGO monitoring of Gap's
:onduct.
ecember 15, 1995, in the midst of the holiday shopping season, Gap agreed
se demands. A "pilot program" using Salvadoran NGOs for external, inde-
monitoring of Gap's corporate code of conduct was set up initially for the
doran factory whose workers' rights violations had sparked the NLC cam-

e among the code initiatives described thus far is the absence of a strong
ntal role. In May 1995, for example, the Clinton administration released
e code titled "Model Business Principles," which merely "encouraged" all
to adopt voluntarily. The U.S. Department of Labor has played essen-
eerleader role in the new corporate codes. In mid-1996, it convened a
mong leaders from the apparel and footwear industries and representatives
an rights and labor rights organizations but then largely stood to the side
berations. In April 1997, the group released its compromise "Workplace
'onduct," which included strong guidelines on workers' rights. Signifi-
agreement included a detailed "Principles of Monitoring" spelling out
gations of companies" and "obligations of independent external moni-

tors." The group continues to work on the details of the monitoring and enforcement mechanisms (Schilling 1997).

As this section has begun to suggest, the generation of corporate codes of the 1990s has had some impact. In several cases, it has begun to change public awareness—witness Kathie Lee Gifford's tears over revelations of child labor in factories producing her own line of clothing or Doonesbury's rendition of Nike's labor infractions in Vietnam. And in some notable cases, with public pressure, code campaigns have moved beyond merely changing awareness to changing corporate behavior. New coalitions have been catalyzed and new actors brought into the third way. As they gather strength and learn from each other, they build momentum toward greater enforceability—a goal still largely unmet. But, when put together, do these campaigns spell out a countervailing power to transnational corporations? That is a question to which we return after a brief look, for comparison's sake, at another set of campaigns within the third way.

LABOR AND ENVIRONMENT IN TRADE AGREEMENTS

While we have chosen to focus on corporate codes of conduct as an example of the third-way campaigns, it is also useful to highlight more briefly another focus of third-way campaigns in the 1990s, social clauses in trade and investment agreements, in part to demonstrate the diversity of tactics and reach of globalization from below.

The 1990s could be dubbed the "decade of free trade and investment agreements," given the flurry of such negotiating activity at both the regional and the global level. Citizen campaigns have attempted, with varying degrees of success, to inject social and environmental concerns into these negotiations so as to influence the behavior of the global firms that are the ultimate beneficiaries of the new agreements. Unlike the 1990s code work, however, this so-called social clause activism focuses on mandatory, regulatory (not voluntary) rules made by governments, not the corporations themselves.

The history of this effort in the United States goes back at least 100 years: Numerous campaigns over the twentieth century targeted government trade policy as a way to address certain negative corporate labor practices. As early as the late nineteenth century, workers and workers' rights advocates in the United States fought successfully to link respect for workers' rights to trade benefits. The U.S. McKinley Tariff Act of 1890 prohibited the domestic trade of goods made by convicts in the United States. Over the ensuing decades, a number of related measures limited U.S. imports of goods made by prison labor.

The movement to link trade to workers' rights, however, was fully launched in the United States in the 1980s, when labor, human rights, and religious activists created the International Labor Rights Fund in Washington, D.C. Working with allies in some key Southern countries, the participating groups studied seventy years of International Labor Organization (ILO) deliberations in order to specify the most basic of internationally recognized workers' rights: freedom of association, the right to collective bargaining, bans on child and prison labor, and minimum standards with respect to wages, working conditions, and health and safety.

The recent wave of activism in the United States began as largely unilateral initiatives. Having this set of core, internationally recognized labor rights significantly advanced the effort and gave it more credibility than some other unilateral legislative initiatives. Working with allies in the U.S. Congress and in unions, human rights groups, and relevant Third World countries, the International Labor Rights Fund and other groups helped craft U.S. legislation to link U.S. trade and investment privileges to other countries' respect for these basic workers' rights. The U.S. corporate community, viewing the legislation as an infringement on its freedom to profit from differences in the respect for rights among countries, fought the linkage. Yet on several occasions since 1984, the U.S. Congress passed legislation linking trade and investment privileges to respect for workers' rights. First, in 1984, the U.S. Generalized System of Preferences, whereby many goods from the Third World enter the United States without paying tariffs, was amended so that if a country was found to be violating internationally recognized workers' rights, it could be denied the duty-free benefits. Similar amendments were attached to the Overseas Private Investment Corporation, the Caribbean Basin Initiative, and the Trade Act of 1988.

This unilateral work linking trade and labor rights was transformed during the four-year debate over the rules of regional integration that followed the 1990 announcement by Presidents George Bush and Carlos Salinas of plans to negotiate NAFTA. This set off a parallel initiative among third-way NGOs in Canada, the United States, and Mexico, part advocacy against the government agenda and part deliberation of an alternative agenda. Many citizens' groups in all three countries opposed the pact outright. Others, including a significant portion of the environmental community, argued for enforceable workers' rights and environmental standards to be part of the agreement. What was new about the NGO response was that it was decidedly trinational and that it was more sophisticated than merely a defensive "reject." In the end, pressure from this broad array of groups led the U.S. government to propose side agreements to NAFTA on the environment and on labor. Hundreds of transnational corporations banded together in a corporate alliance (USA/NAFTA), which opposed the side agreements. In the final document, the linkage between trade and labor and environmental rights was quite weak. But NAFTA and its side agreements opened a door to green and labor-friendly trade agreements and NGO involvement in trade agreements—a door that is unlikely to be closed.

Third-way NGOs are also pushing the trade–workers' rights–environmental rights linkage at a multilateral level in the WTO. This too has a historical precedent: From the initial deliberations over the General Agreement on Tariffs and Trade (GATT) and the ill-fated International Trade Organization over fifty years ago, debates over the content of global trade rules have included fights over whether trade benefits should be linked to countries' respect for core workers' rights. Indeed, under pressure from their trade unions, the United States and some other Northern governments continue to argue for a linkage in the WTO.

THE THIRD WAY AS A COUNTERVAILING POWER: CHALLENGES

We stand at a critical juncture in the backlash against corporate globalization. A quarter century ago, governments of the South, with some support from northern European governments, began to create governmental mechanisms to check the power and direction of corporate-driven globalization. Much of this government sensibility was eroded in the 1980s, especially after the fall of the Berlin Wall, as free-market ideology reigned in the West and was imposed on much of the South through World Bank and International Monetary Fund programs. Since 1995, however, the pendulum appears to have begun to shift back away from the magic of the marketplace as the great panacea.

The momentum of globalization from above versus the backlash from below depends on many factors. Economic crises—such as the one that hit Mexico in 1994 or the 1997–1998 Asian crises—are notable cases in point. It is our contention, however, that the ultimate success of third-way globalization from below and its ability to confront effectively corporate-led globalization from above—will depend on the ability of its leading protagonists to grapple with certain tensions and address certain large issues. How the third way handles key challenges will, in large measure, determine whether it ultimately is able to serve as an effective countervailing power. We address six of the most important challenges.

1. *The success of the third way depends on its ability to come together as a movement that crosses myriad campaigns and sectors and different strategic goals.* Far from working together toward a common strategic goal, globalization-from-below forces do not typically even perceive themselves as part of an overall movement. Rather, the "movement" features thousands of campaigns around globalization and global corporations that have been launched by thousands of different groups. With few cross-cutting campaigns to link various campaigners together, the third way is fragmented along lines that reflect the main tactic, method, or instrument of given campaigns: direct actions, lawsuits, ethical competitors, shareholder resolutions and actions, dialogue, legislative instruments, and actions to influence consumers (for more detailed descriptions of these, see Broad and Cavanagh 1997). Many campaigns at a given moment in history seem unaware of their historical antecedents. An example is the current work on codes of conduct, much of which is uninformed by the UN code work that preceded it.

Beyond tactics, the movement separates into two camps, reflecting a difference of strategic goals concerning what should be done with globalization's most dynamic actor, the corporation. Some work builds on a strategic goal of changing the behavior of corporations, most often individual abusive cases. Other campaigns are constructed to change the nature of the corporation itself. A "corporate democracy" movement in United States, for example, seeks to return to the public the ability to shape the charters of corporations and ultimately to revoke those that no longer advance the public good (Grossman 1996).

While, arguably, a multitude of tactics and different strategic goals could serve as a strength, the hard reality is that third-way groups with different strategic goals often view one another as adversaries or competitors. The speed with which the antiglobalization movement grows will depend in part on the ability of groups with different strategic goals and tactics to collaborate and appreciate one another's role in the overall scheme. With sufficient consultation, groups deploying different tactics can often reinforce one another; indeed, confrontational groups often seem to create space for more reformist groups.

2. *The movement's strength depends on effectively basing its work on North-South alliances—a challenge that not only implies working out logistical difficulties of cross-country dialogue, coordination, and campaigns but also requires working through some key debates.* Although there is a recognition that most effective third-way campaigns have involved North-South alliances, there are still too few fora in which activists in one country working on corporate issues can meet their counterparts from around the world. There are even fewer examples of campaigns that are coordinated at a global level. Moreover, to the extent that campaigners in the North reach out to Southern colleagues, at times the Southern side of these alliances is brought in only after Northern groups have already launched the work. The challenge is not simply to consult with Southern groups but, in relevant campaigns, to accept the leadership of Southern groups—as Hong Kong groups led in the toy campaign.

Part of the reason that such coordination is the exception rather than the rule is that North-South campaigns are more complicated and expensive than those based in one country. In addition, there are inadequate fora for cross-country discussions and debates before campaigns are launched. There are some fairly recent attempts at building such space, notably the San Francisco–based International Forum on Globalization, which, since 1994, has brought together thousands of third-way activists from around the world for frank discussions and debates that should lead to better campaign coordination.

This open space is needed in part because there are still areas of disagreement that would benefit from greater discussion. One such crucial debate is a disagreement over attaching labor and environmental "social clauses" to trade agreements. While there is widespread support in the North and South for creating corporate codes of conduct to advance workers' rights, there is more controversy around linking enforcement of these rights and standards to trade sanctions. Despite far-reaching support for this linkage among trade unions in the North and South (Asian and Pacific Regional Organization 1994; Egge and Shumperli 1996), a number of citizens' groups in Asia led by the well-respected Third World Network are deeply concerned that Northern governments could use the linkage as a form of disguised protectionism (Khor 1994; Compa 1995). Discussion is crucial to understanding the basis for both positions and to finding compromise. Such a process evolved in the NAFTA case as a result of a three-year discussion among Mexican, U.S., and Canadian groups that concluded in a compromise document titled "A Just and Sustainable Trade and Development Initiative for North America" (Alliance for Responsible Trade 1993).

3. *The third-way movement needs to better harness the potential powers of its various strands.* Many social forces within the third way—led by unions and environmental groups—have far greater potential power to influence corporations than they currently exercise. Part of this enhanced power lies in their using their power as investors more creatively. Here the rich experience and knowledge of investor–activists, who have for years put pressure on pension funds, insurance companies, and mutual funds to operate in a socially responsible fashion, need to be shared. With short-term financial flows accelerating their reach, speed, and fickleness, the third-way work on investor responsibility deserves to spread. A hopeful sign is the interest shown by the "new" AFL-CIO in engaging in these investor and related debates; it has created a new division of corporate affairs to spearhead such efforts.

Meeting this third challenge also necessitates better crosscutting work between labor and environmental groups. Work on advancing workers' rights and standards with corporations and through trade agreements is more advanced than the work on environmental rights and standards. Until there is a multilateral attempt to delineate core environmental rights and standards, work on environmental codes and linkages to trade agreements is unlikely to advance significantly. Once such international environmental rights are delineated, the challenge is for campaigns to more consistently merge social and environmental issues.

4. *The third way will be inhibited in its anticorporate campaigns until it addresses the growing corporate control of politics.* As their campaigns pick up momentum, third-way activists are gaining understanding of the reach of corporate power. Some activists have already termed the growing corporate influence over governments and multilateral institutions as "corporate rule" and are shifting their campaign focus from individual corporations and antiglobalization work to the issue of corporate control of politics and political institutions. A case in point is Canadian anti-NAFTA leader Tony Clarke, who is leading an International Forum on Globalization effort to pull together activists in several countries around the theme of "challenging corporate rule," by which Clarke means challenging not only corporate abuse of workers and the environment but also their growing grip over political agendas all over the world (Clarke 1996).

5. *While continuing their campaigns and media exposes on high-profile companies, third-way campaigns have yet to demonstrate significant on-the-ground results across economic sectors, companies, and countries.* A major test of the movement is to demonstrate its ability to move beyond "easier" countries and "better" companies in "easier" sectors. Thus far, the momentum of codes of conduct, for example, is largely in the apparel, footwear, and toy sectors, and the codes focus primarily on sweatshop conditions. Campaigns that target corporations with some claim to social responsi-

bility (e.g., Gap, Levi Strauss, and Liz Claiborne) have been more successful both in engaging the corporation and in changing corporate behavior than campaigns targeting those corporations that deny a broader social mission (e.g., Shell in Nigeria). And, to a certain extent, the reality has been that the *somewhat* more socially responsible firms have been targeted by activists since they are more likely to engage. This has led to the current arguably perverse situation in which the more responsible companies have "voluntary" codes and thus are more vulnerable to criticism for noncompliance while less responsible companies without codes may be able to escape unscathed.

Similarly, for U.S.-based campaigns, it has proven understandably easier to succeed when campaigns focused on countries that are less "strategically" important to the United States (e.g., Burma and El Salvador). This may, however, mean that the more "effective" campaigns have either failed in or avoided more strategic countries, notably China (where the dearth of independent trade unions and NGOs also limits third-way initiatives and alliances). But, given the logic of global capital, unless third-way campaigns can demonstrate an ability to succeed in a country such as China, which has wooed corporations by offering the lowest of labor and environmental costs, third-way campaigns will be limited in their influence on corporate-driven globalization.

While third-way activists should expect that corporations will opt for voluntary rather than regulatory initiatives, the challenge is to test the limits of corporate self-regulation while simultaneously having at least one of the movement's feet solidly grounded in regulatory campaigns such as social clauses. In the code work, "testing the limits" means not only forcing effectiveness on the codes through independent, external monitoring but also developing an accountability process that is participatory.

6. *The movement also needs better to delineate a role for global governance.* At this moment, much of the third-way work on global governance involves critiquing and confronting the current set of multilateral institutions. The WTO, the World Bank, the International Monetary Fund, NAFTA, and the proposed Multilateral Agreement on Investment are all perceived by corporate activists to be part of a set of global rules that is badly skewed in favor of the corporation.

Yet global governance is another issue on which globalization-from-below forces need space to iron out differences in strategic goals. Some, such as Ralph Nader, view any initiative that takes power away from nation-states as being an affront on sovereignty and are against most forms of global governance. Others, such as Pharis Harvey and other proponents of social clauses, believe that the current institutions are deeply flawed but that, in the final analysis, new institutions of global governance are necessary for third-way initiatives to be effective.

CONCLUSION

The concentration and global reach of large corporations will continue to grow rapidly over the next decade, spreading benefits to a minority and a host of social and environmental problems to the majority. Citizens' groups, many searching for a new internationalism based on values of social justice, ecological sustainability, and economic well-being, are likewise growing as a countervailing force. They face increasing competition from another group of antiglobalization forces that are isolationist in nature. The next decade is likely to feature ongoing battles among these three approaches to globalization. The promise of globalization from below as an effective countervailing power both to globalization from above and to the more nationalistic antiglobalization forces depends on its becoming self-conscious enough as a movement to collectively meet a series of daunting challenges. The outcome of these battles will shape the social, economic, and environmental landscape of the twenty-first century.

14

Enforcing Norms and Normalizing Enforcement for Humane Governance

Robert C. Johansen

Of the many influences contributing to peace within what Richard Falk (1995) has aptly called "humane global governance," the capacity to ensure compliance with fundamental international norms constitutes an essential element. Readily available technologies of destruction, peoples' capacity for social disruption, and environmental fragilities combine to make all societies highly vulnerable—even the militarily most powerful. Because people have no choice but to live within permeable territorial boundaries, peace and human security can no longer be achieved without ensuring that all people everywhere obey at least a few rules prohibiting severely threatening actions, whether of a military, migratory, or environmental nature. Difficult though it may be to accomplish, peace and security can be substantially enhanced only through taking further steps to domesticate the international system (Johansen 1996). Perhaps the most significant of these steps would be to increase the international community's capacity to hold individuals accountable to fundamental international norms of peace and human rights (defined below).

Experience with the enforcement of law in domestic societies demonstrates that, in societies congenial to human life, people comply with basic legal norms out of habit, convenience, conviction, or some combination of these but not primarily because they cower before heavily armed law enforcers. They feel a sense of commitment to the legal order and live amidst a pervasive culture of compliance. Moreover, when explicit enforcement mechanisms *do* determine behavior, the most frequent enforcement consequences arise from suffering embarrassment, social opprobrium, and monetary fines. Only those whom we label as socially deviant seek to escape fundamental legal norms through drastic means that invite the risk of arrest at gunpoint and prolonged imprisonment.

Although most people willingly comply with most laws most of the time, some instruments for coercive enforcement *are* necessary to ensure respect for human rights and a minimal level of social and economic predictability, cooperation, and personal and official security. Enforcement is especially difficult in international relations because of weak social bonds, ethical constraints, and political institutions across ethnic, religious, and state boundaries. Since ancient times, most people—although not all—have considered wars to be legitimate instruments for settling intersocietal disputes because governing functions have been nonexistent or extremely unreliable between societies. Even the best effort of the human species to prohibit aggressive war and institute community-wide enforcement, expressed in the UN Charter, "governs" international conflicts primarily by asking the major powers, through the Security Council's collective security mechanism, to employ war if diplomacy fails in settling disputes. The problems with collective security are legion, and even when faced with the most obvious of enforcement needs, such as addressing unconscionable deeds in the early 1990s in Bosnia or Rwanda or Somalia, the international community has not cooperated well to halt collective violence and vast human suffering.

Political leaders have given little attention to establishing a rule of law in world affairs that would hold *individuals* accountable to fundamental norms prohibiting aggressive war and genocide. To illustrate, only states (not individuals) may be brought before the International Court of Justice (World Court). A permanent international criminal court that is legally competent to try individuals has not even existed, although the Rome Treaty of 1998 enables the international community now to make significant breakthroughs in this regard, setting the stage for further domestication of the international system.

Few people disagree with the idea that the prohibitions against genocide and war ought to be enforced. Yet most governments and individuals have never committed themselves to measures of international domestication that could effectively enforce fundamental norms of peace and human rights. To counter the inertia sustaining today's violence-prone, international system, we need to question the widespread assumption that it will be impossible to hold individuals accountable to international law until *after* it is possible to hold states accountable to law through collective security mechanisms. The international community's difficulty in holding national governments accountable to fundamental legal norms is not sufficient reason to remain indifferent to imaginative efforts to hold individuals, including officials, accountable to international law. Even imperfect initiatives to hold *individuals* accountable can be normatively preferable to a focus on enforcement against *states* because the former efforts focus responsibility on the violators of specific norms in a way that wars of enforcement against entire societies never can. An emphasis on *individual* accountability also contributes to *state* compliance and to the political education and precedent building that are essential to constructing a more just and peaceful world community in the long run.

PURPOSE

The purpose of this chapter is to demonstrate that steps to enforce law on individuals can be taken immediately, without jeopardizing any society's legitimate security interests, if more citizens' organizations and progressive governments in the international community would commit themselves to two goals: (1) to hold individuals accountable, insofar as possible, to fundamental norms of peace and human rights, and (2) to strengthen UN capabilities for employing legal instruments of individualized enforcement, including highly trained UN police and police trainers, conflict experts, internationally sponsored judicial proceedings, and "smart" sanctions. This strategy would encourage and, where necessary and possible, *require* individuals, regardless of rank or position in society, to honor widely agreed-on international norms of peace and human rights. If the international community were to pursue this strategy, it would mean taking war crimes investigations, indictments, and extraditions far more seriously. It would also lead international agencies to attend sensitively to local people's needs and thereby to encourage local consent to and participation in the administration of a UN "justice package" (UN police monitoring with penal and judicial reform) with the goal of transforming conflicts from lethal to nonlethal modes of resolution based on positive social change.

After explaining several concepts essential for this analysis, I briefly describe the normative contributions of various UN enforcement instruments—military operations, economic sanctions, peacekeeping, and civilian police—to holding individuals accountable to international standards. The discussion then turns to the need for expanded UN civilian police functions and the benefits of a permanent UN police force.

CONCEPTS AND DEFINITIONS

The "norms of peace" refer collectively to crimes against humanity (e.g., genocide), crimes against the peace (e.g., aggressive war), war crimes (e.g., mistreatment of civilians or prisoners in warfare), and gross violations of human rights that constitute a threat to the peace or that cause scores of civilian deaths, such as "ethnic cleansing" in Bosnia-Herzegovina or the obstruction of efforts by relief agencies to avert mass starvation in Somalia in 1993. Although these international norms govern human rights as much as matters of war and peace, I will refer to them as the "norms of peace" for the sake of simplicity and to reflect the Security Council's preference for rationalizing its enforcement actions by relating them to the council's primary responsibility for maintaining peace.

"Enforcement" will be used to mean UN actions, ranging from positive inducements to military coercion taken under Chapter VII of the Charter, to ensure that states comply with the norms of peace and any legally binding Security Council decisions that may be made to maintain peace and security. The term may refer to economic sanctions or military action against a country, but it can also include war crimes tribunals or the use of domestic courts to enforce international law on individuals. The distinguishing feature of enforcement is that it does not wait for the consent of a lawbreaking state or official for the United Nations to take action.

Successful enforcement in the global arena, as in the local community, often is nested within what might be called a "culture of compliance"—beliefs, values, norms, symbols, institutions, and sanctions—rather than relying entirely or even primarily on sheer physical force. Unless the shaping of cultural factors is given more serious attention in international diplomacy, the inertia of the existing "culture of military enforcement" will overshadow suggestions to implement a new multilateral strategy of enforcement, as the lack of serious response to Boutros Boutros-Ghali's *Agenda for Peace* (1995) has made clear. The point is not that military thinking is unimportant but that it is often a distracting part of a broad spectrum of enforcement instruments within a culture of compliance.

A "culture of compliance" is manifested where a constabulary or police agency representing the community is authorized by the community to enforce norms established by the community on members within the community—and to conduct such enforcement within prescribed procedures guaranteeing a maximum of fairness and a minimum of violence. In contrast, a "culture of military enforcement" (or, more simply, "culture of combat") is encouraged when, in normal international relations, one country threatens or uses force to enforce norms that it interprets in a manner that it unilaterally deems appropriate to advance its interests against another party. A culture of compliance can easily degenerate into a culture of combat if an enforcing agent does not represent the entire community, if the norms to be enforced have not been established by the community, if disputes over the meaning of the norms are not settled impartially and by a legitimate authority, if the enforcement mechanism itself denies equal respect for human lives, or if a pattern of enforcement develops in which the norms are applied to some but not to all members of the community. Of particular relevance to this discussion, today's culture of military enforcement can develop into a culture of compliance if the conditions noted here are increasingly met.

Enforcement by the United Nations has functioned at the interface of these two cultures, authorizing the use of military force in some cases—Korea (1950), Congo (1960), Iraq (1991), Somalia (1992), Bosnia (1992), and Haiti (1993)—but attempting to make such an authorization only after recognized international norms have been impartially applied to a government's conduct and the conduct is found wanting. Military action and a culture of combat reinforce each other. On the other hand, effective police enforcement and a culture of compliance reinforce each other. Existing preoccupation with and support for military instruments, even in UN peacekeeping contexts, impedes the domestication of international conduct that is essential if the international community seeks to make enforcement more reliable at acceptable moral and financial costs.

The police enforcement proposed here differs sharply from the role that police have played in colonial administrations and authoritarian societies. In the latter, police forces and military forces can hardly be differentiated because both focus on maintaining control by the rulers rather than on safety for people in society. In these cases, police have often reported directly to military authorities. Military forces have viewed security threats as primarily internal and have employed both military and police forces in a military mode as if the people were the enemy.

For purposes of this analysis, police are sharply differentiated from military forces. Police, at their best, enforce law on individuals; in contrast, military forces seek to overcome or dominate and control entire societies. Police aim to arrest or capture only those individuals who allegedly have broken the law; soldiers in combat target all opposing military personnel, many of whom are personally innocent of wrongdoing. Police use force only as a last resort, in a limited way, and only to apprehend those to be arrested; soldiers use unlimited force with only modest discrimination and often with the intent to produce maximum social devastation to break the will of the enemy. Police have no enemy, aiming to uphold the law against any individual violator regardless of nationality; military forces oppose another nationality in thought, word, and action. Police are governed closely by rules of operation and subject to grievance procedures designed to protect people from police abuse; soldiers are less closely governed by rules protecting the innocent, and those victimized by military forces in combat have little recourse for redress of injuries. Police implement and abide by rules established by the community; soldiers usually implement policies and follow procedures established primarily by their side in making war on others. Police perform most of their duties openly and with community support; soldiers frequently employ secrecy and deception to overpower an adversary. Police seek to be impartial in upholding the law and requiring all individuals' conduct to meet that standard; soldiers are usually partial in opposing a particular nationality or other group identity.

Much confusion arises from the tendency of some observers to believe that the UN desire for impartiality necessarily means doing nothing to halt illegal behavior, especially in the context of UN peacekeeping. To avoid confusion, I use the term "neutrality" to refer to UN peacekeepers who passively do nothing in the face of clear violations of fundamental norms because they want to avoid taking a stand for or against a particular adversary. I use "impartiality" to refer to UN personnel who attempt to uphold, even forcefully, fundamental norms by holding all actors equally accountable to a norm without regard for the nationality or citizenship of wrongdoers. A neutral observer is passive and refuses to alienate either of two sides in a dispute; an impartial official is active and adheres impartially to established rules even if so doing alienates one or more violators of the rules. Both terms can be distinguished from "partiality" in which UN personnel may (inappropriately) impose rules on one nationality but not on another. In my parlance, UN peacekeepers may often remain *neutral* because they seek to perform valuable buffering functions while operating within a state-centric frame of reference, aiming to maintain good diplomatic relations with all concerned, even offenders. Good civilian police normally apply law *impartially* on individuals regardless of their origin and without expecting the alleged offender to be pleased with arrest. Although police may be unarmed or less heavily armed than peacekeepers, they also may be less neutral and more impartial.[1]

"Peacekeeping" includes (1) traditional cease-fire monitoring and buffering activities of UN forces and (2) expanded activities, such as election monitoring, demobilizing belligerents, retraining indigenous police, and administrative functions facilitating transition from war to peace. These activities may be carried out by contingents of armed forces or civilian police, often referred to as CIVPOL, contributed by member nations for special UN duty. United Nations peacekeeping forces are deployed with the consent of the adversaries, carry only light arms, do not fire their weapons except as a last resort in self-defense, usually maintain a neutral posture between two or more adversaries, and do not perform generally coercive functions.

With these concepts in mind, I turn now to discuss how UN military combat, UN peacekeeping, and UN economic sanctions influence a culture of compliance. Then I examine the potential impact of an enhanced UN civilian police.

THE CONTRIBUTIONS OF UN MILITARY ENFORCEMENT TO A CULTURE OF COMPLIANCE

Regardless of where one stands on the spectrum of opinion about the UN's use of military force in intrastate and interstate conflicts, it seems unlikely that the UN will establish its own military capability in the foreseeable future. Moreover, even if military combat receives UN endorsement, it frequently threatens to exact unbearable political, military, and moral costs. Indeed, that is precisely why governments rejected more intense UN military action in many conflicts in the early 1990s, allowing mass killings to proceed. Because UN members are frequently reluctant to support military enforcement,[2] whether for good or dubious reasons, it might be wise to utilize some creative space that lies outside the realm of both traditional peacekeeping and the resort to large-scale military force, such as occurred in Operation Desert Storm. There is an enforcement option that lies between doing nothing and sending in the troops. It is to hold individuals accountable to the norms of peace by attempting to use a police rather than a military mode of enforcement.

Most UN enforcement experience demonstrates the need to examine possible alternatives to past practice. This was underscored in 1997 by the failure of NATO troops to arrest those indicted for war crimes in Bosnia and in 1999 by the unpreparedness of UN and NATO governments to provide public safety in Kosovo, both before and after NATO bombing, when first Albanians and subsequently Serbs were forced to flee for their lives. First, it is extremely difficult and costly to enforce international law collectively against an entire society, especially if it is well armed and unified in resisting external military efforts to coerce the entire society. Second, the military instrument lumps most people together in a target society, implicitly imposes collective guilt on them, and harms many relatively innocent people during combat. In contrast, the legal instrument imposes penalties by differentiating those who have committed misdeeds, regardless of nationality, from those who did not. United Nations police enforcement seeking to apprehend only alleged law violators would be seen as far more legitimate and politically acceptable throughout the world than military enforcement. Third, the emphasis on individual accountability increases the prospects, often exceedingly dim, for reconciling adversaries because it refuses to condemn or bless all people on the basis of their identity or nationality. Fourth, the emphasis on individual accountability may be more effective than war in deterring future misdeeds because it is a reminder to every individual contemplating illegal acts that he or she may one day be held accountable. The drawback of international police enforcement, of course, is that police may be unable to attain immediate access to indictees without sparking a war that UN civilian police cannot fight. They can, however, maintain legal and police pressure until a time when conditions for arrest may improve.

Although UN military enforcement comes closer to contributing to a climate of compliance than does use of military force by one or more national governments, many negative consequences have attended UN use of force. It has been difficult to obtain or retain the support of the world community for military operations. Because the United Nations is not equipped to oversee military action, it may be forced to assign command of UN military enforcement to a major power, such as the United States in the war against Iraq or NATO against Yugoslavia in 1999. Offering a blank check to a nationally led military coalition, which pursues its own goals, may discredit the United Nations. In such a case, the United Nations then loses both the benefits associated with the neutrality of peacekeeping and the impartiality of police enforcement. Almost inevitably, the United Nations becomes a partisan, unable to use the potential strength of its transcendent legitimacy as an expression of cross-cultural ideals.

Even when it may appear to do so, UN military combat does not work well as an enforcement instrument. In the U.S.-led Operation Desert Storm, for example, despite the worldwide condemnation of Saddam Hussein's invasion and annexation of Kuwait, he began to receive new support as soon as the military destruction of Iraqi society mounted. Even in those countries such as Pakistan, where people had an interest in siding with Kuwait against Hussein because overseas Pakistanis in Kuwait contributed 40 percent of Pakistani remittances from abroad, the initial sympathy for Kuwait dwindled. Although Pakistan committed 10,000 troops to fight against Iraq, soon after the UN-endorsed bombs began to fall, so did the popular mood. President George Bush and Prime Minister John Major were burned in effigy in demonstrations against UN-endorsed military action. The idea spread that deliberately ambiguous U.S. diplomatic signals had lured Iraq into Kuwait so that the West could destroy Iraq's power. Soon some began to side with Hussein because he stood up against the Western-dominated United Nations. Many began to feel that he championed the poor against the rich, powerful states despite his previous failures to use many of his own resources on behalf of the poor. Because of the military nature of the enforcement instrument—not because of the intrinsic merits of his behavior—he became more popular among the poor in many countries. "What mattered in the thick of the fray was heroic resistance, being with one's own people, being of the faith, and attacking those who had humiliated the poor of the world" (du Preez 1994, 128).

The UN operation against Iraq probably was the most propitious context for UN military enforcement that one can expect to find. Almost no one questioned the UN justification for intervention. Iraq had clearly engaged in military aggression and annexed a recognized UN member. A universal UN coalition arose to reverse this misdeed, and wealthy countries offered large-scale financial support for the war. Iraq's terrain was highly vulnerable to aerial bombardment and surveillance, and the target was a small, isolated country of only 17 million people. If in such an instance the political costs of UN military enforcement rose alarmingly, then such an enforcement instrument will usually ring alarm bells. The problem is rooted in the bluntness of the military instrument and the target's ability to gain sympathy because military combat harms the entire target society (rather than only wrongdoers). What occurs in this mode of enforcement is an almost instant redistribution of hatred against the rich. The poor have suffered so much at the hands of world markets and the geostrategic machinations of the major powers, and they are treated so shabbily by their own elites, that to redistribute hatred toward those employing high-tech weapons of war, even in the name of the United Nations, will be likely to recur if military enforcement is attempted.

For all the foregoing reasons, the military instrument, even in UN hands, does not contribute to a culture of compliance.

THE CONTRIBUTIONS OF UN ECONOMIC SANCTIONS TO A CULTURE OF COMPLIANCE

The rapid growth in the number of instances in which economic sanctions have been considered or employed in recent years attests to the difficulties of employing military force for enforcement and the lack of imagination in developing other Article 41 enforcement instruments. The Security Council employs economic sanctions to show that it wants to react more strongly than through words alone while finding the military instrument inappropriate. Economic sanctions have several merits: They exert coercive power so that, when coercion is needed, they offer the world community leverage to encourage a noncomplying country to change its behavior. Because they are usually less costly than war in human and financial terms, political support for them can more readily be generated than for military enforcement. And they are morally preferable to military enforcement if they result in less loss of life than war.

On the other hand, they have limited effectiveness and may inflict a heavy toll of suffering on innocent people who already have been victimized by their own governments. As the economic sanctions against Iraq and Haiti in the 1990s have shown, they do contribute to death for many already living on the margins of subsistence.[3] They may be little more than an instrument of the strong (seldom sanctioned) against the weak (often targeted). These valid criticisms of economic sanctions do not, however, lead to the conclusion that their potential has been fully explored. Sanctions might be made more effective by applying them more strictly, by focusing their impact on elites rather than on entire populations, by utilizing a longer-term strategy when sanctioning government officials who have broken the law, and by attempting to focus them on holding *individuals* accountable, such as happens with freezing overseas assets of a ruler such as Raoul Cèdras or in pressing indicted persons to appear before an international tribunal.

The prevailing wisdom has been that economic sanctions, like military operations, can be most effective if they impose heavy costs very quickly. However, in some cases a nearly opposite strategy may have merit.[4] If one is attempting to extradite a handful of individuals who have been indicted for war crimes, for example, economic sanctions may be more likely to influence behavior positively if they seriously inconvenience only a relatively small elite located in the areas shielding an indictee and are maintained, if necessary, for a long time. Such an approach has a better chance of avoiding (1) severely negative consequences for a large number of people and (2) the "rally round the flag" phenomena that *increase* support for the government of the target state. United Nations authorities also could provide assurances that sanctions would immediately be lifted if the targeted misbehavior, such as refusal of indictees to stand trial, would end. The goal, of course, is to affect those wanted for crimes without harming the entire population. Sanctions that freeze assets and stop international travel of elites, for example, are not a way of bringing a society to its knees, but they can bring pressure on elites to quit shielding indictees, to allow extradition of the accused for a fair trial, or to discourage future crimes. For such an approach to succeed, willingness to maintain pinpointed financial measures indefinitely is required. The "smarter" and more precise sanctions can become, the larger the step toward individual accountability and the more powerfully the instrument will nurture a culture of compliance.

THE CONTRIBUTIONS OF UN PEACEKEEPING TO A CULTURE OF COMPLIANCE

No multilateral practice has contributed more to understanding the possibilities and pitfalls of attempting to establish an effective UN civilian police corps than the experience of UN peacekeeping. Occasionally, peacekeepers themselves have engaged in a modest form of enforcement, even while acting under Chapter VI mandates, insofar as peacekeepers attempt to prevent individuals or small groups of people from violating a cease-fire that peacekeepers have been deployed to uphold—even while maintaining overall neutrality toward the primary parties to the cease-fire. Peace-keepers have demonstrated the global legitimacy arising from a force symbolically representing the entire world community and the benefits of a strategic doctrine that deliberately eschews use of military force even by military personnel. Negative factors in peacekeeping experience also have demonstrated the need for better training, for an ombudsman and grievance procedure for local people to bring complaints against UN personnel if their behavior is inappropriate, and for a more reliable form of financing.

Whereas the main deficiency of military enforcement lies in its failure to nurture a culture of compliance and to delegitimize collective violence and national partisanship, a primary deficiency of peacekeeping is its failure to move beyond neutrality when necessary to act against gross violations of the norms of peace. More effective use of UN police can address each of these deficiencies, at least in part.

THE CONTRIBUTIONS OF UN CIVILIAN POLICE TO A CULTURE OF COMPLIANCE

Because the United Nations cannot conduct combat well, because combat is not normatively desirable, and because economic sanctions and peacekeeping do not sufficiently pinpoint individual responsibility for misdeeds or require individuals to be internationally accountable, the international community has good reasons to explore an expanded role for police. A UN police and law-enforcement option, including help in penal and judicial reform, illustrates how a UN operation could nurture a culture of compliance. The activities of UN civilian police are less likely than military forces to produce a political backlash within the UN community. If the law to be enforced is widely agreed on, such as to prohibit "ethnic cleansing," substantial support for UN police enforcement and international court action could be generated. The police/legal option will not be immediately or always effective, of course, but it can frequently be effective in part, and it is better than doing nothing to reaffirm challenged norms. In establishing this enforcement instrument, the UN stance against genocide can clearly exist before, during, and after a crisis. If some persons are indicted for wrongdoing, they stand stigmatized before the world until they have appeared for trial. A UN coalition can continue to ask for investigations and trials until they occur. The police and law-enforcement option also does not threaten legitimate interests of people in the target state, thus decreasing the prospect that a political coalition will arise against UN operations out of empathy for the wider society. All that is asked of the individuals under scrutiny is to obey the law. Although some opposition to UN civilian police may arise within the domestic society in which officials are targets of enforcement, it is likely to be neither as widespread nor as unified as a UN military operation would generate.

Past Experiences with UN Civilian Police

Although the United Nations has experience with civilian police on which to build, its significance is often overlooked. Yet it illustrates how the United Nations could, in partnership with other law-abiding people locally and globally, conduct enforcement effectively at local levels; it also suggests ways in which local enforcement could open the door to an expanding culture of compliance and more effective enforcement of international norms on officials at increasingly high levels of government. A dozen peacekeeping missions have deployed small numbers of police, including operations in Namibia (1,500 officers), Cambodia (3,600), Haiti (900), Mozambique (1,000), and Bosnia (1,700) in recent years. In Cyprus (35 civilian police and 370 internationally and locally recruited civilian staff), the UN Civilian Police (UNCIVPOL) first demonstrated that well-trained civilian police in peacekeeping operations could play a valuable role dampening violence between hostile nationalities (Brown et al. 1984, 160, 166). In Namibia, UN civilian police monitored South African police performance on human rights, defused incidents, and induced local police administrators to perform in a way that made the elections there highly successful (United Nations 1989, 7–8). United Nations police also monitored political gatherings, voter registration and polling stations, and guarded ballot boxes together with local police. The UN police curbed intimidation by local police and collaborated with the UN High Commissioner for Refugees (UNHCR) to repatriate approximately 58,000 refugees (Fortna 1993, 365, 371). In the UN Transition Authority in Cambodia (UNTAC), civilian police were mandated not only to monitor but also to "supervise and control" the police of the existing Cambodian government. This police experience was hampered by poor training, coordination, and readiness for the complexities of their mission. The UN police suffered from difficulties in communication and cooperation among the different nationalities contributing police officers. Lack of training in international contexts, lack of experience in working together, inability to speak Khmer (more detrimental for effective functioning of police than of soldiers), lack of equipment, and lack of knowledge about driving police vehicles all made the CIVPOL operation, in Michael Doyle's (1995) characterization, "nothing short of quixotic" (48). The civilian police were not prepared to carry out their ambitious mandate "to ensure that law and order are maintained effectively and impartially, and that human rights and fundamental freedoms are fully protected."[5]

Nonetheless, the police did give briefings on human rights and responsible policing to Cambodian police. In at least one province, UN police training "had a substantial impact and united all four [political] factions" (Doyle 1995, 48). Although limited in scope, this was a remarkable achievement given the extreme adversarial nature of the factionalism, suggesting what could be done by UN police if they were well prepared for their work and deployed in adequate numbers over a sufficient length of time. The occasionally successful UN efforts in training Cambodian police enabled CIVPOL to develop rapport with local police and officials as well as encourage good communication with appreciative citizens at the local level. This in turn facilitated UN monitoring of human rights. The UN presence "contributed to a general reduction in the most blatant forms of state intimidation" (Doyle 1995, 47–48).

Of special relevance to our search for nurturing enforcement through a culture of compliance, Doyle (1995) reports that the "single largest cause" of UNTAC failures in the realm of public security "lay in the absence of an independent judicial framework" (49). United Nations police possessed the authority to make arrests, and they acquired a building to use as a UN prison, but the UN operation had no acceptable way to prosecute. Without the authority to establish a UN court or to take prisoners to an international tribunal (none existed), no system of legal order could come into being. United Nations police might take prisoners to protect human rights, but ironically neither the prisoner's rights nor the victim's rights could be upheld because there was no adequate judicial system ready to receive them. This deficiency, which member governments did nothing to correct, easily discredits the genuine possibilities that could exist for using UN police more effectively and for deterring future misdeeds. The UNTAC special prosecutor, Mark Plunkett, recommended that any future UN peace-building operation include a "justice package" with carefully prepared agencies for prosecution, policing, and judicial proceedings. These should be established along with a mandate to train local people in the use of these and similar institutions (Plunkett 1994).[6]

To the extent that UNTAC achieved success, it was by communicating directly to the people about the meaning and importance of the election. Lieutenant General Sanderson, UNTAC commander, said that the strategy became to "bypass the propaganda of the Cambodian factions" and forge an "alliance with the Cambodian people" (Doyle 1995, 55). To this end, the United Nations had its own radio broadcasting facilities. Despite continued violence and efforts to intimidate voters, 90 percent of Cambodian citizens turned out for their first national election. After the UN mission left, Cambodians again became vulnerable to intimidation by corrupt military forces, police, and other officials. Much of this backsliding could have been prevented if an adequate UN operation had been available to develop new police and local judicial mechanisms after the election was over.

A remarkable development in reestablishing the police in Somalia further illustrates the enormous unrealized potential that lies in differentiating police and military instrumentalities in enforcement. A revealing study by the International Peace Academy demonstrates that "the military mindset" guiding the UN Unified Task Force (UNITAF) and continuing through the UN Operation in Somalia II (UNOSOM II) exacerbated local factionalism and lawlessness. The UN force committed many errors in what "should have essentially been a civilian operation, in large part because UNOSOM II was led by former and serving officials from the U.S. military establishment and the U.S. National Security Council." Indeed, all international civilian efforts "were subsumed by the military objectives of the U.S. and the UN. . . . By the time these military objectives changed in October 1993, UNOSOM II had become too discredited to be seen as an honest broker in the political process."

For a time at least, the UN "had become too discredited to play an effective role in Somalia" (Jan 1996, 3–4). A more effective, legally stabilizing approach "would have been to help create civilian authorities in areas controlled by a unified clan and endorsed by the faction that served as the military arm of that clan. In this way, indigenous and authoritative clan-based civilian authorities could have been fostered" (Doyle 1995, 49).

After the "can-do" military forces had departed without achieving success in restoring order, and despite the years of brutal fighting among heavily armed Somali clans, an indigenous police force has been gradually reconstituted in some local communities and has helped reestablish the rule of law in parts of Somalia. To institute this process, a political committee composed of members of the more powerful Somali clans met and decided that a security force was needed to deal with refugee problems but that clan military personnel were not appropriate for that task. To create a new local police force, many former members of the Somali police, who had not functioned since 1991, were willing to put clan differences aside to uphold the law for their fellow citizens. In areas where UN personnel coordinated, worked with, and supported the reconstituted police forces, they were the most effective. A crucial factor in the cooperative success was the willingness of the United Nations to let the local community control the police, an approach that was not possible when external military forces, even under the UN umbrella, were present. Initial police functions included traffic and crowd control, patrolling neighborhoods, securing food at distribution centers, and providing security at airports and the major port. Police did not try to carry out missions for which they lacked training, personnel, and equipment, such as demobilizing the militias (Sismanidis 1997, 10–11).

The Peace Academy study emphasized that the Security Council should have developed an overall plan for peace building focused centrally on "how to demilitarize or 'civilianize,' inter-clan politics. . . . Efforts should have concentrated on restarting civilian-led political processes, rather than supporting reconciliation at the faction level" (Jan 1996, 17). Yet this strategy, congenial to a culture of compliance, did not unfold in the prevailing culture of combat that influenced U.S. and UN decisions.

The preceding examples demonstrate both the success of modest policing efforts in which heavy-handed military operations had failed and the ability of UN civilian police to work cooperatively with local community leaders to elicit "consent" for a UN involvement when meaningful consent had previously been lacking.[7] This is an extremely important lesson because the scope and effectiveness of UN enforcement can be increased at acceptable cost *if* a society consents to the UN presence. Without host consent, UN police can operate only at a distance, and they are far less likely to meet with success. In some cases, the United Nations has performed a delicate balancing act in deploying civilians with the consent of national authorities yet tactfully bypassing these authorities to forge an alliance with and to serve the local people, receptive to the protection of international norms administered by their own indigenous police, monitored and encouraged by UN civilian police. Each case of UN police operations in Namibia, Cambodia, Somalia, El Salvador, Bosnia, and

Haiti is different, yet all show the enormous unrealized potential of collaborative enforcement efforts in which UN law-enforcing civilians work in partnership with local and national officials.

The Need for Expanding the Role of UN Civilian Police

The historical experience with UN enforcement suggests four important needs for UN civilian police. First, there is a need to provide an impartial, professional constabulary that could be used when indigenous police forces are severely partial or fundamentally inadequate in maintaining public safety, implementing peace accords, or upholding international norms of peace and human rights.[8] In fulfilling this function, UN police might conduct their own patrols but preferably should work with existing or reconstituted local police. In Brycko, for example, UN police performing joint patrols with local police substantially increased UN capacities to monitor human rights and helped reduce abuses by local police. This success, however, merely illustrates what could have been done in Bosnia, given adequate support, rather than constituting the norm there. The prospect for successful implementation of the Dayton Accords would almost certainly have looked far brighter if well-prepared UN police had been provided in adequate numbers immediately following the signing of the agreement.

Second, in societies with a complete breakdown of law and order, UN personnel are needed not only to conduct joint patrols but also to develop, organize, and reconstitute indigenous police forces from the ground up. Of course, this task, which requires quite different talents than patrolling, should be done in concert with local citizens and authorities. For this purpose, UN personnel should help screen, train, equip, monitor, and communicate with local police as well as serve as a feedback channel or complaint mechanism for citizens. United Nations civilian police would also be needed subsequently to monitor the practice of local police as the latter gradually establish a desirable code of conduct and external monitoring can be phased out. The UN experience in Namibia, Cambodia, El Salvador, and Haiti has demonstrated that UN civilian police trainers are invaluable for educating local police units that have in the past lacked respect for human rights.

Training by UN police can establish important communication with local officials and citizens, inform the latter of procedures to protect their rights as the United Nations phases out its presence, and establish a reputation to encourage governments in the future to grant consent for a UN police presence even though they might not give consent for a UN military presence (Kosovo). These activities, if sensitively carried out, can enable the United Nations to establish appropriate influence in war-torn societies or to maintain positive roles in societies where peace building is under way but external monitoring is still needed. Training by the United Nations "can ensure that a UN operation leaves institutions behind that, with the proper domestic and international support, help carry forward a commitment to impartial justice and human rights" (Doyle 1995, 49).

Third, UN police are needed to gather information for possible criminal prosecutions and to assist the work of international tribunals or truth commissions. United Nations personnel could conduct specialized investigations, guard prisoners, monitor prison administration, and provide witness-protection programs. The need to assist the international criminal tribunals was demonstrated in the UN court in Arusha, Tanzania, where a Dutch policeman needed protection to conduct a forensic investigation to provide evidence for the trial of a Hutu militia leader accused of genocide in 1994.[9] If UN police were available to conduct systematic investigations and maintain accurate records, the prospects of indictments and arrest warrants might deter some misdeeds because there is no statute of limitation for those accused of war crimes, even when there is no immediate prospect of bringing the accused to trial (Meron 1993, 122–35). Most prosecution witnesses giving evidence to the UN tribunal in Arusha have done so at great risk of being targeted for revenge.[10] United Nations civilian police are urgently needed to safeguard the lives of prosecution witnesses if the international community is to take seriously the task of holding individuals accountable to international law.

A fourth need is to establish a UN police capability and appropriate strategy to enforce, insofar as possible, the arrest warrants and decisions of the ad hoc International Criminal Tribunals for the former Yugoslavia and Rwanda and of a permanent international criminal court as soon as one is established. Failure to make more serious efforts to bring indictees to trial hurts the credibility of the International Criminal Tribunal, undermines the possibility that trials might clear a path for later reconciliation between adversaries, and weakens the prospect that the entire process will deter future lawbreakers because of widespread knowledge that the international community will act against war crimes.

The Need for a Permanent UN Police Force

A careful study of past UN peacekeeping and enforcement experience reveals a profound need for a *permanent* UN civilian police force that is highly educated, well trained to perform a wide variety of diverse tasks, well integrated and disciplined, well commanded, multinational, individually recruited from among people of all nationalities who may volunteer for UN duty, immediately available for deployment, and responsive only to the United Nations rather than to possibly confusing signals from national capitals.[11]

Such a force has many advantages. It could be deployed when needed without arousing the hesitations that now arise in member states because they are reluctant to mandate UN activity that would place units of their own military forces in risky situations.[12] It could also be more skilled in relating to local populations in difficult and confusing humanitarian emergencies, with sensitivity to local culture and without inflaming national passions in the target state or among contributors to UN forces. It could be deployed in larger numbers, addressing the disadvantage that UN police operations have never enjoyed the larger number of forces that are usually "regarded as indispensable to traditional law enforcement" (Brown et al. 1984, 1). The excellent study by the Ministry of Foreign Affairs and the Ministry of National Defense of the Canadian Government (1995), *Towards a Rapid Reaction Capability for the United Nations,* notes that the "most obvious advantage of a permanent, standing UN civilian police unit is reliability." With such a force, the United Nations would not be forced "to await the lengthy domestic processes of each Member State before a critical mass of police forces is assembled" (Government of Canada 1995, 59). Strikingly, the Canadian study concluded that "a UN rapid-reaction capability can be truly reliable only if it no longer depends on Member States of the UN for the supply of personnel for peace operations. If the UN is to build a rapid-reaction capability which is fully reliable, the challenge in years ahead will be to develop its own personnel, independent of state authority."[13] Other observers have similarly concluded that only through the development and training of the United Nations' own civilian police can a solution be found (Brown et al. 1984, 59).

Perhaps most important, UN police open the door to turning an "us-them" enforcement relationship associated with external military occupation into an "us-us" relationship of police on the ground, helping local communities sort out their problems while cultivating a culture of compliance with international norms of peace and human rights. This symbolic and real transformation of the enforcement relationship constitutes one of the United Nations' strongest assets and least utilized potential strengths. To capitalize on this strength, the United Nations should prepare to offer war-torn societies a judicial package that includes not only the United Nations' own permanent civilian police and police trainers but also personnel skilled in establishing professional penal and judicial systems. Transforming the enforcement relationship is a necessary condition for constructing a culture of compliance.

Making UN Peacekeeping Forces More Effective

Because of their special training and professionalism, availability, and willingness to enter high-risk situations, UN civilian police could also enable traditional and expanded peacekeeping, blended with some Chapter VII enforcement measures, to become far more effective. Increased effectiveness would grow not only from the capacity to deploy a well-trained *police* force more quickly when needed. If UN civilian police could help local police maintain order in war-torn societies, they would also enable *peacekeeping* operations to avoid some of the pitfalls that they have faced with domestic lawlessness. The presence of civilian police might also enable the United Nations to reduce the heavy-handedness that occurs when it farms out enforcement duties to great powers. A good UN police force would add much needed UN capacity in the domain of conflict transformation and peace building, along the lines suggested by John Paul Lederach (1995) and others (Fetherston 1994; Fetherston and Parkin 1997; Peck 1998). Police can perform more tasks than they have been asked in the past to carry out, including some of the tasks that peacekeepers now undertake. Although peacekeepers are more heavily armed than police, this capacity to employ more violence is not the most significant difference between them. As Brian Urquhart (1991) has noted, "The principle of nonviolence sets the peace-keeping forces above the conflict they are dealing with; violation of the principle almost invariably leads to the peacekeepers becoming part of the conflict and therefore part of the problem" (7). This principle suggests that police, who ideally are trained to operate by the same principle, might be even more successful than military personnel retrained for peacekeeping, especially when carrying out functions that are obviously useful to local people. A UN police force might induce a government to give consent to UN police operations even when it would be unwilling to admit UN military personnel.

Arresting Indictees and Deterring War Crimes

A standing UN police force is also needed to be constantly prepared to assist in arresting indictees wherever UN police gain entrance to a society in which alleged international criminals reside or whenever indictees lose the shielding effect of a pro-criminal governing sanctuary. Once the Security Council has authorized police enforcement and an international tribunal has prepared an indictment and authorized an arrest, any persons who oppose police efforts could be considered to be obstructing the Security Council's legally binding mandate and thus also be considered to be committing crimes against the peace. United Nations civilians could also help educate governments and local police about the international obligation for individuals to honor the prohibition of genocide and the other norms of peace. The Security Council could require all military organizations throughout the world to instruct their soldiers in the obligation not to commit war crimes.

Even when a society refuses a UN presence, UN police can play an important role from a distance. In such cases, the international community should gather information to use in prosecuting people after the crisis has passed. Eventually, with foreknowledge of serious investigative police work, some people would be deterred from misdeeds. With no statute of limitations for war crimes, indictees would be minimally penalized even if not tried. Still others might later face trials, especially as political tides change in countries shielding alleged war criminals or indictees, as has happened in Cambodia, Rwanda, and to a lesser degree Croatia. In cases in which the UN police might attempt to arrest indicted persons, these actions communicate that the entire society is *not* being targeted, a difference that is obscured by military action and clarified by police enforcement. The police emphasis recognizes the reality of civil society even in the state where arrests are warranted. Thus, the beneficiaries of arrest warrants include even the local people living in a war-torn society where only the indicted may be targeted for arrest.

Where UN police can enter a war-torn country, they can offer a society some positive inducements, such as social stability and multiethnic integration, more effectively than military agents of enforcement. This is important for establishing the consent of the war-torn society to a UN presence. United Nations civilian police might be invited into a society by government officials (Rwanda), by all parties to a civil conflict (Cambodia), by factional leaders (Somalia), or by democratically elected but ousted officials (Haiti). In some cases, even citizens' groups suffering gross violations of human rights might request a UN police monitoring presence (Kosovo). In such cases, the government might reluctantly consent to the monitoring, in part to demonstrate its self-proclaimed innocence. In other cases, the UN Security Council might mandate monitoring where possible even without the consent of national authorities. The possibility that pressure for UN police monitoring might be difficult to resist could make rulers reluctant to commit crimes or to refuse a UN presence, as has happened in some requests for a UN presence to confirm the fairness of elections. Although marginal, such a potential influence could be sufficient to avert crimes in some cases. It would be more difficult for a reluctant government to oppose the introduction of UN police observers than to oppose the introduction of UN military personnel because by opposing a UN police presence one seems to be condoning license to commit crimes. Deploying what usually are unarmed police monitors would also produce less political volatility in local communities than sending in UN military units.

To enhance nonmilitary enforcement, it is imperative to establish the international criminal court now under discussion within the UN system. Only a permanent court can signal that *all* alleged crimes, committed by people of *any* nationality, acting at *any* time in the future, will be under scrutiny. Anything less than a permanent, independent court and investigative capacity will give the impression that the international community wants only victor's justice or intends to penalize only a particular people acting in a specific conflict. This will not have the deterring effect needed to nurture a culture of compliance. On the other hand, if a permanent international criminal court is established and a UN prosecutor brings indictments against officials, regardless of nationality, because of alleged violations of the laws against genocide or aggression, indictees could face some penalties, such as constraint on travel and foreign interactions, for the rest of their lives if they refuse to stand trial. Confession within a certain length of time could mitigate those penalties and possibly more severe punishment if convicted. The prospect that lower-level persons may implicate higher officials can aid investigations and, over time, increase pressure for good behavior.[14] Officials would begin to have a vested interest in maintaining a meritorious image, even if their government is not democratic, because of the prospect that they could face lifetime penalties, which would be irritating if not more seriously damaging, unless they faced trial once they had been indicted. The modest pretrial and preconviction penalties suggested here would presumably not matter to some leaders, but they could make a difference to others. For those not in leadership positions, the prospects for an embarrassing investigation could motivate them to act more cautiously simply to avoid any possibility that an enforcement process could eventually come home to haunt them because they had endorsed illegal killing. Once some officials refuse to commit such misdeeds, others are put on notice that their behavior will stand out more clearly as normatively deficient if they violate norms that others chose to respect. The keys to this dynamic process are a permanent international criminal court with general jurisdiction and permanent UN police powers impartially administered.[15]

Deterrence is far from certain in specific cases, of course, but eventually the deterring instruments could be quite strong. Those indicted could face a lifelong stigma for refusing to stand trial, lifelong freezing of all overseas assets, lifelong inability to travel and to have normal interactions with organizations located outside a shielding society, and lifelong fear that the shielding society may lose interest in forever shielding an indictee from a fair trial, especially at continuing cost to the shielding group. If the international community would do its utmost to make clear that penalties would be imposed and would be continued throughout the lifetime of the lawbreaker and any accomplices shielding indictees from a fair international trial, the deterring impact could be significant in the long run.[16]

HOLDING INDIVIDUALS ACCOUNTABLE: A PROBLEM FOR COLLECTIVE SECURITY

Studies of intergroup hostilities show that genocide occurs because people attribute collective guilt to an outgroup considered to be evil or inferior or inhuman. Indeed, most of the violent ideologies of the twentieth century "are chiefly about the redistribution of hatred," channeling it toward a collective identity. "Fascism, Nazism, nationalism, communism, and religious fundamentalism are about the [collective] punishment of those who are to blame" (du Preez 1994, 123). Collective security responses using military instruments to oppose another society usually do not encourage the dismantling of such hostility or bigotry. On the contrary, enforcement based on military instruments tends to reinforce collective hysteria. Collective security operations, even when in the form of UN Chapter VII military enforcement, are far less able than UN police enforcement to dampen people's impulses in a targeted society to project hostility on the enforcer. Collective security in practice seems to impose collective guilt on the targeted society and reinforces counterhostility.[17] Police responses, in contrast, can be focused on individual wrongdoers. Unlike collective security military action, the refusal of police to attack an entire nationality or group identity calls into question the human impulses underpinning collective violence and genocidal impulses, thus making rationales for mass killing less tenable and genocidal acts less likely.

Perhaps the most important contribution of UN civilian police is to help the international community turn the corner toward making *individuals* the focus for international responsibility. In assigning individual accountability for crimes, new opportunities arise for achieving enforcement within a culture of compliance. Tension reduction is far more likely if the enforcer seeks to differentiate individual wrongdoers from the rest of a society and if the rest are encouraged to differentiate themselves from the wrongdoers. The need to enforce law on individuals demands the proper instrument to do it: UN civilian police. All other instrumentalities presently at the disposal of the United Nations—collective security enforcement through military means, peacekeeping, and general economic sanctions—are severely limited in their ability to enforce law on individuals. Their most justifiable function today may be to provide incentives to force reluctant parties to let the proposed UN police do their work. Indeed, "the time has come to rethink collective security within the UN setting, associating UN uses of force with ideas of policing and reconciliation, not as a species of war-making" (Falk 1995, 248).

For those raising legitimate questions about whether *any* UN interventionary policies are justifiable at all,[18] it is relevant to note that, in the absence of new efforts to employ police in holding individuals accountable to the law, the international system will continue to rely on collective security mechanisms in which the militarily most powerful will dominate the rest. Enforcement of norms will be from the top down and carried out by the strong against the weak. These mechanisms will, to the degree possible, probably maintain the existing international code of conduct with all its present unreliability and inequity. Moving toward a larger role for police enforcement can transform not only conflict formations but also the international system from within and from below, if the proposed role for UN civilian police is wisely implemented, with transnational citizens' groups, intergovernmental organizations and UN agencies, and progressive states working together. The international community could discover that what civilian police lack in their incapacity to overpower a hostile military force they more than make up for normatively because their positive inability to inflict collective violence on others encourages them to build trust within societies where they operate, to transform the code of international conduct within a culture of compliance, and to domesticate international relations.[19]

STRENGTHENING A CULTURE OF COMPLIANCE IN THE MIDST OF A CULTURE OF COMBAT

Close scrutiny of the functions already performed by UN civilian police and the temporary war crimes tribunals confirms that progress in holding individuals accountable to international law can begin within the existing configuration of military power, although further progress would be enhanced by gradually reducing the role of military power. Even while the culture of military enforcement exists, legal processes taking root in a culture of compliance need not be moribund. Just as the Nuremberg and Tokyo war crimes precedents, although flawed as victors' justice, were better than no precedents at all, so some police enforcement, in some conflicts, with some indictments and trials, is likely to be more helpful than none at all.

The opportunity now exists for progressive governments, citizens' groups, and UN agencies to launch a comprehensive approach to enforcing the norms of peace by establishing a highly professional, permanent civilian police capability and impartial judicial proceedings. Although no panacea, civilian police would enable a partnership between the United Nations and victimized peoples at precisely the point at which public security and peace are most needed and at which UN capacities are best able to make an enforcement contribution, using instruments that admirably fit its highest moral aim of respect for all human life. This approach realistically recognizes both the United Nations' unlimited duty to keep peace and its limited yet politically vital capacity to contribute to peace and security while nurturing a broader culture of compliance within international law. The humanitarian crises of the past decade and the echoes of victims' voices cry out for ushering in this promising way of deterring individuals from unconscionable misdeeds and serving peoples' legitimate security needs.

NOTES

1. In this usage, "neutrality" and "impartiality" may sharply diverge. For example, if almost all illegal acts are committed by one party in a two-sided conflict, a neutral observer who does nothing to stop illegalities fails to uphold the law with impartiality. Such an observer shows partiality for the wrongdoer and against the victim.

2. The Iraqi aggression in Kuwait and the UN response constitute an exceptional case.

3. For insightful analysis of these issues, see Eland (1995), Lopez and Cortright (1995), and Weiss et al. (1997).

4. For a discussion of the determinants of success, see U.S. General Accounting Office (1993).

5. See the Report of the Secretary-General, February 19, 1992, S/23613, para. 124.

6. See Plunkett (1994), quoted in Doyle (1995, 49).

7. Similarly, in El Salvador, both the government and the guerrilla forces Frente Farabundo Marti de Liberacion Nacional (FMLN) were extremely skeptical about the prospects for reconstituting a police force that either side would find acceptable. Yet they expressed a hesitant willingness to try the idea, thus giving their reluctant consent for the UN experiment. The program to completely reconstitute the police proved surprisingly successful, and within two years the public attitude toward police was radically transformed, and respect for human rights dramatically improved. See Costa (1995) and Montgomery (1995).

8. The need for expanded UN police functions is thoroughly documented by Call and Barnett (1997).

9. Reuters report from Arusha, Tanzania, February 1997.

10. A woman and her entire family were killed in early January before she was scheduled to testify against a former town mayor on trial for the massacre of 2,000 people in 1994 (Hrvoje Hranjski, Associated Press, report from Arusha, Tanzania, January 19, 1997).

11. For an excellent discussion of the need for a permanent UN police force specifically dedicated to enforcing the prohibition of genocide, see Mendlovitz and Fousek (1996). For possible functions of a police force, see Chopra (1996, 355).

12. Officials of the United States have used strong rhetoric advocating an international police force to arrest indicted war criminals. General John Shalikashvili, chairman of the joint chiefs of staff, has discussed the idea with Canadian and European allies (Reuters report from Washington, January 18, 1997). Although allied governments reportedly have agreed that such a force is needed, they could not agree on who should lead it or participate in it (Lekic

1997). This hesitation to employ police could be more easily addressed if a UN police force were readily available.

13. Even though the logic of the Canadian study calls for the establishment of a standing UN police force, the study falls short of recommending it at this time because of political and financial problems (Government of Canada 1995, 59–60).

14. The stunning consequences of this dynamic have been demonstrated in 1996–1997 in the proceedings of the South African truth commission.

15. The influence and degree of success resulting from this type of police and law enforcement depend on how strongly a would-be lawbreaker wants to violate the norms of peace and what the international community asks of people seeking to avoid indictment, pretrial irritants, and possible arrest. To ask people to forgo genocide is a minimal expectation.

16. Of course, the United Nations would be asking merely for a fair trial as a condition for ending secondary penalties, not for an admission of guilt.

17. To be sure, if and when military enforcement does occur, a UN collective decision to authorize it provides greater legitimacy than unilateral national military action, but UN endorsement is far from ideal, as Desert Storm has demonstrated.

18. These are discussed in Falk (1995).

19. Of course, police are far from a panacea, as evidence of police corruption, victimization, and abuse of power in almost every land underscores. The most stringent checks and watchdog roles would need to accompany the creation of any permanent police force. The potential problems remind us that the noncoercive elements of a culture of compliance and enforcement are also essential and preferable to coercive enforcement, necessary though the latter sometimes may be.

15

The Underside of Peace: Reflections on Aum Shinrikyo

Robert Jay Lifton

The most extreme perversion of peace is the practice of genocide and mass killing. These practices become increasingly possible as the world continues to develop weapons of mass destruction and encourages some of its people to find comfort in apocalyptic narratives. I find this malignant combination in my ongoing explorations of Aum Shinrikyo—the cult movement originating in Japan committed to poisoning vast numbers of people in an attempt to accelerate the destruction of the world. By studying Aum Shinrikyo through a psychohistorical lens, my work aims to uncover the character of apocalyptic violence and to penetrate the profound mystery that lies underneath impulses toward mass killing. In this chapter, I provide an early statement of themes that I have encountered with Aum Shinrikyo. The chapter must be read, then, as the opening of a type of exploration rather than a completed research project.

In my work, I have a model or paradigm of issues of death and death equivalents, on the one hand, and of a larger human connectedness, or the symbolization of immortality, on the other. The latter principle is necessary to a scientific psychology and should not be a concern of only theologians and philosophers. I think that one really needs such a death-centered and life-continuity-centered model or paradigm to even touch these apocalyptic issues, especially the issue of apocalyptic violence. One has to take into account the worldwide reverberations of any significant event, so that collective acts of killing have ramifications throughout the world system within which we all live. Such was the case of Timothy McVeigh's bombing of the federal building in Oklahoma City. It was true, certainly and chillingly, of the murder of Yitzhak Rabin in Israel. It is also true of Aum Shinrikyo and its attempt to kill very large numbers of people with sarin gas. Thus, our own perceptions of collective death—and indeed of our individual death—are becoming increasingly related to the world system.

Aum Shinrikyo connects with my most morbid preoccupations, starting with Chinese thought reform and ideological totalism, with the psychology of genocide, and also with a certain kind of proteanism. It embraces proteanism both in a perverse way—proteanism gone berserk, so to speak—and in its fundamentalist and violent antagonism to constructive forms of protean exploration. Aum also relates to my work with Nazi doctors and the whole principle of killing to heal. One cannot understand large-scale killing of any kind, or the attempt at large-scale killing, without positing the killer's claim to virtue and, in this case, spiritual elevation by means of killing.

Let me mention a few details about what Aum members did. They released their sarin gas on five different Tokyo subway trains—the trains all converging on the most populated downtown area and the seat of the national Japanese government. Twelve people were killed and 5,000 injured. Before that there had been trial runs: in 1993 in Australia (where gas was apparently released in an isolated area) and in 1994 in Matsumoto, a Japanese city, where a sarin gas release killed seven people and injured 200.

More followed the March 20, 1995, incident. On May 5, they deposited plastic bags containing cyanide gas in Shinjuku Station (also in Tokyo) at a shopping mall, where only the alertness of a few station attendants prevented a large number of deaths. This incident sparked a series of "copycat" releases of gas in different subway stations and department stores, some of which are believed to be done by Aum members. In addition, Aum members were definitely responsible for an attempt at assassinating the head of the National Police Agency on March 30 and for sending a parcel bomb to Tokyo City Hall on May 16.

However, Aum had ambitions of much greater violence, associated with a vision of the end of the world. Their extensive stockpiles of sarin gas were such that, had the March 20 operation been conducted more efficiently, they could have killed thousands or even hundreds of thousands of people. They were also developing deadly biological weapons, notably anthrax and *Botulinus bacilli*. In addition, they were making active inquiries, especially in Russia, about uranium technology and possibilities for purchasing or building nuclear weapons. Aum engaged in a number of individual murders, mostly by strangulation, of recalcitrant members who, for one reason or another, opposed the cult. All this was preliminary to a plan, fortunately never realized, for a November release of enormous amounts of sarin gas from helicopters as a means of bringing about World War III, which in turn would be a path to Armageddon. To accomplish all this, Aum had branches not only throughout Japan but also in such cities as Moscow (there were reported to be 30,000 Russian members, as opposed to only 10,000 Japanese), Bonn, Sri Lanka, and New York.

The question that haunts this work, even in its early stages, is this: What factors brought about the crossing of a terrible threshold from merely *anticipating* the end of the world to engaging in large-scale violence aimed at *bringing about* that world ending? Aum is not just some arcane or distant cult from an alien society but rather a manifestation of precisely the kind of issues that haunt us in our everyday lives. Indeed, at the heart of the issues addressed in this chapter is this end-of-the-world expectation and its relationship to the end, or death, or envisioned rebirth, of the individual self.

Aum Shinrikyo follows a profile of extreme religious and political cults in the United States, a profile that has to do with issues of ideological totalism. I have tried to lay out such issues in earlier work (Lifton 1961, 1987). I will not go into them now in any detail, except to mention two of the basic characteristics of ideological totalism. The first is that of total *milieu control*—control of all information exchange and imagery in an environment that seeks to extend itself to internal controls of every kind. The second is the ultimate and most significant dimension of ideological totalism, the *dispensing of existence*, the presumption of the right to decide who has the right to exist and who does not. Sometimes this last dimension is symbolic in terms of recognition or nonrecognition, and sometimes it is literal in terms of individual or mass murder, as we saw with Aum.

The extremity of guru worship was crucial here in developing Aum's particular expressions of milieu control and the dispensing of existence. Asahara, the cult leader, carried the idea of guru worship to a new degree. His guruism is a more complex and puzzling phenomenon than meets the eye. It is true that guruism is more culturally accepted in East Asian societies—especially in the esoteric Buddhism that Asahara drew on—as compared to the United States. However, there is something very extreme and bizarre and unlimited in Aum's guruism. For example, guru worship reached such heights that it extended to creating or claiming to create actual connections to the brain waves of Asahara through technological attachments. It was Asahara's person and presence that had held his disciples, according to former Aum members whom I interviewed. He offered his disciples, as must always be the case, immortality, transcendence. Now, he was not exactly a beautiful-looking man by most standards, as many Japanese pointed out to me. Somehow, in the way he conducted religious practices, especially his yoga and his version of Buddhism, he could inspire a sense of immortality and transcendence in what they considered to be genuinely mystical experiences. So we cannot just dismiss Asahara or Aum as psychopathic, although indeed psychopathic he and it did become.

In terms of the guru's relation to violence, Asahara understood *poa*, or killing as a way to elevate the status of the victim. *Poa* is a practice of tantric Buddhism, enabling the dying to enhance their journey to Buddhahood or at least achieve a higher and more desirable form of reincarnation. It is really a version of what you find in most premodern cultures—the individual soul merging with the collective soul, transforming death into a relationship with immortality. But in Asahara's and Aum's hands, *poa* became killing enemies; murder was justified in the name of *poa*. They killed people whom they considered their enemies (e.g., a lawyer and his family), and sometimes they *poa* recalcitrant members. The person who is killed by spiritually advanced beings is elevated into immortality, and the person who does the killing gains further spiritually by enhancing the immortality of the victim. So you never actually kill anyone; rather, you offer your victim *poa,* or killing in the name of healing.

Such a theory of killing reminds me of my work with Nazi doctors, who also killed in the name of healing. The difference is that the Nazis were trying to heal the Nordic race by killing Jews, who were an "infection," as well as Gypsies and some other groups, but mainly Jews, which had to be extirpated. But with *poa,* you are not really killing, you are elevating the victims. You are not healing your own group, as the Nazis were doing, but rather healing the victims themselves. The Nazis did not claim that they were healing Jews by killing them. They were healing the Nordic race because the Jews were evil and subversive to Nordic power and Nordic existence or survival. In *poa* you devictimize the victim.

One person's cult is another's religion. There is no clear scientific distinction between them. In my work, I consider the behavior of a "new religion" to be cultlike when it displays three particular characteristics. First, there is the shift from the worship of spiritual ideals into the worship of the guru figure, as in Aum with the headsets that ostensibly connected the listener to the brain waves of Asahara. Second, there is the combination of genuine spiritual search from below—on the part of ordinary disciples—and extreme exploitation—economic and sexual—from above, mostly on the part of the guru himself. Third, there are thought-reforms, or brainwashing-like methods, actively employed. In Aum these methods included total immersion in the guru's words and images, along with intense exercises combining extreme isolation and a variety of pressures and threats that manipulate guilt, shame, and fear having to do with the threat of inner death as opposed to the promise of immortality.

Aum Shinrikyo is not just a new religion in Japan but what is sometimes called a "new-new religion," a term meaning that it has been around not for 100 or 200 years but rather since 1970. Significantly, these new-new religions tend to emphasize techniques directed less toward responsible social behavior than toward the disciplines of personal salvation. In the case of Aum, the focus was on what was called *gedatsu,* or emancipation, and *satori,* or illumination, to the exclusion of concerns about the well-being of the tainted masses outside the cult. These practices were bound up not only with primal issues of life and death but also with the pervasive end-of-the-world theme that so dominated Aum's existence.

Shoko Asahara came early to his apocalyptic preoccupations. The son of a poor *tatami* mat maker, resentful at being sent as a child to a school for the blind (while his vision was considerably impaired, he has always had a certain amount of sight), he was always aggressive and ambitious in his failures. As a young man, he was arrested on two occasions, once for causing physical injury and once for selling fake Chinese medicines.

His apocalyptic plunge took many forms. His focus on yoga in creating Aum in the mid-1980s, when he was about thirty years old, involved what he called the "awakening of mystical *kundalini,*" or divine energy, thereby carrying yoga to a transcendent level. More specific to his world-ending vision was his particular image of

Shambala (as appropriated by Asahara for his own purposes), derived from Hinduism and early Buddhism and influenced by Islam. *Shambala* was seen as a mysterious valley somewhere in northeastern Asia and as a symbol of apocalyptic struggle, with some resemblance to Armageddon. Asahara was to report a vision he had in 1985 in which he was called upon by Shiva, the Hindu god, to become "the God of light who leads the armies of the gods" in a struggle of light against darkness. *Shambala* stood for an ideal utopian community of perfect virtue that would emerge from the apocalyptic struggle. Asahara also embraced a pre–World War II Japanese visionary who plumbed "ultra-ancient history" for a version of Armageddon, followed by the emergence of a Japanese spiritual leader.

In addition to all these Eastern influences, Asahara went on to encompass Western Christian traditions of the end of the world. He fiercely embraced the Book of Revelation, which he connected with his earlier vision of Shiva, and came to see himself as the Christ. He also immersed himself in the writings of Nostradamus, the early sixteenth-century French physician-mystic who predicted that the world would end in the year 2000 and added something that could be interpreted as a suggestion that the post-Armageddon spiritual leader would come from the East. Thus, for Asahara and Aum, Armageddon became something of a generic term that included all these religious images of the end of the world as well as the imagery of ultimate weaponry in a large-scale war. They all became blended.

In discussing these issues with an articulate, strongly anti-Aum lawyer, I was told that the lawyer too believed in Armageddon, "just like Asahara." Given his antipathy to Aum, I was surprised by the remark and said, "Well, doesn't Asahara have a whole religious structure?" He answered, "Oh yes, but those are just words. Look, these missiles could explode on all of us." What he was saying was that the nuclear culture in which we all grow up creates an Armageddon-like expectation or sets of images in all of us that can be seized upon by a person with the right "words." Thus, Asahara, on behalf of world ending, became an avatar of Shiva, a Jesus figure from the Book of Revelation, a Nostradamus-imagined savior, and a Japanese-imagined savior as well. I believe that he carried an impulse toward ending the world further than anyone else has, creating a kind of calendar of Armageddon that seemed to have a combination of Herman Kahn (remember Herman Kahn's scenarios of how many people would be killed in a nuclear Armageddon) and the atomic scientist's clock (ticking away toward Armageddon). Thus, at a certain point he would say, "If we mobilize enough true believers, we will hold off Armageddon." Then later he would say, as former disciples recalled during our interviews, "No, things are much worse in the world. There is no possibility of holding off Armageddon. It is already impossible to limit the victims to less than one-fourth of the population of the world." He said the latter in 1989. Later he shifted to the idea that everyone in the world would be killed except a tiny remnant of Aum Shinrikyo people who would respiritualize the world.

He was obsessed with nuclear annihilation. One of the places (in the Tokyo subway) where the gas was planted was a very deep subterranean area, which he had described as the best nuclear shelter available in Japan. He also spoke of building the perfect nuclear shelter for his group. He also insisted that Armageddon could be survived only by carrying out Aum's spiritual practices—though he also urged his disciples to be prepared for death at any time.

What we need to realize, psychologically, is that what happens in a man such as Asahara is that self and world become combined. Instead of the self becoming, so to speak, a part of the world, the world becomes an aspect of the self. The projection of Armageddon, buttressed by various forms of ideology, becomes, in a psychological sense, a reading of the self, a projection of the self and an assertion of the self, which contains the world. One cannot understand the ebbs and flows and violent explosions of Aum behavior or the decisions made without recognizing the state of the guru's self. A totalistic group process develops, but it is the guru who takes the group into the Armageddon-like series of events.

Another unique feature of Aum Shinrikyo was its involvement of professionals, which reminded me very much of my work with Nazi doctors. Aum had a kind of shadow government in which they had a ministry of health, a ministry of science, and a ministry of construction. All this had a certain absurdity, of course, but they took it seriously; they had trained scientists, physicians, builders, and architects, all of whom were involved in these so-called ministries. There is a mystery among many Japanese about how they could attract well-educated people, and there is no simple answer. When I looked into it initially, people said to me, "Oh these people didn't believe. They're just given a lot of money and opportunities to practice their craft. They could do medical research or certain things in science and be paid for it better than they could otherwise." However, it was not that simple. In some cases, people left promising positions in the society—although it was also true that many of the professionals were floundering and confused before joining Aum. But, as in the case of Nazi doctors, these people were drawn to the Aum message.

They were, like all Aum members, critical of existing Japanese society. Aum mounted a powerful critique of Japanese materialism, of the corrupt consumer society, of the authoritarian educational system and the lockstep requirements for moving up the ladder—and, above all, of the absence of a sense of meaning. I would say that Aum tapped an immortality hunger, or a hunger for meaning and for larger human connectedness. Aum could provide for some a believable sense of immortality, and that could be decisive. We find similar patterns in American society and in relation to cult behavior. But the hunger may be especially great in contemporary Japan—a society that has recently been undergoing extraordinary tensions: the earthquake in Kobe, the Hiroshima and World War II commemoration, mass media confusions, and Aum Shinrikyo itself—all of these in the context of significant economic recession.

To deepen our appreciation for the inner psychological dynamics of Aum, let me relate a three-and-a-half-hour encounter with a former Aum member. He is a university-educated young man in his early thirties who was a practitioner of several of the arts but had received some setbacks in his career and was floundering. He had always been spiritually inclined, was unsure about his future, and was very critical of the existing Japanese society. He encountered Aum at a public ceremony, was deeply drawn to it, and underwent a total immersion. He describes intense exercises to overcome the "the polluted data" of the outside world (computer language is frequently used in this way by Aum). He and others would repeat endlessly words written or spoken by Asahara, sometimes having them at the same time flashed visually before him even as they were being spoken into his earphones. These and related exercises, some of them drawn from esoteric Buddhism, had to be repeated in accordance with one's age: If under twenty, 300 times, if between twenty and thirty, 500 times; if between thirty and forty, 700 times; if over forty, 1,000 times—the idea being that the older one is, the more severe the pollution. In the process, he had a number of mystical experiences in which he saw magnificent images and bright lights, these in turn resonating with an earlier pre-Aum mystical experience while acting in a play. Thus, one can speak of a thought-reform-like process, but there was also, for him and many others, opportunities for experiences of transcendence, of high states and a sense that one was part of something in the way of cosmic meaning. Aum told him that one does not choose the means of salvation: It is given to you. He said that he had some doubts about Aum, especially concerning their insistence upon the conspiratorial manipulations of the Freemasons, as endangering the whole world and threatening to bring about Armageddon. However, he remained intensely bound to the group because "I needed Aum." It gave him the kind of spiritual anchor he had sought. He was admitted into an "Armageddon seminar," as it was called. Intensely and for many hours a day, they would see the effects of all sorts of weapons. They had videotapes from all over the world. These videotapes consisted of wars everywhere, and they were told that the next war and the next set of weapons would be much worse. That, of course, would be Armageddon. That Armageddon seminar intensified this disciple's desire—indeed, hunger—for Armageddon. "I wanted to destroy this world," he said, "to make a new world." He came to believe more in Asahara through the Armageddon seminar because only Asahara could help save him and the other followers. You could be best saved by Asahara by renouncing the world and becoming an Aum monk (or *shukke*), which he did. If that was not possible, the next best thing was to acquire the brainwave headgear, which was extremely expensive if you were not a monk (Aum charged exorbitantly for its offerings) and which was said to give you the most desired kind of contact with Asahara from the outside, so to speak.

They were told to train themselves to become supermen. That was part of the message from the Armageddon seminar and from Aum more generally. With the release of gas, there was some confusion in this disciple's mind and in many disciples' minds because most Aum members knew nothing about what was going on (only a small group of trusted top disciples had full knowledge of weapons stockpiling and Aum violence). As to who released the gas, they did not know. The Aum Shinrikyo story, which was vague but put forward, was that it was released by the United States—or the Japanese government—in any case through the machinations of the Freemasons. He did not know whether to believe that. But what he felt was only excitement: "I didn't ask who did it. . . . I didn't care who did it. . . . This was Armageddon. . . . We're going to be the savior of the world!" In retrospect, he compared it to "the feeling of being a star." He was telling me that the only thing that mattered was that the much-yearned-for world ending was occurring.

However, after that he began to have doubts. Media reports, especially those including confessions of high-ranking Aum members, eventually convinced him that it was Aum Shinrikyo that had released the gas. It took him a few months to make his way out of Aum, with the help of media people whom he had met. But for those interim months after the sarin incident, he had a double mind-set. He served as a spokesman to the media, putting forth the official Aum explanation that others had done it, while at the same time thinking that there was "something fake" about this explanation and about Aum Shinrikyo in general. While he now has no doubt about Aum's responsibility for the event and other violence, he still struggles with his own earlier attraction to Asahara and plunge into Aum mysticism.

At the end of our talk, I asked him why he thought Aum Shinrikyo had released the gas and why Asahara particularly had initiated the order. He said that they made the gas because "they wanted to make their own world." He was suggesting a key aspect of a beginning explanation for how Aum came to cross the threshold that I mentioned at the introduction to this chapter. You must create your own Armageddon (that was part of Asahara's sense of self and, by extension, the others in the cult) in order to control and believe in your claim to be a savior of others. Otherwise, you are an object of someone else's Armageddon. In that sense, crossing the line meant reestablishing a claim to meaning and to immortality as opposed to being vulnerable to death, meaninglessness, and fragmentation.

The dynamic of the actual release of the gas emerges from a prior habit of violence—and a pervasive evil—that had evolved quite quickly over the relatively few years of the cult's existence. As is typical when a cult breaks out in some form of violence, it does so when under duress. There was threat from the authorities (the police were about to close in), and there were threats from within, both losing cult members and Asahara becoming ill. Thus, the gas event was initiated, ironically and paradoxically, in order to reassert, call it the integrity, the vitality, or the immortality of the cult itself, all of which were enormously threatened by these processes. There was also an attempt to cast Aum in the role of victims of a gas attack from the outside and thereby to undermine the police investigation. The Gulf War played a part here too because during the Gulf War there was much talk of poison gas, and Asahara identified with Saddam Hussein as a victim of Western high-tech transgression. However, all this occurred in connection with a long-standing preoccupation with the end of the world and with weapons capable of bringing about that end.

Once you embrace "end time," there is a preoccupation with survival. In addition, the myth is always that everything will always be destroyed in order for the world to be renewed. Every single myth about end time or about death and rebirth involves renewal. The very idea of renewal is dangerous, I would say, when you connect it with ultimate weapons, which now exist in the world, which is our new situation. The weapons had a tremendous psychological attraction for Asahara. Thus, the weapons are dynamic elements in the psychological process. Asahara was obsessed with nuclear weapons. He said Japan would be atom bombed again and would be destroyed. He wanted to create a war with the United States. The weapons were for him a psychological organizing force. We do not know how to talk about this; we talk only about weapons as destroying everything. But the weapons can encourage megalomania or encourage the individual tendency to imagine being able to destroy the world single-handedly. That is another reason why their very existence is doubly dangerous.

To be sure, there are certain elements here specific to Japan. I will just mention them, without diminishing the universal importance of this cult. The degree of Japanese dislocation and confusion may be greater than that of any other country, given the rapidity with which the culture has moved from a feudal culture (from the time of the Meiji Restoration in the late nineteenth century) to a modern and postmodern one and then the extraordinary defeat, humiliation, and millions of deaths in World War II. The millions of dead could not be mourned in any significant way because of the dishonoring of the whole system for which all of those people died. There is also another Japanese dimension here—the Japanese embrace of the impossible heroic task. It is sometimes referred to as "jumping off *Kiyomizu,*" referring to a temple on a high hill outside of Kyoto. The image suggests a plunge into an extreme action, even if the effort will almost certainly fail. Admiral Tojo is said to have used the phrase when ordering the attack on Pearl Harbor. There is a relationship here to the samurai spirit and the kamikaze principle.

Notwithstanding the cultural context of Aum, the cult has enormous significance for all of us. It is like a kind of intense, almost exaggerated and caricatured statement on the pathology of our time, as well as on the danger of destroying ourselves in the name of renewal, an impulse that end-of-the-world imagery creates.

Normative political thought must wrestle with this almost perennial and universal impulse. It can best do so by confronting the dark and psychosocial dimension of apocalyptic violence. By exploring and addressing the dangers posed by weapons married to apocalyptic narratives, we can look into the abyss and find a modicum of hope. We can see and articulate alternative orientations that respect long-standing human impulses by translating them into more humane enterprises. By appreciating Aum Shinrikyo, we empower ourselves toward better self- and collective understanding.

16

An Axial Age? Imagining Peace
in the New Millennium

Elise Boulding

INTRODUCTION: AXIAL AGES—AN ALTERNATIVE
READING OF HISTORY

History can be read as the story of axial ages. These are periods when people, ideas, and cultural traditions from widely different regions interact with one another in a sustained manner. At such times, there is a flowering of human creativity as people generate new cultural understandings and develop shared sensibilities. Normative international relations, to the degree that it focuses on human civilization throughout the world and aims to enhance human well-being, needs to be mindful of axial ages. Axial ages represent moments of transformation. They stand as historical opportunities for the emergence of more humane and peaceful world orders.

In this chapter, I provide a reading of history that focuses on the emergence of axial ages in the past and asks whether humanity is at the beginning of a new axial age in the relatively near future. My purpose is to demonstrate that progressive, large-scale change has taken place in the past and thus to justify a hope in future progressive change. Moreover, I analyze the elements that activate the emergence of axial ages and evaluate the degree to which these elements presently exist. Overall, I aim to investigate the tectonic-like shifts in world history that sit in the mind's eye of normative thinkers as they envision the possibility and contemplate the forces that can bring about widespread change. For those of us committed to imagining peace in the new millennium, a focus on axial ages can provide useful conceptual guideposts.

EARLY AXIAL EXPRESSION

The first axial age we can document comes about 3000 B.C.E. with the establishment of the first great central empires of Africa and the Mediterranean, Egypt, and Sumer.

New population densities, mixing of cultures and lifeways, and intersettlement networks produced the social and technological innovations that made cities and civilizations possible. The wandering from the familiar to the unfamiliar and the experiencing of different social patterns confronted humans with the startling fact that there was more to the world than had previously been thought and initiated new social imaginings about the human prospect. However, the power differentials that developed with the first great ventures in urban centralization severely limited the two-way flow of ideas and resources that might have produced liberating ways of life for all the peoples involved. What emerged were warrior-maintained bastions of privilege for the elite. Such power differentials have continued to limit the human potential for peaceful sharing in succeeding axial ages.

The beginning of the first millennium of the common era marked the midpoint of a second prolonged axial age. Previously isolated peoples in Asia, Africa, Europe, and the Americas encountered one another in a continual process of a discovery of cultures, technologies, religions, and lifeways of steppes, plains, forests, coastal lands, and cities of new and competing "universal empires." During these centuries, venerated teachers and their followers—small bands of Zoroastrians, Buddhists, Jainists, Israelites, and later Christian and Muslim holy men and women—walked their continents, trade routes, and byways, carrying the message that there was a cosmic order of which the earth was a mirror; that a human community of shared abundance, peaceableness, and universal harmony was possible; and that human beings not only could envision the better but also could act on their visions.

The carriers of these visions, often vowed to simplicity and powerlessness, were also the carriers of the growing knowledge stock itself and so were critically important to the civilizational flowering that they nurtured and spread. The rulers and aristocracy who received their messages, however, envisioned abundance for themselves, not for everyone. The economic, political, and technological infrastructures of empires developed apace, moving boundaries, expanding frontiers with the aid of powerful armies to push ever further into new territories. The more powerful they became, the less they learned from the people they conquered. The axial age petered out. Meanwhile, the foot wanderers had their own path, went their own ways, and never stopped at boundaries.

The beginning of the second millennium hardly seemed to offer conditions for a new axial age. A Europe newly freed of the Viking scourge came to life by launching the invasions of the Middle East known as the Crusades. Ironically, these invasions ended the prolonged isolation of Europe from the great Islamic scientific and cultural flowering of preceding centuries and in fact produced more cultural than military activity, leading to the next axial age. Andalusian Spain nurtured the cultural symbiosis of Christian, Jewish, and Muslim cultures under the dialogue-promoting rule of Islam. Scholars from Mediterranean lands helped European monasteries become centers of science and learning. Craft guilds all over Europe developed their own transnational networks as journeymen traveled from workshop to workshop sharing inventions and copying designs.

Utopian visions were everywhere. This was, Joachim de Fiore was to write later, the postbureaucratic "Age of the Holy Spirit." Locally rooted communal experiments flourished by the 1300s, as did revolutionary networks of chiliasts, Anabaptists, and monastics. This was indeed an axial age, exploring new terrains, learning from hitherto unknown cultures, and generating new human possibilities. However, the exploding new technologies of this preindustrial era led to new imperial capabilities and the expansion of the West to all continents through exploration and conquest. This brought the interaction of cultures in a learning mode to an end. The axial age petered out. Only the foot wanderers remained to carry out contacts on a human scale, crisscrossing continents, knowing no boundaries.

THE RISE OF WESTERN UNIVERSALISM

One-way expansion, a highly competitive cultural penetration of new territories, and increasing internecine warfare, could not continue indefinitely. The states of the imperial West began to feel the toll of their military burdens, making them responsive to the call of Czar Nicholas II for a peace conference at The Hague in 1899. The impetus for establishing arrangements to replace war with diplomacy was as much economic as political. Indeed, the subsequent International Court of Justice, the League of Nations, and its successor, the United Nations, all came into being as the "concert of nations" struggled for the structure and order necessary for economic prosperity for individual states. The need for that order has pushed the old UN "founding club" of fifty states to nearly quadruple its membership, laying the somewhat shaky groundwork for possible symmetrical interaction among societies, that most elusive aspect of an axial age.

None of these structural arrangements could have come into being if another significant set of conditions had not been present: the gradual formation of a global civil society that began arguably with of the first World's Fair in London in 1851, followed by three World's Fairs in Paris (1855, 1867, and 1900) and one each in Chicago (1893) and in St. Louis (1904). Here was a new pattern for the age-old encounter with new terrains and new lifeways: a planned coming together of people with previously identified common interests in one or another aspect of human culture—science, technology, medicine, the arts, humanities, and human welfare. Although spurred by excitement over new scientific wonders, these fairs were not simply occasions for scientific show-and-tell. They were gathering places for people at work on similar problems (Boulding 1991).

The 122 international congresses that met in Paris during its World's Fair of 1900 represented the birth of the era of transnational nongovernmental organizations (NGOs), boundary-crossing people's associations brought together by common concern for human betterment. Communities of faith had always had boundary-crossing structures, but now the entire range of human enterprise and concern entered the global arena.

However, if the communication networks for these new transnational peoples associations multiplied rapidly, two-way dialogue did not. The old *mission civiliatrice* of the West evolved into a premature assertion of universalistic values: secular individualism for all. Communal identities and the sense of the sacred were treated as evidence of backwardness, laying the groundwork for profound mistrust of the cultures of the West by many non-Western peoples.

This premature Western assertion of universalism was accompanied by an unfortunate skewing of the work of national scientific communities toward military research and development, thus creating a powerful military system that undercut nascent efforts to replace war by diplomacy.

Yet the possibility that the fragmented, technologized, and militarized globalism of the twentieth century may yet grow into an axial age grounded in new understandings of the planet as still alive. The possibility lies in changes in ecological consciousness that shift the emphasis from "universal" to "global," understood as a vast set of interdependent physical and social systems, and offering new ways of seeing reality. The emergence of general systems thinking has been part of that movement and included studies of arms races as causes of war in the late nineteenth and early twentieth centuries (Richardson 1960). Eventually, the movement gave rise to the formation of the Society for General Systems in 1955. A social science version of general systems thinking based on the original arms race analyses led to studies of how the international system could function without war. In the late 1940s, a generation of idealistic graduate students and their professors in Europe, Asia, and the Americas—interdisciplinary in focus and representing all the social sciences—helped create the peace research movement that led to the formation of the International Peace Research Association in the mid-1960s. This body currently has members and associated peace research institutes in over seventy countries.

The late 1960s witnessed the birth of another international interdisciplinary group of scholars under the name World Order Models Project. These scholars expanded the peace research agenda to include economic well-being, social justice, ecological balance, and positive identity, an agenda that infuses much of the thinking in this book. The peace research community was expanding its agenda along similar lines, as it moved from its starting point of war avoidance—negative peace— toward identifying the conditions of peace—positive peace.

This was an exciting period for social scientists. They were coming to see the world as made up of interrelated sets of bounded social and political wholes, an approach that developed side by side with ecological analysis of the world as made up of interrelated ecosystems and bioregions. These holistic approaches contravened realpolitik conceptions of the world as an international military system containing opposed alliance systems and generated new visions of interrelatedness and the possibilities of widespread and human well-being.

These efforts offer great promise. They represent nascent forces that may help usher in a new axial age. Our ability to nurture their potential rests, in my view, on our capacity to see the world a particular way. We must be able to look at phenomena holistically, envision new maps, and appreciate multiple spheres. Let me outline each of these.

SEEING WHOLES

In general, modern science does not encourage us to see wholes since most of its advances have come from intensive specialization within the fields of chemistry, physics, biology, and the geologic and atmospheric sciences. Yet there is also the view of the planet as Gaia, as a self-regulating system of geochemical and geophysical interactions of the materials of earth, including atmosphere, oceans, and rocks, in a constant flux and flow of matter and energy, most eloquently expounded by Lovelock (1979, 1991). This conception has been steadily growing since the 1860s, when both Russian and American geographers began raising questions about long-term deterioration of soils and forests in the Mediterranean world (Mather and Sdasyuk 1991). By the 1920s, a global ecological conception of the biosphere had developed, and the term "noosphere" was introduced to describe the impact of human thought and activity on the biosphere. By the mid-1950s, a monumental interdisciplinary enterprise was organized on "Man's Role in Changing the Face of the Earth" (Thomas 1956), and the social and natural sciences began working together on issues of global environmental change. A culmination of that work came in the UN Geosphere-Biosphere Decade, 1985–1995, during which member associations of the International Council of Scientific Unions and the International Social Science Council undertook both separate and collaborative studies of environmental change and its human dimension.

While ecosystem theory and practice has been spreading among certain groups of interdisciplinary scientists and also in a growing community of international non-governmental organizations (INGOs) focused on the environment, development, and peace, our educational, political, and economic systems have not been overly supportive in developing this kind of thinking. The globes and wall maps of the world we see in classrooms, libraries, and centers of political and economic decision making are usually representations of the political boundaries of the 185 states of the international system, with pastel-colored landmass patchworks separated by blue oceans, crowned by white ice caps at the poles. How can we relate the flesh-and-blood realities of the communities we know firsthand with this one-dimensional representation of odd-shaped states with governments and armies continually threatening one another in the name of national security?

NEW MAPS

Axial age thinking begins with new maps—not maps on paper, but a multidimensional globe understood and felt in our bodies, hearts, minds, and spirits. The following exercise of the imagination illustrates what is involved in this new mapmaking in the context of Gaia.

First, imagine the geosphere with its unimaginably hot molten liquid surrounding a firm core, periodically erupting with hot lava through the many-layered crust of earth. Here is the primal matter of earth, contoured at the planet's outer face in peaks and valleys and plains, in rich soil, bare rock, and sandy desert. Then see the hydrosphere with the inward eye: the great heaving oceans of earth, the glistening lakes, the majestic rivers and streams connected to vast underground bodies and veins of water. Now turn the mind's eye to the cryosphere—the vast gleaming sheets of ice that advance and retreat in slow majesty over eons at the earth's poles. Still turning, see the biosphere blooming out of that earth, out of those waters, yes, even in the crevices of the ice, the great mass of flora and fauna. Here is life that is rooted in soil and life that moves: the two-legged, four-legged, and the winged, the crawlers and the swimmers. Now look up to imagine the wonderful layers of life-giving atmosphere that swirl around the planet, generating storms and calm, letting in the light of the sun but shielding earth from the sun's deadliest rays. Finally, move the inward eye back to earth. See weaving in and out of the biosphere a two-legged species at work generating still other spheres. First is the sociosphere, a vast, intricate, and busy web of humans, their structures, their interactions, their patterns of culture. Hovering luminously over the sociosphere is the noosphere, the invisible net of human thought, containing the wisdom and the mental follies of the species, its aspirations, its loves, and its fears, interlaced with the generative spirit that is also present in every part of Gaia as she moves to unheard music, circling her star in one of the many universes that stretch beyond imagination.

Our ignorance of this totality is vast, but at the metaphoric level, our species can know our interrelatedness with all of creation. It is the ability to imagine this world as an interactive, interdependent whole that opens the possibility of visualizing another, more peaceable future for the planet.

THE SOCIOSPHERE

The notion of the sociosphere is in itself an axial age concept. There are the five and a half billion human beings, female and male of many races and tongues, alive today. Each goes about her daily business, moving through her own life space and that of many others as she weaves her threads into the social fabric. These human beings live in well over one billion households. It is in and from these households that most of the daily business of humans gets done—the rearing of children, the personal care of humans of all ages, planting and crafting according to the seasons, managing recurrent events of birth, death, drought, earthquake, flood, war—and celebrating life itself in times of respite. Households, which can be of many types, including communes, monasteries, and single individuals, with or without a sheltering roof overhead, are the countable and ultimately adaptable units of every social system.

These one billion households are clustered in thousands of societies scattered across the planet—the tribal, ethnic, and other identity groups that carry on the work of community nurturance and passing on of traditions that give continuity to human experience.

The 185 states plus territories and dependencies comprising that part of the planetary social system most familiar to us through textbook maps are primarily boundary-maintaining units. While in theory responsible for the general well-being of their citizens, governments specialize in defending their peoples from external threats, with increasingly sophisticated military force. The arbitrariness of state boundaries is somewhat mitigated by the more than 2,000 intergovernmental organizations that have come into existence to solve economic, environmental, and resource problems that individual state cannot manage alone. Interstate cooperation is further assisted by the roughly 63,000 treaty agreements that bind states regionally and globally in mutual aid agreements. The United Nations adds another layer of cooperative networks though its twenty operating organs, sixteen specialized agencies, twenty-plus institutes and special programs, a growing number of peacekeeping missions, and fifty worldwide information systems.

All these state-related systems are severely hampered by centralism, bureaucratic inefficiency, and lack of knowledge of the actual social terrains for which they are responsible. This is not any less true in capitalist than in socialist countries. In fact, these days, states are being overshadowed by another kind of entity: the global corporation. Of the 100 largest economic units in the world, only forty-nine are countries, and fifty-one are multinational corporations. Crossing all state borders, they are a law unto themselves, accountable to no other bodies and with profit as their primary goal.

There is one more, essentially two-part system that overlays all the rest, being both more inclusive and more local. One part is the 20,000 INGOs, or peoples' organizations, that span all continents and (unlike multinational corporations) link households, communities, and states in networks based on the common interests of their members. Covering the whole range of human interests—economic, culture, religion, science, politics, the arts, and sports—they represent global civil society (Boulding 1990; Falk 1995). The most rapidly growing transnational associations in recent years have been those focused on peace, the environment, development, and human rights. These are the problem-solving networks of the planet. They command knowledge, competence, and historical memory as no state does and are committed to the world interest rather than national interest. Their primary weakness is that the majority originated in the West and have Western perspectives on world interests, often violating the axial age principle of dialogue between equals. However, this is changing as non-Western INGOs grow stronger and as the Two-Thirds World members within the older INGOs become more articulate about the diversity of interests and values that characterizes human thought on the planet. It is also changing as rapidly growing feminist networks are introducing new dimensions of holistic thinking and creating a global sisterhood rooted in practical on-the-ground knowledge of the relationship between victimization of women, violence in all its forms (including war), and maldevelopment (Morgan 1984; Brock-Utne 1989; Boulding 1992a).

The other part of the system consists of the many thousands of grassroots organizations (GROs) that have arisen locally to deal with local problems. Sometimes they link with INGOs, but often they remain distinctively local. Whether in the One-Third World or Two-Thirds World, these GROs deal in their own ways with problems of poverty and destruction of natural resources. Through these networks, individuals, households, and a great variety of identity groups have a voice in planetary affairs that their national governments cannot offer them. For the first time in history, global bodies of physical and social scientists are looking at questions the concerned citizen can at best approach only intuitively. In addition, for the first time in history, global bodies of indigenous peoples are pooling their wisdom about how to live peacefully with Gaia and offering alternative lifeways to societies that have lost their understanding of their place in nature.

INTERNATIONAL NGOS AND PEACE BUILDING

International NGOs are in fact social interface networks, the global human resource available both to states and to the UN, that hold the potential for a reversal of global militarization and the nurturance of local and regionally based peace cultures. Coalitions of these INGOs have provided, for example, the primary impetus for the creation by states of zones of peace (initially Nuclear Weapon Free Zone Treaties) in the Antarctic, Latin America, the South Pacific, and most recently in Africa, with more zone proposals in process for other areas, including Europe and the Middle East (Boulding 1992b). Zone-of-peace initiatives represent a very slow but steady process of modeling future demilitarization that continues to wear down state resistance to that demilitarization. A related phenomenon is found in the growing numbers of INGOs that focus on training in conflict resolution and problem solving. In coalition with environmental, women's human rights, and scientific INGOs, they are contributing nonviolent peace-building personnel to work in ethnic, environmental, and resource conflict situations in which national and UN armies are present but lack the skills for a problem-solving approach to peacemaking and peacekeeping. Often they are present as unarmed "peace teams," such as Peace Brigades International, working with local peacemakers to resolve conflicts that are often poorly understood by would-be peace forces from outside the region (Boulding and Oberg 1996).

Other groups work with former soldiers and guerillas, including child soldiers, to develop occupational and social skills for reentry into civilian life, and still others work with both victims and victimizers in postgenocide situations, always with the goal of seeking reconciliation and transformed relationships in fractured societies. Increasingly, educational INGOs are focusing on peace studies to help teachers develop the skills of conflict resolution and mediation for the classroom, from kinder-garten to the university. Conflict resolution professionals, working with intergovern-mental bodies, are forming new INGOs to provide the services of preventive diplomacy, including the maintenance of continually updated maps of high-risk zones around the world. Peace organizations, in addition to constant lobbying for nuclear and conventional disarmament, hold workshops to imagine a world without weapons as a way of generating new strategies for moving toward a disarmed world (Boulding 1988).

One important set of transnational actors, historically the bearers of new insights in past axial ages, is the communities of faith. Many new peace-building INGOs have been established both within and between faith communities. The recently founded international interfaith Committee for a Peace Council, an offshoot of the 1893 World Parliament of Religions and its 1993 successor, is committed to support the work of peace building in every local temple, synagogue, church, and mosque of each of the faiths it represents, with particular attention to areas presently experienc-ing violent conflict.

CONCLUSION: TOWARD A NEW AXIAL AGE

The many types of peace-oriented INGOs described here represent a trend away from militarism and toward a more peaceful international order. They are working to create a culture of peace to replace the culture of violence that has cast such a pall over many aspects of life in the twentieth century. Yet peace building is only in process, with no major breakthroughs guaranteed. Similarly, with the zones-of-peace movement and the many other efforts to introduce nonviolent problem solving in conflict arenas, the pace of change is not always as we would hope it to be. Demili-tarization, and even limited arms control, is proceeding far too slowly, as always held back in the name of "national security." Inevitably, this makes it easier for states to resort to force when diplomacy founders.

Knowing that we live in dangerous times, with the still real possibility that hu-mans can destroy the planet, does it make sense to talk of an axial age? I said at the outset that axial ages emerge out of a particular cluster of patterns of human adventurousness: the exploration of new terrains; intersection in a sustained way with strangers, thus generating new conceptions of the world; and images of another and better future. The new image of earth as a living entity of interacting spheres is clearly a result of the exploration of new terrain. The new peoples' globe-spanning networks provide for sustained interaction with strangers, and many of these net-works generate images of a human community of shared abundance and peaceable-ness.

But there are many obstacles. Conflicts within the INGO community, the limited power of INGOs, the expanding power of socially insensitive corporate entities, and the persistent parochial vision of states within a state system pose significant challenges. In my view, the best hope remains in our ability to conceptualize the world through more humane lenses and to work to realize our visions. Seeing phenomena more holistically, envisioning new maps, and appreciating the existence and relationships among multiple spheres of human experience are critical to inching the world into a new axial age.

17

From a Twentieth Century of War to a Twenty-First Century of Peace?

Johan Galtung

THE TWENTIETH CENTURY: FROM BORDER WARS TO FAULT-LINE WARS

Too optimistic? Oh yes, especially when written under the shadows of Western civilization at its worst: Orthodox killing Muslims, Protestants and Catholics bombing Orthodox—old patterns reenacted. But let us try some visions of goals and processes, more for December 31, 2099, than for January 1, 2000. Being located near the watershed between two centuries, even two millennia, a way to start would be to look back at the twentieth century. A century of horrors: wars, genocide, torturism and terrorism, and repression, exploitation, alienation, and ideologies such as colonialism, Bolshevism, Nazism, Dai-to-a, and Maoism. But what were the major conflict formations? What was it about?

Coming out of the nineteenth century, there were considerable residues from feudalism and slavery and, indeed, colonialism. All over the world, the struggle against the suppression of women and the young and against the exploitation of the nonwhites and the workers set the tone for a century focused on *gender and generation, race and class,* and the liberation of the suppressed, including their right to vote and to be elected.

And then there was that fifth fault line in the human construction, the *nation,* the struggle for equal citizenship, including becoming an independent country, like my own country, Norway, separating nonviolently from Sweden in 1905.

In most of the world, the ruling *states* were instruments of a tiny, male, old, white bourgeois (MOWB) minority from Anglo-Saxon and other Western nations ruling through vast imperialist systems. Women, youth, workers, Gandhi, Mao, Tojo, and African leaders stood up against the MOWB syndrome. But the struggle continues. That fault line between Anglo-Saxon and MOWBs and the rest generated the two major conflict formations of the twentieth century: first, race wars, as in the struggle for decolonization, for the liberation of the nonwhite, pitting countries in the world's Northwest—the United States and northwestern Europe—against most of the rest of the world (including, in the eighteenth century, the Atlantic seaboard colonies that became the United States) and, second, class wars, as in the struggle against forces threatening MOWB domination, such as Nazis in central Europe, fascists in southern Europe, and communists in Eastern Europe (in the Balkans all three) and Gandhians in India, Maoists in China, and militarists in Japan.

There was also World War I, between the Northwest (the United Kingdom, France, and the United States) and central and southeastern Europe (Prussia, Austria, and Turkey). But that was a classical interstate war, as defined by the 1648 Peace of Westphalia, with MOWB elites from Anglo-Saxon and other nations pitting their states and their armies against each other and adjusting some borders.

There was an element of this in World War II. But typical of the twentieth century were the massive category wars (genocides) as opposed to interelite wars. Governments killed categories of peoples that stood in their way (Armenians, Jews, and "kulaks") like the West had done earlier in the colonies, including on the Atlantic seaboard. States went to war against states run by the other class. That nineteenth-century transplant into the first half of the twentieth century, Sir Winston Churchill, and his class hated the working class (often called "populist") elements in Germany, Italy, and Russia. From Munich onward, the policy was clear: let the lower classes fight each other in a European civil war of communists against Nazi-Fascists.

In the end, MOWBs turned out to need the help of the Soviet Union against Nazism, and vice versa as "allies," and the Soviet Union got a short lease on life. The Cold War then became the second confrontation within this syndrome. The basic crime of the Soviet Union, from a MOWB point of view, was neither genocide nor colonization of others, as MOWBs had done that for centuries. The Soviet Union had done something worse: raising the popular masses from misery to poverty, with basic material needs satisfied, at the expense of the bourgeois freedoms to use capitalism for their own enrichment regardless of the costs.

In the late twentieth century, the Soviet Union imploded as an absurd society. That major challenge to Northwest and MOWB submitted to capitalism. Yugoslavia, Cuba, North Korea, and China submitted less, placing them next in line for structurocide. No alternatives are permitted in the New Neuordnung (new world order).

But what happened to gender, generation, and nation? They are there. We would expect nations of all kinds to try to break out of states that they consider prisons. They will get the support of the Northwest to the extent that they represent the upper-tier interests mentioned, otherwise not (e.g., Israel/Palestine). And we would expect ugly backlashes against women, for example, by decreasing their numbers through selective abortion and against the old, maybe through patterns of euthanasia. Some of this may be avoided if the level of awareness is high enough.

To summarize, the twentieth century was about fault lines in general and race and class in particular. The new aspect was the globalization of the struggle to race and class wars in the interstate system, with genocides within and between states. And that leads us to the obvious question: What next?

THE TWENTY-FIRST CENTURY:
FROM INTERSTATE TO GLOBAL WARS?

History moves slowly. No agenda has been completed; in fact, human agendas rarely are ever completed. They linger on. We would expect the Northwestern corner of the world, under the leadership of the United States and its assistant, the United Kingdom, to continue the pattern of race and class exploitation and to continue preparing for the Big Battle with exploited races and classes. In other words, we would expect class conflict between colored, very poor people and MOWB from Anglo-Saxon and kindred Western nations to deepen. And we would expect interregional formations, such as the U.S. quest for control of Eurasia by NATO's expanding eastward[1] and AMPO[2] westward, to be a key to the twenty-first century.

In short, we expect the following conflict formations: geoeconomic (the world economic crisis), geomilitary (NATO/AMPO expansion), geopolitical (the state/nation controversy), geocultural (Christian-Muslim antinomy), and the three Europes (Catholics/Protestants, Orthodox, and Muslim). In all five of these, class and/or race are prevalent. These are not the classical formations with elites using states to move borders. States are used, but they are used to fight categories across fault lines within and among states. Mobilization is along global lines.

The general absence of solidarity with the poor is remarkable, and the gap in purchasing power between the top and the bottom 20 percent expands at a rate above 3 percent annually (world economic growth is, on average, less than 3 percent). Three persons own more than the 48 percent of the world's countries.

That the poor mainly are women, children, very old, colored, and/or working class goes without saying. They live not only in Eurasia, however. But their large states are in Eurasia—Russia, China, India (with 40 percent of the world's people), and Pakistan—and the states designated by the United States as "rogue" or "pariah"—Iran, Iraq, and Syria. Assuming that there are four or more nuclear powers among them and that there is coordination to the point of de facto alliance formation, the NATO/AMPO system headed by the United States has produced an awesome enemy for a clash of superregions (not civilizations, as Eurasia is very pluralistic).

The only positive point is that this pincer movement against Eurasia probably will lead to a solution of the Kashmir problem. The United States, on the other hand, will need and use, to the utmost, the Balkan and Korea conflicts and supply its NATO/AMPO allies with missiles.

The last three conflict formations transcend the classical state system completely. Two of them are global: 2,000 nations fighting for recognition within 200 states and the world's two largest religions pitted against each other. One is European, at present enacted in Yugoslavia and some parts of Russia.

The parallel that comes to mind is Hitler's use of the national conflict between Sudeten Germans and Czechs. The pressure on Czechoslovakia also had the support of England.

Japan's attack on Manchuria in 1931–1945 and Italy's attack on Ethiopia in 1935–1941 were also against the Kellogg-Briand Pact of 1928 (Briand got the Nobel Peace Prize in 1926, Kellogg in 1929): sixty-two states, among them all major powers, agreed to renounce war as political instrument and to settle all international disputes by peaceful means. The exceptions were wars of self-defense or military obligations from the League Covenant, the Monroe Doctrine, or alliance obligations—very similar to the UN Charter, Article II(4), with exceptions.

The three dictatorships were above the law and the League Covenant. They brushed all resolutions aside. Their propaganda was as massive as the NATO propaganda. The power on the side of those "above the law," using a criterion of their own choice—the will of the strong—was overpowering. There may actually have been more popular will behind those dictatorships in the 1930s than behind the democracies sixty to seventy years later: Dictatorships were more honest, and democracies more manipulatory, concealing intentions.

The dictatorships followed up what they started, launched a second world war for Neuordnung/Nuovo Ordine/Dai-to-a, and lost: Newton's third law. The democracies, headed by the United States and using NATO, AMPO, and TIAP, may be tempted to do the same, starting with North Korea and Colombia, to implement the "new world order."

The outlook is ominous. Is there any light? In order to find some clarification, we have to go beyond these projections, however warranted they are, to attempt to identify some inherent weaknesses in these forces and some countervailing forces.

THE HORRORS OF THE TWENTIETH CENTURY
AND THE ROLE OF THE STATE

All these phenomena have one thing in common: the state is the key instrument for internal and external power, making the ownership of the state a key issue (MOWBs in the central states, their trusted clients in the periphery, and anti-MOWB in the evil states). The state was certainly used for the world wars, as classical wars, as category wars, and for genocide. The state was used for colonial, racist wars, including genocide. The state has been used for torture; nonstate torture is a trifle in comparison. The state is the ideal instrument for repression, depriving everyone under its sway of civil and political human rights, including their lives under capital punishment. Cooperating with capital forces, the state can also sustain patterns of exploitation, depriving everyone under its command of economic, social, and cultural rights. And, inspired and informed by its cultural elites, the state can engage in massive alienation, such as depriving groups under its command of their own idiom, their myths, and their belief systems.

But one thing the state is not good at: abolishing itself. Nonstates often fight states, as in the struggle against colonialism, against MOWB (white); or as in the struggle against capitalism, against MOWB (bourgeois); as women fighting MOWB (males); or as younger people fighting MOWB (old). But they all tend to end up sharing the state or founding a new state after a secession struggle or after a revolution. The state/nonstate dialectic tends to strengthen the state system at the expense of the breakdown of some of them. Anti-MOWB movements conquer states, turn them into their instruments, and even go to war against MOWB states. But chances are that they end up as neo-MOWB states.

Why? Very simple: The state system has a certain logic and is capable of shaping different people the same way, as could be seen in the 1999 war of social democrats against Serbia. The adage "To he who has a hammer the world looks like a nail" holds also for social democrats when they become statesmen. They may also be more sensitive to Serbian blatant infraction of human rights and more sensitive to the calls for Atlantic solidarity than conservative, state/nation-centric MOWBs.

Being the successor to the absolute monarchies or to the monarchs or princes themselves, with their monopoly on force, states tend to see conflict as raw material for their own power aggrandizement. A conflict solved is an opportunity forgone. Conflicts shake the system, as some parts loosen and are up for grabs. Big states, like big vultures, circle in the air, waiting for the opportunity. They may bomb, a little or a lot, softening the web of smaller states and nonstates, prying some parts loose, rearranging and often calling the cemetery/desert "peace" (Tacitus).

So, how can I retain a minimum of optimism after a war over a conflict that it would even have been easy to solve[3] and with such dark visions for the twenty-first century? Because of an analytical category I have found interesting: *absurdity.*

I define absurdity as the decoupling between culture and structure. An example is the Soviet Union. That culture contained visions of utopia, eliminating not only misery but also classes, war, violence, and repression. What they got was poverty but also a new class society, war, violence, and repression. The culture contained a major cognition, predicting that capitalism would collapse. Capitalism failed to live down to the prediction; what collapsed was their system. There are limits to absurdity.

The classical case of absurdity as a category is, of course, Andersen's emperor with no clothes. Only a child was adult enough to voice the decoupling. The adults were all brainwashed by the culture to live in virtual rather than real reality, like people breathing the thin air of finance economy (culture), blind to the crisis in a productive economy of overproduction and underconsumption (structure). Absurdity constitutes a very unstable equilibrium. In the Soviet Union, I date the absurdity crisis from the early 1970s. From that point on, the system could be kept alive only by the stepped-up threat from the United States (the "theater" missiles). NATO gave the system an additional decade.

The absurdity of saving lives through bombing and of protecting the rule of law by breaking it does not pass unnoticed. Bombing/destroying Iraq, bombing/destroying Serbia, bombing Sudan, bombing Afghanistan—all of this after having destroyed Korea and then Vietnam and in all cases with results very different from what was announced—does not pass unnoticed. Of course, there is no assumption that MOWBAS (here adding U.S. and U.K. Anglo-Saxons) will pay attention; autism is a condition for being the world's most belligerent countries.

But the rest of the world starts paying attention and may one day arrive at a conclusion: The world has a major problem—not terrorism, not small scale local potentates, although all such problems have to be taken seriously and creatively. The name of that problem is the United States and its mother-turned-little-daughter. From that point on, alliances will start withering, and the blind allegiance under the spell of U.S. charm, opulence, intellectual creativity, and leadership will fade away. A turning point is coming, quickly; United States beware.

But the United States may also be lagging behind, as happened in the case of slavery. Even more important than the United States is a deeper phenomenon that we witness every day: the absurdity of the state system. Interestingly, the demise of the state as the guardian of welfare, as an economic actor and protector of distribution, went extremely quickly, using the absurdities of the late Soviet system for political leverage. That may easily pave the way for more basic questions: How about the capacity of the state to protect its citizens against violence relative to its capacity to kill, including its own people? How about the capacity of the state system to solve its own conflicts? Could it simply be that state system and peace system are mutually incompatible?

A basic thesis is that *we may be witnessing the beginning of the end of the state system, not the end of the beginning.* The feudal system ended because it killed, repressed, exploited, and alienated more people than it provided with survival (secure lives), well-being (a reasonable livelihood), freedom, and identity. There were and are islands and niches where these four basic needs are reasonably met, but certainly not for the system as a whole.

That means that we are probably heading for the "big turning point," as we did for monarchy, slavery, colonialism, and patriarchy. All four may continue in softer forms. Centuries of struggle against an English monarchy of absolute powers led to a turning point, as did the English antislavery campaign, Gandhi's anticolonial struggle, and the feminist revolution. Ultimately, the antinuclear movement will reach even the U.S. government, the only place from which the instruments of nuclear holocaust may finally be delegitimized. So will the antiwar movement. With neither wars nor peace, the state is as absurd as the emperor with no clothes.

THE MIXED WORLD: WANING STATES WITH VEXING NONSTATES

Global governance is defined here as the concerted action for meeting human needs by territorial and nonterritorial actors together. The capacity of the state system to put constraints on itself being very limited, world government by a concert of, say, nineteen states is not what we are talking about. One additional reason is that the road seems to pass through regions that develop into superstates conducting superwars, in other words, what we may be heading for in the relation between the Catholic/Protestant, Slavic-Orthodox, and Turko-Muslim blocs in Europe. A Russo-Chinese bloc may, as mentioned, join with India/Pakistan, brought into being by the synchronized expansion of NATO eastward and AMPO westward. But these can also be the absurd phenomena that will lead us closer to the turning points.

Does this mean that nonstates take over? Not if we want global governance, concerted state-nonstate action. Nonstates are corporations, transnational corporations (TNCs), and civil society. Civil society has three components: international people's organizations (IPOs), also known as nongovernmental organizations (NGOs) (nonterritorial); local authorities (LAs) (territorial and nonterritorial, some kind of archipelago); and just people—a lot of them. They cannot govern alone.

Thus, civil society should not be romanticized. Nations, or groups of people with a strong sense of what is sacred in space and time, are also NGOs—often of a vicious, exclusivist, dualist sort, yearning to creep into the hide of their own state to wreak havoc on earth or at least on their neighbors. However, these are exceptions. One fact stands out: nonstates, TNCs, NGOs, LAs, and people, do not have legitimate armies. The first task of global governance is to keep it that way.

We can now distinguish five phases in the evolution of the state/nonstate dialectic in the total world system.

Phase 1. In Europe, the modern *state system* dates from the *Treaty of Westphalia* of October 24, 1648, 350 years ago, with the *right of war in the interest of the state* as one characteristic. In China, that was the system at the axial time, from 500 B.C., the time of Confucius, Lao-Tse, the Buddha, and the warring states, until 221 B.C., when China became unified in the Chin dynasty. There is a tacit coordination in the system defined by the culture of the warrior castes. Thus, in that system, values such as honor, courage, and dignity were shared across borders, limiting the violence.

Phase 2. The state system with its right of war has to coordinate itself, starting at the top. International governmental organizations (IGOs) emerge, starting with the Vienna Concert of five countries against Napoleon, following up with the League of Nations in 1920 (against Germany-Austria) and on October 24, 1945, with the United Nations and a Security Council of the leading states against Nazi Germany and militarist Japan. Today we are almost back to Vienna: The "Contact Group" against Yugoslavia consists of the Security Council minus China plus Germany and Italy. The idea of coordination by concert remains, bypassing the UN General Assembly (Article XII), even the Security Council.

Phase 3. Social protests start building up as social revolutions against excessive state power and as social movements against Clausewitzian war or in favor of softening war (e.g., Henri Dunant and the Red Cross in Geneva). Typically, each group exercises some pressure on its own government. Less war-prone countries emerge in the process.

Phase 4. Some of these people's movements come together, as did the *Hague System* of 1899, with *ius ad bellum/in bello,* and the international peace organizations after World War II (e.g., War Resisters' International, the Women's International League for Peace and Freedom, and the International Peace Bureau) and the numerous NGOs and international nongovernmental organizations (INGOs) after World War II. In the Prevention and Management of Violent Conflict European Platform for conflict mediation, no less than 475 organizations, the overwhelming majority of which are NGOs, are listed. The growth rate is well above 10 percent per year, meaning a doubling every seven years. In this field, the sky is the limit. Nonterritorial space knows no limits.

Phase 5. The INGOs start exercising direct pressure on the IGOs, starting with the UN Environment Conference in Stockholm 1972; making UN NGO fora major features of world politics. At this point, the UN contribution to the development of democratic practice cannot be overestimated. Democracy is only partly, not even mainly, about elections (and especially not about a choice between only two, and almost identical, parties, with participation well below 50 percent). Democracy is about participation. And the United Nations made that possible, providing the infrastructure for a super-IGO to interact with a super-INGO.

Hundreds of thousands have participated in this, as they also would have done had states organized NGO fora in parallel with the sessions of their national assemblies (and not only basing the interaction on the very limited perspectives of political parties). This is a major pointer to a more democratic future.

Phase 6. But even more important is the next phase. Nonstates—NGOs, LAs, TNCs—start substituting for the world politics of governments. They are usually not operating secretly, they have more contact with people, and they do not have armies but rather normative and contractual power. No doubt there will be terrorists and militias roaming around, and no doubt there will be the need for a world police. But there will not be states with the legitimate right to be armed to the brim and to go to the brink and beyond, investing enormous amounts in a weapons technology, which in turn is one of the driving forces in the arms races.

In this phase, the NGOs no longer work primarily as pressure groups on their own governments or on the IGOs or even on the United Nations. They start doing the job themselves, as conflict mediators, reconstructing after disasters, often in fierce competition with one another, but generally without violence. The NGOs coming in after an earthquake often do what not even the local or national governments are able to. The NGOs have an enormous advantage: They can draw on expertise from all over the world where local and national governments have to give priority to their own experts and often only from their own party. The NGOs and TNCs are the parents and offspring of a truly globalizing world, not a power concert by self-appointed states.

The six phases outlined here can also be used to tell the story of domestic history, from territorial entities, principalities, states, and regions vying for power until non-territorial entities (such as parties) become strong and experienced enough to run the country. Territory wanes, nonterritory vexes. The world has come quite far in recent years. Oversized, overpowered states start looking like dinosaurs. Their time is up.

SOME GLIMPSES OF A MORE PEACEFUL WORLD

This is my utopia: a world territorially rooted in local communities, woven together by dense networks of IPOs and NGOs around values and/or interests and serviced by TNCs that have discovered ways of giving first priority to the needs of those most in need. These three points are related: TNCs that fail to live up to this basic premise will be boycotted by NGOs and deprived of their permits to operate by LAs. It would be best to cooperate.

The key to the transition from a *twentieth century of war to a twenty-first century of peace* lies in the transition from state to nonstate as the point of gravity for world politics, as it has been for a long time, in many countries, for domestic politics. People live in their communities, relate through organizations (including families), are serviced by business, and are protected by governments. What we need is equally good global governance.

Only a democratic state system can today provide the world setting that would make this possible.[4] The state as we know it, like the city-state within the nation-state earlier, would then gradually wither away not because it is "no longer needed to protect capitalism" but because it has reached its level of absurdity, being more of a threat than a benefit to most people. In its place comes a combination of the LA/NGO/TNC system, and an improved United Nations softening and democra-tizing the state system.

The task, then, is to make this package of nonstate world politics as rich, dense, and peace building as possible, noting that such cooperation is, in and by itself, peace building. But there is no anarchist illusion that a "world setting" is not needed, nor any Hobbesian delusion about enormous amounts of coercive power that has to be assembled at the top.

What we have in mind is, of course, an improved version of the United Nations, liberated from the veto power, with a UN Peoples' Assembly (based on NGOs, LAs, and direct vote with one representative per million inhabitants, using states as elec-tion districts) open only to members who do not break international law and do pay their dues and not located in countries capable of exercising political pressure.

The UN power at the top should, in addition to the police forces mentioned, be based on normative and contractual power. Just to mention one example of many: the globalization of human rights. Human rights had a double function: to check the power of the state ("freedom from") and to turn the power of the state in a positive direction for the citizen ("freedom to"). We keep the former as a constraint on the United Nations and then turn to the United Nations rather than to a vanishing or illegitimized state system. The world system, through the LAs, using NGOs to a large extent as conduits (as they already do), can provide what is needed for people to survive, with their basic material needs guaranteed, with freedom and with their identity intact. The setting for the latter would be the local rather than the state community, the 200 states being a very inadequate setting for 2,000 nations seeking their identity through statehood. The protected local community may work better.

The reader will have noticed that the thesis is not to abolish the war system by abolishing the military, although the increasing number of states without armies is a trend that certainly should be encouraged. The problem is that such states tend to be small and that big powers are more to offer them a "protection" that they cannot reject.

The point here is that the state system, especially at its top, especially at its most self-righteous (which used to be Christian or Muslim self-righteousness; democracy/human rights self-righteousness may now have taken over), is inherently belligerent in its motivation; they also have the capability of amassing the arms needed. World politics should be more in the hands of actors, more motivated for peace, and less capable of launching wars. Is that transformation feasible?

In centuries past, the world has witnessed two highly successful transformations: the abolition of slavery and the abolition of colonialism. Both institutions were seen as normal, natural, and indispensable. If the slaves or the colonies were let loose, anarchy would surely follow. They both needed that firm disciplinary hand from above, being only semihuman. Even if not semihuman, even if granted status as humans, abolition of slavery and/or colonialism would ruin a Western civilization based on the economic fruits derived from those institutions.

We are programmed by the same type of ideology today: Strong states with "muscle" are needed at the top to discipline all those rogues further down. Slavery and colonialism were by and large abolished. The MOWBs somehow managed to remain in power, and the world income gap is broader than ever. Very much was achieved, but there may also be much truth in that old adage "*plus ça change plus c'est la même chose.*" The enormous cultural, structural, and direct violence of the twentieth century may twist any soft global governance into a caricature of itself.

On the other hand, this utopia has the advantage of being a mirror of successful processes at the domestic level and to be based on global trends that have already come quite far.

NOTES

1. As an example, see Brzezinski (1997). For background, such as the Joint Chiefs of Staff Memorandum 570/2 of 1943, see Hayes et al. (1986, 19–30).

2. AMPO is the Japanese acronym for the Japan-U.S. Security Treaty (Nichibei Anzen-hosho Joayku).

3. Consult Yugoslavia at www.transcend.com.

4. In line with Article XXVIII of the Universal Declaration of Human Rights: "Everyone is entitled to a social and international order in which the rights and freedoms set forth in this Declaration can be fully realized."

18

The Normative Promise of Nonstate Actors: A Theoretical Account of Global Civil Society

Paul Wapner

A number of chapters in this book express skepticism regarding the ability of states to address some of the more pressing contemporary global challenges and point to the realm of global civil society as a domain possessing normative promise. The argument goes something like this: The state system encourages an egoistic perspective that forces states to care foremost about their own well-being and attend to common challenges only when it is clear that their individual interests will be enhanced or at least not diminished in the act of doing so. Global civil society, as a transnational domain in which people form relationships and develop elements of identity outside their role as a citizen of a particular state, represents a sphere that thus transcends the self-regarding character of the state system and can work in the service of a genuinely transnational, public interest. Activities emerging out of global civil society, then, hold promise for overcoming the many impediments associated with statist politics.

Connected with this argument is a pessimistic attitude regarding the world economy. Economic globalization is not heralding in a new age that is responsive to widespread human suffering but rather is advancing the profit-making potential of corporate actors. It is often the case that such potential comes at the expense of global problems. Again, for many authors in this book and for many normative thinkers in general, global civil society appears as a promising alternative domain of collective life. Aside from developing an identity outside one's role of a citizen of a particular state, global civil society is also a sphere in which one thinks and acts independently of one's role as a consumer and producer. It thus represents a sphere of collective life that is free from the structural impediments not only of the state system but also of the world economy. Global civil society, like its domestic counterpart, is that domain in which people voluntarily associate to express themselves and pursue various noneconomic aims in common, and it is in the practice of such association that one can look for progressive political activity.[1]

The promise of global civil society rests on the normative commitment toward humane governance. At bottom, humane governance is about managing the affairs of public life in a democratic fashion by which the energies of people are coordinated to solve certain dilemmas and realize the many virtues that are possible in a collective setting. Global civil society represents a domain that, if properly tapped and sufficiently exercised, can provide both the democratic dimension of governance and the pertinent substantive focus. To be sure, global civil society, in and of itself, is not the embodiment of humane governance. As will be shown, it is populated by forces that have less benign intentions. Indeed, it is a complicated arena marked by competition among various groups that uphold conflicting interests and work to advance them. In addition, it is comprised of many who believe that they have humanity's well-being in mind when, in fact, they are operating from a purely private, self-interested perspective. Nonetheless, for all its complexity and impure characteristics, global civil society *does* represent a domain of global collective life that can contribute to a more humane world order, and this accounts for the attention accorded it by normative scholars.

While many thinkers look to global civil society for political promise, there is very little understanding of why and how it can operate in the service of global governance. Aside from noting its independence from the state system and the world economy, few studies explain the mechanics by which activities in global civil society engage the structures that govern global collective life; few studies present a theoretical understanding of power in global civil society and analyze it in a way that clarifies its ability to shape widespread thought and behavior. Most studies see global civil society as the place where nongovernmental organizations (NGOs) arise and carry out their activities. And, insofar as these studies tend to focus on politically progressive NGOs, there is an implicit assumption that global civil society itself works automatically as a reformist domain. But how is it that NGOs themselves can participate in global governance? How does their location in global civil society enable them to operate with any degree of success? What mechanisms in global civil society work to shape widespread thought and behavior?

This chapter provides a theoretical account of why and how the efforts of NGOs influence and participate in global governance. By understanding NGOs as part of global civil society and theorizing about the political impact of this domain, the chapter explains how efforts undertaken outside the state system (and separate from the world economy) nonetheless shape world collective life. My aim in undertaking this study is to provide theoretical and analytical support for the normative move toward global civil society. It should be emphasized that I do not believe that global civil society is a panacea for the many tragic dimensions of contemporary global life, if for no other reason than, as mentioned, its normative quality is complex and often compromised. But it nevertheless holds *some* promise for progressive world politics, and the ability of this promise to be realized can be enhanced, in my view, through greater understanding of its structure and overall quality. Thus, this chapter participates in the conversation about humane governance by specifying the governing promise of global civil society.

The chapter proceeds in the following fashion. The first section reviews understandings of civil society at the domestic level. By tracing the evolution of the term's meaning and reviewing one of the more plausible accounts of how such a realm actually emerges, the section aims to provide a conceptual grounding for understanding civil society at the global level. The second section outlines the meaning of global civil society. It draws an analogy between domestic and global collective life and describes the emergence and dynamics of a realm that fosters transnational activity above the individual and below the state. This entails specifying the nature of NGOs and explaining how they constitute global civil society. The third section explicates how global civil society participates in global governance. It does so, first, by providing a theoretical account of the political dimension of global civil society and then by illustrating it with a number of empirical examples. Global civil society participates in global governance in both an unintentional and a deliberate manner. The section mentions the unintentional dimension but focuses specifically on calculated efforts by NGOs to politicize global civil society and use it to create institutions of global governance. The final section presents a concise rendition of the overall argument and draws out a number of implications for the study of world politics.

CIVIL SOCIETY

The concept of civil society has a long history that has been well documented by a number of scholars (Cohen and Arato 1992; Seligman 1992; Kumar 1993). This history is almost wholly confined to reflection on domestic collective life but holds relevance for conceptualizing global civil society. Indeed, to understand the meaning of civil society at the global level, it is useful to appreciate, at least in broad outline, some of the more important developments in the evolution of the concept's relevance at the domestic level.

To begin, it is worth noting that until roughly the eighteenth century the term "civil society"—from the Latin *societas civilas*—was synonymous with the state or political society (Cohen and Arato 1992, 83ff; Kumar 1993, 376). Civil society referred to a community of citizens that regulated their relationships and settled disputes according to a system of law. This was in contrast to human relations at large. A lawful society enjoyed a "civilized" existence: civility, not barbarism, governed human affairs. Civil society, as such, demarcated a domain separate from the so-called natural relations existing in the "state of nature" outside the polis, republic, or well-ordered state (Cohen and Arato 1992, 86ff).

Central to early notions of civil society is that the legal code, according to which citizens interacted with one another, was supported by a broader set of norms and values (ethos) that permeated throughout society. Governance was not simply a matter of governmental statutes but operated in a more holistic manner. Social mores complemented legal codes, and thus civil society denoted an all-encompassing social system.[2] Civil society, then, was not simply differentiated from the state of nature; it was also distinguished from systems of government in which political rule operated through despotic decree. In short, the idea of civil society originated in an attempt to articulate the experience of living as a citizen in a well-ordered community. Civil society denoted lawfulness, in both the legal and social senses, compared to the capriciousness of human communal life at large.

Starting in the eighteenth century, for reasons well outlined by others, the equation between political rule and society began to break down (Keane 1988). The state, a dominant form of political organization at the time, began to be seen as separate from society, which had a form and dynamic of its own. The thinker most closely associated with the distinction is Hegel,[3] who saw civil society as a domain above the family but below the state wherein free association takes place between individuals and corporate groups.[4] Civil society, as such, was seen as an arena in which people pursued their own aims in the course of everyday life and thus was associated with particular needs, private interests, and often divisiveness. The state was seen as analytically separate from civil society—although, in classic Hegelian form, mutually constitutive of it—in that it possessed the quality of publicness or "legality." That is, it accentuated universalist, in contrast to particularist principles, and thus organized the energies of civil society to realize the general good. Hegel represents a turning point in the history of civil society insofar as he articulated the character of civil society in dialectical relation to the state and thereby enabled theorists to think about the two spheres as analytically distinct.[5]

Building on Hegel's view, most modern and contemporary theorists understand civil society in contrast to the state, although the justification for the distinction and its meaning for collective life assume different emphases. Arguably the most significant trajectory of thought is the liberal one that sees civil society as a function of a market economy and limited government although eventually with enough institutionalization to constitute a realm of its own.[6] Taking the latter aspect first, it is often pointed out that the rise of the modern bureaucratic state brought with it a system of rights that constituted human beings as legal entities, and it was these rights that established a domain of private, horizontal interaction (Lewis 1992, 37; Blaney and Pasha 1993, 8ff; Perez-Diaz 1995). As the state established itself as a material object possessing military, police, juridical, and administrative power, citizens necessarily organized themselves in opposition to, and independent from, its prerogatives and directives. This involved both increased participation, to the degree that civic associations directed their energies toward the state, and a developed associational sphere in which commerce, common enterprise, social trust, and other horizontal experiences could be cultivated in their own right. The development of the idea of civil society arose in this context insofar as the state itself often recognized and legitimized citizen interaction and the bonds and interests that develop as a result. The liberal state acknowledged that citizens in fact possess a certain degree of freedom from state authority and particular rights to hold the state accountable.[7] The theoretical articulation of this notion of civil society finds its origins in the thought of writers such as Montesquieu (1989), Tocqueville (1969), Paine (1982), and Smith (1993). Concerned in part with the debilitating effects of despotism, each of these thinkers reflected on the extent and character of state rule and ways of accentuating antidespotic tendencies. Each tried, in his own way, to justify the significance of a domain free from state regulation wherein people could experience the quality of associational life and concomitantly form networks that would structurally obstruct the domineering tendency of state authority. Additionally, they supported this domain since it possessed an innate rationality that could, contra Hegel, help realize the general good. The notion of civil society that emerged from this thought saw it as a sphere in which social groups could interact independently of the state— and thus form their own codes of conduct—yet also influence the dynamics of the polity. Key to such a domain was the existence of the modern, liberal state.

The second aspect of the liberal notion sees the rise of civil society tied to the emergence of a particular form of economic life, namely, a market-driven economy based on private property. Private property and market relations generate a distinct domain that is autonomous from the state and other social spheres. Private property enables people to concentrate their productive energies on genuinely personal, self-interested enterprises and, in doing so, create and mobilize significant, autonomous sources of wealth. The spread of market relations accentuates this as it creates extensive networks between producers and consumers that pull successive members of society into a privately coordinated mode of economic life.[8] Together, the rise of private property and the spread of market relations give way to a rich, commercial associational life independent of the state (Calhoun 1992).

Civil society, from this perspective, is characterized by the quality of human experience and relations that arise from commercial interaction. A market system of exchange is based on individuals and their associations engaging in countless contractual transactions that are uncoerced. Sellers and buyers are on their own, as it were, to find each other, devise prices, and so on. This model of interaction accentuates the autonomous quality of human interaction, the experience of individual prerogative. Civil society is associated with a market economy, then, insofar as it involves the freedom to buy and sell all kinds of goods as one sees fit. This sense of prerogative provides a foundational experience for noncommercial, horizontal relationships and joint actions.

This second component of the liberal notion of civil society is connected to the first in that the state plays a key role in the formal codification of private property and often sets the terms of market exchange. The so-called rights of property, articulated by Locke and others, are preserved by government, as is the legal obligation to respect contracts (Locke 1965; Mardin 1995). Private property and market relations are not autonomous but rather are wrapped up in and partially constituted by the liberal state. Taken together, the conjunction of a limited state that respects citizen rights and a market economy that allows people to engage privately in exchange underpins the liberal concept of civil society. The two form the structural foundation of a nonstate domain of collective life.

What makes certain horizontal interactions "civil," and thus what distinguishes civil society from the economy and the state, is the quality of intrasocietal relations. In its modern sense, the notion of civil denotes cordiality. This comes from the Scottish Enlightenment idea that manners, education, and the experience of so-called civilization encourage people to treat one another with a certain degree of decency and tolerance. It recognizes that people have certain sensibilities and that these can be both harnessed for the good of society and preserved for individual enrichment through widespread mutual respect (Bryant 1995). At a more general level, civil refers simply to the bonds and allegiances that arise through sustained, voluntary, noncommercial interaction. Such bonds need not always be cordial but, nonetheless, provide the material out of which citizens organize their aspirations and advance projects that emerge spontaneously in the course of everyday life. Activities associated with the state, then, are not civil per se because they follow preordained patterns emanating from official authority. Likewise, economic interactions are not specifically civil because they have to do with the purely instrumental activity of enhancing monetary gain. Civil society is different in that it is about voluntarily experiencing the virtues of sociality and self-consciously representing oneself in a group in a social context. Churches, unions, movements, and clubs of all sorts constitute the organizations of civil society. Together they establish a domain of associational life above the individual and below the state marked by affiliation and social solidarity.

THE EMERGENCE OF GLOBAL CIVIL SOCIETY

Transposing the concept of civil society to the global level is fraught with difficulties. As many scholars point out, the idea of civil society evolved within the Western tradition of political thought and finds its empirical mooring paradigmatically in the liberal regimes that arose in the West during the latter part of the seventeenth and eighteenth centuries. From this perspective, civil society today is said to exist only in those countries with a rich liberal tradition, distinguished by a stable conjunction of limited government and private economic enterprise. Civil society, in other words, is historically specific, or at least contextually dependent, and thus impertinent to most settings. According to this line of thinking, it makes no sense to talk about civil society in, for example, Africa (Lewis 1992), India (Blaney and Pasha 1993), China (Wank 1995), or even Poland (Seligman 1992). It makes even less sense to speak, then, of *global* civil society.

While the historicity of civil society is important to keep in mind, one is nonetheless attracted to the concept when one notices that the same type of space and similar affections and relations that define civil society at the domestic level are prevalent at the global one. Human interaction throughout the world is not contained within the territorial borders of the state. People communicate, collaborate, and build relationships across national boundaries. In doing so, they establish modes of interaction and generate affiliations that constitute rich transnational networks. While perhaps less coherent than domestic social and cultural networks, sustained cross-boundary practices generate a domain unto itself. And, because of conceptual similarities, it makes analytical sense to understand this domain as global civil society. Global civil society, then, is that domain of associational life that exists above the individual and below the state yet across state boundaries through which people experience the virtues of sociality and represent themselves in a social context.

The liberal account, although developed through reflection on collective life at the domestic level, partially explains the emergence of global civil society. At one level, there is a state system under which much collective life is organized, and this has the trappings of a governmental structure that can foster transnational civil relations. Since at least the seventeenth century, the state system has expanded to include all parts of the world. All regions are under the jurisdiction of the state, even if individual territories do not enjoy territorial sovereignty. States recognize one another's authority and interact in the attempt to realize their individual aims and to address public goods problems. The state system represents a public authority of sorts, then, that establishes a modicum of governmental presence at the global level. To be sure, the governance involved is partial, continually contested, and often ineffective, as states often fail to cooperate or honor their commitments; nonetheless, it provides a structural component to global governance.

While certainly not liberal in character, the state system recognizes, legitimizes, and encourages transnational citizen interaction. International regimes, for example, lay down the groundwork for much transnational cultural and social networks. They set the terms of much transnational practice and thus lower transaction costs for all actors. One indicator of this is the profusion of transnational associations that emerged in tandem with the expansion of the state system. According to John Boli and George Thomas (1995), the presence of nonstate actors "jumped to a far higher level than ever before at exactly the time that the nation-state form was adopted or imposed on practically all the remaining land mass of the world" (18). Such associations expanded in the interstices of interstate activities, often taking advantage of the resources states devote to their own interactions. Additionally, the state system has done much to acknowledge formally the rights and practices of nonstate actors. The United Nations, for example, officially recognizes thousands of organizations that operate transnationally, as do other international governing bodies, such as the Antarctica Treaty System (Clark, 1994; Conca 1995; Gordenker and Weiss 1995). While global civil society is not reducible to the state system, it is partially a product of it. Private and voluntary transnational relationships can and do arise partially because there is a state system to support them.

The second feature of the global system that fosters civil society is the degree to which an integrated world market continues to extend itself to all areas of the world. While many regions have possessed market economies for centuries, there is now a globalized marketplace in which individuals and corporations produce, transport, and sell products and services the world over. The globalization of markets circumscribes a domain across national boundaries in which people can interact free from complete governmental penetration and extends the experience of private economic activity.

The nonstate quality of globalization is partly indicated by the rise of multinational corporations (MNCs)—businesses that undertake production, sales, and investment within multiple countries and across national boundaries. While such entities have existed for centuries in some form, the sheer quantity and extent of such firms have grown tremendously in recent decades (see generally Held et al. 1999). What marks MNCs is their quasi-detachment from the particular interests and values of their country of origin. Although they arise in a particular country, they often jump its borders when labor costs, regulations, or tax conditions within it disfavor their operations; MNCs function transnationally.

Like the analogy with the state system, the existence of a globalized market is not the same thing as a national economy based on private property and organized according to the market. Free markets do not exist everywhere, and there are not always smooth, integrative connections between separate free-market systems. Nonetheless, there is a thin, if not heterogeneous, economic system that spans the globe and is animated, primarily, by market relations based on private property. This, like the globalized state system, provides a component of the structural preconditions for global civil society. It allows individuals and corporate bodies to experience free association across state boundaries; it provides the ground for individual and corporate action based on prerogative rather than coercion or necessity. Considered along with the state system, the global economy sculpts a sector of global life that is transnational and in which allegiances, solidarities, and codes of conduct can arise.

While the state system and the global economy provide a space for global civil society, as a phenomenon its existence rests on the activities of certain actors that actually constitute it and the quality of relations that emerge between them. Nongovernmental organizations, including international scientific bodies, transnational political activist groups, religious associations, and all other voluntary affiliations that organize themselves or that at least project their energies across national boundaries, instantiate global civil society. Their activities actually establish horizontal transnational networks. If, for some unimaginable reason, they stopped operating, the potential for global civil society would still exist, but the actual phenomenon would not.

The term "NGO," to be sure, is unwieldy insofar as it represents a vast diversity of actors.[9] The term is relevant in this context, however, because it is the diversity that needs to be emphasized. Global civil society is not populated simply by politically progressive organizations that concentrate on issues such as human rights, environmental protection, and peace issues, as many analysts implicitly suggest.[10] Rather, it includes all voluntary organizations that operate across state boundaries. The

Catholic Church is as much an actor in global civil society as the International Chess Association; the transnational group Aryan Nations is as much a part of it as Greenpeace. What links these groups together is that, on the one hand, they are not tied to the territoriality of the state and thus focus on issues and pursue aims free from the task of preserving and enhancing the welfare of a given, geographically situated population. Following James Rosenau's lead, one could call them "sovereignty-free" actors.[11] On the other hand, they are nonprofit in the sense that they are not businesses seeking economic gain but rather are animated by social, cultural, or normative concerns.

GLOBAL CIVIL SOCIETY AND GOVERNANCE

As a domain of transnational collective life, global civil society is not necessarily political, and thus its contribution to global governance can be obscure. If global civil society operates simply as a sphere in which private individuals and groups engage in activities that affect only themselves—for example, international chess clubs—the political component is quite hidden.[12] Global civil society, however, is more than this. Like its domestic counterpart, it supports activities that shape widespread behavior and influences the way public issues are addressed. As such, it plays a role in governing the world polity. To appreciate this, it is useful to delineate the role that civil society plays in governing domestic affairs and then transpose that analysis up to the global level.

It will be remembered that, in its classical form, the idea of civil society (*societas civilas*) denoted a system of rule within a given community. It designated a domain in which laws regulated relationships among, and helped settle disputes between, citizens. Law, in this context, did not mean simply governmental directives but also included a social dimension. Norms, mores, and values were consistent with and found embodiment within the legal codes of society. The social order was conceived as an all-encompassing domain animated by a system of rules and norms as well as legal edicts.

While the term "civil society" eventually came to mean a distinct sphere within a social order—a domain above the individual and below the state (and distinct from the economy)—it never lost its political character. That is, while it came to designate an unofficial domain within collective life, there has always been the sense that it contributes to the overall quality of the polity. Although separate from the state, civil society has an element of political agency to it. It partially governs public affairs. One sees this most clearly in the attempt by thinkers to articulate the exact relationship between the state and civil society.

According to Gramsci, the distinction between the state and civil society is fundamentally analytic. In certain contexts, for example, the state and civil society are practically indistinguishable insofar as both operate according to a unified ideology. For Gramsci this means that a given class presents its own interests as universal and thus is capable of eliciting the consent of schools, churches, the press, councils, unions, and so on as well as the state (Gramsci 1971, 181–82). In these so-called hegemonic social orders, civil society is not subordinate to the state, nor is it superior to it. Rather, an integrated system of governance is at work, reinforcing itself through multiple institutions and organizations. The state and civil society represent two aspects of social order. One recognizes the agency of civil society here insofar as it is essential to the unity and coherence of hegemonic social orders.

One also recognizes such agency in cases in which the state and civil society are not integrated. At times, the state is captured by a given class that fails to define its interests universally and thus is unable to win consent of the organizations and institutions of civil society. In these cases civil society does not disappear but plays a particular role in governing society and in, at least theoretically, transforming political rule. In their governing role, the norms, codes of conduct, and prevalent values of civil society organize and shape the everyday affairs of citizens insofar as such affairs are free from the dictates of the state. In their transformative role, the institutions of civil society can be successively enlisted in a counterhegemonic effort to shift the social foundations of power and, eventually, topple the state. Schools, councils, the press, and so on become organized to resist state ideological-cultural imperatives and generate their own vision of social life—a situation that Gramsci calls a "war of position." The presupposition of such ideas is that certain modalities of power exist in civil society and that their activation and mobilization are potent forms of governance (see, generally, Gramsci 1971, 210–78).

While imprecise, Gramsci's insights are relevant at the global level. The global polity has a semblance of order, and this is constituted not simply by the state system but also by global civil society. In the same way that domestic civil society is always enacting order within a national polity—under both hegemonic and nonhegemonic settings—global civil society is always influencing the institutions of global life. This happens in two ways. First, global civil society conditions world order in an unintentional and largely unfocused manner. Many, if not most, NGOs populating global civil society eschew political affairs and pursue their transnational relations unaware of the political effects of their actions. Their activities in the aggregate, however, have public consequences insofar as they shape widespread understanding and behavior. That is, through the sheer multiplicity of NGOs, institutions inadvertently arise that guide collective life. To use postmodern language, the manifold force relations of global civil society create dominant discourses that consolidate and advance certain understandings and practices. In this first way, then, global civil society exerts influence on the world polity simply by existing.

The second way global civil society governs world order, and one more germane to the topic of this chapter, is through the deliberate efforts of politically motivated NGOs. A significant number of NGOs form for purely political reasons. They are part of transnational social movements aimed at advancing particular normative agendas. The most obvious of these include Amnesty International, Greenpeace, European Nuclear Disarmament, and Oxfam International, but, as mentioned, organizations such as Aryan Nations, the World Anti-Communist League, and the World

Union of National Socialists must also be included. These organizations devote themselves exclusively to setting up institutions to guide behavior with regard to public issues, and it is here that one can appreciate the social function of governance in global civil society.

One witnesses the governing efforts of politically motivated NGOs in the way in which they, for example, directly pressure states to undertake specific actions.[13] This entails persuading state officials—through lobbying, protest, and so on—to adopt policy recommendations. Nongovernmental organizations recognize that states are the main actors in world affairs and thus can most easily reach into and influence the lives of citizens. States, in other words, represent the quickest means for establishing effective institutions. Nongovernmental organizations expend tremendous effort trying to win the ear of states so that states will set up or remain in compliance with institutions that advance NGO aims. Examples of such activity abound.

Amnesty International and Human Rights Watch, for example, constantly lobby states to promote stricter international standards for the protection of human rights. This includes defining human rights in greater specificity and encouraging states to identify and punish violating states. In this latter regard, Amnesty International and Human Rights Watch publicize specific cases of human rights abuses and organize international censure. Such effort has had significant impact on the activity of states and on the further institutionalization of respect for human rights (see, e.g., Forsythe 1989; Goldman 1993; Sikkink 1993; Keck and Sikkink 1998). Similar efforts have been taken by transnational environmental groups with equal effect. Greenpeace and the Antarctic and Southern Oceans Coalition (ASOC), for example, work to influence international negotiations concerning protection of the oceans and Antarctica. In the former case, Greenpeace successfully convinced states to phase out industrial dumping in the North Sea and northeastern Atlantic as part of the London Dumping Convention—a policy recommendation initiated solely by Greenpeace (Stairs and Taylor 1992, 128). In the latter case, Greenpeace and ASOC orchestrated the defeat of the Convention on the Regulation of Antarctic Mineral Resources Activity (CRAMRA), which originally aimed to regulate mineral exploration on the continent, and advanced the idea of and won support for the 1991 Environmental Protocol, which prohibits mineral exploration for at least fifty years and establishes a framework for preserving the continent as a world park (see Deihl 1991; Wapner 1996, 136–37). In both cases, Greenpeace and ASOC pressured states to adopt certain policies that, through international cooperation, became institutionalized. Key to notice here is that, while states ultimately institutionalized these policies, the initiation and articulation of them arose outside the state system, that is, in global civil society.

One also witnesses the way in which NGOs engage in global governance by noticing how they mobilize means of governance that operate independently of the state system. It is fair to say that NGOs would prefer to work through the state system and enlist state capability in the construction of institutions. This route is often unavailable, however, in that many NGOs have little access to state officials—a situation prevalent in both democratic and nondemocratic settings. In these cases, NGOs make a strategic decision to identify and mobilize mechanisms of governance strewn throughout the nongovernmental sphere, a practice called *world civic politics* (Wapner 1995). In this capacity, NGOs target existing social and cultural institutions and seek to construct new ones in the service of advancing a particular cause. To be sure, this practice is difficult and often ineffective and produces results that are difficult to evaluate. Nonetheless, to the degree that NGOs successfully shift, for example, the standards of good conduct or fundamental understandings that animate particular widespread activities, it represents an important strategy for establishing institutions to govern widespread behavior. Examples of this type of activity also abound.

For years, European Nuclear Disarmament (END) not only sought to influence European governments with regard to the deployment of nuclear weapons but also aimed to create, what END members took to be, more peaceful societies. This latter objective involved demystifying traditional understandings of one's supposed enemy, propagating expressions of nonviolence, and combating widespread faith in the infallibility of one's society (see Thompson 1990 and more generally Joseph 1993; Galtung 1989). In such a case, END attempted to bend social and cultural discourses about peace and war to support its objectives; it sought to reconfigure the existing ideational institutions to promote its goal of reducing the threat of nuclear war. In a similar fashion, Friends of the Earth and a host of other national and international environmental groups have been working for years outside the domain of governments to reconfigure institutions that inform corporate practices. One of the more dramatic efforts along these lines is the establishment of the CERES Principles (referring to the Coalition for Environmentally Responsible Economies [formally the Valdez Principles]), which specify a set of guidelines for corporate practices based on a code of conduct that would minimize corporate contribution to environmental degradation (see Coalition for Environmentally Responsible Economies 1990). To date, a number of Fortune 500 MNCs, including General Motors and Sun Company, are signatories to the principles, as are a large number of less prominent MNCs. The principles represent a new set of institutional constraints on companies and thus another case of going outside the state system to institutionalize guidelines for widespread and transnational behavior (Ann-Zondorak 1991; Wapner 1996, 129–30). In both cases, NGOs turn their gaze away from the state system and concentrate on other entities within global society to win support for and the instantiation of their goals. Both cases illustrate an effort by NGOs to influence and construct institutions or, put differently, to practice world civic politics.

CONCLUSION

Many normative thinkers look to global civil society as a domain able to generate progressive political energy in the service of global well-being. To help realize the positive potential of global civil society, one needs to go beyond being a mere cheerleader of the domain and investigate the dynamics by which global civil society engages structures of power and thus is able to participate in global governance. This chapter aims to contribute to such an understanding insofar as it provides a theoretical account of global civil society. It tries to specify the quality of power operative in global civil society and the way in which it positions itself vis-à-vis other forms of global governance. The chapter's main point is to explain how global civil society provides a terrain on which actors can organize material and ideational resources to shift the institutional matrix that shapes widespread behavior. Institutions, as Oran Young (1994) reminds us, are "sets of rules of the game or codes of conduct that serve to define social practices, assign roles to the participants in these practices, and guide the interactions among occupants of these roles" (3). As such, they need not arise simply through the efforts of states but can emerge and be built by nonstate actors. To be sure, such entities are often less effective in establishing institutions, but nonetheless they engage in such activity.

A number of scholars have documented the effectiveness of NGOs in establishing institutions (see, e.g., Stairs and Taylor 1992; Sikkink 1993; Princen and Finger 1994; Klotz 1995; Keck and Sikkink 1998). This work focuses on NGO efforts to persuade national governments to pursue certain policy recommendations with regard to international negotiations and to work outside the state system to create norms, principles, values, and so on that influence the thinking and behavior of individuals and collectivities throughout the world. This chapter presents a theoretical account of why such NGO efforts matter or, put differently, why such efforts actually establish specific institutions. By explaining the nature of global civil society and explicating its role in global governance, the chapter analytically places NGOs within a particular realm of collective life and clarifies why their activities within it have political effect.

Humane governance is one of those idealized values that both broaden the political imagination and provide an orientation for assessing contemporary political conditions. Like peace, ecological balance, social justice, and economic well-being, it sits in the mind's eye as a dream, but one that can provide a posture for critique and a trajectory along which to correlate future-oriented action. There seems to be some consensus that global civil society is part of the equation of what would ultimately constitute humane governance at the global level and that global civil society is one of the most promising places to look for emerging progressive political thought and action. By providing an understanding of the character of global civil society at this point in history, this chapter implicitly works for humane governance. It was undertaken in the belief that analysis is an important part of normative international relations and motivated by the dream of a world governed by arrangements that have human well-being at the center of concern.

NOTES

A shorter and less developed version of this essay appeared as "Governance in Global Civil Society," in *Global Governance: Drawing Insights from the Environmental Experience,* ed. Oran Young (Cambridge, Mass.: MIT Press, 1997).

1. For this view of domestic civil society, see Cohen and Arato (1992) and Walzer (1995).

2. This broader understanding of civil governance extends back to the Aristotelian notion of *koinonia politike,* the forebear of *societas civilas* (Cohen and Arato 1992, 85) and helps account for later understandings associated with Locke, Kant, Rousseau, and others that conflate the state and civil society (Kumar 1993, 376).

3. According to John Keane, Hegel's role in distinguishing the state from civil society is exaggerated. Between 1750 and 1850, scores of political thinkers wrestled with the distinction through reflection on the limits of state action (see Keane 1988, 63).

4. It should be noted that, while Hegel characterizes civil society taking place outside the *household* and below the state, I locate it above the *individual* and the state. I do so because I am persuaded by arguments that claim that the household is a part of civil society. See Pateman (1988) and Singerman (1998).

5. The relationship between the state and civil society in Hegel is admittedly abstract. As I understand it, the state makes apparent what already exists in civil society by disciplining the particularist dynamics of civil society to more universalist, public aims. Put differently, as a moment of social organization, civil society sits at an intermediate stage between the family and the state. The state's job, as it were, is to enable universal interest—in contrast to private interest—to prevail. In Hegelian terminology, it allows for the realization of ethical life in contrast to the abstract morality available in civil society. See Hegel (1942).

6. The liberal account of civil society, to which I refer, is a particular strain of liberal thought that sees civil society arising in relation to the economy and the modern state. This strain of thought differs from liberal accounts that see the economy as essentially equivalent to civil society or at least the central dynamic at work in civil society.

7. This acknowledgment was part of a broader development of rationalized law that eventually circumscribed such freedom and codified such rights. See Mardin (1995, 279–80).

8. To be sure, the result of this is not a homogeneous private domain but a stratified one wherein separate classes possess only circumscribed interests and partial social affiliations. Nonetheless, a coherent domain is, in fact, created where people can pursue private aims. See Lewis (1992, 37–38).

9. For a discussion of problems associated with the term "nongovernmental organization," see Gordenker and Weiss (1995), Korten (1990, 95), and Rosenau (1990, 36).

10. See, for example, Lipschutz (1992). Although they do not use the term "global civil society," Princen and Finger (1994) and Boli and Thomas (1995) suggest that NGO activity is undertaken primarily by politically progressive organizations.

11. James Rosenau persuasively argues that the term "NGO" unduly places too much attention on states and thus perpetuates the state-centrism of international relations scholarship. He suggests using the term "sovereignty-free" actors. I prefer the term "NGO" simply because of its common currency, although I realize that there are certain costs involved with employing it. See Rosenau (1990).

12. Implicit in this formulation is the idea that what is of concern to the public is necessarily political. For background on this idea of the public and the conjunction between it and politics, see Dewey (1954, 15–16).

13. For a comprehensive study of how environmental NGOs engage in world political activity, see Wapner (2000).

19

Technological Underdevelopment in the South: The Continuing Cold War

Ali A. Mazrui

It is not often realized that the most obstinate line of demarcation between North and South is not income (criteria of wealth) but technology (criteria of skill). The entire international system of stratification has come to be based *not* on "who owns what" but on "who *knows* what." Kuwait and Saudi Arabia may have a higher per capita income than some of the members of the European Union, but the Gulf states are well below Western Europe in skills of production and economic organization. Indeed, members of the Organization of Petroleum Exporting Countries (OPEC) do not even have adequate skills to control or drill their own oil.

Nowhere is this caste system of skill demonstrated more clearly than in southern Africa and the Middle East. Less than five million whites in South Africa were able to hold to ransom a black population in the subregion twenty times their own. They held neighboring blacks to ransom both economically and militarily. The main explanation was not simply that South Africa was rich but that its wealth had been extracted through African labor and *European* expertise. South Africa's neighbors, such as Mozambique, had African labor as well. Some of them, such as Angola and Botswana, were also rich in minerals. There was also well-endowed Zaire (Congo). What the blacks lacked indigenously was the superior technology of production and the accompanying culture of efficient organization.

The Middle East is a clearer and more staggering illustration of the power of skill over income. At least since the 1970s, parts of the Arab world have become significantly richer than Israel in sheer income. Indeed, the Israeli economy would have suffered severe shrinkage but for the infusion of billions of dollars from the United States and from world Jewry. Yet, despite being outnumbered and outmoneyed, the Israelis have retained the upper hand militarily against the Arabs. The supremacy of skill over income and numbers has been dramatically illustrated in one Middle East war after another.

275

In both South Africa and Israel, the cultural variable is critical. Had Israel consisted entirely of Middle Eastern Jews, the Arabs would have won every war. Indeed, it would not have been necessary to have more than the 1948 war. After all, Middle Eastern Jews are not very different from their Arab neighbors in culture and skill. In a war against fellow Middle Easterners, the numeric preponderance of the Arabs would have triumphed against Jews long before the numeric advantage was reinforced by Arab petro-wealth.

What has made the Israelis militarily preeminent is not the Jewishness of 80 percent of the total population but the European-ness of less than half of that Jewish sector. It is the European and Western Jews who have provided the technological foundations of Israel's regional hegemony.

If, then, the ultimate basis of international stratification is skill rather than income, what is the Third World to do in order to ameliorate the consequences of this technological underdevelopment? How can the Third World "skill" itself to overcome its weak status in the international system and resist the hegemonic power of the North? These questions sit at the heart of contemporary normative international relations, especially since the power gap between the North and the South provides a central dynamic of world politics.

The obvious prescriptive response to these questions is for the Third World to obtain expertise from the Northern Hemisphere as rapidly as possible. However, there are difficulties. Countries of the Northern Hemisphere are often all too eager to transfer certain forms of technology, especially through transnational corporations, but the South's need for certain technological transfers only helps deepen relationships of dependency between the two hemispheres.

On the other hand, there are other areas of technology that the North is not at all keen to transfer. Preeminent among the taboos is the transfer of certain branches of nuclear physics and technology. The computer is part of the phenomenon of dependency through technology transfer; the nuclear plant or reactor is a symbol of dependency through technological monopoly by the North. The transnational corporations are often instruments of Northern penetration of the South through technological transfer; nuclear power, on the other hand, is a symbol of Northern hegemony through technological monopoly.

Behind the Western fear of the spread of nuclear expertise to Third World countries is the fear of nuclear weapons proliferation. There is anxiety in Western capitals that what begins as the peaceful use of nuclear energy may become something more ominous—thus the repeated attempts by the United States to pull back Russia from any kind of nuclear cooperation (however peaceful) with a country like Iran.

Keeping these challenges in mind, this chapter outlines a number of actions that the South can undertake to resist its inferior status and begin to "skill" itself in a manner that would advance its own well-being. Key in the following discussion is the idea of the South undertaking its own initiatives and not relying on the North. While it may presently lack technological prowess vis-à-vis the North, it certainly possesses the wherewithal to pursue effective strategies toward greater technological capability and development. Solidarity within the South is essential for realizing this potential.

SKILL TRANSFER AS A GLOBAL STRATEGY

The best strategy for the Third World (including China) is both to learn from the North and to share expertise among themselves. Those aspects of technology that are being freely transferred by the North should be "decolonized" and stripped of their dependency implications as fast as possible. Those aspects of technology that are deliberately monopolized by the North should be the targets of Southern industrial espionage in a bid to break the monopoly. Pakistani scientists have been on the right track in their reported efforts to subject the Northern nuclear monopoly to Southern industrial spying. Now that Pakistan has more openly become Islam's first nuclear power, if it decides to share nuclear secrets with select fellow Muslims, that trend will be in the direction of enhanced technological cooperation among Third World countries.

The foregoing is one reason that the brain drain from the South is *not* an unmitigated disaster. It is vital that the South counterpenetrate the citadels of technological and economic power. The counterpenetration can take the form of Southern engineers, teachers and professors, medical doctors and consultants, and businesspersons and scientists working in the North. The North needs to be more sensitized to Southern needs not only through the speeches of Southern statesmen and ambassadors but also through the influence and leverage of Southerners resident in the North, provided that these retain residual Southern characteristics and commitments.

In any case, there is no law of gravity that says that expertise can only flow from the North to the South. There is no gravitational logic that says that a European teacher teaching African children is natural, but an African teacher teaching European children is not. The structure of scientific stratification in the world should cease to be a rigid caste system and allow for social mobility in both directions. Of course, a major brain drain from the South northward could deeply hurt the South. The trouble with the present level of the brain drain is not that it is too great, however, but that it is grossly underutilized. Professor Edward S. Ayensu, a Ghanaian research director at the Smithsonian Institution in Washington, D.C., has argued that there is a large potential pool of Third World experts resident in the Northern Hemisphere who would be only too glad to serve for a year or two in developing societies if only their services were solicited. What is more, the Northern institutions in which they work would, according to Professor Ayensu, be sympathetically inclined toward facilitating such exchanges from time to time if so requested by Third World authorities.[1]

If that were to happen, Southern expertise would be tapped on the basis of a triangular formula. The flow of expertise would be first from South to North, then

North to South, and then South to South—often involving the same Southern experts or their equivalents, sharing their expertise across hemispheres.

Unfortunately, while the North may indeed be willing to share with the South some of its newly acquired Southern experts, the South itself has shown more enthusiasm for borrowing "pure" Northern experts than for borrowing Southern experts resident in the North. The psychological dependency of the South is such that the South is less likely to be impressed by an Indian or Nigerian expert coming from the United States than by an American expert with far less understanding of the Third World. The American is regarded as "the real thing" in expertise, while the Indian statistician or Nigerian engineer is deemed to be a mere Southern imitation. The technological prestige of the North has undermined the South's self-confidence and sense of independence.

Fortunately, all is not bleak. There is some movement of expertise among Third World countries. Boutros Boutros-Ghali, when he was minister of state for foreign affairs of Egypt before his days at the United Nations, assured me in an interview in Cairo in 1983 that Egypt had "two million experts" working in other countries, mainly Africa and the Middle East. The number has not declined. South Asia also exports a considerable corps of experts to other parts of the Third World.[2]

Political instability and economic problems at home cause some of the traffic in expertise across Third World frontiers. Qualified Ugandans are scattered in almost all four corners of the Third World as well as in the North. So are qualified Lebanese, Palestinians, southern Africans, Ethiopians, and others.

Then there is the inter–Third World traffic of experts caused by the magnetism of petro-wealth: The Gulf states have a particularly impressive wealth of human talent from different lands. Two Ghanaian scholars visited the University of Petroleum and Minerals in Dhahran in Saudi Arabia in the summer of 1984. They were impressed by the Ghanaian presence in the research complex of the university. They were also surprised to learn about "twenty-four highly qualified Ghanaian medical officers working in and around this University town of Dhahran."[3] Dhahran continues to be a magnet for foreign skills.

To summarize, there is a *push-out factor* in some of the less fortunate Third World countries that forces many of the native experts to search for opportunities in other countries. These push forces include political instability, tyranny, lack of research facilities, and poor economic rewards. However, there is also a *pull-in factor* in the wealthier Third World societies that attracts workers and specialists from other lands. The pull-in factor includes greater freedom, better infrastructure, professional recognition, and better financial rewards. Together these two forces are helping lay the foundations for future organic solidarity within the Third World in the field of expertise.

Organic solidarity is a process of integration among Third World countries themselves. Strategic solidarity is Southern unity in policy to face the North. What is lacking is an adequate linkage between organic and strategic solidarity in this field of evolving Third World expertise. A systematic program that would enable the

South to borrow some of the Southern experts now resident in the North could become an important stage in the evolution of a merger between organic and strategic solidarity.

SOUTH-SOUTH SOLIDARITY: ORGANIC AND STRATEGIC

In order for skill transfer to lead to greater Southern empowerment in North-South relations, the South has to explore other areas of leverage. Although *the power of skill* is, at the moment, overwhelmingly in the hands of the North, there are other areas of power that the South possesses but has underutilized. In several of those areas, South-South solidarity is an imperative.

Two forms of solidarity are critical for the Third World if the global system is to change in favor of the disadvantaged. *Organic solidarity* concerns South-South linkages designed to increase mutual dependence between and among Third World countries themselves. *Strategic solidarity* concerns cooperation among Third World countries in their struggle to extract concessions from the industrialized Northern world. Organic solidarity concerns the aspiration to promote greater integration among Third World economies. Strategic solidarity aspires to decrease the South's dependent integration into Northern economies. The focus of organic solidarity is primarily a South-South economic marriage. The focus of strategic solidarity is either a North-South divorce, a new marriage settlement, or a new social contract between North and South. The terms of the North-South bond have to be renegotiated.

Economic flows are currently far deeper between North and South than between South and South. Overall, Southerners do far greater trade with the North than with each other and have more extensive relations of production with industrialized states than with fellow developing countries. However, those economic relations between North and South are distorted by a tradition of dependency involving unequal partnership. The structural links give undue advantage and leverage to the North, leaving the South vulnerable and exploited.

What, then, is the way out? How can organic and strategic solidarity help ameliorate the Third World's predicament of dependency and its persistent economic vulnerability? In fact, the Third World has many sources of power, among them producer power, consumer power, and debtor power.

OPEC is an illustration of producer power. From 1973 to 1983, OPEC grossly underutilized its leverage. Instead of using that golden decade to put pressure on the North for fundamental adjustments in the patterns and rules of the world economy, OPEC concentrated almost exclusively on the prices game, a game of short-term maximization of returns. The South needs skills of long-term strategizing in this area.

There is a crying need for other "producer cartels," no matter how weak in the short run. Cobalt has more promise as a mineral of leverage than does copper and would involve fewer countries. Experimentation with a cobalt cartel could pay off if the Democratic Republic of the Congo (formerly Zaire) asserted itself more decisively as an independent power. After all, Congo (Kinshasa) has the credentials to be the Saudi Arabia of cobalt when the market improves in the years ahead.

The Third World has also underutilized its consumer power, regionally specific and patchy as it is. The Middle East is especially important as a consumer of Western civil and military hardware and technology and household products. Occasionally, individual Middle East countries flex their muscles and threaten to cancel trade contracts or to refuse to renew them. However, such muscles are flexed usually for relatively minor issues, such as protesting against the television film *Death of a Princess* or when an Arab delegation is snubbed by a Western power. The consumer power of the Middle East could be used as leverage for more fundamental changes in the exchange patterns between North and South. The South should sharpen its skills of negotiations and exerting pressure. Malaysia has used its trading muscle with England to punish the *Sunday Times* (London) for irresponsible allegations against Malaysia's prime minister. Malaysia's action posed a question: Can the South's economic muscle help create a New International Information Order? Malaysia won the battle, but the South has yet to win the war.[4]

The third form of power currently underutilized by the South is *debtor power*. Some years ago, President Julius Nyerere of Tanzania, on being elected chairman of the Organization of African Unity, identified development, debt, and drought as the three leading concerns of the current African condition. Of course, African debts are modest compared with those of Latin America, but Nyerere identified debt as a source of power and not merely as a source of weakness. At his press conference after his election, he lamented that the Third World was not utilizing the threat of defaulting more efficiently to induce Western banks to make more fundamental concessions to the indebted.[5]

It is indeed true that if I owe my local bank a few thousand dollars, I am vulnerable, but if I owe the bank millions of dollars, the bank is vulnerable. Tanzania owes so little that the country is very vulnerable. However, Nyerere virtually declared that if he owed as much as some huge debtor countries, he would simply refuse to pay and demand a reappraisal.[6]

In reality, Tanzania would still be vulnerable unless there was substantial strategic solidarity among both African and Latin American countries. The utilization of debtor power requires considerable consensus among the indebted. The Western banks have evolved a kind of organic solidarity of their own as well as mechanisms of almost continuous consultation. The creditors of the North are united, but the debtors of the South are in disarray. Sustained solidarity needs skills of perseverance.

Africa and Latin America need to explore the possibility of creating a strategic solidarity of the dispossessed and the indebted to help induce the sharks of the North to make concessions on such issues as rates of interest, schedules of payment, methods of payment, and the conditions for a moratorium where needed.

Fundamental as all these areas of strategic solidarity are, they are no substitutes for organic solidarity in terms of greater trade, investment, and other interactions among Third World countries themselves. Here the "Less Developed Countries" (LDCs) are caught up in several contradictions. In their relations with the North, LDCs need to diversify their economies. However, in their relations with one another, LDCs need to specialize in order to increase mutual complementarity. Uganda could revive its cotton industry and sell the fiber to Kenya to process into a textile industry. This specialization would help the two countries develop in the direction of complementary specialization. However, the imperatives of Uganda's relations with the world economy as a whole dictate diversification of Uganda's industry rather than specialization. This is an acute dilemma that Third World countries need to resolve as a matter of urgency. They need to find a suitable balance between diversification for North-South relations and specialization for South-South trade. Such a balancing act needs skills of its own.

Related to this is the imperative of finding alternative methods of payment in South-South trade. The principle of using Northern currencies for South–South trade has been very stressful. The bogey of "foreign exchange" has bedeviled Southern economies. Tanzania, Zambia, and Zimbabwe have been exploring possibilities of reviving barter as a basis of at least aspects of their economic relations. The new détente among Uganda, Rwanda, and Congo (Kinshasa) also envisages areas of barter trade among the three countries in the years ahead. Moreover, if Uganda's cotton were to feed Kenya's textile industry more systematically in the future, it would not be unrealistic for Kenya to pay back Uganda in shirts and processed military uniforms rather than in hard foreign exchange. Even modest manufacturing skills can be used to good advantage.

Another area of organic solidarity among Third World countries concerns the issue of sharing energy. There have been years when Kenya has needed to get a third of its electricity from the dam at Jinja in Uganda. Uganda is still a major supplier of power to Kenya. The Akasombo Dam on the Volta River in Ghana was also designed to be a major regional supplier of electricity in West Africa. Unfortunately, the level of water has sometimes been so low that far from supplying power to neighbors, Ghana has periodically had to ration power domestically. Ghana has sometimes needed electrical cooperation from the Ivory Coast. The 1990s have witnessed considerable improvement. Southern African dams, such as Kariba, have had more successful regional roles. They all symbolize a kind of pan-Africanism of energy—organic solidarity through interlocking structures of hydroelectric power.

An integrated European steel complex once served as midwife to the birth of the European Economic Community. Indeed, the integrated steel industry was envisioned as insurance against any future fratricidal war in Europe. If European steel production was interlocked, industrial interdependence was at hand, and separate military aggression in the future would therefore be less likely.

In the same spirit, interlocking electrical systems among Third World countries should deepen mutual dependence and create incentives for cooperation in other areas. Learning from other people's history is itself a valuable skill. Inter-African trade on a large scale will not be easy since most African countries produce similar primary commodities and raw materials. Major inter-African traders have been countries such as Kenya, Zaire (now Congo), and, increasingly, postapartheid South Africa. However, if organic solidarity is to achieve fundamental change, African economies need to plan for future complementarity. If Zambia already has a factory for manufacturing bicycles, neighboring Malawi should specialize in the manufacture of, say, such farm implements as ploughs, hoes, and lawn mowers, which are more modern. Ideally, Zambia would be selling bicycles to Malawi (and others), and Malawi would be selling farm implements to Zambia (and others).

In other parts of the world, the struggle for a more integrated Southeast Asia is more of a success story, as the Association of Southeast Asian Nations (ASEAN) has emerged as a major economic and diplomatic force in the affairs of the region, while the struggle for a more integrated Arab world is mixed, ranging from the positive promise of the Gulf Cooperation Council to the negative internecine squabbles of Arab politics.

In Latin America, regional integration is also a mixed record. Central America is emerging from under the clouds of war. Chile and Argentina, through the mediation of the Vatican, have diffused the sensitive issue of the Bege Channel. Economic cooperation has had its ups and downs throughout the region, but the ideal of greater integration is alive and well; the North Atlantic Free Trade Area may be extended to cover the hemisphere as a whole in the years ahead.

CONCLUSION

In sum, in the Third World, technological illiteracy is an Achilles' heel. Countries of East and Southeast Asia have shown remarkable progress in economic performance, but the central divide between North and South continues to be fundamentally technological. As I have argued, in international affairs stratification is based not on "who *owns* what" but on "who *knows* what."

The Third World must think of strategies for overcoming its technological handicap and economic vulnerability. I have distinguished between organic solidarity, which is designed to increase mutual dependence among Third World countries themselves, and strategic solidarity, which is South-South cooperation in the struggle to gain concessions from the North. I have also pointed out that while *skill power* is overwhelmingly in favor of the North, the South does have *producer power* (based on its resources) and *consumer power* (based on its purchasing ability). Perhaps more risky are the potentialities of unified *debtor power*. Ultimately, the foundations of international stratification are not income differences, military gadgets, or demographic variations. Ultimate power resides neither in the barrel of the gun nor in the barrel of oil but rather in the technology that can produce and use both efficiently. A "new international economic order" would be void without a "new international technological order." The South needs strategies of solidarity to realize both.

NOTES

1. Ayensu (1984).

2. Indian professors, doctors, and consultants are part of the labor markets of Africa, the Middle East, Southeast Asia, as well as the West. South Asia is also well represented on the staff of the World Bank and the International Monetary Fund.

3. The two Ghanaian visitors were Professor Alexander Kwapong, vice rector of the United Nations University in Japan, and Professor Edward Ayensu of the Smithsonian Institution in the United States. See Ayensu's lecture in Note 1.

4. When I discussed the affair of the *Sunday Times* with the prime minister of Malaysia in 1995, Dr. Mahathir Mohamed assured me that the offending editor of the British newspaper has been relocated to New York and that the issue had been discreetly resolved. The prime minister was satisfied that Malaysia's economic pressure had paid off.

5. The Voice of America's African Service broadcast a recording of both Nyerere's speech and Nyerere's press conference. One such broadcast by the Voice of America was on Saturday, November 24, 1984.

6. Africa's leading debtor nations include Nigeria, Egypt, and Congo (Kinshasa).

20

Governance, Legitimacy, and Security: Three Scenarios for the Twenty-First Century

Mary Kaldor

The short twentieth century, as Eric Hobsbawm (1995) calls it, began in 1914 and ended in 1991. It was a tumultuous, violent period in which powerful groups of states contended for control over people, territory, and resources. The system of governance was determined largely by the dominant conflicts between groups of states, most notably during the Cold War period.

The collapse of the Soviet Union and of communism has been followed by a pervasive sense of uncertainty about the future. The dominant stream of political science rooted in the twentieth-century experience is able to predict only a new variant of the past or else the descent into chaos. Precisely because it was directed toward the existing system of governance, providing at the same time a form of justification or legitimation of that system and a basis for offering advice about how to operate within the system, conventional political science is characterized by a kind of fatalism or determinism about the future. In contrast, critical or normative approaches to political science, as exemplified in the work of Richard Falk, allow for human agency. They are based on the assumption that people make their own history and can choose their futures, at least within a certain framework that can be analyzed.

By governance, I mean the process of managing human affairs and how this is organized through political institutions. Nowadays, the pattern of governance includes layers of institutions: nation-states; regional organizations, such as the European Union or NATO; and wider transnational institutions, including the United Nations, the General Agreement on Tariffs and Trade (GATT), or the International Monetary Fund (IMF). Central to the future of governance is provision of security, which, I would argue, is inextricably bound up with legitimacy. I define security in the narrow sense to mean the control of organized violence and to include the security of the individual and not just the state. By legitimacy, I mean the extent to which people consent to and even support the framework of rules within which political institutions function, either because political institutions are viewed as having gained their authority through some legitimate process and/or because they are seen to represent ideas or values that are widely supported.

Nowadays, there is a lot of talk about what is known as the "security vacuum," especially but not only in the postcommunist states. What this means is the absence of institutions to guarantee security, and this view informs the debate, at least in Europe, about the extension of NATO, the role of the Organization for Security and Cooperation in Europe (OSCE) and so on. There is a security vacuum today, but it is not merely an institutional security vacuum; it is a real security vacuum. That is, over the last two decades there has been an erosion of the ability of states and transnational institutions to maintain order; this is reflected in both the rise of violent crime and the number of civilians killed or expelled from their homes in wars.[1] This real security vacuum has to be explained, I would argue, in terms of a growing loss of legitimacy in the aftermath of the Cold War and in the context of globalization.

In what follows, I elaborate on this argument about the link between patterns of governance, sources of legitimacy, and ways of maintaining security and then, in the light of the analysis, consider three scenarios for governance in the twenty-first century. The first is Samuel Huntington's "The Clash of Civilizations?", an attempt to extrapolate future arrangements for security in a more or less linear direction from the past. (Huntington 1993, 1997). The second is Robert D. Kaplan's "Coming Anarchy," which is a counsel of despair, an admission of our inability to analyze global developments (Kaplan 1994, 1997). The third, is Richard Falk's "Humane Governance," which courageously offers a normative vision of the future (Falk 1995).

POLITICAL INSTITUTIONS, LEGITIMACY, AND SECURITY

The control of organized violence is an essential precondition for effective governance. It is inseparable from another essential precondition: legitimacy. On the one hand, the ability to maintain order, to protect individuals in a physical sense, to guarantee the operation of justice and the rule of law, are the primary functions of institutions from which they derive legitimacy. Moreover, the character of these institutions is defined largely in relation to the way in which these functions are undertaken and which aspects of security are accorded priority. On the other hand, it is not possible to provide security in the sense just defined without some underlying legitimacy. There has to be some mechanism, whether it is religious injunction, ideological fanaticism, or democratic consent, that explains why people obey rules and why, in particular, agents of organized violence (e.g., soldiers or policemen) follow orders.

The Westphalian era is usually said to mark the rise of a states system in Europe characterized by a gradual monopolization of legitimate violence by individual states. Anthony Giddens (1985) points out that Max Weber's definition of the state as the organization that "successfully upholds the monopoly of legitimate organised violence" actually applies only to the modern state, which came into being somewhere between the fifteenth and eighteenth centuries and which he contrasts with traditional states. The rise of modern states and, more particularly, nation-states that emerged in the nineteenth century involved a centralization and secularization of power within a given territory together with the development of absolutist notions of sovereignty. This process was intimately linked to the growth of war-making capacities encapsulated by Tilly's (1990) famous remark that "the state made war and war made states." On the one hand, the success of modern states as institutions was the consequence of their ability to win wars and to protect territory. On the other hand, the ability to win wars depended on the development of centralized administration and revenue-raising capacity as well as increased legitimacy. Michael Mann (1988) has shown that in the case of England, military expenditures were the main component of state expenditures up to the nineteenth century and that taxation was increased and regularized, as was state borrowing, during times of war. The process of monopolization of legitimate violence entailed the elimination of private armies, the establishment of law and order, and the rise of regular professional armies that were sharply distinguished from the civilian police.

Essentially, the modern state could be said to be the organized entity through which violence was contained. It was contained geographically in that violence was pushed outward against other states. The implicit contract through which a rule of law and civil society was established legitimized the state as the embodiment of an emergent national identity in exchange for external protection. As the absolutist state of the seventeenth and eighteenth centuries gave way to the nineteenth-century nation-state, a concept of citizenship was developed that was based largely on civil and political rights. Citizens acquired the right to participate, through voting or through being able to organize or express opinions freely without fear of intimidation, and they also acquired the duty to pay taxes and, if necessary, to serve in the armed forces. Patriotism linked to a notion of rights became the primary source of legitimacy. Ultimately, the readiness to die for one's country expressed the strength of the new patriotism.

With the emergence of the European states system, security came to be seen as the preserve of the state, involving a dual character of territorial defense externally and law and order domestically. As R. B. J. Walker (1990a) points out, a binary opposition between inside and outside was established in which the outside was characterized by fragmentation and anarchy and the inside by centralization and legitimate authority. "The principle of state sovereignty refers neither to just the fact of fragmentation nor to the fact of centralised authority, but to a specific claim about both tendencies. State sovereignty is in effect an exceptionally elegant resolution of the apparent contradiction between centralisation and fragmentation, or phrased in more philosophical language, between universality and particularity" (10). The defense of territory against external enemies that came to be largely identified with security during the era of the nation-state was at one and the same time seen as defense of nation building internally, involving the emergence of, if not always democracy, at least the concept of citizenship.

Among political thinkers, there has always been a tension between the realist Hobbesian view of human nature and the liberal idealist conception. The former assumes that human beings naturally tend toward aggression and that strong political institutions are required to tame or "civilize" human society. Thus, the realists strongly emphasize the key role of the state in providing security. The latter have a much more rationalist view of human nature and are more concerned about how to constrain the violence of political institutions and how to construct legitimacy on which law and order can be based.

In the era of the states system, it was realist thinking that became dominant in the study of international relations because of the fragmented character of the "outside" world. According to the realists, the most important mechanism in maintaining order among the separate fragmented units of the states system was the balance of power. Because there was no ultimate arbiter, war was seen as the mechanism used to reestablish order when rules broke down. States pursued their interests unilaterally, and since there was no constraint or limitation on this pursuit, war was understood as a rational instrument of geopolitics.

Liberal ideas were always on the margins of international thought and were generally treated as naive or "utopian." For the liberals, the states system was not immutable. They pointed to the various mechanisms that were developing in Europe to increase interaction among states—international law, diplomacy, congresses—and they developed schemes for "perpetual peace" that anticipated the international institutions that exist today. Liberal thinkers tended to be skeptical about the balance of power. They saw war, and indeed the concept of balance of power, as a mechanism for sustaining undemocratic rule at home by turning quarrels outward. In his critique of the Abbé Saint Pierre's peace project, J. J. Rousseau asks why schemes for perpetual peace are not adopted. If we can establish a civil society in a given territory, why is it not possible to extend the rule of law? A legal framework for settling conflicts of interest at an international level is a much more rational way to pursue national interests than costly and tragic wars. His answer is that states need wars to justify their rule, for legitimacy:

> Again, anyone can understand that war and conquest without and the encroachments of despotism within give each other mutual support; that money and men are habitually taken at pleasure from a people of slaves, to bring others beneath the same yoke; and that conversely war furnishes a pretext for exactions of money and another, no less plausible, for keeping large armies constantly on foot, to hold people in awe. In a word, anyone can see that aggressive princes wage war at least as much on their subjects as on their enemies, and that the conquering nation is left no better off than the conquered. (Rousseau 1991, 90–91)

In the second half of the twentieth century, the states system was supplanted by the bloc system. After two terrible wars, which affected most parts of the world, a new international pattern of governance was established in which groups of states were brought together under the ideological label of blocs. While at its most rigid in Europe, the bloc system was, in fact, global in scope. Every state defined its international position in relation to the blocs: pro-West, pro-Soviet, or neutral or non-aligned. The bloc system was shaped by the experience of two world wars, especially World War II. This was a total war in which mobilization went beyond anything hitherto experienced. The scale of resources required and the commitment demanded of the populations involved in the war were qualitatively different from the wars of the eighteenth and nineteenth centuries. A secular national identity was no longer a sufficient basis on which to appeal for sacrifice. To the sense of nationhood was added an ideological dimension: To be British or American meant to have certain rights, to be free and democratic, and indeed, in contrast to Germany, humane; to be Soviet was to be socialist—the last great secular religion, as Ernest Gellner (1994) puts it. The war brought about a huge increase not only in taxation levels but also in the redistribution of income and in degrees of social equality, and this resulted in an expansion in the notion of rights. In the West, the right to social security was added to the right to physical security; in the Soviet Union, social rights came to have priority over civil and political rights. Thus, political ideology was added to national identity as a form of legitimacy. But unlike national identity, this ideology was universalistic; it had no territorial limits and consequently could be extended to groups of nations. People risked their lives not simply for patriotism but for certain ideals: freedom and socialism.

The Cold War reproduced the experience of World War II and grouped nations together under the ideological labels of democracy or of socialism. The bloc system in effect produced a profound change in the character of states. In Europe especially, nation-states, by integrating their military forces into alliance command structures, effectively abandoned the claim to the monopoly of organized violence. Their armed forces were transnationalized and, except in the case of England and France—and even in these two countries there were limitations—European countries were, for the most part, no longer able to wage war unilaterally. Outside Europe, the dependence of non-European armed forces on patron states, mainly the United States and the Soviet Union, curtailed the unilateral ability to wage war and meant that interstate war became less frequent and was limited by outside intervention of various kinds.[2]

Within this security framework, this period was characterized by the proliferation of transnational institutions—the United Nations; various economic institutions, including the IMF or GATT; and regional institutions, such as the European Community, the Organization of African Unity (OAU), or the Association of Southeast Asian Nations (ASEAN). While these institutions were primarily intergovernmental and depended on the consent of individual states, the bloc system established an ethos that allowed for cooperation and meant, in effect, that many functions typically associated with sovereignty were gradually pooled or taken over. By establishing bloc identities based on a shared ideological commitment, a transnational public space was also created in which extended cooperation became possible. Internal pacification was extended across groups of nations, thus the finding so widely quoted that democratic countries do not fight each other. Quarrels were pushed further outward. The inside/outside character of state sovereignty, described by Walker, was extended to groups of nations.

For the realist, the key mechanism in the new international order was deterrence. The basic argument was a variant of the old balance-of-power thesis. Beyond, the cozy felicity of the shared public space of those who go under the same ideological label is a world of anarchy. What prevents anarchy, what stops aggression, is the threat of a war so terrible that it cannot be contemplated. The proof that nuclear weapons kept the peace in Europe was the fact that war did not take place, at least in Europe, during the Cold War period.

For the idealists, however, this was an alarming argument. The only way to disprove the argument was the annihilation of the world. Suppose, however, that neither side actually wanted war. Then the function of deterrence was quite different. It was a way of imagining a war similar to but worse than World War II; it was thus a way of reinforcing political identity, of ensuring loyalty and cohesion. It was a profoundly undemocratic instrument since politicians literally held the power of life and death. It created a permanent atmosphere of fear, a polarization of attitudes and of dissent that limited constructive democratic debate (Kaldor 1990).

The way in which differing patterns of governance are associated with different sources of political legitimacy and different constructions of security are depicted in Table 20.1. In the case of both the nation-state system and the blocs, security was

Table 20.1 Patterns of Governance

Patterns of Governance	Political Institutions	Source of Legitimacy	Mode of Security
States System	Nation-states	Patriotism	External defense; internal pacification
Cold War	Nation-states; blocs; transnational institutions	Ideology; freedom or socialism	Deterrence; bloc cohesion
Clash of Civilizations	Nation-states; civilizational blocs	Cultural identity	Civilizational defense at home and abroad
Coming Anarchy	Pockets of authority	Very few	Pervasive violence
Humane Governance	Transnational institutions; nation-states; local government	Humane values	Global civic security; elimination of interstate war; peace intervention

still defined in terms of defense of "core values" (Baylis 1997), but it was implemented through territorial defense. Thus, legitimacy based on consent to and support for a particular institution or set of institutions was at the same time identified
with security, meaning defense against an external threat, an "other." It should be
emphasized that, in both cases, legitimacy derived from forward-looking projects,
even if this was in defense of the existing order. The emergence of a national identity
was linked to nation building, which was conceived, at least in popular terms, as an
optimistic nineteenth-century project for democracy and prosperity; patriotism was
linked to a notion of rights. Likewise, the Cold War was understood as an ongoing
struggle for a way of life even if, from time to time, its virtues could be hailed only
in relation to the vices of an enemy. And in both cases, these forward-looking projects were drawn from experience, especially, but not only, during wars.

Effectively, the Westphalian system had broken down in 1914. The bloc system
represented an important modification of state sovereignty, even though this became
apparent only in the aftermath of the Cold War. The discourse of bipolarity effectively concealed the processes that are now widely described as globalization and that
undermine the inside/outside character of states and blocs. On the one hand, processes of integration at a transnational level call into question the identification of
security with the defense of territory. The monopoly of legitimate organized violence
is eroded from above as a result of the processes of military integration that took
place during the Cold War period and that have been extended through a range of
new mechanisms for cooperation, such as arms control, the exchange of technology,
or joint peacekeeping tasks. Both the fact of interdependence in a range of fields—
economic, political, military—and the moral prohibitions against the unilateral use
of force that have become enshrined in international law since the two world wars
mean that threats to territory are increasingly remote. On the other hand, the end
of the Cold War has called into question the sources of legitimacy on which political
institutions depended. Socialism was discredited; Western countries lost an "other"
against which they could assess their positive achievements; nonaligned or neutral
countries lost their distinctive positions within the international system. If the fragmentation of state sovereignty at an international level is challenged by globalization,
the centralization of state authority domestically is challenged by increasing fragmentation and privatization. In particular, the monopoly of organized violence is
also eroded from below as a consequence of emergence of paramilitary groups, criminal gangs, and private security firms.

Attempts by orthodox political thinkers to reconstruct the sources of legitimacy
have tended to be backward looking because they cannot escape the link between
legitimacy and the defense of territory. In the West, the 1989 revolutions were
greeted with triumph—they were perceived as the final victory of democracy after
the long years of struggle. Terms such as the "end of history" seemed to suggest that
the Western project had been achieved; there was nothing more to look forward to,
for which to struggle.[3] This (temporary) euphoria concealed the very real problems

within the Western sphere of influence and, indeed, within the newly democratic postcommunist space for which it was possible to offer recipes only from the past.

Elsewhere, it can be argued, the dominant trend is to construct apparently essentialist identities—nation, race, tribe, religion—based on nostalgia for the past. In this postmodern environment, these identities are mostly labels as opposed to projects for the future. To be Muslim in Bosnia or to be Catholic in Ireland is a national label; it is something that an individual is born with and cannot change. The claim to political power on the basis of a label is justified in terms of some often mythical past—a victory in a great battle, an ancient kingdom, a particular blood lineage. To be sure, in the case of Islam, there are missionary projects for a society ordered along Islamic lines, as, for example, in Iran or Afghanistan. These are inclusive in the sense that people can convert to Islam although they are backward looking. But in most ethnic conflicts, the struggles for political power are based purely on identity and do not offer a project for government other than the exclusion of those with a different identity.

These backward-looking identities seem unable to confront the plight of the post–Cold War world. The supposed "peace" of the Cold War era represented a kind of apology for wars that was taking place throughout the period. Some five million people were killed every decade after 1945 in wars that did not "count" because they were "limited"; that is, they did not involve all-out nuclear war. Promises of social citizenship were abandoned in the 1970s and 1980s, and the redistributive commitments of the World War II period were abandoned in favor of a reversion to nineteenth-century neoliberalism by elites who had grown overconfident of the Cold War formula for legitimacy. Despite the machinery for transnational governance—the array of international organizations left over from the Cold War period—and the opportunities for co-operation in addressing global predicaments, pessimism, skepticism, and apathy seem to face those who have to make decisions about the future.

Huntington and Kaplan to a large extent represent differing examples of the backward-looking approach to an understanding of the present. I discuss each in turn before coming to Falk's forward-looking project.

THE CLASH OF CIVILIZATIONS

Huntington's thesis is a variant of the bloc system in which a culture is substituted for ideology. His book has received so much attention because it expresses what many believe is in the hearts and minds of those whose livelihood depended on the Cold War—an attempt to re-create the comfortable certainties of the bipolar world and to construct a new threat to substitute for communism. The Persian Gulf War represented the paradigm for this approach; Saddam Hussein was literally built up in the communist image. The plan rolled out by the Pentagon had originally been designed to contain a Soviet thrust southward to the Persian Gulf. By following organizational routine and mobilizing on a scale commensurate with a Cold War scenario, Saddam Hussein was transformed into a formidable enemy equivalent to his Soviet predecessor (Kaldor 1991).

Huntington argues that we are entering a multicivilizational world in which culture rather than ideology will be the bonding mechanism for societies and groups of states. As many critics have pointed out, he is rather vague about what is meant by culture, although clearly, for him, religion is a key defining element of culture. Thus, the West is Christian, but only Catholic and Protestant. He is adamant that Turkey cannot be allowed to join the European Union because it is Muslim, and he considers that the membership of Greece, an Orthodox country, is a mistake; according to Huntington, Greece is definitely not part of Western civilization. It is also clear that, for him, states are the key guarantors of civilizations. He emphasizes the role of "core states" (e.g., the United States for the West and China for Asia).

He defines some six or seven civilizations (Sinic, Japanese, Hindu, Islamic, Western, Latin American, and possibly African). But he sees the dominant cleavage that shapes global order between the West and either Islam or Asia. Islam is viewed as a threat because of population growth and what he sees as the Muslim "propensity for violence." Asia is viewed as a threat because of rapid economic growth organized around what he calls the "bamboo network" of ethnic Chinese. For Huntington, the West is defined as American political creed plus Western culture. He takes the view that Western culture is decaying and must defend itself against alien cultures; in particular, the United States and Europe must stick together as they did in the Cold War period.

The main source of violence are what Huntington calls "fault-line wars." He argues that communal conflicts are a fact of contemporary existence. They are increasing in scale partly because of the collapse of communism and partly because of demographic changes. When communal conflicts involve different civilizations, as in Bosnia-Herzegovina, they become fault-line wars calling into being what he calls the kin-country syndrome. Thus, Russia was brought into the Bosnian conflict on the Serbian side, Germany on the Croatian side, and the Islamic states on the Bosniak side. (He is a little puzzled by U.S. support for Bosnia, which does not quite fit the thesis, but this can be explained away in terms of the mistaken legacy of a universalizing political ideology).

Huntington is at the same time highly critical of a global universalizing mission, describing himself as a cultural relativist, and deeply opposed to multiculturalism. He argues that the United States no longer has the capacity to act as a global power, citing the overstretch of U.S. forces at the time of the Gulf War and that its task is to protect Western civilization in a multicivilizational world. He also considers that human rights and individualism are purely Western phenomena and that we have no right to impose Western political values on societies to whom this is alien. At the same time, he argues that the United States has the task to preserve Western culture domestically. Thus, what he envisages is what might be described as a kind of a global apartheid in which relatively homogeneous territorially based civilizations held together from above by core states become mutual guardians of international order helping one another through their mutual confrontation to preserve the purity of their respective civilizations. Thus, his vision reproduces the combination of universality and particularity that Walker identifies with state sovereignty.

> In the greater clash, the global *"real* clash" between Civilization and barbarism, the world's great civilizations . . . will . . . hang together or hang separately. In the emerging era, clashes of civilization are the greatest threat to world peace, and an international order based on civilizations is the surest safeguard against world war. (Huntington 1997, 321)

A major problem for Huntington is the fact that the Muslim world has no core state capable of keeping order. Just as the United States needed the Soviet Union to sustain the bipolar order of the Cold War years, so the Huntington scenario requires a stable enemy. Huntington's project is awash with nostalgia for the Cold War years. It reproduces the "Great Contest," as Isaac Deutscher (1960) called it, in a new distorted form in which the place of political ideology is taken by a kind of exclusivist culturalism. Yet the absence of a core Muslim state is more than just a problem for the argument, for it has something to do with the fragility of the entire theoretical framework. For Huntington, it is geopolitics as usual. In his framework, states retain the monopoly of legitimate organized violence. Civilizational security is provided by core states and, at least implicitly, provides the basis for the legitimacy of civilizational blocs. But is this realistic?

Huntington does not ask why the Soviet Union collapsed or what the factors are that characterize the current transition period. Words such as "globalization" or "civil society" simply do not enter the Huntington vocabulary. For him, history is about changing state relations; models of state structures can be constructed without any relation to changing state-society relations. Seemingly random developments such as population growth or urbanization are invoked to explain particular phenomena, such as the growth of fundamentalism or the strength of China. But there is no questioning of the content of governance, of how political institutions change in character, and little explanation about how the world moves from today's uncertainty to the new civilizational order.

Certainly one scenario for the future could be of a fortress West in which prosperous countries close their minds and their borders against the victims of poverty and oppression; in such a scenario, the Huntington thesis might find fertile ground as a tool of legitimization. Fundamentalisms of various kinds might breed in the excluded areas of the world. But this scenario is not new. It is, in fact, a rerun of the Cold War period seen from a different perspective. What is new is the difficulty of sealing territory off from global developments. The collapse of communism can, at least in part, be explained in terms of the inability to sustain closed societies in the new age of travel and communication. The concept of homogeneous blocs or states as envisaged by Huntington is, fortunately, the most unconvincing part of his thesis because it ignores contemporary realities.

THE COMING ANARCHY

In contrast, the strength of Kaplan's argument is his compelling descriptions of social life as it exists today on the ground. His book *The Ends of the Earth: A Journey at the Dawn of the Twenty-First Century* is full of valuable insights. He draws attention to the erosion of state authority in many parts of the world and the myopia induced by a state-centric view of the world:

> What if there are really not fifty-odd nations in Africa as the maps suggest—what if there are only six, or seven, or eight real nations on the continent? Or, instead of nations, several hundred tribal entities? . . . What if the territory held by guerrilla armies and urban mafias—territory that is never shown on maps—is more significant than the territory claimed by many recognized states? What if Africa is even further away from North America and Europe than the maps indicate? (Kaplan 1997, 6)

In Sierra Leone, Kaplan discovers the breakdown of the monopoly of organized violence—the weakening of the distinction between "armies and civilians, and armies and criminal gangs" (45). In Pakistan, he discovers a "decomposing polity based more on criminal activities than effective government" (329). In Iran, he speculates about a new type of economy based on the bazaar. His journey gives him scope to describe the growing scarcity of resources, widespread environmental degradation, the pressures of urbanization, and the new class of restless unemployed young urban dwellers attracted to the certainties of religious fundamentalism. He talks about global inequalities of wealth and about the global communications revolution, which has made these disparities so visible. He describes the growth of nongovernmental organizations (NGOs) "the international army of the future" (432). He dwells on the impact of modern technology in traditional societies, for example, the radio as magic in Africa.

In his original article in the *New Republic,* Kaplan coined the phrase the "coming anarchy" to depict a world in which civil order had broken down. In West Africa, he observed a return to nature and to Hobbesian chaos, which he argued prefigured the future elsewhere in the world. Kaplan told a BBC interviewer in March 1995,

> You have a lot of people in London and Washington who fly all over the world, who stay in luxury hotels, who think that English is dominating every place, but yet they have no idea what is out there. Out there is that thin membrane of luxury hotels, of things that work, of civil order, which is proportionately getting thinner and thinner and thinner. (quoted in Keen 1996, 14)

In Kaplan's book, the thesis is somewhat modified. He also finds islands of civility in Eritrea, in Risha valley in India, or in the slums of Istanbul, where local people have succeeded in establishing or maintaining new or traditional forms of self-management. He is doubtful about whether these relatively isolated examples can provide models for other regions, arguing that their success depends largely on whether they have inherited certain civic-minded traditions, on what is or is not inherent in local culture. Henceforth, he argues,

> The map of the world will never be static. The future map—in a sense, the "last map"—will be an ever-mutating representation of cartographic chaos: in some areas benign, or even productive, and in some areas violent. Because the map will be always changing, it may be updated, like weather reports, and transmitted daily over the internet in those places that have reliable electricity or private generators. On this map, the rules by which diplomats and other policymaking elites have ordered the world these past few hundred years will apply less and less. Solutions in the main, will have to come from within the affected cultures themselves. (Kaplan 1997, 327)

Kaplan's argument is essentially determinist. While he rightly dismisses geopolitical solutions of the Huntington type drawn on the state-centric assumptions of the past, he implicitly shares Huntington's assumption that the prospects for governance depend on essentialist assumptions about culture. For him authority is possible only in situations in which local culture involves habits and traditions of self-organization derived from a long historical evolution. Because he witnesses collapsing states and because he cannot envisage alternative forms of authority at a global level, his scenario contains no security and no legitimacy except in certain arbitrary instances in which those local traditions of authority exist.

Both arguments are curiously ahistorical. Both Huntington and Kaplan frequently make use of classical allusions; both seem happy to explain contemporary behavior in terms of events that happened hundreds or even of thousands of years ago. But there is remarkably little analysis of the recent past. Like Huntington, Kaplan laments the passing of the Cold War, suggesting that we may, in the future, come to see the Cold War as an interlude between violence and chaos, like the golden age of Athenian democracy.

Kaplan concludes his book with an admission of helplessness:

> I would be unfaithful to my experience if I thought we had a general solution to these problems. *We are not in control.* As societies grow more populous and complex, the idea that a global elite like the UN can engineer reality from above is just as absurd as the idea that political "science" can reduce any of this to a *science.* (Kaplan 1997, 436)

HUMANE GOVERNANCE

In contrast to Huntington and Kaplan, Richard Falk starts from a normative vision of the future. He does not claim to offer a science, in the sense implied by Kaplan; at the same time his approach assumes that a search for solutions is possible. A normative vision has to be situated in an analysis that is capable of pointing toward solutions at both global and local levels, although these can never be absolute. The normative vision, as it were, guides analyses that can be changed and adapted according to circumstance:

> The normative project in its essence is constantly identifying and re-establishing the various interfaces between the specific and the general in each and every context, yet also keeping its borders open for entry and exit, being wary of any version of truth-claim as the foundation of extremism and political violence. (Falk 1995, 242)

Falk uses the term "geogovernance" to describe the integration of governance at a global level. Geogovernance exists in the contemporary period, driven, on the one hand, by global market forces and, on the other hand, by geopolitics—the realist pursuit of interests by dominant states. Contemporary ills so vividly described by Kaplan, or the indictments of inhumane governance as laid out by Falk, are not viewed as natural or inevitable. They are largely the consequence of the erosion of state authority, at least in part under the impact of this dual phenomenon of geopolitics and global capital. I would add that globalization cannot be reduced merely to economic processes in which uncontrollable market forces cut through traditional forms of livelihood and authority; it is also the consequence of political processes. "Structural adjustment" in the Third World, "transition" in Eastern Europe, "convergence criteria" in Western Europe, or even "flexible labor markets" in the United States are all expressions of a political outlook that currently dominates geogovernance.

Humane governance is the contemporary variant of the idealist project. As Falk (1995) puts it, it is a "preferred form of geo-governance. It is both a process and a goal" (8). Whereas the Huntington scenario is based on an elitist orientation, searching for solutions from above, humane governance is a project that derives from the countervailing forces of "global civil society"—the spread of transnational NGOs and social movements that constitute a form of "globalization from below"—and of the popular demand for democracy expressed in so many parts of the world, what Falk calls the "democratizing imperative." Unlike Huntington and Kaplan, Falk does not mourn the Cold War. On the contrary, the end of the Cold War offers an opportunity to eliminate the barbarism of nuclearism and war. The end of bipolarity and its rigid ideological imperatives has opened up possibilities for political pluralism that are not confined to the postcommunist world.

As is the case with the other scenarios, it can be argued that security is basic to the project of humane governance. In the Falk vision, political legitimacy has to be reconstructed around the principles of humanity—a universalistic goal of comprehensive rights for everyone and the elimination of war. The implication of my argument is that if "core values" are to be a widely shared reality and not confined to humane-minded civil society groups, they have to mean something in practice; in particular, it has to be self-evidently linked to the control of organized violence. But in the context of globalization, the control of organized violence can no longer be identified with the defense of territory. As we have seen, the state's monopoly of organized violence has been eroded from above through the transnationalization of organized violence that began during the Cold War as a result both of military alliances and of the interdependence of the global military sector. It has also been eroded from below, as described by Kaplan, through the privatization of violence—the breakup of armies and the spread of interlinked paramilitary and criminal gangs. The former offers real possibilities for the elimination of interstate war, and Falk offers a number of proposals about how this might be done. The latter limits the capacity of local communities to solve their own problems; local level solutions as proposed by Kaplan may be severely circumscribed by the prevalence of violence, both local and transnational. The challenge for the project of humane governance is how to develop a form of peace intervention that can enforce international norms while at the same time enabling local solutions. Such an intervention has to involve a form of transnational policing, which removes the distinction between the "internal" (police) and the "external" (military) and which reconstitutes control over organized violence at both local and transnational levels. At the same time, to be legitimate, it would have to be seen as acting on behalf of a humane project in which the comprehensive rights envisaged by the Falk project are granted in exchange for new forms of global taxation and the will to take risks, which might even include life itself, for the sake of humanity.

This is not a project for a single world government. Essentially, what is proposed is a form of "global overwatch." It is possible to envisage a range of territorially based political entities from municipalities to nation-states to continental organizations that operate within a set of accepted rules—standards of international behavior. The job of international institutions is to ensure implementation of those rules, especially as regards human rights and humanitarian law. Just as it is increasingly accepted that governments can intervene in family affairs to stop domestic violence, so a similar principle would be applied on a global scale.

In some senses, a humane governance is already coming into being. Transnational NGOs monitor and draw public attention to abuses of human rights, to genocide and other war crimes, and international institutions do respond in different ways. What has been lacking up to now has been enforcement. The argument here is that some form of international law enforcement would have to underpin effective humane governance. In effect, it would fill the security vacuum and enhance the legitimacy of international institutions, enabling them to mobilize public support and to act in other fields, for example, the environment or poverty. Of course, international institutions would need to increase for accountability and transparency, to develop democratic procedures for authorizing the use of legitimate force.[4] My concern is less with the exact procedures than it is with the process. Just as the development of the modern state involved a symbiotic process through which war, administrative structures, and legitimacy evolved, so the development of humane governance is already taking place through a similar although evidently fragile process involving growing administrative responsibility for upholding comprehensive rights and eliminating war.

What are the implications of this approach for the debate about European security? Any security organization has to be inclusive rather than exclusive. An organization with boundaries is one that implicitly emphasizes external defense against a similar enemy rather than cosmopolitan law enforcement. The advantage of NATO was that it became the instrument through which military forces were transnationalized; it provided a basis for transnational pacification. This is probably the most important reason that a war between France and Germany is now unthinkable. The disadvantage was that it kept alive the prospect of bloc war. The proposed enlargement of NATO will include Hungary but not Romania, the Czech Republic but not Slovakia, and Poland but not most of the former Soviet Union. External defense of NATO will not protect its member countries from the spread of new wars, but it will treat those countries outside the boundaries as potential enemies. Those countries that are poorer with less well established political institutions, that are perhaps Muslim and/or Orthodox, are designated as outsiders. This is unlikely to create a new civilizational order on the Huntingtonian model. On the contrary, exclusion is likely to contribute to the conditions that give rise to Kaplan-type anarchy.

A humane approach to European and, indeed, global security would try to bring together potentially conflicting countries and to spread as far as possible the transnationalization of armed forces. This could be under the umbrella of NATO, including Russia, the OSCE, or the United Nations. The important point is not the name of the organization but how the security task is reconceptualized. Insofar as these organizations are responsible for coordinating the agents of legitimate organized violence, their task is not external defense, as was the case for national or bloc models of security, but the enforcement of humane law.

It can be argued that geogovernance driven by geopolitics and market forces will inevitably come face-to-face with limits of its own making. What is widely dubbed as an absurdly utopian project, like all the idealist international projects of the past, may turn out to be the only realistic option if it is the case that human beings can choose their own futures. Traditional statist concepts of security assumed a fragmented world order and an integrated domestic order. Today, integration at a global level has been accompanied by fragmentation at a local level. Any effort to reconstruct statist notions of security is likely to represent a brake on global integration while failing to halt local fragmentation because the new locally based essentialist sources of legitimacy have no forward-looking project to offer. Only a vision along the lines of Falk's humane governance, which places the emphasis on the reconstruction of legitimacy at both global and local levels, can sustain the integration process and overcome local fragmentation. Otherwise, some version of Kaplan's chaos or even Huntington's civilizational barbarism could very well come true.

NOTES

1. Some measures of the scale of recent violence are provided in Kaldor and Vashee (1997).
2. An exception was the long Iran-Iraq war of the 1980s. But the huge losses and the

continuing stalemate of the war offered yet another proof of the futility of interstate war in contemporary conditions.

3. Huntington himself argues that civilizations at their peak, when they are about to decay, tend to think that struggle is over. He quotes Arnold Toynbee on the English middle classes in 1897: "History for them was over. . . . And they had every reason to congratulate themselves on the permanent state of felicity which this ending of history had conferred on them." (Huntington 1996, 301).

4. Archibugi et al. (1999). See especially David Beetham's chapter, "Human Rights as a Model for Cosmopolitan Democracy" (58–71).

21

The Age of Relativization: Toward a Twenty-First Century of Active Civil Society

Yoshikazu Sakamoto

THE AGE OF ABSOLUTIZATION AND THE AGE OF RELATIVIZATION

The twentieth century, especially the 1917–1991 period, can be called "the age of absolutization." The era began when the Bolsheviks came to power in Russia, followed by the Fascists in Italy, the Nazis in Germany, and the militarists in Japan, and continued through the Cold War. It ended when the Soviet communist regime crumbled. The age was characterized by a forceful tendency. The state, which embodied organized power and organized ideology, whether it was a party-state, class-state, or ethnonational state, demanded that its members accept its value standard and even its conceptual standard as absolute, commanding the absolute loyalty of its members.

A new phase of history that has begun to manifest itself since 1992 can be called the "age of relativization."[1] This change is closely connected with a transition during which the United States went from being the standard bearer of the post–Cold War absolutization (i.e., the promoter of the "new world order") to a state animated primarily by domestic concerns. Since the early 1990s, the United States has receded from the arena of world politics and has taken largely an inward-looking orientation. I see this as a matter of *self-relativization* with respect to the international role of the United States. This is part of a larger trend whereby many states are no longer confident in their ability to provide universal principles for thinking about world affairs and in their capacity to dictate world events.

The age of relativization represents a profound shift in world affairs. As a result, it deserves sustained analytical reflection by all students of world politics. Moreover, to the degree that the age of relativization provides the backdrop against which normative theory must operate, it is essential for the discipline of normative international relations to come to terms with it.

This chapter provides an analysis of the shift to a relativized world and outlines what the shift means for advancing the human prospect. One of its main themes is to argue that citizens throughout the world must recognize how world affairs are becoming relativized and begin acting in ways that can humanize such a situation. To put the matter differently, the chapter argues that an active civil society in the twenty-first century must participate in the relativization process but steer it in humane directions.

To begin, let me say a bit more about the process of relativization. The onset of the age of relativization can be examined from the following three angles: pluralization of the international power structure, relativization of ideology, and relativization of the issues.

PLURALIZATION OF POWER

Structure of Power

In the brief period of post–Cold War absolutization, the United States acted as the only superpower with global interests. Precisely because the rival global superpower had ceased to exist, however, the United States itself began to reduce its global commitments. In this respect, the end of bipolarity has not led to lasting unipolarity but rather has tended to come close to nonpolarity.

This shift was dramatically illustrated by U.S. policy toward Somalia. If it had been the continuing bipolar Cold War, the United States would have intervened in the internal strife of Somalia, even at a high cost, in order to deprive the Soviet Union of any opportunity to increase its strategic influence over the Horn of Africa. Despite its unrivaled global hegemonic military capabilities and relatively few casualties, however, the United States soon withdrew its troops. Apart from the general constraint that U.S. military supremacy does not mean military omnipotence capable of maintaining order in every corner of the world, more relevant is that the United States no longer has vital global interests. As a consequence, American global hegemony has been, in effect, localized and therefore relativized, thus the trend toward depolarized pluralization of the international power structure.

The United Nations

The same trend has manifested itself in the way in which the world public began to relativize the authority and competence of the UN Security Council—a change closely related to the self-relativization of the United States.

The relations between the United States and the United Nations are often torturous, reflecting their complexity. In the post–Cold War transition period, especially at the time of the Persian Gulf War, the United Nations had the luster of reactivated authority; but it had this because the UN's performance was a function of U.S. hegemony. Ironically, when the United Nations appeared, in the eyes of the world public, to have been dramatically reactivated, UN high officials were privately complaining that the organization had been, in reality, "hijacked by the United States." Then, as the U.S. presence in the United Nations diminished as a result of growing self-relativization on the part of the United States, the United Nations weakened. The conscious self-relativization of the United States was illustrated by its unilateral bombing of Iraq in September 1996 instead of resorting, as in the case of the Gulf War, to multilateral legitimation. It was clear that the relativization of U.S. hegemony would be made embarrassingly manifest if the action was put to a vote in the Security Council.

In short, the wavering presence of the United States in UN affairs expresses the age of relativization. It illustrates the changeable dynamic in contemporary world politics whereby political life reflects the inward-looking, parochial orientation of key actors such as the United States and, thus, the pluralization and relativization of international power.

Nuclear Proliferation

The pluralization and the corresponding relativization of the international power structure can also be observed in another issue area, that is, nuclear proliferation. The fact that, despite its rhetoric of displeasure, the United States virtually approved the last-minute nuclear tests of France and China in 1995–1996 indicates not only that the United States found them not threatening to its nuclear supremacy but also that it virtually recognized the relative constellation consisting of the five nuclear powers. More important, the United States had to accede to the Comprehensive Test Ban Treaty of 1996 even though, because of the relative limits of its influence, it had failed to include at the time India, Pakistan, Israel, and other de facto nuclear powers in the test ban regime.

Since nuclear proliferation is a prominent indicator of the pluralization and relativization of the structure of international power, the primary task for the United States as the holder of nuclear hegemony is to minimize the danger of proliferation. Further, nuclear weapons technology is probably the area in which the United States will continue to command supremacy and maintain, with a relatively small amount of additional input, the most favorable comparative advantage of all military capabilities at its disposal. It is natural that prevention of nuclear proliferation should be a matter of primary concern for the United States, as illustrated by the elaborate policy that it has been pursuing toward North Korea. The shrewd maneuvers over nuclear proliferation that will continue to be exchanged between the United States and "potential" nuclear powers are a constant reminder of the persistence of the political forces for further pluralization and relativization of the structure of international power.

RELATIVIZATION OF IDEOLOGY

Closely related to the pluralization of the international power structure is the depolarization of ideology that is under way in the postabsolutization era.

Conflict of Cultures

Subsequent to the end of the Cold War, an ideology of a new Cold War was formulated in terms of the "clash of civilizations" (Huntington 1993), reflecting the sense of crisis that the Western values that had just appeared to have prevailed over the communist ideological challenge were perceived to be confronted with the deeper threat of cultural relativization posed by non-Western civilizations.

I happened to be present at the international conference where Samuel Huntington presented his well-known paper. I expressed my reservations as follows:

> Although there are obviously significant differences among cultures and civilizations, cultural difference is not the same as cultural conflict, let alone violent conflict between different ethno-cultural groups. The question that can meaningfully be asked in social scientific terms is: Under what conditions will groups of different cultures and civilizations come into conflict? And under what conditions will the conflict between these groups turn into violent conflict? (quoted in Clesse et al. 1994, 784–85)

In fact, there are groups and individuals of different cultures and civilizations who coexist in peace. This coexistence is a topic of as much scientific importance as the "clash of civilizations." Today, no one would doubt that Catholics and Protestants as religious groups can coexist. Thus, the chronic violent conflict in Northern Ireland, for example, cannot be accounted for in terms of the difference in the belief in religious orthodoxy. It is rooted in the persistent political and economic structural conditions of that region. The equation of major contemporary international or internal conflict with the "clash of civilizations" is untenable. At the same time, it is true that, as a result of the end of the Cold War, civilization, culture, or ethnicity, in place of the Eastern and Western ideologies, began to carry greater weight than before as the dominant framework for defining collective identity.

In the United States, where the doctrine of the "clash of civilizations" was advanced regarding the Islamic and Confucian countries as the new sources of external threat, challenges have been raised *from within* by "multiculturalism" and the politics of difference. Proponents of "multiculturalism" are committed to the intellectual and political relativization of the "homogenizing" hegemony of the Anglo-Saxon tradition of "liberal democracy" (Young 1990; Benhabib 1996). Contrary to the Cold War ideologies geared to the universalization of an absolute ideology, the challenge of "multiculturalism" is oriented to the universalization of relativist perspective through the mutual recognition of the plurality of cultural values. Similar intellectual and social movements for cultural relativization have come to the surface in many other countries, raising the issue of relativized collective identity that will have to be tackled by every society in the twenty-first century.

Development Models

Another manifestation of the relativization of ideology is the ambiguity and confusion concerning the idea and policy of the welfare state in the North. What should be the role to be played by the state in meeting the requirements of the market economy on the one hand and those of social well-being on the other? How should the antinomies of economic efficiency, social welfare, and citizens' autonomy be resolved? The welfare state that has been legitimized through the relativization of both free competitive capitalism and centrally planned socialism now faces the challenge of its own relativization. No Western social democratic parties have responded to this challenge in a convincing, systematic way.

In a similar vein, the oscillation of the development model is widely observable in the developing countries. As a result of the demise of the state-socialist model, the newly industrializing economies (NIE) model was at one time considered the only uncontested alternative for the developing countries. Although the NIE model is still potent, it has demonstrated its incapacity to solve, in addition to serious environmental degradation, the problem of the widening gap between rich and poor. Further, it has become questionable whether, under the condition of globalizing market economy, a developing *state* can ever have the capacity to ensure equity and well-being on a national basis. In fact, recognizing the failure of the state in this respect, numerous projects for peoples' autonomous development and mutual aid have been put into practice at the grassroots level. The declining confidence in the state's social policy in the South also points to the relativization of the idea of the welfare state.

Democratic Models

The relativization of ideology has also been directed to the concept of democracy, as exemplified by the stand taken by some Asian NIE regimes that espouse the ideology of the plurality and relativity of the principles of democracy and human rights. Former Prime Minister Lee Kuan-yew of Singapore and Prime Minister Mahathir bin Mohamad of Malaysia are the most vocal proponents of "Asian values," which they argue are different from, or even superior to, the values that underlie the Western concepts of democracy and human rights. Though in a different context of socialist market economy, Chinese authorities subscribe to a similar view. What is common is their argument that the very insistence on the *universality* of the principles of democracy and human rights is an indication of the *specificity* of the Western ideology of democracy. Universalization of human rights is rejected as the "interference with domestic affairs."

This view is problematic and is not really "Asian" because it is not accepted by all peoples in Asia, as illustrated by the rebuttal of Kim Dae Jung (Kim 1994). It must be noted that East and Southeast Asia consists of both those societies where democratization of the regime was achieved by citizens' movements from below, such as South Korea, the Philippines, and Taiwan, and those countries where the regime has not been so transformed, such as Singapore and Malaysia. It is no accident that, while the elites in the latter category emphasize the importance of Asian specificity, the elites as well as the people in the former category recognize the essential universality of democracy and human rights.

What is notable is the fact that a sizable number of informed people in the West show interest in this notion of Asian values, revealing their suspicion that there may be an "Asian brand of democracy" different from the Western model. The apparent credibility of the idea of Asian values stems, in part, from the success of the Asian NIEs in achieving high economic growth up to 1997 in contrast with the generally low growth of the North. Perhaps the important factor that makes this idea plausible is the declining self-confidence of Western democracies, which derives from the social disorder exemplified by crimes, drugs, disintegration of school and family life, and so forth; this sense of crisis has urged them to look for a key to orderly society in Asian values with their emphasis on moral discipline. Thus, it may be a manifestation not so much of the relativization of the political legitimacy of Western democracy as of the self-relativization of the *social* foundation of Western democracy.

RELATIVIZATION OF ISSUES

The age of relativization is characterized by the relativization of fundamental issues as well.

Nuclear Issues

First, regarding the relativization of the issue of nuclear war and nuclear weapons, that the danger of nuclear world war has to any extent diminished is one of the most important positive results of the end of the Cold War. The prevention of nuclear war, which was the absolute imperative at the height of the Cold War, has ceased to be the matter of highest priority on the global agenda. Drastic nuclear disarmament has not materialized, and the United States and Russia retain a stockpile of nuclear weapons that could exterminate humankind many times over. Yet, while nuclear *weapons* have not been appreciably reduced, the probability of nuclear *war* has been substantially reduced.

The relativization of the issue of nuclear war was illustrated by the international popular reactions against a series of French tests in 1995–1996. The voice of protest against the tests, especially strong in the Pacific region, was no longer primarily a manifestation of the fear of nuclear war but of anger at a test that instantly "killed" a beautiful tropical sea near Tahiti. Moreover, Greenpeace, long the most radical protagonist of the antinuclear peace movement, has steadily shifted its main focus from the war/peace issue to the environment.

The relativization of the nuclear war issue also came to the fore during an incident at the Smithsonian Institution in Washington, D.C., in 1995. In commemoration of the end of World War II fifty years before, the Smithsonian planned special exhibits in order to reflect on the historical and human implications of the nuclear age, including the ethical dilemmas involved in the bombings of Hiroshima and Nagasaki. Relevant materials from Hiroshima as well as from the United States were to be displayed. These plans gave rise to impassioned opposition from veterans' associations and some congressmen who insisted that the program should be for the celebration of the American victory over militarist Japan, especially in view of the fact that the atomic bombings saved, according to Harry Truman and Henry Stimson, "one million" American casualties and an even larger number of Japanese. Because of such pressures, the original plans were canceled in favor of a program to celebrate the American victory by demonstrating its overwhelming military power, dramatically represented by the atomic bombs (Lifton and Mitchell 1995, 276–97; Harwit 1996). The incident caused perplexity, disillusionment, and even indignation on the part of the Japanese public, who looked at nuclear weapons as a matter of absolute primary concern for the survival of the whole of humankind, transcending any enmity between particular nations.

It is true that there was nothing new in the veterans' reactions. The atomic bombings have long been relativized by most Americans in relation to Pearl Harbor. Yet, if the debate had occurred during the Cold War, it might have centered not only on whether the use of atomic weapons was justifiable but also, or even more, on whether nuclear arms and nuclear deterrence were appropriate means to ensure the survival of humankind, including the American people. This was exactly the question that the voices from Hiroshima and Nagasaki sought to address by evoking a common concern about the present and future of humanity. Unfortunately, the discourse in the United States was focused on 1945, relative to Pearl Harbor in 1941, a prenuclear incident.

An even more profound relativization of the spirit of Hiroshima and Nagasaki came from those Asian people who rejoiced at the two atomic bombings in 1945 that dealt a fatal blow to the Japanese militarism that occupied Asia. A number of Asian people took the bombings as the herald of liberation. During the Cold War, however, their voices were muted because they felt that they and Japan confronted common enemies: the threat of communism and the danger of nuclear war between the superpowers. The end of the Cold War removed these constraints on the uninhibited pronouncement of their views on the atomic bombing of the two cities. Thus, the voice of Hiroshima/Nagasaki has been relativized by the critical voice of Asian war victims who say that Hiroshima and Nagasaki should not forget their war responsibility as the perpetrators of aggression.

Should the "Hibakushas," who barely survived the hell of atomic holocaust and were destined to live the rest of their lives suffering from incurably deep wounds of mind and body, be held accountable as victimizers of other peoples? In the face of relativization through this "unreason" of history, Hiroshima/Nagasaki today finds itself obliged to undergo an agonizing self-reappraisal.

Still another form of the relativization of the issue of nuclear weapons and nuclear war can be observed in the advisory opinion of the International Court of Justice delivered in July 1996. This advisory opinion is of dual character. On the one hand, it makes the important judgment that "the threat or use of nuclear weapons would generally be contrary to the rules of international law applicable in armed conflict." On the other hand, it states that "the Court cannot conclude definitively whether the threat or use of nuclear weapons would be lawful or unlawful in an extreme circumstances of self-defence, in which the very survival of a State would be at stake" (International Court of Justice 1996, 36).

Inconclusive on the legality of the threat or use of nuclear weapons, this opinion is one form of relativizing the issue of nuclear weapons and nuclear war. If it had been handed down during the Cold War period, the opinion of the judges would, in all likelihood, have been more sharply polarized, with the result that the court might have suspended judgment on this highly sensitive political issue by making a procedural statement that the matter was not within its competence. In this sense, the end of the Cold War enabled the court to make substantive deliberations but led it to a dual conclusion, each argument claiming relative validity.

War/Peace Issues

Decrease in the danger of nuclear war implies decrease in the danger of world war, which, in turn, has brought about the relativization of war or armed conflict in the form of its localization. Practically all wars, of course, begin at a certain locality; what is crucial is whether the states concerned or the international community at large will respond by seeking to keep them localized or to generalize them. In the age of post–Cold War relativization, there is a clear trend toward localizing armed conflict. This is a consequence not of an active localization policy but of a negative policy of noninvolvement due to lack of vital interest. Whether to intervene is a matter of choice left in the hands of individual states.

In the Cold War period, if one of the two superpowers intervened in local conflict, the other was almost automatically also bound to intervene. If the superpowers intervened, many other big and small powers were also bound to be involved. But today, if the sole superpower, the United States, should intervene, other powers might remain uninvolved, as in the case of the unilateral U.S. bombing of Iraq in 1996. Or, if one of the big powers should intervene, no other states might be interested, as in the case of the French intervention in the civil war in Rwanda in 1994. In short, to the extent that response to local conflict has been relativized depending on the selective policy of intervention or nonintervention of individual states, the conflict itself has also been relativized in the form of localization.

Thus, intervention has become a matter of concern mainly of those countries that have relatively direct interest in, and are relatively directly affected by, local conflict;

and since, unlike in the Cold War context of globalization, these countries generally are in geographic proximity and/or economically linked, "regional" interests are likely to carry greater weight than global interests. This was dramatically illustrated by the armed conflict in the former Yugoslavia. Arguably, the peoples of Western Europe have had gravest concern about the spread of the conflict, borne the financial and social burden of admitting refugees, and harbored greatest anguish over the daily gross violations of human rights. It is natural that the primary direct diplomatic and military interest was shown by West European countries through the regional frameworks of the European Union and NATO. The U.S. involvement would not have taken place but for the existence of NATO. In the absence of a similar regional framework with effective capacity for implementation, local conflicts and human tragedies in Africa have failed to evoke a comparable regional, let alone global, response.

As a result of the relativization of armed conflict and its localization, the coexistence of war and peace has become a "normal" state of the world. This is a condition that cannot be lightly dismissed. In the 1930s, Soviet Foreign Minister Maxim Litvinov made a famous remark: "Peace is indivisible." He said this in support of the League of Nations, which was expected to play the role of collective security system in opposition to fascist states. Collective security was predicated on the recognition of the historical change that the days of selective local or national response to local conflict were over—an idea that underlies the League of Nations and the United Nations. But, contrary to this vision or understanding, the present practice is increasingly governed by the idea that "peace is divisible." Thus, the world is partly divided into peace zones and war zones that can be mutually isolated.

If relativized local peace and local war are accepted as the basic pattern of global security, the principle of collective security on which the United Nations was founded would inevitably cease to work. In fact, the idea of "peace enforcement" was put forward in 1992 by UN Secretary-General Boutros Boutros-Ghali in *An Agenda for Peace* (1995), which reflected the aura of the multinational force for the Gulf War. It instantly evoked strong worldwide interest; yet it quickly fell into oblivion since few states would run the risk of sacrificing their own soldiers beyond noncombatant peacekeeping operations unless they had direct vital interests. Even the less vulnerable mission for "preventive diplomacy" depends on states with relatively strong direct interests.

To localize war and conflict is to localize peace. If the people of a state feel that the perceived threat has been substantially decreased as far as the peace of the region in which they have a stake is concerned, it is natural that the state should become inward looking. The primacy of domestic politics that major powers, including the United States, acknowledge today has much to do with the relativized localization of war-and-peace issues. Thus, the unipolar "new world order" has been relativized not only at the international level but also from within each state, giving priority to the articulation of domestic interests.

CONCLUSIONS

We have seen the contemporary trend toward relativization in terms of power, ideology, and issues. This trend indicates the historical dynamics of depolarization and pluralism as against the absolutization of polarization, whether bipolar or unipolar. Depolarization of the international power structure has taken the form of self-relativization in the United States, relativization of the United Nations, and diplomatic exchange over nuclear proliferation. Although this process of depolarization is limited to the interstate level with the semblance of multipolarization, it is different from the time-honored balance-of-power system in which major powers took general war for granted as a last resort to maintain or restore "balance." Today, the likelihood of general war between the major powers represented by the big five is minimized, partly because of the inhibiting strategic calculation of the consequences of general war. But if this is the only reason, the avoidance of general war will not rule out the possibility of a continued worldwide arms race geared to "deterrence," mutual or unilateral, as we saw in the later phase of the Cold War.

This danger has been mitigated by another factor: ideological similarities in terms of political democracy and market economy (as in the case of the West's relations to the former East) or at least the market economy (as exemplified by China's relations to other major powers). And what characterizes the ideological similarity is a common pluralist appreciation of values as a source of legitimation. While depolarization at the interstate level concerns the redefinition of the dominant international power structure alone, pluralist depolarization in ideological terms points to the redefinition of the much deeper question of legitimacy, as illustrated by the redefinition of community values, development models, and democratic models discussed here. The redefinition of these models of society refers, in the final analysis, to the search for a new identity on the part of social forces and individual citizens.

We must conclude, then, by asking, Who has generated and promoted the dynamics of relativization? This is a question of crucial importance because the mode and meaning of relativization significantly varies, depending on who is promoting relativization and for what purposes. Depending on who defines citizens' collective identity, and how, depolarization of world order may signify its fragmentation. For example, as we observed here, relativizing nuclear issues but leaving the fundamental problem of nuclearism unresolved and localizing war/peace issues but leaving the problems of terror and genocide unresolved amount to the fragmentation of world order. This fragmentation reflects the lack of vital interest in such matters on the part of the major powers and the global market forces and is also a consequence of insufficient counteraction by transnational democratic forces rooted in civil society.

Finally, it must be noted that the "age of relativization" by no means implies that we live in an era in which everything is relativized with no fundamental point of reference in sight. It is true that the nation-state, which has been "imagined" as the basic framework for the polity, economy, and citizens' identity in modern times, is being relativized by globalized market forces. It is also true that citizens and civil society are exposed to the relativizing power of the market. However, a civil society that has been struggling to relativize the state in modern history is now also posing a challenge to the power of the globalized market with a view to relativizing it in defense of the dignity and equal rights of human beings. The world of the twenty-first century will be quite different, depending on which forces of relativization prevail. If it is to be a more humane and just world, our preference should be for activating civil society, which, unlike the market, is grounded in the commitment to humanized end values.

NOTES

1. The concept of "relativization" used in this chapter, in contrast to "absolutization," refers to the act of giving meaning to events and problems in terms (1) not of immutability but of changeability and (2) not of incomparability or irreplaceability but of comparability and choosability. This is a paradigm shift as an integral part of political struggle and transformation. The act of giving meanings in these terms presupposes the existence of the "subject" that cannot be the object of relativization.

22

The Emergence of WOMP in the Normative Tradition: Biography and Theory

Saul Mendlovitz

The preceding chapters of this book aim to contribute to the study of normative international relations. Organized under the rubric of values articulated by the World Order Models Project (WOMP) and under the category of "Critical Perspectives on International Relations," the chapters provide substantive reflection on the challenges of thinking carefully about, and working to usher in, a world marked by greater social justice, peace, economic well-being, and humane governance. Together, they provide, as the book's introduction says, a "portrait" of some of the most innovative and insightful contemporary normative international relations scholarship.

My own contribution to this book takes a different approach. The occasion for undertaking this volume was to honor the work of Richard Falk, Albert G. Milbank Professor of International Law and Practice at Princeton University. Richard has had a long and distinguished career that many of us felt deserved recognition. This book is the culmination of the effort to express our appreciation to him for his pathbreaking and inspiring scholarship. As authors, we felt that the best way to honor Richard was to present original research that would advance the project of normative international relations. It is hoped that the preceding chapters have made small steps toward that end. For my own part, I have chosen to depart from that agenda with the aim of concentrating on Richard's work itself and explaining how it fits into the tradition of normative international relations. Richard has been a guiding light over the last decades for pursuing a type of scholarship that is mindful of the immense challenges to a more just world order and motivated fundamentally toward improving the quality of life for all living beings. I have had the good fortune to travel along with him through many of the byways of normative scholarship and felt it appropriate to de-

311

scribe his contribution to the normative tradition. For, as I see it, the discipline of normative international relations has been significantly fashioned through Richard's work and the students and colleagues who he has inspired. It is only fitting then, in a book on new normative approaches, to focus directly on Richard's work and situate it within the broader normative effort.

Richard Falk's life has quintessentially been that of an engaged scholar. His contributions to maintaining, deepening, and enriching the normative tradition in international law and activist progressive politics throughout the globe have been extraordinary. Falk blends superb technical craft with deeply held moral commitments and a nuanced sensibility for natural law. His formulation of the Grotian quest epiphanizes the manner in which Grotius theory and methodology can and should be used for this era of history. His depiction of a shadowland—cast backward by the future to the present moment—has informed the work of many scholars, jurists, and practitioners throughout the world, as evidenced by the distinguished authors in this book. That we must participate in shaping the emerging human polity—more just, more peaceful, more sustainable, and more humane—building on the empirical and normative strands of our time, is a lesson we have all learned from him.

Richard and I have been friends and colleagues for four decades. During this time we coedited and authored twelve volumes and a series of articles and were involved in many political enterprises—enough, one might think, for any individual. However, Richard is not just any individual. In this same period, he also published an additional thirty-five volumes and 500 articles, held leadership positions and was active in over 100 professional associations, participated in many conferences and consultationships, and had some 1,000 speaking engagements while responsibly carrying a full teaching schedule—all of this in pursuit of understanding and promoting a just world order.

In this chapter, therefore, I do not attempt to cover the full panoply of scholarly and activist roles in which Richard has been engaged. It seems appropriate, however, to report on some of our joint work, especially as it relates to insinuating a just world order perspective within both scholarship discourse and political processes of global collective life. In particular, I report on Richard's contribution to the World Order Models Project (WOMP) and, more generally, world order inquiry and action. A brief description of Richard's participation in two major transnational civil society movements—resistance to U.S. involvement in Vietnam and opposition to nuclear weapons—is also sketched. I conclude with a discussion of his recent work developing the concept of humane governance, including some matters on which we have had intense dialogue. Permit me first to indulge in some personal reminiscences.

BEGINNINGS

Richard Falk and I first met in the basement of Langdell Hall, Harvard Law School, Cambridge, Massachusetts, in the fall of 1958. We were assistant professors on leave

from Ohio State and Rutgers, respectively. Richard was pursuing a Doctor of Juridi-
cial Science (S.J.D.) degree, and I was a visiting scholar under a Ford grant. We
consider it to have been our very good fortune that a brilliant young Egyptian
scholar, Georges Abi-Saab, also completing an S.J.D., was a member of the basement cohort. The three of us became fast friends and have remained so. (Georges
has gone on to a distinguished career as scholar, publicist, and more recently as a
judge on the ad hoc tribunal for former Yugoslavia. He has attended many WOMP
conferences, and the three of us have been in close contact over these four decades.)
Our relationship was so intense that the basement colleagues dubbed us, perhaps
blasphemously, the trinity, namely, father (myself, I am oldest), son (Georges, he is
youngest), and the holy spirit (Richard).

In retrospect, I realize that Richard was aptly named the holy spirit for two reasons. He possesses a questing spiritual aura, constantly attempting to answer the
question, "What's it all about, Alfie?" More earthbound, the cliché "many irons in
the fire" certainly fits him. Trained at the Wharton School, including somehow the
study of Sanskrit; possessing an encyclopedic knowledge of humanities, social sciences, and international law; and exercising a daily physical regimen—squash, ten-
nis, basketball, Ping-Pong (which I regret to say he excelled at; that is, I never won
a match from him)—made him elusive even then. Furthermore, constant travel frequently made it difficult to locate him.

That having been said, Richard was and is firmly rooted and located in terms of
moral and ethical commitment. His passion to make the world a better place—and,
not so incidentally, an abiding, profound exploration of what a "better place" might
mean—has guided his feeling, thinking, and acting about the human condition,
Gaia, universe, and *mysterium tremendum* (all, it should be noted, with suitable
ironic deference).

WORLD ORDER MODELS PROJECT

Richard Falk is a foundational figure in the development of world-order inquiry.
His understanding that the realist paradigm carries a normative view (sometimes
explicitly denied by practitioners) as well as an analytic frame informs his exploration
and construction of an alternative world-order value perspective on international
relations, international law, and global order. His contribution to the formulation
of this perspective has its origin in the early 1960s, when he was a consultant to a
major educational project, the Fund for Education Concerning World Peace
Through World Law (FECWPTWL). His substantive input on issues facing that
project was crucial in development of the world-order value scheme and even more
directly to the WOMP enterprises. Over the past four decades, he has carried on
sustained research in this area and trained two generations of students in world-
order inquiry. It seems sensible, therefore, to provide a narrative describing how
WOMP evolved, detailing Richard's significant contributions.

WOMP antecedents can be traced to efforts of a small number of U.S. citizens who, in 1960, retired from the private sector and committed themselves to the movement to abolish war. These individuals exhibited the commitment associated with abolitionists against slavery and groups involved in dismemberment of colonialism and imperialism. In particular, the role of Harry Hollins should be noted. A former successful Wall Street broker, Hollins initiated and assumed a full-time leadership role of FECWPTWL—a very unique, worldwide education program. His dedication, thoughtfulness, and generosity for two decades were a constant source of inspiration and energy in the movement to abolish war.

During this period, the Cold War, with its threat of mutual nuclear annihilation, was at its peak (i.e., the Cuban missile crisis). At the same time, there were a number of new initiatives—the Pugwash Conferences, the Peace Research Institute of Oslo, and the Center for Conflict Resolution at the University of Michigan—in their start-up phase. These "informal" contacts between prestigious U.S. and Soviet scholars and the initiation of basic research, vis-á-vis conflict and international violence, helped ease Cold War tensions and initiated serious investigation of war as a human institution. However, a survey of education programs throughout the world revealed almost no curricula dealing with the abolition of war. It was this absence that was the guiding animus for this effort, based on the following rationale.

With the exception of a small number of nonviolent practitioners and some peace churches, almost all individuals throughout the world—including, perhaps even especially, political leadership—were encapsulated in a worldview in which war, although considered unfortunate, was a permanent structure of human society. It was to dispel this view that the decision was made to produce instructional materials for colleges and universities throughout the world. It was hoped that these materials would stimulate faculty to initiate research and teaching, recruit students, and, in so doing, provide academic legitimacy for the topic of war prevention and the abolition of war.

In undertaking this effort, we were very much aware that the abolition of war did not fit easily into existing curricula or disciplines. In addition, there was still intense debate on "value-free" social sciences, casting doubt on the validity of the subject matter as an appropriate academic venture. It was necessary then to produce materials and texts that would pass muster of the most stringent academic standards (as defined by scholars who headed traditional academic associations). In 1962, the Institute for International Order (successively, the Institute for World Order and the World Policy Institute) published Legal and Political Problems of World Order (LPPWO) which utilized World Peace Through World Law (WPTWL) as an instructional model. Coauthored by Grenville Clark and Louis Sohn, WPTWL articulated a major revision of the UN Charter, recommending the establishment of a limited world government for security matters. The provisions of WPTWL call for a disarmed world, establishment of a global police force, mandatory jurisdiction before the International Court of Justice for state disputes, an International Criminal

Court for individuals on crimes of aggression, an expanded Security Council with supermajorities replacing permanent membership veto, a revised General Assembly based on population criteria possessing legislative capacity on security and international conflict, and a global tax scheme. The LPPWO materials, on which Richard was an active consultant, were designed to question the necessity, feasibility, and desirability of the changes recommended in WPTWL. In the following three years, some 10,000 volumes of LPPWO were adopted in 350 courses and seminars in the United States. On the basis of this encouraging response, Richard and I were commissioned to produce a more comprehensive work. In 1966, a four-volume work, *The Strategy of World Order,* was published. These volumes also used WPTWL as an instructional model and were directly related to war prevention. They comprehended materials on basic problems of world order and security, international law, the United Nations, and disarmament and development. Forty thousand volumes were adopted for classroom and library use, mostly in the United States, with some modest distribution in other regions of the world as well.

Three points should be noted concerning Richard's collaboration in these volumes. Richard was much more skeptical than I of the desirability, let alone feasibility, of limited world government. (Neither of us have been members of the World Federalist Movement, although we were very familiar with its program and had cordial relations with many of its leading figures.) Nevertheless, he did not shy away from the subject: abolition of war. While he felt that WPTWL standing on its own was overly legalistic and presented a too-Western view of the world and a political transition that he considered apolitical, he found merit in its overall aim, its comprehensiveness, and its significance as a pedagogical tool. Perhaps more important, Richard was aware that there would be serious questioning, perhaps derision, of such a venture within the academic community. Yet he believed that it was possible and necessary to study, provide insight, and recommend actions for this abolition movement. And finally, his participation was crucial to the success of the undertaking. His commitment, competence, intelligence, and congeniality were superb.

In the summer of 1966, Professors Louis Sohn, Thomas Frank, and I conducted a two-week workshop on world order and justice issues in Dar-es-Salaam. Participants were from eight East African societies and included policy officials, social activists, religious leaders, and journalists. The syllabus was made up of materials authored by African, Asian, and Latin American scholars that highlighted problems and issues that were of primary concern to these areas. At the same time, WPTWL and materials questioning validity of the WPTWL model were also included. Nevertheless, the response to this syllabus ranged from skepticism to hostility; it was seen as another insinuation of Western ideology on the African continent. On returning to the United States, I discussed this experience with Harry Hollins. It was he who suggested that if the workshop participants had presented their own model of world order, this probably would have led to a more fruitful dialogue.

This experience and discussion made up the background from which WOMP evolved. We decided to organize the small group of scholar/activists from various regions of the world, inviting them to produce their own models (images or perspectives) on world-order problems. It was hoped that these individuals would agree on the major issues facing humanity but that they would be given free rein in defining their weight and, more important, policy resolutions. These models would then be evaluated and compared, and the areas of agreement and disagreement could be highlighted. It was hoped that after publication and sufficient discussion throughout the world, as well as WOMP participants, a consensus model might then be achieved.

Richard and I were in close contact on these matters, and once we had proper funding (the Carnegie Endowment for International Peace), we initiated the enterprise. As a first step, I was fortunate enough to be able to recruit a distinguished group of scholar activists from various regions of the world. The initial participants included the following: Edward Arab-Ogly, Richard Falk, Johann Galtung, Gennadi Gerasamov, Horazo Godoy, Rahjni Kothari, Gustavo Lagos, Paul Linn, Ali Mazrui, Yoshikazu Sakamoto, Lev Stepanov, and Carl-Friedrich von Wiezaker. (It is clear that male chauvinism prevailed here. It was some two or three years before Elise Boulding, Randy Forsberg, and a number of other women were invited to participate.) In recruiting these individuals, it was apparent that Richard's membership on the project was a significant factor in their decision to join.

In the process of selecting these individuals and honing the project, it became clear that focusing on the abolition of war was insufficient—indeed, biased—from a "Third World" viewpoint. The participants from Asia, Africa, and Latin America stated forcefully that the overwhelming issues of the day confronting humanity were poverty, maldevelopment and oppression, colonialism, imperialism, and social injustice. International conflict, and especially the threat of nuclear weapons, were problems for the first and second world to resolve within their bipolar embrace. In the ensuing discussion, these matters were clarified, and an analytic and normative framework was formulated. Utilizing a set of interacting values—peace, economic well-being, and social justice—the participants organized research teams to deal with the problematique of world order: war, poverty and maldevelopment, and social injustice, also seen as interactive domains, from the perspective of their regional and cultural locations.

The first of some thirty meetings of WOMP was held in January 1968 and continue to the present day. Richard, in what I consider to be a remarkable show of commitment and loyalty, participated in all these conferences. For each of these meetings, he was present for the entire time (and almost on time for each individual discussion). He frequently presented a major paper and was a conscientious, thoughtful discussant. He introduced into WOMP deliberations the subject matters of environment and feminism, both of which were initially met with skepticism and negativism (another illustration, it was alleged, of either North American hegemony or a fey agenda). It is to his persuasive capacities and intellectual and moral authority that these two areas are a prominent aspect of WOMP inquiry. His volume *A Study of Future Worlds,* along with the *Creation of a Just World Order,* were the first to appear in 1972, soon followed by four other volumes. It is fair to say then that Richard was both a foundational figure and a guiding light in WOMP's work. And to the extent to which this normative perspective has seriously confronted the realist paradigm over the past three decades, his leadership made it so.

ADVANCEMENTS

During these past four decades, Richard has been engaged in many significant social and political actions throughout the world. He has done so as scholar, legal practitioner, and activist. Some of the more significant enterprises include the following: promoting the Nuremberg Code and genocide treaty; anti-apartheid; anti–Vietnam War; environmental concerns; inappropriate and illegal use of armed forces, especially by major powers; justice for indigenous people; East Timor; Palestinian rights; feminism; and human rights. Here I wish to describe briefly two significant political/legal enterprises in which he was involved: the anti–Vietnam War movement and the abolition of nuclear weapons.

Richard's activities opposing the Vietnam War were persistent, powerful, and visible. As a member of the Lawyers Committee on UN Policy in Vietnam, he collaborated in developing the arguments on illegality, imprudence, and immorality of U.S. military forces in that tortured area of the world. He was legal counsel for many individuals who challenged the Selective Service Act, engaged in civil disobedience, and fled to Canada; he was first to use the Nuremberg defense in this context. (Richard also practiced civil disobedience, including a day in a municipal Washington, D.C., jail for lying down before the Senate doors, petitioning that body for a redress of grievance to stop the war.) He developed research programs; wrote articles; participated in teach-ins, workshops, and conferences throughout the world; and visited North Vietnam during the war. He was a recognized global figure in the effort to halt U.S. intervention in that part of the world.

At the same time, Richard was very much concerned with global security matters—running the gamut from the Cold War and deterrence through national liberation movements and humanitarian law. In particular, he was a leader in highlighting the threat to the human race of nuclear weapons. Richard's awe and horror at the advent of nuclear weapons—and their use at Hiroshima and Nagasaki—has been a compelling motif of his work over these four decades. He has published six volumes and fifty articles dealing with nuclear weapons. His 1981 article "Nuclear Weapons and International Law" (coauthored with Meyrowitz and Sanderson) is frequently cited as a seminal piece for the moral, intellectual, and political movement prohibiting the threat or use of nuclear weapons. With a number of New Zealand activists, he contributed to formulating the World Court Project, culminating in the Advisory Opinion from the International Court of Justice on the illegality of the threat or use of nuclear weapons (July 1996). He coauthored a model brief with members of the

International Association of Lawyers Against Nuclear Arms, which was utilized as a basic resource by many states that argued the illegality of nuclear weapons. To the present moment, he has pursued the objective of eliminating nuclear weapons and has been forceful in using the Advisory Opinion both for scholarship and for political activities.

HUMANE GOVERNANCE

In the fall of 1986, Georgi Shaknazarov, special assistant to Mikhail Gorbachev and president of the International Political Science Association, visited WOMP. His purpose was to discuss matters of "common concern," especially reviewing security doctrines undergirding Cold War tensions. Very much aware of the changes that President Gorbachev was introducing within the Soviet Union and of the implications for global polity processes, Shaknazarov advanced the thesis that "a new way of thinking" needed to be introduced for understanding global polity and to promote human values (his term). He explained that a group of colleagues and he had carefully studied the WOMP "holistic–organic" approach as well as the policy objectives that stemmed from these materials; it was their view that they provided a sound basis both for "scientific" research and progressive political action. A dialogue on these matters during the following year resulted in the initiation of a project "Global Civilization: Challenges for Democracy, Sovereignty and Security" (GCP). A Steering Committee representing scholarly, diplomatic, mass media, and religious concerns from the major regions of the world was organized. (This time women were part of the original group; we followed the Ali Mazrui rule—30 to 50 percent of the participants in WOMP conferences should be women.) In the early discussions establishing GCP, Richard introduced the notion of humane governance that was ultimately adopted as the conceptual rubric establishing the research agenda. And since no good deed goes unpunished, Richard accepted the rapporteur's role—a task that he has characterized as "the most difficult intellectual undertaking" of his career. There is a significant sociology of knowledge narrative of the context for Richard's statement that is helpful in understanding some of the formidable difficulties in pursuing inquiry on a just world order.

The GCP was a five-year project with annual workshops devoted to the principal domains: The Common Global Civilization: What Kind of Sovereignty (Moscow, 1988); Deepening and Globalizing Democracy (Yokohama, 1990); Global Political Economy: Trends and Preferences (Cairo, 1990); Shaping Global Polity (South Bend, 1991); and Toward a Just World Order for the 21st Century (Harare, 1993). In addition to the Steering Committee, such personages as Bibi Anderson, Jagdish Bhagwati, Robert MacNamara, Evgeni Primakov, Nathan Shamuyarira, and others participated in our discussions. From all of this, there was a wide range of publications: four volumes, various journal articles, and a series published by the Center for International Studies, Princeton. As rapporteur, Richard was intimately familiar with internal memos, drafts, the ongoing dialogue, and final publications. He wrote a number of preliminary drafts and attempted to prepare a final document on behalf of the Steering Committee. After some excruciatingly difficult meetings, it became clear to the Steering Committee and Richard that the complexity and richness of the issues that GCP was investigating defied a group product. To write a report that would fairly state the panoply of insights, nuances, and differences within the Steering Committee was simply not possible. This underscores how difficult it is to create a common vision by and for the progressive intelligentsia of the world; that is, WOMP had not met its goal of a consensus document. At the same time, Richard was asked to prepare a report stating his understanding of what GCP had been about with the latitude of putting forward his own position on matters we had discussed. It is fair to say that the result was outstanding.

Humane Governance: Toward a New Global Politics is a landmark statement for inquiry on a just world order. The title of the first chapter, "From Geopolitics to Humane Governance: A Necessary Journey," states the major thesis of the work in a very synoptic form (perhaps overly so). The range, depth, and intricacy of analysis contained in *On Humane Governance* precludes an easy summary. However, Richard and a number of us prepared a statement for use in a series of WOMP workshops on the United Nations and Humane Governance. An adaptation of that statement follows.

THEORETICAL FRAME AND DEFINITION OF HUMANE GOVERNANCE

World politics as generally understood up to now has been dealt with mainly from a state-centered geopolitical perspective. However, with an emerging global civil society facing problems of a planetary scale, outstripping the capacity of the existing state system, the time has come for a move from geopolitics toward a broader notion of transnational governance: *geogovernance.*

Geopolitics has as its central focus a global security system in which the leadership and management role is played by a few dominant states and in which recurrent conflict tends to be resolved through wars and their outcomes. It often is associated with "realism," a world view that looks upon international warfare and wide economic disparities as inevitable ingredients of any political order that lacks a governmental center. It is, however, a viewpoint which, while claiming to be objective and scientific, is as normative as any other postulate about political behavior and potentiality.

Geogovernance reflects an erosion of this centrality of statist forms of world order. The State remains focal for many purposes; but overall, non-state actors, non-territorial socioeconomic forces, and globally organized media and communications networks are exerting a defining influence on large-scale social behavior. The interplay of complexity and fragility, combined with the elusiveness of transnational capital and environmental challenges to the health and survival of the peoples of the earth, is pushing world order in cooperative and integrative directions. The result of these pushes will be, we believe, the emergence of some form of geogovernance.

Such integrated coordination and control is indispensable and probably inevitable, although its normative orientation and behavioral implications is by no means determined. The transition from geopolitics to geogovernance is an adaptive, evolutionary period with many tendencies seeking to preempt the moment for a particular kind of geogovernance. Market forces, associated with corporate, financial, and banking activity, have been particularly active in projecting a type of geogovernance that aims, above all else, at sustaining high levels of economic growth and at promoting the most efficient frameworks for return on capital investments. Such geogovernance is not at all dedicated to policies of redistribution designed to achieve greater equity between different regions in the world; nor is it particularly concerned about high levels of unemployment or large concentrations of poverty and despair.

Our stress is upon humane governance—that is, a type of governance that is people, human rights (including basic needs), and sustainable development oriented—rather than statist and market-oriented; demilitarization, including disarmament and peaceful resolution of disputes are also a central focus. On an analytic level, this perspective recognizes that power analysis is essential to understanding the organization of human society. At the same time, humane governance inquiry and its political activity counterpart use human security as an axiological premise. Its frame of reference involves the values of peace, social justice, economic well-being, ecological balance, and positive identity. These values are the analytical as well as normative parameters. Humane global governance seeks to achieve these values for all human beings and groups throughout the globe.

(Mendlovitz and Weston 1995)

In addition to the analytic effort in this statement, Richard has also suggested a political agenda in the final two chapters, "In Pursuit of Humane Governance" and "The Essential Vision: A Normative Project to Achieve Humane Governance." They are closely reasoned, combining vision and political opportunity.

APPRECIATION

Over these four decades of close collaboration, Richard and I have found ourselves in agreement—sometimes after intense and long dialogue—involved in research or promoting a political agenda for a just world order. There are two matters on which we still tend to, if not disagree, place different emphasis and importance: world government and military or police intervention for humanitarian purposes. For example, Richard writes,

> Adherence of humane governance should not be dogmatically opposed to world government. Nevertheless, skepticism is in order. The only elites that are likely to contemplate world government favorably in the foreseeable future are those that currently seem sensitive to the most acute forms of human suffering. The abstractions of world government, even a phrase with a sensitive awareness of the plight of the poor and vulnerable, are not likely to produce beneficial results unless tied to a democratic political movement that includes the establishment of world government as an integral role. (Falk 1995, 7)

A careful parsing of this paragraph demonstrates that Richard is aware of the possibility and perhaps necessity of world government. Nevertheless, it is the initial posture of "not . . . dogmatically opposed to world government" that causes some concern. As I see it, government is an aspect of good governance, and therefore I would argue that establishing a "good" world government is crucial for achieving humane governance for the people of the world.

Similarly, Richard is opposed to constabulary, let alone military, forces for humanitarian purposes *under present circumstances*. It is his view that intervention in the contemporary world is either done at the behest of the superpower, the United States and its allies, with deleterious impact on people and governments or the global community lacks the political will to engage in these actions in an effective and beneficial fashion, engendering disappointment and disillusionment. Notwithstanding, it is my view that serious efforts to construct appropriate interventionary models—authoritative invocation, size, weapons systems and location of forces, clear mandates, and adequate funding—is the more desirable posture. One should, of course, be aware of the dangers that Richard points to. Yet, in the spirit of combining vision with political possibility, I urge him once more to review this matter.

But this is not the occasion for full rehearsal of these differences. Rather, it is the moment to celebrate Richard's presence and contributions. It is clear that when the pantheon of significant figures who contributed to the dismantling of the war system is chronicled by historians in the middle of the twenty-first century, Richard Falk will undoubtedly be in the first tier. Indeed, I look forward to the next two decades with full expectation that Richard Falk will be in the forefront of the movement to establish a world polity in which humane governance has been established for the people of the world. I join with friends, colleagues, and the academic and broader community in expressing our admiration and appreciation and in wishing him well.

23

Culture, Politics, and the Sense of the Ethical: Challenges for Normative International Relations

Lester Edwin J. Ruiz

> Our age is one in which the very activities of their own states—combined re-
> gimes of sovereignty and governmentality—together with the global capitalism
> of states and the environmental degradation of many populous regions of the
> planet have made many millions of people radically endangered strangers in
> their own homes a well as criminalized or anathemized strangers in the places
> to which they have been forced to flee. The modern age's response to the
> strangeness of others, indeed, the scale of its politically instrumental, deliberate,
> juridical, and governmental manufacture of estrangement, necessarily calls into
> question, therefore, its very ethical and political foundations and accomplish-
> ments—particularly those of the state and of the international state system.
> (Dillon 1995, 357–58)

INTRODUCTION: NORMATIVE INTERNATIONAL
RELATIONS AT CENTURY'S END

As the world moves into the twenty-first century, scholars and activists have been
forced to deal with the fundamental transformations in the political, economic, cultural, technological, and ecological processes that have occurred worldwide in the
last quarter of this century. They have especially been forced to respond to the trans-
nationalization/globalization of capitalism as well as to the market-driven constitu-
tionalisms and the normative, conceptual, and institutional discursive practices associated with it.[1] Nowhere is this more clearly seen than in the ways in which
normative international relations scholars and activists have addressed the questions
of peace and security or struggled to make sense of the broader themes of culture,
democracy, governance, and the contingent but central place of ethics in their work.

322

In this concluding chapter, I want to provide some kind of cartography of these themes in the context of both the specific contributions to this book and some currently influential political debates. I especially want to meditate on their significance from a perspective that is self-consciously concerned with, and committed to, struggles for peace, security, and identity.

Peace, Security, and Identity

One way of interpreting the contestation between what Richard Falk calls the "normative" and the "realist" consensus of international relations (Falk 1992, 214–27) is as "wars of position" around the meaning and significance of peace and security. While there are generally assumed to be profound differences between the practices of peace and security, I want to insist that both are inextricably related. This is so because, first, both are often used interchangeably in "everyday language"; second, both touch on the common concerns of violence, insecurity, and avoidable harm; third, in the continuing "wars of position" among those concerned with the previously noted issues but especially among the pundits and disciples of the "realist consensus," the notion of peace is actually subsumed under the notion of security, interpreted largely as the "obsession for absolute invulnerability"; and, finally, I understand peace in terms of the need and desire both to overcome avoidable, untimely harm and to adopt principles of nonviolence both as a strategy and as a philosophy of life. In this context, not only has the pursuit of peace and security become profoundly difficult, but speaking clearly of peace and security itself has also become almost impossible—as Mary Kaldor, Robert Jay Lifton, and Radmila Nakarada have demonstrated in this book.

Part of the difficulty of speaking about peace and security is no doubt a consequence of the always and already intensely contested, contradictory, and indeed conflictual character of human life. This is a consequence not only of the inherent plurality of human existence but also, as the essays of Michael Doyle and Rajni Kothari in this book suggest, of the profoundly assymetrical character of modern social structures. Moreover, claims about peace and security have long thrived on what R. B. J. Walker calls "a denotative imprecision that has been carefully calibrated," by which he means that much of the rhetorical force and political legitimation expressed through modern discourses of peace and security rest ultimately on the "simultaneous appeal to the hard and the vacuous, the precise and the imprecise, the exaction of blood and sacrifice in the name of the grand generalization" (Walker 1997, 61–82). A further part of the difficulty lies in the fact that the dominant "realist consensus" on peace and security, as well as on what might be called "state making" and "wealth making," retain a certain plausibility, not only because some of their claims remain adequate to contemporary circumstances but also because of the absence of any sustained agreement about alternatives to them (Kothari 1993, 119–39). This dominant consensus or, more precisely, this consensus of the dominant and the challenges to this consensus have been systematically circumscribed and arbitrarily defined by global capitalism's seemingly unchallenged understanding of what is good, or true, or beautiful (Fukuyama 1992).

To put the matter in this way is to suggest that activists and scholars alike are confronted not only by profound transformations, dilemmas, and questions that call for both interpretation and action but also with the task of articulating practices of peace and security that are adequate not only for the particular historical moment but, equally important, also for the particular spaces and places in which they find themselves today. The authors in this book may all agree that we are now moving through a post–post–Cold War period, but such a period is experienced differently depending on one's spatiotemporal location. Thus, as Robin Broad, John Cavanagh, Ali Mazrui, and Vandana Shiva have suggested here, there is a need to explore alternatives to the specific, contingent and plural practices that have characterized the most violent century in the history of this planet.

The critical question, it seems to me, and paraphrasing Walker, is this: Under what conditions is it now possible to think, speak, and make authoritative claims about what is referred in the language of modern international relations as "peace and security"—given not only the consensus of the dominant but, more specifically, the proliferation of multiple practices of violence, insecurity, and avoidable harm under the sign of global capitalism? Can activists and scholars alike, in fact, envisage a "normative international relations" that embraces the realities of contemporary change; attend to our world's contending plurality of spaces, times, and places; and engage creatively and imaginatively in this profoundly divided world without destroying it?[2]

Rethinking Peace and Security: Reconstituting the Practices of the Subject

To pose the question of "normative international relations" in this way, both in general and in relation to peace and security in particular, Walker notes, is not only to direct our attention to the importance of immediate historical and structural contexts, nor merely to demand broader understandings of what peace and security involve, nor simply to require expanded notions of whose peace and security is at stake, at the same time that one insists on ensuring their "security" (Walker 1997). Rather, it is to suggest that any discussion of peace and security—and, for that matter, of normative international relations—cannot be detached from even more basic claims about human identity, claims, that is, about who we are, what we hope for, and how we can get from where we are to where we hope to be.

Here there are at least three inextricably related aspects of the politics of identity that are critical to any rethinking of peace and security as well as of (normative) international relations:

1. Those involving the character and location of political life. Because it is so widely claimed—not least by James Mittleman and Ashwini Tambe, Yoshikazu Sakamoto, Vandana Shiva, and Paul Wapner in this book—that the state (or

the system of states) is no longer the exclusive locus of political identity, conventional accounts of the "political" need to be rethought so that the question of peace and security can be rethought as well.

2. Those involving questions about whose peace and security is being assumed and under what conditions, that is, the question of the subject and of subjectivity. It is no longer possible to simply assume that peace and security is mainly about the peace and security either of particular individuals or of specific states. Demands are now commonplace, for example, that we think in relation to "nonviolence, safety, and well-being" for those who historically have been rendered insecure. This is part of the significance of discourses that raise the question of the marginalization and proletarianization of peoples of color (Marable 1983), the pauperization and feminization of poverty (Mies 1986), the sexual division of labor and even sexual slavery (Truong 1990), the commodification of sex (*AMPO Japan-Asia Quarterly Review* 1995), domestic violence, and enforced prostitution and trafficking of women and children (O'Grady 1992; Cook 1994; Davies 1994). These peoples are the ones harmed, rendered "insecure," and made to pay for the costly obsessions and rituals of repetition of the realist consensus.

3. Those involving the languages (or discourses) of peace and security itself.[3] It is no longer possible to make facile assertions about the separation of knowledge and power, reason and desire, fact and value, language and institutions. As the essays by Fritz Kratochwil, James Rosenau, and R. B. J. Walker insist, there is a need to attend to the language, to the discursive formations and strategies shaping our practices of peace and security as well as our understanding of normative international relations. The point, of course, is that language not only shapes the political agenda but also, as Michel Foucault (1980) and others have amply demonstrated, is productive—it produces an effect: "God said, 'Let there be light' and there was light" (Genesis 1:14). George Soros or Alan Greenspan speak, and the Japanese yen or the German mark rises and falls. Asia Pacific Economic Cooperation (APEC) speaks, and Manila's traffic lanes are rerouted.

RETHINKING THE PRACTICES OF INTERNATIONAL RELATIONS: CRITICAL DIMENSIONS OF POLITICAL IDENTITY

Extending to international relations Walker's suggestion that rethinking and reconstituting peace and security require analyses of the ways in which modern political subjects and subjectivities are today being reconstituted, thereby enabling analyses of the possible meaning of peace and security for emerging political subjectivities, I want to explore some challenges to international relations in terms of the question of political identity. In particular, I want to explore four critical dimensions of contemporary identity politics: "culture," "democracy," "governance," and "ethics," especially in relation to the specific conditions of global capitalism.[4]

Culture(s)

Like "democracy," "governance," and "ethics," the concept of "culture" has become not only contested but one of the critical sites in which issues of life and death have been and are being "fought" today. Raymond Williams (1983) has reminded us that culture is "one of the two or three most complicated words in the English language" (87). Similarly, Walker has pointed out that the notion of culture gestures toward universality—and does so in grand style—while at the same time reminding us of the highly specific, localized, even chauvinistic and deeply fragmented character of human experience. Walker goes on to argue that culture refers to complex accumulations of theoretical speculation about human affairs as well as embodies assumptions and contradictions arising from specific historical contexts. What we have inherited, in fact, has been an understanding of culture that is articulated on the basis of philosophical claims and analytical methods that presume a fundamental ontological difference between, for example, idea and matter, language and world, or fact and value and that simultaneously challenges and reaffirms the universalizing claims of the Enlightenment.

More recently, Mahathir bin Mohammed and Shintaro Ishihara, in their book *The Voice of Asia,* have noted with candidness, if not veiled contempt, that the differences between "Pacific" Asia, "Western" Europe, and the North Atlantic, not only in their practices of democracy and capitalism, are largely the result of critical "cultural differences" between the so-called East and West. They also suggest that the successes of Asian capitalist economies and, conversely, the failures of their Western counterparts may be explained by these critical "cultural differences" (Mohammed and Ishihara 1996).[5]

Setting aside for the moment what specifically these cultural differences are and whether, in fact, they are truly geographically distinct or unique, what is abundantly clear in Mahathir's and Ishihara's work is that "culture" has now become an important, if not strategic, arena in defining identity, development, and the role of "Pacific" Asia in the coming century.[6] However one defines *substantively* or views *methodologically* the idea of "culture"—whether as a "superstructure," as in certain construals of Karl Marx (1975), or as "webs of interpretive meaning," as in Clifford Geertz (1973), or as "knowledge/power," as in Foucault (1980)—it is important in the articulation of alternative practices to current perspectives on peace, security, development, and education—in short, to international relations.

Moreover, Mahathir and Ishihara may also be read as suggesting that Asian capitalism is not only about trade liberalization, or capitalist globalization, or even "Pacific" Asia's rights to economic, political, and, cultural self-determination; nor even is it only about the role that cultures can and do play in these practices. Global capitalism, they seem to suggest, is the sign under which political, economic, and cultural practices are today organized. Indeed, global capitalism is a specific cultural form. More precisely, as a historical conjuncture of specific (cultural) practices, global capitalism is the principle of articulation for most, if not all, of the practices of modern life in general.

By "cultural practice" I mean, following Michael Ryan, those multiplicities of discursive and rhetorical forms, gestures, procedures, modes, shapes, and genres of everyday life that are "radically contingent arenas of imagination, strategy, and creative manoeuvre" (Ryan 1989, 97). More than demarcations of time and place (as "culture" is so often (mis)recognized), I understand "culture," following Foucault, as referring to the vast institutionalized manifold of persons, theories, projects, experiments, and technologies that characterize and specify human life. At century's end, this understanding may be assigned to the realities of global capitalism as well: from the more conventional notions of surplus value, modes of production, falling rates of profit, to notions such as deregulation, liberalization, structural adjustment, and, most important, to the practices of everyday life. Thus the importance of the fact, for example, that as a result of the so-called successes of the "free-trade ideologies" of the General Agreement on Tariffs and Trade (GATT) and the World Trade Organization (WTO), imported corned beef is less expensive in the Philippines today than its local counterpart or that apples from California are less expensive than mangoes from Laguna, the Philippines.

To read global capitalism as a specific cultural form is neither new nor especially compelling; it is so obvious as to border on banality and is consequently often overlooked. Both Antonio Gramsci (1971) and Karl Marx (1967) understood the "economic" as articulating itself dialectically in politics and culture. How else can one understand the persistent marginalization of cultural discourses in supposedly political and economic discourses of mainstream social science? Why do some among us, academics and activists alike, for example, still offer comprehensive analyses and strategies of politics and economics as if cultures were mere "epiphenomena," separating, in many instances, fact from value, language from thought, political institutions from "cultural" production? Why do many in "the guild" still look askance on *academic* aspirations toward "principled commitment and scholarship" in international relations theory and practice?[7]

In fact, to suggest that global capitalism can be appropriately and productively understood as a conjuncture of specific cultural practices is to reject the conventional wisdom that "culture" (including art, philosophy, and theology) is, at best, the legitimizer, if not inspirer, of economic and political interests. It is to affirm the need for comprehending matters of polity and economy precisely as if they were matters of culture. They are not only descriptively amenable empirical materials—cold, hard facts rendered transparent by reason and manipulatable through sophisticated technologies or surveillance, observation, normalization, calculation, evaluation, and differentiation—but also have to do with meaning and significance and are understandable only through a shared interpretive process, which is always and already historical, contingent, and fragile.

At the same time, it is to suggest that what Josef Lapid and Fritz Kratochwil (1996a) have called the "return of culture and identity in international relations theory," far from simply being an admission that "cultural factors" are important variables for the study of politics or economy, is about the recognition that practices such as intellectual property rights, tariff reductions, nontariff measures, and so on, as well as regional arms races, balances of power, multilateral security arrangements, the multilateral trade agreements of the WTO or the Organization for Economic Cooperation and Development (OECD) "direct foreign investment," and "full equity ownership," are cultural as much as they are political or economic artifacts. Thus, it is crucial for any international relations theorizing to track, to the best of its abilities, how the structures and processes of global capitalism—especially as they are embodied in its institutions, such as APEC, the European Union (EU), the North American Free Trade Agreement (NAFTA), the International Monetary Fund (IMF)/World Bank (WB), the WTO, and its ideologies, such as "globalization" or "neoliberalism"—discipline the very structures, institutions, behaviors, and meanings of planetary life (see, e.g., Barnet and Cavanagh 1994; Bello 1997; Lim 1998; Shiva n.d.).

Moreover, it is extremely important that those who aspire to a normative understanding of international relations track these movements in the context of a commitment to the global South. They must do so at the level of *how* ideas that are embodied in the specific discursive strategies and logics of, for example, APEC[8] or of the existing and envisioned regional security systems, such as the U.S.-Japan Security Treaty, the Association of Southeast Asian Nations (ASEAN) Regional Forum, and the U.S.-Philippine Visiting Forces Agreement, and of our educational institutions are *experienced* by the people most affected by them and in whose name peace and security, or trade liberalization, or modernization, are invoked. These, of course, are often the majority of our countries' populations—the poor (Gutierrez 1983), the colonized (Fanon 1968), the subaltern (Spivak 1988), the dispensable (Kothari 1993), and the forgotten (Nakarada; see chap. 5 in this book). Whether in the North or the South, we must demand an accounting of the social totality at the level of cultural meaning and situate the issues of social justice, economic well-being, peace, and humane governance at the level of "everyday life."

Marx understood the dynamics of capital very well. As R. B. J. Walker and Warren Magnusson put it some time ago, Marx understood capital not as a thing-in-itself but as a relation, a principle of articulation, that manifests itself in all aspects of human life (Walker and Magnusson 1988, 37–71; cf. Ollman 1976; Gould 1988). One such manifestation is the fetishism of commodities—the establishment within capitalist societies of particular identities conducive to the reproduction of capital; the bourgeois individual, the citizen, the consumer, is another. The globalization of the market and the regionalization of capital, as well as the marketization of human experience accompanied by a market morality that "stigmatizes others as objects for personal pleasure and bodily stimulation," is yet another (West 1993).

Capital, in its money form, which circles the world endlessly pursuing the scent of power and profit, touching ground when and where it is needed and vanishing when it is threatened, is perhaps the classical metaphor for global capitalism today. The restructuring of labor on a global scale, the migration of peoples in search of meaningful and productive work, is yet another. Moreover, once allied with the state, capitalism has refused to be controlled by conventional political forms, reducing the state, for example, to a "local authority," not even any longer to the "executive committee of the bourgeoisie." Not only do states and peoples have little power to control capital flight; but capital today is also more elusive and mobile.[9] In fact, capitalism in its multinational, global form seems to be transforming into a polyarchic, decentered reality, making it very difficult to contain by conventional practices of resistance and solidarity. One way of putting it, provisionally, is that global capitalism has been transformed from matter into spirit,[10] although the effects or costs of this transformation of capital into spirit is inversely proportional to the costs that it exacts at the level of concrete, sensuous reality, not least in alienation, commodification, the dispensability of vast sectors of humanity, ecological degradation, and the feminization of poverty.

Such a reading suggests that those who would challenge "the spirit of global capitalism" must offer something more than an ideological, even "spiritual," challenge—not to mention be dissatisfied with its economic critiques. Here, one could explore some kind of "spectral challenge," a "haunting" as Jacques Derrida (1993) put it, by which I mean the articulation of a critical and creative practice that refuses, on the one hand, the temptation of a disembodied transcendence (a legacy of some critical theories) and, on the other hand, one that rejects the seduction of a totalizing embodied immanence (a legacy of some Marxist theories). Here, one focuses on the *effects* of capitalism, recognizing the reversibility of its origins and consequences without yielding to the temptation of returning to some self-validating, self-evident "ground" for its definition or explanation. The Derridean "ghost" is illuminating: One recognizes the ghost because one knows the person who now returns as a ghost; but the ghost is not a replica (or even a copy) of the latter—not in its materiality— and the ghost is not without actual, historical "effect" (cf. Laclau 1996; Matustik 1998). In this context, we can see that the "practical" question today is not only "What is to be done?" or "Who gets what, when, where, and how?" but also "What is the nature of spirit?"

Capitalism has also managed to accommodate itself to already existing hegemonies constructed around the discourses of race and gender. Indeed, Marable and Mies have pointed out long before it was fashionable to do so that both racism and gender oppression have played decisive roles in capitalist accumulation on a world scale, have reinforced the capitalist division of labor, and have contributed to the marginalization and proletarianization of peoples of color as well as to the pauperization of women and the feminization of poverty. Capitalism on a world scale has legitimized not only the exploitative relations of production and reproduction but also the capitalist control of the bodies of both women and men and nature (Butler 1993; Grosz 1994). Equally important, but often unacknowledged, this "writing and rewriting" on/of women's, men's, and children's bodies occurs as capitalism creates and re-creates space, time, and place in its own image (see, e.g., Giddens 1990; Soja 1996; Casey 1997).

In this context, the irony, if not the paradox or anomaly, of the pursuit of capitalist globalization by states or economies is not lost to those of the global South—nor even to a George Soros (1998): On the one hand, wealth making within a global capitalist framework requires "free trade" in order to guarantee unhampered competition and accumulation of wealth; on the other hand, state making, at least within the present system of states, requires that state sovereignty be held sacrosanct (Walker and Mendlovitz 1990). Not surprisingly, one of the sites of struggle within and between states has to do with how economies can secure maximum efficiency and profitability while preserving state sovereignty. Here we are brought face-to-face with some of the profound contradictions inherent in capitalism: The pursuit of power and profit requires that authoritarianism and inequality be sustained; power, as Max Weber demonstrated, requires domination, while profit, as Marx explained, presupposes exploitation.

I want to suggest, however, that "free trade" is only one of the "Trojan horses" of capitalist, neoliberal wealth making. While its proclaimed *telos* is undeniably maximum profit and hedonistic pleasure, the *arche* of its pursuit of power and profit is competition and the survival of the fittest, and, therefore, its operative *telos* is insecurity. Today it can no longer be denied that capitalism's logic of the accumulation of power and profit structurally and fundamentally generates a profound insecurity, if not violence. Here, Thomas Hobbes, not Adam Smith, is global capitalism's prophet and patron saint: not the "invisible hand" of a benign and benevolent capitalism but rather the perpetual war of each against all in the pursuit of power and profit (Hobbes 1946; cf. Huntington 1968, 1997). Thus, for example, if one wants to understand global capitalism more fully in general and Philippine capitalist development as a creature of global capitalist development in particular, one will have to rearticulate, if not reconnect, conventional economic analyses within the Hobbesean political and philosophical legacy. Not only are peoples of the global South up against an economic and political Leviathan, but this Leviathan is constituted by dispersed and mobile practices whose controlling assumptions are rooted in the values and meanings of the Western European cultures of the seventeenth century (see Macpherson 1962; cf. Unger 1975; Laclau 1994).

In this context, it will be necessary to deflate the ideology of competition: first, that competition is economically desirable; second, that competition under the sign of global capitalism is possible; and, third, that competition is necessary because it is rooted in the human condition. Is it true, for example, that competition ensures the quality of production? Does "fair competition" actually exist under the conditions of combined and uneven development, if not monopoly capitalism? Is competition an inescapable, necessary fact, or is it socially constructed reality just like cooperation? In this context, we must also more fully and explicitly establish the connections between capitalist competition and its sexualized and racialized assumptions (see, e.g., Enloe 1993; Goldberg 1993; West 1993).

Equally important, it will be crucial to demystify the rational illusions of capitalist accumulation. Weber was, indeed, correct in linking the emergence of capitalism to the "spirit of Protestantism," thereby underscoring the "cultural" origins of capitalism on the one hand and the "economic" implications of Calvinist Protestantism on the other. Even more incisive was his analysis of the different forms of rationality and how the rationalities of modernity (including instrumental rationality) create an "iron cage" from which there is no escape. One way to read the Weberian analysis of capitalism, then, is as an analysis of the logic of (capitalist) accumulation: its rationality, necessity, and, calculability. Not only, it is argued, are power and profit—the twin goals of capitalism—desirable, if not necessary, but power and profit can be accumulated since, through the logic of accumulation, they have been transformed into "calculable subjects which operate in calculable spaces." What becomes clear in the Weberian analysis is that capitalist accumulation is not only about the rationality of capitalism or of accumulation as such. Rather, it is about the dynamics of domination: the subjection of nature and human beings to calculative and instrumental rationality (cf. Leiss 1972; Heidegger 1977; Habermas 1989).

Finally, it would be important, indeed critical, to rethink—as many already have, from M. K. Gandhi (1945) to E. F. Schumacher (1973) to Herman Daly and John Cobb (1982) and from the International Labor Organization (ILO) and the UN Development Program (UNDP) to the IMF/WB and WTO—our notions of work as vocation, not only what work has become under the sign of global capitalism but also what work ought to be as human activity (UN Development Program 1996). Marx can be credited for pointing to the fundamentally alienated and flawed character of (wage) labor in capitalist societies (Marx 1967). However, it is left to those inspired by Marx to track the dynamics of labor today, especially in the context of the restructuring of the global economy and of the migration of peoples and populations following the scent of capital (see, e.g., Dillon 1995). In fact, the widespread devolution and devaluation of work into jobs reveal the depth of global capitalism's exploitation and transformation of both human life and nature. Not only is there a burgeoning sector of the world's population that is unemployed or underemployed even as it is being overworked, underpaid, and devalued, but this sector is being rendered redundant or superfluous by the so-called inexorable march of modern technology at the same time that it is confronted by its unsustainability and the limits of nature's renewability as well as its degradation (Daly and Cobb 1982).

Economies are about human (productive and reproductive) activity—work—and global capitalism, at its core, may be understood as one form of this activity. In the light of the preceding "cultural argument" about capitalism, it is clear that work cannot be reduced to wage labor alone. Nor can the migration of peoples and populations only be about following the scent of capital. On the contrary, it is about the pursuit of meaningful, profitable, and dignified work (Fox 1995; Lerner 1996). As

332

Lester Edwin J. Ruiz

Thomas Aquinas put it, "To live well is to work well or to display a good activity" (*Summa theologica,* I–II, q. 57, a. 5).

Democracy

Whatever its technologies or classifications—representative, constitutional, or authoritarian; liberal, national or socialist; as "the rule of the people" or "the power of the people"—democracy is about the question of who the subject is and what is entailed in being a subject. It is about identity and subjectivity: who we are, what we hope for, what we need to do.

As "the power of the people" especially, democracy raises at least three interrelated and critical issues for normative international relations theorizing: (1) "power," (2) "people," and (3) "civil society." Contemporary politics is the heir to at least two competing interpretations of power that now must be revisited, not least because it has become profoundly contested. On the one hand, modern political theory and practice, especially that drawing on Hobbes and Locke, understands power primarily as the capacity to gain precedence over others. While understood and achieved in a variety of ways, this "precedence" often finds its clearest expression in the subjection of reality to a calculative, instrumental, and legal rationality. In fact, power, in this tradition, is "coercion" or "domination" (*Herrschaft*), that is, the unilateral assertion of the will of (autonomous) subjects.

In contrast to this monologic, unilateral understanding of power is a "relational and dialogic" interpretation of power: "the ability both to produce and to undergo an effect . . . to sustain a mutually internal relationship" (Loomer 1976, 20–23). Hannah Arendt locates this relational understanding of power in a wider political context by suggesting that it is always and only *potestas in populo* (Arendt 1970, 44; cf. Tillich 1954). In fact, power is a public and intersubjective activity, inevitably located in particular communities that act in concert to bring about what they deem to be "the good, the true, the beautiful." In other words, power is inextricably related to production, to the "bringing forth" or "letting come forth" (poiesis) of human life, which, in turn, is a constitutive dimension of what Martin Heiddeger (1977) called "human dwelling" (praxis).

In this context, power shows itself to be of a profoundly dynamic, if contested, character not only in the theories of culture, politics, and ethics but also in the manifold practices of everyday life, which include multiple and overlapping forms of coercion, resistance, and, struggle as well as of production and reproduction, representations, and transformations—in short, wherever the practices of power play on, in, and through each other. Unfortunately, both perspectives of power noted previously fail to comprehend adequately the origins and destinations of power precisely because both are embedded in traditional discourses that have hewed more in the direction of the *what* of power and less in the direction of its *how*. Thus, for example, the ways in which power circulates in a "postmodern" informational society are significantly different from their counterparts in a "feudal" society.

Foucault offers an "analytic of power" that directs our attention not to power as such but to its mechanisms. Foucault (1980, 93) suggests that in any society there are "manifold relations of power which permeate, characterize, and constitute the social body, and these relations of power cannot themselves be established, consolidated, nor implemented without the production, accumulation, circulation, and functioning of a discourse." "There can be no possible exercise of power," Foucault continues, "without a certain economy of discourse of truth which operates through and on the basis of this association. We are subjected to the production of truth through power and we cannot exercise power except through the production of truth." In short, power is a relational term that cannot be defined, understood, or comprehended apart from its consequences and effects.

Thus, rather than ask how the discourse of truth is able to fix the limits of power (thus, for example, the truism "speaking truth to power"), one ought to ask "what rules of right are implemented by the relations of power in the production of discourses of truth, or, alternatively, what type of power is susceptible of producing discourses of truth that in a society are endowed with such potent effects?" (Foucault 1980, 93). For Foucault, then, any analysis of power must move away from the "traditional, noble, and philosophic question of power" and towards a "more down-to-earth and concrete" exploration of those practices in which and through which power is produced and/or reproduced. Moreover, precisely because power is always and already intimately and inextricably implicated in the structures and processes of knowledge and discourse, it requires rethinking not only at the institutional level but, equally important, also at the conceptual, analytical, epistemological, and normative levels.

Precisely because of its dynamic *practical* character, power can be comprehended only in terms of its productive effects, that is, in terms of practice—which includes questions of coercion, resistance, and struggle. Thus, the question of power turns on the question of "people." In this context, the fundamental challenge is not only about *who* the people are but also *what* is entailed in being a people and, most important, *how* a people are brought into being (Benhabib 1996). As Simona Sharoni demonstrates in this book, this coming into being of a people is an essentially long, intensely contested, and fundamentally protracted struggle. Here, feminist struggles are illustrative of what I understand is fundamental to what "becoming a people" entails: from struggles to render the invisible visible, to creating and nurturing cultures of resistance and solidarity, to shaping and transforming gendered histories. Women in the body politic, becoming a people, if you will, in fact go to the heart of the democratic project. In the first place, the many forms of feminism, as theory and practice, are practices of rendering visible the fact not only that culture and politics are gendered practices but also that feminist practices are struggles that problematize conventional notions of political identity in the modern world. In so doing, they not only open the possibility of resurrecting excluded and buried voices but also provide the grounds for challenging the historically specific, and often invisible, accounts of political identity within, say, the spatial and temporal boundaries of community (i.e., state and sovereignty)—accounts that govern the theory and practice of politics and that are constitutive of modern life.

In the second place, feminist practices are cultures of resistance and solidarity. As a politics of resistance, they are both deconstructive and reconstructive. The former involves, among many things, the dismantling of male-centric, technostrategic discourses, for example, militarized and decontextualized rationalities (Runyan and Peterson 1993); the latter involves the articulation of compelling alternative visions of possible futures, including alternative conceptions of rationality and imagination (hooks 1984). By "listening to all voices of subjugation and hearing their insurrectionary truths [they] make us better able to question our own political and personal practices. . . . And if another term and a different politics emerge from this questioning, it will be in the service of new local actions, new creative energies, and new alliances against power (Diamond and Orenstein 1990, 126ff).

In the third place, women's and feminist struggles, far from being adaptive or remedial mechanisms within an otherwise acceptable polity, are practices of cultural transformation that are aimed at eradicating structures and processes of domination. They articulate different understandings of community and identity; they describe and delineate, indeed celebrate, the full range of women's experiences—mother, sister, theorist, wife, lover, comrade, artist, worker, companion, peasant, warrior—which can shape and transform the male-centric, hierarchical, often misogynist practices in social and political life. Indeed, feminist struggles problematize the full range of commanding (often dominating) gendered ways of thinking, feeling, and acting: from the exploitation of women in the home to the feminization of poverty worldwide, from the inequality between the sexes to the subordination of women through male-defined social roles, from the marginalization and/or exclusion of women to their being rendered invisible or dispensable.

Democracy and the democratic project have been construed mainly within a framework of the state and of state sovereignty as the fundamental principle constituting modern political life. At the same time, as Elise Boulding notes in this book and elsewhere, the proliferation of nongovernmental organizations (NGOs), peoples' movements, and international NGOs has challenged the very boundaries of the state system, forcing the rethinking of the fundamental categories of political life (cf. Toulmin 1990). Thus, the question of "people" also raises the question of "civil society," not merely what civil society is but especially which part of civil society, in fact, builds or destroys human communities—which is the question about the criteria by which to discern the critical and necessary differences as to who it is that are the bearers, if not the keepers, of transformation. Yoshikazu Sakamoto, Vandana Shiva, and Paul Wapner point us in this direction in their contributions to this book.

At the same time, there are at least two critical problem areas associated with civil society as an idea and a set of practices related to the question of democracy. In the first place, there is nothing inherently transformative or desirable about civil society. There are many elements of civil society that are racist, sexist, and antidemocratic:

from fundamentalist, "right-wing" groups to elitist and hierarchical, not to mention gender-biased, associations to state-centric, capitalist-driven organizations—to mention only a few. In the second place, the notion of civil society presupposes the discourses of the modern state and of (global) capitalism (Keane 1988; Cohen and Arato 1992). Circumscribed both by the state and by global capitalism, civil society cannot be understood apart from them. Thus, any claim to it being the agency for change cannot avoid the contradictory realities of the state and of capital as an inextricable part of what that agency means. The question of citizenship, whether in its cosmopolitan or national form, suffers a similar fate.

Today it is the state *as a particular practice* under the sign of global capitalism that is intensely problematic—from the theoretical formulations about what the state is to the empirical tracking of what the state actually does. Walden Bello (1994), among others, for example, has argued that one way to challenge global capitalism is to strengthen the state (cf. Barber 1984). Such an argument makes sense only if one recognizes the importance of the *state apparatus* as being genuinely representative of an *empowered* citizenry. Even more important is the recognition of the empirical fact that the state today cannot be reduced to its apparatus, nor to a "thing-in-itself." Like capitalism, the state must be understood as a principle of articulation—concrete, contingent, and fragile—which is implicated conjuncturally in the everyday practices of civil society and which for this very reason makes of the state and its apparatus extremely resilient, if not relatively permanent, and therefore of continuing significance to any rethinking of (normative) international relations.

Thus, the theoretical and political move to "civil society," if it is to be genuinely transformative, must be articulated at the level of "resistance," solidarity, and inclusive vision. In short, the critical issue is not just civil society as such but *democratic* civil society. Normative international relations theorists must ask the question not only of identity, of subjecthood and subjectivity, but of *political* subjectivity as well, that is, what is entailed in being a member of "civil society" (see, e.g., Cadava et al. 1991; Mouffe 1992; Critchley and Dews 1996).

In the Philippine context, as well as in the Asia-Pacific one, normative international relations theorizing will need to recognize the democratic deficits of our respective societies and identify those elements of these civil societies that contribute to the creation of what Smitu Kothari (1996) calls a "vibrant and democratic civil society." However, in my view, it is not enough to identify these groups. It is important that their practices be interrogated by and survive the scrutiny of the "democratic norm"—not only whether they are participatory in character but also whether they create, enhance, and sustain the capacities of peoples in their struggles for a "good life": from enhancing the purchasing power of peoples; to resisting those practices that displace, dispossess, and marginalize peoples; to widening and deepening the economic and political choices of peoples; to empowering people to hold corporate capitalism, governments, and international institutions accountable for their policies. As much is suggested by Robin Broad and John Cavanagh, David Held, and Robert Johansen in this book.

In fact, despite the rhetoric about equity, sustainability, and participation emanating from the flagships of global capitalism, such as the IMF/WB, as well as from so-called progressive governments of both the global North and the global South, these institutions have often, if not systematically, excluded that part of civil society that is critical of, uninformed by, or apathetic to their initiatives. They have also insisted, in practice, on keeping the assumptions of power and profit as the fundamental starting point of their definitions of "the good, the true, and the beautiful." And despite all their rhetoric that "all ships will rise with the capitalist tide," what is clear thus far, in the Asia-Pacific region, for example, and also in the global North and South, has been the displacement, dispossession, and marginalization of vast, "unproductive" sectors of their populations in the name of global capitalism's "free trade" and economic liberalization (see Falk 1995). In this sense, not only is global capitalism going to be economically disadvantageous to the marginalized and the dispossessed, it is going to be antidemocratic.

Indeed, the logic of capitalism, its drive not only toward power and profit but also toward the *freedom* of capital, requires of its leadership and institutions an undemocratic, if not antidemocratic, modus operandi—this is one of the "lessons" of modern political and economic history, from Suharto to Lee to Marcos; from the Japanese *keiretsu* to Wall Street to the IMF/WB. These exclusions inhibit the realization of a vibrant and democratic civil society, which means that if activists and scholars want to challenge, not to mention oppose, global capitalism, they must work toward a vibrant (global) civil society. However, NGOs and/or citizens' groups alone cannot carry any genuine revolution even if they are integral to it; and civil societies are more than peoples' organizations. Thus, the question of civil society must also be a question about which other elements of civil society are part of democratic civil society and, most important, in what ways these elements are connected.

The question of "connections" is especially important when one understands that "civil society" cannot be fully understood apart from what has been called "the greening of the 'social.'" Drawing on the insights of "ecological movements," I understand the "social" to be the reflection of an expanded notion of the ecological self, which "responds not only to human actions but also to the actions of plants, animals, stones, rivers, and mountains. These nonhuman members of the ecological web are themselves relational and influential" (Kaza 1993, 128).

One need not capitulate to the metaphysical assumptions of "deep ecology" to understand the far-reaching implications of this ecological understanding for a fuller appreciation of "civil society," not to mention of the state. In fact, Vandana Shiva has demonstrated in this book that political subjectivity is always and already ecological subjectivity (cf. Sajor and Resurreccion 1998). By this I mean that subjectivity is constituted not by reason (*logos*) alone—not even a reflexive rationality—but through the confluence of the full range of human and nonhuman realities: from sources of food, water, livelihood, energy, and materials to friends, ideas, recreation and sports, and sacred inspiration—not to mention economic, political, and cultural interests and/or concerns. The struggle, then, to discover or evaluate the role of civil society in the construction of a viable democratic polity must also attend to the ways in which these realities shape the structures and processes of political, economic, and cultural life. This is yet another way of saying that the "democratic project" for the coming century must also be about the creation of "sustainable democratic civil societies" (cf. Orr 1992; Gare 1995).

Governance

The question of governance is complicated further by the fact that it is accompanied by questions about other practices, also deeply contested, through which forms of governance are constituted: sovereignty, authority, and the state (Walker 1993; Falk 1995). These three practices, along with their own respective, relatively autonomous logics, are part of the puzzle of governance. In specific historical circumstances, their conjunctures or effects are not the same, nor are they overdetermined. This is one of the lessons learned not only from Gramsci but also from the experiences of the last ten years: the unexpected fall of Marcos, of the Berlin Wall, or of apartheid in South Africa. What the elements of this puzzle have in common, especially within the realist consensus, is what Michael Dillon, following traditions associated with Weber and Foucault, calls a juridical conception of power, that is, of "command and will, largely concerned with rights relating to the exercise of coercion and constraint, traditionally enframed within political discourse by reference to subjectivity, territoriality, and the problematic of sovereignty" (Dillon 1995, 324; cf. Weber 1958). Governance, in fact, is still understood today as the "art of government," that is, "how to rule": how to secure territory, control populations, maintain legitimacy, and ensure the monopoly of violence. Under the sign of global capitalism, it is not a surprise that, on the one hand, global capitalism continues to organize itself around governments and the legitimacy, if not the desirability, of their ministers and heads of state to formulate and enact policy. Nor is it surprising, on the other hand, that global capitalism undermines these governments and/or states by valuing "free trade," "economic liberalization," and the marketization of politics, economies, and cultures, with their accompanying sanctions, "structural adjustments," and legitimations.

However, there is something less visible and, perhaps, more insidious about governance, especially market-driven governance. Drawing on Foucault's notion of "governmentality," Dillon points out, governance operates in the form of sophisticated technologies of surveillance, observation, normalization, calculation, evaluation, and differentiation or classification. In contrast to the idea of a "unitary, discrete, and willing political subject" who rules and the logics and practices that such an assumption presupposes, governance, in this sense of governmentality, is of the order of "knowledgeable practices, norms of conduct, and elaborate protocols of behavior" whose object is to "produce calculable subjects operating in calculable spaces." In other words,

Men in their relations, their links, their imbrication with those other things which are wealth, resources, means of subsistence, the territory with its specific qualities, climate, irrigation, etc.; men in their relations to that other kind of things which are customs, habits, ways of doing and thinking, etc. (Foucault 1979, 5–22)

Governance as governmentality works in ways that specify and organize populations, and it does so through the rituals and operations of knowledge/power. It *enframes* peoples, nature, things.[11] What this involves is the transvaluation of people into things and then, within a capitalist framework, into commodities: Land is remade into real estate, women are turned into objects of male hedonistic pleasure, "use value" is converted into "exchange value." What this does, of course, is not only to allow for the administration of things but also to enable government at a distance and, in the absence of any credible responses and/or resistance to this particular level of governance, the authorization, if not tolerance, of existing government practice.

It is this level at which I view the insidious character of the state, not to mention global capitalism, especially in the absence of transparency and a widespread genuine and unhampered discussion of what global capitalism and its institutions and practices are and their consequences for peoples in both the global North and the global South. What these institutions in particular and global capital in general are doing, as much by design as by accident, is not only making decisions about matters that affect people's lives, not only setting the limits for what can and cannot be said, thought, or done (i.e., setting the limits of the discussion), but also redefining structurally and fundamentally needs and values, priorities and strategies, problems and prospects. Most important, it does these not only through law and therefore through coercion and violence but also through knowledge, information, and the discursive strategies and formations of market-driven trade and investment liberalization and facilitation, free trade, global competitiveness, and structural adjustment.

NORMATIVE INTERNATIONAL RELATIONS AND THE SENSE OF THE ETHICAL[12]

Ethics, or the "ethical relationship," that is, its structure, is primarily that of the relationship between a mutually constituted and constituting Self and Other. Beyond the *modern* notion of ethics as a set of rules and regulations adopted by pregiven, autonomous subjects or of responsibility grounded in a command or imperative, ethics is primarily responsibility to/for the Other and *others* (cf. Caputo 1993). In fact, without capitulating to some of the dangers of a metaphysics of total otherness of which he is often accused, Emmanuel Levinas may be read, quite appropriately, as arguing that ethics ought to be understood as something insinuated within and integral to subjectivity itself: Ethics "does not supplement a preceding existential base; the very node of the subjective is knotted in ethics and understood as re-

sponsibility" (Levinas 1985, cited in Campbell 1994). In other words, one's identity, one's subjectivity, one's responsibility—that is, the "self"—are always and
already *ethically situated*. Making judgments about conduct depend less on what
rules are invoked as regulations and more on how the interdependencies of our relations with others are appreciated (Campbell 1994, 459ff; Dillon 1995, 349–50).

However, extending Campbell's argument, this "self" is not only ethically situated but also and already *ecologically situated*. By this I do not mean to highlight
only the multiple "ecological therapies" that underscore the importance of ecology
for ethics and politics: from ecotechnology to ecopolitics, from human and social
ecology to mental ecology, from ecological ethics to radical or deep ecology.[13] To be
sure, these critical therapies call for "ethical practices," such as speaking out on behalf of those nonhuman voices that are not included in human decision making or,
following Aldo Leopold's early lead, for example, redefining community to include
"soils, waters, plants, and animals, or collectively: the land" (Leopold 1949) or
adopting "environmentally sustainable" lifestyle choices (e.g., restraint, simplicity,
reduced consumption). Rather, I want to suggest that this "ethical relationship" is
largely about new ways of knowing and understanding, of engaging and being, of
perceiving and communicating with Self, Other, and World. The insight on corpo-
reality shared by feminists bears repeating here, namely, that human beings have
more than logos. They also have *eros* (life and passion), *pathos* (affectivity and sensitivity), and the *daimon* (nature's inner voice). "Reason," Leonardo Boff (1997)
writes, "is neither the primary nor ultimate moment of existence. We are also affectivity, desire, passion, turbulence, communication, and the voice of nature speaking
inside us" (12). This is the sense in which I read the notion that to be ethically
situated is at the same time to be ecologically situated and that to be ecologically
situated is to gesture unavoidably toward a *planetary community*—which is not to
assume that such a community already exists historically or is "pregiven" metaphysi-
cally but rather to indicate only what the trajectory and reach of the conditions of
possibility for ethics today are and to suggest the need for cultivating an ecologically
situated, *fully corporeal* ethical sensibility.

In this context, because ethics has to do primarily with this situated responsibility,
a responsibility for the Other whom we encounter face-to-face, the question "Who
is my neighbor?" becomes a question about the relationship of ethical responsibility
to community (cf. Habermas 1985, 1989). In fact, ethics has always gestured both
toward and away from "community." That is, ethics, as a "responsible, nontotaliz-
ing relation with the Other," has not, and cannot, end with the individual; indeed,
it does not even begin with the individual but rather is always and already in community (Dussel 1988). Here, the primarily one-on-one structure of ethics gestures
toward the communicative and therefore a political relationship, that is, a "relation
to . . . all others, to the plurality of beings that make up the community" (Critchley
1992, 220). Ethics may not be synonymous with politics, but politics is inescapably
ethical. With the constant aggregation, disaggregation, and reaggregation of these
communities due, in large part, to the transformations of space, time, and place

brought about by (economic and political) migrations, "border crossings," "foot wanderers," and exiles, the reality of a territorially circumscribed community is no longer self-evident. Thus, the question "Which community and therefore which ethics?" or "Whose ethics?" becomes a profound issue (see, e.g., Rawls 1989, 1996; Taylor 1991; Sandel 1998).

Moreover, this question is of particular importance not only because what Levinas calls "the third party" always and already interrupts the primary ethical relation of the face-to-face and, by virtue of this interruption, renders the relationship "political" but also because this "third" who is simultaneously other than the other makes one one among others (Levinas 1981). Thus, when Levinas asks, "When others enter (the relationship), each of them external to myself, problems arise. Who is closest to me? Who is the Other?" he may be read as asking not only "To which community do I belong?" nor simply "To whom and for whom am I responsible?" nor even "Which community bears responsibility for 'the world'?" but, rather, "Why are this Other and others conditions of possibility for politics and ethics—or the pursuit of the 'body politic'?"

There is no doubt that difference is central to any politics and that plurality is intrinsic to the ethical relation. When situated not only in a deeply divided, contested world but also in a *globalizing* world under the sign of transnational capitalism, the question "How then shall I live?" which is another way of posing the (normative) ethical question, challenges, and is challenged by, those who, by their very existence, demand it in the first place, namely, those who have become "radically endangered strangers in their own homes as well as criminalized or anathemized strangers in the places to which they have been forced to flee" (Dillon 1995, 357–58). These are the Other and others in the contemporary world. "For the stranger," Dillon writes,

> by his or her very nature as stranger, is out of the settled modes of questioning, and the received understandings of truth and identity, as well as the laws, of which the community is comprised. And yet, the stranger is there not only in all of the mystery that provokes the question, but also in all of the inescapable and shared facticity that demands a response. (Dillon 1995, 358–59)

These questions and challenges are rendered even more problematic when one understands that the "interruption" of the ethical relation is not exhausted by the political relation. In fact, the question of community is also "interrupted" by what may be called the "ecological relation." Moreover, since ethics is tied mainly to human subjectivity—although it is an ecologically situated subjectivity—the burden of the ethical relation, that is, the responsibility for the Other and others, still rests with humankind (Foucault 1997). In this sense, ethics is thrown back on itself, only now it turns out to be less of a set of rules and regulations—whether tradition, law, or common practice—to which one commits oneself by implementing its demands. Rather, ethics turns out to be a fundamental structural relationship, among subjects and subjectivities—ecologically situated—that has to do not only with the capacity to decide but, perhaps even more important, with the (ecological) conditions under which one is able to decide. Here, the question of difference becomes central to the ethical relation, for without genuine alternatives or choices, there can be no genuine decision, only the implementation of an already existing or preexisting "technology." To put the matter differently, justice, nature, and difference are constitutive of the ethical and political relation (Laclau 1990; Young 1990; Harvey 1996).

Indeed, the aggregation, disaggregation, and reaggregation of political subjectivities, in short, the reality of human community under the conditions of global capitalism's dissolution of communities—for example, in the context of immigration and emigration, cross-border and internal refugees (economic or otherwise), or ecological disasters and degradation—is what is at stake here. Such political subjectivities are not overdetermined; nor is it possible to reduce them to mere particular and discrete subjects. Rather, the corollary to this particular view of ethics, in this specific instance, is a multiplicity of subjects and subject positions, each relatively autonomous, even antagonistic, of the other but all connected by virtue of their respective struggles against violence, insecurity, and avoidable harm and each constituted not a priori but in the context of these very struggles—a theme to which many in this book return in their work.

More than the multiplicity of subjects and subject positions is at stake here, however, for one's space, time, and place is of fundamental significance not only to the question of ethics but also to transformation, that is, the creation and nurture of the fundamentally new that is also fundamentally better (Halpern 1987, 1993). Pluralism, even a normative pluralism, has no inherent virtue or efficacy. Who the subjects are, what they hope for, and how they get there are decisive not only to the nature and character of ethics but also to any normative international relations theorizing. This, to my mind, is what the discourses that go under the sign of postcolonialism, understood broadly as "oppositionality which colonialism brings into being" (Ashcroft et al. 1995, 117), are addressing, as when Gayatri Spivak (1988) asks, "Can the subaltern speak?" International relations theory is tirelessly and relentlessly reminded that ethics, in this context, is inextricably related to the singular and specific opposition to all forms of domination by concrete "subjects of history" and struggle. That is, ethics is a "concrete, sensuous" practice that both "refuses to turn the Other into the Same" and challenges those that would deny Otherness (During 1987; cf. Said 1993; Manzo 1997).

Critical to this "oppositional challenge" is an affirmation of the necessary, though insufficient, role that transgression plays in any ethical practice. In her essay "A New Type of Intellectual: The Dissident," Julia Kristeva (1986) argues that it is only in becoming a stranger to one's own country, language, sex, and identity that one avoids "sinking into the mire of common sense." "Writing," she adds, "is impossible without some kind of exile . . . [which is] already itself a form of dissidence" (292–99). At the heart of dissent—as exile and sites of difference and contestation—is both the recognition of limits and the practice of transgression of those limits. Borrowing from Richard K. Ashley and R. B. J. Walker (1990), one might therefore suggest that ethics is about

> the questioning and transgression of limits, not the assertion of boundaries and frame-
> works; a readiness to question how meaning and order are imposed, not the search for
> a source of meaning and order already in place; the unrelenting and meticulous analysis
> of the workings of power in modern global life, not the longing for a sovereign figure
> . . . that promises deliverance from power; the struggle for freedom, not a religious
> desire to produce some territorial domicile of self-evident being that men of innocent
> faith can call home. (265)

In the concreteness, contingency, and oppositionality of their differences, this plurality of subjects and subject positions widen and deepen not only the challenge to global capitalism and provide normative international relations with a larger ethical/political perspective but, more important, creates a fundamental structure of undecidability, which makes possible genuine political choices. The joining and conjoining of different movements in civil society, for example, speak eloquently to this aggregation, disaggregation, and reaggregation of political communities and so with those communities of resistance and solidarity: the excluded, the marginal, those rendered redundant. Without genuine, even antagonistic, perspectives that admit their contingency and recognize the desirability, if not the necessity, of fundamental transformation, there is no possibility of what Derrida (1993) calls the "theoretico-ethical decision." And without the recognition not only of the alterity of these different struggles but especially of what Ernesto Laclau (1996) underscores as the *contingency* of their connections and the contingency of their *connections,* there can be no possibility of constituting our own political identities. For Laclau, this "theoretico-ethical decision" stands between the undecidability, which lies at the heart of plurality and which is the "terrain of the radicalization of the decision," and the undecidability, which is the "source of an ethical injunction." Without it, there can be no ethics or politics. As Derrida (1988) puts it, "There can be no moral or political responsibility without this trial and this passage by way of the undecidable" (116). Indeed, if everything were reduced to the decidable, and if the undecidable were avoided, there would be no ethics, politics, or responsibility—only a program, technology, and its irresponsible application (Campbell 1994, 477).

However, while "the passage by way of the undecidable" is necessary, it is not sufficient. There is no virtue as such in plurality or difference. Moreover, the profound problems confronting normative international relations today—violence, insecurity, avoidable harm—will not be resolved by mere appeals to formal notions of the ethical, political, and ecological relation. Indeed, borrowing from Simon Critchley, I want to suggest that the context and challenge for normative international relations theorizing today is whether it can "navigate the treacherous passage from ethics to politics" (Critchley 1992, 189)—since the ethical is for the sake of politics, that is, for the creation of the fundamentally new, which is also fundamentally better. As Campbell (1994) observes, "The theme of undecidability gives us the context of the decision, but in and of itself undecidability does not provide an account of the (ethical) decision" (471). Indeed, "decisions have to be taken. But, how? And in virtue of what? How does one make a decision in an undecidable terrain?" (Critchley 1992, 199).

To this question there can be no satisfactory answer, save the cultivation of a particular ethical and political sensibility, that is, in the words of Campbell (1994, 477), to struggle for—and on behalf of—alterity and not a struggle to efface, erase, or eradicate alterity, to gesture, as Derrida would, in opposite directions at the same time, without capitulating to quietism, to resist the intolerable, to experience and experiment on the possibility of the impossible, to recognize and respect the limits and possibilities of the *aporia,* of the decision within the undecidable (Cornell et al. 1992).[14] In other words, there can be no politics of resistance, solidarity, and vision without the existence not only of multiple struggles but also of a recognition and affirmation, if not celebration, of a *structural unrepresentability* at the very heart of these struggles. However, precisely because of this basic unrepresentability, it therefore becomes necessary

> to ecologize all that we do and think, to reject closed ideas, mistrust one-way causality, to strive to be inclusive in the face of all exclusions, to be unifying in the face of all disjunctions, to take a holistic approach in the face of all reductionisms, and to appreciate complexity in the face of all over-simplifications. (Boff 1997, 13).

In fact, part of the *sense of the ethical,* what this book has called "normative commitment in the study of international relations," is the recognition of what I understand Radmila Nakarada, also in this book, is clearly and poignantly expressing, namely, the limits of one's territorially defined identities; the dangers of unrepentant, not to mention unbridled, religious and secularized eschatologies and apocalypticisms; and the indomitable human yearning for justice, peace, and security throughout the planet.

Finally, this *sense of the ethical* includes the following:

1. The realization that normative international relations must travel through the "passage by way of the undecidable," even as it admits to the "uncertain reach of (its own) critical theory."
2. The insistence on the limits of human thought and action as constitutive of the activist and scholarly commitment, even as it refuses the luxury of hopelessness for the sake of those without hope.
3. The recognition not only of the inextricable relationship between politics and ethics but also of their fundamental "estrangement," that is, their rootedness in "dissidence and exile" and their inscription on human bodies, which is the condition of politics and ethics as it faces the coming century.[15]
4. The passionate refusal to capitulate to the nihilism that accompanies the so-

called triumph of global capitalism, even as it risks a decision to discern, create, and nurture the connections among the different communities of resistance, solidarity, and, vision—not only of the global South but of the global North as well—that today are exploring ways in which these differences are constitutive of the very struggles against global capitalism and its discursive strategies as well as alternative human and humane pathways into the future.

NORMATIVE INTERNATIONAL RELATIONS AND THE PURSUIT OF THE "BODY POLITIC": AN IMPOLITIC CONCLUDING POSTSCRIPT

What does this kind of ethical sensibility require of international relations theory and practice?

First, such an ethical sensibility requires that international relations theory and practice continue to recognize, affirm, and articulate different ways of producing and reproducing knowledge (epistemology). Here, this is not only about situated knowledges and partial perspectives but also about subjugated and insurrectionary knowledges and agents of knowledges—and the ways in which they are related. In contrast, ethical discourses of the kind noted previously have consistently focused, among other things, on the fundamental situatedness and partial character of our ways of organizing thinking, feeling, and acting and on the necessity, if not desirablity, of rethinking "the relationship between knowledge and emotion and construct[ion of] conceptual models that demonstrate the mutually constitutive rather than oppositional relationship between reason and emotion" (Jaggar 1994). On face value, this may be a straightforward, even simplistic if not obvious, statement about the nature of knowledge. However, when one understands that these claims are set in the context of the historical pretensions about the universality of (masculinist) reason as opposed to, say, feminist desire and of the reality that emotion is associated with subordinate groups—especially women—and deployed to discount and silence those realities deemed to be irrational, then one begins to realize how these epistemologies actually explode patriarchal myths about knowledge (Harding 1991, 1998).

Second, such an ethical sensibility requires that international relations theory and practice continue to recognize, affirm, and articulate different modes of being (ontology). Here, this is not only about thinking, feeling, and acting—as relational practices but also about "volatile bodies," that is, of refiguring and reinscribing bodies, of moving through and beyond the conventional divide of gender as socially contructed on the one hand and of sex as biologically given on the other to "our bodies our selves." Elizabeth Grosz (1987) has suggested that the "male (or female) body can no longer be regarded as a fixed, concrete substance, a pre-cultural given. It has a determinate form only by being socially inscribed" (2). "As a socio-historical 'object,' " she continues, "the body can no longer be confined to biological determinants, to an immanent 'factitious,' or unchanging social status. It is a political object par excellence; its forms, capacities, behaviours, gestures, movements, potential are primary objects of political contestation. As a political object, the body is not inert or fixed. It is pliable and plastic material, which is capable of being formed and organized" (2). This profound insight is shared by Foucault (1984), who argues himself that the body is an "inscribed surface of events" (83). Thus, the body becomes "malleable and alterable," its surface inscribed with gender, appropriate behavior, standards of, for example, femininity. The significance of such an understanding cannot be underestimated, for this means not only that politics, for example, is about who gets "what, when, where, and how" but also that its "what, when, where, and how" are inscribed—written on, embodied—in our very bodies.

Third, such an ethical sensibility requires that international relations theory and practice continue to recognize, affirm, and articulate new forms of "consciousness" (subjectivity). Here, this is not only about consciousness arising out of concrete and sensuous reality but also about spirituality as always and already *embodied* experience—not only what subjectivity is but also what is entailed in becoming subjects. I have already noted what a feminist reading of "becoming subjects" might look like. Here, let me underscore what this has to do with consciousness. If it is true that human beings are more than logos but also eros, pathos, and the daimon, then consciousness, and the structure of spirituality that accompanies it, must also be redefined in terms of touching, feeling, smelling, tasting, eating. Theoretically put, *spirituality* on the one hand refuses the temptation of a disembodied transcendence and on the other rejects its articulation as a totalized immanence. To say that "spirituality" is about "touching, feeling, smelling, tasting, eating" is not only to acknowledge the inadequacies of the received traditions of "spirituality" but also to affirm that this "spirituality" is about a peoples' concrete and sensuous *experience* of self, of other, and, for the religiously inclined, of God.

Fourth, such an ethical sensibility requires international relations theory and practice to recognize, affirm, and articulate different *empowering* practices (politics). Here, this is not only about the importance and power of self-definition, self-valuation, or self-reliance and autonomy but also about transformation and transgression, of finding safe places and voices in the midst of difference. Chandra Mohanty (1991) summarizes this point well:

> Third World women's writings on feminism have consistently focused on (1) the idea of the simultaneity of oppressions as fundamental to the experience of social and political marginality and the grounding of feminist politics in the histories of racism and imperialism; (2) the crucial role of a hegemonic state in circumscribing their/our daily lives and survival struggles; (3) the significance of memory and writing in the creation of oppositional agency; and (4) the differences, conflicts, and contradictions internal to third world women's organizations and communities. In addition, they have insisted on the complex interrelationships between feminist, antiracist, and nationalist struggles.(10)

Of course, the argument for "relationality" is not new. Beverly Harrison (1986), in her critique of domination, has argued persuasively, long before it was fashionable to do so, on the basis of what might be called the "interstructuration of domination." Likewise, Dorothee Soelle (1984) and Matthew Fox (1995) reconstruct Christian theology and politics through a "creation theology/ spirituality" that underscores the inextricable connections between work, love, and politics. Nor is the argument about "difference" exclusively feminist. What is specifically "feminist," in my view, is that the complex and interdependent relationship between theory, history, and struggle is now being emphasized in the light of women's (re)reading and (re)writing of international relations theory and practice, focusing on the intricate connections between systemic and personal relationships and the directionalities of power. Thus, Dorothy Smith introduces the concept of "relations of ruling," by which forms of knowledge and organized practices and institutions, as well as questions of consciousness, experience, and agency, are foregrounded. Rather than positing a simple relation between, say, colonizer and colonized, capitalist and worker, male and female, this perspective posits "multiple intersections of structures of power and emphasizes the process or form of ruling, not the frozen embodiment of it" (Smith, cited in Mohanty 1991).

Indeed, (re)reading and (re)writing international relations theory and practice in the context of an ethical sensibility returns us to its heart, namely, the *body* politic, which, I have argued, albeit indirectly, has been forced into exile by the patriarchal rituals, racialized Eurocentricities, and classist pretensions of modernity itself.[16] To insist on its return as *normative* international relations theory and practice is to imply that politics as we know it today, not only in the Philippines but elsewhere, has failed to bring forth the good, the true, and the beautiful, especially for the majority of the peoples of the world. It is also to suggest that the kind of ethical sensibility discussed in the preceding section challenges international relations theory and practice on at least four grounds—epistemology, ontology, subjectivity, and politics—which, taken together, turns out to be a work of culture, politics, and ethics in the context of the pursuit of the "body politic." If nothing else, this may be the most serious challenge that (normative) international relations theory and practice faces in the coming millennium.

NOTES

1. The term "global capitalism" used throughout this chapter is intended to be imprecise. My concern is less with a substantive definition of capitalism—clearly an impossibility given the plural forms of capitalism today—and more with specifying a region of discursive practices characterized by the globalizing trajectories of *modern* capitalism. See, for example, Giddens (1990). In fact, it might be argued that "multinational capitalism" could very well be the more useful term to describe the many capitalisms at the end of the twentieth century.

2. I am deeply indebted to R. B. J. Walker for the perspective on peace and security that I appropriate freely in this chapter. However, my interpretation of that perspective is situated differently and gestures toward specific practices in the so-called global South.

3. Walker discusses the three areas of identity noted here as well. See Walker (1997, 61–82).

4. I have explored some of these connections in "The Subject of Security is the Subject of Security: APEC and the Globalization of Capital" (Ruiz 1997b).

5. The well-publicized "war of words" between George Soros and Prime Minister Mahathir over the currency crisis during the World Bank/IMF meeting in Hong Kong in September 1997 followed by a flurry of "verbal exchanges" in the same vein between the United States and Japan and between Malaysia and the United States, to mention only two, underscores what might be called a "conflict of cultures"—even a "culture war"—in the context of competition and antagonism within global capitalism, although carried under the guise of, for example, concerns about "democracy" and "human rights."

6. The importance of "culture," especially in the way I understand it, is also manifested in the academic/scholarly literature. See, for example, Chay (1990) and Lapid and Kratochwil (1996a). See also the proliferation of "readers," four of which I find extremely useful: Ashcroft et al. (1995), Grossberg et al. (1992), Jordan and Weedon (1995), and Storey (1996).

7. On this theme, see, for example, Smith et al. (1996).

8. For example, the IAPs and MAPAs, the friendship lanes, and the logic of APEC as Filipino *fiesta*—to borrow the insightful characterization of one Manila taxi driver in my conversation with him during the November 1996 APEC meetings in Manila.

9. The discussions around the WTO's Multilateral Investment Agreement and the OECD's Multilateral Agreement on Investment are as illuminating and instructive as they are cause for alarm. See Ruiz (1997a).

10. Jacques Derrida (1993) develops this theme of "spirit" as *revenant.*

11. Heidegger uses the term *Ge-stell,* translated here as "enframing."

12. The following section draws on the work of David Campbell, who seeks to articulate an ethics sensitive to the profound challenges to conventional ethics posed by the poststructuralist, postempiricist, postpositivist insights of Emmanuel Levinas and Jacques Derrida, among others. My own desire is to situate this kind of ethics within the context of global capitalism's transformation of our world, but from the "perspective" of one committed to the concerns of the global South.

13. For a discussion of these "ecological therapies," see Boff (1997).

14. Citing Derrida, Campbell (1994) notes, "With neither of the two available options being desirable, one confronts an *aporia,* an undecidable and ungrounded political space, where no path is 'clear and given,' where no 'certain knowledge opens up the way in advance,' where no 'decision is already made . . .' 'I will even venture to say that ethics, politics, and responsibility, *if there are any,* will only ever have begun with the experience and experiment of aporia . . .' where there no aporia there could be no politics, for in the absence of the aporia, every decision would have been pre-ordained, such that 'irresponsibly, and in good conscience, one simply applies or implements a program' " (475).

15. Thus, Dillon (1995) writes, "Just as there is no identity without difference, so there can be no politics without this estrangement; that is to say, without the difference we bear within and in respect of our own selves as well as that between ourselves. It does so because that estrangement is a difference that, in both separating and joining (individuating yet also combining), poses the very problematic of the belonging together of human beings in their individuation and of the ordering of the relations between individuals so constituted. Quite simply, it poses the issue of human being's belonging together in its very apartness, and so of how it is itself to assume responsibility for that way of being" (359–60).

16. Modernity, against which most feminisms are (re)read and (re)written, may itself be read as a *masculinist* idealism. At the heart of this originary Eurocentric practice is what Jacques Derrida calls a "principle of reason," which is often believed to be autonomous from the ensemble of relations in which it is implicated and which not only is construed as the ground, the grand narrative, that legitimates modern life but also is understood, often uncritically, as instrumental and technological rationality. Because it has been argued persuasively elsewhere, often by feminists, that the triumph of this type of rationality has led to the eclipse of the gentler, more human passions of life and therefore has become destructive of humanity and nature, it is sufficient to be reminded of it here.

What is important to understand about the idealism that resides in the modernist narrative is its logocentric disposition, which Ashley describes as having the tendency to regard all thought, feeling, and action as being grounded in some fundamental identity, principle of interpretation, or necessary thinking substance that is itself regarded as unproblematic, non-historical, and thus in no need of critical accounting. Crucial to this logocentric disposition is that the principle of interpretation and practice is conceived as existing in itself, as a foundation or origin of history's making, not a contingent effect of political practices within history. Where patriarchy is concerned, its logocentrism lies in its (masculinist) phallocentricity.

Bibliography

Adamson, W. L. 1990. Economic Democracy and the Expediency of Worker Participation. *Political Studies* 38.

Addison, J. T., and W. S. Siebert. 1993. *Social Engineering in the European Community.* London: Institute of Economic Affairs.

Alger, Chadwick, and David Hoover. 1975. Regional Participation in International Organizations. *Proceedings of the Fifth International Peace Research Association Conference.* Varanasi, India: International Peace Research Association.

Alger, Chadwick F., and Saul Mendlovitz. 1987. Grass-Roots Initiatives: The Challenge of Linkages. In *Towards a Just World Peace: Perspectives from Social Movements,* edited by R. B. J. Walker and Saul Mendlovitz. London: Butterworths.

Allen, J. 1992. Post-Industrialism and Post-Fordism. In *Modernity and Its Futures,* edited by S. Hall, D. Held, and T. McGrew. Cambridge: Polity Press.

Alliance for Responsible Trade, Citizens Trade Campaign, and Mexican Action Network on Free Trade. 1993. A Just and Sustainable Development Initiative for North America. Draft, September 18.

Alvares, Norma. 1996. Panchayats vs. Multinationals: The Case of Dupont in Goa. *Lawyers' Collective,* March.

Amdur, Robert. 1977. Rawls' Theory of Justice: Domestic and International Perspectives. *World Politics* 29, no. 3 (April): 438–61.

Amnesty International. 1997. The "Enron Project" in Maharashtra: Protests Suppressed in the Name of Development. *Amnesty International Report,* July.

AMPO Japan-Asia Quarterly Review. 1995. Special issue on The Women's Movement at a Crossroads. *AMPO Japan-Asia Quarterly Review* 25, no. 4 and 26, no. 1.

Amsden, Alice. 1989. *Asia's Next Giant: South Korea and Late Industrialization.* New York: Oxford University Press.

Anderson, Sarah, and John Cavanagh. 1996. *The Top 200: The Rise of Global Corporate Power.* Washington, D.C.: Institute for Policy Studies.

Ann-Zondorak, Valerie. 1991. A New Face in Corporate Responsibility: The Valdez Principles. *Boston College Environmental Affairs Law Review,* no. 18 (spring).

Appadurai, Arjun. 1996. *Modernity at Large: Cultural Dimensions of Globalization.* Minneapolis: University of Minnesota Press.

Arato, A. 1981. Civil Society against the State: Poland 1981–82. *Telos,* no. 47 (spring): 23–47.

Archibugi, Danielle, and David Held, eds. 1995. *Cosmopolitan Democracy: An Agenda for a New World Order.* Cambridge: Polity Press.

Archibugi, D., D. Held, and M. Kohler, eds. 1999. *Re-Imagining Political Community: Studies in Cosmopolitan Democracy.* Cambridge: Polity Press.

Arendt, Hannah. 1970. *The Human Condition.* Chicago: University of Chicago Press.

———. 1994. *Truth and Politics* (Serbian translation). Belgrade: Filip Visnjic.

Aristotle. 1951. *Nicomachian Ethics,* translated by J. A. K. Thompson. Harmondsworth: Penguin Books.

———. 1956. *The Metaphysics,* translated by Hugh Tredennick. London: W. Heinemann.

Ashby, W. Ross. 1960. *Design for a Brain,* 2nd ed. New York: John Wiley & Sons.

Ashcroft, Bill, Gareth Griffiths, and Helen Tiffin, eds. 1995. *The Post-Colonial Studies Reader.* New York: Routledge.

Ashley, Richard, and R. B. J. Walker, eds. 1990. Speaking the Language of Exile: Dissidence in International Studies. *Special Issue, International Studies Quarterly* 34, no. 3: 259–69.

Asia Monitor Resource Center. 1996. Feature: Toys. *Asian Labor Update* (April/July).

Asian and Pacific Regional Organization of the International Confederation of Free Trade Unions. 1994. Social Charter for Democratic Development. Position paper, August.

Ayensu, Edward S. 1984. Natural and Applied Sciences and National Development. Lecture delivered at the Silver Jubilee Celebration of the Ghana Academy of Sciences, Accra, November 22.

Bakhtin, Mikhail. 1981. *The Dialogic Imagination: Four Essays by M. M. Bakhtin,* edited by Michael Holquist. Austin: University of Texas Press.

Balls, E. 1994. Looking beyond the Flexibility Rhetoric. *The Guardian,* June 6.

Barber, Benjamin. 1984. *Strong Democracy: Participatory Politics for a New Age.* Berkeley and Los Angeles: University of California Press.

Barlow, Maude. 1997. Speech at Teach-In on Economic Globalization. International Forum on Globalization, Berkeley, California, April 11.

Barnet, Richard J., and John Cavanagh. 1994. *Global Dreams: Imperial Corporations and the New World Order.* New York: Simon and Schuster.

Barnet, Richard, and Ronald Muller. 1974. *Global Reach: The Power of the Multinational Corporations.* New York: Simon and Schuster.

Bar-On, Mordechi. 1985. *Peace Now: The Portrait of a Movement* (in Hebrew). Tel-Aviv: Hakibbutz Hameuchad.

Barry, Brian. 1982. Humanity and Justice in Global Perspective. In *Ethics, Economics and the Law, Nomos XXIV,* edited by J. Roland Pennock and John W. Chapman. New York: New York University Press.

Bassiouni, M. Cherif, and Christopher Blakesley. 1992. The Need for an International Criminal Court in the New International World Order. *Vanderbilt Journal of Transnational Law* 25: 151–79.

Basu, Amrita. 1990. *Two Faces of Protest: Contrasting Modes of Women's Activism in India.* Berkeley and Los Angeles: University of California Press.

Baylis, John. 1997. International Security in the Post-Cold War Era. In *The Globalization of World Politics: An Introduction to International Relations,* edited by John Baylis and Steve Smith. Oxford: Oxford University Press.

Becker, Avihai. 1998. Sarah Would Have Told God, "Forget It." *Ha'aretz,* January 2 (Internet ed.).

Beetham, D. 1993. Liberal Democracy and the Limits of Democratization. In *Prospects for Democracy: North, South, East and West*, edited by D. Held. Cambridge: Polity Press.

Beitz, Charles. 1975. Justice and International Relations. *Philosophy and Public Affairs* 4, no. 4 (summer): 282–311.

Bellah, Robert N., et al. 1991. Breaking the Tyranny of the Market. *Tikkun* 6, no. 4 (July/August).

Bello, Walden. 1994. *Dark Victory: The United States, Structural Adjustment and Global Poverty.* San Francisco: Food First.

———. 1997. Addicted to Capital: The Ten-Year High and Present Day Withdrawal Trauma of Southeast Asia's Economies. *Focus-on-Trade*, no. 20 (November). http://www.focusweb.org.

Bello, Walden, and Stephanie Rosenfeld. 1990. *Dragons in Distress: Asia's Miracle Economies in Crisis.* San Francisco: Institute for Food and Development Policy.

Benhabib, Seyla. 1995. Cultural Complexity, Moral Interdependence and the Global Dialogical Community. In *Women, Culture and Development*, edited by Martha Nussbaum and Jonathan Glover. New York: Oxford University Press.

———, ed. 1996. *Democracy and Difference: Contesting the Boundaries of the Political.* Princeton, N.J.: Princeton University Press.

Berlin, Isaiah. 1969. *Four Essays on Liberty.* New York: Oxford University Press.

Berman, Jessica. 1996. Bike-Aid: Focus on Environment and Development. *Global Links: Newsletter of the Overseas Development Network* (spring): 9.

Best, Michael. 1990. *The New Competition.* Cambridge, Mass.: Harvard University Press.

Bietz, Charles. 1979. *Political Theory and International Relations.* Princeton, N.J.: Princeton University Press.

Blaney, David L., and Mustapha Kamal Pasha. 1993. Civil Society and Democracy in the Third World: Ambiguities and Historical Possibilities. *Studies in Comparative International Development* 28, no. 1 (spring).

Block, Fred. 1977. *The Origins of International Economic Disorder.* Berkeley and Los Angeles: University of California Press.

Boff, Leonardo. 1997. *Cry of the Earth, Cry of the Poor.* New York: Orbis Books.

Boli, John, and George Thomas. 1995. The World Polity in Formation: A Century of International Non-Governmental Organization. Unpublished manuscript.

Boulding, Elise. 1988. Image and Actions in Peace-Building. *Journal of Social Issues* 44, no. 2.

———. 1990. *Building a Global Civic Culture: Education for an Interdependent World.* Syracuse, N.Y.: Syracuse University Press.

———. 1991. The Old and the New Transnationalism: An Evolutionary Perspective. *Human Relations* 44, no. 8.

———. 1992a. *The Underside of History: A View of Women through Time.* Vol. 2. Thousand Oaks, Calif.: Sage Publications.

———. 1992b. The Zone of Peace Concept in Current Practise: Review and Evaluation. In *Prospects for Peace: Changes in the Indian Ocean Region*, edited by Robert H. Bruce. Monograph No. 1. Perth: Indian Ocean Centre for Peace Studies.

———. 1993. Hope for the Twenty-First Century: NGO and Peoples Networks in the Middle East. In *Building Peace in the Middle East: Challenges for States and Civil Society*, edited by Elise Boulding. Boulder, Colo.: Lynne Rienner Publishers.

Boulding, Elise, and Jan Oberg. 1996. *UN Peacekeeping and NGO Peace Building—Towards Partnership.* Lund, Sweden: Transnational Foundation for Peace and Future Research.

Boutros-Ghali, Boutros. 1995. *An Agenda for Peace 1995*, 2nd ed. (with a new supplement). New York: United Nations.

Bowring, Philip. 1998. Improving the Flow of Information in a Time of Crisis: The Challenge to the Southeast Asian Media. Monograph, Subic, Philippines, October 29–31.

Boyd, Charles. 1995. Making Peace with the Guilty. Foreign Affairs, September/October, 27.

Bratton, Michael. 1991. Beyond the State: Civil Society and Associational Life in Africa. *Transnational Associations* 3 (May–June).

Brewin, Christopher. 1978. Justice in International Relations. In *The Reason of States*, edited by Michael Donelan. London: Allen and Unwin.

Broad, Robin, and John Cavanagh. 1993. *Plundering Paradise: The Struggle for the Environment in the Philippines*. Berkeley and Los Angeles: University of California Press.

———. 1995. Don't Neglect the Impoverished South. *Foreign Policy* 101 (winter): 18–35.

———. 1997. The Corporate Accountability Movement: Lessons and Opportunities. Report for the World Wildlife Fund and World Resources Institute Project on International Financial Flows and the Environment, Washington, D.C.

Broad, Robin, and Christina Melhorn Landi. 1996. Whither the North-South Gap? *Third World Quarterly* 17: 7–17.

Brock-Utne, Birgit. 1989. *Feminist Perspectives on Peace and Peace Education*. New York: Pergamon Press.

Bronfenbronner, Kate. 1997. We'll Close! Plant Closings, Plant-Closing Threats, Union Organizing and NAFTA. *Multinational Monitor*, March, 8–13.

Brookes, Bethan, and Peter Madden. 1995. *The Globe-Trotting Sports Shoe*. London: Christian Aid.

Brown, Chris. 1992. *International Relations Theory: New Normative Approaches*. New York: Columbia University Press.

Brown, Gavin, Barry Barker, and Terry Burke. 1984. *Police as Peace-Keepers*. Victoria: UNCIVPOL.

Brown, Michael E., Sean M. Lynn-Jones, and Steven E. Miller, eds. 1996. *Debating the Democratic Peace*. Cambridge, Mass.: MIT Press.

Brown, Lester, et al. 1999. *State of the World 1999*. New York: W. W. Norton.

Bryant, Christopher G. A. 1995. Civic Nation, Civil Society, Civil Religion. In *Civil Society: Theory, History, Comparison*, edited by John A. Hall. Cambridge: Polity Press.

Brzezinski, Zbigniew. 1997. A Geostrategy for Eurasia. *Foreign Affairs* 76, no. 5 (September/October): 50–64.

Bull, Hedley. 1977. *The Anarchical Society: A Study of World Order*. New York: Columbia University Press.

Buscemi, William. 1993. The Ironic Politics of Richard Rorty. *The Review of Politics* 55 (winter): 141–57.

Butler, Judith. 1990. *Gender Trouble: Feminism and the Subversion of Identity*. New York: Routledge.

———. 1993. *Bodies That Matter: On the Discursive Limits of "Sex."* London: Routledge.

Cadava, Eduardo, Peter Connor, and Jan-Luc Nancy, eds. 1991. *Who Comes after the Subject*. New York: Routledge.

Calhoun, Craig. 1992. Introduction: Habermas and the Public Sphere. In *Habermas and the Public Sphere*. Cambridge, Mass.: MIT Press.

Call, Chuck, and Michael Barnett. 1997. Looking for a Few Good Cops: Peacekeeping,

Peacebuilding and U.N. Civilian Police. Paper presented at the annual meeting of the International Studies Association, Toronto, March 20–24.

Callinicos, A. 1993. Liberalism, Marxism and Democracy: A Response to David Held. *Theory and Society* 22.

Campbell, David. 1994. The Deterritorialization of Responsibility: Levinas, Derrida, and Ethics after the End of Philosophy. *Alternatives: Social Transformation and Humane Governance* 19, no. 4.

Campbell, Horace. 1987. Challenging the Apartheid Regime from Below. In *Popular Struggles for Democracy in Africa,* edited by Peter Anyang' Nyong'o. London: Zed Press.

Caputo, John D. 1993. *Against Ethics.* Bloomington: Indiana University Press.

Carens, Joseph. 1989. Membership and Morality. In *Immigration and the Politics of Citizenship in Europe and North America,* edited by William Brubaker. Lanham, Md.: University Press of America.

Casey, Edward S. 1997. *The Fate of Place: A Philosophical History.* Berkeley and Los Angeles: University of California Press.

Cavanagh, John, and Robin Broad. 1996. Global Reach: Workers Fight the Multinationals. *The Nation,* March 18, 21–24.

Cavanagh, John, Lance Compa, Allan Ebert, Bill Goold, Kathy Selvaggio, and Tim Shorrock. 1988. *Trade's Hidden Costs: Worker Rights in a Changing World Economy.* Washington, D.C.: International Labor Rights Education and Research Fund.

Chay, Jongsuk, ed. 1990. *Culture and International Relations.* New York: Praeger Publishers.

Chicago Council on Foreign Relations. 1983. *American Public Opinion and US Foreign Policy.* Chicago: CCFR.

Chin, Christine B. N., and James H. Mittelman. 1997. Conceptualising Resistance to Globalisation. *New Political Economy* 2, no. 1 (March): 25–37.

Chomsky, Noam. 1994. *World Orders Old and New.* London: Pluto Press.

Chopra, Jarat. 1996. The Space of Peace-Maintenance. *Political Geography* 15, no. 3/4: 335–57.

Clark, Margaret. 1994. The Antarctica Environmental Protocol: NGOs in the Protection of Antarctica. In *Environmental NGOs in World Politics: Linking the Local and the Global,* edited by Thomas Princen and Matthias Finger. London: Routledge.

Clarke, Tony. 1996. *Dismantling Corporate Rule: Towards a New Form of Politics in the Age of Globalization.* San Francisco: International Forum on Globalization.

Clean Clothes Newsletter, *News from IRENE* (International Restructuring Education Network Europe), Tilber, the Netherlands.

Clesse, Almand, Richard Cooper, and Yoshikazu Sakamoto, eds. 1994. *The International System after the Collapse of the East-West Order.* Dordrecht: Martinus Nijhoff.

Coalition for Environmentally Responsible Economies. 1990. *The 1990 CERES Guide to the Valdez Principles.* Boston: CERES.

Coates, D. 1980. *Labour in Power.* London: Longman.

Cobb, John. 1994. *Sustaining the Common Good: A Christian Perspective on the Global Economy.* Cleveland: Pilgrim Press.

Cohen, G. A. 1991. The Future of a Disillusion. *New Left Review,* no. 190.

Cohen, J. 1988. The Material Basis of Deliberative Democracy. *Social Philosophy and Policy* 6, no. 2.

Cohen, Jean L., and Andrew Arato. 1992. *Civil Society and Political Theory.* Cambridge, Mass.: MIT Press.

Cohen, Margot, and Murray Hiebert. 1997. Where There's Smoke. *Far Eastern Economic Review,* October 2, 28–29.

Cohen, Stan. 1993. More Vigilant Than Ever. *Challenge* 4, no. 6 (November/December): 16–17.

Cohen, William. 1997. DOD News Briefing. *Tribunal Watch,* March 3, 1.

Collingsworth, Terry, J. William Goold, and Pharis Harvey. 1994. Time for a Global New Deal. *Foreign Affairs* 73 (January/February): 8–13.

Collins, Joseph, and John Lear. 1995. *Chile's Free Market Miracle: A Second Look.* San Francisco: Institute for Food and Development Policy.

Commission on Global Governance. 1995. *Our Global Neighborhood: The Report of the Commission on Global Governance.* New York: Oxford University Press.

Compa, Lance. 1995. A North-South Controversy over Labor Rights and Trade. *Labor Research Review* 23: 51–65.

Compa, Lance, and T. Hinchliffe-Darricarrere. 1995. Enforcing International Labor Rights through Corporate Codes of Conduct. *Columbia Journal of Transnational Law* 33: 663–89.

Conca, Ken. 1995. Greening the United Nations: Environmental Organisations and the UN System. *Third World Quarterly* 16, no. 3.

Connolly, William. 1981. *Appearance and Reality.* Cambridge: Cambridge University Press.

———. 1983. *The Terms of Political Discourse,* 2nd ed. Princeton, N.J.: Princeton University Press.

Contee, Christine. 1987. *What Americans Think: Views on Development and U.S.-Third World Relations.* New York: Interaction.

Cook, Rebecca J., ed. 1994. *Human Rights of Women: National and International Perspectives.* Philadelphia: University of Pennsylvania Press.

Cooper, Richard. 1977. A New International Economic Order for Mutual Gain. *Foreign Policy* (spring): 65–120.

Cornell, Druscilla, Michel Rosenfeld, and David Gray Carlson, eds. 1992. *Deconstruction and the Possibility of Justice.* New York: Routledge.

Costa, Gino. 1995. The UN and Reform of the Police in El Salvador. *International Peacekeeping* 2, no. 3: 365–90.

Cox, Robert. 1996. *Approaches to World Order.* Cambridge: Cambridge University Press.

———. 1986. Social Forces, States and World Orders: Beyond International Relations Theory. In *Neorealism and Its Critics,* edited by Robert Keohane. New York: Columbia University Press.

Critchley, Simon. 1992. *The Ethics of Deconstruction: Derrida and Levinas.* Oxford: Blackwell.

Critchley, Simon, and Peter Dews, eds. 1996. *Deconstructing Subjectivities.* Albany: State University of New York Press.

Cumings, Bruce. 1987. The Origins and Development of the Northeast Asian Political Economy. In *The Political Economy of the New Asian Industrialism,* edited by E. C. Deyo. Ithaca, N.Y.: Cornell University Press.

———. 1993. The End of the Seventy-Years' Crisis: Trilateralism and the New World Order. In *Past as Prelude,* edited by Meredith Woo-Cummings and Michael Loriaux. Boulder, Colo.: Westview Press.

Dahl, R. A. 1985. *A Preface to Economic Democracy.* Cambridge: Polity Press.

Daly, Herman, and John Cobb. 1982. *For the Common Good: Re-Directing the Economy toward Community, the Environment, and a Sustained Future.* Boston: Beacon Press.

Danaher, Kevin, ed. 1996. *Corporations Are Gonna Get Your Mama: Globalization and the Downsizing of the American Dream*. San Francisco: Global Exchange/Common Courage Press.

Davies, Miranda, ed. 1994. *Women and Violence*. London: Zed Books.

Deihl, Colin. 1991. Antarctica: An International Laboratory. *Boston College Environmental Affairs Law Review* 18, no. 3 (spring).

Deleuze, Gilles, and Felix Guattari. 1986. *Nomadology: The War Machine*, translated by B. Massumi. New York: Semiotext(e).

Der Derian, James. 1997. Post-Theory: The Eternal Return of Ethics in International Relations. In *New Thinking in International Relations Theory*, edited by Michael Doyle and G. John Ikenberry. Boulder, Colo.: Westview Press.

Derrida, Jacques. 1988. *Limited, Inc*. Evanston, Ill.: Northwestern University Press.

———. 1993. *Spectres of Marx: The State of the Debt, the Work of Mourning, and the New International*, translated by Peggy Kamuf. New York: Routledge.

Dessler, David. 1989. What Is at Stake in the Agent/Structure Debate. *International Organization* 46 (summer): 441–74.

Deudney, Daniel. 1995. The Philadelphia System. *International Organization* 49 (spring): 191–228.

Deutscher, Isaac. 1960. *The Great Contest: Russia and the West*. Oxford: Oxford University Press.

Devine, P. 1991. Economy, State and Civil Society. *Economy and Society* 20, no. 2.

Dewey, John. 1954. *The Public and Its Problems*. Chicago: Swallow Press.

Diamond, Irene, and Gloria Orenstein, eds. 1990. *Reweaving the World: The Emergence of Eco-Feminism*. San Francisco: Sierra Club Books.

Dillon, John. 1997. *Turning the Tide: Confronting the Money Traders*. Ottawa: Canadian Centre for Policy Alternatives.

Dillon, Michael. 1995. Sovereignty and Governmentality: From the Problematics of the "New World Order" to the Ethical Problematic of the World Order. *Alternatives: Social Transformation and Humane Governance* 20, no. 3.

Disquieting Signs in Mozambique One Year On. 1995. *Southern Africa Report* 13, no. 44: 11–13.

Doyle, Michael. 1986. International Distributive Justice. *PS*, fall, 857–59.

———. 1995. *UN Peacekeeping in Cambodia: UNTAC's Civil Mandate*. Boulder, Colo.: Lynne Rienner Publishers.

———. 1997. *Ways of War and Peace*. New York: W. W. Norton.

Dryzek, John S. 1997. *The Politics of the Earth: Environmental Discourses*. Oxford: Oxford University Press.

du Preez, Peter. 1994. *Genocide: The Psychology of Mass Murder*. New York: Boyars/Bowerdean.

Durfee, Mary, and James N. Rosenau. 1996. Playing Catch-Up: International Relations Theory and Poverty. *Millennium: Journal of International Studies* 25, no. 3 (winter): 521–45.

During, Simon. 1987. Postmodernism or Postcolonialism Today. *Textual Practice* 1, no. 1.

Dussel, Enrique. 1988. *Ethics and Community*, translated by Robert Barr. New York: Orbis Books.

Dworkin, Ronald. 1986. *Laws Empire*. Cambridge, Mass.: Harvard University Press.

Economic Intelligence Unit. 1996. *Country Report: Mozambique, First Quarter 1996*. London: EIU.

Egge, Michel, and Catherine Shumperli. 1996. Social Clause: Survey among NGOs and Trade Unions of the South. Declaration de Berne and Pain Pour Le Prochain.

Eland, Ivan. 1995. Economic Sanctions as Tools of Foreign Policy. In *Economic Sanctions: Panacea or Peacebuilding in a Post-Cold War World?*, edited by David Cortright and George A. Lopes. Boulder, Colo.: Westview Press.

Elson, Diane. 1994. People, Development and International Financial Institutions: An Interpretation of the Bretton Woods System. *Review of African Political Economy* 21, no. 62 (December): 511–24.

Elster, Jon. 1978. *Logic and Society: Contradictions and Possible Worlds*. Chichester: John Wiley & Sons.

Enloe, Cynthia. 1993. *The Morning After: Sexual Politics at the End of the Cold War*. Berkeley and Los Angeles: University of California Press.

Escobar, Arturo. 1992. Imagining a Post-Development Era? Critical Thought, Development and Social Movements. *Social Text*, no. 31/32: 20–56.

Esping-Andersen, G. 1990. *The Three Worlds of Welfare Capitalism*. Cambridge: Polity Press.

Evans, R. W. 1992. *Coming to Terms: Corporations and the Left*. London: Institute for Public Policy Research.

Eviota, Elizabeth Uy. 1992. *The Political Economy of Gender: Women and the Sexual Division of Labor in the Philippines*. London: Zed Press.

Falk, Richard. 1971. *This Endangered Planet: Prospects and Proposals for Human Survival*. New York: Random House.

———. 1975. *A Study of Future Worlds*. New York: The Free Press.

———. 1983. *The End of World Order: Essays on Normative International Relations*. New York: Homes and Meier.

———. 1992. *Explorations at the Edge of Time*. Philadelphia: Temple University Press.

———. 1993. The Making of Global Citizenship. In *Global Visions: Beyond the New World Order*, edited by Jeremy Brecher, John Brown Childs, and Jill Cutler. Boston: South End Press.

———. 1994. Regionalism and World Order after the Cold War. WIDER/IPSA Workshop, Berlin.

———. 1995. *On Humane Governance: Toward a New Global Politics*. Cambridge: Polity Press.

———. 1996. Our Millennial Challenge. *Humanity*, July.

———. 1997. Resisting "Globalisation-from-Above" through "Globalisation-from-Below." *New Political Economy* 2: 17–24.

Fanon, Franz. 1968. *The Wretched of the Earth*, translated by Constance Farrington. New York: Grove Press.

Fetherston, A. Betts. 1994. *Towards a Theory of United Nations Peacekeeping*. New York: St. Martin's Press.

Fetherston, A. Betts, and A. C. Parkin. 1997. Transforming Violent Conflict: Contributions from Social Theory. In *Issues in Peace Research 1997–8*, edited by L.-A. Broadhead. London: Cassells.

Findlay, Ronald. 1982. International Distributive Justice. *Journal of International Economics* 13: 1–14.

Fischer, Stanley. 1997. Capital Account Liberalization and the Role of the IMF. Paper presented at the Asia and the IMF Seminar, Hong Kong, September 19.

Fisher, Julie. 1993. *The Road from Rio: Sustainable Development and the Nongovernmental Movement in the Third World.* Westport, Conn.: Praeger Publishers, 1993.

Food and Agriculture Organization. 1996. FAOSTAT Database Results. http://www.fao.org.

Forsythe, David. 1989. *Human Rights and World Politics,* 2nd ed. Lincoln: University of Nebraska Press.

Fortna, Virginia Page. 1993. United Nations Transition Assistance Group in Namibia. In *The Evolution of UN Peacekeeping,* edited by William J. Durch. New York: St. Martin's Press.

Foucault, Michel. 1979. Governmentality. *Ideology and Consciousness* 6 (autumn): 5–22.

———. 1980. *Power/Knowledge: Selected Interviews and Other Writings, 1972–1977,* edited by Colin Gordon. New York: Pantheon Books.

———. 1984. Neitzche, Geneology, History. In *The Foucault Reader,* edited by Paul Rabinow. New York: Random House.

———. 1997. *Ethics: Subjectivity and Truth,* edited by Paul Rabinow. New York: The New Press.

Fox, Matthew. 1995. *The Re-Invention of Work: A New Vision of Livelihood for Our Time.* New York: HarperCollins.

Friedman, M. R. 1980. *Free to Choose: A Personal Statement.* Harmondsworth: Penguin Books.

Frost, Melvyn. 1986. *Towards a Normative Theory of International Relations.* Cambridge: Cambridge University Press.

Fukuyama, Francis. 1989. The End of History? *National Interest,* no. 16 (summer 1989).

———. 1992. *The End of History and the Last Man.* New York: The Free Press.

Gaddis, John L. 1992–93. International Relations Theory and the End of the Cold War. *International Security* 17 (winter): 5–58.

Galtung, Johan. 1989. The Peace Movement: An Exercise in Micro-Macro Linkages. *International Social Science Journal* 40, no. 117 (August).

Gandhi, M. K. 1945. *An Autobiography: The Story of My Experiments with Truth.* Ahmedabad: Navajivan Publishing House.

Gandhi, Maneka. 1995. The Crimes of Al-Kabeer. *People for Animals Newsletter,* May.

Gapper, John, and Denton Nicholas. 1996. *All That Glitters: The Fall of Barings.* London: Penguin Books.

Gare, Arran E. 1995. *Postmodernism and the Environmental Crisis.* New York: Routledge.

Gargan, Edward A. 1996. Man Dies during Protest over Asian Islets. *New York Times,* September 27, A8.

Geertz, Clifford. 1973. *The Interpretation of Cultures.* London: Hutchinson.

Gellner, Ernest. 1994. *The Conditions of Liberty: Civil Society and Its Rivals.* London: Hamish Hamilton.

Giddens, Anthony. 1985. *The Nation State and Violence.* Cambridge: Polity Press.

———. 1990. *The Consequences of Modernity.* Stanford, Calif.: Stanford University Press.

Gill, Stephen. 1996. Structural Change and Global Political Economy. In *Global Transformation,* edited by Yoshikazu Sakamoto. Tokyo: United Nations University Press.

Gill, Stephen, ed. 1993. *Gramsci, Historical Materialism and International Relations.* Cambridge: Cambridge University Press.

Gilpin, Robert. 1986. The Richness of the Tradition of Political Realism. In *Neorealism and Its Critics,* edited by Robert Keohane. New York: Columbia University Press.

Gleckman, Harris. 1995. *The Social Benefits of Regulating Transnational Corporations.* Geneva: United Nations Research Institute for Social Development.

Gleckman, Harris, and Riva Krut. 1994. *Business Regulation and Competition Policy: The Case for International Action.* London: Christian Aid, Catholic Institute for International Relations, World Development Movement, and World Wide Fund for Nature–United Kingdom.

———. 1994. Transnational Corporations, International Regulation and Competition Policy: The Next Arena for International Action. Study by Benchmark Environmental Consulting, Maine.

Goldberg, David Theo. 1993. *Racist Culture: Philosophy and the Politics of Meaning.* Cambridge, Mass.: Blackwell.

Goldman, Robert. 1993. International Humanitarian Law: Americas Watch's Experience in Monitoring Internal Armed Conflict. *The American University Journal of International Law and Policy* 9, no. 1 (fall).

Goldsmith, Edward, et al. 1990. *Imperiled Planet: Restoring Our Endangered Ecosystems.* Cambridge, Mass.: MIT Press.

Gordenker, Leon, and Thomas G. Weiss. 1995. Pluralising Global Governance: Analytical Approaches and Dimensions. *Third World Quarterly* 16, no. 3.

Gordon, David, and Michael O'Hanlon. 1996. Sparing Foreign Aid. *Brown Journal of World Affairs* 3, no. 2 (summer–fall): 347–54.

Gotz-Rechter, Stephan. 1996. How America Stiffs the Third World. *New York Times,* August 27, A17.

Gould, Carol. 1988. *Re-Thinking Democracy: Freedom and Social Cooperation in Politics, Economy and Society.* Cambridge: Cambridge University Press.

Government of Canada. 1995. *Towards A Rapid Deployment Capability for the United Nations.* Report by the Government of Canada, September.

Gramsci, Antonio. 1971. *Selections from the Prison Notebooks of Antonio Gramsci,* edited and translated by Quintin Hoare and Geoffrey Nowell Smith. New York: International Publishers.

Greenberg, Joel. 1996. Dashed Hope Fed Arab Fury against Remaining Strictures. *New York Times,* September 27, A1.

Grossberg, Lawrence, Cary Nelson, and Paula Treichler, eds. 1992. *Cultural Studies.* New York: Routledge.

Grossman, David. 1993. To Imagine Peace. *Yediot Acharonot,* 5–6 (in Hebrew).

Grossman, Richard. 1996. Corporations, Accountability and Responsibility. Paper of the Program on Corporations, Law and Democracy, Provincetown, Massachusetts.

Grosz, Elizabeth. 1987. Notes towards a Corporeal Feminism. *Australian Feminist Studies* 5.

———. 1994. *Volatile Bodies: Toward a Corporeal Feminism.* St. Leonard's: Allen and Unwin.

Guastello, Stephen. 1995. *Chaos, Catastrophe, and Human Affairs: Application of Nonlinear Dynamics to Work, Organizations, and Social Evolution.* Mahwah, N.J.: Lawrence Erlbaum Associates.

Gurr, Ted, and James Scarrit. 1989. Minorities Rights at Risk: A Global Survey. *Human Rights Quarterly* 2.

Gusfield, Joseph. 1981. Social Movements and Social Change: Perspectives of Linearity and Fluidity. *Research in Social Movements, Conflict, and Change* 4: 317–39.

Gutierrez, Gustavo. 1983. *The Power of the Poor in History.* New York: Orbis Books.

Habermas, Juergen. 1985. *The Theory of Communicative Action: Reason and the Rationalization of Society.* Vol. 1. Boston: Beacon Press.

——. 1989. *The Theory of Communicative Action: Lifeworld and System: A Critique of Functionalist Reason.* Vol. 2. Boston: Beacon Press.

——. 1992. What Does Socialism Mean Today? In *After the Fall,* edited by R. Blackburn. London: Verso.

Hall, P. 1986. *Governing the Economy.* Cambridge: Polity Press.

Halpern, Manfred. 1987. Choosing between Ways of Life and Death and between Forms of Democracy: An Archetypal Analysis. *Alternatives: Social Transformation and Humane Governance* 12, no. 1: 5–35.

——. 1993. Transformation: Essays for a Work-in-Progress. Unpublished manuscript, Princeton, New Jersey.

Hardin, Garret. 1974. Living on a Lifeboat. *Bioscience* 24, no. 10 (October): 561–68.

Harding, Sandra. 1991. *Whose Science? Whose Knowledge?: Thinking from Women's Lives.* Buckingham: Open University Press.

——. 1998. *Is Science Multicultural?: Postcolonialisms, Feminisms, and Epistemologies.* Bloomington: Indiana University Press.

Harrison, Beverly Wildung. 1986. *Making the Connections: Essays in Feminist Social Ethics,* edited by Carol S. Robb. Boston: Beacon Press.

Harvey, David. 1996. *Justice, Nature and the Geography of Difference.* Oxford: Blackwell.

Harwit, Matin. 1996. *An Exhibit Denied: Lobbying the History of Enola Gay.* New York: Springer-Verlag.

Hawthorne, Geoffrey. 1991. *Plausible Worlds.* Cambridge: Cambridge University Press.

Hayden, Robert. 1997. Schindler's Fate. *NIN* (Belgrade weekly), August 15.

Hayek, F. A. 1960. *The Constitution of Liberty.* London: Routledge and Kegan Paul.

——. 1976. *The Road to Serfdom.* London: Routledge and Kegan Paul.

——. 1978. *New Studies in Philosophy, Politics, Economics and the History of Ideas.* London: Routledge and Kegan Paul.

——. 1982. *Law, Legislation and Liberty.* Vols. 2 and 3. London: Routledge and Kegan Paul.

Hayes, Peter, Lyuba Zarsky, and Walden Bello. 1986. *American Lake: Nuclear Peril in the Pacific.* New York: Penguin Books.

Hegel, G. W. F. 1942. *Hegel's Philosophy of Right,* translated with notes by T. M. Knox. Oxford: Oxford University Press.

Heidegger, Martin. 1977. The Question Concerning Technology. In *The Question Concerning Technology and Other Essays,* translated by William Lovitt. New York: Harper and Row Publishers.

Held, D. 1993a. Anything but a Dog's Life?: Further Comments on Fukuyama, Callinicos and Giddens. *Theory and Society* 22.

——. 1993b. Liberalism, Marxism and Democracy. *Theory and Society* 22.

——, ed. 1993c. *Prospects for Democracy: North, South, East, West.* Cambridge: Polity Press.

——. 1995. *Democracy and Global Order: From the Modern State to Cosmopolitan Governance.* Cambridge: Polity Press.

——. 1996. *Models of Democracy,* 2nd ed. Cambridge: Polity Press.

Held, David, Anthony G. McGrew, David Goldblatt, and Jonathan Perraton. 1999. *Global Transformations: Politics, Economics and Culture.* Palo Alto, Calif.: Stanford University Press.

Hepple, B. 1993. *The European Social Dialogue.* London: Institute of Employment Rights.

Herodotus. 1954. *The Histories,* translated by Aubrey de Selincourt. Harmondsworth: Penguin Books.

Hettne, Bjorn. 1994a. *The New Regionalism: Implications for Development and Peace.* Helsinki: United Nations University/World Institute for Development Economics Research.

———. 1994b. Regionalism and World Order after the Cold War. World Institute for Development Economics Research/IPSA Workshop, Berlin.

Hexter, Jack. 1961. *Reappraisals in History.* London: Longman.

Hirst, Paul. 1990. *Representative Democracy and Its Limits.* Cambridge: Polity Press.

———. 1993. *Debating the Constitution: New Perspectives on Constitutional Reform,* edited by Anthony Barnett, Caroline Ellis, and Paul Hirst. Cambridge: Polity Press.

Hobbes, Thomas. 1946. *Leviathan: Or the Matter, Forme and Power of a Common-Wealth Ecclesiasticall and Civill,* edited by Michael Oakeshott. London: Basil Blackwell.

Hobsbawm, Eric. 1995. *Age of Extremes: The Short Twentieth Century 1914–91.* London: Abacus.

Hoffman, Mark. 1994. Normative International Theory: Approaches and Issues. In *Contemporary International Relations: A Guide to Theory,* edited by A. J. R. Groom and Margot Light. London: Pinter Publishers.

Hoffmann, Stanley. 1977. An American Social Science: International Relations. *Daedalus* 105, no. 3.

Holland, John H. 1995. *Hidden Order: How Adaptation Builds Complexity.* Reading, Mass.: Addison-Wesley Publishing.

Holsti, K. J. 1985. *The Dividing Discipline: Hegemony and Diversity in International Theory.* Boston: Unwin Hyman.

hooks, bell. 1984. *Feminist Theory: From Margin to Center.* Boston: South End Press.

Hughes, Helen. 1992. East Asian Export Success. Research School of Pacific Studies, Australian National University, Canberra.

Huntington, Samuel P. 1968. *Political Order in Changing Societies.* New Haven, Conn.: Yale University Press.

———. 1993. The Clash of Civilizations? *Foreign Affairs* (summer): 22–49.

———. 1996. *The Clash of Civilizations and the Remaking of World Order.* New York: Simon & Schuster.

———. 1997. *The Clash of Civilizations and the Remaking of World Order.* New York: Simon and Schuster.

Hutton, W. 1993. Tokyo Must Curb Rogue Capital Flows. *The Guardian Weekly* 142, no. 2 (July): 11.

Ibn Batutah. 1958. *Journals,* translated by H. A. R. Gibb. London: Hakluyt.

International Court of Justice. 1996. Legality of the Threat or Use of Nuclear Weapons. Advisory Opinion, July 8.

International Forum on Globalization. 1995. South-North: Citizen Strategies to Transform a Divided World. Draft, San Francisco, November.

Islam, Shada. 1996. If It's Broke, Fix It. *Far Eastern Economic Review,* June 20.

Jaggar, Alison M. 1994. *Living with Contradictions: Controversies in Feminist Social Ethics.* Boulder, Colo.: Westview Press.

James, Valentine Udoh, ed. 1995. *Women and Sustainable Development in Africa.* Westport, Conn.: Praeger Publishers.

Jan, Ameen. 1996. Peacebuilding in Somalia. New York: International Peace Academy, Policy Briefing Series.

Johansen, Robert. 1980. *The National and the Human Interest.* Princeton, N.J.: Princeton University Press.

———. 1996. The Future of United Nations Peacekeeping and Enforcement: A Framework for Policymaking. *Global Governance* 2, no. 3 (September–December): 299–333.

Johnson, George. 1997. Researchers on Complexity Ponder What It's All About. *New York Times,* May 6, C7.

Johnston, Hank, Enrique Larana, and Joseph R. Gusfield. 1994. Identities, Grievances, and New Social Movements. In *New Social Movements: From Ideology to Identity,* edited by Enrique Larana, Hank Johnston, and Joseph R. Gusfield. Philadelphia: Temple University Press.

Jordan, Bill. 1985. *The State.* Oxford: Basil Blackwell.

Jordan, Glenn, and Chris Weeden, eds. 1995. *Cultural Politics: Class, Gender, Race, and the Postmodern World.* Oxford: Basil Blackwell.

Joseph, Paul. 1993. *Peace Politics.* Philadelphia: Temple University Press.

Kahler, Miles. 1993. International Relations: Still an American Social Science. In *Ideas and Ideals: Essays on Politics in Honor of Stanley Hoffmann,* edited by Linda Miller and Michael Joseph Smith. Boulder, Colo.: Westview Press.

———. 1997. Inventing International Relations: International Relations Theory after 1945. In *New Thinking in International Relations Theory,* edited by Michael Doyle and G. John Ikenberry. Boulder, Colo.: Westview Press.

Kaiser, Robert G. 1997. Forests of Borneo Going up in Smoke. *Washington Post,* September 7, A18.

Kaldor, Mary. 1990. *The Imaginary War: Understanding the East-West Conflict.* Oxford: Blackwell.

———. 1991. *Marxism Today* 13 (February).

Kaldor, Mary, and Basker Vashee, eds. 1997. *Restructuring the Global Military Sector: Volume I. New Wars.* London: Cassell/Pinter.

Kaminer, Reuven. 1989. The Protest Movement in Israel. In *Intifada: The Palestinian Uprising against Israeli Occupation,* edited by Zachary Lockman and Joel Beinin. Boston: South End Press and Middle East Research and Information Project.

———. 1996. *The Politics of Protest: The Israeli Peace Movement and the Palestinian Intifada.* London: Sussex Academic Press.

Kant, Immanuel. 1963. *On History,* edited by Lewis Beck. New York: Bobbs-Merrill.

———. 1970. Perpetual Peace. In *Kant's Political Writings,* edited by Hans Reiss. Cambridge: Cambridge University Press.

Kaplan, Robert D. 1994. The Coming Anarchy. *The Atlantic Monthly,* February.

———. 1997. *The Ends of the Earth: A Journey at the Dawn of the Twenty First Century.* London: Papermac.

Karliner, Joshua. 1993. Confronting TNCs: Some Thoughts on Strategies. *Third World Resurgence,* no. 40 (December): 34–36.

Kauffman, Stuart. 1995. *At Home in the Universe: The Search for Laws of Self-Organization and Complexity.* New York: Oxford University Press.

Kaza, Stephanie. 1993. Conversations with Trees: Toward an Ecologically Engaged Spirituality. *ReVision* 15, no. 3: 128–36.

Keane, John. 1988. Despotism and Democracy: The Origins and Development of the Distinction between Civil Society and the State, 1750–1850. In *Civil Society and the State.* London: Verso.

Keck, Margaret, and Katherine Sikkink. 1998. *Activists across Borders.* Ithaca, N.Y.: Cornell University Press.

Keen, David. 1996. Organised Chaos: Not the New World We Ordered. *World To-Day,* (January).

Kelly, Kevin. 1994. *Out of Control: The New Biology of Machines, Social Systems, and the Economic World.* New York: Addison-Wesley Publishing.

Kennedy, Paul. 1993. *Preparing for the Twenty-First Century.* London: Fontana Press.

Khor, Martin. 1994. Why GATT and the WTO Should Not Deal with Labour Standards. *Third World Network,* April.

Kim Dae Jung. 1994. Is Culture Destiny? *Foreign Affairs* 73, no.6: 189–94.

Klein-Beekman, Chris. 1996. International Migration and Spatiality in the World Economy: Remapping Economic Space in the Era of Expanding Transnational Flows. *Alternatives: Social Transformation and Humane Governance* 21, no. 4.

Klotz, Audie. 1995. Norms Reconstituting Interests: Global Racial Equality and US Sanctions against South Africa. *International Organization* 49, no. 3.

Kohler, Gernot. 1982. Global Apartheid. In *Toward a Just World Order,* edited by Richard Falk, Sam Kim, and Saul Mendlovitz. Boulder, Colo.: Westview Press.

Korpi, W. 1978. *The Working Class in Welfare Capitalism.* London: Routledge and Kegan Paul.

Korten, David. 1990. *Getting to the 21st Century: Voluntary Action and the Global Agenda.* West Hartford, Conn.: Kumarian Press.

———. 1995. *When Corporations Rule the World.* West Hartford, Conn.: Kumarian Press.

Koselleck, Reinhart. 1985. *Futures Past: On the Semantics of Historical Time.* Cambridge, Mass.: MIT Press.

Kothari, Rajni. 1989. *State against Democracy: In Search of Humane Governance.* New York: New Horizons.

———. 1993. The Yawning Vacuum: A World without Alternatives. *Alternatives: Social Transformation and Humane Governance* 18, no. 2: 119–39.

Kothari, Smitu. 1996. Rising from the Margins: The Awakening of Civil Society in the Third World. *Development 1996* 3.

Kovacevic, Slobodanka, and Putnik Dajic. 1997. *The Chronology of the Yugoslav Crisis 1996.* Belgrade: IES.

Krasner, Stephen. 1993. Westphalia and All That. In *Ideas and Foreign Policy,* edited by Judith Goldstein and Robert Keohane. Ithaca, N.Y.: Cornell University Press.

———. 1985. *Structural Conflict: The Third World against Global Liberalism.* Berkeley and Los Angeles: University of California Press.

Kratochwil, Friedrich. 1989. *Rules, Norms, and Decisions: On the Conditions of Practical and Legal Reasoning in International Relations and Domestic Affairs.* Cambridge: Cambridge University Press.

Kriesberg, Louis. 1974. Organizational Membership and Structure: International Non-Governmental Organizations and Co-Membership from Adversary Nations. *Journal of Voluntary Action Research* 3, nos. 3–4 (July–October).

Kristeva, Julia. 1986. A New Type of Intellectual: The Dissident. In *The Kristeva Reader,* edited by Toril Moi. New York: Columbia University Press.

Kreuger, Anne. 1993. East Asia: Lessons for Growth Theory. Paper presented at the Fourth Annual East Asian Seminar on Economics, National Bureau of Economic Research, San Francisco, June 17–19.

Kumar, Krishan. 1993. Civil Society: An Inquiry into the Usefulness of an Historical Term. *British Journal of Sociology* 44, no. 3 (September).

Laclau, Ernesto. 1990. *New Reflections on the Revolution of Our Time.* New York: Verso.

———, ed. 1994. *The Making of Political Identities.* New York: Verso.

———. 1996. *Emancipation(s).* New York: Verso.

Lakatos, Imre. 1970. Falsification and the Methodology of Scientific Research Programs. In *Criticism and the Growth of Knowledge,* edited by A. Musgrave and I. Lakatos. Cambridge: Cambridge University Press.

Lapid, Yosef. 1989. The Third Debate. *International Studies Quarterly* 33 (September): 235–54.

Lapid, Yosef, and Kratochwil Friedrich, eds. 1996a. *The Return of Culture and Identity in IR Theory.* Boulder, Colo.: Lynne Rienner Publishers.

Lapid, Yosef, and Kratochwil, Friedrich. 1996b. Revisiting the "National": Towards an Identity Agenda in Neorealism? In *The Return of Culture and Identity in IR Theory.* Boulder, Colo.: Lynne Rienner Publishers.

Lebrun, J.-F. 1990. Towards an Economic and Social Area. *Social Europe* 1.

Lederach, John Paul. 1995. *Preparing for Peace: Conflict Transformation across Cultures.* Syracuse, N.Y.: Syracuse University Press.

Leiss, William. 1972. *The Domination of Nature.* Boston: Beacon Press.

Lekic, Slobodan. 1997. Associated Press report from Washington, No. 1833, March 26.

Leopold, Aldo. 1949. *Sand Country Almanac.* New York: Ballantine Press.

Lerner, Michael. 1996. *The Politics of Meaning: Restoring Hope and Possibility in an Age of Cynicism.* Reading, Mass.: Addison-Wesley Publishing.

Levinas, Emmanuel. 1981. *Otherwise Than Being or Beyond Essence,* translated by Alphonso Lingis. The Hague: Martinus Nijhoff.

———. 1985. *Ethics and Infinity: Conversations with Philippe Nemo,* translated by Richard Cohen. Pittsburgh: Duquesne University Press.

Levinson, Jerome. 1996. *NAFTA's Labor Side Agreement: Lessons from the First Three Years.* Washington, D.C.: Institute for Policy Studies and International Labor Rights Fund.

Lewin, Roger. 1992. *Complexity: Life at the Edge of Chaos.* New York: Macmillan.

Lewis, Peter. 1992. Political Transition and the Dilemma of Civil Society in Africa. *Journal of International Affairs* 46, no. 1 (summer).

Lifton, Robert J. 1961. *Thought Reform and the Psychology of Totalism.* Chapel Hill: University of North Carolina Press.

———. 1987. Cults: Religious Totalism and Civil Liberties. In *The Future of Immortality.* New York: Basic Books.

Lifton, Robert Jay, and Greg Mitchell. 1995. *Hiroshima in America.* New York: Putnam's Sons.

Lim, Joseph Y. 1998. The Social Impact and Responses to the Current East Asian Economic and Financial Crisis: The Philippine Case. Unpublished Philippine Country Paper for the UN Development Program/Regional Bureau for Asia and the Pacific.

Lindblom, C. E. 1977. *Politics and Markets.* New York: Basic Books.

Lipietz, A. 1992. *Towards a New Economic Order.* Cambridge: Polity Press.

Lipschutz, Ronnie. 1992. Restructuring World Politics: The Emergence of Global Civil Society. *Millennium: Journal of International Studies* 21, no. 3 (winter).

Little, Ian D. 1982. *Economic Development*. New York: Basic Books.

Locke, John. [1965] 1988. *Two Treatises on Government*, ed. Peter Laslett, Cambridge: Cambridge University Press.

Loehr, William, and John Powelson. 1983. *Threat to Development: Pitfalls of the New International Economic Order*. Boulder, Colo.: Westview Press.

Loomer, Bernard. 1976. Two Conceptions of Power. *Criterion* 15 (winter): 2–29.

Lopez, George A., and David Cortright. 1995. Economic Sanctions in Contemporary Global Relations. In *Economic Sanctions: Panacea or Peacebuilding in a Post-Cold War World?*, edited by David Cortright and George A. Lopez. Boulder, Colo.: Westview Press.

Lovelock, J. E. 1979. *Gaia: A New Look at Life on Earth*. New York: Oxford University Press.

———. 1991. *Healing Gaia, Practical Medicine for the Planet*. New York: Harmony Books.

Luhmann, Niklas. 1984. *Soziale Systeme*. Frankfurt: Suhrkamp.

Lyotard, Jean-Francois. 1984. *The Postmodern Condition: A Report on Knowledge*, translated by G. Bennington and B. Massinni. Minneapolis: University of Minnesota Press.

Macpherson, C. B. 1962. *The Political Theory of Possessive Individualism: Hobbes to Locke*. New York: Oxford University Press.

Mander, Jerry, and Edward Goldsmith, eds. 1996. *The Case against the Global Economy: And for a Turn to the Local*. San Francisco: Sierra Club Books.

Mann, Michael. 1988. State and Society 1130–1815: An Analysis of English State Finances. In *States, War and Capitalism: Studies in Political Sociology*. Oxford: Basil Blackwell.

Manzo, Kate. 1997. Critical Humanism: Postcolonialism and Postmodern Ethics. *Alternatives: Social Transformation and Humane Governance* 22, no. 3: 381–408.

Marable, Manning. 1983. *How Capitalism Underdeveloped America*. Boston: South End Press.

Mardin, Serif. 1995. Civil Society and Islam. In *Civil Society: Theory, History, Comparison*, edited by John A. Hall. Cambridge: Polity Press.

Marshall, Judith. 1990. Structural Adjustment and Social Policy in Mozambique. *Review of African Political Economy* 47 (spring): 28–43.

Marx, Karl. 1967. *Economic and Philosophical Manuscripts of 1844*. Moscow: Progress Publishers.

———. 1975. *Early Writings*. London: Penguin Books.

Mather, John, and Galina Sdasyuk, eds. 1991. *Global Change: Geographical Approaches*. Tucson: University of Arizona Press.

Mathews, Jessica T. 1997. Power Shift. *Foreign Affairs,* January/February: 50–66.

Matustik, Martin J. Beck. 1998. *Specters of Liberation: Great Refusals in the New World Order*. New York: State University of New York Press.

Mazrui, Ali. 1993. Global Apartheid? Paper presented at the Ninetieth Anniversary Nobel Jubilee Symposium, Oslo, December.

McDougal, Myres. 1966. Some Basic Theoretical Concepts about International Law: A Policy Oriented Framework of Inquiry. In *The Strategy of World Order: Volume 2. International Law*, edited by Richard Falk and Saul Mendlovitz. New York: World Law Fund.

McDougal, Myres, and Harold Laswell. 1966. The Appraisal of Diverse Systems of Public Order. In *The Strategy of World Order: Volume 2. International Law*, edited by Richard Falk and Saul Mendlovitz. New York: World Law Fund.

Mearsheimer, John. 1990. Back to the Future: Instability in Europe after the Cold War. *International Security* 15 (summer): 5–56.

Melucci, Alberto. 1980. The New Social Movements: A Theoretical Approach. *Social Science Information* 19.
———. 1994. The Process of Collective Identity. In *Social Movements and Culture*, edited by Hank Johnston and Bert Klandermans. Minneapolis: University of Minnesota Press.
Mendlovitz, Saul, and John Fousek. 1996. Enforcing the Law on Genocide. *Alternatives* 21: 237–58.
Mendlovitz, Saul, and Burns Weston. 1995. The United Nations at Fifty. In *Preferred Futures for the United Nations*. Irvington-on-Hudson, N.Y.: Transnational Publishers.
Meron, Theodor. 1993. The Case for War Crimes Trials in Yugoslavia. *Foreign Affairs* 72 (summer): 122–35.
Mies, Maria. 1986. *Patriarchy and Accumulation on a World Scale: Women in the International Division of Labour*. London: Zed Press.
Miller, D. 1989. *Market, State and Community: Theoretical Foundations of Market Socialism*. Oxford: Clarendon Press.
Mische, Gerald, and Patricia Mische. 1977. *Toward a Human Order: Beyond the National Security Straightjacket*. New York: Paulist Press.
Mittelman, James H. 1991. Marginalization and the International Division of Labor: Mozambique's Strategy of Opening the Market. *African Studies Review* 34, no. 3 (December): 89–106.
———. 1996. The Dynamics of Globalization. In *Globalization: Critical Reflections*. Boulder, Colo.: Lynne Rienner Publishers.
———, ed. 1996. *Globalization: Critical Reflections*. Boulder, Colo.: Lynne Rienner Publishers.
———. 2000. *The Globalization Syndrome: Transformation and Resistance*. Princeton, N.J.: Princeton University Press.
Mittelman, James H., and Mustapha Kamal Pasha. 1997. *Out from Underdevelopment Revisited: Changing Global Structures and the Remaking of the Third World*. London: Macmillan.
Mohammed, Mahathir, and Shintaro Ishihara. 1996. *The Voice of Asia*. Tokyo: Kodansha.
Mohanty, Chandra. 1991. Cartographies of Struggle: Third World Women and the Politics of Feminism. In *Third World Women and the Politics of Feminism*, edited by Chandra Mohanty, Ann Russo, and Lourdes Tunes. Bloomington: Indiana University Press.
Montesquieu, Baron de. 1989. *The Spirit of the Laws*, translated by Ann Cohler et al. Cambridge: Cambridge University Press.
Montgomery, Tommie Sue. 1995. Getting Peace in El Salvador: The Roles of the UN Secretariat and ONUSAL. *Journal of Interamerican Studies and World Affairs* 37, no. 4 (winter): 139–72.
Moore, Barrington Jr. 1972. *Reflections on the Causes of Human Misery and upon Certain Proposals to Eliminate Them*. Boston: Beacon Press.
Morgan, Robin. 1984. *Sisterhood is Global*. New York: Anchor Press/Doubleday.
Mouffe, Chantall, ed. 1992. *Dimensions of Radical Democracy: Pluralism, Citizenship, Community*. New York: Verso.
Mozambiquefile. 1993a. Food Aid Rots in Maputo. *Mozambiquefile* (Mozambique News Agency Monthly) 200 (March): 21.
———. 1993b. Food Aid Stolen. *Mozambiquefile* (Mozambique News Agency Monthly) 201 (April): 21.
Murphy, Craig. 1994. *International Organization and Industrial Change: Global Governance since 1850*. New York: Oxford University Press.

Nakarada, Radmila. 1995. Disintegration of Yugoslavia: A New Challenge to the International Peace Movements. In *The Blocked Civil Society,* edited by Vukasin Pavlovic. Belgrade: EcoCenter.

Nardin, Terry, and David Mapel, eds. 1992. *Traditions of International Ethics.* New York: Cambridge University Press.

National Academy of Science Commission on Human Rights. 1993. Scientists and Human Rights in Syria. Pamphlet. Washington, D.C.: National Academy Press.

National Labor Committee. 1995. Gap Agrees to Independent Monitoring of Its Contractors, Setting a New Standard for the Entire Retail Industry. Press release, New York, December 19.

Nerfin, Marc. 1989. Neither Prince nor Merchant: Citizen—an Introduction to the Third System. *IFDA Dossier* 56 (November/December).

Nozick, R. 1974. *Anarchy, State and Utopia.* Oxford: Basil Blackwell.

Ofreno, Rene. 1995. Globalization and the Filipino Working Masses. *Proceedings of the Sixth Annual Lecture of the Civil Liberties Union.* Greenhills, Philippines.

O'Grady, Ron. 1992. *The Child and the Tourist: The Story behind the Escalation of Child Prostitution in Asia.* Bangkok and Auckland: ECPAT and PACE Publishing.

O'Laughlin, Bridget. 1995. Past and Present Options: Land Reform in Mozambique. *Review of African Political Economy* 22, no. 63 (March): 99–106.

Ollman, Bertell. 1976. *Alienation: Marx's Conception of Man in Capitalist Society,* 2nd ed. New York: Cambridge University Press.

O'Neill, Onora. 1975. Lifeboat Earth. *Philosophy and Public Affairs* 4, no. 3 (spring): 273–92.

Orr, David. 1992. *Ecological Literacy: Education and the Transition to a Postmodern World.* Albany: State University of New York Press.

Paine, Thomas. 1982. *Common Sense,* edited by Isaac Kramnick. Harmondsworth: Penguin Books.

Passell, Peter. 1990. So Much for Assumptions about Immigrants and Jobs. *New York Times,* April 25, E4.

Pateman, Carole. 1985. *The Problem of Political Obligation: A Critique of Liberal Theory.* Cambridge: Polity Press.

Pateman, Carole. 1988. Feminist Critiques of the Public/Private Dichotomy. In *Public and Private in Social Life,* edited by S. Benn and G. Gauss. Canberra: Croom Helm.

Pauly, Louis. 1995. Capital Mobility, State Autonomy and Political Legitimacy. *Journal of International Affairs* 48 (winter): 369–83.

Peck, Connie. 1998. *Sustainable Peace: The Role of the UN and Regional Organizations in Preventing Conflict.* Lanham, Md.: Rowman & Littlefield.

Pennock, J. Roland. 1993. Equality and Inequality. In *The Oxford Companion to Politics of the World,* edited by Joel Krieger. New York: Oxford University Press.

Perez-Diaz, Victor. 1995. The Possibility of Civil Society. In *Civil Society: Theory, History, Comparison,* edited by John A. Hall. Cambridge: Polity Press.

Pierson, C. 1993. Democracy, Markets and Capital: Are There Necessary Economic Limits to Democracy? In *Prospects for Democracy: North, South, East, West,* edited by D. Held. Cambridge: Polity Press.

———. 1995. *Socialism after Communism: The New Market Socialism.* Cambridge: Polity Press.

Pincus, J. J. 1975. Pressure Groups and the Pattern of Tariffs. *Journal of Political Economy* 83 (August): 757–78.

Piore, M., and Sabel, C. 1984. *The Second Industrial Divide.* New York: Basic Books.

Plato. 1973. *Republic.* New York: Anchor.

Plunkett, Mark. 1994. Law and Order Institution Building: The Establishment of the Rule of Law in Post Conflict Peacebuilding. In *International Peacekeeping—a Regional Perspective.* ADF/DFAT Seminar, Canberra, May 3.

Pogge, Thomas. 1994. An Egalitarian Law of Peoples. *Philosophy and Public Affairs* 23, no. 3 (summer): 195–224.

Polanyi, Karl. 1957. *The Great Transformation: The Political and Economic Origins of Our Time.* Boston: Beacon Press.

———. 1968. *Primitive, Archaic and Modern Economies,* edited by George Dalton. Garden City, N.Y.: Anchor Books.

Polkinghorne, Donald. 1988. *Narrative Knowing and the Human Sciences.* Albany: State University of New York Press.

Popper, Karl. 1957. *The Poverty of Historicism.* New York: Harper.

———. 1965. *Conjectures and Refutations.* New York: Harper.

———. 1968. *The Logic of Scientific Discovery.* New York: Harper and Row.

Posen, Barry. 1993. Nationalism, the Mass Army and Military Power. *International Security* 18: 80–124.

Princen, Thomas, and Matthias Finger. 1994. *Environmental NGOs in World Politics: Linking the Local and the Global.* London: Routledge.

Putnam, Robert. 1993. *Making Democracy Work: Civic Traditions in Modern Italy,* Princeton, N.J.: Princeton University Press.

Raghavan, Chakravarthi. 1995. *Recolonization: GATT, the Uruguay Round and the Third World.* New Delhi: Third World Network.

———. 1997. Europe: Life vs. TNCs—and TNCs Win. *SUNS,* July 21.

Rawls, John. 1989. *A Theory of Justice.* Cambridge, Mass.: Harvard University Press.

———. 1993. The Law of Peoples. In *On Human Rights,* edited by Stephen Shute and Susan Hurley. New York: Basic Books.

———. 1996. *Political Liberalism.* New York: Columbia University Press.

Reich, Robert B. 1993. *The Work of Nations.* London: Simon and Schuster.

Research Foundation for Science, Technology and Ecology. 1997. The Enclosure and Recovery of the Commons. Research report, New Delhi.

Research Foundation for Science, Technology and Natural Resource Policy. 1995. Patents: Violating Dignity of Life. *Bija,* no.14 (December).

———. 1996. Hands Off: Forbidden Seeds. *Bija Newsletter,* no. 17–18 (November).

Reuters. 1998. Confidence Returning to Asia, Says Report. November 11.

Rich, Bruce. 1994. *Mortgaging the Earth: The World Bank, Environmental Impoverishment, and the Crisis of Development.* Boston: Beacon Press.

Richardson, Lewis. 1960. *Arms and Insecurity: A Mathematical Study of the Causes and Origins of War.* Pittsburgh: Boxwood Press.

Richburg, Keith. 1996. Free Trade Helps Lift World Poor. *Washington Post,* December 29, A1, 26.

"Richie Rich." 1997. *The Nation,* October 13.

Rodney, Walter. 1981. *How Europe Underdeveloped Africa.* Cambridge, Mass.: Harvard University Press.

Rogers, J., and W. Streeck. 1994. Productive Solidarities: Economic Strategy and Left Politics. In *Reinventing the Left,* edited by D. Milibard. Cambridge: Polity Press.

Rorty, Richard. 1989. *Contingency, Irony and Solidarity.* Cambridge: Cambridge University Press.

Rosa, Kumudhini. 1994. The Conditions and Organizational Activities of Women in Free Trade Zones, Malaysia, Philippines and Sri Lanka, 1970–1990. In *Dignity and Daily Bread: New Forms of Economic Organizing among Poor Women in the Third World and the First,* edited by Sheila Rowbotham and Swasti Mitter. London: Routledge.

Rosenau, James N. 1971. *The Scientific Study of Foreign Policy.* New York: The Free Press.

———. 1981. *The Study of Political Adaptation.* London: Frances Pinter Publishers.

———. 1983. "Fragmegrative" Challenges to National Security. In *Understanding U.S. Strategy: A Reader,* edited by Terry L. Heyns. Washington, D.C.: National Defense University.

———. 1989. The Scholar as an Adaptive System. In *Journeys through World Politics: Autobiographical Reflections of Thirty-Four Academic Travelers,* edited by Joseph Kruzel and James N. Rosenau. Lexington, Mass.: Lexington Books.

———. 1990. *Turbulence in World Politics: A Theory of Change and Continuity.* Princeton, N.J.: Princeton University Press.

———. 1992. Normative Challenges in a Turbulent World. *Ethics and International Affairs* 6: 1–19.

———. 1995. Distant Proximities: The Dynamics and Dialectics of Globalization. In *International Political Economy: Understanding Global Disorder,* edited by Bjorn Hettne. London: Zed Books.

———. 1997a. *Along the Domestic-Foreign Frontier: Exploring Governance in a Turbulent World.* Cambridge: Cambridge University Press.

———. 1997b. Many Damn Things Simultaneously: Complexity Theory and World Affairs. In *Complexity, Global Politics, and National Security,* edited by David S. Alberts and Thomas J. Czerwinski. Washington, D.C.: National Defense University.

Rosenau, James N., and Ernst-Otto Czempiel, eds. 1992. *Governance without Government: Order and Change in World Politics.* Cambridge: Cambridge University Press.

Rosenau, James N., and Mary Durfee. 1995. *Thinking Theory Thoroughly: Coherent Approaches to an Incoherent World.* Boulder, Colo.: Westview Press.

Ross, G., S. Hoffman, and S. Malzacher. 1987. *The Mitterand Experiment.* Cambridge: Polity Press.

Rothstein, Richard. 1996. The Starbucks Solution: Can Voluntary Codes Raise Global Living Standards? *The American Prospect* 27 (July–August): 36–42.

Rousseau, J.-J. 1968. *The Social Contract.* Harmondsworth: Penguin Books.

———. 1991. Abstract and Judgement of Saint-Pierre's Project for Perpetual Peace. In *Rousseau on International Relations,* edited by Stanley Hoffman and David P. Fidler. Oxford: Oxford University Press.

Rubin, Robert. 1998a. Remarks at the Sasin Institute of Business Administration. Chulalongkorn University, Bangkok, June 30.

———. 1998b. Strengthening the Architecture of the International Financial System. Speech delivered at the Brookings Institution, Washington, D.C., April 14.

Ruggie, John. 1983. Continuity and Transformation in the World Polity: Toward a Neo-Realist Synthesis. *World Politics* 35 (January): 261–85.

———. 1994. Trade Protectionism and the Future of Welfare Capitalism. *Journal of International Affairs* 48 (summer): 1–12.

Ruiz, Lester Edwin J. 1990. Sovereignty as Transformative Practice. In *Contending Sovereignties: Redefining Political Community,* edited by R. B. J. Walker and Saul Mendlovitz. Boulder, Colo.: Lynne Rienner Publishers.

———. 1997a. Re-Thinking Democracy, Revitalizing Civil Society under the Sign of Global Capitalism. *Conjuncture* 9, no. 4: 10–12.

———. 1997b. The Subject of Security Is the Subject of Security: APEC and the Globalization of Capital. *Pacifica Review* 9, no. 2 (October–November): 3–17.

Runyan, Anne, and Spike Peterson.1993. *Global Gender Issues.* Boulder, Colo.: Westview Press.

Rutland, P. 1985. *The Myth of the Plan: Lessons of Soviet Planning Experiences.* London: Hutchinson.

Ryan, Michael. 1989. *Politics and Culture: Working Hypotheses for a Post Revolutionary Society.* Baltimore: The Johns Hopkins University Press.

Sahlins, Peter. 1984. *Boundaries: The Making of France and Spain in the Pyrenees.* Berkeley and Los Angeles: University of California Press.

Said, Edward. 1993. *Culture and Imperialism.* New York: Alfred A. Knopf.

Sajor, Edsel, and Babette Resurreccion. 1998. Constellations of Power: Philippine Ecopolitics Re-Examined. *Alternatives: Social Transformation and Humane Governance* 23, no. 2 230–43.

Sakamoto, Yoshikazu. 1997. Civil Society and Democratic World Order. In *Innovation and Transformation in International Studies,* edited by Stephen Gill and James Mittelman. Cambridge: Cambridge University Press.

Saker, Neil. 1996. Guest Viewpoint: Thailand Update: Market Pessimism Is Overblown. *BOI Investment Review* 2 (December 31).

Salamon, L., and J. Siegfried. 1977. Economic Power and Political Influence. *American Political Science Review* 71 (September): 1026–43.

Sandel, Michael J. 1998. *Liberalism and the Limits of Justice.* 2nd ed. Chicago: University of Chicago Press.

SC Bans Import of Hazardous Wastes. 1997. *Times of India,* March 6.

Scarlett, Prunella. 1992. The Unofficial Commonwealth. *Transnational Associations* 1 (January–February).

Schilling, David M. 1997. A Step towards Eliminating Sweatshops: The White House Apparel Industry Partnership Report. *The Corporate Examiner* 25, no. 9 (May 9): 1–8.

Schmidheiny, Stephan. 1992. *Changing Course: A Global Business Perspective on Development and the Environment.* Cambridge, Mass.: MIT Press.

Schmidt, Brian. 1995. Lessons from the Past: A Reconsideration of the Great Debate between Idealism and Realism. Paper presented at the annual meeting of the American Political Science Association, August 31–September 3.

Schroeder, Paul. 1994. Historical Reality vs. Neo-Realist Theory. *International Security* 19 (summer): 18–48.

Schumacher, E. F. 1973. *Small Is Beautiful.* London: Abacus Press.

Schumpeter, J. 1976. *Capitalism, Socialism and Democracy.* London: Allen and Unwin.

Seligman, Adam B. 1992. *The Idea of Civil Society.* New York: The Free Press.

Sharoni, Simona. 1993. Conflict Resolution through Feminist Lenses: Theorizing the Israeli Palestinian Conflict from the Perspectives of Women Peace Activists in Israel. Ph.D. dissertation, George Mason University.

————. 1995. *Gender and the Israeli-Palestinian Conflict: The Politics of Women's Resistance.* Syracuse, N.Y.: Syracuse University Press.

————. 1997. Motherhood and the Politics of Women's Resistance: Israeli Women Organizing for Peace. In *The Politics of Motherhood: Activist Voices from Left to Right,* edited by Alexis Jetter, Annelise Orleck, and Diana Taylor. Hanover: N.H.: University Press of New England.

Shaw, Martin. 1994. Civil Society and Global Politics: Beyond a Social Movements Approach. *Millennium: Journal of International Studies* 23, no. 3 (winter).

Shiva, Vandana. 1995. *Globalisation and Localisation: Citizen Power in a Period of Global Corporate Rule.* New Delhi.

————. 1996. Of Spies, Crime and IPR. *Hindustan Times,* November 21.

————. n.d. Globalization: Gandhi and Swadeshi. Unpublished manuscript, Research Foundation for Science, Technology and Natural Resource Policy, Dehr Dun, India.

Shnitzer, Shachar. 1993. Catch 21. *Challenge* 4, no. 5 (September–October): 36–37.

Sikkink, Kathryn. 1986. Codes of Conduct for Transnational Corporations: The Case of the WHO/UNICEF Code. *International Organization* 40 (autumn): 815–40.

————. 1993. Human Rights Issue-Networks in Latin America. *International Organization* 47, no. 3 (summer).

Simon, Herbert A. 1945. *Administrative Behavior: A Study of Decision-Making Behavior in Administrative Organization.* New York: Macmillan.

Simons, Marlies. 1996. Scandals Force the 2 Belgiums to Explore Inner Ills. *New York Times,* October 10, A3.

Singer, Peter. 1972. Famine, Affluence, and Morality. *Philosophy and Public Affairs* 1, no. 3 (spring): 229–43.

Singerman, Diane. 1998. Civil Society in the Shadow of the Egyptian State: The Role of Informal Networks and the Construction of Public Life. Monograph series, G. E. von Grunebaum Center for Near Eastern Studies, University of California at Los Angeles.

Sismanidis, Roxane D. 1997. UN Police Functions in Peace Operations. Policy paper, United States Institute of Peace, Washington, D.C.

Smiley, Marion. 1992. *Moral Responsibility and the Boundaries of Community.* Chicago: University of Chicago Press.

Smith, Adam. 1993. *An Inquiry into the Nature and Causes of Wealth of Nations,* edited by Kathryn Sutherland. New York: Oxford University Press.

Smith, R. David. 1995. The Inapplicability Principle: What Chaos Means for Social Science. *Behavioral Science* 40.

Smith, Steve. 1992. The Forty Years' Detour: The Resurgence of Normative Theory in International Relations. *Millennium: Journal of International Studies* 21, no. 3 (winter).

Smith, Steve, Ken Booth, and Marysia Zalewski, eds. 1996. *International Theory: Positivism and Beyond.* Cambridge: Cambridge University Press.

Smoker, Paul. 1992. Possible Roles for Social Movements. In *Restructuring for World Peace on the Threshold of the Twenty-First Century,* edited by Katharine Tehranian and Majid Tehranian. Cresshill, N.J.: Hampton Press, 90–110.

Snyder, Jack. 1990. Averting Anarchy in the New Europe. *International Security* 14: 5–41.

Social Weather Station. 1994. Social Weather Report Survey. Social Weather Station, Quezon City.

Soelle, Dorothee. 1984. *To Work and to Love: A Theology of Creation.* Philadelphia: Fortress Press.

Soja, Edward W. 1996. *Thirdspace: Journeys to Los Angeles and Other Real-and-Imagined Places.* Oxford: Blackwell.

Soros, George. 1998. Can There Be a Global Economy without a Global Society? Lecture, Stockholm, Sweden, June 11.

South Commission. 1990. *The Challenge to the South.* Oxford: Oxford University Press.

Sparks, Allister. 1994. The Secret Revolution. *The New Yorker,* April 11, 56–78.

Spiro, Gideon. 1988. The Israeli Draft Refusal Movement: Yesh Gvul. Unpublished paper (in Hebrew).

Spivak, Gayatri. 1988. Can the Subaltern Speak? In *Marxism and the Interpretation of Culture,* edited by Cary Nelson and Lawrence Grossberg. London: Macmillan.

Spretnak, Charlene. 1999. *The Resurgence of the Real: Body, Nature and Place in a Hypermodern World.* New York: Routledge.

Stairs, Keven, and Peter Taylor. 1992. Non-Governmental Organizations and the Legal Protection of the Oceans: A Case Study. In *The International Politics of the Environment,* edited by Andrew Hurrell and Benedict Kingsbury. Oxford: Oxford University Press.

Storey, John. 1996. *What Is Cultural Studies? A Reader.* London: Arnold Press.

Strange, Susan. 1993. *States and Markets,* 2nd ed. London: Pinter.

Summers, Larry. 1998. The Global Economic Situation and What It Means for the United States. Remarks to the National Governors Association, Milwaukee, Wisconsin, August 4.

Taylor, Charles. 1991. *The Ethics of Authenticity.* Cambridge, Mass.: Harvard University Press.

Tetlock, Philip, and Aaron Belkin, eds. 1996. *Counterfactual Thought Experiments in World Politics.* Princeton, N.J.: Princeton University Press.

Thiele, Leslie. 1997. *Thinking Politics: Perspectives on Ancient, Modern and Postmodern Political Theory.* Chatham, N.J.: Chatham House.

Third World Network. 1997. The Multilateral Agreement on Investment: Impact on Sustainable Development. Briefing papers prepared for the Earth Summit Plus Five, New York, June 23–27.

Thomas, W. L. Jr., ed. 1956. *Man's Role in Changing the Face of the Earth.* Chicago: University of Chicago Press.

Thompson, E. P. 1990. E.N.D. and the Beginning: History Turns on a New Hinge. *The Nation,* 250, no. 4 (January 29).

Thomson, Janice E., and Stephen D. Krasner. 1989. Global Transactions and the Consolidation of Sovereignty. In *Global Changes and Theoretical Challenges: Approaches to World Politics for the 1990s,* edited by Ernst-Otto Czempiel and James Rosenau. Lexington, Mass.: Lexington Books.

Tilly, Charles. 1990. *Coercion, Capital and European States* AD 990–1990. Oxford: Basil Blackwell.

Tillich, Paul. 1954. *Love, Power, and Justice: Ontological Analyses and Ethical Applications.* New York: Oxford University Press.

Tocqueville, Alexis de. 1969. *Democracy in America,* edited by J. P Mayer, translated by George Lawrence. Garden City, N.Y.: Anchor Books.

Toulmin, Stephen. 1990. *Cosmopolis: The Hidden Agenda of Modernity.* New York: The Free Press.

Truong, Thanh-dam. 1990. *Sex, Money, and Mortality: Prostitution and Tourism in Southeast Asia.* Atlantic Highlands, N.J.: Zed Books.

Tschirley, David L., and Michael T. Weber. 1994. Food Security Strategies under Extremely Adverse Conditions: The Determinants of Household Income and Consumption in Rural Mozambique. *World Development* 22, no. 2: 159–73.

Tucker, Robert C. 1981. *Politics as Leadership*. New York: Columbia University Press.

Tucker, Robert W. 1975. *The Inequality of States*. New York: Basic Books.

United Nations. 1989. *United Nations Document S/20883*. New York: United Nations, October 6.

UN Conference on Trade and Development. 1996. *World Investment Report 1996*. New York: United Nations.

UN Development Program. 1996. *Human Development Report 1992*. Oxford: Oxford University Press.

———. 1993. *Human Development Report 1993*. Oxford: Oxford University Press.

———. 1996. *Human Development Report 1996*. New York: Oxford University Press.

UN Economic and Social Council. 1997. Report on the World Social Situation. E/CN5/ 1997/8, January.

UN Fund for Population Activities. 1992a. *Population and the Environment: The Challenge Ahead*. New York: United Nations.

———. 1992b. *State of the World Population 1992*. New York: United Nations.

Unger, Roberto. 1975. *Knowledge and Politics*. New York: The Free Press.

UNICEF. 1992. *The State of the World's Children*. Oxford: Oxford University Press.

———. 1993. *The State of the World's Children*. Oxford: Oxford University Press.

Urquhart, Brian. 1991. Foreword. In *United Nations Peacekeeping and the Non-Use of Force, International Peace Academy Occasional Paper Series*, edited by F. T. Liu. Boulder, Colo.: Lynne Rienner Publishers.

U.S. General Accounting Office, U.S. Senate, Committee on Foreign Relations. 1993. U.N. Peacekeeping: Observations on Mandates and Operational Capability. Statement of Frank C. Conahan, assistant comptroller-general, national security and intern.

U.S./Guatemala Labour Education Campaign. Various issues (updates). Published by US/ Labor Education in the Americas Project (formerly US/GLEP), Chicago.

Vajda, M. 1978. The State and Socialism. *Social Research* 4 (November).

Vander Stickele, Myriam, and Peter Pennartz. 1996. Making It Our Business: European NGO Campaigns on Transnational Corporations Briefing, Catholic Institute for International Relations, London, September.

Vichyanond, Pakorn. 1994. *Thailand's Financial System: Structure and Liberalization*. Bangkok: Thailand Development Research Institute.

Wade, Robert. 1990. *Governing the Market: Economic Theory and the Role of Government in East Asian Industrialization*. Princeton, N.J.: Princeton University Press.

———. 1992. East Asia's Economic Success: Conflicting Perspectives, Partial Insights, Shaky Evidence. *World Politics* 44, no. 2 (January): 270–320.

Waldrop, M. Mitchell. 1992. *Complexity: The Emerging Science at the Edge of Order and Chaos*. New York: Simon and Schuster.

Walker, R. B. J.. 1988. *One World/Many Words*. Boulder, Colo.: Lynne Rienner Publishers.

———. 1990a. Security, Sovereignty and the Challenge of World Politics. *Alternatives* 25.

———. 1990b. Sovereignty, Identity, Community: Reflections on the Horizons of Contemporary Political Practice. In *Contending Sovereignties: Redefining Political Community*, edited by R. B. J. Walker and Saul Mendlovitz. Boulder, Colo.: Lynne Rienner Publishers.

———. 1993. *Inside/Outside: International Relations as Political Theory.* Cambridge: Cambridge University Press.

———. 1997. The Subject of Security. In *Critical Security Studies: Concepts and Cases,* edited by Keith Krause and Michael C. Williams. Minneapolis: University of Minnesota Press.

Walker, R. B. J., and Warren Magnusson. 1988. De-Centering the State: Political Theory and Canadian Political Economy. *Studies in Political Economy* 26 (summer): 37–71.

Walker, R. B. J., and Saul Mendlovitz, eds. 1990. *Contending Sovereignties: Redefining Political Community.* Boulder, Colo.: Lynne Rienner Publishers.

Wallerstein, Immanuel. 1974. *The Modern World System.* Vol. 1. New York: Academic Press.

———. 1991. *Transforming the Revolution: Social Movements and the World System.* New York: Monthly Review Press.

Walter, Andrew. 1983. Distributive Justice and the Theory of International Relations. *Australian Outlook* 37, no. 2 (August): 98–103.

Waltz, Kenneth. 1979. *Theory of International Politics.* Reading, Mass.: Addison-Wesley Publishing.

Walzer, Michael. 1992. *Just and Unjust War: A Moral Argument with Historical Illustrations,* 2nd ed. New York: Basic Books.

———. 1995. The Concept of Civil Society. In *Toward a Global Civil Society.* Providence, R.I.: Berghahn Books.

Wank, David L. 1995. Civil Society in Communist China? Private Business and Political Alliance, 1989. In *Civil Society: Theory, History, Comparison,* edited by John A. Hall. Cambridge: Polity Press.

Wapner, Paul. 1994. On the Global Dimension of Environmental Challenges. *Politics and the Life Sciences* 13, no. 2 (August): 173–81.

———. 1995. Politics beyond the State. *World Politics* 47, no. 3 (April): 311–40.

———. 1996. *Environmental Activism and World Civic Politics.* Albany: State University of New York Press.

———. 2000. The Transnational Politics of Environmental NGOs: Governmental, Economic and Social Activism. In *The United Nations and the Global Environment in the 21st Century: From Common Challenges to Shared Responsibilities,* edited by Pamela Chasek. Tokyo: United Nations University Press.

Weaver, Ole. 1994. Insecurity and Identity Unlimited. Centre for Peace and Conflict Research. Monograph, Copenhagen.

Weber, Max. 1922. *Schriften zur Wissenschaftslehre,* Tübingen: J. C. B. Mohr.

———. 1958. Politics as Vocation. In *From Max Weber: Essays in Sociology,* edited by Hans Gerth and C. Mills Wright. New York: Oxford University Press.

———. 1978. *Economy and Society.* Vol. 1, edited by Guenther Roth and Claus Wittich. Berkeley and Los Angeles: University of California Press.

Weiss, Thomas G., David Cortright, George A. Lopez, and Larry Minear, eds. 1997. *Political Gain and Civilian Pain: Humanitarian Impacts of Economic Sanctions.* Lanham, Md.: Rowman & Littlefield.

Wendt Alexander. 1992. Anarchy Is What the Agents Make of It. *International Organization* 46, (spring): 391–425.

West, Cornel. 1993. *Race Matters.* Boston: Beacon Press.

Wijkman, Anders. 1996. Stumbling Blocks on the Road to Sustainable Development. *Brown Journal of World Affairs* 3, no. 2 (summer–fall): 177–86.

Williams, Raymond. 1983. *Keywords,* rev. ed. London: Fontana.

Wolf, Susan. 1982. Moral Saints. *Ethics* 79 (August): 419–39.

Wolfsfeld, Gadi. 1988. *The Politics of Provocation: Participation and Protest in Israel.* Albany: State University of New York Press.

World Bank. 1989. *World Bank Development Report.* Washington, D.C.: World Bank.

———. 1990–99. *World Development Report.* New York: Oxford University Press.

———. 1993. *The East Asian Miracle.* New York: Oxford University Press.

———. 1996. *Poverty Reduction and the World Bank: Progress and Challenges in the 1990s.* Washington, D.C.: World Bank.

———. 1997. *Global Development Finance: Volume 1. Analysis and Summary Tables.* Washington, D.C.: World Bank.

———. 1998. *Poverty Reduction and the World Bank: Progress in Fiscal 1996 and 1997.* Washington, D.C.: World Bank.

Yishai, Yael. 1997. *Between the Flag and the Banner: Women in Israeli Politics.* Albany: State University of New York Press.

Young, Iris Marion. 1990. *Justice and the Politics of Difference.* Princeton, N.J.: Princeton University Press.

Young, Oran R. 1994. *International Governance: Protecting the Environment in a Stateless Society.* Ithaca, N.Y.: Cornell University Press.

Zacher, Mark W., and Richard A. Matthews. 1995. Liberal International Theory: Common Threads, Divergent Strands. In *Controversies in International Relations Theory: Realism and the Neoliberal Challenge,* edited by Charles W. Kegley Jr. New York: St. Martin's Press.

Zuckoff, Mitchell. 1994. Taking a Profit and Inflicting a Cost. *Boston Globe,* July 10.

Index

Abi-Saab, Georges, 313
absolutism, 61, 300–301, 310n1
access avenues, 158, 162
accountability, 101, 104, 155; corporate, 17;
    global sources of, 131; individual, 210,
    215, 217, 227–28; state, 265
adaptation, 42–43, 48n7
AFL-CIO, corporate affairs division of, 205
agency, 41, 284; crisis of, 74–77; political,
    11, 19, 66, 164
Agenda for Peace, An (Boutros-Ghali), 212,
    308
age of absolutism, described, 300–301
age of relativization, 302, 309–10; described,
    300–301
age of uncertainty, 107–9
"Age of the Holy Spirit" (Fiore), 242
agribusiness, devastation by, 195
Akasombo Dam, 281
Albrecht, Josef: Seed Act and, 134
al-Kabeer Slaughterhouse case, 141–44
Allende regime, undermining, 159
AMF. *See* Asian Monetary Fund
Amnesty International, 14, 270, 271
AMPO, 252, 253, 256, 260n2
anarchy, 28, 54, 61, 294–95
Anderson, Bibi, 318
Antarctic and Southern Oceans Coalition
    (ASOC), 271
Antarctica Treaty System, 267
Anti-Enron Committee, 139
antiglobalization, 204, 207

anti-MOWB movements, 253, 254
apartheid: corporate support for, 198; eco-
    nomic, 193; environmental, 135–37;
    global, 66
APEC. *See* Asia Pacific Economic Coopera-
    tion
apocalypse, 231, 239
aporia, 343, 347n14
Aquinas, Thomas, 332
Arab-Israeli conflict, 112–13; identity crisis
    and, 113, 114–15
Arab-Olgy, Edward, 316
Arafat, Yassir, 119
Arendt, Hannah, 74, 332
Aristotle: householding and, 169; polis and,
    24; telos by, 53
Armageddon, Asahara and, 236, 237, 238
Arthur, Brian: economics and, 40
Aryan Nations, 268, 270
Asahara, Shoko, 237; apocalyptic preoccupa-
    tions of, 234–35; guru worship of, 233;
    mysticism and, 238; nuclear annihilation
    and, 235–36, 239
ASEAN. *See* Association of Southeast Asian
    Nations
Ashley, Richard K., 342, 348n16
Asian financial crisis, 187–89, 203; end of,
    187, 190; IMF and, 183–84; interpreta-
    tion of, 181, 184; speculative/bank capi-
    tal and, 183
Asian Monetary Fund (AMF), 182, 328
Asian Wall Street Journal, 186, 187

Asia Pacific Economic Cooperation (APEC), 186, 325, 347n8
Asia Week, 185, 187
ASOC. *See* Antarctic and Southern Oceans Coalition
assets, freezing, 217, 227
association, 262; global civil society and, 267
Association of Southeast Asian Nations (ASEAN), 25, 110n5, 282, 288 Regional Forum of, 328
At Home in the Universe (Kauffman), 40
Aum Shinrikyo: cultural context of, 239; guruism of, 233, 234; as new-new religion, 234; profile of, 231, 233, 236, 238; proteanism of, 232; psychological dynamics of, 235–37; violence by, 237–38
authority, 61; sources/agencies of, 25
axial ages, 243–44; early expression of, 240–42; growth of, 240, 243, 248–49; history reading and, 240; maps for, 244–45
Ayensu, Edward S., 277, 283n3

Bak, Per, 40
balance of power, 287, 289, 309
bamboo network, economic growth and, 292
Bank for European Construction and Development, 162
barbarism, 74; civilization and, 293
Barlow, Maude: corporate bill of rights and, 191
Barry, Brian, 83–84
Basel International Convention, 139, 140
Bataan EPZ, 176, 177
Bat-Shalom, 120, 126
Batutah, Ibn, 81
Bege Channel, negotiation over, 282
Begin, Menachem: protest activities and, 116
Beitz, Charles, 86, 95n6
Bello, Walden: on global capitalism, 335
Berlin, Isaiah, 96n10
Bhagwati, Jagdish, 318
Bharatiya Janata Party, 135
biodiversity, 144; commercialization of, 18;

IPRs and, 146–47; protecting, 10, 145–46, 147
biological wealth, exporting, 141–44
biopiracy, 144–45, 148
bipolarity, 111n5, 290; multipolarity and, 54–55
bloc system, 289, 290, 291
body politic, 340; normative IR and, 344–46
Boff, Leonardo: on reason, 339
Boli, John, 267
Bonior, David, 196
border wars, fault-line wars and, 250–52
Boulding, Elise, 316, 334
Boutros-Ghali, Boutros, 308; agenda of, 212; on Egyptian experts, 278
Bowring, Philip: on economic journalism, 186
Boyd, Charles, 73, 74, 78n8
Bretton Woods, 132, 159
Briand, Aristide, 253
Brittany, Leon: GATT and, 132
Broad, Robin, 324, 335
Buchanan, Pat, 196, 197
Buddhism, 143, 241, 256; Aum Shinrikyo and, 233, 235
Bush, George, 215; free market and, 198; NAFTA and, 202
business press, Asian financial crisis and, 185, 187
Business Week, 186
Butler, Judith: on identity deconstruction, 129

Cafruny, Alan, 96n7
Campbell, David, 339, 343, 347nn11, 14
Canadian Ministry of Foreign Affairs/ Canadian Ministry of National Defense (Canada), study by, 224
capital: flexibility of, 170; flight, 162, 329; international, 162; ownership/control of, 164
capitalism, 24, 29; betrayal of, 68; contradictions in, 330; corporate, 155; cultural argument about, 331–32; democracy and, 155–56, 158, 161; global, 33, 34, 330, 347n5; logic of, 336; monopoly, 330; na-

tionalization/globalization of, 322; polis and, 26; race/gender and, 329; rationalism of, 24; substantive definition of, 346n1; transnational, 340; Weberian analysis of, 331. *See also* crony capitalism
Cargill, 191
Caribbean Basin Initiative, 202
cartels, 279–80
cash-crop sales, in Mozambique, 173, 174
casino economies, 193, 194
cattle: breeds of, 143; waste from, 141–44
Cavanagh, John, 324, 335
Cèdras, Raoul: freezing assets of, 217
Center for Conflict Resolution, 314
Center for International Studies, 318–19
CERES. *See* Coalition for Environmentally Responsible Economies
change: conceptualization of, 53; extreme wrongs and, 69–70; normal/system-transforming, 53; political, 114–21; post-Cold War, 55; problem of, 53–59
"Charter on the Safe Production of Toys," 199
Churchill, Winston: working class and, 251
citizens' groups, 207, 305; global firms and, 201
citizenship, 33, 80, 250, 287; democracy and, 164; global, 14, 30–31; overlapping, 25; social, 291
civilization: barbarism and, 293; clash of, 291–93, 303
civil society, 13–14, 102, 106, 256, 342; abstract morality in, 274n5; churnings of, 107–8; civil society and, 293; defining, 94, 105, 263–66, 267, 269, 270, 336–37; ecological movements and, 336; harmony in, 109; move to, 335; new conception of, 103–6; NGOs and, 268; notion of, 265–66; political promise of, 15; problems with, 103, 104, 334–35; rule of law and, 286; significance of, 13; state and, 106, 155, 269–70, 274n3, 274nn4, 5, 6, 310, 335; sustainable, 337; transnational, 267, 312; understanding, 336; vulnerable sections of, 104. *See also* global civil society

civitas, 103
Clark, Grenville, 314
Clarke, Tony, 205
Clash of Civilizations and the Remaking of World Order, The (Huntington), 111n5, 285
Clinton, Bill, 196; fast track and, 197
Coalition for Environmentally Responsible Economies (CERES), 272
cobalt cartel, 279–80
codes of conduct: developing, 197, 198–201, 228; labor rights and, 200, 204, 205
Cohen, Stan: on peace agreement, 119
Cold War: bipolar, 301; duties following, 93–95; end of, 1, 2–3; globalization of, 308; legitimacy and, 291; MOWB and, 251; national groupings during, 288; new world order and, 3; as ongoing struggle, 290; peace movement and, 75; peace of, 291
collective experience, 8, 152
collective guilt, 215; genocide and, 227
collective identity, 114, 115; developing, 227; relativized, 304; Yesh Gvul and, 123
collective life, 13; civil dimension of, 15; domestic level, 267; NGOs and, 270; violence/poverty and, 5
collective rights, protecting, 145–46
collective security, 308; problems for, 227–28; rethinking, 228
colonialism, 33, 83, 104, 250, 255; abolition of, 259; violence and, 131
"Coming Anarchy" (Kaplan), 285
Commission on Transnational Corporations, 198
Committee for a Peace Council, 248
Common Global Civilization: What Kind of Sovereignty, The (GCP), 318
common law, global, 81–84
communitas, 103
community, 26, 114, 132–35; destruction of, 193, 194–95; understanding of, 334
community rights, 146–47
competition, 153; fair, 330; globalization and, 137, 198, 330, 338
complexity theory, 36, 40; disillusionment

with, 37; limits to, 37, 44–48; normative commitments and, 48; policy problems and, 42; premises of, 41, 42, 47; strides in, 37, 41–44; value concerns and, 48; world affairs and, 41
compliance. *See* culture of compliance
Comprehensive Test Ban Treaty (1996), 302
computer simulations, 45, 48
conceptual frameworks, 39, 40, 60, 344
conflict formations, 69, 252–53
conflict resolution, 76, 248
conservation culture, 144; globalization and, 141
constitutional law, 86, 143
consumerism, 135, 282; neoliberalism and, 178
Contact Group, 256
contestation, 75; dilution of, 76
Convention on the Regulation of Antarctic Mineral Resources Activity (CRAMRA), 271
cooperation, 153; interstate, 246
core states, 292, 293
core values, 290, 296
corporate behavior, changing, 201, 203
corporate bill of rights, 191
"corporate democracy" movement, 204
counterfactuals, 52, 57, 62; importance of, 64
Cox, Robert, 27
craft guilds, work of, 241
CRAMRA. *See* Convention on the Regulation of Antarctic Mineral Resources Activity
Creation of a Just World Order (Falk), 317
Critchley, Simon: normative IR and, 342
critical theory, 65–66, 68, 69–70, 73; challenge of, 66; international law and, 71; reach of, 74; realism of, 76; rule of law and, 74; tasks of, 70, 76–77
crony capitalism, 182–85; Asian financial crisis and, 188; criticism of, 183
cultural difference, 33, 90, 109, 326
cultural factors, 212, 328
cultural practices, 276; global capitalism and, 327; plurality of, 303; transformations in, 322

culture, 322, 326–32, 347n6; conflict of, 303–4; epiphenomenal, 327; understanding, 326
culture of compliance, 209; culture of combat and, 212, 228–29; enforcement and, 214–16, 220; expanding, 219, 224; individual accountability and, 217; sanctions and, 216–17; UN and, 214–16, 217–18

Daly, Herman, 331
Dayton Accords, UN police and, 222
death-centered/life-continuity-centered model/paradigm, 231
Death of a Princess (film), protesting, 280
debtor power, 280, 282
decent government, limited government and, 152–53
decision-making centers, transnational, 165
decolonization, 110n4, 251, 277
deconstruction, 17, 21n14, 52; relativism and, 59
deep ecology, 336
DeKlerk, F. W., 48n7
democracy, 26, 107, 322, 326, 347n5; Asian brand of, 305; capitalism and, 155–56, 158; challenge of, 157; citizenship and, 164; community boundaries and, 164; concept of, 304, 332–37; cosmopolitan, 165; deepening of, 164; deterioration of, 193; as double-sided process, 164; economic life and, 153–61; equal interest in, 160; free market and, 151; future of, 164; globalization and, 135, 139, 195; growth of, 94, 158; legal, 153, 157; participation and, 257; redistribution and, 92; social justice and, 99–102; sphere of, 163; state sovereignty and, 334; threats to, 153–54; universalization of, 305
democratic age, transformation to, 106
democratic autonomy, 156, 157, 158
democratic conditions, delimiting, 161
Democratic law, international, 159
Democratic models, 304–5
Democratic Party, globalization and, 196
democratic political economy, 161
democratic processes/outcomes, 154, 155; distorting, 157

democratic rights/obligations, entrenchment of, 159, 163
democratization, 75, 296; potentialities of, 24
depolarization: historical dynamics of, 309; pluralist, 309
Derrida, Jacques, 329, 343, 347n12; on moral/political responsibility, 342; principle of reason and, 348n16; on theoretico-ethical decision, 342
Descartes, René, 29
Deutscher, Isaac: Great Contest and, 293
development, 304; alternative, 99; globalization and, 36, 131; poverty and, 102; profit-by-plunder, 194; vision of, 103
difference principle, 86, 87, 90, 92
Dillon, Michael, 337; on identity/difference, 347n15; on stranger, 340
distributive justice, 4, 9, 96nn7, 15; international, 79, 84, 87, 91–92; neoliberal globalization and, 166
Dole, Bob: globalization and, 196
double movement, 65, 66, 71, 76
double standards, 70–71, 74
Dow Jones, *Far Eastern Economic Review* and, 185
Doyle, Michael, 219, 323
Dunant, Henri, 256
Dunkel, Arthur: DDT and, 132
DuPont, Thapur and, 138–39
Durfee, Mary: on poverty, 166

Earth Summit, 130
East Asian Miracle, The (World Bank), 182–83, 188
ecological issues, 25, 148, 191, 322, 329, 339, 340; globalization and, 10, 130–31
ecological sustainability, 131, 207
Economic and Rehabilitation Program (PRE-2), Mozambique and, 174
economic globalization, 3, 12, 15, 39, 130, 162; social dislocation of, 17
economic growth, 3, 5, 12, 36, 99, 154, 162, 163, 169, 261; bamboo network and, 292; in Philippines, 176–77; in South, 81

economic journalism, problems with, 185–86
economics, 171, 253; concentration/centralization of, 153; democracy and, 157–61; interstate, 9; political intervention in, 151, 157; society and, 168; transformations in, 322
economic welfare, 164, 207
Economist, 186
ecopolitics/ecotechnology, 339
Eddie Bauer, 199
Ehrlich, Paul: population growth and, 95n5
Elliot, Dorinda, 186
Elson, Diane: on poverty, 174
embeddedness, Polanyi on, 169
emergent order, 38, 42; contradictions/ambiguities in, 39
eminent domain, 133
empirical, 53; normative and, 36
emplotment, 56, 63
END. *See* European Nuclear Disarmament
End of History, The (Fukuyama), 108
Ends of the Earth: A Journey at the Dawn of the Twenty-First Century, The (Kaplan), 294
end time, embracing, 232–33, 238–39
Enlightenment, 102, 266, 326
Enron power project, 135
environmental concerns, 135–37, 141, 157, 187–88, 194, 209, 247, 294, 322, 339; economics and, 136–37; Falk and, 317; globalization and, 137–39; trade and, 202
environmentalists, 196; labor groups and, 205
Environmental Protocol (1991), 271
EPZs. *See* Bataan EPZ; export-processing zones
equal rights, 90, 91, 156, 160, 310
equilibrium, 43, 53, 54
Essex's rebellion, 57
Estrada, Joseph, 182
ethics, 58, 326, 332, 338–40, 347n14; normative IR and, 338–44; politics and, 343; structural relationship and, 340
ethnic cleansing, 72, 73, 211, 218

ethnoscapes, landscapes and, 38
European Community, 25, 27, 33, 288; steel complex and, 281
European Nuclear Disarmament (END), 270, 272
European Union (EU), 12, 13, 76, 135, 275, 284, 308; decision-making by, 165; globalization and, 328
export-processing zones (EPZs), 168–69; women in, 176–77, 178
extreme wrongs, 66–70; change and, 69–70; extreme rights and, 67

failed states, symptoms of, 33
Falk, Richard, 79, 155; orientation of, 5–7; on values/scholarship, 5; work of, 4, 21n3, 311–13, 316–17
Fallows, James, 187
Far Eastern Economic Review, 185, 186, 187
fault-line wars, 292
FECWPTWL. *See* Fund for Education Concerning World Peace Through World Law
Federal Ministry of Environment, DuPont and, 138
Feketekutty, Gaza: DuPont and, 138
Fellowship magazine, metaphor in, 80
feminism, 116, 255, 333, 334; Falk and, 317; Israeli, 124–26; modernity and, 348n16; political mobilization of, 126; Third World writing on, 345
feudalism, 250, 332
Financial Times, 186, 187
finanscapes, landscapes and, 38
Fiore, Joachim de, 242
Fischer, Stanley, 184
fledgling theory, familiar premises and, 36–37
FMLN. *See* Frente Farabundo Marti de Liberacion Nacional
food insecurity, pricing mechanisms and, 173–74
foreign aid, 93, 95
foreign finances/markets, 182–85; moving away from, 189
Forsberg, Randy, 316
Foucault, Michel, 11, 325, 345; on analysis

of power, 333; on culture, 326, 327; governmentality and, 337
Four Mothers, 120–21, 126
Fox, Matthew, 346
fragmegration, 38, 47, 48, 48n1
fragmentation, 286, 290; social, 105
Frank, Thomas: workshop by, 315
free association, 264, 268
free market, 151, 159, 198, 268
Freemasons, 237, 238
free trade, 159, 201, 327, 330, 337, 338; obstructions to, 133; protectionism and, 196; TNCs and, 138
FRELIMO. *See* Mozambique Liberation Front
Frente Farabundo Marti de Liberacion Nacional (FMLN), skepticism of, 229n7
Friends of the Earth, 272
Fukuyama, Francis, 108, 109
fundamentalism, 104, 107, 294
Fund for Education Concerning World Peace Through World Law (FECWPTWL), 313, 314

Gabriel, Daniel: on market saturation, 172
Gaia, 244, 245, 247, 313
Galtung, Johann, 316
Gandhi, M. K., 331
Gandhi, Mahatma, 143, 145, 250; anticolonial struggle of, 255; Satyagraha and, 148
Gap: code of conduct by, 197, 206; monitoring of, 200
GATT. *See* General Agreement on Tariffs and Trade
GCP. *See* "Global Civilization: Challenges for Democracy, Sovereignty and Security"
Geertz, Clifford: on culture, 326
Gell-Mann, Murray, 40
Gellner, Ernest, 288
gender, 167, 177; food security and, 174; generation and, 250; globalization and, 172, 175, 178–79; in Israel, 127; marginalization and, 178–79
gender ideology, 168, 178; food cultivation

and, 174; hiring policies and, 177; production and, 171–72
General Agreement on Tariffs and Trade (GATT), 202, 284, 288; free-trade ideologies and, 327; multilateral treaties and, 132; Uruguay Round of, 130, 131
General Motors, 133, 196; CERES and, 272
genocide, 35, 73, 74, 211, 223, 231, 250–53; collective guilt and, 227; NGOs and, 297; prohibitions against, 210, 218, 226; silent, 66; treaty on, 317
geogovernance, 319, 320; Falk on, 209, 296; geopolitics and, 298
geopolitics, 252, 287, 296, 319, 320; geogovernance and, 298; speed/temporality and, 33, 34
Gephardt, Richard, 196
Gerasamov, Gennadi, 316
Giddens, Anthony, 286
Gifford, Kathie Lee: child labor and, 201
Gilpin, Robert, 92
global capitalism, 296, 322, 328, 329, 337, 338, 346n1; challenging, 335, 342; communities and, 341; competition and, 330; cultural practices and, 327; life/nature and, 331; North-South and, 336; state and, 335; triumph of, 344
"Global Civilization: Challenges for Democracy, Sovereignty and Security" (GCP), workshops by, 318
global civil society, 13, 15, 246, 293, 296, 319; associational life and, 267; character of, 262, 273; emergence of, 14, 266–69; global well-being and, 272–73; governance and, 263, 269–72, 273; NGOs and, 262, 270; skepticism about, 261–62; space for, 268; world order and, 270–71
global corporations. *See* multinational corporations
global economy, 13, 172
global factories, 193, 195
global governance, 209; defining, 255–56; global civil society and, 263; NGOs and, 262; soft, 259; structural component of, 267; third-way movement and, 206

globalization, 15, 18, 26, 28, 31, 65–66, 105, 107, 290, 328, 340; appeal of, 133; backlash against, 10, 191–92, 195–96, 203–6; capitalist, 326–27, 330; challenges of, 8–9, 19, 193, 196–98; corporate-led, 191–93, 195–201, 203, 206; dynamics of, 137, 148, 192, 197; as environmental apartheid, 135–37; ideology of, 134–35, 168; impact of, 24, 148; intersocietal dimension to, 13; public interest and, 135, 167; as quasi-universalization, 32; social implications of, 10–11, 130–31; understanding, 171; violence of, 148–49; waves of, 131–32; *See also* economic globalization
globalization from above, 203; challenging, 198
globalization from below, 206; Falk on, 191, 192; promise of, 207
Global Political Economy: Trends and Preferences (GCP), 318
global processes, double movements of, 65, 76
global reach, 192, 206–7
global wars, interstate wars and, 252–53
GNP. *See* gross national product
Godoy, Horazo, 316
Golde, Dr.: Mo-cell line and, 134
governance, 322, 326; effective, 12, 285, 337; existing system of, 284; future of, 284; global civil society and, 269–72; as governmentality, 338; international pattern of, 288; market-driven, 337; mechanisms of, 11, 13; pattern of, 284, 285, 289–90, 289 (table); question of, 337–38
Gramsci, Antonio, 337; economic and, 327; on state/civil society, 269–70; war of position and, 270
grassroots organizations (GROs), 247
Greenpeace, 14, 268, 270, 271, 305; hazardous wastes and, 140, 141
Greenspan, Alan, 325
Grossman, David, 113
gross national product (GNP), 67; in East Asia, 183; in Mozambique, 172, 180n2; in Rwanda, 180n2

Grosz, Elizabeth, 344
Grotius, Hugo: Falk on, 4
Group of Seven, 25, 162; Asian financial crisis and, 181
Guatemalan Labor Education Project, Starbucks and, 199
Gulf Cooperation Council, 282
Gulf War, 238, 291–92; aftermath of, 119; legitimation and, 302; UN and, 301–2; women's peace movement and, 125
Guru worship, 233, 234, 236

Hague System (1899), 257
Hardin, Garret, 95n6; lifeboat of, 87; population growth and, 95n5
Harim-al-Sharif massacre, 119
Harrison, Beverly: on domination, 345–46
Hart, H. L. A., 84
Hayakawa, S. I.: Panama Canal and, 84
Hayek, Friedrich, 151, 155, 156, 157; on free market, 152; on free society, 152; market relations and, 153; on neoliberalism, 153
Hegel, Georg Wilhelm Friedrich, 264, 265; on state/civil society, 274nn3, 4, 5
hegemony, 102, 276, 301, 302
Heidegger, Martin, 347n11; on human dwelling, 332
Held, David, 335
Hibakushas, 306
Hidden Order (Holland), 40
high-performing Asian community (HPAE), 183
Hiroshima, 307, 317; voices from, 306
historical understanding, 58, 62, 63; emplotment/interpretation and, 56
history: abuse of, 54, 57–59; axial ages and, 240; denial of, 54–57; neorealists and, 55; theory/struggle and, 346
Hitler, Adolf, 57, 253
Hobbes, Thomas, 29, 31, 61, 330, 332
Hobsbawm, Eric, 284
Holland, John H.: mathematical theory by, 40
Hollins, Harry, 314, 315
homogenization, 14, 99
householding, 169, 274n4

HPAE. *See* high-performing Asian community
human capital, investment in, 161, 163
humane governance, 23, 262, 273, 295–98, 311; development of, 297, 312; Falk on, 165, 285, 298, 320; global civil society and, 263; searching for, 7–10; theoretical frame/definition of, 319–20; workshop on, 318
"Humane Governance" (Falk), 285
Humane Governance: Toward a New Global Politics (Falk), 318
humanitarianism, 93, 223, 229; global, 82
human rights, 4, 9, 58, 98, 107, 118, 209, 210, 246; codes of conduct and, 199; Falk and, 317; function of, 258; infractions of, 254; NGOs and, 297; norms for, 211; peace movements and, 75; protecting, 71, 219, 220, 222; respect for, 210, 222, 271; South African police performance on, 219; universalization of, 304, 305; violations of, 135, 226, 308; women's, 247
Human Rights Watch, 271
Huntington, Samuel, 109, 187, 285, 291, 295, 296, 303; on civilizations, 108, 298, 299n3; on civil society/globalization, 293; legitimization and, 293; model by, 298; on multicivilizational world, 292–93; on universalizing mission, 292
Hussein, Saddam, 215, 291–92; and Asahara compared, 238
hydroelectric projects, 101, 281
hypothesis testing, self-correcting process of, 51

idealism, 16, 27, 31
identity, 26, 114, 323–24; communal, 243; deconstruction of, 129; defense/reassertion of, 121; essentialist, 291; ethnic, 75, 105, 291; peace movement and, 123; statehood and, 259; understanding of, 324, 334. *See also* collective identity; national identity; political identity
identity politics, 113–14; Israeli-Jewish collectivity and, 128–29; Israeli peace move-

ment and, 127–28; social movements and, 121–27
ideology, 99, 233; depolarization of, 303; relativization of, 301, 303–5
ideoscapes, landscapes and, 38
IGOs. *See* intergovernmental organizations
ILO. *See* International Labor Organization
IMF. *See* International Monetary Fund
immigration, 82, 92
income: average per capita, 67, 81; basic, 158; gaps, 188, 259; redistribution of, 87, 91, 97n16; skill and, 275
India International Center, 147
Indian Cultural Heritage, 143
individuals: accountability for, 210, 211, 215, 217, 227–28; rights of, 91
Industrial Development Act, 139
inequality, 153, 191; economic, 79, 80–81; increase in, 94, 193; neoliberalism and, 178
INGOs. *See* international nongovernmental organizations
Institute for International Order, 314
Institute for Policy Studies, on billionaires/wealth, 193
Institute for World Order, 314
intellectual property rights (IPRs), 133, 328; biodiversity and, 146–47; claims to, 144; private funding/public institutions and, 134; TNCs and, 144–45; trade-related, 145
interdependence, 25, 297
intergovernmental organizations (IGOs), 246, 257
International Association of Lawyers Against Nuclear Arms, 318
International Council of Scientific Union, environmental change and, 244
International Court of Justice (World Court), 210, 242, 315; Advisory Opinion from, 317–18; nuclear war and, 307
International Criminal Court, 223, 226–27, 315
International Forum on Globalization, 197, 204, 205
international governmental organizations (IGOs), 256

International Labor Organization (ILO), 331; workers' rights and, 193, 202
International Labor Rights Fund, creation of, 201–2
international law, 20, 86, 287; accountability to, 70–71, 210, 212, 223; critical theory and, 71; double movements in, 71; global elite and, 70; nuclear weapons and, 307; sanctions and, 73; TNCs and, 159; violation of, 139
International Monetary Fund (IMF), 132, 136, 162, 206, 284, 288, 331, 336; Asian financial crisis and, 183–84, 189; development and, 160; free-market ideology and, 203; globalization and, 328; Mozambique and, 172, 174
international nongovernmental organizations (INGOs), 244, 246, 334; conflict within, 248; educational, 247–48; limited power of, 248; peace building and, 247–48; scientific, 247; super-, 257
international organizations, 12–13, 161; redistribution and, 85, 90
International Peace Bureau, 257
International Peace Research Association, 243
international people's organizations (IPOs), 256, 258
international relations (IR), 35; antecedents for, 6; challenging, 325–38, 346; culture/identity in, 328; domesticating, 228; ethical sensibility and, 344; interest in, 1–2, 3, 287, 343; international law and, 86; normative/realist consensus of, 323; skepticism about, 1, 2–3, 9; as social science, 6; state-centric character of, 9; theories of, 31; U.S. foreign policy and, 6. *See also* normative international relations
international relations theory, 30, 36; poststructural/postpositivist, 35; problematic analogies of, 52; rereading/rewriting, 346; tradition of, 20
International Social Science Council, environmental change and, 244
International Trade Organization, 202
international tribunals, 223, 227

interstate war: elimination of, 297; global wars and, 252–53
intervention, 9, 307–8; forms/levels of, 161–62; political, 151, 157
intifada, 115, 116–19, 124
IPOs. *See* international people's organizations
IPRs. *See* intellectual property rights
IR. *See* international relations; normative international relations
Iraq: sanctions against, 217; UN operation against, 216
Ishihara, Shintaro, 326
Islamic Confucian Connection, struggle against, 187
Israeli economy, world Jewry and, 275, 276
Israeli-Jewish collectivity, 126–27; identity politics and, 128–29; Israeli-Palestinian conflict and, 112, 121; Palestinian women prisoners and, 125
Israeli-Palestinian conflict, 118; centrality of, 112–13; Israeli-Jewish collectivity and, 112, 121
Israeli peace movement, 114, 115; identity crisis and, 127–28; Oslo Accords and, 120–21; political reality and, 121; slogans of, 117–18. *See also* peace movement; women's peace movement
Israeli Women Against the Occupation, 117
Israeli Women's Peace Net, 117
issues, relativization of, 301, 305–8
IT&T, Allende coup and, 198

Jafri, Afsar H., 147
Jaramillo, Fernando, 131, 132
Jerusalem Center for Women, 120
Jerusalem Link, 120
jobs/wages, erosion of, 191, 193
Johansen, Robert, 335
"Just and Sustainable Trade and Development Initiative for North America" (NAFTA), 205
justice, 99, 103; as fairness, 84, 85–87; global, 82, 98
justice package, 211, 220
just-war theory, 4, 9

Kahn, Herman, 235
Kaldor, Mary, 323
Kant, Immanuel, 31, 89, 97n15, 274n2; spirit of commerce and, 9
Kantor, Mickey: GATT and, 132
Kaplan, Robert D., 285, 291, 296, 297, 298; argument of, 294–95
Karnataka Assembly, 146
Kaufmann, Stuart, 40; on self-organization, 48n4
Keane, John, 274n3
Kellogg-Briand Pact (1928), 253
Kennedy, Paul: on Africa, 78n3
Keohane, Robert, 64n1
Keynesianism, global, 94
Kim Dae Jung, 304
Kothari, Rahjni, 316, 323
Kothari, Smitu, 335
Krasner, 56, 58, 63
Kratochwil, Fritz, 325; on culture/identity, 328
Krishna Iyer, V. R., 147
Kristeva, Julia, 341
Kwapong, Alexander, 283n3

labor: child, 101; codes of conduct and, 200; flexibility/mobility of, 170; gender division of, 168; trade and, 202. *See also* trade unions
Labor Party, 120, 125
Laclau, Ernesto, 342
Lagos, Gustavo, 316
Lapid, Josef: on culture/identity, 328; on pluralism, 52
LAs. *See* local authorities
Lawyers Committee on UN Policy, 317
LDCs. *See* Less Developed Countries
League of Nations, 242, 253, 256, 308
Lebanon invasion (1982), 115–16; opposition to, 125
Lederach, John Paul, 224
Lee Kuan-yew, 304
Leeson, Nick, 186
Legal and Political Problems of World Order (LPPWO), 314, 315
legitimacy, 23, 50, 61; Cold War and, 291; gap in, 93; Gulf War and, 302; patrio-

tism and, 286; political institutions and, 285–91; relativization of, 305; war and, 287

Leipzig Conference on Plant Genetic Resources, 134

Leopold, Aldo, 339

Less Developed Countries (LDCs), North and, 281

Letzter, Irit: Four Mothers and, 126

Levinas, Emmanuel, 338, 340, 347n12

Levi Strauss, Claude: corporate behavior and, 199, 206

liberalism, 16, 26, 46, 84, 303; criticism of, 287; economic, 145, 337, 338; redistribution and, 85–92, 93

life expectancy: in Africa/Japan compared, 68; increase in, 94

Lifton, Robert, 323

Likud Party, 113, 125

Lincoln, Abraham: sovereignty and, 61

Linn, Paul, 316

Litvinov, Maxim: on peace, 308

"Living on a Lifeboat" (Hardin), 87

Liz Claiborne, 199; corporate behavior change for, 206

local authorities (LAs), 256, 257, 258, 329; freedom/identity and, 259

location, ownership and, 62

Locke, John, 89, 274n2, 332; civil society and, 265; common law and, 82; radical interpretation of, 83–84

Long-Term Capital, 183, 184

Looking at the Sun (Fallows), 187

Lovelock, James: Gaia and, 244

LPPWO. *See* Legal and Political Problems of World Order

Lyotard, Jacques: on poststructuralism, 16

MacNamara, Robert, 318

Madrid peace process, 119, 125

Magnusson, Warren, 328

Mahathir bin Mohamad, 182, 283n4, 304, 326; Asian financial crisis and, 189; Soros and, 347n5

MAI. *See* Multilateral Agreement on Investments

Major, John, 215

male, old, white bourgeois (MOWB), 252, 253, 255, 259; Anglo Saxon and, 250–51; Cold War and, 251; fighting, 250, 254; ruling states and, 250

Mandela, Nelson, 43

Mann, Michael, 286

Mao Zedong, 96n7, 250

maps, axial-age, 244–45

Maquiladora zone, 194

Marcos, Ferdinand, 185, 336, 337; crony capitalism and, 182

marginalization, 325, 334, 336; gender and, 178–79; globalization and, 167–68, 171, 178–79, 193; poverty and, 171; sustaining, 171; women and, 178

markets, 10, 11–15, 171; reframing, 157–61; neoliberalism and, 153, 169; nonmarket social factors in, 153

Marx, Karl, 24, 27, 70, 103, 330, 331; on culture, 326; economic and, 327

Matsumoto, gas release at, 232

Mazrui, Ali, 316, 318, 324

McDougal: on human dignity, 57; policy science and, 63

McKinley Tariff Act (1890), 201

McVeigh, Timothy, 231

mediascapes, landscapes and, 38

Melucci, Alberto, 121, 127

Mendlovitz, Saul: on Falk/WOMP, 20

Meretz Party, 119, 120

Merriwether, John, 184

military enforcement, 216; culture of, 228; deficiency of, 218

Milosevic, Slobodan, 69, 77

Ministry of Agriculture (Mozambique), on women/transport, 175

mission civiliatrice, 243

Mittleman, James, 324

Miyazawa Plan, 181

MNCs. *See* multinational corporations

"Model Business Principles," 200

modernity, 24; challenging, 32–39; failures/betrayals of, 110n4; feminism and, 348n16

Mohanty, Chandra: on feminism, 345

money: accumulating, 82; tacit and voluntary establishment of, 82

Monroe Doctrine, 253
Montesquieu, civil society and, 265
Moore, Barrington, Jr.: world-order values
  and, 5
Moore, John, 134
moral issues, 80, 90, 92
Morgenthau, Hans, 20–21n1
Mothers Against Silence, 116
MOWB. *See* male, old, white bourgeois
Mozambique: farming sector in, 168–69;
  GNP in, 180n2; growth spurts in, 169;
  hunger in, 173; neoliberal reform in,
  174; poverty in, 172–75, 178; skill in,
  275
Mozambique Liberation Front (FRELIMO),
  172
Mozambique National Resistance Movement (RENAMO), 172
multilateral Agreement on Investments
  (MAI), 198, 206, 347n9
multilateralism, 105, 108, 132
multinational corporations (MNCs), 246;
  CERES and, 272; collaboration with,
  96n7; globalization and, 268; influence
  of, 155, 191; opposition to, 192–93; political action and, 158
multipolarity, 33, 111n5, 309; bipolarity
  and, 54–55
Murdoch, Rupert, 185
mutual aid, development and, 304

Nader, Ralph: corporate-led globalization
  and, 196; global governance and, 206
NAFTA. *See* North American Free Trade
  Agreement
Nagasaki, 307, 317; voices from, 306
Naik, Nilesh, 139
Nakarada, Radmila, 323, 343
Nation, The, 250; Israeli identity crisis and,
  113
National Front for Tribal Self-Rule, 145
national identity, 125, 288; nation building
  and, 290
nationalism, 26, 30, 77, 96n7
National Labor Committee (NLC), 200
National Police Agency, Aum and, 232

national security, 91, 122, 248; primacy of,
  123, 129
nation-states, 286, 287, 289–90, 297
NATO, 75, 76, 252, 253, 256, 284, 298,
  308; in Bosnia, 214; France and, 43;
  transformation of, 42, 285
Navdanya, 148
Neo-Kantians, 89–90, 91
neoliberal globalization, 179; distributive
  justice and, 166; poverty and, 168
neoliberalism, 151, 170, 328; consumerism
  and, 178; globalization and, 166, 169; inequality and, 178; markets and, 153,
  169; poverty and, 178–79; utopia and,
  151–53
neorealists, 51, 64n2; history and, 55; policy
  recommendations by, 55–56
Nerfin, Marc, 132; on state/economy/civil
  society, 13
Netanyahu, Benjamin, 128
Neuordnung, 251, 253
New Institutional Trinity, 132
New International Economic Order, 79, 282
New International Information Order, 280,
  282
New Livestock Policy, 141
newly industrializing countries (NICs),
  187–88
newly industrializing economies (NIEs),
  304, 305
New Republic, 294
"New Type of Intellectual: The Dissident,
  A" (Kristeva), 341
new world order, 107, 189–90, 251, 300;
  Cold War end and, 3; unipolar, 308
NGOs. *See* nongovernmental organizations
Nicholas II, 242
NICs. *See* newly industrializing countries
NIEs. *See* newly industrializing economies
Nike: citizen campaign against, 199; code of
  conduct by, 197; labor infractions by,
  201
NLC. *See* National Labor Committee
Nongovernmental organizations (NGOs),
  91, 104, 105, 256, 257, 258, 296, 297,
  336; civil society and, 262, 268, 270; ef-

forts of, 242, 262, 273; freedom/identity and, 259; Gap/code of conduct and, 200; global governance and, 262, 271–72; growth of, 93–94, 199, 294; hazardous waste importation and, 141; lobbying by, 271–72; NAFTA and, 202; networks of, 258; redistribution and, 90; third-way movement and, 202, 206. *See also* international nongovernmental organizations

normative, 26, 109; character of, 7–19, 70; empirical and, 36

normative international relations, 17, 65, 301, 335; advancing, 3, 7, 16, 19, 23; axial ages and, 240; body politic and, 344–46; challenge of, 66, 342; civil society and, 332; ethical and, 338–44; Falk and, 3–7, 19–20, 311–12; future of, 322–25; marginalization of, 15; poststructuralists and, 181; rethinking, 15, 324–25; strands of, 4; study of, 311, 325, 343; WOMP and, 5. *See also* international relations

normative theory, 7, 239; empirical observations and, 35; engaging in, 23; globalization and, 8–9; political practice and, 20; state and, 9

North: debtor power and, 280; global capitalism and, 336; hegemonic power of, 276; LDCs and, 281; South and, 276, 344

North American Free Trade Agreement (NAFTA), 25, 196, 206; debate over, 191, 197; globalization and, 328; plan by, 205, 282

northern finance capital, 184; Asian financial crisis and, 188

North-South relations, 67, 79, 98, 204, 275; diversification for, 282; Southern empowerment in, 279

Northwest: challenge to, 251; leadership from, 252; support for, 251

Nozick, Robert, 151, 155; market relations and, 153; on utopia, 152

nuclear issues, 235–36, 239, 302, 305–7, 309

Nuclear Weapon Free Zone Treaties, 247

nuclear weapons, 35, 317; eliminating, 318; international law and, 307

"Nuclear Weapons and International Law" (Falk, Meyerowitz, and Sanderson), 317

Nuremberg Code, 317

Nussbaum, Martha, 96n11; distributive justice and, 97n13

Nyerere, Julius, 280, 283n5

OAU. *See* Organization of African Unity obligation, 26, 87, 95

Occupied Territories, 119, 120, 122, 123; intifada and, 117

OECD. *See* Organization for Economic Cooperation and Development

official declared aid (ODA), 67

Ogata, Sadako, 74, 78n8

O'Neill, Onora, 95n6

One-Third World, 247

On Humane Governance (Falk), 79, 318

OPEC. *See* Organization of Petroleum Exporting Countries

Operation Desert Storm, 214, 215

Organization for Economic Cooperation and Development (OECD), 162, 198, 328; toxic waste and, 140

Organization for Security and Cooperation in Europe (OSCE), 285, 298

Organization of African States, 12

Organization of African Unity (OAU), 280, 288

Organization of Petroleum Exporting Countries (OPEC), 88, 275, 279

organizations: invasive role for, 13; proliferation of, 39

OSCE. *See* Organization for Security and Cooperation in Europe

Oslo Accords (1993), 113, 115, 125, 127; aftermath of, 119–21; interpretation of, 121, 128; Israeli peace movement and, 120–21

Other, 340; Same and, 341; Self and, 338, 339

Overseas Private Investment Corporation, 202

OXFAM, 14, 90, 270

Pacific Union, 91
PACs. *See* political action committees
Paine, Thomas: civil society and, 265
panaceas: appeal of, 47–48; searching for,
    39–41
Panchayati Raj Act, 139, 146
parachute journalism, problems with,
    185–86
Parents Against Silence, 116, 124
particularity, universality and, 30, 32, 34,
    293
patriarchy, 177, 255, 348n16; institutional-
    ization of, 168
patriotism, 288, 290; legitimacy and, 286
Pattuvam Panchayat, 146–47; biodiversity
    register of, 147
Pauly, Louis: on capital mobility, 61
peace, 209, 255, 307–8, 323–24; century of,
    258; crimes against, 211, 225; culture of,
    248; divisibility of, 308; local, 308, 309;
    norms for, 211, 228; by peaceful means,
    76; positive/negative, 243; rethinking,
    324–25; security and, 324; upholding,
    222; war and, 308
Peace Academy, on Security Council, 221
Peace Brigades International, 247
peace building, 92, 95, 113–14; INGOs
    and, 247–48; monitoring, 222
peacekeepers/peacekeeping, 228, 246, 247;
    culture of compliance and, 217; defined,
    214; global legitimacy for, 218; negative
    factors in, 218; police and, 219; UN,
    213, 224–25
peace movement, 76, 116, 248, 305; human
    rights movements and, 75; identity and,
    123; international, 257. *See also* Israeli
    peace movement; women's peace move-
    ment
Peace Now, 115
Peace of Westphalia (1648), 251
Peace Research Institute, 314
People's Commission on Biodiversity and
    Indigenous Knowledge and People's
    Knowledge, 147
peoples' movements, 105, 246
Peres, Shimon, 119

Perot, Ross, 197
"Perpetual Peace" (Kant), 97n15
Philippines: economic growth in, 176–77;
    export-processing industries in, 168–69;
    growth spurts in, 169; poverty in, 176–
    78, 178–79
Plato, 18
Plunkett, Mark: on justice package, 220
pluralism, 52, 105, 106, 107; historical dy-
    namics of, 309; normative, 341
Pluto, 44
poa, understanding, 233–34
Pogge, Thomas, 86
Polanyi, Karl, 27, 169, 179
police, 209, 210, 212–14, 230n15; establish-
    ing, 228–29; and military forces com-
    pared, 213; monitoring by, 211; peace-
    keeping missions by, 219; problems with,
    215, 230n19; "us-us" relationship with,
    224. *See also* United Nations Civilian Po-
    lice; United Nations police
political action committees (PACs), 183
political identity, 114, 289; critical dimen-
    sions of, 325–38
political process, 154; globalization and, 15,
    130–31; transformations in, 32, 322
politics, 5, 332, 339, 340; changing charac-
    ter of, 7–8; concepts of, 24, 26, 50, 58,
    163; corporate control of, 205; ethics
    and, 343; legitimacy/security and,
    285–91; limits of science of, 50; marketi-
    zation of, 337; modern, 28, 30, 190;
    problematic of, 30; re-imaging, 23, 25–
    26, 34, 38, 53; self-interest and, 24; sov-
    ereignty and, 28; women's issues and,
    125. *See also* geopolitics; identity politics;
    world politics
Politika, on average per capita income, 67
polity, 312, 321; centralizing tendencies of,
    107; decomposing, 294; global, 91; mac-
    rostructures of, 105
pollution, 89, 136–37, 237; importation of,
    137–39; rights violation and, 83; Third
    World, 137
poststructuralism, 11, 21n13; challenge of,
    17, 18, 19; metanarrative and, 16; nor-
    mative IR and, 19, 181

Pot, Pol, 57
poverty, 106, 110n4, 254, 316; absolute, 81; alleviation of, 68, 88, 94, 169, 179; collective life and, 5; conceptualization of, 171; crime and, 101; decrease in, 166, 167, 171; defined, 166, 170–71; development and, 102, 173; globalization and, 137, 167, 169, 178; marginalization and, 171; in Mozambique, 172–75, 178; neoliberalism and, 168, 169–72, 178–79; persistence of, 101; in Philippines, 176–79; prevailing approach to, 102; reconceptualizing, 169–72; social, 102, 170–72, 179; state spending and, 174–75; as static category, 170; subjective dimensions of, 166; underplaying problems of, 100; understanding, 167; unemployment and, 101; women and, 173, 175, 176–78, 329, 334
Poverty (World Bank), 171
power, 338; analysis of, 333; centralization/secularization of, 286; internationalization/relativization of, 302; logics of, 24; pluralization of, 301–2; practical character of, 333–34; relational/dialogic interpretation of, 332; rule of law and, 70–74; structure of, 301
pragmatism, 46, 64
praxis, understanding, 59–63
PRE-2. *See* Economic and Rehabilitation Program
Preservation and Management of Violent Conflict European Platform, 257
preventive capacity, 68, 308
pricing mechanisms, food insecurity and, 173–74
Primakov, Evgeni, 318
primitive commodities, value of, 82
prisoners, mistreatment of, 201, 211
private property, 265; free market and, 151
problem solving, 50, 108–9
producer power, 282
production: gender ideology and, 171–72; organization/segmentation of, 172; poverty and, 170–72
Progressive Technologies Corporation, 134

property, 59; international, 82, 89, 90
protectionism, 130, 133; free trade and, 196; linkage and, 204; nationalistic, 196
Provisions of the Panchayats (Extension to the Scheduled Areas) Act (1996), 146
Public Interest Research Group, hazardous wastes and, 141
public investment, 161–62; globalization and, 167; support for, 162
Pugwash Conferences, 314
pull-in factor/push-out factor, 278

quota refugees, EPZs and, 176

Rabin, Yitzhak, 119; assassination of, 128, 231; Oslo Accords and, 113, 128
Radical Lockeans, 83–84
Rawls, John, 96n11; contractarian solution of, 58; maximum equal liberty, 89; veil of ignorance and, 86
realism, 46, 87–88; Aristotelian, 29; logic of, 91–92; obligation and, 87; political, 2–3, 31; redistribution and, 93; science and, 21n1
redistribution, 69, 96nn7, 16, 153; debates for/against, 81–93; just, 91; liberals and, 81–87; mixed views of, 92–93; morality of, 81; standard of living and, 82
relativization, 52, 303–8, 310n1; cultural, 303; deconstruction and, 59; dynamics of, 309; issue, 301, 305–8; nihilistic, 60; self-, 300, 302. *See also* age of relativization
RENAMO. *See* Mozambique National Resistance Movement
Republican Party, globalization and, 195–96
Research Foundation for Science, Technology and Ecology (RFSTE), 147; hazardous wastes and, 141; litigation by, 140
Reuters, 186
RFSTE. *See* Research Foundation for Science, Technology and Ecology
Rio agenda: GATT/WTO and, 130; sustainability agenda and, 130
Rodney, Walter, 83
Rome Treaty (1998), 210

Rosenau, James, 269, 325; on NGOs, 274n11; on poverty, 166

Rosenberg, Robert: on intifada, 116

Rousseau, Jean-Jacques, 24, 274n2 on civil society, 287

Rubin, Robert: on Asian financial crisis, 184; on good information, 182

rule of law, 221, 254–55; accountability to, 210; civil society and, 286; critical theory and, 74; power and, 70–74; preservation of, 152; social justice and, 155

rural life, 175; decentralization of, 106

Rwanda: civil war in, 307; GNP in, 180n2

Ryan, Michael: cultural practice and, 327

Saint Pierre, Abbé: peace project of, 287

Sakamoto, Yoshikazu, 316, 324, 334

Saker, Neil, 186, 187

Salinas, Carlos: NAFTA and, 202

sanctions, 228; acclaim for, 72–73; culture of compliance and, 216–17; effective, 211, 217; international law and, 73; UN, 72, 214

Santa Fe Institute, complexity theory and, 40

Sarkaria, R. S., 147

"Scheme of Global Social Cooperation," 90

Schumacher, E. F., 331

Schumpeter, Joseph: on unbounded politics, 163

science, 29, 36; realism and, 21n1; self-correcting process of, 51

Sears, code of conduct by, 199

security, 229, 298, 323–24; civilizational, 293; defining, 284–85; humane governance and, 296; institutions and, 290; peace and, 324; political institutions and, 285–91; redistribution and, 92; rethinking, 324–25. *See also* collective security

"Seed Keepers" (poem), 149, 149n1

Seed Satyagraha, 148

Selective Service Act, 317

Self, Other and, 338, 339

self-determination, 71, 89, 90, 128, 159, 160; accommodation and, 152; national, 112; Palestinian, 124; principle of, 72, 76; struggle for, 116

self-organization, 48, 295; emergency properties and, 42

self-regulating markets, 169, 170

self-rule, 145, 146

Sen, Amartya, 96n11

Shaknazarov, Georgi: WOMP and, 318

Shalikashvili, John, 229n12

Shambala, 235

Shamuyarira, Nathan, 318

Shani, demonstrations by, 117

Shaping Global Polity (GCP), 318

Sharoni, Simona, 333

Shell, corporate behavior change for, 206

Shinjuku Station, cyanide gas in, 232

Shiva, Vandana, 324, 334

simultaneity, challenge of, 33, 34

Singer, Peter, 84, 85, 95nn4, 6; on Northern expenditures, 95n3

Singh, Kuldeep, 147

skill, 276, 282; caste system of, 275; income and, 275; power of, 279; transfer of, 277–79

slavery, 250, 255, 259

small events, power of, 43

Smiley, Marion: on ethics, 58

Smith, Adam, 265, 330

Smith, Dorothy: on relations of ruling, 346

Smith, Steve: on normative discussions, 21n12

Smithsonian Institution, nuclear exhibit at, 306

social change, 103, 114

Social Chapter of the European Maastricht Agreement, 159

social contract, 86–87, 88

social cooperation, 14, 86

social interdependence, redistribution/ products of, 86–87

social investment, management of, 161, 162

socialism, 26, 156, 290

social justice, 91, 106, 131, 207, 311, 316; democracy and, 99–102; global, 87, 98; rule of law and, 155

social movement, 21n9, 98; constraints on, 115; identity politics and, 121–27; Israeli peace movement and, 120; political change and, 114–21

social practices, 58, 241

social rights, 253; civil/political rights and, 288

social systems, 53–54, 246
social texts, deconstruction of, 17
social welfare, 97n16, 164, 304
societas civilas, 263, 269, 274n2
society, 11–15; economy and, 168
Society for General Systems, 243
sociosphere, 245–47
Soelle, Dorothee, 346
Sohn, Louis, 314, 315
solidarity: erosion of, 76; organic/strategic, 279, 280–81; South-South, 279–82
Somalia: police in, 220–21; rule of law in, 221
Soros, George, 184, 325, 330; Mahathir and, 347n5
South: brain drain from, 277; capitalist globalization and, 330; dependency of, 278; expertise in, 277–78; global capitalism and, 336; initiatives by, 276; long-term strategizing for, 279; negotiations skills for, 280; North and, 139–41, 344; solidarity in, 277, 278–82
South Commission, 79, 93
sovereignty, 56–57, 63, 322, 337; democracy and, 334; development of, 61; as dualism, 26–28; erosion of, 38; globalization and, 26–27, 31; language of, 61; misconceptions about, 30; paradoxical/dialectical character of, 27; politics and, 28; principle of, 28, 29; territorial, 128. *See also* state sovereignty
Soviet Union, collapse of, 43, 284
spatiality, 31; speed/temporality and, 33, 34
spirit of commerce, 9; globalized economy and, 10
Spivak, Gayatri: on IR theory, 341
Srishti, hazardous wastes and, 141
standardization, 86, 99
Starbucks: code of conduct by, 197; Guatemalan Labor Education Project and, 199
Star Television, 185
state, 11–15, 132–35; changes for, 38; civil society and, 155, 269–70, 310, 335; cultural community and, 27; deligitimation of, 103; globalization and, 9, 27, 34, 335; identity and, 259; legitimacy/authority and, 109; as particular practice, 335; twentieth-century horrors and, 253–54
state sovereignty, 31, 293; decline of, 23–24; politics of, 33, 34; preserving, 330; principle of, 286
state system, 54, 322; alternative to, 9–10; end of, 255
Stimson, Henry, 306
Strategy of World Order, The (Falk and Mendlovitz), 315
Strauss, Leo, 24
structural adjustment, 54, 173, 175, 327, 337, 338; Third World, 296
struggle, theory/history and, 346
Study of Future Worlds, A (Falk), 316–17
subjectivities, 26, 29, 30, 31; embodied experience and, 345; multiple, 32, 33; political, 341; within/without, 32
subjects/subject positions, multiplicity of, 341, 342
Summers, Lawrence, 138; crony capitalism and, 182, 183; World Development Report and, 136
Sun Company, CERES and, 272
Sunday Times, Malaysia and, 280
suprastatism, IR and, 12
Supreme Court of India: Al-Kabeer Slaughterhouse case and, 141; toxic waste and, 140
sustainability, 79, 130, 145, 148, 320; livestock and, 143

Taborsky, Peter, 134
Tambe, Ashwini, 324
Tamil Nadu, nylon 6, 6 plant and, 138
technology, 104, 341; dependency on, 188; transformations in, 322
technoscapes, landscapes and, 38
terrorism, 250, 255
Thai economy, Asian financial crisis and, 184, 186, 189
Thapur, DuPont and, 138–39
theory, 50; crisis of, 102–3; history/struggle and, 346; process and, 59; reality and, 63–64
Theory of Justice, A (Rawls), 86

"There Is a Limit to the Oppression" (petition), 117

Theresa, Mother, 85

Third way, 202; as countervailing power, 203–6; global governance and, 206

Third World: abolition of war and, 316; cooperation within, 279; democracy/globalization and, 135; electrical systems among, 281; globalization and, 132, 193; Northern Hemisphere and, 276; pollution in, 137; skill in, 277; structural adjustment in, 296; technological illiteracy for, 282

Third World Network, 204

Thomas, George, 267

TIAP, 253

Tikkun, 113

Time Warner, 192; *Asia Week* and, 185

Tito, Josip Broz, 72

TNCs. *See* transnational corporations

Tocqueville, Alexis de, 153; civil society and, 265

Tojo, 239, 250

Toward a Just World Order for the 21st Century (GCP), 318

Towards a Rapid Reaction Capability for the United Nations (Ministry of Foreign Affairs/Ministry of National Defense), 224

Toxics Link Exchange, 141

Toynbee, Arnold: on middle classes, 299n3

trade, 62; deficits, 188; fair, 196; inter-African, 281–82; labor/environmental rights and, 202; liberalization, 326; market-driven, 338; South-South, 281. *See also* free trade

Trade Act (1988), 202; free trade and, 131

trade agreements: environmental codes and, 204, 205; labor/environment in, 197, 201–3; workers' rights and, 201–2

trade unions: environmental groups and, 205; linkage among, 204; pressure from, 203; third-way movement and, 206. *See also* labor

transformations, 25, 39, 50, 68; historical/structural, 26

transnational associations, profusion of, 267

transnational corporations (TNCs), 132, 135, 136, 256, 257, 258; biodiversity and, 147; countervailing power to, 201; free trade and, 138; globalization and, 192; growth/reach of, 192–93; international law and, 159; IPRs and, 144–45; overcoming, 138–39

transnationalization, 8, 14, 65–66, 288

Treaty of the Pyrenees, 56

Treaty of Westphalia (1648), 256

Truman, Harry, 306

truth: discourses of, 333; problematic understanding of, 60

Tucker, Robert W.: international economic justice, 88; on state/global life, 9

Two-Thirds World, 246, 247

UN. *See* United Nations

uncertainty, 37–39, 107–9; cult of, 108

UNCIVPOL. *See* United Nations Civilian Police

UNCTAD. *See* United Nations Conference on Trade and Development

underemployment, 153, 171

UNDP. *See* United Nations Development Program

unemployment, 153, 171, 294, 320; economic disruption of, 92; persistence of, 94, 101; poverty and, 101; in South, 81

UNHCR. *See* United Nations High Commissioner for Refugees

UNICEF, 90, 91; on GNP, 67

unipolarity, 55, 107, 108, 111n5

UNITAF. *See* United Nations Unified Task Force

UNITE, 200

United Nations (UN), 13, 27, 28, 256, 284, 288, 298, 308; codes of conduct and, 198, 199; cooperative networks by, 246; culture of compliance and, 216, 217–18; democracy and, 257; economic sanctions by, 72, 216–17; enforcement by, 211, 212, 214–216, 221, 222–23, 227; Gulf War and, 301–2; peacekeeping by, 213, 214, 219, 224–25, 228, 246; police operations by, 219–22; rapid reaction capability for, 224; role of, 301–2; third way and, 203; U.S. hegemony and, 302

United Nations Charter, 73; Article II(4) of, 253; Article XII of, 256; Chapter VII of, 211; revision of, 314
United Nations Civilian Police (UNCIV-POL), 211, 214, 217; advantage of, 224; Cambodian police and, 219–20; culture of compliance and, 218–27; functions of, 222–23, 228; opposition to, 218; past experiences with, 219–22
United Nations Conference on Trade and Development (UNCTAD), on average per capita income, 67
United Nations Development Program (UNDP), 331
United Nations Environment Conference (1972), 257
United Nations General Assembly, 256, 315
United Nations Geosphere-Biosphere Decade, 1985–1995, 244
United Nations High Commissioner for Refugees (UNHCR), 219
United Nations Operation in Somalia II (UNOSOM II), 220
United Nations Peoples' Assembly, 258
United Nations police, 222–27, 229n11
United Nations Resolution 827, 78n6
United Nations Security Council, 73, 256, 301–2; expanding, 315; mandate of, 210, 211, 216, 225, 226; Peace Academy on, 221
United Nations Transition Authority in Cambodia (UNTAC), 219, 220
United Nations Unified Task Force (UNI-TAF), 220
U.S. Department of Commerce, 62
U.S. Department of Labor, corporate codes and, 200
U.S. Federal Reserve, Long-Term Capital and, 183
U.S. Generalized System of Preferences, 202
U.S.-Japan Security Treaty, 328
U.S. National Security Council, UNOSOM II and, 220
U.S.-Philippine Visiting Forces Agreement, 328
Universal Declaration of Human Rights, Article XXVIII of, 260n4

universality, 31, 241, 242–44, 292; globalization and, 30; particularity and, 30, 32, 34, 293
University of Petroleum and Minerals, Ghanian scholars at, 278
UNOSOM II. *See* United Nations Operation in Somalia II
UNTAC. *See* United Nations Transition Authority in Cambodia
urbanization, 101, 241, 294
Urquhart, Brian: on nonviolence, 225
Uruguay Round (GATT), 130, 131, 132
USA/NAFTA, 202
utilitarianism, 24, 84–85
utilization, 57, 144
utopia: framework for, 151–52, 153; neoliberalism and, 151–53

Valdez Principles, 272
Vatican, mediation by, 282
Vienna Concert, 256
violence, 104, 248; collective life and, 5; control of, 285, 286; privatization of, 297; transnationalization of, 297
Voice of America, African Service of, 283n5
Voice of Asia, The (Mahathir and Ishihara), 326
Vonnegut, Kurt, 67

Walker, R. B. J., 289, 323, 324, 325, 326, 328; on ethics, 342; on state sovereignty, 286
Wallerstein, Immanuel, 27
Wal-Mart, 196
Waltz, Kenneth, 55, 64n1
waning states, nonstates and, 255–58
Wapner, Paul, 324, 334
war, 286, 307–8; abolition of, 259, 314, 316; legitimacy and, 287; local, 308, 309; peace and, 308; relativization of, 308
war crimes, 211, 217; in Bosnia, 214; deterring, 225–27; investigation of, 73, 223; NGOs and, 297; punishing, 73–74; tribunals, 212, 228
War Resisters' International, 257
Warsaw Pact, 43
wastes: disposal of, 140, 141; importation of,

139–41; Lockean, 89; rights violation and, 83

WB. *See* World Bank

Weaver, Ole: on sovereignty, 61

Weber, Max, 31, 286, 330, 337

Westphalian system, 52, 56, 63; collapse of, 290

Wiezaker, Carl-Friedrich von, 316

Williams, Raymond, 326

Winterboer, Dennis and Becky, 134

Wittgenstein, 59, 152

WOFPP. *See* Women's Organizations for Women Political Prisoners

women: body politic and, 333; food claims by, 174; globalization and, 178; health concerns for, 174; marginalization of, 172, 175, 178, 334; poverty and, 172, 173, 175, 176–78; victimization of, 247

Women Against the Invasion of Lebanon, 116, 124

Women and Mothers for Peace, 120–21, 126

Women and Peace Coalition, 117, 120

Women in Black, 119, 120; criticism of, 124; demonstrations by, 117, 118

Women's International League for Peace and Freedom, 257

Women's Organizations for Women Political Prisoners (WOFPP), 117, 118; Palestinian women prisoners and, 125

women's peace movement: collective identity and, 128; emergence of, 124–25, 127–28; Gulf crisis and, 118, 119, 125; political reality and, 121. *See also* peace movement

WOMP. *See* World Order Models Project

workers' rights, 193; codes of conduct and, 204; trade agreements and, 201–2

"Workplace Code of Conduct," 200

World Anti-Communist League, 270

World Bank (WB), 91, 132, 136, 162, 194, 206, 331, 336; Asian financial crisis and, 188, 189; development and, 160; East Asian Miracle and, 182–83; free-market ideology and, 203; globalization and, 328; Mozambique and, 172, 174, 180n2;

on poverty, 170–71; study by, 80–81, 171

World Court, 210, 317

World Development Report (World Bank), 171

World Federalist Movement, 315

world government: machinery for, 291; opposition to, 321

world order, 5, 20, 50, 313–14, 316; global civil society and, 270–71

World Order Models Project (WOMP), 77, 311; environment/feminism and, 316; establishment of, 5, 243; Falk and, 5, 20, 312–18; normative IR and, 5; participants in, 316

World Parliament of Religions (1893), 248

World Peace Through World Law (WPTWL), 314–15

World Policy Institute, 314

world politics, 6, 52, 80, 115, 272; principled, 19–20; state sovereignty in, 114

World's Fairs, 242

World Trade Organization (WTO), 132, 136, 192, 196, 198, 206, 328, 331; environment and, 137; establishment of, 130; free-trade ideologies and, 327; linkage issue and, 203; Multilateral Investment Agreement of, 347n9; trade recipes of, 138; trade/workers' rights/environmental rights and, 202

World Union of National Socialists, 270–71

WPTWL. *See* World Peace Through World Law

WTO. *See* World Trade Organization

WWF-India, hazardous wastes and, 141

Yesh Gvul, 113–14, 120; challenges for, 115, 123, 129; collective identity and, 122, 123, 128; intifada and, 117; Israeli-Jewish collective identity and, 129; peace movement and, 123; political mobilization of, 127–28; political reality and, 121

Yishai, Yael: on women's movement, 123–24

Young, Oran, 273

zones-of-peace movement, 247, 248

About the Contributors

Walden Bello is professor of sociology and public administration at the University of the Philippines and codirector of Focus on the Global South at Chulalongkorn University Social Research Institute in Bangkok. He is the author or coauthor of ten books and numerous articles on Asian political and economic issues, including *A Siamese Tragedy: Development and Disintegration in Modern Thailand* (Zed Books, 1998) and *Dragons in Distress: Asia's Miracle Economies in Crisis* (Penguin Books, 1991). He is also currently a columnist for the *Far Eastern Economic Review*.

Elise Boulding is professor emerita of sociology at Dartmouth College and former secretary-general of the International Peace Research Association. A scholar-activist, she has undertaken numerous transnational and comparative studies of conflict and peace, development, family life, and women in society as well as studies of the future. She is the author of many books, including *The Underside of History: A View of Women through Time* (Sage Publications, 1992), *The Future: Images and Processes* (with Kenneth Boulding; Sage Publications, 1995), and *Cultures of Peace: The Hidden Side of History* (Syracuse University Press, 2000).

Robin Broad is an associate professor at American University and has been active in numerous citizen organizations. She is the author of *Plundering Paradise: The Struggle for the Environment in the Philippines* (with John Cavanagh; University of California Press, 1993) and *Unequal Alliance: The World Bank, the International Monetary Fund, and the Philippines* (University of California Press, 1988).

John Cavanagh is director of the Institute for Policy Studies in Washington, D.C. He is the author of numerous books, including *Global Dreams: Imperial Corporations and the New World Order* (with Richard Barnet; Simon and Schuster, 1994) and *Plundering Paradise: The Struggle for the Environment in the Philippines* (with Robin Broad; University of California Press, 1993). He serves on the boards of six activist organizations.

Michael W. Doyle is Edward S. Sanford Professor of International Affairs and director of the Center of International Studies at Princeton University. He is the author of numerous books, including *Ways of War and Peace: Realism, Liberalism, and Socialism* (Norton, 1997) and *Empires* (Cornell University Press, 1986). He is coeditor of *New Thinking in International Relations Theory* (with G. John Ikenberry; Westview Press, 1997).

Johan Galtung is director of the Transcend Peace and Development Network and professor of peace studies at American, Granada, Ritsumeikan, Tromsö, and Witten/ Herdecke Universities. He is also founder of the International Peace Research Institute, Oslo, Norway. His books include *Theory and Methods of Social Research* (Columbia University Press, 1967), *The True Worlds: A Transnational Perspective* (Free Press, 1980), *Essays in Peace Research* (Ejlers, 1974–88), and *Human Rights in Another Key* (Polity Press, 1994).

David Held teaches at the Open University in England. His books include *Democracy and the Global Order: From the Modern State to Cosmopolitan Governance* (Stanford University Press, 1995) and *Models of Democracy*, 2nd ed. (Stanford University Press, 1996). He has recently coauthored *Global Transformations: Politics, Economics and Culture* (Stanford University Press, 1999). His many edited collections include *Prospects for Democracy: North, South, East, West* (Stanford University Press, 1993).

Robert C. Johansen is interim director of the Kroc Institute for International Peace Studies and professor of government and international studies at the University of Notre Dame. He is the author of *The National Interest and the Human Interest: An Analysis of U.S. Foreign Policy* (Princeton University Press, 1980), coeditor of *The Constitutional Foundations of World Peace* (SUNY Press, 1996), and author of numerous articles on UN peacekeeping, global security, and world order.

Mary Kaldor is director of the Programme on Global Civil Society at the Centre for the Study of Global Governance at the London School of Economics. She is the editor of *Dealignment: A New Foreign Policy Perspective* (with Richard Falk; Basil Blackwell, 1987) and the author of *The Imaginary War: Understanding the East-West Conflict* (Basil Blackwell, 1990). Her most recent book is *New and Old Wars: Organised Violence in a Global Era*. She has been an active leader of the European peace movement.

Rajni Kothari is chairman of the Centre for the Study of Developing Societies, Delhi, India, which he founded in 1963. He was instrumental in starting the journal *Alternatives: Social Transformation and Human Governance* and is currently president of the International Foundation of Development Alternatives (IFDA). He is the author of *Rethinking Development: In Search of Humane Alternatives* (New Horizons Press, 1989) and *Poverty: Human Consciousness and the Amnesia of Development* (Zed Books, 1995). He has been active in the human rights movement in India and is past president of the People's Union for Civil Liberties (PUCL). He has been most recently associated with the movement against India's decision to go nuclear.

Friedrich V. Kratochwil is professor at the Ludwig-Maximilians-Universitaet Muenchen, Germany, and has served on the editorial boards of *World Politics, International Organization,* and *International Studies Quarterly* and is presently the editor of the *European Journal of International Relations.* His books include *Rules, Norms, and Decisions: On the Conditions of Practical and Legal Reasoning in International Relations and Domestic Affairs* (Cambridge University Press, 1991). He is coeditor of *The Return of Culture and Identity in International Relations Theory* (with Yosef Lapid; Lynne Rienner Publishers, 1996) and *International Law: A Contemporary Perspective* (with Richard Falk and Saul H. Mendlovitz; Westview Press, 1985).

Robert Jay Lifton is distinguished professor of Psychiatry and Psychology at John Jay College, City University of New York. His most recent book is *The Protean Self: Human Resilience in an Age of Fragmentation* (Basic Books, 1993). He is the coauthor of *Indefensible Weapons: The Political and Psychological Case against Nuclearism* (with Richard Falk; Basic Books, 1982), and *Hiroshima in America: Fifty Years of Denial* (with Greg Mitchell; Putnam's Sons, 1995).

Ali A. Mazrui is director of the Institute of Global Cultural Studies, State University of New York at Binghamton. He is the author of over twenty books and of the television series *The Africans: A Triple Heritage* (BBC/PBS, 1986). His latest book is *The Power of Babel: Language and Governance in Africa's Experience* (with Alamin M. Mazrui; University of Chicago Press 1998).

Saul Mendlovitz is Dag Hammarksjold Professor of Peace and World Order Studies at Rutgers University School of Law and codirector of the World Order Models Project (WOMP). He is a member of the board of directors of the Arms Control Association, a former consultant for the Social Science Advisory Board of the U.S. Arms Control and Disarmament Agency, and vice president of the Lawyers' Committee on Nuclear Policy and represents a number of organizations at the United Nations, including the International Association of Lawyers Against Nuclear Arms (IALANA). He has written extensively on security matters and issues relevant to promoting a just world order. His publications include the four-volume *Strategy of World Order* (with Richard Falk; World Law Fund, 1966), *The United Nations and a Just World Order* (with Richard Falk and Samuel Kim; Westview Press, 1991), and *Preferred Futures for the United Nations* (with Burns Weston; Transnational Publishers, 1995).

James H. Mittelman is professor of International Relations at American University. His most recent books are *The Globalization Syndrome: Transformation and Resis-*

tance (Princeton University Press, 2000) and *Innovation and Transformation in International Studies* (with Stephen Gill as coeditor; Cambridge University Press, 1997).

Radmila Nakarada is a senior research fellow at the Institute for European Studies, Belgrade, Yugoslavia. She is the editor of *The Post-Bipolar World: The North/South Antinomies* (Institute for European Studies/WOMP, 1995) as well as other books and articles on world affairs.

James N. Rosenau is university professor at George Washington University. His books include *Along the Domestic-Foreign Frontier: Exploring Governance in a Turbulent World* (Cambridge University Press, 1997) and *Turbulence in World Politics: A Theory of Change and Continuity* (Princeton University Press, 1990). He is also the author or editor of numerous other volumes.

Lester Edwin J. Ruiz is director of the Doctor of Ministry Program at New York Theological Seminary and a professor of theology and culture. He is coeditor of *Christian Ethics in Ecumenical Context: Theology, Culture, and Politics in Dialogue* (with Shin Chiba and George R. Hunsberger; W. B. Eerdmans, 1995) and the author of articles on peace and world order studies, politics, ethics, and theology. He is on the editorial committee of *Alternatives: Social Transformation and Humane Governance*.

Yoshikazu Sakamoto is professor emeritus of international politics at the University of Tokyo. He is the editor of *Global Transformation: Challenges to the State System* (United Nations University Press, 1994) and coeditor of *Democratizing Japan: The Allied Occupation* (with Robert E. Ward; University of Hawaii Press, 1987). He has also written extensively in the area of politics, peace research, and world order affairs.

Simona Sharoni teaches at Evergreen State College in Olympia, Washington. She has also been involved in a number of solidarity initiatives and grassroots community development and action research projects in Israel/Palestine and the north of Ireland. She cochairs the board of directors of the Consortium On Peace Research, Education & Development (COPRED) and is the author of *Gender and the Israeli-Palestinian Conflict: The Politics of Women's Resistance* (Syracuse University Press, 1995).

Vandana Shiva is director of the Research Foundation for Science, Technology and Natural Resource Policy in Dehra Dun, India. She is the author of numerous books, including *Biopiracy: The Plunder of Nature and Knowledge* (South End Press, 1997) and *Staying Alive: Women, Ecology and Development* (Zed Books, 1988). She is one of the leading spokespersons for ecological and social justice movements in the global South.

Ashwini Tambe is comleting her doctoral dissertation, "Codes of Misconduct: Legal Discourse on Prostitution in Colonial Bombay," for the School of International Service at American University. Her areas of specialization include gender studies, political economy, and international communication. Her forthcoming publications concern the state and sexual reform, and gender and communication technology.

R. B. J. Walker is a professor at the University of Victoria, Canada. His books include *Inside/Outside: International Relations as Political Theory* (Cambridge University Press, 1993) and *One World/Many Worlds* (Lynne Rienner Publishers, 1988). His edited volumes include *Contending Sovereignties: Rethinking Political Community* (with Saul Mendlovitz; Lynne Rienner Publishers, 1990). He is associate editor of *Alternatives: Social Transformation and Humane Governance.*

Paul Wapner is an associate professor at American University. He is the author of *Environmental Activism and World Civic Politics* (SUNY Press, 1996), which was the recipient of the Harold and Margaret Sprout Award, as well as numerous articles on environmental politics, international relations theory, and environmental ethics. He is associate editor of the journal *Global Environmental Politics* and is on the editorial board of *International Studies Quarterly.*